Letters of Eugene V. Debs

Letters of
EUGENE V. DEBS

VOLUME 2   1913-1919

Edited by
J. Robert Constantine

University of Illinois Press

Urbana and Chicago

© 1990 by the Board of Trustees of the University of Illinois
Manufactured in the United States of America
C 5 4 3 2 1

This book is printed on acid-free paper.

Library of Congress Cataloging-in-Publication Data

Debs, Eugene V. (Eugene Victor), 1855-1926.
    Letters of Eugene V. Debs / edited by J. Robert Constantine.
        p.   cm.
    Includes bibliographical references.
    Contents: v. 1. 1874-1912—v. 2. 1913-1919—v. 3. 1919-1926.
    1. Debs, Eugene V. (Eugene Victor), 1855-1926—Correspondence.
2. Socialists—United States—Correspondence.   3. Socialism—United
States—History—Sources.   4. United States—Politics and
government—1865-1933—Sources.   I. Constantine, J. Robert.
II. Title.
HX84.D3A4   1990   335'.3'092   89-5135
ISBN 0-252-01742-0 (set : alk. paper)

Contents

Illustrations

Symbols and Abbreviations

Repository Symbols

CaOOA   Public Archives of Canada, Ottawa, Labour Archives
CLobs   California State University, Long Beach
CLSU   University of Southern California, Los Angeles
CLU   University of California, Los Angeles
CSmH   Huntington Library, San Marino, Calif.
CSt   Stanford University, Archives
CSt-H   Stanford University, Hoover Institution on War, Revolution, and Peace
CtU   University of Connecticut, Storrs
CtY   Yale University, New Haven, Conn.
CU   University of California, Berkeley
DCU   Catholic University of America
DLC   Library of Congress, Washington, D.C.
DNA   National Archives, Washington, D.C.
DebsH   Debs Foundation, Debs Home, Terre Haute, Ind.
IaH   State Historical Society of Iowa, Iowa City
IaU   University of Iowa, Iowa City
ICarbS   Southern Illinois University, Carbondale
ICIU   University of Illinois, Chicago
ICN   Newberry Library, Chicago
IHi   Illinois State Historical Library, Springfield
ILGWU   International Ladies' Garment Workers' Union, Archives, New York City
In   Indiana State Library, Indianapolis
InGrD   DePauw University, Greencastle, Ind.
InH   Indiana Historical Society, Indianapolis
InTI   Indiana State University, Terre Haute
InU   Indiana University, Bloomington, Lilly Library
IGR   Knox College, Galesburg, Ill.
IU   University of Illinois, Champaign
KPT   Pittsburg State University, Pittsburg, Kans.
KU   University of Kansas, Lawrence

MH	Harvard University, Houghton Library, Cambridge, Mass.
MHi	Massachusetts Historical Society, Boston
MiDW	Wayne State University, Detroit, Mich., Reuther Library
MiU	University of Michigan, Ann Arbor
MnHi	Minnesota Historical Society, St. Paul
MoH	Missouri Historical Society, St. Louis
MoU	University of Missouri, Columbia
NcD	Duke University, Durham, N.C.
NhD	Dartmouth College, Hanover, N.H.
NIC	Cornell University, Ithaca, N.Y., Labor-Management Documentation Center
NjP	Princeton University, Princeton, N.J., Seeley G. Mudd Manuscript Library
NN Kars	New York Public Library, Karsner Collection
NNC	Columbia University, New York City
NNU Tam	New York University, Tamiment Library
NNWML	Wagner College, Staten Island, N.Y.
NRAB	American Baptist Historical Society, Rochester, N.Y.
NNYI	YIVO Institute for Jewish Research, New York City
NRU	University of Rochester, Rochester, N.Y.
NSyU	Syracuse University, Syracuse, N.Y.
OT	Toledo-Lucas County Public Library
OClWHi	Western Reserve Historical Society, Cleveland, Ohio
PHi	Historical Society of Pennsylvania, Philadelphia
PST	Pennsylvania State University, University Park
PU	University of Pennsylvania, Philadelphia
TxArU	University of Texas, Arlington
TxLT	Texas Tech University, Lubbock
TxU	University of Texas, Austin, Barker Texas History Center
WHi	Wisconsin State Historical Society, Madison
WM	Milwaukee Public Library

Document Symbols

A	Autograph
AL	Autograph letter, not signed or signature missing
ALc	Autograph letter, copy
ALS	Autograph letter, signed
AN	Autograph note, not signed
ANS	Autograph note, signed
AS	Autograph, signed
EVD	Eugene Victor Debs
MS(S)	Manuscript(s)

PLS	Printed form letter, signed
T	Typed
Tc	Transcript copy
TDc	Typed document, copy
TDS	Typed document, signed
TL	Typed letter, not signed
TLc	Typed letter, copy
TLS	Typed letter, signed
TLSc	Typed letter, signed copy
TS	Typed, signed
(Y)	Initial of Bart Young, Debs's secretary

Letters

1913-1919

EVD to Fred D. Warren

January 3, 1913
Terre Haute, Indiana

My dear Fred:—

Yours of 1st. received. Its contents are mighty good to me. You came home from the West[1] just in time. You certainly were confronted by a condition that taxed all your resources. Of course I am heartily glad you have won out. It would have been a calamity if the C.N. had been forced to suspend.[2] With the shape you have things in now financially you will be able to do your work along other lines with some show of doing justice to yourself. I hope you may never again have to worry about the financial end. I wish some way could be found to fix that so that you would not be harassed by it again.

You were up against a combination that must have tried you to the very marrow. And then Wayland's death on top of it all![3] Few men could have stood up under it and it is a wonder it had not crushed you. But having survived the ordeal you are now the bigger and stronger and better for it. Had you been less than true metal, without a "blowhole," you could not have stood it, and I for one want you to know that I have some understanding of what you have passed through and I hope a full appreciation of the Spartan courage which sustained you in that terrible hour of trial.

I note what you say about coming to Girard and it is very gratifying to me. I am taking a course of osteopathic treatment and I am also dieting and doing everything else I know how to help nature to put me in fighting form. I have been thoroughly examined by a specialist who tells me that I am an organic marvel; that there is not the slightest flaw or defect in any vital organ. He tells me that my trouble is in the back which I strained severely at heavy work in my youth, but that this can be pretty fully corrected. This trouble is made somewhat acute, he says, by exhaustion which prevents proper digestion and assimilation. As a consequence I lack blood, my hands and feet are always cold and I sleep by jerks or not at all. But I don't want to annoy you with my ailments. I do not think they are serious. I am resolved to get well because I have got to. If I don't succeed in improving and at least showing favorable tendencies within the next two or three weeks I am going to resign temporarily at least and go away for three or six months, perhaps a year, cut myself off from the world of activity and live in a hut and work with an ax in the backwoods and play savage for recreation, scalping anything that shows up, until nature makes me whole again. Daily work of that kind out in the fresh air and a hominy diet will have its effect and nature will do the rest. I have fifteen years more work in me[4] and I want it to be the best work of my life.

Note what you said about the Typographical Union trying to hold you up. Whatever you do don't allow them to do that. Put your foot down and look them in the eye {& tell them} that it don't go. There are any number of socialists you can get to do the work. Insert an ad in the Appeal and you can get all the good men you want. That union is a closed corporation and is all for itself. Its scabbing record makes it contemptible in the eyes of every honest man. This union does not care a damn about anybody but itself. It is all hog and has not a bit of sympathy for other workers. If its members can only tie themselves up in a good wage agreement they are perfectly willing to see all other workers ground down to starvation and if they strike take their places and scab on them in the name of unionism as they did in Chicago. Damn such unionism to hell. It is the worst kind of scabbing. Lynch[5] who is at the head of this union is a prime favorite with the Civic Federation gang and with the newspaper trust. He is a man after their own heart and they openly avow themselves as the champion of his union. And why? Because it is their union and they use it to beat out the brains of other workers, and it is no wonder they are willing to pay them well for their treachery.

All you have to do is to call the bluff and give them to understand in a few words that you mean business. Don't palter with them, don't make any defense or apology when they try to hold you up but give them an emphatic no and that will end it. If they threaten to go out on strike tell them that you will fill their places in thirty minutes and then make a statement of the facts in the case in the following issue of the Appeal. You are paying more now than anyone else in that section and if you can afford anything in the the way of increase let it go to some of the rest who are just as important as the printers. I have been informed that there are two or three printers who are at the bottom of this and who are determined to take advantage of your position, feeling sure that you won't risk a strike. Well, by god, you will have to disabuse their minds of that sooner or later and the sooner the better. Tell them that you are a union man but if they think they can use their union to hold you up and to compel you to submit to outrageous terms they are against the wrong man and the wrong institution, and tell them too that if they want to strike on that issue they can't get out of the office too quick to suit you. That will end the matter and you will be troubled no more. These fellows are not socialists and they are not unionists. They are self-seeking grafters with the spirit but lacking the nerve of highwayman. Do the square thing by them, as I know you will, and then draw the line and give them to understand once for all that you will stand on your rights and that bulldozing unionism of the variety they represent don't go.[6]

Have delivered the poke in the beak to Theo. as directed. Later— Theo. has just attempted to reciprocate with a return poke with instructions to deliver to you when I go to Girard.

Latest—we are both doing as well as could be expected.

Yes, Glenn and Boydie[7] would make a great firm. Hope some day Boydie may go with me and Mrs. Debs also when I go out to Girard.

Will have copy with you for the special[8] in ample time.

Yours always
Debs

TLS, CtU, Fred Warren Papers.

1. Warren had been in Los Angeles collecting material for a series of articles to counter the "lies" being printed about the *Appeal* in the *Los Angeles Times*. Probably the most damaging charge made in the *Times* articles was the accusation that Wayland and Warren used the *Appeal* as a money-making engine that had made both men very rich.

2. The *Coming Nation*, edited in Girard by Algie M. Simons, struggled for survival throughout 1912, and its removal to Chicago in February 1913 merely postponed its demise. The last issue of the magazine appeared in June 1913. The failure of the *Coming Nation* led to a bitter controversy between Warren and Simons in which the latter claimed that Warren had deliberately scuttled the magazine.

3. Julius A. Wayland, publisher of the *Appeal*, committed suicide on November 10, 1912.

4. Debs died in October 1926.

5. James Mathew Lynch (1867-1930) was president of the International Typographical Union from 1900 to 1914.

6. Warren apparently did "the square thing" by the printers. There was no strike at the *Appeal*.

7. Glenn Warren, Fred Warren's son, and Oscar Baur, Katherine Debs's nephew.

8. Debs's "Story of the Indictment," which described the indictments against him and Warren and Jake Sheppard for attempted bribery of a witness as "perfectly infamous," appeared in the *Appeal*'s special indictment issue on January 18, 1913.

EVD to Grace D. Brewer

January 25, 1913
Terre Haute, Indiana

Personal

My dear Comrade Brewer: —

Yours 23rd. enjoyed muchly. Theo. and I roared on seeing Walker's[1] Turkeytrotting Fred and George.[2] Talk about masterpieces of art. This takes the candy. The picture gives Fred a soulful expression as if all his heart were in his heels. I'd give at least fo' bits to see that performance but I'd need half a dozen ripe bananas or tomatoes or henfruit for the applause. I should not be able, I know, to restrain my enthusiasm.

Some one, presumably you, sent us a couple of hundred of the new circulars about the Arsenal.[3] Many thanks! They come just right and we will make good use of them.

Was walking on the street with Mrs. Debs yesterday and I remarked that things were running a little quiet and smooth and that something was due to happen. An hour later I was gobbled up [by] the deputy marshals. You see that long experience has given me a keen sense of coming events and I can feel the weight of the shadow when the hand of fate is about to caress or cuff me.[4]

Note what you say about George and Theo. Alas, my cup is full on that subject. God alone knows what I now suffer in the way of tyranny and oppression since Theo. is my bondsman.[5] All my previous experience was paradisiacal. Hourly he threatens to deliver me up [to] the sheriff. I now have to have a written permission to leave his sight and I have to report to him in all meekness and humility three times a day to satisfy him that I am not seeking to make my escape. A hot rebellion is brewing within me and you must not be surprised if you hear of an outbreak. The situation is growing very tense.

I am so glad to hear that Mrs. Lovejoy is deputy clerk.[6] She is worthy and true in the highest degree. Did not know the Wilsons[7] had moved to Joplin. Hope they will do well. But as long as you are at Girard they will soon be back again. Hope I may get out there one of these days. Would give much to see you all. But somehow I am crowded here every minute. Have written to Tom Grant's sister.[8]

Love to you all.
E. V. Debs

Don't answer

TLS, EVD Foundation, Debs Home.

1. Ryan Walker, *Appeal* cartoonist.

2. Fred Warren and George Brewer.

3. *The Arsenal of Facts,* a handbook brought up to date annually and sold by the *Appeal.*

4. Debs was arrested in the witness-bribery case by the Indiana federal marshal in Terre Haute on January 24, 1913. He was immediately released on bail.

5. Theodore Debs posted bond for Debs at the time of his arrest.

6. In the November 1912 elections in Crawford County (Girard), Kansas, a socialist, Guy E. Turner, was elected county clerk. He appointed Debs's Girard friend, Mrs. A. W. Lovejoy, to serve as deputy clerk.

7. Benjamin Franklin Wilson, a field organizer for the Socialist party in Kansas, was elected to the Kansas state legislature from Crawford County in 1912.

8. In "Vale, Tom Grant" (*Appeal,* February 1, 1913) Debs described his first meeting with Grant, a printer on the *Appeal* who died on January 18, 1913. After hearing Debs's speech in Muscatine, Iowa, in 1807, Grant claimed that he was converted to socialism and lent Debs five dollars "for a train ticket to the next point." Debs repaid him and later encouraged him to move to Girard to work for the *Appeal.*

Lucien Sanial[1] to EVD

January 27, 1913
New York City

Dearest Debs:—

Yesterday I read—with my daughter's eyes—the news of your arrest and release on bail. Well said the ancient poet, "Quos Jupiter vult perdere prius dementat" (Those whom Jupiter wills to destroy he first makes mad). Demented Capitalism is indeed madly running to perdition. With all our might let us urge it on, even at the cost of such bruises as we may get from the kicks of its political legs and from the blows of its judicial arms.

Your welcome card of the 18th reached me a week ago at my new quarters. Please note, as above, my change of address).

It may seem rather late to acknowledge also, and reciprocate your New Year's wishes so kindly joined in by your brave companion in ~~such~~ sunshine and storm; but you know by this time that in your every motion on the hard road you travel my heart and thought go to you, anxiously and sympathetically.

I would have much to say to you and intend to write you at some length within the next ten days, but would like to know as soon as possible if a letter addressed to Terre Haute will surely reach you promptly or where else I should send it. The chief object I have in view is to call your attention to the *now* imminent collapse of the Banking fabric, which ~~I had already~~ in two articles published in The

NY Call[2] I had already shown to be inevitable; (namely, one sixteen months ago ~~May~~ Sept 3, 1911, a copy of which I sent you, and the other nine months ago, May 5, 1912, which may have escaped your attention).

In those articles I showed that Capitalism, through the conversion of its banking power into a vast reservoir of trustification water, had driven itself into a corner from which there was no possible outlet and that the real issue of the Presidential Campaign could only be "Socialism or General Bankruptcy."

I had hoped that the S. P. would take up the facts, figures, and conclusions which I had presented, and that there would be in ~~the~~ its National platform a strong plank on that subject. Had this been done the capitalist parties would have been forced to discuss publicly the financial situation—that is, the very subject which they, were all most anxious to ignore—as glaringly shown by Pujo's[3] adjournment of his so-called "Money Trust" investigation until the campaign was over, on the ground that he did not want to inject party politics into the financial question.

I am now preparing a 16-page pamphlet[4] in which I shall give figures of tremendous import now held back by Pujo and no doubt to be passed over lightly in his report if they appear at all in it, his obvious intention being to divert public attention from the situation itself by concentrating it on the personalities of a few men.

Looking over the battlefield with growing confidence in the victory of Man over the Beast I remain

Most affectionately yours
Lucien Sanial[5]

ALS, InTI, Debs Collection.

1. Lucien Delabarre Sanial (1836-1927) was born in France and came to the United States at the outbreak of the Civil War as a correspondent for *Le Temps* of Paris. Sanial edited a number of socialist publications and was the author of scores of books and pamphlets on socialism and related economic subjects.

2. Excerpts from Sanial's *Call* articles on banking were printed in the *Appeal* (February 15, 1913).

3. Arsene Paulin Pujo (1861-1939) was a congressman from Louisiana whose committee's investigation of the money trust in 1912 is credited with promoting banking reform through the Federal Reserve and Clayton acts, passed early in the Wilson administration.

4. Sanial's *General Bankruptcy or Socialism* was published in 1913.

5. Debs inserted parts of this Sanial letter in the *Appeal* (February 15, 1913).

EVD to H. M. Hyndman[1]

January 31, 1913
Terre Haute, Indiana

My dear Hyndman:—

I have just read your splendid editorial in the current issue of Justice[2] and I wish to drop you this line of thanks and appreciation not only for myself but in behalf of the many thousands of socialists on this side who love you and hold you in highest respect for your uncompromising loyalty to the socialist movement through all the years of your active life.

It is wonderful what a clear understanding you have of the situation on this side; much clearer I must admit than that of many of our own comrades.

Syndicalism has swooped down upon us and the capitalist papers and magazines are giving it unlimited space but the Socialist party is in no danger on account of it. Just at present there are some sharp divisions and some bitter controversies on account of it but the Socialist party will emerge all the stronger after syndicalism has had its fling.

The anarchists are all jubilant over the prospect that syndicalism may disrupt the Socialist party, but they will again be disappointed. There are many of our socialists who favor syndicalism and sabotage, or think they do, but the party is overwhelmingly opposed to both[3] and will stick to the main track to the end. We are with you in your position and in due time you will be once more triumphantly vindicated. Revolutionary political action and revolutionary industrial organization will finally win out against all opposition both from without and within.

With love and greeting and warmest wishes I am, my dear old comrade,

Yours always
E. V. Debs

TLc, InTI, Debs Collection.

1. Henry Mayer Hyndman (1842-1921) was an English journalist, social reformer, and founder of the Social Democratic Federation (1881), which was the nucleus of the socialist movement in British politics.

2. Excerpts from Hyndman's Justice article, in which he hailed Debs's popular vote in the 1912 election as one of the "great events for socialism" during the past year, were printed in the Appeal (February 15, 1913).

3. As noted, at its 1912 convention the Socialist party amended its constitution to provide for the expulsion of members who opposed political action or advocated "crime, sabotage, or other methods of violence." One of the first victims of the new

order was William D. Haywood, IWW leader, who was removed from the party's
national executive committee for a December 1912 speech in New York in which he
called for direct action as "the shortest way home." Debs agreed with the antisabotage,
antiviolence changes in the constitution but disliked the expulsion clause as an in-
fringement of free speech.

William English Walling to EVD

March 2, 1913
Cedarhurst, Long Island, New York

Dear Comrade Debs,

Items like the enclosed (from Perkins organ)[1] have appeared in
every one of the Capitalist papers of New York. Does this not show
that Haywood's recall is taken as a victory of capitalism within the
Socialist Party?

Do you approve of the statement on the recall ballot that Haywood
was guilty of an untried charge against the Socialist Party (repudiation
of political action)? Is not Montana right in demanding a new ballot?[2]
As we Socialists approve of proportional representation, ought it not
to apply to party affairs? Even if Haywood only represents a third of
the party is not this third entitled to some voice?[3]

Do you not advocate {or approve} *some* of the practices that now
go under the name of sabotage? Do you not approve of law-breaking
under certain exceptional circumstances?

I have consulted with nobody in writing this and shall mention it
to nobody. I am confident that your own judgement and initiative
will lead you to the right action. I only trust that letters like mine
may help to hasten any public statement you have in mind.

I sent you my "Socialism As It Is"[4] and received no acknowledgment. Enclosed find some press notices. If you have not received it
I shall send another copy.

Fraternally,
Wm English Walling

P.S. Are you aware that Haywood's supposed repudiation of
political action lay in the exact use of your words "I do not ask the
workingman for his vote"?[5]

ALS, InTI, Debs Collection.

1. George Walbridge Perkins (1862-1920) was the J. P. Morgan & Co. specialist
in corporate mergers and reorganization and was a strong supporter of Theodore

Roosevelt in the Bull Moose campaign of 1912. During the campaign, Perkins founded the *Progressive Bulletin,* which was continued as a monthly publication after the campaign.

2. Haywood's supporters complained that the preamble to "Referendum D, 1912," canvassing the party membership regarding the recall of Haywood from the national executive committee, assumed that Haywood was guilty of calling for direct action and sabotage and then asked the members whether or not he should be recalled. Montana was one of several states demanding that the preamble be deleted and a new referendum ballot sent out, but the demand was ignored.

3. Haywood was removed from the national executive committee by a vote of 22,000 to 11,000. *Socialist Party Monthly Bulletin,* March-April 1913.

4. Walling's book was published in 1912.

5. Quotation attributed to Debs during the 1912 campaign by *International Socialist Review,* 8 (November 1912).

EVD to William English Walling[1]

March 5, 1913
Terre Haute, Indiana

Dear Comrade Walling:—

It does not matter to me what the capitalist papers think is going on in the Socialist party as long as we can keep the party as it ought to be.

I regretted to see Haywood's recall but it was inevitable. He brought it on himself. I should not have put section 6[2] in the constitution but it is there and put there by the party and Haywood deliberately violated it. Is this not the fact?

The question of what sabotage means has nothing to do with the matter. Its advocates have shown that it means anything, everything, or nothing at all. If I had been in Haywood's place and had felt bound to advocate sabotage as he did I would have withdrawn from the party to do it. If I had deliberately violated the constitution I would have expected to be called to account for it. Else why a constitution at all?

The constitution also prohibits fusion with other parties. Suppose certain members fuse with other parties, would they have any fault to find if they were expelled from the party?

I am not now judging Haywood, I am answering your questions. I am free to confess, however, judging from some of the reports I have seen, that Haywood has been talking a good deal more like an anarchist than a socialist.

The I.W.W. for which Haywood stands and speaks is an anarchist organization in all except in name and this is the cause of all the trouble. Anarchism and socialism have never mixed and never will. The I.W.W. has treated the Socialist party most indecently to put it very mildly. When it gets into trouble it frantically appeals to the Socialist party for aid, which has always been freely rendered, and after it is all over the I.W.W. kicks the Socialist party in the face. That is the case put in plain words and the Socialist party has had enough of that sort of business and I don't blame them a bit. There are I.W.W. anarchists who are in the Socialist party for no other purpose than to disrupt it and the Socialist party is right in taking a decided stand against them.

Answering your questions specifically, (1) The statement on the recall ballot you refer to should in my opinion {have been} omitted. (2) I have not seen Montana's demand but so far as the right of it is concerned, whatever it may be, that is for the party to decide. (3) Certainly I approve of some of the practices that now go under the name of sabotage, for almost everything goes under that name. (4) The same answer as to law-breaking. There are certainly circumstances under which I advocate it but I must know what the circumstances are. (5) I think you know there is a very wide difference between the kind of political action Haywood advocates and the kind I advocate, even if we happen to use identical words.

I received the copy of your book and sent you quite an extended acknowledgment of it from Girard where it reached me. Sorry this letter did not get to you. Allow me to thank you now for it.

Pardon these hurried words as I am extremely busy. This letter is not private and you can use it as you wish.

Yours fraternally
[Eugene V. Debs]

TLc, InTI, Debs Collection.

1. This letter, under various titles, was widely reprinted in the socialist press. See, e.g., "Plain Words from Debs," *Indiana Socialist*, April 12, 1913.
2. The antisabotage, anti–direct action amendment to the party constitution.

EVD to Frank P. O'Hare[1]

March 8, 1913
[Terre Haute, Indiana]

Dear Comrade O'Hare: —

A thousand thanks to you for your kindness! You will find the answer to the fellow Davis'[2] falsehood enclosed. He has lied to you from start to finish. He is not a socialist and has never voted the socialist ticket in his life. He is [a] republican ward heeler and was kicked out of the Central Labor Union for being caught in the act, while a member of that body, of attempting to deliver the endorsement and support of that body to the Republican County Central Committee. He got his price without a doubt but was kicked out bodily, expelled in disgrace, before he could deliver the goods.

The Labor News[3] he speaks of has not been in existence for several years. It died of its own corruption. The editor of it who was Davis' pal in circulating these lies about me, for which they were doubtless paid, absconded with the funds of the Printer's union of this city. Both are thieves, grafters and heelers.

I do not think the fellow is any longer a member of the carpenters' union. I shall make inquiry, not on my account but on the union's account and if he is a member I am going to make him face me before its next meeting.[4] I will put an end to that fellow's career as a libeller and blackmailer, you may be sure. I have just had a talk with the president of the Central Labor Union[5] who knows the scoundrel well and at the next meeting of the central body I will be there with his letter and so will he if he can be induced to attend, and if not he will be put on record in a way that will silence his slanderous tongue and prevent him from libelling and blackmailing others. If I have time before leaving I shall go to his house[6] and give him a chance to look me in the face and ask him what he thinks of himself.

But the answer you made him is so crushing that it would seem unnecessary to add another word. The idea of this self-confessed scab charging me with giving a job to a non union man. He gave himself dead away and your clear eye saw through him instantly and turned him inside out, or rather had him turn himself inside out to expose his deceit and treachery.

One cannot help wondering what such serpents were ever created for. I suppose I ought not to pay the least attention to this creature and I certainly should not if it were not for the hurt he can do the cause. I would not be at all surprised if he were a detective as well as a blackmailer.

I note that Mrs. O'Hare[7] is to be here Sunday and hope I may be able to see her before leaving. I am glad she is coming and am sure the comrades will give her a good meeting and a warm welcome.

Thanking you again and again and with all affectionate remembrances to you all I am

Yours always
Eugene V. Debs

P.S. If you can without inconvenience give space to enclosed article in the Rip-Saw I should much appreciate it, but go to no trouble about it.

TLc, InTI, Debs Collection.

1. Francis Patrick O'Hare (1877-1960) was at the time manager of the *National Rip-Saw*, a St. Louis socialist monthly for which Debs wrote editorials from 1914 until 1917. A native of Iowa, O'Hare married Kate Richards in 1902 and for the next fifteen years Frank and Kate O'Hare were among the most popular socialist speakers in the West, especially in Kansas, Oklahoma, and Missouri. Much of Debs's correspondence with O'Hare centered on O'Hare's role as manager of Debs's lecture tours on behalf of the *Rip-Saw* and on the trial and imprisonment of Kate O'Hare for violation of the wartime Espionage Act. Two of the O'Hare children, twin boys born in 1908, were named Eugene Robert and Victor Edwin.

2. Philip I. Davis was listed in the 1908 Terre Haute city directory as a carpenter and president of the carpenters' local. On September 25, 1908, the *Indianapolis News* reported that Davis had been expelled from the Terre Haute Central Labor Union for unduly trying to influence the union's position in the state and local elections that year and for spreading the rumor that Debs had "employed nonunion labor in repairs on his house." The rumor "was given a wide circulation . . . all over the country."

3. The *Labor News* was published in Terre Haute from 1905 to 1910. It was edited by William H. Terrill.

4. In "Nail the Liar" (*Appeal*, March 29, 1913), Debs described his appearance "within the last two weeks" at the Terre Haute carpenters' union meeting, at which he "challenged anyone to accuse him in his presence or to ask him any question in reference to his union record." There was, Debs said, "not an accuser nor a question asked."

5. Debs's close friend Phil K. Reinbold.

6. The 1913 Terre Haute city directory lists Davis as a contractor.

7. Kate O'Hare spoke to the Terre Haute Seventh Ward socialists and to the city's Woman's Franchise League on March 9, 1913. *Terre Haute Star*, March 8, 1913; *Terre Haute Tribune*, March 9, 1913.

EVD to John M. Work[1]

April 4, 1913
Terre Haute, Indiana

Dear Comrade Work:—

Referring to enclosed letter from West Virginia I wish to give it my hearty endorsement and to urge that the matter of which it treats be brought to the attention of the N.E.C.

The most important situation in all this country at the present hour is West Virginia[2] and along with many others I deem it strange that the N.E.C. has thus far taken no action. It would be the greatest pity to allow this great opportunity for propaganda and organization to go by unimproved. I think the N.E.C. should issue a clear cut statement in reference to this situation and in connection with this make a ringing appeal to the working class of the country.[3] The comrades who are in the military prison in West Virginia are among the most loyal, active and efficient in the party and the party owes it to them to espouse their cause in this hour of their incarceration and to use all its powers to effect their rescue. There are a good many wondering why this has not been done, or at least why something has not been attempted in behalf of these imprisoned comrades of ours, and it has been more than once hinted that if it were Hillquit or Spargo or Berger in the clutch of the military power and threatened with military brutality, instead of Mother Jones,[4] action would have been taken by the N.E.C. long ago, and I do not hesitate to say that this expresses my own opinion.

I have been doing the little I could through the Appeal to Reason[5] to urge the party to action but if there has been any encouragement from national headquarters I have not heard of it.

It is altogether probable, it seems to me, that the bankrupt condition of the national party treasury has something to do with the inaction of the N.E.C.

For my own information will you kindly let me know just what the present debt of the national party is, and how much of this debt is due to the national campaign of last year? I shall very likely have occasion to use these figures soon and wish to have them accurate. Please let me know the amount advanced to the campaign committee from the national treasury by order of the N.E.C. and the amount of debt left by the campaign committee to be liquidated from the national party treasury when it wound up its affairs. In a word, I wish to know the amount for which the national campaign committee "went into the hole"; the difference between its receipts and expenditures, which bankrupted the national party treasury.[6]

There is no good reason on earth why the national campaign of last year should have made such a record and should have wound up as a financial millstone about the neck of the party. In no previous national campaign was there any deficit, so far as I know, and there would have been none in this if the party had not been cut in two at the start about the campaign manager, and those who are responsible for that affair are responsible for the present bankrupt condition of the national treasury and the consequent inaction of the party at a time when it should have the fullest command of its resources.

All this I knew very well and could not help knowing from the hour this matter was precipitated at the national convention. I knew it would arrest contributions to the campaign fund as well as paralyze other activities and I was not in the least surprised when comrades and sympathizers who had in previous campaigns been our largest and most liberal contributors indignantly refused to put up a cent.

I am not now recalling this matter because I am fond of raking up unpleasantnesses of the past, but only because it seems that things are shaping to make it necessary to have the causes of some of the present conditions confronting us made clearly known to the party.

The financial bankruptcy of the party is in a large measure responsible, without a doubt, for the inertness that seems to have crept upon it and for the lack of systematic agitation and corresponding enthusiasm which are absolutely essential to the militancy and to the very life of the party organization.

I have been told that during the last six months the party has lost 35,000 dues paying members.[7] Please let me know if this is true. I would like to be advised as to the present number of dues paying members in the national party and also the number and the date when the party membership was at its maximum.[8]

All the conditions throughout the country are in the most favorable possible condition for the socialist propaganda but the national party does not seem to be able, for some reason, to organize and properly direct the work of efficient organization and to inspire and enthuse the rank and file of party membership.

I am sorry not to be able to go to West Virginia in response to the call from there at this time. I would do so gladly if it were not impossible in my present situation. I am down with a severe attack of the grip and am dictating this letter under difficulties, and besides, my own trial will begin soon in the federal court in Kansas and I shall have to leave for there as soon as I get on my feet and clear the decks here of accumulations which require attention.

In closing I earnestly hope you can bring this matter of West Virginia to the early attention of the N.E.C. and that it may not be long before our national party gives to the country some evidence of having interest in Mother Jones and other comrades who while fighting the battles of the working class have fallen into the clutches of a military tyranny.

Yours fraternally
[E. V. Debs]

TLc, InTI, Debs Collection.

1. Work was national secretary of the party from 1911 to 1913.

2. The Paint Creek–Cabin Creek coal miners' strike in West Virginia in 1912-13 was one of the most violent in American labor history. Debs had begun to write

regularly on the strike in the *Appeal* in February 1913, beginning with two articles, "Mother Jones Arrest" and "West Virginia's Disgrace" in the February 22 issue, and before the conclusion of the strike he became embroiled in a bitter intraparty controversy centering on the role played by the party during the strike and the report on the strike made by the party's special three-man investigation committee, composed of Debs, Victor Berger, and Adolph Germer.

3. In a letter dated May 11, 1913, and addressed to President Wilson, the national executive committee denounced the suppression of free speech and free assemblage in West Virginia, the imposition of martial law and imprisonment of "citizens . . . by drumhead court martial," and the destruction of newspapers that had "presented favorably the claims of the striking miners." The letter demanded an investigation of "the condition of civil war in West Virginia" and announced the selection of the above-mentioned three-man committee, which was instructed to "wait upon [Wilson] at your convenience to voice further our indignant protest." *Appeal,* May 24, 1913.

4. In a letter from "Pratt, W. Va. Military Bastile, April 25, 1913," Mother Jones reported that she had been imprisoned "for about eleven weeks" and that among "we poor devils" were "the editor of the socialist paper in Charleston . . . and one of our speakers, John Brown." *Appeal,* May 10, 1913.

5. The *Appeal* had in fact made the West Virginia situation its chief interest, printing Debs's essays on the subject and running on its front pages a series of articles by John Kenneth Turner.

6. The party incurred a deficit of $11,390 in the 1912 campaign. Work attributed the deficit to J. Mahlon Barnes's mismanagement. *Monthly Bulletin,* January 1913.

7. The average monthly dues-paying membership of the party declined about 22,000 in 1913. In February 1913 there were about 110,000 dues-paying members; in June, 80,795.

8. In April 1912 the number of dues-paying members reached 135,436.

John M. Work to EVD

April 8, 1913
Chicago, Illinois

Dear Comrade: —

Your favor of the 4th is at hand. The communication from Charleston, West Virginia,[1] was transmitted to the National Executive Committee on the 3rd inst.

Under separate cover I am sending you copies of the Monthly Bulletin from January, 1912, to date, giving all of the financial statements covering the period of the campaign, and since, also the period of highest dues. The amount of obligations turned over by the Campaign Committee to the National Office proper after election was $11,390.12. You will notice that each monthly statement since then includes some Campaign Receipts and some additional items of deficit. The amount of cash, rent and literature etc., advanced to the Campaign Committee before election amounted to $952.91. The National

Office also paid something over a thousand dollars for office furniture, typewriting machines, etc., which reverted to the National Office after election.

Since election, most of the surplus income, over and above the regular expenses, has been applied toward the payment of the campaign debts. On April first, the amount of obligations (exclusive of the Lyceum Department) was $7395.79. Of this amount, something over three thousand dollars is the remaining portion of the campaign debt. $1,100.00 is money advanced by the State Committee of Washington for dues. The remainder consists of current obligations. The largest amount of dues we ever received in any one month was in April, 1912, the amount being $6799.15, indicating a membership of 133,746. Of course, it is impossible to draw conclusions from the dues for any given month. The average membership for the year 1912 was 118,045. The average membership for the first three months of 1913 is 108,080. I trust that the average membership for the entire year 1913 may equal that of 1912. In the year 1909, the year succeeding the previous presidential campaign, the average membership was slightly less than in 1908.

I am sorry to hear that you have been having an attack of the grip, and hope that you are on your feet again by this time. I have no doubt that you will find the Kansas court anxious to let go.

Fraternally yours,
John M. Work
National Secretary

TLS, InTI, Debs Collection.

1. Presumably the letter written by Harold Houston, state secretary of the Socialist party in West Virginia, criticizing "the paralytic apathy of the national organization" in the West Virginia miners' strike. Cited in David A. Corbin, "Betrayal in the West Virginia Coal Fields: Eugene V. Debs and the Socialist Party of America, 1912-1914," which ignores Debs's efforts on behalf of the West Virginia miners in general, and Mother Jones in particular, before his appointment to the three-man investigating committee in May 1913.

EVD to Sen. James A. Reed[1]

April 22, 1913
[Terre Haute, Indiana]

Dear Senator Reed:—

Allow me, as one of the defendants in the action referred to in your letter to the Attorney General,[2] which I have just read in the

Appeal to Reason,[3] to thank you heartily for the kindly interest and the spirit of fairness evinced by you in the matter of the prosecution of said Appeal to Reason during the last seven years by the several departments of the federal government. We are quite aware that you are not in accord with our economic and political views and therefore appreciate all the more the attitude so clearly indicated in your letter of a square deal even to socialists.

If the Attorney General and the Department of Justice be moved by your appeal to institute an impartial and thorough investigation of this case—and that is all we ask—and he fails to find that his so-called prosecution is as infamous and shameless an instance of persecution to subserve corrupt and selfish interests as ever disgraced the annals of American jurisprudence, each of us defendants will not only accept without complaint but insist upon the maximum penalty of a fine of five thousand dollars and five years in the federal prison.

Thanking you again in behalf of my defendant brothers and myself, and with all kind regards and good wishes, I am

Sincerely yours
E. V. Debs

TLS, InTI, Debs Collection.

1. James Alexander Reed (1861-1944) was United States senator from Missouri from 1911 to 1929.
2. James Clark McReynolds (1862-1946) served as Wilson's attorney general from 1913 to 1914 when he was appointed to the Supreme Court.
3. The *Appeal* (April 26, 1913) printed on its front page Reed's letter to McReynolds, in which Reed said that he did not "agree with the editors of the *Appeal* in most of their utterances" but cited the numerous federal government cases against the paper and asked McReynolds to check carefully to be certain that the pending bribery case against Debs, Warren and Sheppard was not an abuse of power.

EVD to Fred D. Warren

April 25, 1913
Terre Haute, Indiana

My dear Fred:—

Yours of the 24th. and 25th., the latter special delivery, received and carefully noted. A thousand thanks! I prefer to remain here for a couple or three weeks yet on account of my health, but I shall be prepared to leave for Girard or Ft. Scott on an hour's notice, and I will be out anyway just as soon as I can get myself in physical shape.

You are extremely kind and considerate in this matter and I will surely make up for it some time.

The explanation you make of the status of our case in court was exactly my view of it. I shall not leave on Thursday next for Girard as I had intended but continue to do my work here for the present unless I receive a telegram from you to the contrary.

Pollock's decision[1] is a great victory. I have dropped Jake a line in regard to it. I have told him it was his victory and your jubilee. Poor Bone![2] I am beginning to feel sorry for him. He is now near his finish and it will be sad and humiliating enough.

You have a copy of the Hollingsworth article.[3] Miss Lallement[4] is right in saying that the original was returned to me. But in returning it you wrote me saying that you had had a copy of it made and that you would retain this for future use. I take it, therefore, that in your desk or in the files you have a copy of this Hollingsworth article and that you will readily find it. If not please let me know and I will at once send you the original or have a copy of it made for you.

Your idea about the confiscation campaign is great.[5] It will win tremendously. You are at your best in what you say about that trump card and the way you propose to play it. Say, old man, when the psychological moment comes we can unmask our battery and dis-charge a broadside that will lift the plutes out of their confiscated boots. Count me in on that fight from the tap of the drum.

You have noticed, doubtless, that the miners have settled in West Virginia.[6] But the settlement settled nothing and we must go on in our fight. It is the kind of a settlement that has been made before and will be all off before the ink is dry. The coal operators have agreed not to discriminate against union men. This is pure rot. A union man will stand as much show as a man of straw in hell. Soon as things quiet down they will weed out the active union men, the fighters, and leave only the weaklings. In any event we have got to get out Mother Jones[7] and the rest of our people and we have got to derussianize West Virginia and re-establish the right of workingmen to live there and to organize for their self-protection. The Appeal can win this West Virginia fight and I know of no fight that is more important to the whole movement and to us all at this particular time.

Thanking you again and again for your generous and devoted consideration which touches me deeply and which I shall never forget, and hoping that you are strong in body equal to the task before you and that Mrs. Warren is renewing her health and that the boys are happy I remain as ever

                                                          Your old pard
                                                          E. V. Debs

P.S. The article headed "Aggressive Tactics"[8] is intended as a circulation article.

TLS, Warren Papers, Schenectady, New York.

1. On April 22, 1913, Judge John C. Pollock sustained the *Appeal*'s demurrer in the case against Warren and Lincoln Phifer for printing obscene materials in the series of *Appeal* articles exposing conditions at the Leavenworth penitentiary. The case had been pending for eighteen months.

2. Harry J. Bone, federal prosecutor for the District of Kansas, who had secured many of the indictments against Debs, Warren, and others connected with the *Appeal* during the preceding half dozen years.

3. A search of the *Appeal* for 1913 turned up no Hollingsworth article, but the reference may have been to the material collected by Debs's Terre Haute friend, the Rev. James Hollingsworth, and published as *What Debs' Neighbors Say About Him* during the 1912 campaign.

4. Effie D. Lallement wrote "The Appeal Army" column for the paper.

5. The *Appeal* was promoting Fred Warren's pamphlet *$2,000 Per Year and a Six Hour Day*, in which he proposed confiscation as the means of "acquiring possession of the property now owned by the capitalist class."

6. The terms of the April 1913 contract between the UMW and the West Virginia coal operators called for a nine-hour day, semimonthly pay, miners' selection of check-weighmen, and no discrimination against union miners, but many of the original demands of the miners were ignored and, as Debs predicted, "the settlement settled nothing." In an effort to force acceptance of the settlement, West Virginia Governor Henry D. Hatfield threatened to deport workers who rejected the settlement and effectively shut down the socialist papers in the state.

7. In "The Appeal to Reason's Greatest Victory" (*Appeal*, June 14, 1913), Debs claimed that the *Appeal*'s relentless exposure of conditions in West Virginia, sent to "every village, every town, and every cross-roads in West Virginia," had forced the release from the bullpen of Mother Jones and some fifty others during the period May 15-22, 1913.

8. An unsigned editorial praising the *Appeal*'s "aggressive attitude and its determination to carry the fight into plutocracy's camp" appeared in the *Appeal* on May 3, 1913.

EVD to Fred D. Warren

April 25, 1913
[Terre Haute, Indiana]

My dear Fred: —

I think the Belgium victory the greatest victory ever achieved by the working class.[1] I am sure that many of our people far underestimate its historic significance. I have written an article that I think fairly states what I believe should be the Appeal's size-up of this great achievement. You can publish this with or without my name as you prefer. It is rather long but it could not be made shorter and do justice. I hope you can give it space in the Appeal and I believe it ought to have first page. I can think of nothing that carries with it a livelier message or more inspiring and awakening tidings to the American people. But if you should think it too long for the Appeal you can if you wish send it to Simons for the C.N. and he will only have to change the words Appeal to Reason to Coming Nation where they appear. But I hope for the Appeal that you can play it up in the Appeal.

Have sent an article on Bouck White's book[2] to Simons for the C.N. and have this morning a wonderfully fine letter from White. He is a great light and has the blood of Christ in his veins and the passion of Christ to serve humanity in his soul.

Yours always
Gene

TLS, Warren Papers, Schenectady, New York.

1. In "Belgium's Great Victory" (*Appeal*, May 10, 1913), Debs praised the equal-franchise victory of the Belgian workers, who had combined their economic and political power with great success and with "no syndicalism, no sabotage, no 'propaganda of the deed,' and no 'direct action.' "

2. Bouck White was pastor of the Church of the Social Revolution in New York City. His book *The Call of the Carpenter*, which portrayed Christ as a revolutionary "proletaire," was praised by Debs in "Bouck White's Great Book" (*Coming Nation*, May 10, 1913) as "the greatest book I have read since *Les Miserables*."

EVD to Claude G. Bowers

May 3, 1913
[Terre Haute, Indiana]

Dear Claude: —

The press dispatches announce that Senator Kern[1] is determined on the West Virginia investigation. This to me is extremely gratifying and I earnestly hope the senator will compell action in spite of the protests of the criminal coal barons represented up to this time in the senate by the Elkinses, Scotts, Watsons and Chiltons.[2]

I have been in West Virginia weeks at a time and the situation there cries to heaven. There is nothing in Russia or Mexico more utterly and damnably despotic and debauching. A thorough investigation would result in disclosures that would shock and horrify this nation. I know whereof I speak. The bullpen rule which now prevails

in West Virginia in flagrant violation of both national and state con-
stitutions, is a burning disgrace to the whole nation.

Every labor organization in the country, I verily believe, will back
up Senator Kern in his fight for a congressional investigation. Entirely
aside from the supreme urgency of this demand on grounds of justice,
decency, and humanity, no act Senator Kern could now perform would
strike a more responsive chord in the breasts of the toiling masses.

I am sending you a copy of the Coming Nation and some copies
of the Appeal containing special articles on the West Virginia situation.
The whole world of labor is aroused over it and especially over the
lawless, brutal, utterly infamous kidnaping and bullpenning of Mother
Jones, eighty years of age, and her associates. They are slowly murdering her and in a few weeks more it will be too late for she will be
beyond help.[3]

The Appeal to Reason has had John Kenneth Turner, whose articles
on "Barbarous Mexico" started the revolution in that country, in West
Virginia several weeks, incog, and he is now preparing a series of
articles that will put in the shade anything and everything heretofore
written exposing corporate greed, rapacity, corruption and crime.[4]

I have just sent a long dispatch to the Appeal to Reason (they go
to press today) urging all its readers and sympathizers to write to
Senator Kern and back him up in his fight. You may be sure that we
will all stand by him to the full extent of our power.[5]

I know the senator is at present under a tremendous pressure and
so I write this to you, asking that you bring my letter to the senator's
attention at a time when he is not harassed by other exactions, and
that at the same time you present to him my sincere personal regards.

Believe me with all good wishes,

Yours faithfully

E. V. Debs

TLc, InTI, Debs Collection.

1. On May 2, 1913, Indiana Senator John Worth Kern, for whom Bowers worked
as an administrative assistant, introduced in the Senate a resolution calling for a
congressional investigation of the West Virginia miners' strike.

2. Stephen Benton Elkins (1841-1911) was United States senator from West Virginia from 1895 until his death; Nathan Bay Scott (1842-1924) from 1899 to 1911;
Clarence Wayland Watson (1864-1940) from 1911 to 1913; and William Edwin Chilton
(1858-1939) from 1911 to 1917.

3. In "To the Rescue of Mother Jones" (Appeal, May 3, 1913) Debs declared that
"the murder of this grand old lady at 80 years of age, in a bull-pen, will be on our
heads" if workers did not support the Appeal's "war on the lawless coal barons of
West Virginia." As noted, Mother Jones was released from the bullpen on May 15,
1913.

4. Turner's articles filled most of the columns of the *Appeal* in the spring of 1913.
5. Debs's "Demand Investigation" appeared in the *Appeal* on May 17, 1913.

Claude G. Bowers to EVD

May 7, 1913
Washington, D.C.

Dear Sir:—

Your letter and telegram to Senator Kern, received; also the resolution adopted at the Mass Meeting in Terre Haute.[1]

The Senator desires me to say that he is really convinced with the information in his possession that conditions in West Virginia are infinitely worse than they have been pictured and that there is no influence which can be brought to bear upon him that can prevent him from pushing the resolution to the utmost. He hopes to get favorable action upon it today or within a few days[2] and desires me to thank you for the support you have given the resolution. I may add for your information, that the Senator has received a very pitiful telegram from Mother Jones and a letter from Brown[3] and the other men now incarcerated in the bull pens of West Virginia.

Your Mass Meeting has brought forth a harvest in the form of a great many letters from Terre Haute, all of which can be used advantageously. It may interest you to know that one representative of Wall Street who is an old time friend of Senator Kern, called him over the phone and asked him to drop the resolution and that Senator Kern's words in reply were "I will see you in h—— first."

With kind regards, I am,

Yours very truly,
Claude G. Bowers

TLS, InTI, Debs Collection.

1. On Sunday, May 4, 1913, a joint meeting of Terre Haute socialists and the Central Labor Union passed resolutions denouncing "the reign of terror" against the workers of West Virginia and demanded a congressional investigation. *Terre Haute Tribune,* May 5, 1913.

2. The Senate voted to approve an investigation on June 7, 1913.

3. John W. Brown was a national organizer and speaker for the Socialist party. He described his experiences in the West Virginia miners' strike in "Military Despotism in West Virginia," *Coming Nation,* May 3, 1913.

EVD to Claude G. Bowers

May 10, 1913
Terre Haute, Indiana

Dear Friend Bowers:—

I have read with keen interest the account of the clash in the senate yesterday in the press dispatches this morning. I drop you this line to tender my congratulations to Senator Kern upon his fearless stand in behalf of the enslaved and outraged workers of West Virginia.

Chilton is notoriously attorney for the mine owners; the same is true of Goff.[1] The former is a democrat and the latter a republican but both are representatives of the railroad and mine-owning interests. There is politically no shadow of difference between them. Neither of them represent West Virginia as a state; both represent corporate property and have feathered their nests good and plenty in that capacity. When Chilton said that all he had against Hatfield[2] was that he was a republican some socialist member ought to have been in that body to ask him to explain the difference between his brand of democratic politics and Hatfield's brand of republican politics.

Chilton's comparison between West Virginia and Indiana[3] Kern should shoot full of holes when the matter comes up on Tuesday. It is true that a number of labor leaders were tried at Indianapolis for alleged dynamiting and rushed to the pen by special train which had been contracted for a month before they were convicted (and this point ought surely to be scored) but that whatever may be said about this, and much remains to be said and will be said, the right of free speech, free press and free assemblage prevail unquestioned in Indiana and no law-abiding labor organizer has ever been slugged and bull-penned, no labor meeting has ever been broken up by a mob of corporation hirelings as was done in Huntington, W.Va. a few days ago, and no martial law has been declared to jail labor unionists who could not be lawfully convicted in any court on earth. It is notorious that for twenty years West Virginia has been in the clutches of the coal trust and the railroad trust and it is equally notorious among the workingmen of the country that when a union man enters West Virginia to preach unionism and to help his fellow-workers out of slavery he does so at the risk of his life. Hundreds have been slugged and driven out of there and if the proof is wanted the United Mine Workers can furnish it.

If the senate declines to investigate in the face of such an overwhelming demand, or if the resolution is emasculated or made abortive so it will fail of its purpose while pretending to serve it, there will be a country-wide protest and the tide of indignation now rising will rise higher and higher until President Wilson and congress are compelled to act in the enforcement of the constitution in West Virginia or there will be a widespread working class revolt and insurrection, with which all liberty-loving citizens will sympathize, and I want to say very frankly that I will do all in my power to incite the revolt and precipitate the crisis. If Mother Jones who has violated no law can be murdered before our eyes at the command of corporate brigands and there is no law to protect her, then I should feel that we are not only a gang of slaves, as Wendell Phillips[4] said, but a gang of contemptible cowards fit only to be trampled down and spat upon if we did not rise in revolt against such tyranny and misrule.

Yours very truly
E. V. Debs

P.S. I see that my dispatch to Senator Kern[5] has been published in the New York Papers.

TLS, InU, Lilly Library, Bowers MSS.

1. Nathan Goff (1843-1919) was a congressman from West Virginia from 1883 to 1889 and United States senator from 1913 to 1919.
2. Henry Drury Hatfield (1875-1962) was governor of West Virginia from 1913 to 1917 and United States senator from that state from 1929 to 1935.
3. In opposing the Kern resolution calling for an investigation of conditions in the West Virginia miners' strike, Senator Chilton compared the imprisonment of socialists and union leaders in the West Virginia coal strike with the December 1912 conviction in the federal court of Indiana of some forty officers of the Bridge and Structural Iron Workers Union in the aftermath of the McNamara case. In "Chilton and Goff" (Appeal, May 24, 1913), Debs called the two senators and Governor Hatfield "tools and allies of the robber coal barons."
4. Debs frequently cited Phillips as having been a profound influence in shaping his early career. See "Wendell Phillips: Orator and Abolitionist," Pearson's, May 1917.
5. Debs's letter to Senator Kern, dated May 5, 1913, assured Kern that "the whole working class will back you" in "turning on the light in West Virginia" and "calling Hatfield's bluff" (New York Call, May 6, 1913).

EVD to Adolph F. Germer

May 14, 1913
Terre Haute, Indiana

Dear Comrade Germer:—
Your telegram dated 10.33 P.M., 13th. inst., has been delivered this morning, 8.15 A.M. It is very strange. On receiving your telegram

yesterday advising me of action of committee[1] I at once wired you acceptance and followed this up with a letter, both in care of Work. I cannot understand why these have failed to reach you, at least the telegram. If you are away from national headquarters I should think they would have sent you the telegram.

You say the national committee desires immediate action. I am glad of it. But the action is two months behind at best. Had the national executive committee acted as it had the power to do and as it was its duty to do two months ago there would today be a different situation in West Virginia. Had it been Berger and Spargo[2] in the bullpen instead of Mother Jones and John Brown the N.E.C. would not have waited until the whole country was seething and action was finally forced upon national headquarters where it should have originated.

Yes, certainly I accept and I shall be ready to leave in a couple of days, as soon as I can possibly get the most important matters I have in hand in shape to leave them. You and Berger will probably go direct from Chicago via B.&O. to Charleston. I shall go from here there. From there we can go into the coal fields together, it being only a few miles.

Please let me know when you expect to leave Chicago and I will know about how to time my schedule. I have a couple of brief stops to make en route but these will detain me but a few hours.

By the way, I wrote Work[3] yesterday asking about my appointment on this committee. I saw a report of it in the press dispatches of the morning papers on Monday but received no notice until your telegram came into my hands Tuesday noon. Thinking it strange I received no earlier notice and not knowing if the reported action of the com mittee as it appeared in the papers was true I wrote to Work for information. I now make this bit of explanation so you may know how I happened to write to Work.

Looking forward with pleasure to meeting you and hoping we may be able in some measure to make up for lost time and render some actual service to our comrades in the bullpen and to the party and to the movement I am as ever

Yours fraternally
E. V. Debs

TLS, WHi, Germer Papers.

1. The special committee to investigate the West Virginia miners' strike, composed of Debs, Germer, and Victor Berger, was appointed at the national executive committee meeting on May 10, 1913. Berger and Germer were members of the five-man committee.

2. John Spargo was a member of the national committee (seventy members) of the party from Vermont.

3. Walter Lanfersiek of Kentucky was elected national secretary to replace John Work at the committee meeting on May 10.

EVD to Theodore Debs

May 17, 1913
Cincinnati, Ohio

My dear Kude:

Arrived here ok. Met Germer at Indianapolis where he got aboard train. Had good nights sleep & we leave at noon for Charleston. Engdahl[1] is to meet us here & serve as correspondent of committee. Berger is not here — told Germer The Leader[2] needed him badly — had to raise money for it. I guess its in hard straits. He probably wants to wait to see if we get slugged & then will show up in time to go to White House to see Wilson.[3]

Will arrive at Charleston at 6 this evening. Frank Hayes[4] is there.

Send my mail, papers & all, to *Charleston W.Va.* till I advise you otherwise. Be sure & send the Monday morning mail to me there so it will get away on the 117 pm noon train — Shall keep in close touch with you. St. Car strike here is on — saw near riot at Fountain Square this am. Hope the poor Devils will win but it's doubtful. No cars are running & the streets are swarming with police mounted & afoot & in patrol wagons

Love & kisses to you all

Your old pard
Eugene

ALS, InTI, Debs Collection.

1. J. Louis Engdahl (1884-1932) was for a time editor of the *Chicago Daily Socialist* and in 1910 was a delegate to the party congress in Copenhagen. He edited the party paper, *American Socialist,* until World War I and was, with Germer, Berger, and others, given a twenty-year sentence (reversed on appeal) for violation of the wartime Espionage Act. After the war, Engdahl joined the left-wing secession from the Socialist party, helped found the Communist party, and later edited the Communist party paper, the *Daily Worker.*

2. Berger's paper, the *Milwaukee Leader.*

3. It was originally intended that the committee would report its findings to the president.

4. Frank J. Hayes (1882-1948) was international vice-president of the UMW from 1910 to 1917 and president from 1917 to 1920. He was at this time directing the union's strategy in the West Virginia coal strike.

W. H. Thompson[1] to EVD

May 19, 1913
Kanawha County Jail, Charleston, West Virginia

On the morning of May 9, between the hours of 1 & 2, George W. Gillespie,[2] R.M. Kephart,[3] F.M. Sturm[4] and myself were arrested by the sheriff of Cabell County,[5] at our respective homes in the city of Huntington and incarcerated in the county jail. The sheriff had as his authority for this action a written order from Governor Henry D. Hatfield.

While the sheriff was carrying out his part in this outrage, a squad of state militia under command of Major Tom Davis and Lieutenants Templeton and Rippertoe proceeded to the plant of The Socialist Printing Co., where they kidnapped Elmer Rumbaugh,[6] a reporter for The Socialist & Labor Star who happened to be in the building at the time. The soldiers then proceeded to wreck the entire plant, presumably because the mechanical work on The Star was done thereat. The printing of The Star is only a small part of the business of The Socialist Printing Co, which, by the [way] was is [sic] a corporation authorized to do business by the state of W.Va. This, however, mattered little to the wreckers who, after beating to a worthless mass of wreckage the "forms" of The Star, which were then ready for the press, they proceeded to demolish the job department, destroying material, breaking presses and even commercial job work ready for delivery was torn open and scattered over the streets. Type and pieces of machinery were picked up the following morning 4 squares from the wrecked office. The militia then proceeded to my home where my sick wife had been left alone by my arrest, and ransacked the entire place, carrying away numerous private papers, letters and books. It may be said to the credit of the sheriff that he protested against both the destruction of the printing plant and the searching of my home, pointing out to the soldiers that no legal papers had been issued ordering this. They, however, told him that they had *secret orders* and so the outrage was consumated. Friday evening the sheriff was ordered, by wire, to deliver us to the militia. We protested vigorously against this last action, claiming, as citizens of Cabell County, the protection of its officials and courts. Our protests were unavailing and we were brought to the Kanawha Co. Jail at Charleston Friday night.

F.M. Sturm, who at one time was business manager of The Star but who had not been connected with the paper for several months, was released Friday night. R.M. Kephart and Geo. W. Gillespie, president and treasurer of The Socialist Printing Co. were released Sat urday night, it being learned that they were in no way responsible for The Star's utterances. Rumbaugh and myself have been held here, absolutely "incommunicado," since our arrest. No mention of a trial has ever been made and in fact we do not know with what crime or crimes we are charged.

The loss to The Socialist Printing Co. is estimated at $2000.00.

It will be noticed that all acts of the officials were committed under cover of darkness—our arrests, the destruction of the plant, the burglary of my home, the release of the other comrades—all in the wee sma hours[7]

W. H. Thompson

ALS, InTI, Debs Collection.

1. Wyatt H. Thompson was editor of the *Huntington* (West Virginia) *Socialist and Labor Star.* His account of the suppression of his paper by the Cabell County sheriff and a state militia unit is substantially corroborated by the contemporary socialist and nonsocialist press and by testimony given to the Senate special committee that investigated the West Virginia coal strike.

2. Gillespie was treasurer of the Socialist Printing Company in Huntington, which published the *Socialist and Labor Star.*

3. Kephart was president of the Socialist Printing Company.

4. Sturm was formerly business manager of the *Socialist and Labor Star.*

5. Bonner Hill.

6. Rumbaugh, better known later as the author of labor songs and leader of the bitter Bisbee, Arizona, strike, was released from jail on May 20, 1913. *Kanawha Citizen,* May 22, 1913.

7. In "Report on West Virginia" (*Appeal,* June 14, 1913), Debs cited "the assault on the Star" as "especially brutal and outrageous" and relied heavily on Thompson's account in describing the episode.

EVD to Theodore Debs

[May 23, 1913]
Charleston, West Virginia

My dear Kude:

Two interviews with Governor yesterday. All the boys out. Martial law will be ended. Everything is settled. Socialist papers will be started up again. No more slugging of organizers. Tremendous victory.[1] We go into Cabin Creek today and tomorrow. Send no more mail here. Hold till I get back. See *June Metropolitan.*[2] Fine as a fox. Expect to be home soon. Kisses

Your old pard
Eugene

ALS, InTI, Debs Collection.

1. In the "Official Report on West Virginia," which was widely published in the socialist press, Debs, Germer, and Berger largely exonerated Governor Hatfield and placed most of the blame for the troubles in West Virginia on Hatfield's predecessor, William E. Glasscock (1862-1925), whose term as governor ended on March 3, 1913, and who was blamed for the imposition of martial law; the creation of the military commission; the court-martial and imprisonment of Mother Jones, John Brown, and some fifty other socialist and labor leaders; and the bloody attacks on miners' tents and cabins by mine guards. As the chief author of the report, Debs was strongly attacked in a number of socialist papers, including the *Socialist and Labor Star*, in which Wyatt Thompson called the report (June 13, 1913) "a weak mass of misstatements" and "a sickening eulogy of dictator Hatfield." In "Vilifiers of the West Virginia Committee Report" (*St. Louis Labor*, June 12, 1913), Debs identified the critics of the report as "Chicago I.W.W.-ites" who, he said, "are seeking to disrupt and drive out the United Mine Workers to make room for the I.W.W."

2. The issue carried a long article by Allan L. Benson, "The Last Families of West Virginia," an indictment of the coal barons of the state and the living standards of workers there.

EVD to Robert B. Sims[1]

May 23, 1913
Charleston, West Virginia

Dear Mr. Sims: —

Pardon this belated acknowledgement of your favor of the 14th inst.[2] which has been forwarded from Terre Haute and has only now reached me here.

I regret that in my present situation it is not possible for me to make such answer to your communication as I would like to do under more favorable circumstances.

The measure now pending in the State of Arizona providing for the abolition of the death penalty is one that should appeal to every just and humane person in the State. Capital punishment is simply a relic of barbarism. There is absolutely no justification for its survival in our present civilization. The taking of human life through criminal impulse or in an hour of passion by an individual is not to be compared to the immeasurably greater crime committed by the State when it deliberately puts to death the individual charged with such crime.

Society may not consistently condemn murder as long as it is itself red-handed with that crime.

We are now sufficiently enlightened to understand that what is known as crime is in a large measure due to unfortunate environment; that crime is in fact a disease, an infirmity, and that every consideration of humanity demands that the unfortunate victim of society's weakness or maladjustment, shall be treated with the same degree of patience, and with all the skill that science has made available, that is bestowed upon other human derelicts and infirmitives.

The people of Arizona have shown themselves to be so progressive and so entirely abreast of the enlightened spirit of the times in so many other matters that I feel safe ~~confident~~ in predicting that she will follow the lead of other progressive States and blot this insufferable stigma from her fame.[3]

Thanking you for your kindness and with all good wishes, I remain

Yours sincerely,

[Eugene V. Debs]

TLc, InTI, Debs Collection.

1. Robert B. Sims (1876-1951) was one of the framers of the Arizona Constitution in 1910 and served as warden of the state prison at Florence from 1912 to 1922.

2. Sims's letter, which was sent to "Authoritative National Leaders," asked Debs to comment on a proposal to "eliminate capital punishment from our penal code."

3. In December 1916, Arizona abolished the death penalty but reinstated it in December 1918.

EVD to Editor,[1] *Pittsburgh Socialist*

June 1, 1913
[Terre Haute, Indiana]

Dear Comrade:—

Your communication with copy of Justice enclosed has been received. I have no time to answer the drivel which the latter contains. I was told at Charleston that Merrick[2] was furious because he had been released from jail, that he denounced and repudiated the efforts of his attorney, his friends and his family in his behalf. It is quite fitting that these silly charges and stupid falsehoods should be corroborated in the same issue by the malicious lies published in the papers owned and controlled by the mine owners.[3] I can pity Merrick but I have no answer to make to his ravings.

In the next few days you will receive, as will all socialist papers, a full report by our committee and then you will be able to judge as to what the foundation there is for these insane rantings. Had our committee utterly failed in its mission and its members had been slugged and jailed besides and the situation in West Virginia were irretrievably disastrous then quite likely the extremists and wild men who would have the working class we have served for forty years regard us as feeble-minded children, would acclaim us as wise and wondrous leaders.

Yours fraternally
Eugene V. Debs

TLc, InTI, Debs Collection.

1. Isador Ladoff.

2. Fred Merrick published *Justice* in Pittsburgh and was a Debs supporter at the 1912 socialist convention. When Charles Boswell, editor of the *Charleston Labor Argus*, was arrested in March 1913, Merrick went to Charleston as temporary editor of the paper and was himself arrested on May 2, 1913. He was released, along with Mother Jones, John Brown, and others, during the week of May 15, 1913. While Debs felt that the investigating committee deserved credit for the release of the prisoners in West Virginia, Merrick was one of the strongest critics of the special report and what he considered its whitewash of Governor Hatfield.

3. As noted, criticism of the West Virginia committee report appeared in a number of socialist publications, notably the *International Socialist Review*, and in labor publications, as well. In the *American Federationist* (October, 1913), Samuel Gompers denounced "the clean bill of health given to the Governor" and wondered about "the sanity or honesty of the Socialist committee."

Mrs. C. D. Merrick[1] to EVD

June 2, 1913
Parkersburg, West Virginia

My dear Mr. Debs:

I am sorry that I have been so slow in getting my thanks off to you. Surely it has been in my heart every day since you left W.Va. The lasting help you have been to our oppressed Commonwealth. You came just at the opportune hour to add and aid us as I view it and I want you to understand how gratefull I shall ever be for the Service rendered.

Ever since a little girl of seven years I heard my Anti Slavery father scorn oppressors, to the day of his death when we wrapped him in his Country's flag which he so loved I have in a peculiar way for a woman shared his interest in State and National affairs—and it has deeply hurt me, the disgrace our Supreme Court[2] has brought upon us. I have an abiding faith that when man reaches his Extremity he has help in prayer—in the Unseen—and I certainly have had re-

course to this Agency during these recent weeks in the U.S. Senate.[3]
So I want to thank you for all you have been, and are to W.Va. and
for the inspiration you have been to Fred[4]—it is not lost and may
the coming days bring you the cheer and Comfort you so richly deserve

Believe me as sincerely

Mrs. C. D. Merrick

ALS, InTI, Debs Collection.

1. Addie H. Merrick, Fred Merrick's mother, whose assessment of Debs's role in
West Virginia at the time differed markedly from Fred's.
2. Possibly a reference to a decision handed down in December 1912 by the West
Virginia Supreme Court, which approved the imposition of martial law and creation
of a military commission by Governor Glasscock in his efforts to deal with the miners'
strike.
3. After prolonged debate, the Senate voted on June 7, 1913, to create a special
committee to investigate the West Virginia miners' strike.
4. In a letter written during Debs's imprisonment (April 25, 1920), Mrs. Merrick
recalled having met Debs in 1906 when Fred Merrick "introduced me to you." Debs
had signed a photograph at the time and it was "framed for Fred," and had had "an
abiding place . . . on our library wall."

EVD to Fred D. Warren

June 2, 1913
Terre Haute, Indiana

My dear Fred:—

Enclosed please find draft for $250. This was handed to me by
Paulsen[1] for the miners when I left Charleston to be sent to the *Appeal*
and credited the same as the amount sent you some days ago. Please
send receipted bill for printing same as before to Paul J. Paulsen, Box
953, Charleston W.Va.

I came back thoroughly tired out. The work at Charleston was one
of the most difficult, trying and delicate I ever had anything to do
with. I was busy from 18 to 20 hours every day and night I was there.
The greatest trouble is not with the mine owners but to keep peace
on our own side. There are a few wild men there who were bound
to tear things wide open and have the union miners and socialists tear
others bowels out. We studied the situation carefully and made individual pleas and brought unfriendly parties together and finally
suceeded, I think, in putting things in shape to promise a better future.
One or two I.W.W.ites are doing their best to set socialists and union

miners at each other's throats but I don't think they will succeed. We had them altogether in meeting but when we were face to face with them they had but little to say. But I am hopeful for the future. If we can prevent outbreaks among our own people the future is secure. We have nothing more to fear from the mine owners or the politicians, but only from ourselves. Strange, isn't it?

We have certainly made staunch friends among the miners in West Virginia. They all love the Appeal and hail it as deliverer.

When I left there the officials all without exception assured me that the service which had been rendered was invaluable and would never be forgotten. Returned so dog tired from the anxiety and excitement and strain and loss of rest that for a couple of days I was limp as a rag. But I am shaping up again and will send you an article on West Virginia and other copy soon.

You will receive a copy of our report within the next two or three days, in time for the next issue.[2] I am satisfied that our mission was entirely fulfilled and that results will prove it. I do not wish to make any boast but all things considered I feel satisfied with what was accomplished. The mine owners and their henchmen, abetted by the few wild men on our side, did all in their power to create open rupture on our side and blow us to atoms in self-destructive strife, and that they were thwarted for the time at least was due, I believe, and so do the miners, to the patient, painstaking and tactful way in which the situation was handled. As for the governor and others in office they gave us no excuse to fight and it would have been madness and utterly destructive on our part if we had denounced them after they had conceded in the most decent manner possible everything the party sent us there to ask for. Merrick is shrieking that we were led into a trap. But Merrick was furious when he was let out of jail and has denounced everybody, including Houston,[3] his lawyer and best friend. He can do no possible good there nor do I think he can do any harm for he is generally regarded as a rampant and reckless mischief-maker. The opinion is freely expressed that he is unbalanced and it certainly seems so.

Yours
E. V. Debs

See enclosed envelope. This puts it over you out of sight and leaves you utterly in the shade and hopelessly distanced.

TLS (with handwritten note and signature by Theodore Debs?), Warren Papers, Schenectady, New York.

1. Paul Jasper Paulsen (1870-1940) was state secretary of the Socialist party in Wyoming from 1908 to 1912 and a member of the UMW international executive board from Wyoming from 1911 to 1918.

2. Curiously, despite Debs's defense of the "West Virginia Committee Report" (*Appeal*, June 14, 1913), the *Appeal* continued to publish John Kenneth Turner's stories on conditions in West Virginia, which seemed to support the position of the critics of the report. See, for example, "Judas Hatfield Unmasked" (*Appeal*, June 21, 1913), in which Turner insisted that Governor Hatfield was "equally guilty with Glasscock" and had gone "to even greater extremes than Glasscock with military rule."

3. Harold W. Houston, socialist attorney and UMW counsel from Charleston, West Virginia.

EVD to Claude G. Bowers

June 7, 1913
Terre Haute, Indiana

My dear friend Bowers: —

Your favor of the 3rd. inst. has been received. The speeches and copies of the Congressional Record requested by me have also come for which please accept my thanks.

I am quite sure that all our people will do their utmost to make the investigation serve its intended purpose and I am also confident that in spite of all the efforts that will be put forth to the contrary the investigation will produce a harvest of good results. The Socialist party and the United Mine Workers will each have competent counsel on the ground, lawyers that are thoroughly familiar with the situation and who know how to have the essential facts incorporated in the testimony and placed upon the record for the public benefit.

The attitude of Senator Kern toward the Socialist party has been exceptionally fair, high-minded and courageous and I am sure that socialists throughout the country give him full credit.

I note what you say in regard to Governor Hatfield. You may be right in your estimate but with all my prejudice against him I am bound to say that he could not have treated our committee more fairly nor shown a more commendable spirit and purpose in protecting the miners and in making possible for the first time the organization of the workers in West Virginia. Of course I am not insensible to the fact that a great change came over him but I am not disinclined to withhold such credit as may be due him {on that account,} without reference to the motive that impelled such change. Not only Hatfield, but almost everybody else in West Virginia official life, civic and military, experienced the same change when Senator Kern announced his determination to force the investigation and backed up his words with actions that will be remembered to his credit for all time.

You may be sure that we are all deeply sensible of the powerful influence this investigation from its inception has had upon the West Virginia situation and how greatly we are indebted to Senator Kern, Senator Reed, Senator Borah and others who forced the measure through in spite of the powerful influences that sought its defeat.[1]

As to our report it contains the facts as we found them and if certain features of it are favorable to Governor Hatfield it is only because the governor's actions were such as to preclude any other kind of report without falsifying the facts. He could not possibly have treated us more courteously or more fairly and as he conceded every solitary thing we contended for, and even tendered us the use of a special train in behalf of the state, which we declined, we could not report otherwise than we did. You will see that we excuse him of nothing he is justly responsible for but hold him to a strict accountability for his acts.[2] The entire report was not handled by the press and I am having the national executive secretary send you a copy of it.

I am glad you are to speak in Boston. You will be delighted with the experience. I never enjoy speaking more than in old Faneuil Hall which is always packed to the doors and full of the spirit and alive with the memory of the old patriots. You will meet with a royal reception there and you will win fresh laurels as an orator.

With kind remembrances to Senator Kern and warmest wishes to you both I am

Yours sincerely
Eugene V. Debs

TLS (typed signature), InU, Lilly Library, Bowers MSS.

1. William Edgar Borah (1865-1940) was United States senator from Idaho from 1906 until his death. In "The Investigation" (*Appeal*, June 21, 1913), Debs praised Kern, Reed, and Borah for pushing for the West Virginia investigation in the Senate but speculated that "such an investigation would have been impossible a few years ago" before "the recent amendment which provides that senators shall now be elected by a direct vote of the people."

2. In "Committee Report on West Virginia" (*Appeal*, June 14, 1913), which was Debs's elaboration of the report itself, he claimed that Hatfield's "gravest official misact" was the suppression of the *Socialist and Labor Star* and the *Charleston Labor Argus*.

William E. Borah to EVD

June 9, 1913
[Washington, D.C.]

My dear Mr. Debs:

The Senate Committee authorized to investigate conditions in West Virginia, particularly in the Cabin and Paint Creek country, will open its meetings tomorrow, and I am writing you as a member of the Committee knowing that you have lately been in that territory. If there is any information which you feel that you can send me which would be helpful in making the investigation I should be very glad to hear from you.[1] We are anxious to get as thorough gathering of the facts as possible, and knowing you had lately been in the territory I thought there might be things which you would be able to give the Committee which might be very helpful. Of course any statement which you make will be treated as confidential unless you state in your letter that it may be used. You can write me at Charleston, W. Va., general delivery.

Very respectfully,
Wm. E. Borah

TLS, InTI, Debs Collection.

1. Debs's letter to Borah (if any) in response to this invitation has not been found, but he wrote to Borah on June 26, 1913, suggesting names of "those participants in the strike who were most relentlessly persecuted" who had not been "permitted to appear before the committee at all." InTI, Debs Collection.

EVD to Editor,[1] *Socialist and Labor Star*

June 16, 1913
Terre Haute, Indiana

Dear Comrade:—

Please give me space for a few words. In your issue of June 13th. you have an article covering several columns entitled "Socialists Failed as Investigators" and sub-headed "Their Report a Weak Mass of Misstatements in Regard to Present Conditions and a Sickening Eulogy of Dictator Hatfield."

You sweepingly condemn the report of the committee, but you do not publish it.

Please publish in your next issue along with this a few of this "mass of misstatements" and also an extract or two from the "Sickening Eulogy of Dictator Hatfield."

If there is in our report a "Mass of Misstatements" and a "Sickening Eulogy of Dictator Hatfield" our report should be repudiated; and if you have brought false charges your paper should be repudiated.

The report speaks for itself. Let the rank and file read and judge.

Yours fraternally
Eugene V. Debs

TLc, InTI, Debs Collection.

1. Wyatt H. Thompson.

W. H. Thompson to EVD

June 17, 1913
Huntington, West Virginia

Dear Comrade Debs:

Upon returning from Charleston today, after spending four days trying to get to tell my story to the Senate Investigating Committee, I find your kind letter of the 13 inst[1] for which I thank you.

One sentence of your letter is such a co-incidence that I can't refrain from writing you again on the subject. You say: "You will, of course, get your story in its entirety before the Senate Committee."[2]

You will probably be surprised when I tell you that despite my best efforts for four days I was unable to get on the stand   nor has anyone of the other comrades who was persecuted under the Hatfield administration ever been put on the stand.

There is some mysterious League of interests, in which the U.M.W. of A. attorneys are an important adjunct, which is protecting this murderous tyrant, and no word of testimony relating to his official acts can be gotten into the record. You have no doubt discovered by now that Mother Jones, Brown, Boswell,[3] Parsons,[4] and others *were tried and sentenced after Hatfield* assumed the governor's robe.[5] He was inaugurated March 4th and their trials began March 7th. Not one of these victims was ever put on the stand.

Boswell and myself had a private talk with Senator Swanson yesterday and one of the first things he asked us was "why is everybody trying to shield Hatfield?" He told us he would try and have us summoned before the committee when it returned to Washington. You see they are hearing here only the witnesses put on by the attorneys for each side and "our" attorneys "excuse" us.

Just what Hatfield "has on" the U.M.W. of A. officials I can't say,
but that they dance when he plays no one can deny.

Yours for the Cause

W. H. Thompson

ALS, InTI, Debs Collection.

1. Debs's June 13 letter to Thompson has not been found, and his June 16 letter
to Thompson (above) apparently had not reached Thompson.
2. The committee, a subcommittee of the Senate Labor and Education Committee,
was composed of Claude Augustus Swanson (1862-1939) from Virginia, William Squire
Kenyon (1869-1933) from Iowa, James Edgar Martine (1850-1925) from New Jersey,
John Knight Shields (1858-1934) from Tennessee, and Borah. The committee held
hearings June 10-18, 1913, in Charleston.
3. Charles H. Boswell, a delegate to the 1912 socialist convention from West
Virginia, edited the *Charleston Labor Argus*. He was arrested and court-martialed in
March; the *Labor Argus* was suppressed on May 2, 1913.
4. George S. ("Fleet") Parson, a socialist organizer in Kanawha County, West
Virginia, was described in the *Kanawha Citizen* (March 23, 1913) as a "leader of the
troubles . . . on Paint Creek" who had been "sent to the Mason county jail at Point
Pleasant . . . to await the findings of the military commission."
5. The "Committee Report on West Virginia" had stated that "it was under the
administration of Glasscock and not Hatfield that Mother Jones, John Brown, C. H.
Boswell and numerous others were court martialed and convicted." In "A Correction
of Error," which appeared in the *Party Builder* (July, 1913), the *Appeal* (August 2,
1913), and in many other socialist, labor, and capitalist papers, Debs acknowledged
that Mother Jones, Brown, Boswell, "and other comrades" were "tried under the
Hatfield administration." Their trials had occurred on March 7, 1913, three days
after Hatfield was inaugurated and Debs claimed that he had "somehow gotten the
impression that they were tried before instead of a few days after the close of the
Glasscock administration."

Henry D. Hatfield to Theodore Debs

June 18, 1913
Charleston, West Virginia

My dear Mr. Debs:

I thank you most sincerely for the copy of the Terre Haute Star,[1]
together with other literature sent me recently by you.

I had quite a nice chat with the Honorable Eugene V. Debs during
his sojourn in Charleston, and I assure you that my interview with
him was refreshing and satisfactory. Mr. Debs, I feel, upon his arrival
in Charleston had the wrong opinion of my attitude, and I was indeed
very glad to have an opportunity to tell him personally of my position

upon all matters that interested him and his mission in the State of West Virginia.

I hope I may have the pleasure of meeting you some time and making your acquaintance.

Again thanking you, and assuring you of my appreciation of your thoughtfulness, believe me

Yours most sincerely,
H. D. Hatfield

TLS, InTI, Debs Collection.

1. The accounts of the West Virginia strike in both the *Terre Haute Star* and the *Tribune* reflected Debs's interpretation of the Socialist party committee's mission and success in West Virginia, including praise for Governor Hatfield, who "did not abuse the strikers" as his predecessor had done and who had released those imprisoned (*Terre Haute Star,* June 4, 1913; *Tribune,* June 14, 1913).

EVD to Adolph F. Germer

June 19, 1913
Terre Haute, Indiana

My dear Germer: —

Many thanks to you for the copy of the "Report of the Ninth International Report of the Trade Union Movement" for 1911. I shall be glad to look over this as soon as time will allow and put it on my book shelf for further reference. I know there is much in this volume that will be of interest and value to me.

Let me suggest that the national committee should take some action on our West Virginia report, either to accept or reject it, and I suggest that a motion to approve be made to bring the matter before that body for action. Suppose you drop Berger a line in regard to it. So far as I know our report is entirely satisfactory to the party at large. You have doubtless seen Merrick's violent attack upon the report in general and myself in particular. Of course this was to be expected. And similar attacks from similar sources must also be expected but they will amount to little except in the possible mischief they may do in deceiving the uninformed. But it is necessary for obvious reasons that the national committee should act on our report. It ordered us to do a certain thing. We did it and reported and the report should now be accepted or rejected. I anticipate future attacks and in anticipation of these and in justice to ourselves we must know if what we have done has the approval of the national committee, representing the national party, or not. Once our report is approved, as I have every reason to believe it will be, our acts become the acts of the party and as such those who are now assailing us for having done our duty will be silenced.[1] You undoubtedly see the point.

The investigation was far too short at Charleston. I am keenly disappointed, especially as the most important witnesses seem to have been shut out. Please tell me if you can why Mother Jones, John Brown, Boswell, Thompson and Merrick, yes Merrick, were not put on the stand by our attorneys. It is utterly inexplicable to me. Why was not Governor Hatfield himself made to testify as to his acts? I am informed that Swanson of the Senate committee asked "why is everybody trying to shield Hatfield?" It has been broadly hinted that the U.M.W. has from first to last sought to shield Hatfield and to prevent anything reflecting upon him and his administration from coming before the committee. If there is anything in this I want to know it and I will fight it from the drop of the hat, no matter who may be defending it. What the country wants is the truth, the whole truth, regardless of who is hit, whether it be Hatfield or anyone else, and if the officers of the U.M.W. and our attorneys are in collusion to prevent any part of the truth from coming out, which I would be very loath to believe, I want to know it. There is certainly something suspicious in Mother Jones and John Brown and Boswell and Thompson having been denied the right to appear before the committee and testify.[2] I am going to demand in the Appeal as loudly as I know how that the committee hear them either at Washington or by returning to Charleston and I know that millions will join in that demand.[3] But first of all I want to know why they were shut out so I may be sure of my ground. The U.M.W. is all at stake in this affair and if any weak-kneed or crooked officials are conniving to keep the truth from being told and to shut out some of the most damnable testimony of all, such as the wrecking of the Star plant, then I propose to turn on them and fight them to a finish, and go into West Virginia to do it. Please write me at your earliest convenience. You can use this letter as you may see fit.

With warmest wishes

Yours always
E. V. Debs

TLS, WHi, Germer Papers.

1. At the following national executive committee meeting, July 12-14, 1913, which Germer attended, motions were approved to send additional organizers into West Virginia and to lend Wyatt H. Thompson $100 for repair of the *Socialist and Labor*

Star plant, but no formal action was taken on the special committee report. *Party Builder,* July 19, 1913.

2. Germer wrote to Debs (July 8, 1913) that he was "not sure we should insist upon them [i.e., Jones, Boswell, Brown, and Thompson] appearing from that fact that their movements are known minutely and their testimony will not only injure the case that has been established before the Committee, but some of the boys might be involved in serious complications." Said Germer: "This is particularly true of Brown and Boswell and neither of them showed any special anxiety to testify."

3. In "In West Virginia" (*Appeal,* July 12, 1913), Debs attacked the Senate committee's exclusion of witnesses and the protection of Governor Hatfield and declared that "only the truth, the whole truth about West Virginia will satisfy the *Appeal.*"

EVD to W. H. Thompson

June 19, 1913
[Terre Haute, Indiana]

Dear Comrade Thompson: —

Your favor of the 17th. inst. has been received. I have been looking in the daily reports for your testimony and that of Mother Jones, Brown Boswell and others and had begun to wonder why none of you comrades were placed on the stand. And now your letter advises me that you sought in vain for a hearing and were denied. This seems strange and mysterious to me and on the strength of your letter I have written to Germer asking why you and the comrades above named were not given a chance to testify. It may be that for some good reason you are to be given a chance to testify before the full committee at Washington or before the sub committee at Charleston when it returns there as it probably will according to the press dispatches.[1]

I am both amazed and disappointed that the committee did not remain longer on the ground and make its investigation more thorough and exhausting. It strikes me that much of the most valuable testimony on our side has not been heard at all. For instance one of the most outrageous incidents in the whole affair was the destruction of the Star plant,[2] and I say this notwithstanding I have no personal reason to feel partial toward the Star. But the outrage is undeniable and every particle of testimony in regard to it ought to have been brought before the committee with a view to fixing the responsibility where it belongs.

I have objected to Hatfield being condemned for what Glasscock[3] was responsible for, but I have insisted also that Hatfield should be held accountable for all his acts. I supposed he would be placed upon the stand and questioned thoroughly as to what has actually taken place under his administration. It now appears that he was not subpoenaed or examined at all and this certainly seems strange to me.

What the country wants is the truth, no matter who is hit or hurt by it. Less than that, whatever the purpose may be in evading or suppressing it, will only result in making matters worse.

The Senate committee could not possibly hear all our hundreds of willing witnesses and get at the bottom facts in the short space of time given to the investigation. I confess that the fact that neither Mother Jones, Brown, Boswell or youself was put upon the witness stand looks suspicious to me and I have so stated in my letter to Germer and told him that if there was anything behind it I wanted to know it and that if it were not straight I would fight it to a finish.

I not only took it for granted that you and your comrades would have a chance to testify in detail as to the destruction of your plant and the burglarizing of your home, but I also supposed you would be eagerly summoned by our lawyers and that every detail would be brought out and put upon record, and I counted much upon the effect the true story of this crime would have upon the general public.

There may be some good reason for all this and if so I shall be glad, but it certainly is inexplicable to me why those who have suffered the bitterest persecution and the cruelest outrages have not been heard at all. You intimate, or rather charge, that there is some league of interest in which U.M.W. attorneys are involved to suppress certain incriminating testimony. I am loth to believe this for it seems impossible to me, but if there is any truth in it I want it known and I have so stated in plain terms in my request for information. So far as I am concerned I want the truth known and I should insist upon that even if I myself were condemned by it. I want no one unjustly condemned and no one unjustly shielded.

There is something wrong with anyone connected with this affair who is not willing that every particle of material testimony shall be brought out and every material fact brought to light.

You inform me that in a conversation you and Boswell had with Senator Swanson he said to you "Why is everybody trying to shield Hatfield?" It strikes me that this has significance. If there was or is any purpose to shield Hatfield I do not know what it can be. You have accused me of this in your columns but without a shadow of justification and you will some day admit it. I wanted Governor Hatfield relieved of the blame where he was not responsible and there I drew the line sharply saying in my statements that I wanted him held responsible for every act of his administration, and I supposed all along he would be placed upon the stand the same as Glasscock was and that our lawyers would examine him thoroughly and put upon record exactly what he did in reference to the strike, that he might be judged accordingly. This has been and is my position and I believe it to be the right position and in fact the only position to be taken if equal and exact justice is to be done to all concerned.

Fred Merrick has treated me outrageously and you have acted anything but fairly toward our committee, but no matter. If I had been at Charleston and had had any influence I should have insisted on both you and Merrick taking the stand and telling your story to the country. Both of you were imprisoned in defiance of your lawful rights and I so stated to Governor Hatfield, and this fact should have been made a part of the report of the Senate investigation.

If there is any collusion to suppress testimony as you charge and I can get satisfactory proof of it, I shall expose it and fight it with all my strength no matter who may be involved.

Yours fraternally
Eugene V. Debs

TLc, InTI, Debs Collection.

1. The committee finished its hearings in Charleston on June 18 and resumed hearings in Washington from September 4 to 13, 1913.

2. In "In West Virginia" (*Appeal*, July 12, 1913), Debs called the destruction of the *Socialist and Labor Star* "one of the most outrageous incidents in the reign of lawlessness and crime in West Virginia" and urged "the senate committee to place Editor Thompson and his associates upon the witness stand . . . to tell their story."

3. William Ellsworth Glasscock (1862-1925) was governor of West Virginia from 1909 to 1913 and was blamed in the "Special Report on West Virginia" for almost all of the offenses against the socialists and miners. Glasscock defended his policies before the Senate committee on June 13, 1913, and Debs acknowledged in his "Correction" statement that Glasscock had been mistakenly blamed for some acts—the trial and imprisonment of Mother Jones, for example—that should properly have been attributed to Governor Hatfield.

W. H. Thompson to EVD

June 21, 1913
Huntington, West Virginia

Dear Comrade Debs:

Many thanks for your kind letter of the 19 inst which I believe requires an answer, to some of the points raised, at least.

In the first place in looking over the many things I have said about the Socialist Investigating Committee's report it appears that I have

used your name in connection therewith and almost totally excluded
Germer and Berger. This would be easily understood by the West
Virginia comrades but might be construed, by those unacquainted
with the real feeling here, to mean that we were deliberately making
a scapegoat of you, and trying to shield the other members of the
committee. This arises from the fact that we never expected anything
from Comrades Berger and Germer. They were hopelessly prejudiced
against the so-called "red-element" and in which they have been
pleased to place us. They were committed to the U.M.W. of A. be it
right or wrong, and we were satisfied that they would see things
through U.M.W. of A. eyes.[1]

Therefore, as I have said before, our one hope was, that you would
get an inkling of what we *knew* so well, and that the report would
give some of what we considered the ~~facts~~ real vital facts—or a
minority report by yourself would result.

Now, to begin at the beginning: Socialism in West Virginia is growing so rapidly that it is becoming a real menace to the "too" old
parties. (90 per cent. of the Union miners are Socialists).[2] Hatfield
being a very astute politician hit upon the brilliant scheme of [setting]
the Mine Worker's organization and the Socialist organization at each
others throats; and I am sorry to say that he succeeded—with the
mine workers, at least. There are numbers of Jesuits[3] high in official
circles of the U.M.W. of A. who love socialism about as well as we
love modern capitalism. These men were willing to accept Hatfield's
rather fickle promise of protection for their organization in exchange
for their "influence" against Socialism—and the deal was made.
Thereupon the persecution of Mine Workers officials ceased abruptly
and the war of extermination upon the Socialists was begun. The
M.W. had been supporting the Argus[4] financially during the strike.
This support was suddenly transferred to the capitalistic and treacherous Kanawha Citizen,[5] and a Catholic priest[6] was employed to contribute articles *against* Socialism. The governor then suppressed The
Argus and when The [Star dropped] into the breach it too [felt] the
"Iron Heel." The day after The Star was suppressed Thomas Haggerty[7]
of the M.W. publicly commended the governor's actions in The Citizen, saying: "I want to say that I heartily approve of Gov. Hatfield's
efforts to restore peace in the coal fields. I believe he has the interests
of the laboring men at heart and is doing the very best an able, strong
and honest man can do." At this time both Socialist papers had just
been put out of business and 20 Socialists were in jail.

The agreement {and arrangement} between the Gov. and the M.W.
officials to crush the Socialists was being actively carried out when

the National Ex. Com. appointed you and your co-workers to come into the state and *co-operate with the U.M.W. of A.*!

[We knew] that a desperate effort would [be made] to prevent you from learning [the] real facts, and with most all of those who knew these facts in jail, they would succeed. The fact that they did succeed is fully bourn out in the report. It doesn't make any difference what interpretation you put on the wording of the report it has been accepted by everybody else as a complete exoneration of Hatfield and this fact remains.

Then comes the Senatorial Investigation and meets with the same reception from the M.W. as did our Committee—a determination to shield their fellow conspirator, Hatfield and to ignore the wrongs done the Socialists. On top of all this comes your letter telling me you have written to Germer *demanding the truth*—why not write Haggerty—or Hatfield?

I am trully sorry that it has fallen to my lot to be compelled to criticize the Socialist Committee's report, but that report can never be accepted by the West Virginia Socialists, as a true and fair representation of conditions here when it was written. We had to attack the report in self-defense for the capitalistic papers were running it as a justification of the things they had said about us and as a complete exoneration of the Dictator.[8] Personally, I have never doubted your sincerity for a monent, but, I do believe, with thousands of other West Virginians, that you permitted youself to be *outrageously deceived and used by as crooked a bunch of "leaders" as ever skuttled a labor union.*[9] Believe me

Fraternally yours
W. H. Thompson

ALS, InTI, Debs Collection.

1. Adolph Germer had been for many years an officer of the UMW in Illinois and a leader in the effort to win over the union to socialism.

2. In the 1912 election, West Virginia socialists had cast more than 15,000 votes for Debs, double the number cast in the 1910 off-year election and three times the number cast in 1908. *Appeal,* January 4, 1913.

3. In both membership and leadership, Roman Catholics played dominant roles in the UMW and more generally in the American Federation of Labor. In the latter by 1918, Catholics made up a majority of the membership, dominated the executive board, and held the presidencies of fifty international affiliates. Mel Piehl, *Breaking Bread* (Temple University Press, 1982), 36.

4. *Charleston Labor Argus.*

5. Published in Charleston, the *Kanawha Citizen* was launched in September 1912 soon after the miners' strike began. It was, to be sure, capitalistic—it regularly warned miners against "the wanton destruction of property" (September 23, 1912)—but it gave considerable space to statements by miners' spokesmen, letters from miners, and

other pro-miner material (see "Both Sides Have Grounds for Their Respective Positions," December 13, 1912) and front-page coverage to the socialist investigating committee ("Eugene V. Debs Talks of the Industrial Situation in West Virginia," May 19, 1913; "Debs Talks of Things of Interest to the American Workingman," May 22, 1913).

6. In West Virginia the Catholic hierarchy's opposition to socialism was led by Patrick James Donahue (1849-1922), who was bishop of Wheeling, West Virginia, from 1894 until his death. Called "the holy hypocrite" by socialists, Donahue had much influence among the miners of the state, whom he warned of the evils of socialism. In May and June 1913 the *Kanawha Citizen* printed a series of articles, "Socialism versus Social Liberty," by Father Thomas H. Collins of Montgomery, West Virginia, and reprinted the series in its June 14, 1913, edition because, it said, the editions in which the articles had appeared had been "bought up."

7. Thomas Haggerty was a member of the UMW national executive board in charge of the miners' strike in West Virginia.

8. Hatfield.

9. In Corbin, "Betrayal in the West Virginia Coal Fields," the Socialist party committee report and Debs's defense of it are blamed for the defection of a number of West Virginia socialists from the party.

John W. Brown to EVD

June 21, 1913
Charleston, West Virginia

Dear Comrade Debs:

I have calculated on writeing you several times since you left here and strange as it may seem this is the first chance I have had when I realy felt like writeing. I think I told you while in Clarksburg two years ago about a weakness or a kind of a doupy spell I passed through. Well, I have had another one. The last few days I was in jail I used to lay down about 23 hours out of 24 and couldnt keep my mind on a colum article even when the subject was the Kern resolution.

I made up my mind that what I needed was a stimulant, and when we were released I went after the "Corn Juce," and made out to get around for a few days. However, I knew something else was the matter, and the day after you left here I called in a physician. I had to cut out tobacco, which I had been chewing ever since I was ten years old, also all beverages that carried any alcohol! which I did, and my boy, — well, let it suffice to say that I had a few cold sweats. However, I am beginning to feel fine now, and if this feeling continues to grow I will be able in six months to clean out the guards myself.

As to the investigation, of cours you have seen by the press reports what came of it, the admission of Quinn Morten,[1] and others, but there are things the investigation has not brought out, and these things puzzel me. Our side has nothing to hide, and couldnt hide it if we wanted to, but there is a deseided efford to screne Hatfield, Sheriff Hill and the whole official machinery of the state. This became very ~~appearant~~ apperent when during the cross examanation of Lee Calvin, an ex. Balwin Guard,[2] it looked as tho Bonner Hill was to be draged in, Belcher,[3] one of the atorneys for the Miners jumped up and reccommended to the Committee that it was not their intention in any way shape or manner to implicate Mr. Hill. In fact, they wanted him held exempt from any responsibility for the shooting up of Holly Grove.[4] Aside from this by-play, there are other devalopments that stagger the emagination at times.

For instance, the "Kanawha Citizen" which has been supporting the strike (for a price, of course) has taken to runing quite lengthy articles against socialisim by a bunch of "Holy Fathers" and it is not hard to diserne the motive back of it. In the meantime the socialists are being eliminated so far as their taking any active part on the fireing line is consirned as fast as it is expediant to do so.

I would not be suprized to see Houston resigne any day, and if he does it simply means that once again the poor miners are to be turned over to the Jesuites. As to the settlement. Comrade, there has been no settlement. Every active man on both creeks is blacklisted. On Paint Creek they are forced to mine a long ton, where prior to the strike they mined a short ton, while as for the Guards they are just as arragant, insolant and overbearing as ever, and ere this letter reaches you I shall be much surprized if a greater strike than ever will not be on.[5]

As for Merrick. Well, there is only one thing to do with a freek and that is to let him run wild. The scrap betwen Boswell and Haggerty[6] is prahaps unfortunate. There is many things transpiring here that smack of the Jesuite, and it would surprize you to know to what extent this thought extends. Many of these miners are Masons, American ~~mechamis~~ mechanics and Junior A.M.[7] and in and out of the mines it is safe to say that 80% of those who are in any way interested are with Boswell. And not only that, but several of the National Board members who have been in here and *Taken out for cause* are writeing Boswell and assuring him of their support. From now on the scrap will be betwen Boswell and Hagerty and will in no way involve the movement. Will advise you as to future devalopments. Hopeing you trip here did not retard your compleat recovery, and with best wishes to all from Mrs. Brown and myself.

I am sincerely yours,
J. W. Brown

TLS, InTI, Debs Collection.

1. Quinn Morton (1858-1925) was president of the Kanawha Coal Operators Association and chief spokesman for the operators before the Senate investigating committee in Charleston. In "Investigation Comment" (*Appeal*, July 5, 1913), Debs described Morton as "insolent, defiant, and arrogant" in his testimony and accused Morton of being responsible for and personally involved in the "Massacre Train"—called the "Bull Moose Special"—episode in which the operators sent an armored train into the coal fields to "shoot up the shacks and tents of women and children under cover of night." When asked by Senator Kenyon if he had ever considered arbitration "if only for humanitarian motives," Morton responded, "Never, sir."

2. The Baldwin-Feltz Detective Agency had its headquarters in Bluefield, West Virginia, but it provided mine guards during strikes throughout the country. In the *Appeal* of June 7, 1913, John Kenneth Turner reported that the agency employed 2,000 men, who were usually called thugs or scabs or worse in the labor and socialist press. On June 14, Lee Calvin, who had been on the Massacre Train, described to the Senate committee "how the armored special train riddled the coal camps." *New York Times*, June 15, 1913.

3. A. M. Belcher, a Charleston attorney who served as counsel to the UMW in the Senate committee hearings.

4. The miners' tent city at Holly Grove, near the mouth of Paint Creek, was the chief target of the Bull Moose Special.

5. Citing "violations on the part of the operators" on Paint and Cabin creeks and in the Coal River field, on June 27 Thomas Haggerty called for a new strike on July 1, 1913. *Kanawha Citizen*, June 28, 1913. A new agreement—"Peace With Honor," the *Kanawha Citizen* called it on July 9—was reached during July 1913, only to be followed by charges of contract violations by both sides the following month. *Kanawha Citizen*, August 24, 1913.

6. On June 4, 1913, Charles H. Boswell, editor of the recently reopened *Labor Argus* and recently released from jail, was arrested on a warrant sworn by Thomas Haggerty, who charged criminal libel against Boswell for describing Haggerty in a May 30 issue of the *Labor Argus* as "a traitor to the miners." *Indiana Socialist*, July 1913.

7. The Order of United American Mechanics and its offspring, the Junior Order of United American Mechanics, were secret fraternal organizations dating from the nativist ferment of the late nineteenth century. Their programs generally called for immigration restriction and for close attention to the "Catholic peril." John Higham, *Strangers in the Land* (Rutgers University Press, 1955), 57-58.

Theodore Debs to Editor, *Our Sunday Visitor*[1]

June 21, 1913
Terre Haute, Indiana

Dear Sir:—

My attention has been called to an article in your paper under date of June 22nd., signed by "Rev. C.J. Kluser."[2] I shall make no attempt to answer all the falsehoods contained in this article but I wish space enough only to point out one specific instance of such falsification that your readers may know the character of the man who makes these charges.

I want to show you conclusively that Mr. Kluser has made false charges and I want to show you quite as conclusively that he knew thay were false at the time he made them.

Mr. Kluser, quoting from the Appeal to Reason of two separate issues, quotes my brother, Eugene V. Debs, as saying: "The Appeal pays me $100. a week" and "It is true that the Appeal has been paying me $100. a week."

But Mr. Kluser—and mark you his disreputable method—quotes that and stops there. If he had been an honest man he would have quoted the rest which showed that out of that one hundred dollars per week my salary, as my brother's assistant is paid, typewriters are employed, office rent, postage, telegraphing and other office expenses are paid, so that as a matter of fact my brother's actual salary, after all these expenses are paid out of his allowance, does not amount to one third of one hundred dollars per week, and does not more than cover the living expenses of his family. This statement was clearly made in both the articles from which Mr. Kluser quotes, but this priest of God, deliberately omits this for the deliberate purpose of deceiving your readers and discrediting Mr. Debs.

This is the actual truth and Mr. Kluser dare not quote from the files of the Appeal without exposing himself as a wilful, wicked and malicious falsifier by charging that my brother's salary is one hundred dollars per week when he knew at the time he made his charge that this allowance of one hundred dollars not only covered my brother's salary, but the salaries of his assistants and all other office expenses.

What do you and your readers now think of the Rev. C. J. Kluser?

If space allowed and I were so inclined I would follow him through his tirade step by step and prove him out of his own mouth to be guilty of the grossest falsification and calumny.

But one more instance will suffice.

Mr. Kluser charges that my brother received $5,000. for his meetings during the presidential campaign last fall. This is another made-to-order, unqualified, deliberate and malicious falsehood. The records at the national headquarters of the Socialist party, 111 N. Market st., Chicago, Ills., are open for inspection. The actual truth is that my brother received just enough to cover his traveling expenses, stenographer's services, postage, telegraphing and hotel bills. He received not one single dollar for his services. The fact is that the entire allowance did not cover expenses and that when the campaign was over my brother was actually out of pocket. Now let Rev. C.J. Kluser produce his proof or stand convicted as a vulgar falsifier and conscienceless slanderer. The ridiculous charge that my brother and I live in mansions is beneath our contempt.[3]

I am not willing to believe, Mr. Editor, that you would knowingly give currency to such malicious calumnies, more especially if they issue from the throat of a professed minister of God.

Yours respectfully
Theodore Debs

TLc, InTI, Debs Collection.

1. John Francis Noll (1875-1956) founded and became editor of *Our Sunday Visitor* in 1912. Founded to respond to *The Menace,* an anti-Catholic paper published in Aurora, Missouri, the *Visitor* was sold to Catholic pastors for a penny a copy and sold for a nickel or given away at churches and quickly became one of the popular and influential Catholic apologetic journals, reaching by the 1920s, it was claimed, more than half the English-language Catholic churches in the country. Noll was bishop of the Fort Wayne, Indiana, diocese from 1925 until his death, a tireless worker in the Midwest and on the national level in the effort to win acceptance of Catholicism by a predominantly Protestant society.

2. The Rev. Charles Joseph Kluser (1856-1939), a Catholic priest from Morgantown, West Virginia, was a leading critic in that state of socialism in general and of Gene Debs in particular. In a letter to Theodore Debs, dated April 17, 1913, Kluser recalled that he had publicly called Debs "an unmitigated liar" in 1911 and said he "still [stood] by my charge." His article in *Our Sunday Visitor* was called "An Open Letter to Theodore Debs."

3. Gene Debs's home (built in 1890) and Theodore's home (built in 1911) were both substantial two-story dwellings with full basements and attics, but neither would have been considered a mansion by the standards of the time or later. In the case of Gene Debs's home, the charges that it reflected aristocratic taste, was too luxurious for a union man and socialist, etc., were frequently raised, especially during his presidential campaigns.

William E. Borah to EVD

June 23, 1913
[Washington, D.C.]

My dear Mr. Debs:
Your letter of the 21st to hand.[1] If you find upon investigation that there were some witnesses who ought to have been placed on the stand who were not I shall be glad to have their names and the subject to which their testimony would be addressed. There were witnesses whom we could have used but their testimony seems to have been wholly cumulative and the Committee felt that after a principle was thoroughly established or a general course of conduct thoroughly established that we might save the cost of merely cumulative testimony. However, I am sure the Committee is desirous of having all the material testimony. I shall be glad to hear from you at any time you have anything to suggest in this matter.

Very respectfully,
Wm E Borah

TLS, InTI, Debs Collection.

1. Debs's letter to Borah of June 21, 1913, has not been found, but it presumably contained his complaint that Mother Jones, John Brown, and others had not testified in Charleston.

EVD to William E. Borah

June 26, 1913
[Terre Haute, Indiana]

My dear Senator Borah:—
Your favor of the 23rd. inst. has been received and noted. Answering your inquiry I beg to say that there are a number of witnesses who should in my opinion be heard by the Senate committee but who were not given the opportunity to present their testimony at the Charleston hearing. It appears that some of those participants in the strike who were most relentlessly persecuted and suffered the greatest wrongs were for some reason I am unable to understand not permitted to appear before the committee at all. I have reference to Mother Jones, who could undoubtedly give testimony that would have weighty influence with the committee and be of interest to the country; also

John Brown, W.H. Thompson, C.H. Boswell, Fred Merrick and others, some of whom were seized outside of the military zone[1] and tried and sentenced under martial law in violation of their constitutional rights. It seems to me that all such testimony as this which comes at first hand from those who were active participants in the troubles under investigation would be of value in arriving at a just conclusion and clearing up this unfortunate situation.

I have taken the liberty in some correspondence with Brown and Thompson in the last day to suggest that they write to you in regard to being heard by the committee. I can give you all their addresses if you should wish to communicate with them, or with any of them, direct.

I have wondered why none of the state and county officials of Kanawha county were placed upon the stand and questioned as to their participation in and knowledge of certain acts and facts in connection with the strike and the trials and convictions under martial law which have been so bitterly condemned and have provoked such widespread resentment.

Complaint has been made in letters I have received that powerful influences have been brought to bear to shield Governor Hatfield, Sheriff Hill and other state and county officials. What foundation there is, if any, for this charge I do not know but certainly I hope that before the Senate committee has concluded its labors it will have brought before it every person of whatever rank or degree, official and otherwise, whose testimony is necessary to have every essential fact brought out that the responsibility may be placed where it properly belongs and that such measures may be taken as may be deemed necessary to prevent a recurrence of the terrible wrongs which the miners of West Virginia and their wives and children have suffered during the past fifteen months.

If there is any well grounded suspicion that any person or set of persons, be they whom they may, are shielding from the consequences of their acts, the confidence the people now have in the fairness, fearlessness and rigid impartiality of the committee will suffer and the effect of its findings and the value of its work will be correspondingly impaired.

I have no reason to believe that the committee has been other than fair and conscientious in reference to the desire to hear all material testimony and this I am certain {is true} in a special sense of yourself and Senator Martine.

I take this occasion to call your particular attention to the case of W.H. Thompson and his associates and the suppression of his paper, The Socialist and Labor Star, at Huntington, the looting and destruction of the newspaper property and the burglarizing of his home and the carrying away of his private papers by a squad of soldiers after midnight. I think this one of the most outrageous affairs that ever occurred under a civilized government and that every one who had to do with it should be ferreted out and punished to the full extent of the law. The soldiers in this instance carried on their work of destruction and pillage over the protest of the sheriff and this can be proved beyond any question of doubt.

And yet I am informed by Mr. Thompson that after vainly waiting for four days at Charleston he was turned away and denied the opportunity to tell his story.

If there is any act of cruelty and outrage and of utter defiance of constitutional and lawful rights in connection with the West Virginia strike it is the wanton destruction of this newspaper property and the midnight sacking of the editor's home after being thrown into jail without warrant and without the least knowledge as to the reason why.

Huntington, bear in mind, was far beyond the military zone when Thompson and his associates were seized and thrown into jail at midnight by a squad of soldiers, their property which was a general publishing concern, destroyed, smashed, torn into shreds and scattered about for blocks, including orders to the general trade ready for delivery, and when Thompson's home was entered, after he was jailed, and his wife, who was ill, subjected to the terrors of such a barbarous attack, while the soldiers went from room to room, searched every drawer and ransacked and carried away with them private papers and letters, with all the brutality and bravado of Russian cossacks. I avouch that I know enough of this particular case to warrant my saying to you that every material fact here stated can be substantiated by incontrovertible testimony before your committee.

Let the members of the Senate committee imagine if they can just how they and their wives would feel if they were seized and torn from their homes at midnight by a squad of soldiers without knowing why, thrown into jail without warrant, their homes sacked and their private letters and papers stolen, what they would think of the United States constitution, and what sentiments of patriotic devotion to their country would be inspired in their breasts!

Enclosed I beg to hand you an article I have written in which this matter is more fully presented.[2]

Pardon me for having written you at such length. I well know how busy you are and I should not have ventured to intrude upon your time under any other circumstances.

Thanking you for your kind and considerate attention and with all good wishes for the success of your work and for you personally I remain

Yours very sincerely
[Eugene V. Debs]

TLc, InTI, Debs Collection.

1. Governor Glasscock's proclamation of September 2, 1912, limited the area in which martial law was imposed to Kanawha County, West Virginia, then further limited its boundary within that county. Some of the arrests were made in Huntington (Cabell County), fifty miles outside the zone.

2. Probably "Investigation Comment" (*Appeal*, June 28, 1913), in which Debs dealt at length with the committee's Charleston hearings.

EVD to John W. Brown

June 26, 1913
[Terre Haute, Indiana]

My dear John Brown:—

I have read your letter of the 21st. and have read it carefully and with deep interest. I knew you were not your physical self when I was at Charleston and for that reason you will remember that I advised a period of quiet and rest and freedom from excitement to give you a chance to recuperate. I now see that something was working on you that, if unchecked, would have undermined your health. If the "spell" you had will be the means of permanently cutting out "the juice" it will be all the better for you, and in this I know whereof I speak.[1] You will be all the better off and so will your wife and children if you will draw the line sharp on the booze and keep it there the rest of your days. It can do you no possible good but it may do you infinite and irreparable harm. This is not intended as a sermon but I could not help saying this much after the opening you made for it. I applaud your pluck in "cutting it out" and all I have to say is, stick to it!

I note what you say about the investigation and I am entirely agreed with you. If there has been any attempt to screen Governor Hatfield or anybody else it is without my knowledge or approval. On the contrary I advised and urged in all I have said and written, privately and publicly, the most searching investigation, regardless of who might be hit or hurt.

I have been unable to understand why you and Mother Jones, Boswell, Thompson and Merrick were not called before the committee to testify. It may be that for reasons I do not understand or on account of possible developments later that you did not want to testify. But anyway it has seemed to me that those who were most persecuted and hounded were the ones who should have been given the fullest chance to present their cases. I have a letter from Thompson telling me that he was anxious to testify but denied the chance. I am taking this matter up with Senator Borah with whom I have been in correspondence since the opening of the investigation. The senator has asked me to make any suggestions I wish and I am writing and urging that you and Boswell and Thompson and Merrick be heard by the committee either at Washington or at Charleston. At the same time I am saying to Senator Borah that Mother Jones' story should be heard in full. If she or any of you have testified there has been no report in any paper I have seen.

You can help in this matter if you and Boswell will write to Senator William E. Borah, Washington, and state your cases briefly and your desire to be heard. I think it very important that the matter of the destruction of the Star plant should go into the record and that Thompson and his associates be heard and I suggest that you also write and urge it upon Senator Borah.

So far as I am concerned I want nobody screened and least of all myself. I want the investigation to be thorough and the facts laid bare, all of them, and the responsibility placed where it belongs.

As to whether there has been any "settlement" that is for the miners to decide and I believe they have intelligence enough and stamina enough to decide it for themselves. Mischievous meddling on the part of those who are not miners and who are interested only in destroying the United Mine Workers can only make matters worse.

If, as you say, "the socialists are being eliminated so far as their taking any active part on the firing line is concerned" and if, as you continue, "the poor miners are once again to be turned over to the Jesuits" the socialists themselves, certain of them at least, will not be without blame. The tactics they are pursuing in their mad denunciation of everything U.M.W., good, bad and indifferent, are utterly suicidal and destructive all around.

From my crown to my footsoles I am an industrial unionist but I am not an industrial anarchist. The spirit of Chicago I.W.W.ism is getting in its deadly work in the name of socialism and if it is permitted to go on it will result in wiping out all organization, the Socialist party included, and finally in wiping out the papers through which it found expression.

I know about these matters by bitter experience for as early as twenty years ago I foolishly tried to do with the trade unions what some of the socialists in West Virginia are trying to do with the United Mine Workers today.[2] It is entirely a matter of tactics. The talk about our committee whitewashing Hatfield is all bosh. If our committee had turned on the U.M.W., denounced its officers as crooks and torn it wide open, to the delight of the mine owners, then those socialists who are just enough for political action to cloak their anarchy, would have shouted our praises. But because we refused to commit such a suicidal, asinine and destructive act, we are denounced by these same I.W.W.ites as traitors. Be it so. I would not have it otherwise. I conscientiously did my duty at Charleston and I have no apology to make {to} anyone on earth on account of it.

Yes, "the scrap between Boswell and Haggerty is unfortunate." That is putting it mildly. I foresaw it and did all in my power to avert it until at least after the investigation was over. If Boswell insists that such a fight at this particular time is best for the Labor Argus and best for the Socialist party and for the enslaved miners of West Virginia, then certainly it is his privilege not only to precipitate it but to keep it up, but in the final reckoning he will bear the consequences.

The way to keep reactionary trade union officials where they are is to attack {them} as Merrick has been doing and their followers adhere to them all the more closely. That is one reason why Gompers is still at the head of the A.F. of L. There is a way to attack crooked union officials but it is not by wild and indiscriminate abuse of the organization and everybody connected with it, and that is one reason why "socialists are being eliminated so far as their taking any active part on the firing line is concerned." How could U.M.W. men help but hate socialists if Merrick is a fair representative of the feeling of socialists toward their union? If the attacks that are made were confined to the particular officials that are accused of being crooked and their crookedness were pointed out and made clear in calm and reasonable language, instead of a torrent of invective and abuse launched against the whole U.M.W. indiscriminately, and this day after day and issue after issue, with all the dark hints of treachery and conspiracy thrown in besides, the crooked officials could soon be gotten rid of by the union men themselves and they would thank the socialists for helping them, but never will the policy of the Argus, so far as I have been able to observe it, accomplish the desired result.

There has got to be more of love and kindness than of hate and suspicion and abuse in our propaganda if we expect to win union men to industrial unionism and socialism.[3]

You say that 80 per cent of the miners who are interested are for Boswell and against Haggerty. You may be right but I do not believe you are. If you are right then by all means have the 80 per cent at once unite in a demand to White[4] for Haggerty's withdrawal. White would not dare to leave him there a day if 80 per cent of the rank and file demanded his withdrawal. This is an easy solution of the difficulty and it will also be a confirmation as well as a test of your claim that 80 per cent of the miners are with Boswell. My personal judgment is that if 80 per cent of the miners are with Boswell the Argus would have never been suppressed and Boswell would never have been sent to jail. I do not doubt a good many miners have full confidence in Boswell, but when you come to a show down you will be surprised to see {how} far short they will fall of being 80 per cent of the whole number. I myself have complete confidence in Boswell so far as honesty and integrity are concerned. But I take decided issue with his judgment and with his tactics and whether he is right or I am right time alone can tell.

You are greatly mistaken, Comrade John, when you say that "from now on the scrap will be between Boswell and Haggerty and will in no way involve the movement." Every such quarrel has its roots in causes that are more impersonal than personal. Boswell's friends will back him and Haggerty's friends will back him and there will be the inevitable tearing asunder of such unity as there is and an ugly, bitter, implacable factional fight, just at the very hour when it will save the mine owners and when it will destroy us. I would have averted that quarrel until at least it could have been fought out under other circumstances than those which now exist and when the present crisis was safely over. For the present and until the crisis is past everything else should be set aside and the miners urged regardless of all dif ferences to stand elbow to elbow and heart to heart in every camp throughout the state. That would be my policy but if another is preferred I can not help it and will have to make the most of it, as will also the poor devils of miners and their wives and babies who suffer the whole burden of our folly and short-sightedness, and this lays on my heart so heavily that I have lain awake many a night on account of it.

Just this final word. You will find that sooner or later you will have to take your stand wholly with the Chicago I.W.W.ites[5] or against them. The very hour they find that they cannot dominate you and use you for their purposes they will denounce you as a traitor, ac cording to their code, as they have denounced everybody else.

But come what may my heart is with you and the miners of West Virginia.

I am wishing you and your dear wife and sweet children all the good there is possible in this world. Mrs. Debs, Theodore and I are all uniting in our affection and loyalty to you all.

Yours always
E. V. Debs

TLS, InTI, Debs Collection.

1. This is perhaps Debs's most candid comment on his own drinking problem, which was a source of concern and controversy to his contemporaries and of disagreement among his biographers. The issue was raised in party affairs, especially at national conventions, and was a matter of anxiety to those arranging Debs's lecture tours. A few years after Debs's death, Theodore Debs wrote to William James Ghent that "Gene was in no sense a teetotaler—he took a drink whenever he cared and for this he made neither excuse or apology. It is not apparent to me what this has to do with his public activities any more than if on occasion he drank coffee." InTI, Debs Collection.

2. Debs believed that the American Railway Union, as an industrial union of all railroad workers, would replace the aristocratic craft unions—the brotherhoods—in that industry.

3. In "An Appeal to the Miners of West Virginia" (*Appeal*, June 21, 1913), Debs repeated much of the material included in this letter to Brown.

4. John P. White (1870-1934) was international president of the UMW from 1912 to 1917.

5. The "Chicago I.W.W.ites," led by William Haywood, included in their "Declaration of Principles" a refusal of "all alliances, direct or indirect, with existing political parties."

EVD to W. H. Thompson

June 26, 1913
[Terre Haute, Indiana]

Dear Comrade Thompson:—

Your letter of the 21st. has been carefully read. If your position is right then you should drive Goebel[1] out of West Virginia instead of advertising him in your paper as you do. He will work in harmony with the U.M.W. and do all other things for which you have condemned our committee.

If the U.M.W. is officially an aggregation of crooks then how about Mother Jones and John Brown who are in their service, working hand in hand with them and being paid their salaries by them?

You did not find in all our report a single, solitary thing that you could commend, did you? It was all just one "mass of mis-statements" and "sickening eulogy of Hatfield."

Say, Thompson, you have had a lot of troubles and far be it from me to add a feather-weight to them, but let me ask you when you are in an even mood to go over our report from beginning to end, purely upon its merits, and see if the manner in which you have treated it does not bring a blush to your cheek.

I do not question your honesty, nor have I any reason to. All the more keenly do I regret that a man of your character and intelligence should be so unfair and show such a spirit toward comrades.

Do not imagine that I believe for one moment that what we said or did not say about Hatfield animated you in what you have had to say of us and our report. It is the U.M.W. and its officials that you would have had us tear wide open in that critical situation and nothing less on our part would have satisfied you and Merrick and Boswell and a few others. Had we turned on the U.M.W. officials and denounced them as traitors and started a row that would have torn the union to pieces we would have met your conception of what it was our duty to do, and it would not have mattered much what we said or did not say about Governor Hatfield.

Please do me the justice to charge me with anything other than that I was deceived. That would have been even worse than treason.

How long have you been in the labor movement as unionist and socialist? I do not know but I do know that I have been actively in the movement for thirty-eight years, before you were born, and I know that my insight was never keener, my vision clearer, nor my intuition more unerring than it was at Charleston and if my advice would have been taken there would not now be the ugly row on between the Socialist party and the U.M.W. which threatens the very life of both and which even threatens the papers that are fanning the flame as evidenced by the very diminished size of the last issue of the Socialist and Labor Star.

By the way, in your last issue, after reiterating your contemptuous repudiation of our report (I think it was the last issue) you close with an eager hail to the senate committee and say: "We will now have a REAL INVESTIGATION," or words to that effect, and now after this REAL investigation has taken place you inform me that you were allowed to cool your heels in the ante room of the committee for four days without being given a chance to open your mouth. The investigation then does not seem to have been so REAL after all.

But no matter. I am not writing to gratify any feeling of resentment. I have none. I only want you to get my view-point long enough, if possible, to see some things as I see them for your own good and the good of the cause you are fighting for. You might not be influenced in the least but I am inclined to think otherwise.

In answer to a long letter received from Brown along this same

line I have written him at considerable length and what I have said
to him seems so apropos in this answer that I am going to quote in
part what I wrote to him:

"... So far as I am concerned I want nobody screened and least
of all myself. I want the investigation to be thorough and the facts
laid bare, all of them, and the responsibility placed where it belongs.

"As to whether there has been any 'settlement,' that is for the
miners to decide and I believe they have intelligence enough and
stamina enough to decide it for themselves. Mischievous meddling
on the part of those who are not miners and who are interested
only in destroying the United Mine Workers can only make matters
worse.

"If, as your say, 'the socialists are being eliminated so far as
taking any active part on the firing line is concerned' and if, as
you continue, 'the poor miners are once again to be turned over
to the Jesuits' the socialists themselves, certain of them at least, will
not be without blame. The tactics they are pursuing in their mad
denunciation of everything U.M.W., good, bad and indifferent, are
utterly suicidal and destructive all around.

"From my crown to my foot soles I am an industrial unionist
but I am not an industrial anarchist. The spirit of Chicago I.W.W.ism
is getting in its deadly work in the name of socialism and if it is
permitted to go on it will result in wiping out all organization, the
Socialist party included, and finally in wiping out the papers through
which it found expression.

"I know about these matters by bitter experience for as early
as twenty years ago I foolishly tried to do with the trade unions
what some of the socialists in West Virginia are trying to do with
the U.M.W. today. It is entirely a matter of tactics. The talk about
our committee whitewashing Hatfield is all bosh. If our committee
had turned on the U.M.W., denounced its officers as crooks and
torn it wide open, to the delight of the mine owners, then those
socialists who are just enough for political action to cloak their
anarchy, would have shouted our praises. But because we refuse
to commit such a suicidal, asinine and destructive act, we are denounced by these same I.W.W.ites as traitors. Be it so. I would not
have it otherwise. I conscientiously did my duty at Charleston and
I have no apology to make to anyone on earth on account of it.

"Yes, 'the scrap between Boswell and Haggerty is unfortunate.'
That is putting it mildly. I foresaw it and did all in my power to
avert it until at least after the investigation was over. If Boswell
insists that such a fight at this particular time is best for the Labor

Argus and best for the Socialist party and for the enslaved miners of West Virginia, then certainly it is his privilege not only to precipitate it but to keep it up, but in the final reckoning he will bear the consequences.

"The way to keep reactionary trade union officials where they are is to attack them as Merrick has been doing and their followers adhere to them all the more closely. That is one reason why Gompers is still at the head of the A.F. of L. There is a way to attack crooked union officials but it is not by wild and indiscriminate abuse of the organization and everybody connected with it, and that is one reason why 'socialists are being eliminated so far as their taking any active part on the firing line is concerned.' How could U.M.W. men help but hate socialists if Merrick is a fair representative of the feeling of socialists toward their union? If the attacks that are made were confined to the particular officials that are accused of being crooked and their crookedness were pointed out and made clear in calm and reasonable language, instead of a torrent of invective and abuse launched against the whole U.M.W. indiscriminately, and this day after day and issue after issue, with all the dark hints of treachery and conspiracy thrown in besides, the crooked officials could soon be gotten rid of by the union men themselves and they would thank the socialists for helping them, but never will the policy of the Argus, so far as I have been able to observe it, accomplish the desired result.

"There has got to be more of love and kindness than of hate and suspicion and abuse in our propaganda if we expect to win union men to industrial unionism and socialism.

"You say that 80 per cent of the miners who are interested are for Boswell and against Haggerty. You may be right but I do not believe you are. If you are right then by all means have the 80 per cent at once unite in a demand to White for Haggerty's withdrawal. White would not dare to leave him there a day if 80 per cent of the rank and file demanded his withdrawal. This is an easy solution of the difficulty and it will also be a confirmation as well as a test of your claim that 80 per cent of the miners are with Boswell. My personal judgment is that if 80 per cent of the miners were with Boswell the Argus would never have been suppressed and Boswell would never have been sent to jail. I do not doubt a good many miners have full confidence in Boswell, but when you come to a show down you will be surprised to see how far short they fall of being 80 per cent of the whole number. I myself have complete confidence in Boswell so far as honesty and integrity are concerned. But I take decided issue with his judgment and with his tactics and whether he is right or whether I am right time alone can tell.

"You are greatly mistaken, Comrade John, when you say that, 'from now on the scrap will be between Boswell and Haggerty and will in no way involve the movement.' Every such quarrel has its roots in causes that are more impersonal than personal. Boswell's friends will back him and Haggerty's friends will back him and there will be the inevitable tearing asunder of such unity as there is and an ugly, bitter, implacable factional fight, just at the very hour when it will save the mine owners and when it will destroy us. I would have averted that quarrel until at least it could have been fought out under other circumstances than those which now exist and when the present crisis was safely over. For the present and until the crisis is past everything else should be set aside and the miners urged regardless of all differences to stand elbow to elbow and heart to heart in every camp throughout the state. That would be my policy but if another is preferred I cannot help it and will have to make the most of it, as will also the poor devils of miners and their wives and babies who suffer the whole burden of our folly and short-sightedness, and this lays on my heart so heavily that I have lain awake many a night on account of it.

"Just this final word. You will find that sooner or later you will have to take your stand wholly with the Chicago I.W.W.ites or against them. The very hour they find that they cannot dominate you and use you for their purposes they will denounce you as a traitor, according to their code, as they have denounced everybody else.

"But come what may my heart is with you and the miners of West Virginia."

And now, Comrade Thompson, let me ask you comrades who are denouncing Haggerty as a crook why you do not, to be consistent, also denounce Mother Jones as a crook? It was Haggerty who had Mother Jones come into West Virginia years ago and who more than any other has been the means of keeping her there. Mother Jones has been working hand in hand with Haggerty all these years and she has repeatedly told me that Haggerty was one of the truest men in the labor movement and that his sufferings and persecution covering many years could never be told.

How about this? Are both crooks? Mother Jones has always stood by Haggerty and does today so far as I know. If he is a crook she certainly knows it and they who denounce Haggerty also denounce

Mother Jones although for reasons quite obvious they do not include her name.

Before we left Charleston I got Brown and Boswell into the same room with our committee, anticipating as I did that after we left there we would be attacked, and sitting face to face with them I demanded that they tell us frankly what they had to say, if anything, in criticism of our work and our actions, but they had not a word to say of any material consequence. They substantially approved our attitude and actions, so far as any protest was concerned.

In my first interview with Governor Hatfield I not only arranged with him to meet our whole committee but also to meet Harold Houston, Brown and others. I intended to go with Brown to the governor to secure his manuscript[2] and to understand certain disputed points but before this arrangement could be carried out we had to leave there. I asked Boswell if he would go with me to Governor Hatfield and meet him face to face and present his complaint, or say what he might have to say, but he answered, "Emphatically No" and said he would not meet Hatfield under any circumstances.

So you will see that in every step we were absolutely above board.

Fred Merrick told me in jail that the U.M.W. officials had connived with the authorities to have him thrown into jail, but he must produce some proof before I will believe that even reactionary union officials would be guilty of such an infamy.

Also, while we were at Charleston, and after you boys were released we held a special meeting with the socialists and asked them to send word to all the comrades. We wanted them to frankly criticise and advise us according to their light. Fred Merrick was specially invited to this meeting but he made the excuse to Berger that he would not attend because he "did not want to make any more trouble," but he didn't lose any time making trouble after we had left there. He would not have dared to face me before the local comrades and make the false and vicious charges he has since made, or if he had I would have had something to say to him he would not soon have forgotten.

The very first request I made of Governor Hatfield {was} that he release Fred Merrick, thinking that he was still in prison the morning I saw the governor. But Merrick did not come near me after he was out. I only heard that he proposed to "cut loose" at our committee. He admits that I have always been his friend, then why did he not come to me like a man and point out my error and give me a chance to explain myself? Is that the way one socialist comrade should treat another after years of friendship? I would have looked him up for his own sake, busy as I was, but I did not know where to find him.

When he was in jail at Pittsburg[3] I took the risk of missing an engagement and went to no end of trouble to get to his jail to bring him fruit and other things I thought he would like to eat, only to be denied admittance when I got there, but he knows I was there, and when he was in trouble I was never too busy to write and encourage him, and an hundred times I have defended him when he was assailed, only to be publicly denounced by him in the most abusive and scurrilous manner.

Fred Merrick's mother knows that I have been his friend even if he does not, and when I think of how he has acted in this affair I wonder how he must feel when he calmly thinks it over, if he is capable of doing so, and stands face to face with himself in the court of his own conscience.

You close your letter in a burst of wholesale denunciation of the U.M.W. officials. There is not, according to you, an honest hair in the head of a single one of them. They are all absolutely crooked just as you and Boswell are absolutely straight. But that is exactly where your weakness lies. Your minds are made up and you prejudge them without knowing them. If Christ himself were a U.M.W. official you would condemn him as a crook without giving him a chance to utter a word. I say to you that these men are not all crooks. I dare say there is no lot of union officials in which there is not some element of honesty.

You contemptuously couple up Germer with Hatfield and ask why I do not write to the latter instead of the former and I dare say that you do not even know Germer. He is a U.M.W. official and that is enough. You have said in your paper that his selection was "unfortunate." How do you know when you are a stranger to the man? I have known him pretty intimately for some fifteen years and I have never known him to be other than straightforward and I would not hesitate to trust him in any manner whatsoever. I do not say that I will stand for all he stands for but I do believe him to be an honest man and anything but a crook and reactionary.

This is all. I have written you fully because I believe you to be worth while. You are a young man. Your years are all before you and I believe you are capable of great usefulness and for this reason I have taken time enough to write you at such unusual length. I have uttered no word in anger. I wish you only well and this I wish you as earnestly as comrade can for comrade.

Yours fraternally
E. V. Debs

TLc, InTI, Debs Collection.

1. George H. Goebel, a national executive committee member from New Jersey, was coordinating the party's recruitment effort in West Virginia.

2. In its May 31, 1913, issue the *Appeal* reported that John W. Brown's manuscript of a book on the strike had been confiscated by his jailer in Harrison County, West Virginia, and had been turned over to Governor Hatfield.

3. See EVD to Fred Merrick, February 5, 1912.

Theodore Debs to John F. Noll

June 27, 1913
[Terre Haute, Indiana]

Dear Mr. Noll: —

Your courteous letter of the 25th. is received. I am glad you confirm my unwillingness to believe that you would knowingly or intentionally spread falsehood and slander through your columns.

Father Kluser has for months told deliberate lies about my brother and me and spread them as far as his slanderous pen would reach and if you have any doubt about it and will come here to this city and bring Father Kluser with you and I do not prove to the satisfaction of any committee of Catholics you may choose in this city that Father Kluser has lied scandalously about my brother and me I will agree to pay the entire expenses of both of you for the round trip and publicly acknowledge through the columns of your paper that Father Kluser's charges are true.

Is this a fair proposition? Will you accept it? Will Father Kluser? I dare say in advance that Father Kluser will not dare to come here to our home and repeat his malicious calumnies. A slanderer is always a coward and Father Kluser is both as you will ascertain before many days.

I may here inform you that this matter has been taken in hand in this city by others than ourselves and that before it is over with Father Kluser will prove his charges or he will retract them.

In previous articles published over his name Father Kluser called my brother and me "rascals," "scoundrels," "liars" and almost everything else that is vile.

I do not know what the object of this foul-mouthed priest can be unless he is being paid from the Wall Street fund that was raised to discredit socialists and socialism.

We never harmed Father Kluser and in fact had never heard of him. When my brother went to Morgantown to lecture a couple of years ago Father Kluser had bought a page of space in one of the papers and had handbills scattered over all the city denouncing my brother in the vilest terms. It was on that occasion that a committee of local citizens came to my brother's lecture manager and stated to him that Father Kluser had seduced and ruined a young woman there, breaking off an engagement and the young man himself was ready to testify to that fact. My brother was asked to use this against Father Kluser but refused to do so. Had my brother been so inclined he could have published this as Kluser certainly would have done without hesitation, if my brother had been so charged by people in his own community, but my brother refused to descend to that level.

If my article has in it the evidence of a somewhat heated temper I do not think that under the circumstances you should expect me to apologize for it. For months we have been silent under Father Kluser's calumnies but patience has ceased to be a virtue and in duty to ourselves and to silence a foul calumniator whose vicious influence ought to be destroyed as a duty to others who may fall victims, we now propose that Father Kluser shall prove his lies or swallow them. My brother and I were both born and we have lived all our lives in this city. We are known here and here is the place to ascertain if we are scoundrels or honest men.

Within the last few days the postmaster of this city received a letter asking in regard to my brother's character and the answer of the postmaster was that for honesty, integrity and good character generally there was not a man in this city who stood higher than my brother. If you doubt this write to him yourself. His name is Thatcher Parker[1] and he is as much opposed to my brother's economic and political views as anybody can be.

I ask you to come here and let me take you among the Catholic neighbors of my brother and myself and ask them to tell you what they know respecting our character and standing in this community.

Father Kluser has charged in your paper that we live in "mansions." If you will come here I will show the mansion in which I live, and which is not yet paid for, and then you shall judge for yourself.

Our father kept a grocery store in this city forty years. Not a man, woman or child will you find in this city who knew him who will say that he was other than an honest, upright man, who never did a human being a harm. He dealt for forty years with Herman Hulman Sr., the head of the largest wholesale grocery house in this city and in the state of Indiana, and one of the largest in the United States. Mr. Hulman is worth several million dollars. He built and endowed the St. Anthony's Hospital in this city.

My brother worked for Mr. Hulman five years when he was a young man. Mr. Hulman has known him since the day he was born and loves him as if he was his own son.

Mr. Hulman is an ardent Catholic. Now I want you to come here with Father Kluser and I will go with you to Mr. Hulman and Mr. Hulman will tell you who my brother is[2] and you can then judge for yourself who is the scoundrel, Kluser or my brother. I will take you to as many other prominent Catholics as you care to meet, and then I will ask you to take time enough to search this town from one end to the other and find any man who will say that my brother or I ever lied to them, deceived them, cheated them or wronged them in anyway whatsoever.

There is not a store in this town in which the credit of myself and brother is not unlimited.

In my article to your paper, which I shall expect you to publish unless you find it to be untrue in any particular, I said that Father Kluser knew he was lying when he stated that my brother received a salary of $100. a week from the Appeal to Reason. The very article he uses as his authority and which he quotes, proves that he lied to deliberately deceive your readers. I have the absolute documentary proof of this in my possession. He also invented the lie that my brother received $5000. last fall for his campaign speeches when as a matter of fact not even all his campaign expenses were paid but part of them were covered from his own private pocket and he personally contributed $50. to the campaign fund besides.

I know what our legal rights are with reference to your publication of these falsehoods and calumnies and I know that you are liable under the law, but believing that you have been imposed upon and that when so convinced you will of yourself repudiate these calumnies and their author, we are not inclined to cause you any trouble.

Yours very truly
Theodore Debs

TLc, InTI, Debs Collection.

1. In his letter dated June 2, 1913, to a Martin Nilsson in Marion, Nebraska, Parker wrote that he had "known Mr. Debs for many years [and] no one in our City stands any higher than he does." Parker sent a copy of the letter to Debs.

2. Herman Hulman, Sr., had contributed an appreciation of Debs to the 1912 campaign booklet, *What Debs' Neighbors Say About Him*. He died on July 4, 1913—a week after Theodore Debs's letter to Father Noll was written.

EVD to Editor, *Socialist and Labor Star*

June 30, 1913
[Terre Haute, Indiana]

Dear Comrade: —

When I said in my last letter to the Socialist and Labor Star that I would not change a word in our committee's report on West Virginia I should have made the exception heretofore noted in reference to the administration under which Mother Jones, John Brown, C.H. Boswell and other comrades were tried by the military commission.

The comrades above named were arrested and put in the bullpen[1] under Glasscock; martial law was declared and the military commission so created was legalized by the state supreme court during the administration of Governor Glasscock, but it was not until after the expiration of the Glasscock administration and the beginning of the Hatfield administration that these comrades were tried by the military commission.

Knowing that it was Glasscock who arrested our comrades and put them in the bullpen and that it was Hatfield who gave them their liberty I somehow got the impression that they were tried before instead of a few days after the close of the Glasscock administration.

This error of dates, for which I alone am responsible, I frankly confess and have set about to correct.[2]

In our report there was but one purpose and that was to set down the facts as we found them. We could have had no possible object in charging anything to Glasscock that Hatfield was responsible for. We wanted each to be held accountable for the acts of his administration, no less and no more, and judgment rendered accordingly.

Yours fraternally
Eugene V. Debs

TLc, InTI, Debs Collection.

1. Detention cell for prisoners awaiting trial.
2. As noted, this letter was sent to and printed in scores of socialist and nonsocialist papers.

Mother [Mary] Jones to EVD

July 5, 1913
Indianapolis, Indiana

My Dear Comrade Debs: —

I so much regretted that I did not see you when you were in West Virginia, but I had so much work to do in Washington, when the pirates let me out of the bull pen that I was unable to meet you. I have been so busy since I got out that I have not had time to write you a line, much as I wanted to.

I very much regret the sad incident [with] that that [*sic*] fellow Simons and the Appeal.[1] I expected nothing else when he went there. I think that Warren will learn when it is a little too late. I told him about Ricker and about Rogers, I told him about Shoaf.[2] You know that we are living in a peculiar economic age, and self interest comes to the front instead of principle or a cause. When I was going into West Virginia, to take up the battle of the poor slaves, I stopped off to see poor Wayland in Girard. He was not there but I saw Warren; Simons said he hoped I would get lost in West Virginia, and never return. When a man is so cold and brutal as that there is nothing in him for a great cause. I have known Simons for some few years, and he has done just what I expected to the Appeal. But there is an unfortunate phase in our movement. That if you undertake to give people any warning they generally put you down as a knocker. I just read in the morning paper which prompted me to write you that you took a girl home when the court said that she would have to either keep off the street or go down to the red light district.[3] If that judge[4] would not have exhibited his ignorance as he did the public might have more respect for him. If he would study the causes that bring those effects into society it would be far more to his credit as a member of the judiciary. That poor girl was a victim of a horrible system that is more brutal than the world has ever known, and God grants that we have more Eugene Debs, to protect such people from the depraved lions of capitalism.

I am on my way to Washington, to work among the Senators, and explain to them the horrors of West Virginia. I shall be going through next month, to Texas, and I shall try to stop off at Terre Haute, and see you.

Give my regards to Mrs. Debs, to Theodore and his family.

I am, always yours in the great struggle for the race,

Mother Jones

TLS, InTI, Debs Collection.

1. In "Assassinating the Coming Nation" (*Appeal*, June 28, 1913), Algie Simons claimed that *Coming Nation*, which he edited, was showing a profit when it was "strangled" by Fred Warren, who, Simons wrote, "wanted all the profits for the *Appeal*."

2. Allen W. Richer, Bruce Rogers, and George Shoaf, all of whom had at one time or another been on the *Appeal* staff.

3. On July 5, 1913, both the *Terre Haute Star* and the *Tribune* reported that Debs was "sheltering in his home, Helen Cox, daughter of a Methodist preacher once prominent in Indiana." Debs had taken her from the city jail, after being told by the police that "she must keep off the streets or go to the red light district." Helen Cox was the daughter of the Rev. James H. Hollingsworth, Debs's Terre Haute friend, and a detailed account of the incident is in "Eugene V. Debs vs. Christianity," *K. Lamity's Harpoon* (Austin, Texas), August 1913. Debs described the act as a "challenge to the Christianity of Terre Haute."

4. Charles S. Batt, Terre Haute city court judge, appointed Debs an emergency probation officer to enable him to take the girl to his home.

EVD to William E. Borah

July 8, 1913
Terre Haute, Indiana

My dear Senator Borah:—

I have a letter this morning from W.H. Thompson, Editor of the Socialist and Labor Star, Huntington, W. Va., who has also written to you, in which he says, referring to an extract from your letter to me which I enclosed to him:

> "The Senator is mistaken when he says "We had upon the witness stand in addition to the governor, the county attorney, the sheriff etc.'. Those he refers to were *Ex-officials* and not the present executives. The new, or present county officials were inaugurated January 1st., 1913. The state officials on March 4th. *None* of the *new* officials were placed on the stand."

This accords with my previous statement to you and my present understanding. The armored train that shot up the villages of the miners was in charge of the present sheriff[1] but he was not placed on the stand to tell what he knows about it. None of the present state or county officials have been examined and it is this that seems very strange to me, seeing that some of the most lawless acts and some of the most cruel outrages were committed under the present county administration which began on January 1st.

I venture to observe that all these persons, including both state and county officials now holding office, should be examined to secure a complete investigation and to bring out all the material facts.

Yours faithfully
E. V. Debs

TLc, InTI, Debs Collection.

    1. Bonner Hill.

William E. Borah to EVD

July 10, 1913
Washington, D.C.

My dear Mr. Debs:

Before replying to your letter of the 8th in full I desire to consult with some of my colleagues on the Committee in order that I may be more certain as to some dates and as to some witnesses who were called. But in any event I can assure you again that your suggestions will all be thoroughly presented to the Committee before final action is taken. Mr. Thompson is right in assuming that I referred to the ex-officials, that is, those who were in office at the time of the occurrence of events which I had particularly for investigation. I was not present when the armored train affair was examined into, being compelled to return to Washington a couple of days in advance of the hearing of this which was under the particular charge of Senator Kenyon. I agree with you fully that every official who was in office at the time anything of that kind took place should be called.[1] But the details of these matters I will undertake to straighten out as soon as I can get to see Mr. Kenyon and the rest of the Committee, Mr. Kenyon now being out of the City.

Very respectfully,
Wm E Borah

TLS, InTI, Debs Collection.

    1. When the Senate committee hearings were resumed in Washington on September 3, 1913, the witnesses who were heard included neither the state officials nor Mother Jones, Boswell, Brown, and the others whose testimony Debs had sought. Instead, "the coal operators gave their side of the story," as the *Kanawha Citizen* put it (September 4, 1913), and the "burden of their testimony" was that the effort of the UMW to unionize the fields "brought about the trouble." For two weeks a string of witnesses testified, including Bishop Donahue, who denied that he had "come to Washington at the request of the operators" but generally sustained the operators' "side of the story." *Kanawha Citizen*, September 5, 6, 9, 11, 15, 1913.

EVD to Fred D. Warren

September 6, 1913
[Terre Haute, Indiana]

My dear Fred:—

Enclosed please find some copy. I call your particular attention to the article on "Capitalism and Marriage"[1] and suggest that you play this up prominently in the next issue. It is the greatest opening for a crushing rejoinder that capitalism has given us for a long time. Capitalism here furnishes the facts which bring down upon it its own damnation.[2] It will forever put an end to the slander about socialism breaking up the home and destroying the marriage relation etc. This vicious charge which has been put in every conceivable form by our enemies, especially Catholic priests, has seriously interfered with the advance of socialism in this country. I believe the enclosed article will deal those hypocrites a crushing blow from which they will not easily recover. I believe this will make the best kind of propaganda matter and suggest that this article after it appears in the Appeal is published in the form of an Appeal leaflet and then advertised at so much per thousand for general distribution, bearing upon its back an advertisement of the Appeal. I believe millions of this leaflet could be distributed. This charge against socialism has worried and in a way thwarted our most energetic propagandists and I believe they will all take hold in sowing the country knee-deep with the facts here presented out of the mouth of capitalism itself and with which we now bury capitalism in its own filth. It will take more gall than even the lying jesuits have to spring the old slander about socialism and free love after the Appeal publishes the enclosed scorching indictment. This particular subject upon which socialists have been so cruelly outraged is one upon which they are especially sensitive and I believe the reading of this article will set the blood of the Army workers tingling and they will not be slow to look up the pious lackeys of capitalism who have been talking about socialism and free love and ramming this refutation down their lying throats. I hope you can give it a good position and play it up in type that will stand out and make it read and sizzle like an avenging flame. You can publish it with or without my name, as you prefer. Perhaps it might have better effect at this particular time to go out over your name.[3] It is certainly a live wire and will show that the Appeal is quick to strike at such a wide opening as capitalism has here given it.

I will have some more copy with you in time for the next issue and I will be at Girard about the 16th. on my way to exile.[4]

Yours always

Debs

TLS, Warren Papers, Schenectady, New York.

1. In "Capitalism and Marriage" (*Appeal*, September 27, 1913), Debs denounced the "made-to-order slander" that socialism had "sinister designs upon marriage" and blamed capitalism for the large number of unmarried men and women in the United States, "countless illegitimate babes," widespread prostitution, and the "bartering off" of the "daughters of the plutocracy" to the "titled vermin" of Europe.

2. In writing "Capitalism and Marriage," Debs drew heavily upon "a capitalistic Associated Press" article, which, in turn, was based on official statistics provided by the New York State conservation commission.

3. The article appeared on page 3 of the *Appeal* under Debs's name. Warren did not print it as a pamphlet.

4. For several weeks the *Appeal* had been carrying notices of Debs's upcoming lecture tour through the Northwest, but Debs, citing poor health, decided to cancel the tour and try to recover on a ranch.

EVD to Fred D. Warren

September 8, 1913
Terre Haute, Indiana

My dear Fred: —

Yours of the 6th. in answer to mine of the 5th. has been received. I am glad things are looking up and only sorry that I am in no shape to lend a substantial hand when it is so much needed. There is good reason for the slump in things just now, totally independent of ourselves, and when I get out there next week we will talk it all over.

You no doubt received my letter of August 30th. advising you of my inability to fill the Western engagements and my intention to spend the next several months on a ranch. That will be the only way I can ever hope to get in fit shape to be of any use. Shall go to work as a ranch "hand," learn to plow and all other kinds of farm work, developing and strengthening every fibre and muscle in my body and taking out all the softness and flabbiness which mutely protest against a man's parasitism, and of which he should be ashamed, and at the same time give my head a rest and stop getting worked up and overheated about everything that goes wrong or about every little quarrel that breaks out in the movement. I have treated with a number of doctors in the last few months but the one I have most faith in told me candidly that my nerves were threatening to put me out of the game and that at my age I would have to let go now if I wanted to live. When I take into account that fact that I have become a total stranger to sleep and that it has been so long since I felt the "balm of nature's restorative" that I have forgotten how it feels, then I must conclude that the doctor is right, and so I am having an outfit made including brogans, overalls etc. and I am going to work outdoors in the sun, get brown as an Indian, earn my daily bread by my own sweat and make my body redeem itself and become once more sufficiently self-respecting to give me a certificate of character and the necessary strength to work for socialism. I will either return well and strong, erect and stalwart and make the socialist speech I have always felt it in me to make, but have never yet made, or I am off the boards for all time.

I will be out for a day or two next week en route to Colorado. We will go all over it together. I don't want to be of any more expense to you or the Appeal. I will be able to tide over until I can get a new grip on myself. You have been more than kind, you have been generous and I shall not forget it. If while I am on the ranch I can help you or the Appeal I shall gladly be at your service.

Enclosed I am sending you a little copy. Tomorrow I will send you a circulation article and some other copy. I am feeling somewhat better these last few days. For two or three weeks I was completely down and out. My body was so limp that I could not stand and my head was so weak that I could not think above an oyster. I hope it will be possible for you to fill the Washington engagements although I know you are already full up.[1] Brewer or Ben Wilson would fill the bill and if they are not available Kirkpatrick[2] would make a splendid man. I hope you are well and strong. More than glad that George Allan England[3] is with you. Remember me to Mrs. Warren and the boys. Shall be happy to see you all.

Yours always
Debs

TLS, Warren Papers, Schenectady, New York.

1. Ryan Walker substituted for Debs at many of the meetings scheduled for Debs's Northwest tour in the fall of 1913.

2. George Ross Kirkpatrick (1867-1937) joined the Socialist Party in 1903 and thereafter lectured on socialism and other economic issues, mostly in the Midwest. His best-known book, *War—What For?*, was published in 1910 and became especially popular after the outbreak of World War I. Kirkpatrick was the party's vice-presidential candidate in 1916.

3. England's *The Story of the Appeal—The Greatest Political Newspaper in the World* (1913) was being run serially in the *Appeal* at the time.

EVD to Theodore Debs

October 2, 1913
Estes Park, Colorado

My Dear old Pard:

Arrived here at 3 PM yesterday after a fine ride through the mountains in a steamer—auto. Left Denver at 8 AM—arrived at Loveland, 60 miles north, at 11. left at 11 in steamer—auto with 6 passengers & arrived here at 3—we passed through a grand canyon & I wished often that you were with me to enjoy it. Am 30 miles from railroad, 7500 ft high & a clear, cold atmosphere. Feel like I shall be greatly benefited. I am temporarily at a nice little hotel here where the Sweets[1] have secured a room for me. Have a cozy room, clean bed, electric light, hot & cold water, closet in house & yet there are hardly 50 people in the little village at present. Thousands come in here in summer months. Yesterday just after leaving Boulder saw a lone prairie chicken—it lit close to the train & seemed very big to me. Shortly after saw a beautiful pheasant & it was a winged glory. The latter are protected by law all the year around.

The people have left the ranch I was to go on so I must find another. Mrs. Sweet[2] gave me several names.

Heavy frost last night & every night. It has already snowed here. The snow-covered mountains are all about me. Wish you were here. Have but one thought here & that is to *get well & strong* & want you to do the same. Don't write much, nor will I. *Get out & get well!* All depends on that. Tell everybody I'm away from railroad & mails, cut off everything *as short* as you can & *answer nothing* that does not positively have to be answered. I shall work early & late every minute, to get into condition. *I can & by the eternal, I will.* That's sure. When I get home we'll make things hum—but we can't do it as *corpses.* Dead men cut sad figures in live roles.

You old hound I shall beat you to a pulp on sight. Kisses to you and Gertrude and Marguerite.

Enclosed find some stamps. Begin sending letters & papers & all my mail here Estes Park P.O.   Colo.

AL, InTI, Debs Collection.

1. Channing Sweet (1846-1932) was an attorney and businessman in Colorado Springs for more than fifty years. A friend of Debs since the Red Special campaign of 1908 (when Debs spent a night in Sweet's home), Sweet was described in his obituary (*Rocky Mountain News*, August 24, 1932) as "a student of economics who held decided opinions on matters in this category." Sweet's "sympathy for the underdog,"

the obituary added, "led him to adopt liberal views not infrequently at variance with current opinions."

2. Emoroy Stevens Sweet (1850-1922), Channing Sweet's wife.

EVD to Theodore Debs

October 30, 1913
[Estes Park, Colorado]

My dear Kude:

Just read a lovely letter from Reynolds. He is indeed a fine loyal soul.

To-morrow I'm to leave here for the village. I have grown to love my little cabin so that I am truly sorry to think that to-morrow I will sweep it out and tidy it up for the last time.[1] You must some time see this place & we'll come together next time.

Mr. Mills[2] took me out to the beaver colonies again & I saw a beaver, the first I ever saw, & was intensely interested in him.

I feel better, clearer, stronger, cheerfuler and more confident, self-reliant and hopeful than for the last five years. This life in the wilds has done me a world of good. My blood is turning red again and I can once more feel it tingling & bubbling in my veins & the old enthusiasm kindling in my soul. As I'm to leave to-morrow we're to have a farewell at the cabin of Mrs. Sherman[3] & her son John, whom I have grown to love as dear old friends. Mrs. Sherman's husband[4] is editor of the Chicago Inter-Ocean.

The secret of health, bodily and mental, is to eat moderately, eat slowly, anything you please, chew it well, & spend every minute you can *out-doors*. Rain or shine, snow or sleet or hail, go out, stay out, take long walks, *breathe in deeply* the fresh air & health is bound to come & stay. If [you can] sleep outdoors all [the] better. *Oxygen is [life-giving & the]* body could not live [five?] minutes without it. The blood & tissue hunger for oxygen & must have it. You & Gertrude must go out daily for long walks & keep it up *every day.* Let nothing prevent. *Neglect everything to be outdoors.* Every minute out in the fresh air is a blood-builder & a life-preserver.

Have just called on Mr. Mills to settle my bill. The regular rate for the accomodations I had would have been $115.00 for 23 days. Mr. Mills said *Nothing* is the amt of your bill. I protested & insisted & finally he agreed to accept $20. to at least cover the cords of fuel I burnt up. Mr. Mills is one of the noblest souls I've ever met & you too must know him. From now on we're friends in the closest bonds and I'll tell you he's a friend worth having.

Can now split wood hours at a time without getting tired — when I first came here 10 minutes used up all my wind & strength & left me limp as a rag. See? My muscles now stand out like whipcords. This means that there's a damn slim prospect for your hide. Do you follow me?

Sunday evening I speak on Socialism at the only church in Estes Park & all the folks will be there.

Friday morning.

Last night Mr. Mills & Mrs. Sherman gave me a little farewell dinner here, one of the sweetest occasions of my life. Mrs. Sherman is an expert cook & you ought to have seen the dinner. A delicious leg of mutton, mashed potatoes, peas, radishes, fruit salad, honey, cakes, coffee etc. etc. After dinner we went to Mrs. Sherman's lovely log cabin & had Grafanola music, stories, etc. etc. Again coffee was served and then we all said a happy good night. All meet here on common ground — pure democracy. The men all had our pants in our boots & were dressed in our corduroys & overalls. The help, including the cook, carpenter and others were as one with the host & hostess. That's my style of society. Never in my life have I spent a happier evening.

At 4 this A.M. I go down to the village[5] — 9 miles & there I will stay till I leave for Denver. They will all come down to hear me speak Sunday evening.

Love & kisses to all!
Gene

ALS, InTI, Debs Collection.

1. In "Debs in Overalls," which appeared in *St. Louis Labor* (November 8, 1913) and in other socialist publications, Debs described his routine at Estes Park. See also EVD to Theodore Debs, October 11, 1913; October 16, 1913; October 20, 1913; and October 26, 1913.

2. Enos A. Mills (1870-1922) was a nationally acclaimed naturalist and the author of half a dozen books, including *In Beaver World*, based on his trips, unarmed, through the Rockies. Known as the father of Rocky Mountain National Park, Mills fought against government policies that would have granted monopolies to private companies in the national parks and had just completed a national lecture tour on that issue at the time of his death. For many years he operated a resort at the foot of Long's Peak, a few miles south of Estes Park.

3. Mary Bell King Sherman (1865-1935) was active in the national-park movement, particularly in the creation of Rocky Mountain National Park, and served as trustee of the National Parks Association. She was later (1924-28) president of the General Federation of Women's Clubs.

4. John Dickinson Sherman (1859-1926) graduated from Hamilton College in 1881 and the following year began a lifelong career in journalism. He was city editor

of the *Chicago Tribune* from 1889 to 1896, and editor of the *Chicago Inter-Ocean* from 1898 to 1914.

    5. Estes Park.

EVD to Theodore Debs

November 10, 1913
Estes Park, Colorado

My old Pard:

    Bunch of letters just read—forwarded by Channing Sweet also your loving birthday telegram[1] which filled my heart. In my far away mountain home I held your message in my hand & thought how sweet it was in you & Gertrude & Marguerite to thus remember me and then my heart beat responsive in gratefulness such as no words can ever express.

    I am terribly distressed about the injury to your back at Geo. Smith's funeral. Take the best of care of yourself & keep me advised. I can easily understand how your back could be ruined in such a contingency, but I shall hope you only recd a sudden wrench from which you will entirely recover in a few days. You are right in what you say about Geo. Smith.[2] He was a decent fellow & of good parts & I am really sorry to hear of his untimely death.

    Your tribute, which I return, was not only fitting & proper, but it was touching & eloquent. [two illegible words] think of society to say except in [his] favor. It was in fine taste, full or heart, tender & sympathetic in every note & it could not have been expressed in tenderer or fitter words.

    Sorry to hear of George Heinl's death[3]—thought he had gotten well. Have written John letter of condolence.

    Have also written Frank & Marguerite Prevey[4] & Ben Wilson, acknowledging birthday cigars etc. How fine and loyal in these dear comrades. They never forget my birthday. You damn rascal, I don't doubt you are sampling the cigars thoroughly. I want you to smoke 'em up, old man, for if you don't they'll be dried up by the time I get back. So smoke 'em & enjoy 'em & that will be fully as good to me as if I smoked 'em myself. It is enough to know that we have such loving, loyal comrades.

    Rec'd the two papers containing the Herron articles & have read 'em & written to Herron.[5]

    Note the letter from Bruce Calvert[6] & on reaching Denver will consult Dr. Tilden[7] the food chemist as he suggests.

Leave here Friday for Denver & reluctantly for I have been treated here with wonderful kindness. Let me know about your back.

Kisses to all
Gene

ALS, InTI, Debs Collection.

1. Debs's birthday was November 5.

2. George C. Smith (1865-1913) was owner of a transfer company in Terre Haute and a longtime friend of the Debs family.

3. George Heinl was the brother of Debs's brother-in-law John G. Heinl.

4. Frank Prevey, Marguerite's husband, was an Akron, Ohio, jeweler who attracted national attention as a leader in the Akron rubber workers' strike in 1913. Describing Prevey as a leading light of the Socialist party in Ohio, *The Rebel* (May 3, 1913) quoted a Prevey speech to the strikers in which he declared that "Jesus Christ belongs to the working class."

5. Beginning in April 1913, *Metropolitan Magazine* ran a series of articles by George Herron, who was living in Italy. The articles—"Socialism and Spiritual Expansion" (April 1913), "Bread and The Soul" (May 1913), and 3 others—were widely reprinted in the socialist press.

6. Bruce Calvert of Griffith, Indiana, was a writer whose articles appeared in *National Rip-Saw, American Socialist,* and other socialist publications before World War I.

7. Dr. John Henry Tilden (1850-1940) was head of Tilden Sanitarium in Denver from 1890 until his death. He was a nationally prominent nutritionist.

Morris Hillquit to EVD

November 15, 1913
New York City

Dear Gene:

I have your two letters written on November 7th and 8th respectively and also copy manuscript of my article on religion[1] which accompanied the former. I am deeply and sincerely grateful to you for the pains which you have taken with the article and for the very valuable suggestions you make. The distinction between the church as a religious institution and the church as a political machine is a very excellent one, and while I have tried to point out that distinction in my article, I realize that I have by far not made it {as} clear and striking as the use of the terms suggested by you make it. I shall look up the article of Mark Hanna in the National Magazine to which you refer,[2] and probably find a way of bringing in the statement which you quote and which can be made very telling.

I have been thinking of quoting pro-slavery clericals in support of our contention that the church is always in alliance with the oppressors of mankind and opposed to all movements for social betterment and civic and economic liberty, but you must realize that I am limited to about five thousand words for each article, and on the subject of religion particularly there are so many phases that must be treated, that I hardly could do more than make a general reference to the attitude of the clergy in the ante-bellum days. Perhaps I will get a chance to return to it in my sur-rebuttal, if Dr. Ryan should deny my general statement in the reply.

The incident described by Bouck White in his "Call of the Carpenter"[3] is certainly very effective, but I must confess I have some doubts about its correctness. The building erected by the Socialist workmen of Brussels and occupied as headquarters for the Socialist, co-operative and trade union movement is the Maison du Peuple. I visited the building some years ago and failed to notice the fresco mentioned by White. It is, of course, quite possible that I overlooked it, all the more that my visit was a very hasty one, but somehow the entire alleged incident does not seem to me to agree with the general spirit and mental attitude of the Belgian workers. I have written to Huysmans[4] to verify this statement, and hope to get his answer in time for use on the revised copy, if he confirms the incident. At any rate, I am very thankful for the suggestion. I hope you will follow the debate from month to month as it appears in the magazine and that you will continue your kind interest in it and have no hesitancy in making frank criticisms and suggestions. I shall have an opportunity to come back at almost every point in the debate in the final summary. Besides, it is expected that the entire discussion will be published in book form[5] after it has run serially through the magazine, and in that event I shall have another opportunity to fortify my arguments to some extent.

I am glad you are picking up again and am somewhat incensed at your over-sensitive conscience, which would not permit you to enjoy your brief recreation without reserve. It seems to me that you have more than earned it by your strenuous work in the past, and that it is a might [sic] sensible investment for the still greater work which is ahead of you.

With very kind regards,

Sincerely and fraternally yours,
Morris Hillquit

TLS, InTI, Debs Collection.

1. Each month between October 1913 and April 1914, *Everybody's Magazine* published an installment of the debate on "Socialism: Promise or Menace" between

Hillquit and Father John Augustine Ryan (1869-1945), a leading Catholic spokesman for social reform and the author of *A Living Wage* (1906), a major statement of Catholic social philosophy in America. As a teacher, writer, and public figure, Ryan was credited with bringing Catholic social thought into the mainstream of American reform.

2. In "Socialism and the Labor Unions" (*National Magazine*, 19:553-58), Hanna described labor unions as "a boon to our country" but considered "the menace of today . . . the spread of socialism," which could be destroyed through "the power of education . . . in politics, religion, and business."

3. To support his contention that workers were generally anticlerical and hostile to organized Christianity and at the same time "ardent in their affections" toward Jesus, White cited "the Labourist party in Belgium," which built the Maison du Peuple and, "behind a curtain" in the main lecture hall, installed a fresco painting of "the Nazarene."

4. Camille Huysmans (1871-1968) was a Labor party member of the Belgian parliament and from 1906 to 1919 secretary of the International Socialist Bureau, which was housed in the Maison du Peuple in Brussels. No exchange of correspondence between Hillquit and Huysmans on the subject has been found.

5. Macmillan published *Socialism Promise or Menace*, the Hillquit-Ryan debates, in 1914.

Elizabeth H. Thomas[1] to EVD

November 26, 1913
Milwaukee, Wisconsin

Dear Comrade Debs:

You have, no doubt, heard of the outrageous verdict given last Saturday against the Milwaukee Leader, Comrade Berger and Comrade Bistorius, the Business Manager of the Leader.[2] A jury packed with Knights of Columbus, Ancient Hibernians and Militia of Christ men[3] rendered a verdict of $17,500 damages for alleged libel.

The suit for libel was brought by the "non-partisan" City Clerk, who had been charged with graft in the Leader. The word "graft" appeared only once in the article, and a judge has decided that this City Clerk was actually guilty of illegal practices in connection with his office. No fair minded jury would have given the plaintiff 6 cents damages. But of course their object was to kill the Leader and stamp out Socialism in Milwaukee.

We are determined that they shall not accomplish this fell purpose. We will fight to the last ditch. It goes without saying, however, that a Socialist daily paper does not have $20,000 laid up in the bank— and with costs this verdict will amount to no less than $20,000.[4] The Leader has had a very hard struggle to get established.[5] The working men of Milwaukee have drawn upon their small resources to the utmost to start the daily. They have sacrificed almost up to the last limit. We cannot ask them to raise the entire $20,000. It would simply be impossible for them to gather this total amount in nickels and dimes.

We, therefore, must appeal to our comrades outside of Wisconsin.

The Milwaukee movement, I believe I may say without any desire to boast, has been an encouragement and inspiration to the Socialists of America. We have worked hard and fought hard. Now we hope that the comrades all over the country will stand by us in this grave crisis.

We do not ask for donations. We ask only that the comrades will purchase our bonds and thus enable us to meet this tremendous emergency. Now may I ask of you, Comrade Debs, to write an appeal to the membership of the Socialist Party, asking them to stand by Milwaukee in the storm?[6]

This would have a great effect and would call the attention of the membership to the gravity of the situation here.

There are now only two English Socialist dailies[7] in the United States. We must not let the enemy put out one of these lights.

Can we count on you, dear comrade, to lend us your voice in this time of trouble?

Hoping to hear from you, I am,
Sincerely and fraternally,

Your old comrade,
Elizabeth H. Thomas

I write this at the request of the Milwaukee Comrades.

TLS, InTI, Debs Collection.

1. Elizabeth Thomas was a longtime ally of Victor Berger in Wisconsin politics and state secretary of the Socialist party there.

2. On November 22, 1913, a Milwaukee jury awarded damages of $17,500 to Peter Leuch, the city clerk, who was accused in a *Leader* story of paying double salaries to his office workers. Leuch sued the *Leader;* Victor Berger, who was majority owner of the paper; and Henry S. Bistorius, business manager.

3. The Knights of Columbus and Militia for Christ were two of the most aggressive Catholic antisocialist organizations at the time.

4. On appeal, the case was finally settled in November 1916. The damage award was scaled down to $2,250 plus $1,000 court costs against the *Leader.*

5. As successor to the weekly *Social Democratic Herald,* the daily *Leader* was launched in December 1911 with substantial financial support from Arthur Brisbane.

6. In "Persecute Socialist Papers" (*Appeal, December 13, 1913*), Debs said the fact that there were "five O'Conners, O'Gormans and O'Briens" on the jury proved its bias and that the damage suit was "in the nature of a plot" to destroy the socialist press.

7. The other was the *New York Call.*

Elizabeth H. Thomas to EVD

December 19, 1913
Milwaukee, Wisconsin

Dear Comrade Debs:

Many thanks for the splendid article![1] It rings like steel and sizzles like red hot iron. Surely, this will arouse the comrades to indignant action.

The case comes up again tomorrow, when we shall demand a new hearing trial. We will, therefore, hold your article until we see what the results of our demand will be. I have little faith in the capitalist courts, but we shall have to try our luck for a second trial.

We shall certainly take great pleasure in sending you a dozen copies of the Leader, containing your magnificent article.

The lines are being drawn very closely here, as they surely will be everywhere when the Socialist movement gains more strength. The Catholic societies[2] are doing great work against us, but in the long run they will help us more than harm. We are not discouraged, and we are going to keep up the fight for the rest of our lives and die in the harness.

Thanking you again most heartily on behalf of all the comrades, and wishing you a Merry Christmas and a most successful New Year in your work, I am,

Sincerely and fraternally yours,
Elizabeth H. Thomas

All the comrades send *kindest regards*.

TLS, InTI, Debs Collection.

1. Debs's "Shall They Kill The Leader" appeared in the *Leader* on February 21, 1914. In it he accused "bosses and grafters" of attempting to kill the paper and asked readers to send aid for its defense.
2. Perhaps Debs's strongest attack on "the Catholic Societies" was "The Knights of Columbus," *International Socialist Review*, April 1915.

EVD to Morris Hillquit

December 20, 1913
Terre Haute, Indiana

Dear Morris:—

Your communication of the 9th. inst. addressed to me at Estes Park reached there after I had left and has followed me from place to place until finally it has overtaken me here. This will explain my belated acknowledgment. I note that Bouck White was right in the matter of the picture of Christ and I am glad of it. I am especially glad to have the verification in the words quoted by you from Huysmans' letter, and I thank you for your kindness in sending me a copy of the post card. I note that you may not be able to use this matter in the present debate, and your reason, which is quite sufficient. You may be able to use it, {and} so may I, on some future occasion.

I was on the point of writing you several times to tell you how thoroughly I enjoyed your December article but concluded that you were busy enough at this time without being diverted with unnecessary correspondence. But I am glad to take this occasion to say that your argument is in my opinion absolutely unanswererable and your manner of presenting it flawless. You covered your opponent's objections so completely and answered him so conclusively that every impartial reader must be convinced that there is but one tenable side to the debate.

You are fortunate in many things in this controversy, especially so in the choice of your opponent. He is weak but fair; or perhaps rather weak because fair. The admissions he makes are unusually candid for an anti-socialist and are of themselves almost fatal to his side. It must be said of Dr. Ryan that he states his premises with exceptional candor and fairness and that he argues in the spirit of one who seeks the truth and would take no mean advantage of an adversary. This is so rare among anti-socialists, especially those of the Catholic and Jesuitic type, that it is all the more refreshing and commendable. Allow me to suggest that it would not weaken your cause if you found it consistent to say something to this effect in your very last article in the debate.

I could not help trying to help the miners in Colorado.[1] It is almost impossible to be near enough the battle to hear the roar of the guns and not have a part in it. It seems like cowardice or desertion or treason. Still I was much improved by running wild in Colorado and doing useful physical work for a couple of months and now I am very confident that with about six weeks more of quiet which I hope to obtain near here I shall be again strong and my nerves sufficiently restored to enable me to get to work again. My life would be reduced to but a few days if it were not for socialism and for the little use I may be to the movement.

Accept my thanks for kind words and the assurance of my appre-

ciation of the splendid work you are doing for our cause and believe
me with best wishes.

Yours fraternally
E. V. Debs

TLS, WHi, Hillquit Papers.

1. The Colorado miners' strike against Colorado Fuel and Iron Company in 1913-14 was, like the strike in West Virginia, one of the most brutal of the era, its brutality dramatized by the Ludlow Massacre of April 1914.

EVD to Helen Keller[1]

December 23, 1913
Terre Haute, Indiana

My dear Comrade Keller: —
     Very sorry am I and so is Mrs. Debs that we missed you on your recent visit here.[2] We are just returned after several months absence and among the first things we heard was of your wonderful address here and its profound impression upon our people. It was a complete conquest and you seem to have captivated the entire community. Please let me tender my hearty congratulations to both you and dear Mrs. Macy.[3]
     This morning I met Mr. Gwinn[4] and he was all aglow with enthusiasm over your visit here. He told me of how you had touched the hearts of all your hearers and won their instantaneous love and admiration. And then he told me of the more than kind words you had spoken of me and coming from no other source could such an expression have touched me more deeply or afforded me greater satisfaction. I need not say to you that the sentiments of appreciation and regard so kindly and generously expressed by you are heartily reciprocated by me, and some good day I hope it may be my pleasure to take you by the hand and make personal acknowledgment of the sense of obligation I feel for the incomparable struggle you have made, in the face of a thousand disheartening obstacles, to serve the cause of humanity.
     Mrs. Debs and the comrades here join in hearty greetings to you and Mrs. Macy and in wishing you a right joyous and prosperous New Year. Believe me always

Your loving comrade
Eugene V. Debs

TLS, American Foundation for the Blind, Keller Collection.

1. Helen Adams Keller (1880-1968) overcame the effects of an illness that left her blind, deaf, and mute at the age of nineteen months and eventually was recognized as one of the world's great women. After graduating cum laude from Radcliffe in 1904, Keller entered a career of writing and lecturing on blindness and other subjects, which took her around the world many times, and her books, including several of an autobiographical nature, were widely read. Her letter to Debs of March 11, 1919, in which she hailed Debs as "an apostle of brotherhood and freedom," was widely reprinted in the socialist press.

2. Keller spoke at Centenary Methodist Church in Terre Haute on November 11, 1913. *Terre Haute Tribune*, November 12, 1913.

3. Anne Mansfield Sullivan Macy (1866-1936) was Helen Keller's teacher, friend, and companion from 1887 until her death. Macy became totally blind in 1935. Her success in teaching Helen Keller is acknowledged as one of the remarkable achievements in American education.

4. Dow R. Gwinn was president of the Terre Haute Young Men's Christian Association, one of the sponsors of Keller's lecture in Terre Haute.

William G. Williams[1] to EVD

January 7, 1914
Cincinnati, Ohio

Comrade:
Your Message to the Children in the Appeal[2] was doubtless sympathetically intended and therefore deserving commendation. Pardon me however to say it was not a rara {avis} in terris on that line of literature for thousands of others, not Socialists, have been just as pathetic towards the children as you. It seems to me (a Socialist) that an analysis shows that as an elucidation of Socialism your essay is entirely ineffective. It is true in part you admit this by stating that it was the "barest outline of what the Socialist party is organized for." But again pardon me distinguished comrade, when I criticize your article of probably over 5000 *words* because it seemed to me so bare of illumination to non Socialists as to any peculiar tenets and special *doctrines.* Your generalities as to what Socialism offers to the children: your lament over *some* of their conditions: your quotations from Jesus & suggestions of his policies cannot be peculiarly & *only* the ideas of modern Socialism. Your suppositions of enthusiasm by some of the Children Socialists who wear red buttons: Your diatribes about certain "old fogies" who never make any *progress* & seem like a "wooden Indian" — these and other expressions are hardly overwise or *directory* [*sic*] *towards* Socialism. You start in the work of illuminating but at once side switch so you finally and exasperatingly to the reader relegate the "little children" and the rest of us to a big task when you

write: "If you want to *know* what the *plans* of the Socialists are read their platform, attend their lectures and study their literature" Yes— I am certain it could be found in such sources *if intelligently* sought and *carefully selected,* but my criticism is that your lengthy essay has not come within the shadow of doing so—and that is what I have written & intended to suggest in the kindest spirit & for the future good of our great cause. *We have the strongest arguments & must abandon mere sentimental or jerky [?] assertions in our journals and by our orators.* Comrade you should be the vanguard in these [one word illegible] methods. Practical politics demands the present {and most} excellent service from Socialists *when in power anywhere.* You unconsciously postpone when in your closing words you seem to indicate that the Kingdom of Heaven will be set up on earth contemporary with your nebulous expression about Socialism.

I invoke your distinguished aid and efficiency in obtaining under patriotic & sane Socialism *somewhat earlier advantages* to the "little children," and the citizenship generally.

Very Truly
Wm G. Williams

ALS, InTI, Debs Collection.

    1. Williams was an attorney in Cincinnati.
    2. In "Message to the Little Children" (*Appeal,* December 27, 1913), Debs compared Christ's teachings with those of modern socialism, urged the young to join the Socialist party and "convert their parents," and predicted that socialism would usher in "the kingdom of heaven . . . here on earth."

Theodore Debs to William G. Williams

January 8, 1914
Terre Haute, Indiana

Dear Comrade Williams:—

In the absence of my brother who is away on account of his health I am having to acknowledge the receipt of your esteemed favor of the 7th. inst., criticising the address of my brother recently issued to the children, which in due time will be brought to my brother's attention and which I am sure will be fully appreciated by him. Permit me to say for my brother that he has always courted criticism and received it gladly when it came in the right spirit, the spirit of candor and fairness so manifest in your communication. Permit me to say further that your criticism of my brother's address is the first of an adverse nature yet received. It is not to be deprecated on that account for possibly this may be its chief virtue. I think my brother has never written anything that has brought him so many letters and met with such genuine enthusiasm and hearty appreciation as this address to the children. Still, this may not be conclusive as to its merits.

The address, you see, was intended for children and not {for} lawyers and critics, and the children at least understand and appreciate it for this office has been fairly flooded with their expressions of enthusiasm and delight since the address went out. Every child who has written a letter here in response to this address has done so to approve it and to thank my brother and send him love for having written it. Not a single expression has been received from any child to the contrary. This, I think, is pretty conclusive evidence from the children for whom the address was intended that it served its purpose even if it was "so bare of illimination" and so "ineffective" as an "elucidation of socialism."

The letters that have come in from the children have been not only from socialist children but from non socialist children as well and to them at least, judging by what they have been moved to say about it, it was a sufficient "elucidation" even though it was such a sad failure from your point of view.

To this it should be also added that some of the most prominent socialists and some of the keenest critics in the movement have pronounced this address the most effective to children ever issued. Comrade A. M. Simons, himself an author and critic of recognized standing, is on record as pronouncing this address the strongest appeal ever issued to children.[1]

Still you may be right and you are certainly entitled to the full benefit of your opinion and I am sure that my brother will receive it in the spirit in which it is offered and give it due consideration.

Pardon me if I suggest that your letter moves me to say that I think you owe it to yourself and to the cause to issue an address to children that shall be effective and serve this very important purpose, and if you succeed where my brother has failed he will appreciate the service you have rendered to him {as} well as the party.

Your fraternally
[Theodore Debs]

TLc, InTI, Debs Collection.

1. Under the title "Suffer Little Children," Debs's "Message to the Little Children" was one of his most widely reprinted essays. In addition to the *Appeal to Reason* and the *Milwaukee Leader* (which Algie Simons was editing), the essay appeared in the *Party*

Builder, the official national-party paper, *Christian Socialist, New York Call, Miners' Magazine, Miami Valley Socialist,* and others.

T. J. McDonald to EVD

January 14, 1914
Christopher, Illinois

Dear Sir

The Miners of Christopher Ill are going to celebrate Labor Day *here* that is miners Labor Day *April* 1st *1914* and a great number of them would like if possible to have you here to speak that day. There is a nice little local here of Socialists, {69,} and timber enough ripe to make 3 or 4 hundred more and a *spring* election for Mayor & *Council* coming on. Now Gene if it is possible We all wish to hve you here that day there is 1500 miners here and we will have 2 or 3 thousand more that day we will also have a number of straight Union Speakers of great note. The kind that tries to Keep politics out of the Union (God bless their simple minds) hoping you may see your way clear to give us that date I remain yours for the Revolution

T. J. McDonald
Christopher, Ill
Sec. Labor Day Association

P.S. Let us know the expense item it wont scare us good stuff is worth buying yours McDonald

ALS, InTI, Debs Collection.

Morris Hillquit to EVD

January 19, 1914
New York City

Dear Gene:

Here is a situation about which I want to consult with you. The "Puck,"[1] the oldest and probably the best known comic weekly in the country, has passed into the hands of the Straus family and is hereafter to be edited by Nathan Straus, Jr.[2] The new proprietors bring practically unlimited resources to the enterprise and they propose to make it a high grade publication. The character of the "Puck" will change considerably under their management, and among other things they propose to introduce several serious features in the magazine. They expect to hire the best talent for all departments and hope to develop a very large circulation.

Among the new features which they propose to introduce is to be a department on Socialism and social problems, and they are offering me the editorial charge of that page. This is to be a standing feature of the magazine, to appear bi-weekly at the start and later on perhaps weekly. Mr. Straus is ready to make a contract for three years or longer and to give me absolute control of the page without the slightest interference on his part. I am to be at liberty to fill the page myself or to print contributions of such other writers as I may choose. The editorial policy of the "Puck" will not be Socialistic, nor will it be anti-Socialistic. I am to be at liberty to criticise the editorial attitude of the magazine whenever I feel like it, including in campaign times. Should the "Puck" editorially support any political party or candidate, I am to be at liberty to attack its choice in my page, and I am besides to have the right to make direct propaganda for the Socialist Party and Socialist candidates during campaigns and between campaigns. I am offered $100 for each page.

I have been thinking over the offer for some time and have come to the conclusion that I should not feel like accepting it unless I had the approval and active co-operation of a group of responsible comrades, you among them, who would consent to share the burden with me. In other words, I do not want to make it an individual, freelance affair of my own. It goes without saying that I would distribute the compensation among the contributors in proportion to their contributions. The questions, then, I should like you to answer are these:

1. Do you advise me to accept the offer?

2. If so, would you permit me to call on you occasionally for contributions?

With very best wishes,

Sincerely and fraternally yours,
Morris Hillquit

TLS, InTI, Debs Collection.

1. Published weekly from 1877 to 1917, *Puck* was a leading journal of humor and satire with strong literature, drama, and art departments.

2. Nathan Straus (1889-1961) began his long career in journalism and communication with the *New York Globe* in 1909. He edited *Puck* from 1914 to 1917, at which time he sold the magazine to the Hearst International Magazine Company, which discontinued its publication in September 1917.

EVD to Fred D. Warren

January 19, 1914
Terre Haute, Indiana

My dear Fred:—

I have made an arrangement with the Rip-Saw,[1] to write their editorial etc. and speak under their auspices, and I think I ought to tell you about it. I had intended and was preparing to organize a little bureau of our own when I got strong enough to work again, believing that I could do my work better, be at home more, and get better results all around. But Phil Wagner[2] and Harry Tichenor[3] came over here and made me a proposition and terms that were so favorable in every way that I concluded to accept them for a time at least. I could not possibly have asked for anything better or more satisfactory than the conditions they proposed and I accepted.

I shall always have the same warm feeling for you personally and for all of the Appeal comrades and workers. All of them treated me at the very best and I can only think of them with feelings of thankfulness and affection.

Hoping that I shall get to see you occasionally and that we can continue to help each other in doing our work as we have in the past, and with kindest remembrances to Mrs. Warren and to the little Warrens who always greeted me so lovingly, I remain as ever

Yours in the cause
E. V. Debs

TLS, Warren Papers, Schenectady, New York.

1. The *Rip-Saw* was published in St. Louis by Phil Wagner from 1904 to 1917, when it became the *Social Revolution,* and in 1919 the *Social Builder.*

2. Phil Wagner was publisher of the *Rip-Saw* and its successors and of the *Melting Pot* and in 1916 edited and published *Labor and Freedom: The Voice and Pen of Eugene V. Debs.*

3. Henry Mulford Tichenor (1858-1922) was editor of the *Rip-Saw,* author of socialist songs and poetry, and a lifelong critic of organized religion, which he attacked in books, such as *The Creed of Constantine,* and in the *Melting Pot,* a monthly magazine that he and Wagner launched in January 1913. The *Melting Pot* was consistently, sometimes rabidly, critical of organized religion in general and of Roman Catholicism in particular.

EVD to Morris Hillquit

January 21, 1914
Terre Haute, Indiana

Dear Morris:—

Your communication of the 19th. in reference to the proposition to you by "Puck" is received and noted with satisfaction and delight. The proposition is exceedingly significant and gratifying, as it appears to me. I have not an instant's hesitation in advising you to accept it. Not to do so would be an egregious error amounting to positive and inexcusable folly. Why should we not take advantage of such a fine opportunity to get our message to the vast and varied clientele of this high grade capitalist publication which, owing to its pictorial and humorous features, has readers among all sorts and conditions of people?

This concession by Puck has been conquered and socialism accepts it standing erect with its hat on its head. It is not a hand-out solicited at the price of principle. There is no compromise about it. At least there need be none on our part.

It is a fair and square proposition made by "Puck" because "Puck" believes it will pay—in dollars, and so I believe it will for a time, but not for a very long time if the right kind of stuff goes into the socialist pages and with you in charge I am quite willing to take the chance.

It is hardly to be expected that capitalism and socialism can dwell in the same house together and I do not look to see this department maintained any longer, or at least much longer, than the Metropolitan Magazine skated on socialist ice.[1] But full advantage should be taken of the opening while it does last for several reasons. First, it will be a surprise of nation-wide interest and its significance will not be lost upon the people. Second, it will open new avenues to our propaganda and many thousands will be reached who will read our message in "Puck" when they would spurn it from any direct socialist source. Third, it will create widespread comment in the capitalist press, provoke general discussion and enliven and energize the socialist propaganda in many ways. Fourth, it will enable a few of our comrades to earn a few dollars which they need and which will help to keep them alive and to give more of themselves to our cause. There are other reasons which need not be mentioned here but there is not a single valid reason for rejecting the proposition. A few hypercriticals will howl.[2] Let them. They are the dogs in the manger of the socialist movement.

The proposition is a flattering personal compliment to you and I congratulate you. The enemy pays respectful homage to your ability, and socialism has become so powerful and influential and respectable that even an ultra capitalist publication of the highest character is compelled to recognize it and give it respectful consideration in its columns.

Of course you can count on me to help you in any way I can if you accept the proposition and you are at liberty to call on me at any time for any service I can render. Only I want no pay for the little I may be able to do. Whatever allowance there may be I wish to go to others who need it more. There is but one condition and that is that the socialist department must be clear socialism, without a trace of truckling, and this, as your letter assures, is a part of the proposition.

Wishing you all success in this new and promising undertaking I am as ever,

Yours fraternally
Eugene V. Debs

TLS, WHi, Hillquit Papers.

1. In July 1912, *Metropolitan* published the first of six articles by Hillquit on "Socialism Up to Date." In "Herron to the Fore" (*Appeal*, February 15, 1913), Debs praised *Metropolitan* for carrying socialist material and for agreeing to publish a series of articles by George Herron, beginning with its March 1913 issue.

2. Citing "several independent sources" who had criticized his writing for *Metropolitan* and accused him of a personal financial interest in the magazine, Hillquit defended "carrying the gospel of Socialism" in "one of the best popular magazines in the country" and denied "any proprietary interest" in it. *Party Builder*, January 3, 1914.

EVD to Carl E. Person[1]

February 14, 1914
Terre Haute, Indiana

My dear Brother:—

I wish to write to you but not being certain about your being allowed to receive mail I drop you this line to ask if a letter from me will reach you. I have read your recent appeal and clearly understand your situation. Count me with you in your efforts to secure a fair trial and a square deal. You are not the first nor will you be the last victim of corporation misrule and you may be sure that we who have had the same experience that you are having now will not desert you but will stand by you to the last.[2]

Believe me with all good wishes,

Yours fraternally,
Eugene V. Debs

TLc, InTI, Debs Collection.

1. Carl E. Person was secretary of Socialist party local in Clinton, Illinois, where he published the *Strike Bulletin* during the bitter strike on the Illinois Central and Harriman lines, which had been carried on since 1911. In September 1913, Person was savagely beaten by a former Clinton police chief, Tony Musser, and Person shot and killed Musser in the fight. Labor and socialist groups raised funds for the Person Defense League and Person was acquitted by a jury in Lincoln, Illinois, on October 4, 1914.

2. In a number of essays in the *Rip-Saw*—"Carl E. Person," March 1914; "Carl Person's Trial," August 1914; "Carl Person Acquitted," November, 1914—Debs sought funds for Person's defense and insisted that Person's shooting of Tony Musser was justifiable self-defense. Person wrote to Debs on August 10, 1914, to thank him "for the many good words you have spoken for me in our cause."

EVD to Morris Hillquit

February 20, 1914
Terre Haute, Indiana

Dear Morris:—

Your favor of the 18th. is at hand. I would rather your decision had been otherwise in the matter of the Puck proposition but I know you gave it your careful consideration and acted in accordance with your mature conviction. I know what that something is that makes us act in certain ways in such situations and you are right in having been finally influenced by your own intuition.

You are very kind to say what you do about the International Congress[1] and I should be glad to go but I guess I shall have to decline the nomination. Pardon these hurried lines as I am to leave on a long speaking tour in the Southwest[2] and shall be extremely busy getting everything in order before I start.

Best wishes to you always!

Yours fraternally,
Eugene V. Debs

TLS, WHi, Hillquit Papers.

1. The congress, which was scheduled for Vienna in July 1914, was rescheduled

for Paris on August 9 and then canceled because of the war. Hillquit's letter to Debs of February 18, 1914, has not been found, but in it Hillquit apparently suggested that Debs be a delegate. The American delegation, which was scheduled to sail for France on August 1, 1914, was composed of Hillquit, Emil Seidel, Victor Berger, Dr. George E. Lunn, Oscar Ameringer, and Charles Edward Russell. However, news of the cancellation of the conference reached them in New York in time for their trip to be canceled.

2. Debs's speaking tours were now arranged by and on behalf of the *Rip-Saw*.

EVD to Claude G. Bowers

April 22, 1914
Terre Haute, Indiana

My dear Friend Bowers: —
Returning here I find the copy of your eloquent and poetic address[1] at Boston on St. Patrick's Day awaiting me, for which please accept my thanks. I have gone through its pages and have found it to be beautiful and elevated in the sentiments expressed as is everything that comes from your pen or tongue, but I fear that addresses and occasions of this kind will be of little real help to the poverty stricken and suffering people of Ireland. The one thing they are suffering from is priestcraft and superstition and as long as they are ruled as they now are by the Roman political machine masquerading as a holy religious institution they will remain where they are and where they have been all these centuries, and no amount of glorification of Irish history and eulogy of Irish patriots will alter their slavish lot.[2]

Look into Italy and Spain, the Philippines and Mexico, where the Roman church has ruled for centuries in holy partnership with the robber kings, barons, plutocrats and other ruling and exploiting classes and you will see what is the matter with Ireland, and this is what ought to be said at a gathering of Irish on St. Patrick's Day but which, if said, would be resented by the Irish politicians of whom there are many in Boston and who are in fact the enemies and not the friends of the oppressed and long suffering Irish people.

As to Irish Home Rule, so-called, about which there has been so much fuss, it is ninety-nine per cent pure humbug and if established tomorrow would be of no earthly help to the peasants and toilers of Ireland, nor make their lot one particle more tolerable than it is today.

Priestcraft is the curse of Ireland, priestcraft in alliance with king-craft and landlordcraft, but the orator who would dare to make this true statement of Ireland's woes at a banquet composed of Irish gentlemen would quite likely be handled pretty roughly by way of applause and appreciation. That smooth and smug cardinal at Boston[3] and that other at Baltimore[4] who are hand in glove with Tammany Murphy,[5] with "Jim" Hill, Andrew Carnegie, Thomas Fortune Ryan[6] and that gang of brigands are the real enemies of the Irish people and they and their hypocritical ilk who hobnob with the rich while they roll their eyes heavenward, perched piously like the blood-sucking leeches they are, on the backs of the suffering poor, will have to be gotten rid of once and for all before poverty and misery, born of ignorance and superstition, relax their grasp upon the toiling and producing masses.

"The Irish Dawn" is in the class-conscious awakening of the Irish toiler class and their marshalling beneath the banner of International Revolutionary Socialism and this thank God sows with stars of hope their otherwise black and starless night.

Thanking you and with all kind wishes I am as ever

Yours sincerely
E. V. Debs

P.S. There are two books I venture to suggest that you ought to read. You will doubtless find them in the Washington library. They are "The Call of the Carpenter" and "The Carpenter and the Rich Man,"[7] both by Bouck White. You will thank me for making the suggestion.

TLS, InU, Lilly Library, Bowers MSS.

1. "The Irish Dawn."
2. Bowers's first book, *The Irish Orators: A History of Ireland's Fight for Freedom*, was published in 1916.
3. William O'Connell (1859-1944) was elevated to cardinal in 1911.
4. James Gibbons (1859-1944) was elevated to cardinal in 1886. His views on social policy were frequently attacked by Debs. Gibbons wrote the introduction to Bowers's *Irish Orators*.
5. Charles Francis Murphy (1858-1924) was chosen head of Tammany Hall in 1902 and retained the position until his death.
6. Thomas Fortune Ryan (1851-1928) was a New York financier who rose from a Baltimore dry-goods store to the boardrooms of more than thirty corporations with interests in public utilities, coal mines, railroads, and Congo diamond mines.
7. White's *Carpenter and the Rich Man*, a "companion book" to *The Call of the Carpenter*, was published in 1914. The material had appeared in serial form in *Coming Nation*, April 5, 1913.

Frank P. Walsh[1] to EVD

May 12, 1914
Washington, D.C.

Dear Sir:

This Commission is arranging for a series of Public Hearings in New York City beginning May 18th.

On May 21st and 22nd, they will conduct a Hearing on the American Federation of Labor, the Industrial Workers of the World and the Socialist Party.

It is the purpose of the Commission to secure from the representatives of these organizations a concise statement of their attitude and aims with relation to industrial problems and the general labor movement.

The participants in this Hearing from the respective points of view will have the privilege and will be called upon for an expression of their views with reference to the others.

The Hearing will be conducted in the form of question and answer, the questions being put to the witnesses by counsel and also by members of the commission, and will deal broadly with the subject.

The witnesses who will probably speak on behalf of the A.F. of L. are Messrs. Gompers, Sullivan,[2] and Gordon;[3] for the Socialist Party Messrs. Debs and Hayes,[4] and for the I.W.W. Messrs. Haywood, Giovannitti[5] and St. John.[6]

I trust that you will waive the formality of service of subpoena, and I will appreciate an immediate reply from you to this effect.

The Government allowance for mileage and attendance upon the Hearings is 5 cents per mile each way from the place of your residence to New York and return and $2.00 per day while in New York.[7]

For your information a copy of the Act creating the Commission is enclosed.

Very truly yours,
Frank P. Walsh
Chairman

TLS, InTI, Debs Collection.

1. Francis Patrick Walsh (1864-1939) was a prominent Kansas City trial lawyer when he was appointed by President Wilson in 1913 to head the Commission on Industrial Relations, which had been created by Congress on August 23, 1912, to investigate the causes of industrial conflict. The commission's hearings, held in various cities throughout the country, did much to arouse public sympathy for labor and hostility toward business during Wilson's first term. Walsh remained chairman of the

commission until 1918, when he became co-chairman, with former President Taft, of the National War Labor Board.

2. James William Sullivan (1848-1938) assisted Gompers as editor of the AFL's *American Federationist* and was one of organized labor's leading critics of socialism and advocates of direct legislation, on which he wrote a book, *Direct Legislation by the Citizenship Through the Initiative and Referendum* (1892).

3. Frederick G. R. Gordon (1860-1944) was one of the founders of the Social Democratic party before becoming a general organizer for the AFL in 1903. He was elected secretary of the American Anti-Socialist League in 1913.

4. Maximilian Sebastian Hayes (1866-1945) founded the *Cleveland Citizen* in 1891 as the official paper (weekly) of the Cleveland Central Labor Union and remained as editor until 1939. Hayes was both a socialist and ardent trade unionist and was from 1898 to 1937 regularly a delegate to the AFL conventions representing the International Typographical Union. Hayes left the Socialist party at the time of the left-wing split in 1919, helped form the Farmer-Labor party, and ran for vice-president on that party's ticket in 1920. By that time he had been for nearly thirty years the leading trade unionist in the socialist movement and the leading socialist in the AFL.

5. Arturo Giovannitti (1884-1959) edited the Italian Socialist Federation's *Il Proletario* for four years before joining the IWW in 1912 during the Lawrence, Massachusetts, textile strike, in connection with which he was charged and acquitted (with Joseph Ettor) of plotting the murder of a striker. Giovannitti left the IWW in 1916 in protest against the centralizing policies of William Haywood but was indicted in 1917 during the federal government's massive attack on IWW leaders. The case against Giovannitti was dropped in 1919 and he worked during the 1920s as an organizer for the Amalgamated Clothing Workers Union, as editor of that union's journal, *Advance*, and as a leader of the Anti-Fascist Alliance of America. Giovannitti was sometimes called "the workers' poet," and a volume of his verse, *Collected Poems*, was published in 1962.

6. Vincent St. John (1876-1929) was one of the founders of the IWW and the organization's chief executive officer from 1908 until his resignation in 1915. St. John published *The IWW: Its History, Structure, and Methods* in 1917.

7. Debs's response to this letter, if any, has not been found. He did not testify at the commission hearings in New York, which lasted from May 18 to June 30, 1913, and were marked by heated exchanges between Samuel Gompers, who charged that socialism "had done nothing to better the condition of the working man," and Morris Hillquit, who cited the Socialist party's 1912 campaign manual as proof that the party sought many of the same goals as the AFL. In addition to Gompers and Hillquit, the commission heard testimony from Gordon, Hayes, Giovannitti, and St. John. *New York Times*, May 21, 22, 23, 24, 1914. Debs was on a *Rip-Saw* lecture tour in New Jersey and New York from May 18 to May 31 and in the Midwest from June 1 to June 17, 1914. *Rip-Saw*, May 1914.

EVD to H. Richter[1]

June 3, 1914
Terre Haute, Indiana

Dear Comrade Richter: —

Some days ago a letter from you reached me while I was on a speaking tour in the Eastern states. It came to me with a number of others and being extremely busy at the time I had no chance to answer. Since then the letter has somehow been misplaced and I am unable to find it but I remember that you asked me to explain a certain reference to the Detroit faction of the I.W.W. in a recent article in the Miners' Magazine.[2] This would require considerable more time than I have now to spare as I am just back from my Eastern trip and have an enormous mass of mail and other accumulations to dispose of with only a couple of days here before having to leave on another long speaking trip in the West.

If I remember your inquiry correctly you wished to know why I think the Detroit faction of the I.W.W. will never amount to more than it does now. To answer fully I would have to go into the past to a considerable extent and go over matters of labor history which would require a deal of writing for which there is unfortunately no time. But briefly, the very name of the I.W.W. is offensive to the great mass of workers in this country and they shrink from it for reasons I think you understand. And the same thing is true in regard to the S.L.P.[3] and anything that has S.L.P. attached to it is simply queered in advance with the great mass of the workers. They will have nothing to do with it and for this sufficient cause can be shown. The spirit which has prevented the S.L.P. from developing into a great party and kept it down to the limits of a small sect will explain in part what I mean when I say there is no future for the faction you represent of the I.W.W.

I could go back over the files of the People[4] and show you falsehoods and slanders without number published about myself and others, which the editor[5] knew were lies and slanders at the time they were published, because they were so proved by members of the S.L.P. itself who knew the truth and who quit the party because of the refusal of the People to publish their articles and retract such falsehoods and slanders. I myself was grossly lied about in the People's columns and the People was convinced of it by good S.L.P. members who knew the facts but never was a line of retraction allowed to appear, but on the contrary the lying went on as before. This has been a long time ago and personally I care nothing about it and harbor no feeling of resentment, but it is this disreputable, mean and hateful spirit which drove hundreds of its best members from its ranks which will account for the stunted growth of the S.L.P. and everything connected with it. Had it not been for this mean spirit the Socialist party would probably never have been organized.

This in brief is my answer to your inquiry. I should not of my own accord have revived these memories. I am doing what I can to have these matters forgotten for I wish the socialists united in one party and in one industrial organization.

With fraternal regards and all good wishes, I remain

Yours fraternally
E. V. Debs

TLc, InTI, Debs Collection.

1. Herman Richter was secretary of the Workers International Industrial Union, which was organized in Detroit in 1909 to preserve the "original principles" of the IWW following the departure of Daniel DeLeon and his supporters from that organization and the IWW's repudiation of political action.

2. In "Industrial Organization" (*Miners' Magazine*, May 7, 1914), Debs called for a new industrial union that should have as its nucleus a merger of the UMW and the Western Federation of Miners. The IWW, he added, could not successfully play a role in the new movement because "the Chicago faction, it now seems plain, stands for anarchy" and "the Detroit faction, for reasons not necessary to discuss here, will never amount to more than it does today."

3. Socialist Labor party.

4. The official paper of the SLP. The daily *People* had suspended publication on April 4, 1914.

5. Daniel DeLeon. Despite their long and often bitter rivalry in the socialist movement, Debs fully acknowledged DeLeon's significance in spreading socialist ideas in "Tribute to Daniel DeLeon" (*Rip-Saw*, August 1914).

EVD to Christian Balzac Hoffman[1]

July 1, 1914
Terre Haute, Indiana

My dear Comrade Hoffman:

Two of the finest young comrades I know are Edna P. Nutter, Industrial Add., R.F.D. 2, Clarksburg, W.Va. and John E. Raikes, Union Heights, R.F.D. 2, Clarksburg, W. Va.[2] They are lovers and sweethearts and engaged to be married but too poor and too many to provide for to get married. She is 20, he is 21. Both yearn with a passion that is marvelous for a chance to be educated and to serve the cause. I have just written her at considerable length and to him also and I am doing the little I can to help and encourage them. I have told them about the College[3] and about you and advised them to write to you. Let me suggest that you mail each of them your prospectus and printed matter and that you drop them a personal line of encouragement. I have told them they would overcome every obstacle because the very spirit of which they gave evidence was unconquerable and bound to win out at last. I have a fourteen page letter from the girl crying aloud for a chance to serve and as Mrs. Debs and I went over it together last night our eyes overflowed with tears. I am going to keep an eye on these two young folks and help them in every way I can and I know you will also give them such encouragement as is in your power. When I think of these two great young souls I can feel more than ever the crying need of such a school as we have in mind and will soon have, I trust, in fact, to confer upon such as these the advantages of which they have been robbed in this unspeakably cruel and pitiless system.

I am just preparing to leave on my speaking tour in the East. Greetings and kind wishes to you and Mrs. Hoffman[4] from Mrs. Debs and

Yours always,
[Eugene V. Debs]

TL (signature missing), KU, Kansas Collection, Hoffman Papers.

1. Christian Balzac Hoffman (1851-1915) was a native of Switzerland who was brought to America in 1854. He amassed a fortune in the milling and banking business in Kansas, retired in 1910, and spent the remainder of his life lecturing on and promoting socialism, for a time as editor of the *Chicago Daily Socialist* and, beginning in July 1914, as president of People's College in Fort Scott, Kansas.

2. Debs spoke at Elkins, near Clarksburg, West Virginia, on May 14, 1914.

3. People's College was founded in Fort Scott, Kansas, in July 1914 to provide "college vocational education" specifically for workers. Debs agreed to serve as chancellor, Hoffman was president, and Jake Sheppard was secretary of the college, which eventually claimed 4,000 "correspondence and residence students" enrolled in courses in law, history, English, mathematics, bookkeeping, and shorthand.

4. Anna Wares Hoffman.

Frank Putnam[1] to EVD

July 1, 1914
St. Louis, Missouri

My Dear Debs:

It was heartening to get your friendly letter. The past year has put me to a hard test—merely to hold the little ground already gained in securing my family against want. As you know, I fought the railroad and political exploiters[2] in Texas with more boldness and severity than one so little protected by property possessions perhaps could wisely fight them. They finally "got me," by shutting me out of employment on the Texas daily papers. So I had to come here to get work to support my boys and girls, temporarily at least. While they continued in school in Houston I have spent most of the past year here, helping campaign for a municipal ownership city charter, opposed by the public utility companies and the big cinch generally. Yesterday the charter was adopted by the voters. The same day my little wife informed me she had been able to trade some idle land for a home—the first we have owned for over twenty years—the "roof of our own" for which we have worked while giving the sons and the daughter such educational opportunity as we could. This means I shall be able, in the fall, to go back to Houston and either find or make employment for myself there, and continue in the field of my choice as a factor advocating democracy—as nearly as possible in all issues pure democracy. At 45 I am more than ever encouraged to believe in the divinity of human nature; in man's ultimate evolution into real civilization. Lacking any talent which would enable me to sustain myself on the outmost firing line, I have done my damnedest, as the cowboy said, helping take outposts, leaving the citadel to be taken by those who will follow.

Here is a page of the P-D,[3] showing you the kind of work I try to get past the watchful guard of the profit-takers, and sometimes do get by them.

You have my love and admiration and sincere friendship, as always since I began following your career of service. My powers are insignificant, but you will please me by commanding me when I can give you any service.

Fatihfully,
Frank Putnam

TLS, InTI, Debs Collection.

    1. Frank A. Putnam (1869-1949) was a newspaperman in Houston, St. Louis, and Chicago before World War I and a regular contributor to socialist publications. In "Three Great Orators" (*Appeal,* June 3, 1911), Putnam called Debs the greatest living orator, to whom "the future belonged."
    2. Putnam's articles appeared regularly in Tom Hickey's *Rebel.* See, e.g., "The Land Question," *Rebel,* January 8, 1912.
    3. *St. Louis Post-Dispatch.*

EVD to Walter Lanfersiek[1]

July 8, 1914
Terre Haute, Indiana

Dear Comrade Lanfersiek: —

Your favor of the 3rd. inst. came in my absence. I note what you say in regard to the time asked for by the campaign committee and I am now communicating with the Rip-Saw comrades in regard to the matter and you will hear from them direct. I surmise that this action of the committee is taken at the suggestion of Comrade Thompson[2] who desires me to have a part in his campaign against the Gompers craft unionist.[3] But I ought to be frank enough to say that even if I could take part in this campaign I am not at all sure that my speeches would meet with the approval of Comrade Thompson unless he has changed his trade union attitude since he left Milwaukee.[4] If I spoke against his opponent I would certainly hammer him hard but I would not stop at him alone, I would hammer without mercy the whole raft of craft union fakers, and hardest of all would I hammer, as I invariably do, rotten craft unionism itself, and this totally regardless of how many trade unionists are offended with what I say. Upon this subject I do not compromise and I would rather lose votes a thousand times than to refrain {from} telling the truth for fear of shooing away some of Gompers' dupes. I cannot change my speeches in a campaign for the sake of getting votes. I despise the politician inside of the Socialist party far more than I do anywhere else. I deem it proper to make this explanation under the circumstances so that there may be no misunderstanding hereafter.

Personally I feel {it would be} hardly fair to the Rip-Saw comrades to set aside their own bookings in campaign time after they have been carrying me during the lean months when the expense was great and there was no campaign on. However I am willing to comply with the request of the national committee if I can do so without doing violence to the Rip-Saw and to the obligation I am under to its management.

Thanking you and the committee and with all good wishes for your success I remain,

Yours fraternally,
E. V. Debs

TLc, InTI, Debs Collection.

1. National secretary of the Socialist party.
2. Carl Dean Thompson was now manager of the information department at the

party's national headquarters. In his unsuccessful campaign for Congress in Chicago's Seventh district in 1914, he ran third behind Democrat Frank Buchanan, who won the election, and Republican Niels Juul. Two years later, Thompson ran third again behind Juul, who won, and Buchanan. Thompson got 13.5 percent of the vote in 1914, 9.0 percent in 1916.

3. Frank Buchanan was international president of the Bridge and Structural Iron Workers from 1901 to 1905 and thereafter was an organizer for that union and others in the Chicago area.

4. Before moving to Chicago, Thompson was an important cog in the Berger machine in Wisconsin, a socialist member of the state legislature from 1907 to 1909 and Milwaukee city clerk in 1910-11.

EVD to Charles H. Kerr

July 11, 1914
Xenia, Ohio

Dear Comrade Kerr:—

The enclosed article on DeLeon was written for the Rip-Saw[1] but in making up the forms it was omitted, to my regret. I shall see that it goes in the August issue and in the meantime I am sending it to the New York People. But I have a personal reason for wishing it to appear in the International Socialist Review and I am hoping you can find room for it in the August issue without imposing on your space. I already have an article with you but you may be able to accommodate this also without asking too much.[2]

A good many members of the Socialist party will not like this article at all and will in fact resent it, but no matter. I think that what I have said is due to DeLeon and therefore I am saying it. Personally I have as good ground as anyone, probably more, for grievance against him, as the paper he edited lied about me outrageously for a long time after the Socialist party was organized; these lies were proven to him to be lies and he knew they were lies but he never retracted a word he had slanderously published about me. He had, moreover, as Lucien Sanial said, "an extraordinary talent for intrigue" and he was anything but scrupulous and honest about a good many things, but when all this is said there still remains his great work for the movement for which we are bound to give him credit and I cannot permit the recollection of any personal wrong he did me interfere with my duty to him and to the cause for which he lived and died. I therefore hope you can do me the kindness to give space to the enclosed article in your August issue.

Yours fraternally,
Eugene V. Debs

TLc, InTI, Debs Collection.

1. "Tribute to Daniel DeLeon," *Rip-Saw*, August 1914.
2. Debs's "Homestead and Ludlow" appeared in the August 1914 issue of *International Socialist Review*, but not his "Tribute to Daniel DeLeon." Nor did Kerr publish it in subsequent issues.

Julius Gerber[1] to EVD

July 20, 1914
New York City

Dear Comrade Debs:

Through my correspondence with the "Rip Saw," in reference to dates in New York, I was informed that while the "Rip Saw" has cancelled the engagement made with Sol Fieldman,[2] that you were to speak for the Church of the Social Revolution on September 13. You, however, agreed to speak at that meeting.

I was rather surprised at your attitude to speak at that meeting in spite of the protest of Local New York, and think that your action is due to not knowing conditions in New York.

For the past few years a number of individuals and several organizations outside of the party, though many of their members are also members of the party, but few are members of Local New York, have made it a point to interfere with the work of the Party Organization as much as possible.[3] If Local New York arranges a meeting in one large hall, they proceed and arrange another a week or so before or after our meeting, with the result that both meetings are failures. We had that last year, and I am afraid that we will have the same this year should you adhere to your decision to speak at the Church of the Social Revolution meeting on September 13.

Local New York is well able to take care of the agitation for Socialism in its territory. We are doing everything, and were it not for the constant interference by outside organizations, we could do much more; but the outside public does not know the difference nor does it care by whom the meeting is held. If the speaker is a well known Socialist, they will flock to that meeting; and if two meetings are held at about the same time in practically the same territory, they get

confused, marvel at the fine system of cooperation among the Socialists, divide their attention, with the result that the meetings are
financially and morally failures.

The Executive Committee of Local New York decided to inform
you of these facts, so that you may know them and act accordingly;
and while we want you here for October 10 at Carnegie Hall and
for a later date in October in the 12th Congressional District, and
we will hold these meetings regardless of what you decide to do about
the meeting of the Church of Social Revolution, we do want you to
know that the Party has no connection with that organization, that
in spite of the fact that the date falls during the campaign, the gentlemen who form that organization, some of whom are party members
and most of whom claim to be Socialists, did not even find it necessary
to inform us about this meeting; and we knew nothing about it until
we got the notice from the "Rip Saw."[4]

We, therefore, think that in the interest of the cause and the organized Party movement, you should not speak here at that meeting;
but we do hope that you will help us by being here on the dates we
want—especially, do we want you for a date at the end of October,
because we are sure we can elect Comrade London[5] to Congress, and
we want your help to do it.

Wishing you success in your work, I am

Fraternally yours,
Julius Gerber
Executive Secretary,
Local New York

TLS, InTI, Debs Collection.

1. Julius Gerber was born in Riga, Latvia, in 1872 and was brought to America
in 1886. He was one of the founders of the Socialist party in New York City and
Kings County and executive secretary of the New York local from 1911 to 1922.
Gerber later (1920-22) served on the party's national executive committee.

2. Solomon Fieldman was a delegate from New York to the socialist convention
in 1908 and for many years was director of the Church of the Social Revolution
(Bouck White's church) in New York.

3. In a letter to Debs on July 17, 1914, Fieldman assured him that the Church
of the Social Revolution was "a bona fide Socialist Church" and charged that certain
members of Local New York were "troublemakers . . . who are attempting to disrupt
this organization."

4. The *Rip-Saw* for September 1914 announced that Debs was booked for seventy
speeches in the Northeast, including a dozen in New York City, from September 6
to November 2, 1914.

5. Meyer London (1871-1926), a native of Poland, came to America in 1891,
studied law, and was admitted to the bar in 1894. One of the founders of the Socialist
party on New York's Lower East Side, he was the second socialist elected to Congress,
where he served from 1915 to 1919 and from 1921 to 1923.

EVD to Julius Gerber

July 22, 1914
Terre Haute, Indiana

Dear Comrade Gerber: —

Your favor of the 20th. inst. has been received and carefully read. Yes, I am to speak for the Church of the Social Revolution in New York, on September 13th., having agreed to do so promptly upon request, and for obvious reasons, not dreaming that any socialist would have any objection to my doing so in the light of the outrageous sentence imposed upon Comrade Bouck White[1] by the New York courts for having attempted in a perfectly {lawful} and orderly way to advance the propaganda of the socialist movement.

It is true that Comrade White's particular method has been criticised by socialists but I am bound to say in his behalf {that} his method in this instance, foolish as it may seem to his critics, is still far preferable to the methods of those who sit back and do nothing but talk and find fault with those who actually do things.[2]

When I heard of Comrade White's infamous persecution my blood ran hot with indignation and I wondered that the socialists of New York were so little inclined to voice their protest or to do anything whatever in his behalf.

Now here was the opportunity for Local New York to hold a protest demonstration and register a protest that would have been loud enough to have been heard by the country, but Local New York failed to act, from what cause is of no consequence here, but now that others have taken the matter up, I am still more surprised that Local New York, having done nothing itself, now objects to anything being done by anyone else.

Now, Comrade Gerber, I think you should know that I have a comradely regard for Local New York and also that I am strong for party discipline, and that it goes against my grain to say or do aught that may even remotely undermine discipline or create dissension, but in this instance I feel no compunction in speaking for the Church of the Revolution in protest against the brutal incarceration of a comrade who lies in jail all these beastly hot months for having served you and me and our cause according to his conscience and his light.

You are quite right in saying that the comrades in New York can rarely be gotten to pull together for the success of a meeting or for the good of the movement, and that what one set of comrades undertakes another promptly throws cold water on. This, alas, is but too true as I know of my own experience in New York for rarely have I spoken there without having to placate some opposition or by personal appeal try to quiet the outbreak of some faction or element that complained that the other set had a machine and was running things to suit themselves. Were it not for this very unfortunate and altogether inexcusable petty jealousy and factional envy New York would long since have a member in congress and the movement would be far in advance of what it is today.

For this, Comrade Gerber, I know that you and many other good comrades like you are not responsible and that you deplore it as much as any one; I know that you are large enough and broad-minded enough to overlook all petty things and work whole-heartedly for the good of the cause, and now let me say that there is a chance here to set an example to the comrades of New York and inspire them all with the desire and imbue them with the spirit to work together on all occasions to make a success of every undertaking and to unite their efforts at all times to build up the movement. Let those who are now objecting come to the front and work for the success of the meeting on September 13th. and put the comrades of the Church of the Revolution and those who sympathize with them under obligation to reciprocate by working for the success of the later meetings to be held during the campaign under the auspices of Local New York. This will insure the success of all the meetings and be for the good of the socialist movement of New York in general.

You need have no fear that the meeting on September 13th. is going to be a failure. I have an intuition about these matters that rarely deceives me. That meeting is going to be a grand success so far as attendance and enthusiasm are concerned and the best thing the socialists can do is to stop objecting and pitch in and lend a hand to make it an epoch-marking demonstration of protest against judicial tyranny and one of the forerunners of the social revolution.

When the request to speak at this meeting was wired to me by such a prominent New York comrade as Sol Fieldman of course I took it for granted that it voiced the command of the socialists of New York and I felt it my duty to accept, which I promptly did,[3] not dreaming, as I have already said, that there would be any objection on the part of socialists but fully expecting them all to join in making the demonstration a great event. I can understand how objections might come from capitalist sources to our protesting against {the} tyrannical persecution and brutal incarceration of one of our comrades for having served our cause, but how any socialist can by any stretch of the imagination find it in his heart to object, it is simply impossible for me to understand.

Now, my dear comrade, I have tried to write to you in explanation of my position in the same comradely spirit in which you have written to me and I earnestly hope that the comrades of Local New York will find it consistent to withdraw any objections they may have entertained and that they may see their way clear to encourage all the comrades in New York to work together in harmony for the success {of this} and all other meetings that are held to further our propaganda and advance the interests of our movement.

With sincere greetings and all kind wishes to you and to your comrades I remain as ever,

Yours faithfully,
[Eugene V. Debs]

TLc, InTI, Debs Collection.

1. On May 13, 1914, Bouck White was sentenced to six months in prison for disrupting the services at Calvary Baptist Church ("Rockefeller's Church") by demanding that the minister answer the question "Did Jesus Teach the Immorality of Being Rich?"

2. Debs praised White and denounced his imprisonment in "Bouck White" (Rip-Saw, August 1914).

3. On July 8, 1914, Debs wrote Fieldman that he would "be very glad indeed to speak for Bouck White and the cause at your proposed Hippodrome meeting if circumstances are such that I am able to do so."

EVD to Comrade[1]

July 23, 1914
Fort Scott, Kansas

COMRADE: —

I have been with you in many campaigns and now I am enlisting your services in the greatest campaign of all—a campaign for education. The results of this campaign will reach every worker, bring freedom and establish equal opportunity in truth. I can conceive of no greater work in which you and I can unite.

The People's College is established. The work is progressing. These loyal comrades, Hoffman, LeSueur,[2] Sheppard, Lowe, Brewer, Wilson, Work, England, McDonald, Kirkpatrick and a host of others whom you know, will devote themselves to the success of your college. Our correspondence work, by which we will reach the workers in the remotest and most isolated parts of the continent, will begin September 15th. The residence college will be under way within the year.

What shall be done depends on the People's College Union.[3] This

Union is the founder and director of the People's College. To build a college, we must build the Union. That is your work and mine.

I am appealing to the men and women who form the fighting squad in the army of the Revolution. It is an honor to be named among them. You have answered every call in the past. You will hear this call as we have heard it and answer in the same spirit—the spirit of service for labor's emancipation. Help given now is help at the crucial moment.

Read this letter to the comrades. If every one of our 6,000 Socialist Locals joins the Union and enrolls members, we will reach the mark we have set for September 1st.

This is our College. Not a dollar of profit is to be made out of the school. It belongs to the people and is only endowed as the people endow it. No master class can endow and control this school. It is ours. Let us make it worthy of the great class to which we belong— the workers of the world.

Shall not we who build all schools have one school of our own? Join with us in building up a great national school for the education of the toiling and producing millions who have always designedly been kept in mental darkness by their exploiters and oppressors.

We await your co-operation. Send your application for membership and join us in the fight for free and universal education.

Yours for the workers,

E. V. Debs

President

People's College Union.

TLS, NcD, Socialist Party of America Papers.

1. This form letter was sent out on People's College Union letterhead.

2. Arthur Le Sueur (1867-1950) was a Minot, North Dakota, lawyer who served as mayor of that city in 1912-13 and as a member of the Socialist party national executive committee in 1915-16. Le Sueur was vice-president of People's College until 1916, when he became president of the school. The others named here, previously identified, were Christian Balzac Hoffman, Jacob Sheppard, Caroline A. Lowe, George Brewer, Jackson Stitt Wilson, John M. Work, George Allan England, Duncan McDonald, and George Kirkpatrick.

3. Funds for People's College came from People's College Union members who pledged to pay a dollar a year for five years as dues and in return received the monthly *College News*.

Upton Sinclair to EVD

July 27, 1914
Croton-on-Hudson, New York

Dear Comrade Debs:

I am making an anthology of Socialist literature[1] for publication. I would like to include one or two extracts from your writings. Would it be putting too much of a burden upon a busy man to ask you to indicate to me what you consider the best? If you have kept any scrapbooks[2] of this sort you might lend them to me.

Fraternally,
U. Sinclair

TLS, InTI, Debs Collection.

1. Sinclair's anthology *The Cry for Justice* was published in Philadelphia in September 1915. Two of Debs's writings, "A Sentiment of Social Reform" ("While there is a lower class . . ."), and "Jesus," which portrayed Christ as "a martyr of the working class," were included in the work.

2. Both Debs and his brother, Theodore, were careful keepers of scrapbooks, which are reproduced as Series III in *The Papers of Eugene V. Debs 1834-1945* (Microfilm Edition, Microfilming Corporation of America, 1983).

John F. Noll to Theodore Debs

July 29, 1914
Huntington, Indiana

Dear Mr. Debs: —

Upon my return home your latest communication[1] was handed to me, and replying to same, would say: —

Our Sunday Visitor certainly wishes to treat everyone, even her enemies, fairly. Father Kluser sent in a series of articles somewhat over a year ago and along with same a couple of letters which had been sent him by your brother or yourself. These he sent in order to show how harsh was the language and how strong the epithets used in the communication, in order to justify his caustic language. I had objected to print his letters because of his harsh expressions and also demanded that he assure me he would substantiate these accusations. Perusing the articles, I discovered that he gave a reference from several Socialistic papers for nearly everything that he charged. The only thing which he did not seem to have reference for, was your brother's home (mansion).

You say that an injustice was done you before our 1,800,000 readers. However, at that time our circulation was no more than one-third
what it is at present, but if you wish us to print in our paper that
portion of your letter in which we are invited to Terre Haute to
inspect your brother's home, I am willing to do so.

Father Kluser sent several other communications to us after that
one series, but we refused to print the same. The fact is, we have
been letting up considerably in fighting Socialism. During several
months we had not a word on the subject; we feel that the Catholic
Church should not shoulder the whole brunt of this opposition herself.
Whilst Catholics in Terre Haute and elsewhere might feel kindly
toward your brother, he certainly does not reciprocate as is evident
from the many severe articles he has in the "Melting Pot."[2]

Assuring you that I, personally, try to be full of charity, I am

Yours very respectfully,
J. F. Noll

TLS, InTI, Debs Collection.

1. In a series of letters dated July 8, 20, and 21, 1914, Theodore Debs renewed
his demand that Father Noll either substantiate or repudiate the charges made against
Gene and him in *Our Sunday Visitor* by Morgantown, West Virginia, priest C. Joseph
Kluser.

2. The *Melting Pot*, published by Phil Wagner and edited by Henry Tichenor in
St. Louis, carried a number of "severe articles" on the church by both Theodore
and Gene. See, e.g., "Where It [the Church] Will Stand," April 1913; "Howl of the
Holy Humbug," June 1913; "The Frocked Fraud of Morgantown," July 1913.

Theodore Debs to Upton Sinclair

August 15, 1914
Terre Haute, Indiana

Dear Comrade Sinclair:—

Your note of the 10th. has just come into my hands. Having just
returned from the southwest there are some pressing accumulations
awaiting me but as soon as these are disposed of in the next day or
two I will try to send you what you want. I note by the circular
enclosed by you about what is desired for your purpose and shall be
glad to send you extracts from Gene's writings as requested and assist
you in any other way I can. With all good wishes I am,

Yours in the cause,
Theodore Debs

TLS, InU, Lilly Library, Sinclair MSS.

EVD to Claude G. Bowers

December 15, 1914
Terre Haute, Indiana

My dear Claude Bowers:—

I read with much appreciation your Washington letter in Sunday's Tribune.[1] You were more than kind in what you had to say about the socialists. You were generous, magnanimous, as you have always been in the treatment of those who differ with you in politics. You were also generous, as you always are, in what you had to say of me, and I need not say that such kindness touches me purely because of the spirit of it. I certainly want no office; I have no use for what are usually called "honors," but I confess that I do love an honest friend and that I love to have an honest friend love me.

But aside from all this we all read your Washington letter with keen interest, and it is the only Washington letter we do read. You have a way of writing, peculiarly your own, that puts life into your lines and makes the words blossom.

In your Sunday article I was particularly pleased with what you said about Meyer London. He deserves every bit of it and you have my word for it that he will not disappoint you. I have taken the liberty to send him your article and also to write him at some length telling him about you and expressing the desire that he know you personally. You will no doubt see him soon after he gets to Washington. You will find him as bright and interesting a chap as you have met in many a day. You will like him and he will like you and you need to know each other. I hope that in this I have taken no undue liberty.

Allow me to wish you and Mrs. Bowers[2] a right joyous holiday season. Please remember me kindly to Senator Kern.

You are very busy. Do not answer.

Yours always,
E. V. Debs

TLS, InU, Lilly Library, Bowers MSS.

1. In Bowers's column, "Washington Side-Lights" (*Terre Haute Tribune*, December 13, 1914) he described a mass meeting in Madison Square Garden in New York on November 11, 1914. He had "hurried to the Garden to hear Gene Debs speak," and while Debs was not in fact on the program, it was "the largest, most enthusiastic, and impressive political gathering" Bowers had ever attended and he promised to "keep the socialist readers of the *Tribune* in touch with their man [Meyer] London after he reaches Washington."

2. Bowers and Sybil McCaslin were married in November 1911 soon after Bowers went to Washington as Senator Kern's assistant.

EVD to Carl D. Thompson[1]

December 16, 1914
Terre Haute, Indiana

Dear Comrade Thompson: —

You are very likely receiving communications similar to the enclosed or hearing reports of the Seidel-Bede debate[2] to the same effect. A doctor who dropped in here after hearing the debate said: "Bede makes a monkey of Seidel, a laughing stock, and makes socialism appear ridiculous and contemptible. If the Socialist party stands for that debate it will not last long." Substantially the same report has come to us from other sources. I have advised that this latest writer write direct to Seidel himself just as she has written to us. I think it is due him as well as the party. That this debate is hurting the cause wherever it is heard I have not the least doubt.

Bede and Seidel have been shrewdly matched by the capitalist bureau to the hurt of socialism. Seidel is no match at all for Bede in a debate. I know them both. Seidel is slow, sincere, a good speaker and would make a good debater with an opponent of his type and mental process. But in Bede he is confronted by a shrewd politician who talks like a house afire, who has wit of lightning, knows all of the tricks of the platform, understands the crowd and is an adept at the game and Seidel has as much chance against Bede in that sort of an arrangement as a hummingbird in a whirl wind.

Seidel's very seriousness becomes a matter of joke and ridicule under Bede's utterly merciless castigation. Bede ought to {go} up against a socialist such as Stanley Clark[3] who would lash him from the platform at his own game in the very first round. Bede doesn't discuss socialism and isn't expected to. He is hired and paid for just what he is doing and that is to make socialism appear as stuff and nonsense to great Chautauqua {and Lyceum} audiences all over the country.

I am writing this to you presuming you to be personally near to Seidel and venturing to suggest that you frankly lay this matter before him. I think it due him. I would want my comrades to be equally frank with me under similar circumstances. You can if you wish hand him this letter or send him a copy of it. It is due him to know just what is being said in such letters as the enclosed, and it is also a matter that concerns the party.

I could have gotten my own price per lecture for doing the Chautauqua stunts under their management, but refused all their offers. Not that I do not think the Chautauqua is alright if we have a fair show in making the arrangements, but I did not propose to be used to give the enemies of socialism a chance to match me with a clown and joker who had no intention of discussing socialism at all but was simply hired for being long on cheap wit, coarse satire, rapid-fire speech, vaudeville jokes and other similar equipment to laugh socialism from the stage under pretense of debate.

Men who are pitted against each other in debate ought to be properly matched. There are men in the socialist movement who would meet Bede on his own ground and beat him to a finish, but Seidel is not one of them. Seidel is capable of holding his own with abler men than Adam Bede but they would have to be of a different type than Bede.

You may think I should have sent this direct to Seidel myself. I would have done so if he felt personally friendly towards me. But he does not. For this {reason} I do not blame him. That is his affair.[4] For this I am sending it to you for such action as you may see fit to take in regard to it. The wonder to me is that there has not been a demand before now upon the party to stop the debate. This would be humiliating to Seidel and certainly not creditable to the party and should if possible be avoided.

It is not agreeable to me to say anything to discourage any comrade whether he is friendly to me or not. I am always glad when I can say or do anything in the way of commending or helping; and it is only from a sense of duty that I now write to you, believing you to be a near friend of Seidel, and ask that you proceed as in your judgment you may think proper in the matter.

With all kind regards and good wishes I remain,

Yours fraternally,
Eugene V. Debs

TLc, InTI, Debs Collection.

1. Thompson was serving as manager of the information department of the national office in Chicago.

2. The debate between James Adam Bede and Emil Seidel on the subject "Is Socialism Desirable in the United States?" was held, according to the *American Socialist* (October 5, 1914), in "100 cities before 100,000 people." Bede (1856-1942) was the editor and publisher of a number of newspapers in Minnesota before being elected to Congress, where he served from 1903 to 1909. Until World War I he was a prominent antisocialist lecturer.

3. Stanley J. Clark, called Preacher Clark, was a radical Texas attorney who was immensely popular on the socialist lecture circuit in the Southwest and was considered particularly effective in debates with antisocialist speakers. Clark was later imprisoned at Leavenworth for his opposition to World War I.

4. Seidel was Debs's running mate in the 1912 campaign. At the party's national

convention that year he ran second to Debs for the presidential nomination and cast
his own vote for Charles Edward Russell.

EVD to Jake Sheppard

December 22, 1914
Terre Haute, Indiana

My dear "Jake":—

I am having to write to you in a way that is nothing less than
painful to me as I am sure you will well understand. Sunday just
passed I gave a lecture at Chicago[1] and at the close Comrade Reynolds[2]
came to my room at the hotel and told me a long story which I would
very much rather not have heard. I should not now write to trouble
you, busy as I know you to be, but for the fact that there is something
brewing that is seriously going to hurt the school[3] unless something
is done to head it off.

As to the merits of the misunderstanding between yourself and
Reynolds[4] I cannot be the judge. I only know that each of you feels
that the other has failed him. This would not be so bad if it remained
purely a personal matter, regrettable as it might be, but unless you
and Stephen come to some kind of an understanding the matter is
going to be placed before the national executive board of the Socialist
party,[5] before Comrade Steinmetz[6] and every one of the persons
connected with the school in any official capacity. Reynolds assured
me that he had not the least personal malice but he felt that it was
his duty to the school and those who were promoting it to lay certain
facts before them and that if then they still wanted to go forward
they could do so and that he at least could feel himself absolved from
all responsibility.

Now let me say for Reynolds that long as I have known him this
is the first time I have ever heard him make a charge or even say an
unkind word about a comrade. He says that a certain man high up
in the Lasalle School,[7] one of its heads in fact, gave him all the inside
facts about your connection with that institution, the exact amounts
of the "enormous monies" you have been paid etc. etc. I will not
repeat the things that this man is alleged to have said about you but
I only want you to know that certain grave charges against you are
being made by men high up in the Lasalle School. I do not know the
name or names of these persons, did not ask, and in fact did not wish
to know.

Reynolds says you and he entered into an agreement, that you put it in your pocket and promised to send him a copy of it, that you made various excuses for not doing so, and that from that day to this he has been unable to get a copy of said agreement.

He says you agreed to furnish him with a stenographer to enable him to do the work he was to do and that you have persistently refused to fulfill this part of your agreement. Notwithstanding this he claims that he went on with his work and did all the work the agreement bound him to do except that you had expressly ordered him not to do. He says the work is ready and has been for some time but that you have contemptuously refused to answer his letters, to examine his work or to do any of the things you were bound to do in the agreement.

Reynolds says moreover that you ordered him to arrange for a certain woman at Chicago, a Normal school teacher of high rank, to take a position with the School, that he made such arrangement and that the women wrote to you twice but that you refused to even answer her letters.

There is a good deal more but I am not going to attempt to put it down here. Reynolds says he has all your letters and that he will prove his case by these alone.

Through all his recital Reynolds betrayed not the least anger or malice, so far as I could see. He said he was brokenhearted because he had loved you and it was impossible for him to believe that you could treat him in such a manner. He says he is still ready to do anything to arrive at an understanding and to be your comrade and friend, but that if there was no disposition on your part to arrive at such an understanding, or even to answer his letters, he says it would be his duty to present the facts to those interested to prevent further breaches of faith and to prevent others who might become connected with the school from having the painful experience he has had.

Now I know you have your side of the story and I told Reynolds about the money you had sent him and everything else I knew favorable to your side, not forgetting to say that you had never said an unkind word against him or even had found any fault with him.

Reynolds said that if you would meet him with me present he felt certain that an understanding could be effected. I need not say that I would gladly do anything in my power to heal the wounds and to bring you two comrades to a happy understanding.

I met a number of the people who are attending Reynolds school, and they are among the finest I have ever met. There are whole families in his classes and he is giving them a course of lessons and delivering a series of lectures covering the season, all drawn from the work he prepared for you and which competent critics tell me is the finest thing that has ever been taught in any school. Reynolds sat in the Chicago library early and late and went deep into the heart of things and far back in the past to the beginnings of history and the people in his classes tell me that the studies under him are the most instructive and fascinating they have ever attended and that the material he has drawn from their hidden sources for his educational work is the most vital yet made accessible to the people by any teacher, lecturer, or by any educational institution.

I hope it is in your heart to drop Reynolds a note of half a dozen lines. A few words of kindness from you at this time would work wonders. His present address is 5344 Greenwood ave., Chicago. This is all. I hope with all my heart that everything may soon come out alright.

With much love and all the greetings of the season I am

Always yours,
[Eugene V. Debs]

TLc, InTI, Debs Collection.

1. Debs spoke at the Oak Theatre in Chicago on December 20, 1914.
2. Stephen Marion Reynolds.
3. People's College in Fort Scott, Kansas.
4. The Reynolds correspondence in the Indiana State Library sheds no light on this misunderstanding. In October 1913 the *Rip-Saw* ran an advertisement that listed Reynolds as dean of the American Correspondence School of Law in Chicago, whose lecturers included such "famous Socialists" as Seymour Stedman, Job Harriman, and James O'Neal. Sheppard was in charge of the law department of People's College.
5. The minutes of the national executive committee meetings, published in *Party Builder*, contain no reference to the Sheppard-Reynolds controversy.
6. Charles Proteus Steinmetz (1865-1923) came to the United States from Germany in 1889 and during the next quarter-century established a world reputation in the fields of mathematics and electrical engineering. In Germany, Steinmetz had joined a student socialist group in Breslau and served for a time as editor of a socialist paper there. In Schenectady, New York, Steinmetz combined his work at General Electric with a continuing interest in socialist affairs, served two terms as a socialist member of the common council, and assisted the city's socialist mayor, George Lunn in 1911-13 and 1915-17. Steinmetz was listed on People's College letterhead and brochures as a member of its advisory board.
7. The La Salle Extension University in Chicago offered a bachelor of laws degree especially tailored for "socialist students," who were told in the school's advertisements (see, e.g., *Rip-Saw*, September 6, 1913) that "Socialist lawyers are coming into greater demand every day" and that "Socialists elected to office should know law." John M. Work, former national secretary of the party, was "secretary of the socialist legal department" at the school at the time.

Carl D. Thompson to EVD

December 23, 1914
Chicago, Illinois

Comrade Debs:—

As I told you at the Oak Theater on Sunday, I have your letter of December 16th concerning the Bede-Seidel debate. I have received some communications and a number of comrades have spoken to me concerning the matter which you discuss in the letter.

I have an impression that the Bede-Seidel debate does not make good from our standpoint. At least I have heard that from a number of socialists. However, I did not realize that it was as serious as your letter and the communication which you enclose would seem to indicate.

At one point, at least, your correspondents are wrong. The Redpath Bureau,[1] I think, made a sincere effort to stage a fairly matched debate. It is not always easy to make good with a proposition of this kind. But I know that the Redpath people tried earnestly to give socialism a fair representative. Seidel was not their first choice, but they took him because they thought it was the best thing to do under the circumstances. I know Harrison[2] quite well, and have worked with the Redpath people for several years, and while none of them are socialists, they have always manifested towards me the spirit of utmost fairness.

I appreciate the confidence that you have shown in bringing this matter to my attention in the way you have. I feel, however, that I would hardly be the right one to take this matter up with Comrade Seidel, in view of the fact that it might seem that I had a personal interest in securing the discontinuance of the Bede-Seidel debate, due to the fact that the Redpath people have frequently called upon me to take the debate, when Seidel was not available.

I do think, however, that the matter should be taken up with Seidel, as you suggest. I will bear the matter in mind, and no doubt the opportunity for such a frank discussion will come, sooner or later, without seeming to bring undue pressure to bear. In this respect, I shall certainly be glad to do my part when the time comes.

And now permit me to draw your attention to a matter which I was very anxious to have an opportunity to discuss with you, namely, the question of the formulation of a peace program for the American socialist movement, and, for that matter, for the international movement.

As a matter of fact, since the outbreak of this terrible war, I have been searching in vain thru the literature of the American and international movement for a real constructive, concrete program on the subject of militarism and war. So far as I can see, there is none. There has been talk of a general strike and insurrection in case of war; there has been discussion of whether the socialists should vote in the parliaments for war credits, etc., but nowhere, so far as I can discover, has there been formulated a real, practical constructive program.

Now, in this tragic hour, nothing seems to me more vital than that we should have for our speakers and our writers such a program. Indeed, it seems strange to me that it has not been developed before.

At the present moment in the United States it is almost impossible to get the attention of the public on any subject beside the war, and yet we are without a real, satisfactory message; and, besides, it strikes me that this occasion offers the greatest opportunity for our propaganda.

Socialism, of course, does have a message and deep significance in the matter of militarism and war. We ought to formulate it in such clear and unmistakable terms that it will draw the attention of the world.

With all of this in mind, and with the help of Comrade Kennedy[3] and others,[4] I have brought the matter to the attention of the N.E.C., with the result that a special committee was appointed, and we are now working upon this program. The first draft of it will appear in the American Socialist this week.[5]

Now, my purpose in writing to you is that I hope to enlist your support in this effort. I wish you would go over the matter carefully, and at your earliest convenience give us the benefit of your suggestions and criticisms, and above all, help us to arrive at and formulate a program that all of us can support and proclaim to the world.

It strikes me that this is one of the great moments in history and a supreme opportunity lies before us.

I sincerely hope that what we are doing may meet with your approval, and, if not, that we may confer with you to the end that united action may be taken against the common enemy.

Shall I keep the letter concerning the Bede-Seidel debate, from Mrs. Judd Lytle,[6] or should it be returned to you?

Hoping to hear from you shortly, and with all good wishes, I am

Very truly yours,
Carl D. Thompson
Director   Information Department

TLS, InTI, Debs Collection.

1. The Redpath Lyceum Bureau, named after James Redpath, a nineteenth-century pioneer in the popular culture movement, was a leading agency for booking public speakers, lectures, debates, etc.

2. Harry P. Harrison (1878-1968) joined the Redpath Lyceum Bureau in 1901, supervised the merger of Redpath with other, smaller bureaus, and became treasurer and general manager of Redpath in 1910. He set down his recollection of the lyceum movement in *Culture under Canvas*, which was published in 1958.

3. John Curtiss Kennedy (1884-1934) was born in Maine, graduated from Cornell in 1904, and moved to Chicago, where he taught for two years at the University of Chicago, wrote for socialist publications, served as state secretary of the party, and ran for governor in 1912. In April 1914 he was elected, as a socialist, a Chicago city alderman.

4. Dan A. White, Walter Lanfersiek, and Winnie Branstetter were the others on a committee calling on the national executive committee to "take up the war situation" in the *American Socialist* (August 19, 1914).

5. "Disarmament and World Peace" (*American Socialist*, December 26, 1914) called for, among other things, a "United States of the World," no indemnities, no transfer of territory, world disarmament, the abolition of secret diplomacy, and political and industrial democracy.

6. Mrs. Lytle was presumably one of Debs's correspondents who had complained about the Bede-Seidel debate, but her letter has not been found.

EVD to Claude G. Bowers

December 28, 1914
Terre Haute, Indiana

My dear Friend Bowers:—

Let me thank you right warmly for the kind letter just received from you. I am glad you and Mrs. Bowers attended the Meyer London meeting in New York.[1] It is at such a time and on such an occasion that one keenly alive and alert as you are can catch the spirit of the oncoming social revolution.

I am glad to note that the press has done some small measure of justice to Jaures.[2] I believe him to have been the foremost orator in Europe, if not the world. I never heard him but know many who have and they were all impressed in the same way by his marvelous power. The last great speech he made was his plea for peace, a noble classic which cost him his life. The poor war-crazed assassin who laid him low was full of the "patriotism" with which the minds and hearts of the ignorant victims of class rule are poisoned by their crafty and designing exploiters.

You do me great honor in giving me so conspicuous a place in your home. You and Mrs. Bowers are certainly kind to me and I hope that when I get to Washington it may be my pleasure and my privilege to see you both. Please remember me kindly to Dr. and Mrs. Cohen[3] and with all good wishes for many happy New Years I remain,

Yours faithfully,

E. V. Debs

TLS, InU, Lilly Library, Bowers MSS.

1. In his "Washington Side-Lights" column (*Terre Haute Tribune*, December 13, 1914), Bowers described the Madison Square Garden meeting of November 9 to honor Meyer London, who had recently won a seat in Congress from New York's Lower East Side.

2. Jean Leon Jaures (1859-1914) was a French socialist leader whose newspaper, *Humanité*, was the party's leading publication. His efforts to prevent the outbreak of war in 1914 were interpreted as unpatriotic by segments of French society, and on July 31, 1914, Jaures was assassinated by Raoul Villain, described in the contemporary press as a fanatic and as demented.

3. Dr. Louis Cohen (1876-1948) was born in Russia, came to the United States in 1889, and received a doctorate in electrical engineering from Columbia University in 1905. A pioneer in the fields of radio transmission and electrical communications, he taught at George Washington University from 1916 to 1929, was a consultant to various government agencies, and wrote a number of books that became standard reference works in his field. His wife, Ethel Slavin Cohen (1876-1959), was a leader in various reform groups seeking equal rights for women and blacks and was a founder of the League of Women Voters. At the time, the Cohens and Bowerses lived in the same apartment building in Washington, D.C. *Washington Star,* September 28, 1948; April 18, 1959.

Fred D. Warren to EVD

[1915?]
Girard, Kansas

Dear Gene:

I am now a private citizen, as you have doubtless noticed by the papers, and it feels mighty good to sit here at home with Max and Karl and Glenn and Hattie, and feel that I can rest and loll about and have a good time.[1] Reilly's "Knee Deep in June" just about describes how I feel.

I have wanted to write to you for some time, but refrained for one reason and another until this morning. I have the impression that you harbor just a tiny bit of ill-feeling towards me, and I don't want you to do that. Our relations in the past were of such a cordial nature that it would grieve me more than words can describe to think that there was to be anything other than the same cordial relationship in the future.

During all the years that you were with me on the Appeal, I tried to make you understand that what you wanted to do was what I wanted you to do. In the closing months of your connection with the Appeal, I labored under the impression that you, for personal reasons, desired to make a change. Feeling this way, I did not want to do or say anything that would lead you to know how anxious I was to have you stay with the paper. I knew that if I expressed this thought you would, because of your generous nature, have remained even though at a great sacrifice.

Again, I had contemplated for some time severing my relationship with the Appeal, and I felt it would have been unjust to you to have persuaded you to pass up some satisfactory arrangement that you might have made, had you not been tied up with the Appeal. I can write you thus frankly without being misunderstood, and I want you to understand how much I appreciate your long years of loyal service to the Appeal and to me.

I know that I shall be charged with "deserting the Wayland boys"[2]— it has already started—but I do feel that after all these years of strenuous effort, I'm entitled to a real vacation. I have been away for three months, most of the time, under the care of a physician, but the trip did me little good—I made the mistake of not relieving myself of the burden of the Appeal before leaving. Its responsibilities and cares were continually with me—exaggerated I believe because of my lonesomeness and homesickness while in Europe. I had not intended staying more than a month, but I got tangled up with a purely commercial deal while in England and time dragged slowly. I shall probably return to England or send some one to look after my affairs before the end of the year.

I had no immediate intention of leaving the *Appeal* in spite of my physical and mental handicap, but on my arrival in Girard I found that Walter and John contemplated taking steps to cancel my lease. As soon as I learned this, I called the boys into my office and told them that such action was not necessary, as I was not only willing but anxious to turn over the Appeal at any time they wished to assume its responsibilities. Their action relieved me of the responsibility of quitting under fire.

Walter has been anxious for some time to try his hand at the Appeal—a very worthy and laudable ambition, and I sincerely trust that he will be equal to the task. It is a big job and a heavy responsibility, but one can never learn to swim unless he gets in deep water!

I had hoped that the National Office would take over the Appeal. Before leaving I left with Goebel[3] a proposal to release my lease in favor of the national organization, but I do not know whether the proposal was presented or considered. I did not know that satisfactory arrangements could have been made with the Wayland boys, but felt certain that some satisfactory plan could be worked out. I was willing to eliminate myself entirely. However, all that is past. I merely relate these facts here that you may know my mind on the matter.

My plans for the future are simple: Get acquainted with my wife and boys. It would have done your heart good to have seen the joy in the Warren household when it was finally and definitely decided that I should quit work on the paper. We are planning great things for our work shop—and I can now hear the snort of the little gasoline engine which Glenn has enstalled in his shop in the back yard to furnish power for his lathe and other machinery. Max is the assistant machinist. The boys faces and hands are the despair of their mother about meal times.

Ben[4] and I will go up on our oil farm near Paola[5] and I expect to put in the fall playing at being a real working man. Fortunately I am in the position financially, through some fortunate investments in Oklahoma and Kansas oil fields, to look the world in the face and tell it to go to hell. In place of doing this, however, I shall try and persuade it to adopt the Co-operative Commonwealth. Just what form my activity will take I have not yet decided.

Please remember me to Mrs. D and to Theodore and his family. Mrs. W and the boys join me in sending love and good wishes.

Sincerely yours,
Fred

P.S.—It has just occured to me that this is the first letter I've written in fourteen years (aside from letters to my family) that somewhere between the lines there did not lurk an invitation to get subs for the Appeal!

TLS, InTI, Debs Collection.

1. Warren announced in the August 8, 1914, *Appeal* that he would be leaving the paper "to recover my health."

2. Julius Wayland's sons, Walter H. (1884-1980), who was cashier of the *Appeal to Reason* Publishing Company, and John (1880-1933), who was a student at Emporia Normal School at the time of their father's suicide in November 1912. When Warren announced his resignation in August 1914, he announced also that "Comrade Walter H. Wayland assumes active charge of the paper."

3. George Goebel was a member of the national executive committee.

4. Fred's brother, Ben Warren, who served as press foreman and later as business manager of the *Appeal.*

5. Paola, Kansas.

EVD to Theodore Debs

January 14, 1915
Great Falls, Montana

Old Pard:

Just arrived—had company all the way—2 & 3 at a time such a day & night as I had at Butte! Of all the situations & feuds & mixups the world ever—heard of that caps them all. Duncan[1] presided—the house was packed—I believe I made one of the speeches of my life. I had been advertised to discuss the Butte situation & all the factions were there & expectation was on tiptoe.[2] I could easily have blundered & started something. But I didn't. God must have inspired me. I spoke two hours. I gave them all hell—the rank & file as well as the Crooked leaders & stoolpigeons. I lit into em fierce & without mercy & it won the day—then I made an appeal with every word white hot from my soul & it set them afire & when I quit, soaked with sweat, they gobbled me up & rushed me to [the] hotel & into my room & all swore it was the most wonderful, thrilling speech they ever heard & that it would surely bring order out of chaos & work a great change in Butte. Most earnestly do I hope so.

Benedict,[3] his wife & boy were there—they live in Butte now. Lou is married again—He's the same noble fellow and his wife is one of the noblest women I ever met. They all send you their love. Lou has got stout & gray—he loves our family as if he were a member of it.

Feel dam bad—have just had to clean up a platter of mountain trout & you may imagine my feelings. When I want to feel like a three year old colt, I think of the hi-kis and the muse of Fred Holt.[4]

Love & kisses to all

Eugene

ALS, InTI, Debs Collection.

1. Lewis Duncan, socialist mayor of Butte, Montana, from 1911 to 1914.
2. In "Martial Law in Butte" (*Rip-Saw*, October 1914), Debs discussed the bitter internal struggle being waged in Local 1 of the Western Federation of Miners, which included the dynamiting of the union hall in Butte on June 23, 1914. In the aftermath the union was torn apart by charges that responsibility for the destruction of the union hall and the theft of its records lay with the IWW, Local 1 dissidents, company union leaders, and the Anaconda Copper Company.
3. Louis Benedict, who had served as Debs's ARU secretary during and after the Pullman Strike.
4. Fred Holt, secretary-treasurer of District 21 (Arkansas, Oklahoma, and Texas) of the UMW, was fined $1,000 and sentenced to six months' imprisonment in January 1915 by the federal court in Arkansas for transporting guns and ammunition from Oklahoma to Arkansas during a coal strike in 1914. In a number of *Rip-Saw* editorials

("The Arkansas Miners," January 1915; "Fred Holt and His Fellow-Prisoners," May, 1915; and others) Debs praised Holt for providing the Arkansas miners with the means of self-defense against the brutality of the mine guards. At Christmas time in 1914, Holt had sent to Gene and Theodore Debs a poem, "Dedicated to the Members of the Hi-Ki Hunting Club," describing an Arkansas hunting trip in which the brothers' participation qualified them for membership in the Hi-Ki Hunting Club.

EVD to Frank P. O'Hare

February 14, 1915
Pocatello, Idaho

Dear Frank:—

Whatever possessed you to put Tooelle[1] into this schedule? The place is almost inaccessible—no earthly way to get from there to Burley[2] and the latter is lost to us, notwithstanding I have been up all night and am about half dead in the vain struggle to get there. There is but one train to Burley and that leaves Salt Lake City at midnight and it is humanly impossible to get back there from Tooele to make that train.

The snow was so deep and the roads so bad that no auto owner would let us have a machine at any price—the only thing we could get was a light open buggy. Naylor[3] of Salt Lake went down with me. I cut off my speech at 9.40 and got into the buggy, steaming hot, in the vain hope of getting to Salt Lake in time to make Burley. In 15 minutes I was half frozen, chilled to the marrow, and my feet soon became like ice. The snow and half-frozen mud from the horses hoofs covered us and we were till midnight on the road—then we had to wait in the cutting cold no depot—for the train—and all for nothing because there was no possible train connection. The buggy was hardly big enough for two, yet three of us were jammed into it taking turns sitting on one another. It was another Kennett ride[4]—enough to kill an ox—and today I'm sick, my throat is raw, my whole body aches, and Burley, where there is to be one of the biggest meetings on the route, sacrificed—no possible way of getting there. I have just wired them a long and detailed explanation expressing regrets etc. etc.

I have now been on the road five weeks[5] and have averaged 18 to 20 hours daily on trains, in the hotels at work, meeting visitors, interviews, comrades etc., but last night alone came nearer knocking me out than the whole rest of the trip. Today I am unfit for anything and ought to cancel the rest of the dates and go home. Must I have such a damned killing dose as {this} administered to me on every trip? I am willing to be killed for the cause but I don't want to die a fool's death. Kennett and Toole each set me back six months. I can stand the work as well as any one but I can't go out of a hot hall, covered with sweat, and climb into an open buggy on a bitter cold, raw night and ride 17 miles over half-frozen roads and then stand waiting for a train until I'm frozen numb—nor can anybody else— and it seems that the only way I can stop it is to do my own booking and that's what I'd better do.

I am so constituted, foolishly perhaps, that I would have taken that ride and made every effort in my power to reach Burley if I had died in my tracks.

They have written me several letters from Burley telling me they were to have the biggest meeting ever held there—people coming in from miles around—and now they are to be disappointed. It cuts me to the quick and makes my heart bleed for those comrades. I feel like a criminal although I am not to blame and have risked my life and outraged my health in the vain and desperate attempt to prevent their disappointment.

I'm not angry and I don't want to find fault—but I can't help but feel keenly the trials of the present hour. To disappoint an audience is to me a crime. It seems that I am fated to be punished and perhaps I ought to be glad that I can stand it. I've had nearly 40 years of it and I'll try my best to be thankfull for it all.

With love,
Gene

P.S. There was no train out of Tooele until Sunday afternoon and if I hadn't taken that midnight ride I would not only have missed Burley but Twin Falls[6] also.

TLc, InTI, Debs Collection.

1. Tooele, Utah.
2. Burley, Idaho.
3. Walter Naylor (1870-1927) was a socialist printer in Salt Lake City. In the *Rip-Saw* (March 1915), it was reported that "against unusual difficulties the faithful band headed by Comrade W. Naylor filled the Garrick Theatre in Salt Lake City" to hear Debs.
4. Kennett, in the bootheel of Missouri.
5. Debs's "Pacific Coast Tour" of 1915 began in Mason City, Iowa, on January 10 and took him to Montana, Washington, Oregon, California, Nevada, Utah, Idaho, and Colorado, closing in Denver on February 17.
6. Twin Falls, Idaho.

Allan L. Benson to EVD

February 21, 1915
Yonkers, New York

My Dear Debs:

Herewith I enclose you the reply that Hillquit made to my challenge in the Call.[1] I also enclose proof of an article I shall run in the next issue of Pearson's[2] which contains the challenge to which Hillquit replied. Two weeks have passed since I printed the article about Hillquit in the Call that I sent you some time ago. He has not replied to it and, I understand, will not do so. It was entirely dignified and good for the party for him to cause his trained eels on the Central Committee to stultify themselves[3] and beat me, but it is apparently undignified for him to debate with me in the party press.

I have been in the party a good many years and I do not think I have been known as a trouble-maker. I never had any taste for the mere politics of the movement, and confined myself to staying at home, minding my own business and doing propaganda work. I should undoubtedly have remained an obscure and peaceful citizen if Hillquit had not seen fit to interfere with my work. I do not object to anyone differing from me on any idea I advance, provided the reasons he gives for opposing me are not scandalously and palpably dishonest. I consider Hillquit's reasons for opposing the war-referendum idea as coming under such characterization. And now that I have been compelled to fight, I intend to make such a fight upon Hillquit that neither he nor anyone else will ever again attack me with unclean hands. I am going to demonstrate that I know a crooked argument from an honest one and that I have enough ability to take care of myself in a controversy. I feel that I must make such a demonstration to prevent gentlemen of this sort from interfering with my work in future. I regret the necessity for it, but I did not create it. I was minding my own business until Hillquit came at me. But if I gain renown for nothing else, I shall at least be known as the gent who put the "quit" in Hillquit.

The Philadelphia resolution,[4] which I sent you a few days ago, will expire by time limitation on April 2. I am doing the best I can to put it over. With your help, if you should feel so inclined, it could be put over. But I am writing a book that the Appeal is now printing serially[5] that will put the idea in the platform some day. I have no doubt of that.

While I should be very glad if you would wire a statement to the Appeal commending the idea and urging locals to second the resolution,[6] I shall feel just as kindly toward you if you do not, because I know that in whatever you do, you will be "on the square." It is these infernal fakers who anger me.

I'll have my book out in six weeks. As soon as I get page proofs, I will send them to you.

Ever Your Friend,
Allan L. Benson

TLS, InTI, Debs Collection.

1. "Benson *vs* Hillquit" (*New York Call Sunday Magazine*, February 7, 1915) summarized Allan Benson's call for a popular referendum before any congressional declaration of war and Morris Hillquit's antipreparedness and peace proposals. Hillquit thought the referendum idea "wild" and said it would "only serve to embarrass the party."

2. Benson's "Shall We Vote on War" (*Pearson's*, April 1915) was a continuation of his "Let the People Vote on War," which had appeared in the December 1914 *Pearson's*.

3. Benson's war referendum proposal was not included in the national executive committee's original statement on the war, which was largely drawn up by Hillquit and adopted at the December 1914 meeting of the committee. *American Socialist*, January 9, 1915.

4. Local Philadelphia's resolution, written by Benson and submitted to the national executive committee, embodied Benson's war-referendum idea. *American Socialist*, January 2, 1915.

5. Benson's series "The Way to Prevent War" began in the *Appeal* on February 20, 1915.

6. In "Debs Praises Benson's Blows at the War Beast" (*Appeal*, April 3, 1915), Debs said that "among all the popular writers against the war Allan Benson takes first place" and called the war-referendum idea "absolutely logical and unassailable." In "Leading Socialists and Peace Advocates" (*Appeal*, May 1, 1915), Debs declared that if Benson's plan were adopted "there will never be another war," and in "What Gene Debs Says" (*Appeal*, April 10, 1915), Debs described the *Appeal*'s serial publication of Benson's *Way to Prevent War* as "an inestimable service."

Fred W. Holt to EVD

February 23, 1915
Fort Smith, Arkansas

My Dear Friend Gene: —

You make me so happy to receive those kind words that are so full of true friendship, and loyalty of purpose.

Coming from one that knows and has felt the sting of Capitalism, woven with the scorn of those of the working class that are to dum to understand; gives me much courage in the thought that the workers may some day understand our mission in life.

I had a beautiful letter from that dear big Brother of yours telling me of your trip west, and that he would posibly join you later. I know you must miss him so much when seperated, for he is so good and kind. My Comrade's and I[1] are making the best of it we can, but Mr. White[2] through his bunch of paid Dis-Organizers are giving us Hell throughout the District stating that we did not get half what we deserved; trying of course to make it appear, that his adminestration condemns all form of violance, but they are meeting with dam poor success before the rank and file. Five of them are here in the city sloping up all the boose that is possible for their degenerated forms to hold, drawing $4.00 per and $3.00 to $5.00 for expenses, with hundreds of hungry striking Miners and their familys here in the midst of this trouble. They are in attendence at all Board meetings, and after we were compelled to make these complimise [compromises] in order to save hundreds of our fellow workers from doing term at Leavensworth,[3] also the District Thousands of dollars in litegation; we were voted Thirty Cents per day per man to eat, and $3.00 dollars per week for our wive's and those depending upon us. As for myself I am not complaining, but some of my comrades are very much agitated.

Knowing that their wive's and babies are unable to visit them for want of funds, but I have shot a few solar plexus blows to the membership and they responded nobly, and we are now able to handle the situation splended from our little den.

Of course this is making our K. C. friends furious,[4] but I will be able to make them moreso before they turn me out of here.

We are not Idle in here I find it one of the finest fields I ever saw to convert men to Socialism I and my Comrade's have organized a Local here with 36 members, and of course I am compelled to make a speack each runaround day, A splended place to distribute literature. The R.S. & M.P.[5] is furnishing me bundles also the American Socialist, along with dear old Dan, and little Freda.[6]

I am enclosing you a list {of} us boys[7] for your files, they are the finest bunch of souls ever housed togather in one Cell.

I wish you could have saw that old pharasite of a Federal Judge[8] foam when I told him why I objected to him passing sentence upon me without imposing like sentence upon the Coal Operator, in as much as both of us had shipped in guns,[9] and the Operator was the first to violate the Law if one had been violated. He was everything but courtious in his reply.

well I must ring of for fear of becoming burdensome to you. My

Comrade's all join me in wishing you good health for that noble heart to continue the fight until victory finally crowns our efforts.

Your Friend, and Comrade to the end,

Fred W. Holt

TLS, InTI, Debs Collection.

1. In "The Convicted Labor Leaders" (*Rip-Saw*, April 1915), Debs named Holt and nine others who were serving time at Fort Smith for "standing up for the rights of union men in the recent mine strikes in Arkansas."

2. In "The Convicted Labor Leaders," Debs attacked UMW President John White for "not lifting a finger" in defense of Holt and the others and for, in fact, siding with "the criminal and conniving operators."

3. In "Letter from Fred Holt" (*Melting Pot*, March 1915), Holt claimed that he and nine others had pleaded guilty in the arms-transportation case to avoid "75 to 100 convictions."

4. Kansas City, Kansas.

5. *Rip-Saw* and *Melting Pot*.

6. Dan and Freda Hogan.

7. Holt enclosed a list of the names of his fellow UMW prisoners, along with their marital status, number of children, term of imprisonment, and fine.

8. Frank A. Youmans (1860-1932) was the federal district judge for the Western District of Arkansas who levied the sentences of six months' prison and $1,000 fines on Holt and his comrades.

9. In "Bravo, Arkansas Coal-Diggers" (*Miners' Magazine*, July 30, 1914) and elsewhere, Debs praised the action of Holt and others in bringing guns and ammunition into the Arkansas strike area, contrasting their defense of themselves with the helpless condition of the miners in the West Virginia and Colorado strikes.

Fred D. Warren to EVD

March 1915
Girard, Kansas

Dear Gene:—

I've received several letters from Socialists similar to the one I received from you.[1] I am making no answer to any of them but yours, as I don't give a damn what they think of me, but I do want to keep your good opinion.

The facts in the Sinclair case are these: I gave Sinclair an outline for a story in 1907. It evolved into the Millenium.[2] Sinclair gave me $300 for the right to make a play of the idea. Then HE WROTE A CONTRACT, which he signed, SETTING FORTH THAT HE WOULD WRITE THE BOOK, MARKET IT, AND GIVE ME ONE-THIRD OF THE ROYALTIES. *Also that the Appeal should have the right to print the story as a serial. FREE.*

That's the contract, signed, sealed and delivered. Now, comes Sinclair and demands $2000[3] for the publication of the story in the Appeal. To quote his own letter to me, Dec. 14, 1914, he says: "I am not demanding anything for writing the story. I AM DEMANDING IT FOR THE SERIAL PUBLICATION IN THE APPEAL."

This after signing a contract, dated Nov. 6, 1909, the last clause of which reads: "IT IS AGREED THAT THE STORY MAY APPEAR SERIALLY IN THE APPEAL AFTER ITS PUBLICATION IN WHATEVER MAGAZINE OR PUBLICATION MAY ACCEPT IT."

Again, some time later, in writing about some disposition he wished to make of the story, he says: "The only obstacle is *OUR contract, which gives the serial rights to the Appeal FREE.*"

The story was completed sometime in 1913, I believe, and on June 9th. of that year I wrote to Sinclair, before I had the story: "I cannot pay you anything for it as a serial."

On Feb. 9, 1914, just before the story appeared, Sinclair wrote to me about it, and this is what I wrote: "I am arranging to print the story (the Millenium) in the Appeal, but aside from that I have no plans. . . . If you cannot find a publisher, it is quite likely that we can arrange to put it out in book form on the same terms you would give to any other publisher."

No protest from Sinclair. It never occured to him that Warren owed him anything until after I had left the *Appeal.* Then he hot foots in, figuratively speaking, to Girard and demands $2000 for the serial rights to the story and a lot more for royalties lost because of the Appeal's failure to print it as a book. And unless Warren settles forthwith, so says Sinclair, he will be under the painful necessity of showing me up and that would be bad for Warren and the Socialist movement. If Warren pays, then of course there will be no exposure and Warren may continue his game of swindling, etc.

It is just a plain game of blackmail.[4] AND I REFUSE TO STAND AND DELIVER. Sinclair's first letters and his threats of exposure make it absolutely impossible for me to consider any plan of settlement with him, without laying myself [open] to the suspicion that I was settling in order to hide something. That game has been tried on me before and it never worked and it will NOT WORK NOW!

I went to New York with the authority from the Appeal to say that the Appeal would print the book on the same terms that would be granted any other publisher—AND SINCLAIR REFUSED TO TALK TO ME. In a letter he explained to Goebel,[5] that "WARREN HAD A LOT OF MONEY AND HE COULD GET SOME OF IT."

I appreciate all you have said, and fully understand the spirit in which you make your suggestions, but I know Sinclair of old and I do not care to have anything more to do with him. He dropped his talk about going into the courts, because in the face of his contract and his correspondence he had nothing to stand upon.

He claims that I verbally promised to publish the book and to sell 100,000 copies.[6] That is absurd on the face of it. I may be all kinds of a scoundrel, but I don't think I ever was so poor a business man as to agree to sell 100,000 copies of any book, much less a book written by Sinclair.

It is curious that if I had made such a promise to him, which he claims was made in 1913, that there was no protest against my letter of Feb 9, 1914, in which I said I had no plans aside from the publication as a serial, until nearly a year after and after I had severed my relationship with the Appeal.

It is just another one of those unfortunate episodes in which it seems my fate to be involved in, but I usually get out on top when all the facts are known.[7] However, in this case, I shall make mighty little effort to make the facts known.

Sincerely Yours,
Fred D. Warren

TLc, CtU, Fred Warren Papers.

1. Like a number of other leading socialists, including Allan Benson, Charles Kerr, and Morris Hillquit, Debs had been drawn into a controversy between Warren and Upton Sinclair, centering on Sinclair's claim that he should be paid for the serialization of *The Millenium* in the *Appeal to Reason* in 1914. In a letter to Warren, dated March 23, 1915, Sinclair appended the opinion of Benson, Kerr, and Hillquit and of Debs, who urged Warren and Sinclair not to take their issue to a capitalistic court but to settle as comrades. The Warren-Sinclair correspondence concerning the dispute is in the University of Connecticut Library at Storrs.

2. Originally written as a four-act play ("a little farce comedy of the future"), *The Millenium* appeared in sixteen consecutive installments of the *Appeal*, beginning on April 19, 1914.

3. In a letter to Warren, dated October 22, 1914, Sinclair said that he "claim[ed] the sum of $2000 as payment for my time" in writing the serial form of *The Millenium* for the *Appeal.*

4. In his October 22, 1914, letter to Warren, Sinclair said he would "wait ten days" before putting the case "in the hand of a lawyer" and he would "regret the publicity" that would follow.

5. In a letter to Warren, dated March 2, 1915, Sinclair said that George Goebel might act as a mediator in the dispute but that Goebel had not responded to Sinclair's proposition.

6. In his October 22, 1914, letter, Sinclair claimed that Warren had promised "to put all the energy of the *Appeal* behind [*The Millenium*] and would sell one or two hundred thousand copies."

7. When *The Millenium* was finally published as a novel in 1924, Sinclair wrote in the foreword that "for the original suggestion of this story the author is indebted to Mr. Fred D. Warren, from whom he purchased the idea."

EVD to Max Ehrmann

March 11, 1915
Terre Haute, Indiana

My dear Max:—

Just as I was about to order a copy of your book on Jesus,[1] concerning which such a fine notice appeared in the local papers[2] a day
or two since, a copy came from your hand, inscribed with your love,
and I thank your for this latest expression of your kindness with all
my heart. I have long been desirous of seeing this book and I shall
examine its pages with deep interest and I am sure with equal satisfaction and profit. I shall not now say more than that my heart is full
and when I see you in person, which I hope may be soon, we will
talk about the book. With all love,

Yours faithfully,
E. V. Debs

TLS, InGRD-Ar, Ehrmann Papers.

    1. *Jesus: A Passion Play.*
    2. In a "Books and Literary Notes" column (*Terre Haute Star,* March 8, 1915),
Ehrmann's *Jesus* was praised as one of his finest works. "The subject," the column
said, "is a big one and it is presented in bigness that almost amazes."

Sidney Hillman[1] to Theodore Debs

March 13, 1915
Chicago, Illinois

Dear Comrade Debs:—

Your favor of the 12th received. If no earlier arrangements can
be made for Eugene V. Debs, to address our meetings, we will take
April 3rd,[2] as satisfactory.

Undoubtedly, you are aware of the position of the Amalgamated
Clothing Workers of America, through the "NEW YORK CALL" and
other Socialist publications.

We are involved in a terrific struggle all over the country to organize
the tailors. Our organization has made wonderful progress within the
last few months.

We have started a campaign in the city of Chicago which may result
in one of the biggest strikes, this city has ever seen.

I should like to convey to your brother that his presence would be

of the greatest benefit, and would contribute at this time a great deal
to our movement.

It is superfluous to say that the name of Debs is beloved among
the tailors in this city, as well as in any other city.

If any earlier date can be made for the arrangement, we will
appreciate it considerably.

Hoping to receive a favorable reply, I remain

Yours fraternally,
Sidney Hillman
General President

Amalgamated Clothing Workers of America.

TLS, In'l'l, Debs Collection.

1. Sidney Hillman (1887-1946) was born in Lithuania, came to the United States
in 1907, and as a Sears, Roebuck and (in 1909) Hart, Schaffner & Marx employee
became deeply involved in union activities. In 1914, under Hillman's leadership, the
United Garment Workers and the Journeymen Tailors Union formed the Amalgamated Clothing Workers of America, of which Hillman served as president until his
death.

2. In the *Rip-Saw* schedule of Debs's speech dates, there is no listing of an April
3, 1915, date in Chicago. April 3, 1915, fell on Saturday before the Chicago city
elections, in which Debs's old friend Seymour Stedman was the party's candidate for
mayor, but the *American Socialist*'s accounts of the day's many rallies, speeches, etc.,
do not mention Debs.

EVD to Upton Sinclair

March 15, 1915
Terre Haute, Indiana

Dear Comrade Sinclair: —

Your communication of the 9th. inst. with copy of your letter to
Fred Warren has been received and both have been carefully read.
Without knowing anything about the merits of the controversy,[1] I
think your proposal a fair one and I am writing Warren to that effect
and urging him to accept it and avoid litigation and possible scandal.
All such matters between comrades ought to be settled among them
selves along the lines suggested in your letter. A suit at law in a capitalist
court would be peculiarly unfortunate in this instance and everything
possible ought to be done by both you and Warren to avoid such an
eventuality.

Sincerely hoping you may come to an understanding[2] and that you
may be mutually satisfied with the result and that the mutual confi-

dence and regard which so long existed between you may be restored
I remain,

Yours fraternally,
E. V. Debs

TLS, InU, Lilly Library, Sinclair MSS.

1. See Fred D. Warren to EVD, March 1915.
2. In his *Autobiography* (New York, 1962) Sinclair mentioned Warren's payment of $500 to Sinclair for serial rights to publish *The Jungle* in the *Appeal to Reason*, but not their controversy concerning *The Millenium*.

Allan L. Benson to EVD

March 19, 1915
Yonkers, New York

Dear Debs:
    I have your letter of the 19th and have read it with interest. I did not know that the German Socialists had ever demanded the democratization of the war-making power. I do not care if they did. I am not trying to be a hero. I am trying to end war. If the German Socialists beat me to it in advancing this idea, I am going to try to beat them in something else. I am going to try to make this idea take root in the popular mind. The German Socialists did not do that. *I am going to do it.* I have the goods. I know how to dress windows. I am going to keep at the job until it is done. I shall make the facts of this so plain that even Socialists will see them. I know that thousands of Socialists already see the facts. You speak of the improbability that I will ever be able to put the question to a vote of the party. Nothing is more certain than that I shall put this to a vote of the party. I am going to come within an eyelash of it this spring. I shall probably fail at that, but I shall not fail in the days that will follow this spring. Nine thousand votes are necessary to put it to a national referendum. I had 7,000 votes last week. I could go out now and speak in a few cities in the middle west and get the votes. I should have won anyway if Hillquit had not upset New York. But I am not going out after votes because I know my book will do the job in the next year or two and do it thoroughly.
    I ask you if you detect any sign of party inability to grasp the idea when one man, in a few months, without the help of anybody who could help, and with the opposition of Hillquit, could start a movement that could command 7,000 votes in so short a time? The slightest

breath of approval from you or from anybody who had power, could turn the scale toward victory now. I don't expect help from anybody who doubts the expediency of the plan, or who does not believe in it. But with or without help, I am going to make the rank and file see it, and I hope even to make the leaders see it. I should have liked to win this spring, but if I can't, I'll win when I can.[1]

I shall keep the letter I have just received from you, as well as the other one in which you made certain observations about the war-referendum and, in a week or two, will endeavor to meet the points you make in a chapter in my book. I shall answer them to your perfect satisfaction. I can see the answers as plainly as I can see this typewriter.

You are entirely too generous in what you say about my work. I have worked under a tremendous inspiration and have done the best I could, but what the effect has been and will be, God only knows— at least I do not.

Whatever you do, don't get the idea that I am in the least irritated because you could not see your way to help. I know that in whatever you do or don't do, you are on the square, and that is all I ask of any man.

Yours Truly,
Allan L. Benson

TLS, InTI, Debs Collection.

1. In 1916, when Benson was the Socialist party candidate for president, the party platform specified that "no war shall be declared or waged by the United States without a referendum vote of the entire people, except for the purpose of repelling invasion."

EVD to Phil Wagner

March 22, 1915
Terre Haute, Indiana

My dear Phil:—

After hearing of your plea of guilty in the federal court I have unhesitatingly advised Harry to do the same.[1] Not only this but I have insisted that there is no other course left open to him. He could not consistently enter court and attempt a defense with the Melting Pot's plea of guilty hanging over him. On the other hand he could not well appeal to the country in a case in which a plea of guilty had already been entered.

I have thought of the case in all its phases and all its possibilities and my conclusion is that if a fight were made at all it must be made entirely upon the basis of the Melting Pot's contempt for the charges and for the gang that instigated them but this is out of the question after a plea of guilty has been entered by you, its publisher and owner.

It would appear very strange to everyone, especially those upon whom we would have to rely for support, if the editor should attempt a defense in a case in which his employer had already entered a plea of guilty. In the legal aspect of the case Harry is but the agent, you the principal, and it would strike our people as nothing short of ridiculous to attempt a fight to prove the agent innocent when the principal, indicted jointly with him upon the same charge, had already confessed guilt and paid the fine imposed upon him by the court. Your plea of guilty would certainly convict Harry in advance before any jury on earth. He would enter the trial handicapped and without the ghost of a show of either getting a favorable verdict or of appealing {effectively} to the revolutionary support of the country.

I should not have advised your plea of guilty in the first instance but now that it is made and the record established there is no other alternative for Harry than to do the same. I would not know upon what ground to make a defense under the circumstances if one were attempted.

Harry himself has protested against what I am now saying to you, feeling that it was his duty to hold out and make the fight, and for this reason I am sending you this written statement of my views.

The Melting Pot has already pleaded guilty to a technical violation of the law under which the indictment was drawn and this ends the matter so far as the present case is concerned. For Harry to attempt to make a fight in the face of this fact would be {not} only foolhardy and expose him to the charge of playing to the gallery in the role of mock heroics, but would waste his time and energy for years to come and finally perhaps land him in [the] penitentiary besides, and all this in a losing fight from the start and with nothing to gain for either himself or for you or for the Melting Pot or the cause, not even the respect of the rank and file for whom he has been fighting. It is well enough to fight and die if necessary but there is neither profit nor glory in "dying as the fool dieth."

Of course you can count on me in any event to stand by you and Harry and to see to it that the case is properly presented to the readers of the Rip-Saw and the Melting Pot.[2] The plea of guilty, bitter a pill as it is for both of you, will not be without its advantages and good results.

With all good wishes,

Yours always,
[Eugene V. Debs]

TLc, InTI, Debs Collection.

1. Both Wagner and Henry Tichenor pleaded guilty to "circulating defamatory and scurrilous literature," as charged in a federal indictment following their publishing in the *Melting Pot* a cartoon depicting Billy Sunday "saving souls at $500 apiece." In "A Fortunate Settlement" (*Rip-Saw*, May 1915), Wagner announced that he and Tichenor were each fined $100 and costs and defended their guilty pleas on the grounds that it avoided a ruinously expensive trial and probably a prison term for one or both of them.

2. Debs's "The Indictment and the Crime" (*Melting Pot*, April 1915) and "The Indictment of Wagner and Tichenor" (*Rip-Saw*, April 1915) called on readers of both publications to "double their circulation" as "our answer to the capitalist class."

EVD to Allan L. Benson

March 22, 1915
Terre Haute, Indiana

My dear Benson: —

Your communication of the 18th. inst.[1] has just been received and carefully read. In the closing paragraph you assure me that you are not in the least irritated and yet I must conclude that you must have been at least a bit "heated" in what you had to say in answer to my letter. If there is not a distinct rebuke in what you have written then I certainly misunderstand you. If, as you say, "the slightest breath of approval" from me would give you victory, my refusing you that breath would certainly justify your rebuke.

Now I am not in the least sensitive when I am dealing with a comrade in whom I have confidence such as I have in you, even though he speak his mind plainly, as you have done, and find fault with me for any real or fancied shortcoming on my part. In fact, I think all the more of him for being frank with me for I would rather be frankly criticised, even condemned, than to be hypocritically commended.

In the scores of times I have commended you and your work against war from the public platform and in the articles I have written and the letters I have sent out to the same effect, it seems to me that I have given you that "slightest breath of approval" which you deny me in the letter now before me.

It would be not only strange but a miracle if you and I were in perfect agreement on this great question upon which scarcely two can be found who hold identical views. You have concentrated all your splendid abilities in the war against war, while I have concentrated the little strength I have in the war against capitalism, the breeder of war, refusing steadily to abandon the main issue and to give myself wholly to secondary issues under any circumstances whatsoever. This has not prevented me, however, from devoting a considerable part of my time to the question of war in every speech I have made not only since the European war began but many years before.

I have never had occasion to criticise you but I am going to do so now for I think you have given me for the first time license to do so. I do not like this last letter from you at all and I excuse it on the ground that notwithstanding your protest to the contrary you were in a state of irritation when you wrote it. You doubtless preserved a copy and if you will look it over and note the number of I's in it you may understand that while such {a} large personal claim might be expected in a letter written by Berger, it appears to me strangely out of place in a letter from Benson.

Reading your letter the conclusion is forced upon one that you feel that this whole anti-war agitation and the responsibility for it has fallen upon your shoulders, and that the whole tremendous task of converting the nation had devolved upon you, that you have been abandoned, deserted of everyone who should have given aid, that you have done and are doing it all, that all others have fluked and that you are going to carry the banner single-handed to victory.

Now I think that an unfortunate mental attitude, to say nothing of the exaggeration of the indictment, and I fear that Hillquit has so lodged in your craw for the moment that you have become splenetic in your attitude toward those who do not agree in toto with your program. You give credit to no single person for a particle of aid or encouragement or co-operation.

Do not understand me as objecting to egotism or to a man's profound faith in himself and his capacity, such as is expressed in your letter, for I know that there are times when even the most intense self-importance and fanaticism are essential in the accomplishment of a task, but in the present instance I do not think you are justified in flouting all others impatiently and asserting the claim that they have done nothing, and that you and you alone are going to put an end to war. In your letter you say very positively, your words underscored: "*I am going to do it.*"

There are personal as well as other reasons why I would be among the last to detract from the value of your service in this crisis or to under-estimate its importance, but when you say that you "have not had the help of anyone who could help" and proceed upon that assumption to claim that you stand alone in the war against war you are saying that for yourself which, if it be true, were better left to be said by others.

You will note by enclosed letter that I have an article with the Appeal on your anti-war crusade.[2] In this poor expression you will see what I have said and have tried to do to help you in all my travels.

This is all. It was my duty to be frank and I have been so. My confidence in your integrity is absolute; my faith in your judgement is great. You are a man and not a god and therefore have a man's liability to err. I know, having erred a thousand times. It may be that you are right and that I am wrong. In either case my respect and affection for you remain undiminished, and when you see a flaw in me I shall expect you to point it out to me and set me right.

It may be that you have been denied support you should have received but I prefer to believe that all good comrades and true, each working along his own line and in accordance with his own ideas of his particular part, are co-operating as efficiently as may reasonably be expected, to put an end to war and to the system that produces war.

With all wishes for your success and all personal regards I remain as ever,

Yours fraternally,
[Eugene V. Debs]

TLc, InTI, Debs Collection.

1. Benson to EVD, March 19, 1915.
2. As noted, Debs's "Debs Praises Benson's Blows at the War Beast" appeared in the April 3, 1915, *Appeal.*

Allan L. Benson to EVD

March 24, 1915
Yonkers, New York

Dear Debs:

I have just this minute finished reading your letter and the smile that began almost with the first paragraph is still on. I do not think your criticism was justified, but I may be wrong. I do not know how

I seem to you. You do not know how I seem to myself. As I look at myself, I do not see the man you described and censured. I do not seem to fit the description. But I realize that the man you described and criticised was the man you saw. Your letter was based upon mine. Mine was rattled off as rapidly as I could strike the keys. I certainly had no thought that I was supporting the universe, and if I gave you the impression that I thought so, I inadvertently misrepresented myself.

You repeated from my letter the underscored sentence: "*I am going to do it.*" You write as if you had gathered the idea that I used this sentence in connection with a determination to "end war." I do not keep copies of my letters, but if you still have this letter and will read it again, I think you will find that this sentence was used in connection with your statement that the German Socialists, in 1870, advocated the war referendum. I said, if I remember correctly, that if they had beaten me to it in evolving the idea, that I was going to beat them in making it take root. It seems to me that this is quite different from declaring I was going to "end war."

I am not at all irritated because you have urged no local, as far as I know, to second the Philadelphia resolution. I certainly expect neither you nor anybody else to think exactly as I do about war or anything else. If you do not agree with the Philadelphia resolution, I could hardly expect you to ask locals to second it. I did not know until you told me that you had ever written or spoken a word with regard to the war-referendum articles I have written.

Now, with regard to my statement that I have "not had the help of anybody who could help." You criticise me for that and draw the conclusion that I am taking myself too seriously. Maybe I am. I have always taken myself seriously and taken my work seriously. But what I meant by this statement was this. The Socialist platform demands the right of the people to pass upon every act of congress by referendum. I singled out war declarations and suggested that the blanket Socialist demand for the referendum was of particular and tremendous importance in connection therewith. When the idea came to me, I had no more idea that any Socialist would oppose me in this than anything in the world. I thought every Socialist would see the point instantly and join in the demand. To my great surprise, only the rank and file have responded by taking affirmative action with regard to the Philadelphia resolution. More than 100 locals have seconded one or another of the 10 war referendum resolutions that have been before the party. The Philadelphia resolution now has endorsements representing more than 7,000 members in good standing. Every week brings more seconds. But up to date, the following men "who could

have helped," have not, so far as I know, uttered one word in behalf
of the Philadelphia resolution:

Berger
Russell,
Simons,
Ameringer,[1]
Seidel,
Thompson,
and any number of others.

Only Hillquit fought it openly—and he is not fighting it any more—
openly at least.

Do you wonder at my amazement that an amplification of our own
platform with regard to so important a subject as war should seem
to strike so many men dumb who have howled for years about the
necessity of democracy both in government and industry?

What in hell is the matter with them? What is my crime? Hillquit
broadly intimates that I am a fool. *If I am a fool it is because I have
taken the words of men at their face value.* I have believed and still believe
that Socialism stands for the complete application of the democratic
principle to representative government. If the Socialist platform means
what it says, it is not "un-Socialistic," as Hillquit says, to demand that
that particular act of congress which we call a declaration of war be
made subject to a referendum. Yet not one man in this country who
"could help" (with the exception of yourself and I have just now
learned for the first time that you have written something perhaps
in general commendation of the principle) has done so much as to
say one word in its favor.

If I am losing my balance, can you wonder at the reason? War has
so cut me to the heart that I, who stood dry-eyed when my father
was lowered into the grave, broke down in December and for an hour
cried until I thought I could never regain my self-control and stop.
I tell you this secret only to lay bare my heart to you. I am shaken
to the soles of my feet with the horror of this war. If I can do anything
to end war I want to do it. I thought I had proposed something that
would be useful; I thought I had kept hand in glove with Socialist
thought. I never doubted that everybody who had a voice or a pen
that would carry would use whatever power he had.

And what happened?

Abuse from Hillquit; silence from everybody except you who could
have helped.

They all say I am a fool. They certainly know that the idea is
rapidly gathering a following in the party. If they are sincere, they
should be trying to head me off. Berger has a daily paper[2] in which

he might attack this "heresy." All the others could speak or write against it. Why in hell don't they fight if they have valid arguments to use against me? Why did Berger and his associates on the N.E.C. adopt my plan in principle—down at the foot of their anti-war program?[3]

They don't dare fight the idea!

Criticise me again if you please. I mean what I say. Hillquit was the only one who was mutt enough to put his neck in the noose— and if his neck hasn't got blisters on it I don't know what blisters are.

That is why I feel sore. If my idea is wrong, these men should have shown me wherein it was wrong. It should hardly be necessary to declare that I make no claims to infallibility. I am always glad to be set right—but I am from Missouri.

. . .

Oh, well, what's the use of talking about it. What is to be will be. I am sorry you think I am an inflated jackass. I cannot help it. I can see only with such eyes as I have been given. I am doing the best I can with such limited intelligence as I have. Not everybody can be a Berger or a Hillquit, or a Seidel or a Goebel.

But, by God, I am going to make it my business, during the remainder of my life, or so much thereof as may be necessary, to learn whether the Socialist party stands for democracy in government or whether it doesn't.

I have some means of communicating with the rank and file of the party, and I am going to use those means.[4]

I note with pleasure that you have written something for the Appeal. If it {is} printed next week, it will appear in the same issue in which I have answered the criticism you expressed of the plan. I quoted your words but did not use your name.

Well, I guess that's all. I am sorry you felt compelled to write as you did, but inasmuch as you felt that way, I am glad you told me. But if I lose every friend I have in the party, I am going to hew to the line as I see it. And, if I have to use the personal pronoun, I shall use it. I am not mealy-mouthed. My manners may be bad, but so far as I know, my intentions are good—which will make me a fit candidate for the place to which some of my "comrades" would doubtless like to consign me.

Yours Truly,
Allan L. Benson

TLS, InTI, Debs Collection.

1. Oscar Ameringer (1870-1943) left his native Germany at fifteen to avoid military

service, came to America, and settled in Cincinnati, where he became active as an organizer for the Knights of Labor. Ameringer returned to Germany from 1890 to 1896 to study art in Munich and returned to Ohio in time to play in a band supporting William McKinley in 1896. Thereafter, he toured the Middle West and Southwest, teaching music and directing bands, until 1903, when he ran for mayor of Columbus, Ohio as a socialist and launched *Labor World,* in which he supported industrial unionism and attacked Gompers and the AFL. In 1907, Ameringer moved to Oklahoma City, which remained the home base for his work as a socialist organizer and speaker, organizer of the Oklahoma Tenant Farmers Union, and editor of a number of papers, including the *Oklahoma Leader.* From 1910 until World War I, Ameringer was closely allied with Victor Berger and the *Milwaukee Leader,* for which he wrote editorials. During World War I he was indicted for obstructing military service but was not brought to trial. In the period between World Wars I and II, Ameringer edited a number of labor papers and in 1932 published the autobiographical *If You Don't Weaken,* his most popular and widely read writing.

    2. The *Milwaukee Leader.*

    3. In the peace program adopted by the national executive committee, the call was for "abolition of secret diplomacy and democratic control of foreign policies." The term "war referendum" was not used. *American Socialist,* May 15, 1915.

    4. Benson's articles appeared regularly in both the *Appeal to Reason* and *American Socialist.*

Allan L. Benson to EVD

April 1, 1915
Yonkers, New York

Dear Debs:

    I was sick yesterday when the *Appeal* containing your article came, or I should have written you at once to tell you how much it pleased me. As to that part of it which was appreciative of my work, I could not have hoped that you would say so much—and probably you did say too much—and as to that part of it which pertained to the war-referendum idea, I could not have asked that you say more. It is enough for me that you accept the general proposition of applying the democratic principle to the war—and holding the war-makers responsible for their votes. I am quite willing to believe that the Philadelphia resolution is not letter-perfect—though I do not know how to improve it—but I am compelled to say that I doubt the sincerity or the sense of any Socialist who opposes an effort to take the war-making power from the minority. That is why I am impatient with Hillquit—I am convinced that he knows better than to talk as he does. I think Morris sent around a little olive branch today as I received from Julius Gerber, Hillquit's man Friday, an invitation to sit on the platform at the Hillquit-Gardner debate in Carnegie Hall tomorrow night.[1] I hope they will not hold up the meeting until they see me.

In the same number of the Appeal in which your article about me appeared was the chapter of my book that I devoted to answering a paragraph in one of your letters.[2] I feel about that chapter as I do about everything I write—a feeling that I should have done it better; but perhaps I did it as well as I could. In my own mind, there is no question as to the facts, and I can only hope that I have made you and others see it as plainly as I do.

Let me thank you again for coming across—*you are the only man who has up to date.* I expected you to, and you have done no more than I believed you would. You are on the square. And, if you will kindly believe that when I once expressed my regret to you that nobody who could help would do so, that I spoke not as a self-seeker might, or as a conceited jackass might, but as one who takes the war horror so seriously that it has perhaps become almost a mania with him—if you will believe these things which are true—you will be patient with me whatever I may do.

Oh, yes. I never saw your Scripps-McRae article.[3] If I had seen it, you can gamble that I would have picked it up and made use of it.

The Philadelphia resolution will die tomorrow—but it will die within a scratch of the victory line with more than 7,000 votes behind it. I will venture to say that in two years no Socialist will oppose it.[4]

Yours Truly,

Allan L. Benson

TLS, InTI, Debs Collection.

1. Augustus Peabody Gardner (1865-1918) was a congressman from Massachusetts from 1902 to 1917, when he resigned to enter the army. He was at this time a leader of the group in Congress demanding more military expenditures and preparedness, which he called for and Hillquit opposed in their debate on April 2, 1915.

2. "Socialism and the War Referendum," chapter 8 of Benson's *Way to Prevent War*, appeared in the April 3, 1915, *Appeal*.

3. As one of "the fifty most representative persons in the United States," Debs was asked by the Scripps-McRae Newspaper Enterprise Association to give his opinion on what Americans could do to bring abut peace. In his reply, "Peace on Earth" (*American Socialist*, January 9, 1915), Debs endorsed Benson's idea of democratizing the declaration of war through a popular referendum.

4. In its section on "Measures to Insure Peace," the 1916 Socialist party platform declared that "no war shall be declared or waged by the United States without a referendum vote of the entire people, except for the purpose of repelling invasion."

Paul J. Paulsen to EVD

April 12, 1915
Cheyenne, Wyoming

Dear Comrade;—

Perhaps I should not write you about the subject I have in mind
were it not that I know you too well, and have known you always to
be on the side of right. I also know that you will not misinterpret this
letter. I dont want to poison your mind against any one who you think
have been wronged.

Yet as a member of the International Executive Board,[1] knowing
what I know of the matters coming before the board, I know that
you are committing a grave injustice against John P. White when you
accuse him as you do in your editorial in the "Rip-Saw" of April
{Issue #2 1915}.[2] If this method is persisted in, it is possible that the
rank and file will be given all the facts in the cases of Howatt and
Holt and if they do it will not be to the glory of these two and things
will {be} exposed that you would hardly believe possible.

It is to be regretted that events in the "South West" have turned
out as they have. The loyal men who fought for the rights of the
miners in the South west are to be commended but dont make the
mistake of mixing the two issues. As to Howatt and Holt, in your
editorial, you say "White not only did not raise a finger in their
defense." Comrade Debs I want to caution you against getting into
something that will be difficult to untangle.

The above is the most unjust statement that was ever made against
President White and some time you will know the truth. I am convinced that you are being used because of your influence. I would
suggest that you see President White and if you do you will sometime
see the wisdom in my suggestion. Not for what Holt and Howatt may
say or do or what has happened to them, I say to you 'Get the facts,
get the truth and then judge'; believe no one, not even me, but get
the facts and undisputed evidence, then judge. You will not have to
take White's word, he will not ask you, he has the documentary
evidence that will show what part he played in the Howatt-Holt controversy at Kansas City.

I know you will not think I am unjust. Holt has always been a
comrade I have admired and I would not do him an injustice. Yet
for the love of the American labor movement I am asking you to
investigate. If you should decide to see White will you let me know
and I will arrange a meeting if possible. Let me know when it would

be convenient for you. In the meantime keep this confidential till you know more.

Hoping to hear from you at an early date.

I am, Sincerely and Fraternally

Paul J. Paulsen

Box 904, Cheyenne, Wyo.

TLS, InTI, Debs Collection.

1. Of the UMW.

2. As noted, in "Ten Convicted Labor Leaders" (*Rip-Saw*, April 1915), Debs applauded Fred Holt, secretary-treasurer, and Alexander Howat (1876-1945), president of UMW District 14, for providing "arms for the miners [in Arkansas] to protect their wives and babies" and criticized UMW President John White "and the other national officers [who] virtually abandoned the men to their fate, fearing, it would seem, to jeopardize their popularity with the operators."

Theodore Debs to Paul J. Paulsen

April 15, 1915
Terre Haute, Indiana

Dear Comrade Paulsen:

Your favor of the 12th has been received and read by Gene but as he is laid up with an injury[1] I am having to answer for him. First of all, he is glad you have written to him; he appreciates your frankness and I need hardly add that he has entire confidence in your judgment, your integrity and your sense of justice. He does not, however, share in the high opinion you express of President White as a union man and wishes me to say that if White is opposed to capitalism and the wage-slave system he is giving no appreciable evidence of that fact.

Answering your inquiry, Gene will be glad to meet President White in regard to the situation in the Southwest, as suggested by you, provided Comrade Fred Holt is also in attendance.

You say that "It is possible that the rank and file will be given all the facts in the cases of Howat and Holt and if they do it will not be to the glory of these two and things will be exposed that you would hardly believe possible." This is an admission not at all calculated to strengthen President White in the confidence of his followers. Why have these facts not already been given to the rank and file? What right has President White or any one else, or what justification, to withhold these facts from the rank and file when thousands of them look upon Holt and Howat as having been deeply wronged and hold to this so insistently that the organization is threatened with disruption of account of it?

President White has done himself no credit by putting a bunch of so-called organizers down in that territory of the character and caliber of ward-heeling thugs and wire-pullers to spread secretly damning reports about Holt and Howat instead of coming out openly and above board like a man and giving the facts, if any he has which condemn these men, to the rank and file and giving the accused a fair and square chance to defend themselves and to bring their counter charges, thus insuring a thorough hearing of both sides and justice to all concerned.

By all means let the truth and the facts be known to the rank and file no matter whether it be Holt or Howat or White himself who is shown up, discredited and removed from any further possibility of harm-doing. As it is now a feeling of ugly discontent smoulders there which will certainly break out in open warfare and possibly disrupt the union if something is not done to relieve it.

The conditions in Illinois and West Virginia are also of a character to excite grave concern among those who are actually true to the United Mine Workers and would see it the great industrial organization it ought to be and accomplish the great work they have been led to expect from it. In West Virginia a socialist is no longer tolerated by the degenerate officialdom in control there, while in Colorado socialist speakers during the campaign were denied admission to or driven out of the strike district after the socialists had done all in their power to help the strikers. At the same time this was going on some of his own official colleagues were circulating the most scurrilous and defamatory reports about Adolph Germer to encompass his defeat,[2] and if President White did anything to prevent this program of persecution in favor of pure and simple unionism I have not heard of it, but if on the other hand he did not himself connive at these same outrages then he has certainly been falsely accused by the members of his own union.

As a matter of course you are at liberty to repeat what is here said to President White if you think proper to do so for nothing is here said that would not be said frankly to White's face if there was occasion to do so.

No member of the organization could have a greater interest in its welfare nor a more earnest desire to see it prosper and grow than Gene has had, but there are certain tendencies clearly marked, especially during the past year, which if unchecked, will lead to disruption and disaster.

With all appreciation of your confidence and all wishes for the success of your labors, I remain,

Yours fraternally,
Theodore Debs.

TLc, InTI, Debs Collection.

1. In a letter from Theodore Debs to Basil M. Manly, April 27, 1915, Debs was said to be "disabled by a torn ligament in his leg, the result of a recent mishap" (see Theodore Debs to Basil M. Manly, April 27, 1915).

2. In his unsuccessful campaign for the presidency of UMW District 12 in November 1914, Germer was accused in an election-eve circular of treason to the miners of Colorado during the bitter and bloody strike against the Colorado Fuel and Iron Company; of having had "illicit relations" with the wife of a Walsenburg, Colorado, merchant; and of having neglected his organizational duties in Colorado. Germer was defeated by Frank Farrington, an antisocialist candidate for the district presidency who was supported by President White.

John P. White to EVD

April 16, 1915
Indianapolis, Indiana

Dear Sir:

I am in receipt of an editorial entitled "Ten Convicted Labor Leaders," which appeared in the "Rip-Saw," and as I understand it the editorial referred to is credited to you.

If this be true, I would like to know from what source you got your information with reference to my conduct in matters in the Southwest affecting Fred Holt, Alex Howat, et al.

This editorial does me, as well as the organization, a rank injustice. There is not one scintilla of truth in it so far as it applies to me.

Before replying to the editorial in a public way, I deem it only fair to ask you for particulars and give you an opportunity to explain what prompted you to write it. I have spent too many years in the service of the United Mine Workers to allow such a statement as this, impugning my good name, to go unanswered. I have entertained a high regard for you and cannot conceive that you would take the liberty to deal with a man's reputation as has been done in this editorial, without at least bringing to his attention some of the alleged misdeeds.

This administration of the United Mine Workers has no alliance with any coal operator. My official acts and my entire record in the labor movement are an open book and I fear no investigation in connection therewith and stand ready to meet my accusers at any time.

I can give a good account of myself in the controversy referred to. I believe you were misinformed, as I happen to know something about the movement to enlist your support in this direction, but I supposed with your experience you would at least weigh matters carefully and permit all parties to be heard before taking the subject up in the public press.

If you care to investigate this matter further, I would suggest that you write to Frank J. Hayes, Vice President, United Mine Workers of America, 1109 Merchants Bank Bldg., Indianapolis, Ind.; James Lord,[1] President, Mining Department of the A.F. of L., 606 Ouray Bldg., Washington, D.C.; Paul J. Paulsen, Member of our International Executive Board, Box 904, Cheyenne, Wyoming; and Jos. Variot,[2] Secretary-Treasurer, District 14, U.M.W. of A., Pittsburgh, Kansas. These men can inform you regarding my conduct and attitude in connection with this controversy.

Trusting I may be favored with an early reply, I am,

Yours very truly,
John P. White
President

TLS, InTI, Debs Collection.

1. James Revell Lord (1878-1948) came to the United States from his native England in 1888, worked in the Illinois coal mines, and was elected to the UMW District 12 executive board in 1909. He was head of the AFL's mining department from 1913 to 1923, during which period he represented the AFL at international labor conferences in England, Mexico, and elsewhere and served on several World War I government boards.

2. Joseph Variot (1875-1942) was head of District 14 for more than twenty years. His tombstone in Pittsburg, Kansas, reads: "Dedicated to the memory of Joe Variot for distinguished service and self-sacrifice in the cause of labor and advancement of the U.M.W. of America."

Theodore Debs to John P. White

April 20, 1915
[Terre Haute, Indiana]

Dear Sir:—

Your favor of the 16th. inst. addressed to my brother, Eugene V. Debs, was forwarded from St. Louis and received here this morning. As my brother is confined to his bed as the result of an injury and unable to give personal attention to his correspondence, I am directed by him to make answer to your communication as follows:

First of all, my brother received a communication from Paul Paulsen some days ago, also criticising the editorial to which you take exception and to this letter my brother directed me to make answer and as this answer covers some of the points of your inquiry I have asked Paulsen, who advises me that he will be in Indianapolis this week, to bring the same to your attention.

My brother wishes me to say that he based the editorial in question upon statements made to him by Holt and Howat, especially the former, and from rank and file members of the United Mine Workers. Your denial raises a question of veracity between yourself and these gentlemen but if your attitude was criticised by any mine owner my brother has not been aware of the fact.

My brother wishes me to say to you that he has known Fred Holt several years and that he has full confidence in his loyalty to the working class and in his personal integrity; that he is now in prison because of such loyalty while men have been placed in his district, presumably to represent the United Mine Workers, who are going about traducing him and doing all in their power to destroy him. The fact that Holt is in jail and that he was put there by the mine owners is in itself prima facia evidence of his loyalty to his union, and my brother has seen and talked with enough union members to satisfy him that they believe in him, notwithstanding the charges made against him by the very mine owners who are responsible for his imprisonment, and if the men who are now spreading slanders about him while he is unable to defend himself are union men then God help the union which stands in need of such base and cowardly service.

At the same time my brother would be the last to make a charge against you not supported by the facts, and if it can be shown that he has accused you wrongly he will be the first to admit it and to make full and ample restitution. He is perfectly willing to meet you personally at any time after he is able to resume his duties, provided only that Fred Holt is also present that he may make the same statements to you that he made to my brother and have the chance to prove them by members in good standing of the United Mine Workers.

My brother well knows that "this administration of the United Mine Workers has no alliance with any coal operator" but judging from what is taking place in West Virginia and other states it would seem that the operators are not without their influence in the United Mine Workers.[1]

You are of course at liberty to reply to the editorial in question in a public way, as you intimate you will do, and this may bring out some further facts in the matter concerning which the rank and file are entitled to full and truthful information.[2]

Hoping this answer may give you the information desired I am,

Yours very truly,

T. D.

TLc, InTI, Debs Collection.

1. In "Industrial Organization" (*Rip-Saw*, December 1914), Debs charged that UMW officials in West Virginia and Illinois were cooperating with capitalist parties and politicians as an antisocialist strategy.

2. In an editorial in the *United Mine Workers Journal* (April 13, 1916), Debs was described as "an active proponent of abortive organizations" who was "always advising division, secession, disruption [with] no compromise."

Basil M. Manly[1] to EVD

April 21, 1915
Chicago, Illinois

Dear Sir:

The United States Commission on Industrial Relations will hold a public hearing in Washington, D.C., during the first two weeks in May at which the principal subject for discussion will be "Labor and Law."

I am directed by the Commission to invite you to appear as a witness on Wednesday, May 12, 1915.

It is desired that your testimony should cover, primarily, your own experiences with the courts and with the officers of the law, but it is desired also that you should be prepared to present to the Commission your opinions and conclusions regarding the law and its enforcement in connection with industrial matters generally.

The Commission will be in session at the Shoreham Hotel, and it is desired that you should be in attendance at ten o'clock A.M. on the date named above, unless otherwise notified. The Government allowance for the expenses of witnesses is five cents per mile each way from your residence to the city in which the hearings are held, and two dollars for each day's attendance upon the hearings.

Will you please acknowledge receipt of this letter at your earliest convenience, and if it should be impossible for you to attend upon the date named above, kindly wire me collect, naming the date which will best suit your convenience.

Yours very truly,
Basil M. Manly
Director

TLS, InTI, Debs Collection.

1. Basil Maxwell Manly (1886-1950) was named director of the Commission on Industrial Relations research and investigation division in 1913 and wrote that part of the commission's *Final Report,* which was approved by the prolabor and rejected by the business or employer members of the commission when it was published in 1915. Manly served on the War Labor Board during World War I, was a close ally of Senator Robert LaFollette in the postwar decade, and was a member of the Federal Power Commission during the New Deal era.

Theodore Debs to Basil M. Manly

April 27, 1915
[Terre Haute, Indiana]

Dear Mr. Manly:—

Your favor of the 21st. addressed to my brother, Eugene V. Debs, inviting him to appear before the Commission on Industrial Relations at Washington has been received, and in reply I beg to say that my brother is at present disabled by a torn ligament in his leg, the result of a recent mishap, in consequence of which he has been confined to his bed during the last three weeks. The injury is mending slowly but at this writing the doctor, while giving assurance of ultimate recovery, is unable to determine how long it may yet be before my brother is able to resume his usual activities.

Allow me in behalf of my brother to thank you and through you the members of the Commission for your kind invitation and to express to you his deep regret with the assurance that but for his physical disability it would afford him the greatest pleasure to appear before your Commission.

Very truly yours,
[Theodore Debs]

TLc, InTI, Debs Collection.

Fred D. Warren to EVD

May 4, 1915
Girard, Kansas

Dear Gene: —

This is strictly a personal note, and for your eye alone. I don't know who else to write to, and I've just got to write to somebody. My soul is filled with anguish and mentally I was never so disturbed and upset in all my life. And with it all is a feeling of desperation that I do not believe I ever experienced before.

I have just read the dispatches announcing the conviction of John R. Lawson[1] and his sentence to life-imprisonment! And here I sit without an opportunity to raise my voice in his defense or do anything for the class he is making this tremendous sacrifice for.

Then there is Pat Quinlan[2] in prison, slowly dying of tuberculosis — his crime merely that he dared raise his voice in defense of the down trodden. Both these comrades convicted on *perjured testimony*. And Gene, the tragedy of it all — that the Socialist party seems divided into petty, almost hostile camps, each afraid the other will accomplish some great work! It makes me heartsick!

The Socialist party, if reports are to be credited, is barely more than beating time — *yet the whole country is seething with Socialist sentiment.* Without being egotistical, I honestly believe that YOU and I are the two men that can crystalize that sentiment into an aggressive active force that will ACCOMPLISH THINGS! We have done it in the past — and certainly there was never greater need of the things which we did in the Moyer-Haywood case, the West Virginia strike, the Coffman case[3] and a host of lesser contests (all of which were fought to a successful issue) being done again.

Pat Quinlan in prison — Fred Holt in a federal jail and John R. Lawson sentenced to the penitentiary for life! What tragedies — and to think that their sacrifices are in vain if we continue as we are doing. No effort, no *concerted effort*, to make people understand that all these things are but incidents in the great class struggle being waged between the working class and the capitalist class.

I know, and so do you, that there is but one thing that will arouse the unthinking public to a sense and to an understanding of the impending conflict — and that one thing is A FIGHT! Abstract propaganda will not hold the attention of the man in the ditch long enough to get the Socialist thought in his brain. IT IS THE CONCRETE ISSUE — "rescue Moyer and Haywood" — "drive a corrupt federal judge from the bench" — "open the prison doors to Coffman" — that rivets attention, and in the doing of this concrete thing the {man in the ditch} gets the abstract principles underlying the class struggle!

I believe, I KNOW, the whole country could be aroused over the terrible injustice of Pat Quinlan in prison—but before we can arouse the people, we must get the FACTS TO THEM. Judge Minturn's dissenting opinion in the Quinlan case,[4] if circulated as we circulated the facts in the W.F.M. case,[5] contains enough dynamite to blow up the Trenton penitentiary and open its doors to its innocent victim!

The secret manipulation of the Rockefellers of the Colorado strike[6] (now merely hinted at by the capitalist press) and its *direct* relationship to the conviction of Lawson would actually paralyze the public mind if these facts were properly presented. BUT ALL OF THIS MEANS A LONG DRAWN OUT PERSISTENT campaign of publicity. No haphazzard hit-and-miss policy will do. Your hands are tied because you can only talk once-a-month,[7] and then to people very largely outside of the industrial centers.

No one knows better than do you, how long and persistently we must hammer on ONE idea to get it riveted in the public mind. And then after the idea is fixed, to get the people to act—BUT IT CAN BE DONE!

People who were inclined to criticize my work on the *Appeal*, attributed to accident the success we had in the big cases. They said there were extraneous causes that contributed to the final and successful outcome. And so I took up the case of Waldo Coffman, an obscure soldier boy. Discredited to start with because very few of our folks have much regard for an enlisted soldier—it took some little maneuvering to get sentiment on his side. He had been tried by court martial—his doom fixed before trial—the trial being held before a tribunal whose authority had never before been called into question, and behind closed doors. YET THE APPEAL REACHED INTO THE FEDERAL PRISON AND TOOK THIS BOY OUT OF HIS CELL AND SET HIM FREE—and there was no other force—no accident—to help in this work. This case demonstrated the power of the ~~people~~ {paper}—it demonstrated the power of a paper to protect the innocent against the hell hounds of capitalism!

All of which made Socialist sentiment, because people were interested in the *FIGHT* and following the successful outcome of the fight, they took up the study of the underlying questions involved, and this lead them to Socialism! This is what happened following the Moyer-Haywood fight, the Federal judge controversy, etc.

The Pat Quinlan case furnishes the same dramatic features as these other cases—~~while~~ {with} this VITAL principle involved: IF THEY CAN SEND QUINLAN TO PRISON ON PERJURED TESTI-

MONY—on the framed-up evidence of private detectives—convict Quinlan of using language that he never uttered—of giving expressions to certain words he never used at a meeting he never attended— then DEBS may be sent to prison in the same way. That this will happen, I have no doubt, if WE SIT DOWN AND DO NOTHING IN A BIG WAY!

I suppose you are wondering why I am writing all this to you. I confess I hardly know myself. No doubt you are saying to yourself: "If all these things are true, then Warren knew that they were [true] months and years ago—then why did he lay down? Why did he allow Debs to quit the Appeal, knowing, as he now tries to point out, that Debs, Warren and the Appeal constituted the combination that *always won!*"

Without trying to apologize for myself, I will only say that my health was shot to pieces—mentally I was a wreck—my physician insisted that I would soon die—my family pleaded with me to quit— and I knew that sooner or later I would, be, by, circumstances, which seemed beyond my control, be forced to give up my work. I could not consistently ask you to give up a certainty on the Rip-Saw for an uncertain position on the Appeal. (After you asked to be relieved from work on the Appeal on account of your health, I held the thought that when you did get ready to go to work again, that you would let me know.)

But no matter, the result has been that the force—the fighting machine that Wayland and Warren and Debs built up, is now being frittered away and dissipated; Debs's hands are virtually tied, because no matter how much liberty you have on a monthly paper, you can't hope to accomplish much against the deluge of daily poison that is vomited forth by the capitalist newspapers; Warren is helpless and our capitalist enemies dancing with glee over the division in our ranks—*divided as to purpose!*

Early in the year, I gave two months of my time to the Call.[8] And I went east with the determination of throwing myself into the fight through that channel. BUT THE CALL IS HOPELESS! I know of no greater tragedy in our movement. After spending $700,000 of the pennies and dimes of the working class, the Call winds up seven years of heart-breaking effort with a debt of nearly $100,000 and a daily circulation of less than 12,000. The comrades on the paper willing and anxious and with the ability to do BIG things—and the Socialists and trade [unionists] of the east ready to support it—but a wet blanket in the shape of a few individuals who seem to be afraid that the Call will make a noise and be heard and get a circulation that will make it self-sustaining, and thus put it beyond their control.

I would have been willing to put up $50,000 of my own money had I seen any prospect of making the paper go—but in the atmosphere and surroundings—NOTHING COULD BE DONE. The task is hopeless.

I have $100,000 and I am tempted, when I see how much there is to be done—AND NO ONE DOING IT—to start a paper, but my judgment is against doing that for the present. I know what it means—a long hard struggle, besides it would be but dividing our forces when there should be unity.

And so today, it occurred to me to write to you and let you pass the word on to Phil[9] to make a weekly of the Rip-Saw—a fighting, militant weekly, such as the old Appeal was. I WOULD BE WILLING TO GIVE MY TIME TO SUCH AN ENTERPRISE, with no compensation save my expenses. Fortunately, I need no more than this. I feel that if I am to maintain my self-respect I must do something more than I am doing.

Any way, my mind is relieved after passing along this suggestion to you, and if nothing comes of it, I will at least have the personal satisfaction of having done my little towards what I believe to be a vitally necessary work.

Sincerely Yours,
Fred D. Warren

TLS, InTI, Debs Collection.

1. John R. Lawson (1871-1945), a board member of UMW District 15 in Colorado, was convicted of murder on charges growing out of the miners' strike in Colorado in 1913-14. He was freed on bail and his sentence eventually was overturned (1917) by the Colorado Supreme Court. Lawson later became president of District 15 and of the Colorado Federation of Labor.

2. In May 1913, Patrick L. Quinlan was convicted of inciting to riot during the Paterson, New Jersey, silk workers' strike. He was fined $500 and given a seven-year sentence. Warren raised $5,000 through the *Appeal* for Quinlan's release on bail pending an appeal to the New Jersey Supreme Court, which in March 1915 upheld the conviction and a two- to seven-year sentence. In "Pat Quinlan's Reward" (*Rip-Saw*, April 1915), "The Quinlan Frame-Up" (*Rip-Saw*, May 1915), and later editorials, Debs cited Quinlan's conviction as continuing evidence of the prejudice of capitalist courts. Quinlan was released from the state prison at Trenton in 1917.

3. In May 1913 the *Appeal to Reason* launched a campaign in support of an "obscure soldier boy," Waldo Coffman, who had been court-martialed and sentenced to two years' imprisonment for "using violent language in reference to the United States flag and speaking disrespectfully of Vice-President Sherman" and for distributing socialist literature. The *Appeal* generated considerable interest in the case, raised money for the Coffman Defense Fund and petitioned President Wilson for Coffman's release, which was granted in October 1914. Debs described the case in "Coffman's Vindication" (*Rip-Saw*, October 1914).

4. Judge James Francis Minturn (1860-1934) was a member of the New Jersey Supreme Court from 1908 to 1929. His dissenting opinions in the Quinlan case and in others growing out of the Paterson silk workers' strike—those of Carlo Tresca and Elizabeth Gurley Flynn—were widely quoted in the socialist and labor press.

5. Western Federation of Miners (the Haywood, Moyer, and Pettibone case).

6. In many of his *Rip-Saw* editorials—"Rockefeller's Republic" (June 1914), "Lexington and Ludlow" (August 1914), "The Ludlow Fiends Acquitted" (October 1914), and others—Debs blamed the Rockefellers, who owned controlling interest in the Colorado Fuel and Iron Company, for the Ludlow Massacre and for the corruption of the state's political system, including its courts.

7. The *Rip-Saw* was published monthly.

8. From late January until mid-March 1915, Warren went on a lecture tour "for the benefit of the *Call*" (*American Socialist*, December 12, 1914). In the *Call* of March 1, 1915, the paper announced that "the $700.00 received on account of the successful Warren Meetings came as a life-saver."

9. Phil Wagner.

Carl D. Thompson to Theodore Debs

May 18, 1915
Chicago, Illinois

Comrade Debs:

"'The Columbiad'"[1] in a recent issue publishes accounts of the lectures of Peter Collins and David Goldstein, and has the following to say with regard to 'Gene:

> "A socialist asked Brother Collins: "Will you agree to debate with our leader, Eugene V. Debs?' The answer came back with such clearness that the socialist was dumbfounded, for Brother Collins replied: 'Will I debate Debs? Why, my friend, I have diligently tried for four years to smoke out the mighty Gene, and I have even gone to the Appeal to Reason, to Debs' editorial den, to get him to debate, but to no avail. So I will make this proposition to you: If you socialists can get Debs to debate with me I will give your socialist local one hundred dollars, and while I am only a workingman I will guarantee to pay E.V. Debs five hundred dollars for his appearance on the public platform to debate with me. He can set the date, and I will guarantee to prove that socialism is the greatest enemy to the progress and welfare of the working people.' "
> (This occurred in Coffeyville, Kansas).

Have you replied to this?[2] If so, we should like very much a have

a copy of your statement for our use and to send to an inquirer.
Thanking you, I am

Yours very truly,
Carl D. Thompson
Director   Information Department

TLS, InTI, Debs Collection.

1. *The Columbiad* was a Knights of Columbus publication. The *Party Builder* (February 21, 1914) described its sponsorship of Peter Collins, David Goldstein, and other antisocialist speakers.

2. In "Peter Collins in the Pillory" (*Rip-Saw*, May 1916), Theodore Debs recalled Peter W. Collins's earlier charges that Debs's home had been built with scab labor and that the *BLF Magazine* had been printed by nonunion labor when Debs was its editor. He called the charges "sewage" and Collins "a liar and blackguard." The *Minutes of the International Brotherhood of Electrical Workers Special Convention* in St. Louis on September 18, 1908, record the "impeachment and discharge" of Collins as grand secretary of that organization on grounds of "gross negligence . . . incompetence, failure to perform his duty [and] assuming the role of a dictator."

EVD to Fred D. Warren

May 18, 1915
Terre Haute, Indiana

My dear Fred:—
   You will excuse my delay when I tell you that for five weeks I have been bed-fast. Broke a tendon in my leg and it laid me low. Snapped like the string of a bass fiddle and the pain was most intense. Fortunately there will be no permanent injury as the wound has mended and the doctor assures me that in good time I shall be entirely recovered. But just about the time I was able to stand on my feet I had an attack of congestion a little after midnight that came very near putting me down. The pain was somthing frightful and only large doses of morphine kept me from going frantic. Seemed as if I could not endure it another moment. But never mind. These are little troubles and I don't want to load you up with them. Only want you to know there was good cause for my silence. I am still weak but feel that I am now on the way to being myself again.
   Your letter has gripped my heart-strings and I am full of the same feeling that prompted it. Only I will not permit myself to be discouraged. Damned if I do! So many things are going wrong at the very time we ought to be at our best but I have made up my mind to keep up my little part of the fight and go straight ahead to the

end. If I were to let go it would be the only way my spirit could be crushed and my hope destroyed. But I cannot let go—and neither can you. God won't let us and I am glad he won't.

You know your views have always been of interest to me and your comment on the general situation does not surprise me, although you shed some light on some point[s] that were obscure to me. Your experience with the Call and your conclusions are of special interest. You are right. I helped launch the Call, spoke for it a number of times and have helped it every chance I have had, but it never seemed able to get on its feet. I hoped when I heard of your campaign in its behalf that your efforts would be successful. But I can understand the weakness and think I can place my finger on the cause of it. New York has always been torn with factional strife. What one faction undertakes the others generally take delight in wet-blanketing. I have never spoken there for socialism without having some faction to placate or some threatening element to pacify. If they would only work together for once they could put the Call on rock bottom in no time.

But the thing in your letter which goes to my heart more than all else is about the way we are frittering away our energies in petty and contemptible scrambles of all kinds while the real big issues that confront us and demand to be dealt with go begging. You are right in reference to the weakness of a monthly. I have felt it a thousand times in the last few months, especially since Pat Quinlan, Fred Holt, John Lawson and other fighting comrades have been sent to prison. Yes, there was a time Fred when we stirred the country and made the powers that be take notice and it can certainly be done today for there are even more vital issues in concrete form confronting us at this hour than ever before. Yes, in that day you speak of you and I worked together with our hearts aflame and so perfectly did we fit each other and so thoroughly were we absorbed in our task that we were one and the messages we sent out were charged with the very fire that burned in our own souls.

I note carefully your suggestion in connection with the Rip-Saw and it is a big one and I appreciate it and I want you to let me know by post card by return mail if you have any objection to my showing this letter to Wagner. He is big, broad and wide-open to a live suggestion. I shall not take this liberty without your assent for you may not wish me to show to others what you have personally written to me.

I would that it were possible to turn the Rip-Saw into a weekly. Perhaps! We shall see.[1] If you and I could get together there I really believe we could sound a clear note at this troubled hour and in this confused situation loud enough to be heard. I believe an appeal could be made and a clearing up campaign could be inaugurated that would bring about some concentration of effort and produce the needed results.

Do not give yourself a thought about my leaving the Appeal. Not a particle of reproach is at your door. I was wholly accountable for the change. For a long time I had not rendered half fit service. I was suffering from a nervous prostration, was worn out and finally had to give up my speaking engagements and during all this time you were kind and generous to me, indulgent beyond expectation, and I have only grateful recollection of the closing weeks of our relations. I had to let go for a time and when I said good bye to you at Girard on my way West to the mountains, I was so weak and worn, and not knowing really where I was going, it seemed as if I might never see you again; and I somehow felt that my work with the Appeal was done and if you remember I wrote you to that effect, so as to be perfectly frank with you, soon after I got to Colorado.[2] If you still have your personal files you will find this letter in them in which I told you that I could be of no further use to the Appeal and that such service as I could render at that time and under the then existing conditions could be quite as well or better rendered by others. I understand your own burden of trouble at the same time and the reason you think that some things might better have been done otherwise. I knew your own health was precarious and that you too were worn down fine and that you were having all you could do to carry your own load.

I never so longed as I now do to have the strength of a giant. The greatest hours in history are now passing us with their tremendous opportunities.

I am giving myself such chance as I can to get strong and well that I may be of some use to the cause. I have no other excuse to be on earth. And I know that it grieves you just as it does me that you cannot do what your heart and soul appeal to you with tongues of flame to do in this tremendous crisis. But be patient. We shall find our place and our duty and we shall be close together and in spirit and enthuse and strengthen one another in our mutual service and devotion to the cause.

Loving regards to Mrs. Warren and the boys.

Yours always,
Gene.

TLS, Warren Papers, Schenectady, New York.

1. The *Rip-Saw* remained a monthly publication.
2. See EVD to Fred D. Warren, September 8, 1913.

Theodore Debs to Carl D. Thompson

May 22, 1915
[Terre Haute, Indiana]

Dear Comrade Thompson: —

Your favor of the 18th. inst. in reference to an article said to have been clipped from "The Columbiad" wherein it is stated that one Peter Collins challenged Gene to debate with him, visited his den at the Appeal to Reason etc., has been received. In reply I have to say that if you know anything about the reputation of said Collins you will not be surprised when I tell you that this statement in the Columbiad is simply another of his ready-made lies. There is not a word of truth in it. Gene never saw Collins, does not know him, never had any communication with him whatever.

The reputation of Collins as a notorious liar discredits him completely and knowing that a decent man would not descend to his low level he feels that he can mouth his challenges when he is at a safe distance with the same impunity that a louse could challenge a lion or a cockroach blackguard an eagle. Collins is too petty and contemptible to attract attention on his own account and make him an asset to his owners and hence his free use of the names of men who are well known and whose reputation he is paid to blacken although he is unfit to blacken their shoes.

For a time Collins peddled the lie that Gene lived in a house built by scab labor and painted and kept in repair by scab labor. Collins peddled this lie, knowing it was a lie, during the presidential campaign and for some time afterward. Then the labor unions of Terre Haute, led by the President of the Central Labor Union, rammed that lie down his black throat and at several points he was faced with the proof of the lie so that he had to discontinue it and proceed to manufacture and deliver others in its place of which the one in the Columbiad is a shining example.

Enclosed I send you the printed proof of the mendacity of this black-hearted, foul-mouthed falsifier and slanderer.

If you want to know how this cowardly bluffer makes good on his challenges ask Fred D. Warren. Collins lyingly boasted that Warren was afraid to meet him and when Warren finally succeeded in cornering him at Pittsburg, Kansas, where an Opera House was packed with people to hear the debate, Collins ran away like a yellow dog.[1] That is Collins. He is not worthy of any decent man's notice and I would not take time to deny his slanders on Gene's account, or on my account, but only because the request comes from you in behalf of the national office.

You are at liberty to use this letter as you may think proper[2] and if you care to send a copy to the Columbiad or to Collins himself you are at liberty to do so.

Yours fraternally,
Theodore Debs

TLc, InTI, Debs Collection.

    1. An account of this episode is in the *Appeal,* April 26, 1913.

    2. As noted, Theodore Debs's response to Collins's attacks on Debs was in the *Rip-Saw* in May 1916. Calling Collins "Windbag Pete," the *American Socialist* (April 8, 1916) printed a letter from Theodore Debs to an unnamed local party secretary in a "western city" in which Theodore called Collins "the biggest liar in America."

Theodore Debs to Adolph F. Germer

June 3, 1915
Terre Haute, Indiana

Dear Adolph:—

Yours of the 30th. ult. is duly received and noted. Gene left on Saturday to fill a long line of speaking engagements.[1] He has not entirely recovered, but the cancelling of a lot of dates causes not only confusion and dissatisfaction but a material loss which the locals, especially in the present hard times, can ill afford and so he concluded that it would be best to make the trip. Following the mishap to his leg, which kept him in bed for five weeks, he had an attack of conges- tion which came nearly putting him under. His condition was so critical that his doctor asked for a conference. He suffered terribly. It was the first time I ever heard him groan. Three or four years ago he had the Mayos cut a tumor out of his side without taking an opiate and he never whimpered during the operation.[2] The doctors had decided as a last resort to operate on him but happily at this juncture the turning point was reached, the crisis was passed, but he was so weak, so terribly exhausted that he had not the strength of an infant. However, from that time on he grew stronger daily until he felt that he could fill his present line of engagements. In a letter from him last evening he says that he is getting along pretty well and feels some stronger than when he left home.

I note with interest what you say of the investigation of your case by the general office.[3] Of course a committee that was not entirely corrupt could bring {in} nothing else but a vindication, but it seems to me that this is not adequate under the circumstances. This report should have carried a recommendation that the perpetrators of this infamous and outrageous attack upon your character, at a time when you had no way of defending yourself, be ferreted out, exposed to the membership and driven from the organization in disgrace. However, such procedure might have cut in too close to the hides of those higher-ups who were most interested in your defeat. I suppose that you are correct in your conclusion that the report on the whole was all or more than you had a right to expect, and that this was due to the honesty of Paulsen and Wilkinson.[4] I do not {know} Wilkinson, but I do know that the integrity of Paulsen is above reproach, and that it must have been galling to White to have the committee bring in so favorable a report. I think it would be a good idea when you go to Oklahoma this summer and talk over the situation with Holt to have Fred gather up all the facts he can relative to the conduct of the organizers that White sent into his district before and during the time he was in jail, names of witnesses etc. There is no doubt but that all these things are going to come one of these days and this data will be most valuable in pointing out the character and methods used to discredit those who have honestly served the organization by White and his lieutenants. The treatment of Holt by officialdom was no less infamous than that accorded you. I know you have all the documents in your own case and you ought to suggest to Holt that he gather up all the facts, as you have done, so that when the time comes he too will have these facts where he can put his hands on them at will.

I hope you and Mrs. Germer are well and in good spirit. We send you our love and our hearty good wishes.

Fraternally yours,
Theodore Debs

TLS, WHi, Germer Papers.

1. Between May 30 and June 23, 1915, Debs was booked by the *Rip-Saw* for twenty-three dates in the Upper Midwest. (*Rip-Saw*, May 1915).

2. In July 1910.

3. In the fall of 1914 a committee of the UMW national executive board investigated and found Germer guilty of most of the charges made against him in the circular, which appeared during his unsuccessful bid for the presidency of District 15 in Colorado in 1914. In May 1915, however, a second committee investigation cleared Germer of the charges.

4. Adam Wilkinson was head of UMW District 27 in Roundup, Montana, and a member of the union's national executive board.

George D. Herron to Theodore Debs

June 4, 1915
Florence, Italy

Dear Comrade Theodore:

It was good of you to write to me about Eugene, and I profoundly hope he has fully recovered. There is no man in this world whose life I more highly and affectionately value than his. I do not want him to think, ~~that~~ even if I imagined he viewed the action of the German socialists differently from myself,[1] that this made the slightest difference in my undying devotion to and admiration for him, — a devotion and admiration in which my beloved always shared, even though she met him but a few times.[2] I wish he could have heard the way in which she has so often spoken of him to European friends.

This week I have been much occupied, serving as the American member of the Mayor's Committee to bid godspeed to the soldiers departing for the frontier. I did so, of course, under the advice and with the permission of our Consul General. I wanted to talk with the soldiers personally, to find out, if I could, the general feeling pervading them. On the whole, I have been highly impressed with a certain exaltation among them which rather eludes definition, but is yet very real. A young peasant, evidently just fresh from his farm, expressed the feeling that this was a holy war, that there could be no freedom or socialism or humanity left in Europe unless Prussia were destroyed. I was much astonished at such an expression from a comparatively ignorant young man, but he seemed to have some understanding of what he was talking about.

I have just received the splendid and stirring message of Eugene about the sinking of the "Lusitania,"[3] and I am giving it to my friends here in Florence to read. Nothing finer or nobler has been said about the subject. It stirs my very bones as well as my soul. Will you give to him and his wife my most loving greetings.

Affectionately Yours,
George D. Herron

TLS, InTI, Debs Collection.

1. After the outbreak of the war in Europe in August 1914, Debs's writings, which appeared regularly in the *Rip-Saw* and were widely reprinted in the socialist press, stressed the ideas that capitalist greed and competition made the war inevitable, that socialists in power would have prevented the war, and that workers were senselessly slaughtering one another to shore up the profits of capitalism. In "Never Be a Soldier" (*Appeal*, August 28, 1915), he argued that "working men are forced into war as working women are forced into prostitution" and asked "working men and working

women of America . . . never to become a soldier and never to go to war!" In "When I Shall Fight" (*Appeal*, September 11, 1915), Debs said he would never violate his socialist principles "for a crazy Kaiser, a savage czar, a degenerate king, or a gang of pot-bellied parasites" but would fight in a war "for the liberation of the workers."

2. Herron's second wife, Carrie Rand Herron, died in 1914.

3. In "The Sinking of the Lusitania" that appeared in the *Rip-Saw* in June 1915, Debs called the destruction of the liner "a fiendish crime . . . but it is no greater crime than many others that are almost of daily occurrence in the present European slaughter" and added that "the system that is responsible for the war is responsible for the crime." However, in "The Sinking of the Lusitania" that appeared in *New Review* on June 1, 1915, Debs blamed "triumphant Prussian militarism . . . the deadliest menace that confronts the modern world" for the sinking and predicted that "the torpedoes that struck the Lusitania sounded the knell of the Hohenzollern-Hapsburg dynasty, the deadliest foe to freedom and progress in all the world." To which of the two articles Herron referred is not known, but, given his strong anti-German stance, the latter would clearly have had a stronger appeal for him.

EVD to Thomas A. Hickey

June 9, 1915
Aberdeen, Kansas

My dear Tom—

Sure thing! No chance to write just now but will have something with you for the anniversary issue.[1] Never too busy to serve you and the Rebel. Success and more of it! In the words of Hogan, the Daniel of the Ozarks,[2] Here's to the Rebel and the Revolution!

Yours always
E. V. Debs

Long live the uncrowned King of the Lone Star State!
In the reign of King Hickey the First

ALS, TxLT, Hickey Papers.

1. In "The *Rebel's* Fourth Anniversary" (*Rebel*, July 3, 1915), Debs called Hickey's paper "a lusty, young giant" and Texas's "organ of revolution."

2. Dan Hogan was state secretary of the Socialist party in Arkansas from 1906 to 1910; an Arkansas delegate to the party's national conventions in 1908, 1912, and 1917; candidate for governor in 1914; and editor of the *Huntington Herald*, the state's chief socialist paper.

EVD to Frank P. O'Hare

July 1, 1915
Millville, New Jersey

Dear Frank:—

I appears that I shall have to quit the Rip-Saw and I guess you had better advise Phil accordingly. I simply cannot stand this kind of booking and that's all there is to it. To fill nine engagements I am racing all over the Eastern states,[1] wasting my time and strength and wearing myself out utterly. You are not to blame—you have done your very best and I have not a word of complaint. But they will not book through the Rip-Saw and that's the cause of the trouble. The R.S. unfortunately, came into bad repute on account of the rotten advertising it used to carry and in this section particularly they will not forget it, and even when they give us a date they do it under protest. At Conneaut Lake[2] they were discussing the R.S. when a woman said she had seen an ad. in it of a sex nature appealing to "sporty socialists" and that she felt so outraged that such a rotten ad. should be allowed in a socialist paper that she never would have anything to do with the R.S. since and has done everything she could to have other socialists boycott it.[3]

Since I have started on this trip I have passed through a hundred places where meetings should have been held and have traveled hundreds of miles to give 9 lectures that should have been covered in a single state.

Monday I was 13 hours getting to Uniontown, making three changes, and one of the trains was so crowded that I had to stand up three hours. It was sweltering hot and I reached Uniontown barely in time to wash the dirt off and get on the platform.[4] I was tired out, used up, full of dust and utterly unfit for my work—there was scarcely any life in me and I could put none in my speech—and under such circumstances I am a loser at every point, the comrades naturally concluding that I am played out. It is not the work that saps my strength and vitality but the eternal riding and jolting on cars all day long and the crazy rush to get from one place to another. Tuesday was about the same as Monday another all day ride in hot, packed cars, and yesterday was quite as bad. I missed the connection at Philadelphia and spent several anxious hours not knowing if there was a later train. The conductor told me the connection at Philadelphia was impossible even if our train was on time, which it was not, as there were but 12 minutes to transfer to the Market st. wharf.

I finally got here late and about as limp as a rag after being packed in a red hot car all day, utterly unfit to get on the platform.[5]

At Philadelphia I shall have to leave at 7 from the North Phila. station, fifteen miles from where I'm to speak[6]—I will not even have time to take off my soaking wet clothes, but will have to be rushed to the train from the meeting, ride all night and then face 25,000 people at Cleveland.[7] They will expect me to [be] fresh and full of fire and instead I will have ridden myself into a stupor on the railroad cars.

I am simply wasting my time and strength under this arrangement. It would be far easier for me to make 3 speeches a day at points 50 miles apart than to make one a day at points a couple of hundred miles apart and reached only after repeated changes and worry about the connections. I am riding myself into exhaustion, using myself up and accomplishing nothing and I think you must see that the net result to both the R.S. and myself does not justify this waste.

On this short Eastern trip alone I will burn up more of myself doing nothing than would be required under fair arrangements to deliver 25 lectures.

Now let me say again that I have no complaint against you or the R.S. On the contrary, my relations with you all have been extremely pleasant and satisfactory and I am deeply sensible of the fact that you have done everything possible to make them so, but after a thorough try-out of a year, the booking business in my case will not work, and for purely physical reasons I shall have to quit the road entirely or make other arrangements. I am willing to break down working for the cause but I can not consent to wrecking myself racing back and forth, day and night, on railroad trains. I can stand my full share of the fatigue incident to the road, but when it comes to an all day and all night strain and struggle to get from one point to another and being utterly worn out each evening before getting on the platform, I simply am compelled to make a change. If the fall bookings you have already made are of this same nature, please cancel them for I shall not undertake to fill them. I can make booking arrangements so that I can fill a dozen engagements in one locality at a time and deliver three or four times as many lectures as now and do it without using myself up and wrecking myself {physically} jolting along day and night in hot and stuffed railroad cars. I shall likely see you before many days. With much love to you all I am as always,

Yours sincerely,
Eugene V. Debs.

TLc, InTI, Debs Collection.

1. The *Rip-Saw* (June 1915) listed nine Debs dates in Ohio, New Jersey, Pennsylvania, and Michigan between June 27 and July 5, 1915.

2. Northeast of Cleveland, Conneaut had a socialist mayor, D. S. Brace.

3. The *Rip-Saw* carried a wide variety of advertisements. The offending ones were perhaps those which promoted a book, *Sex Force* (March 1914), promised larger busts (illustrated, "The Charm of a Full, Firm Bust Is Worth More to a Woman than Beauty," February 1913), or portrayed women in seductive poses who were being cured of kidney trouble or bathing in "folding Bath Tubs" (December 1914). The *Sporty Joke Book* (January 1915) promised that "your friends will laugh until they cry."

4. Debs spoke at Uniontown, Pennsylvania, on June 28, 1915.

5. On June 30, 1915.

6. Easton, Pennsylvania.

7. July 4, 1915.

Arthur M. Lewis[1] to Theodore Debs

July 5, 1915
Chicago, Illinois

Dear Comrade Debs:

Comrade Gene has always been celebrated for the nice things he does, and I greatly appreciate his leading off his editorial with a quotation from my little book.[2]

There is one thing I wish to take up with you as you are Gene's representative in all things and I wish you to help me out as far as you possibly can. For nine years I have held the stage at the Garrick Theater and this last season we had the greatest crowds in our history. One thing I have always admired about Comrade Gene's work is that even in the hottest campaign times he never forgets to sound a clear note as to the value of education and study for working men.

I have often thought I should like Gene to talk to my crowd some Sunday afternoon. I could afford to pay $100.00 for the lecture. He could select his own subject, but what I should like and what would specially fit with my work and my audience would be a goodly admixture of something about the value and desirability of working class education in the great truths of science in order to better grasp and solve their own social problems. This is the burden of my song and I know it fits exactly with Gene's ideas, and while he need not of course make it the theme of the lecture, he could drive the idea home sometime during his talk and thus cement the work I am trying to do. Any Sunday afternoon in December, January, or February would serve me.

Drop me a line or two and tell me what you think of this. I can promise you an audience that will listen closely and appreciate the arguments no matter how complex or difficult and that nobody will leave the theater until the last word has been spoken. My meeting is altogether different from a political campaign meeting in which the audience begins to tramp out after the enthusiasm of the reception has cooled, as is so frequently and regrettably the case. The audience I will give Gene is simply a large student body.[3] If you think this can be arranged, I should like you to pick me out a date as early as possible,[4] so as not to conflict with a probably [*sic*] date I am trying to arrange with Jack London. Jack London and Gene and Charles Edward Russell are the only three men in the country that I consider really big enough to take up the time of my splendid student assembly.

Yours fraternally,
Arthur M. Lewis

TLS, InTI, Debs Collection.

1. Arthur Morrow Lewis (1873-1959) for many years gave Sunday lectures on "scientific socialism" and other subjects at the Garrick Theatre in Chicago. Lewis and his guest lecturers attracted hundreds to the theatre each Sunday and he was a frequent contributor to *American Socialist* and other socialist publications.

2. In "Industrial and Social Democracy" (*American Socialist*, June 19, 1915), Debs quoted from Lewis's *Introduction to Sociology*, which was published by Charles Kerr in 1912.

3. Lewis conducted his Garrick meetings as "Sunday schools." The variety of subjects covered is suggested by the title of his lecture on December 19, 1914: "What Brought the End of the Dark Ages." (*American Socialist*, December 12, 1914).

4. Debs spoke at the Garrick on December 5, 1915, Clarence Darrow on December 12, and Scott Nearing on January 30, 1916.

EVD to Kendrick P. Shedd[1]

July 12, 1915
Terre Haute, Indiana

My dear Comrade Shedd: —

Thank you a thousand times for the very kind and appreciative letter from you I have in my hands. You will not consider me remiss when I tell you that I have been gone almost two months filling speaking engagements and that this is my first chance to drop you a line of acknowledgment. All the sentiments expressed by you have the stamp of your splendid personality and are radiant with your beautiful spirit.

You are to be most heartily congratulated and commended for the amazing success you have achieved in Milwaukee under not too en-couraging circumstances. I have both heard and read of your work and I believe in some measure at least appreciate its value. There are those comrades at Milwaukee who would rather see you fail than succeed. There are but few of these, fortunately, and their influence is not great enough to thwart your vigorous and determined efforts. There are others who are lukewarm and indifferent except as your efforts promote their own plans. Then there is the great body of comrades who are actually and honestly in sympathy with your work in behalf of the children upon the merits of the work itself, and with their co-operation you are certain, in spite of all obstacles, not only to build up the child movement at Milwaukee but to widen indefinitely the field of your operations.

Yes, dear comrade, the Cherdrons[2] are of the true nobility and we have for them sincere regard and deep affection. Their vision is clear, they are ever on the alert and they have the true socialist spirit. Both are of exceptional ability and force and they are uncompromisingly true to the revolution. They are especially alive to the question of schools and education from the socialist point of view and their ideas upon matters educational are the result of their own keen observation, practical experience and philosophical training. Then, too, they are comrades loyal, generous and true. There is not a trace of the mean envy or jealousy that not infrequently mars and distorts otherwise good comrades in their noble nature. They certainly appreciate you and your work and if only others gave you the enthusiastic and in-telligent support they so freely give you there would be no bounds to your success.

No, I am not one bit afraid that honest praise will spoil you. You are not what and where you are today because you can be spoiled by having your brave efforts and your unselfish services commended instead of condemned.

Theodore very thoroughly appreciates your warm-hearted re-membrance. The fine feeling you have for him he also has for you. Often do we speak of you and when your name is mentioned it is always with regard and love.

Heartily wishing you the full measure of success you are so loyally laboring for I remain,

Faithfully yours,
Eugene V. Debs

TLS, NRU, Shedd Papers.

1. Kendrick Philander Shedd (1866-1953) was born in Lima, New York, graduated from the University of Rochester in 1889, joined the faculty there in 1891, and taught

modern languages until 1912, when he was asked to resign because of his socialist activities. Shedd joined the Socialist party in 1910 and organized a socialist Sunday school in Rochester, which was a model for many others throughout the country. Following his dismissal from the University of Rochester in 1912, Shedd was invited to Milwaukee to head and coordinate a number of socialist Sunday schools in that city, where he remained until 1918 when he left the party in opposition to its war policies.

2. Frank and Eliza Taylor Cherdron of Milwaukee. Eliza Cherdron's articles appeared occasionally in the *American Socialist* (e.g., "Woman and War," September 26, 1914), and she worked for Debs in his 1916 congressional campaign, which she described in "November 4 in Terre Haute" (*American Socialist*, October 28, 1916).

Noble C. Wilson[1] to EVD

July 13, 1915
Terre Haute, Indiana

My Dear Comrade Debs:

The Speakers Committee of Branch Terre Haute Wrote to the Rip Saw asking for a date from you on a flat rate. We did not feel that we could make good with the subscription plan and besides we wanted to make a little on the meeting to pay off on our new home[2] which our branch has recently bought.

Comrade O'Hare suggests that we stage something big. He asked us to arrange for a "Chautauqua." He informed us, however, that any arrangement that you make with us will be satisfactory. He says that he knows your are interested in the possibilities of success, here, and feels that you will give us a date on a flat rate.

We should like to have a date the last of August or the first of September.

Hoping to hear from you soon,
I am,

Yours' Fraternally,
Chairman   Speakers Com.
Noble C. Wilson

TLS, InTI, Debs Collection.

1. Noble C. Wilson was a Terre Haute piano tuner and in 1916 was chairman of Debs's campaign for Congress in Indiana's Fifth District.

2. Socialist Hall at 1534 Eighth Avenue in Terre Haute.

EVD to Noble C. Wilson

July 17, 1915
Terre Haute, Indiana

Dear Comrade Wilson: —
Your favor of the 13th. inst. addressed to me at St. Louis has been forwarded to me here. I have been out speaking during the past two months and am now clearing away the accumulations consequent upon my long absence. Answering your inquiry regarding a date here, the Rip Saw had already written me of your request and I had meant to drop you a line or see you but have been so busy that I have had no chance.

I am sorry to say that I shall be away from here, in the far West most of the time between now and September and that on account of other arrangements it will be impossible for me to arrange a date here before autumn.

I note particularly the suggestion of Comrade O'Hare that something large be arranged here and I quite agree that this ought to be done but I do not believe it possible under the present unfortunate local circumstances. I am informed by a number of comrades who in the past have been most active and energetic that a bitter quarrel has been raging here and that an ugly feeling prevails between comrades and this to an extent that they could not and in the present situation would not work together to make such a meeting as we ought to have here a success. I am told that the number of members now in good standing has been greatly reduced and that quite a number have withdrawn from all activity and have declared that they will have nothing more to do with the local while it is under its present control. I am deeply grieved to hear these reports and not a little distressed to think that comrades here who ought to be working together hand in hand to build up the party are engaged in the bitterest kind of a factional quarrel, such a quarrel as should have no place in the Socialist party and certainly can have no place in counsels where the socialist spirit prevails. I am not pretending to judge for I am in no position to know the facts except as they are reported to me. Unfortunately I have no chance to attend local meetings or to do my part of the work necessary to keep the local in active operation. I am away on long speaking tours and when I get back there is such an accumulation here, so many demands of all kinds, and I am so tired and worn that I have no chance to give attention to local affairs, and usually what time I have here is completely taken up in getting even with the work that is behind and preparing for the next trip.

Now I hope it may be possible in the near future to come to a better understanding here and get the comrades who are now at odds into harmonious co-operation for the upbuilding of the party and the movement. We ought to have a great local movement here in Terre Haute. This city and vicinity teem with socialist sentiment and if we had our local machinery in perfect working order we could be enrolling new members at every meeting and forging to the front rapidly as a factor in the city's and county's affairs. All that is required is that our comrades should unite and pull together and encourage and support one another instead of pulling apart and calling one another names. If the spirit of socialism had prevailed among comrades who have fallen out with each other, if those who have been charged with offenses had been approached in a comradely spirit in the first instance and there had been such consideration shown to those accused as one comrade should always have for another the present unfortunate condition would not now exist.

But I need not now go into particulars. I hope I may have a chance to talk over the situation with you and go over the differences calmly with those who are most immediately concerned and if this be done I am sure it will not be long before an understanding is reached and the local is once more harmonious and united and on the road to prosperity and success. Then we shall have no trouble in arranging about a meeting and the terms shall be made entirely satisfactory to the comrades. For my part there is nothing I will not gladly do to help you and the local comrades in any effort you may put forth in behalf of the local movement.

In this connection I should say to you that a couple of years ago, about the time the Terre Haute Labor Temple Association[1] was launched I agreed that on some suitable occasion I would give a lecture the entire proceeds of which should go to the Temple Fund. It is probable, as I am informed, that arrangements may be made by those in charge to have the lecture given this fall and in that event {I} shall of course fulfill my promise.

Thanking you for your kind invitation and earnestly hoping to see the local situation cleared up at an early day and the comrades all working together in harmony and good will to build up the party and speed the day of victory I remain,

Yours fraternally,

E. V. D.

TLc, InTI, Debs Collection.

1. The Terre Haute Labor Temple Association was formed in 1912 to raise funds for the purchase of land and construction of "a permanent home for the industrial

crafts in the city." It had, according to the *Terre Haute Tribune* (May 15, 1915), raised only $7,000 of the $117,000 needed for the project by 1915. In October 1926 at the time of Debs's death, his body lay in state at the temple, which was completed in 1922.

Frank P. Walsh to EVD

July 18, 1915
Kansas City, Missouri

Dear Mr. Debs:

Your kind letter of the 12th inst. was duly received. It was a very great disappointment to me that we did not have the opportunity of hearing you before the Commission. At the time we received the letter from your brother, notifying us of your inability to appear on account of your serious accident, I fully intended to write you a letter, but my intention became mislaid in the rush of affairs which were on at that time.

If you ever have the opportunity of looking over our work, you will find that yourself and your cause were put forth by many of the witnesses.

The Commission is holding continuous session in Chicago, endeavoring to agree upon its report to Congress. It is my sincere wish that it will be a document of enough depth and vitality to assist, at least, in a small way, toward the institution of a decent industrial basic system.

In the discussion of the report last week, one of the employing members of the Commission, in commenting upon the report of one of our experts, who suggested the necessity of industrial organization of workers, said: "According to this report, Eugene Debs was right, and his only mistake was in being about twenty years in advance of the times." Commissioner Garretson,[1] whom you, of course, know, retorted: "He was not the first great man charged with the same mistake." I cite this to show that your personal absence did not eliminate the spirit of your sacrifices and what you have stood for.

I sincerely appreciate all of your kindly and sympathetic support. I trust you have entirely recovered from the effects of your accident.

With my warm good wishes, I am

Sincerely yours,
Frank P. Walsh

TLS, InTI, Debs Collection.

1. Austin Bruce Garretson (1856-1931), a labor member of the Commission on Industrial Relations, was grand chief conductor and president of the Order of Railway Conductors from 1906 to 1919 and editor of the union's journal, *Railway Conductor.*

EVD to Arthur Le Sueur

July 24, 1915
Terre Haute, Indiana

My dear Arthur: —

For a long time I have been meaning to send you an article for the College News[1] but I have been kept so strenuously on the jump that nothing has come from my good intentions. Each day brings more "immediate demands" than can possibly be complied with. You and "Jake"[2] and Comrade Wharton[3] have been extremely considerate and kind to me and you may be sure that I am keenly alive to it all, even though I may seem to be insensible to your generous and considerate treatment.

You are getting out a rattling good College journal. Each issue bristles with the virile nature and revolutionary purpose of the cause it represents. The July number cuts clean as a rapier and its appeal is as stimulating as a cold shower on a sultry day.

Tell "Jake" that I'll very likely drop in on my next trip West, provided he furnishes a written guarantee that when we meet there'll be no "hurling of epitaphs" and that "no names will be named and no reflections cast."

We'll just indulge ourselves in what our old friend Bill Nye used to call "a pleasant bit of cast-irony."

Love to all!

Yours in full and right along,
[Eugene V. Debs]

TLc, InTI, Debs Collection.

1. The *People's College News.*
2. Jake Sheppard.
3. Marian Wharton (1877-1954) was secretary of the People's College Union and author of the college's book for workers, *Plain English.* She and Arthur Le Sueur were married in 1917 and soon thereafter moved to St. Paul, Minnesota, where both played active roles in the Non-Partisan League and Farmer-Labor party.

Theresa S. Malkiel[1] to EVD

July 26, 1915
New York City

My Dear Comrade Debs:

Your splendid article in the American Socialist as well as your good, farsighted letter in the same issue have given me the courage to write this letter to you.[2]

You know how little our men comrades realize the seriousness of the "Woman Question." Not that they do not know what is coming, but what is even worse, they do not want to know. And yet—something has to be done. We women, who have the cause of Socialism at heart, must, therefore, increase our demand on those few men comrades who comprehend the sign of the times, those who are and have always been willing to take up the cudgels in behalf of woman's freedom.

The campaign in the Four Eastern States[3] this year could be made a great victory for Socialism, if our comrades would once for all make up their mind to turn their sole attention to the suffrage issue. But they are far from making up their mind. Whatever little we women succeed in doing is done. One of the burning needs is suitable literature dealing with the suffrage question from the Socialist point of view. We want two short leaflets of about five hundred words each which we could print by the hundreds of thousands and spread broadcast, forcing the issue before the eyes of the voters.

Our Committee, the Woman's National Committee[4] knows full well your ability to say a whole lot in a very few words, hence our appeal to you to please write one, or, if possible, both of these leaflets for us at your earliest convenience. We hope, My dear Comrade Debs, that you will not refuse to come to the aid of your women comrades in the hour of need.[5]

Fraternally
Theresa S. Malkiel

TLS, InTI, Debs Collection.

1. Theresa Serber Malkiel (1873-1949) and her husband, Leon Andrew Malkiel, a prominent New York attorney, were two of the founders of the *New York Call*. Her book *Diary of a Shirtwaist Worker*, published after the Triangle fire in 1911, helped to stimulate the reform of New York's laws on the conditions of women in industry, and she was a popular speaker on the socialist and feminist lecture circuits. Her later career was given over largely to the education and naturalization of immigrant women.

2. Debs's "Women and Their Fight for the Franchise" (*American Socialist*, July 24, 1915) criticized "socialists who regard the matter of equal suffrage with indifference"

and urged them to join enthusiastically in the woman-suffrage movement as "a distinct advance toward democracy" and, as a practical matter, to increase the number of socialist voters significantly.

3. Voters in New York, New Jersey, Pennsylvania, and Massachusetts were scheduled to vote on the suffrage amendment to the U.S. Constitution in the fall of 1915. It was defeated in all four states.

4. The women's national committee of the Socialist party, composed of six members, was abolished by referendum vote in 1916.

5. Debs continued to write frequently on the "Woman Question" in the *Rip-Saw* ("The Women and Their Fight," October 1915; "Triumph for Equal Suffrage," December 1915) and his pieces were widely reprinted, but the two leaflets requested by Mrs. Malkiel have not been found. On October 25, 1915, in what the *American Socialist* (October 30, 1915) called "the greatest suffrage parade ever held in America," Debs marched at the head of the "Socialist section of 5,000 women" in a New York City parade.

Elizabeth Gurley Flynn[1] to EVD

ca. August 18, 1915
New York City

Dear Comrade Debs:—

I write to you on behalf of a valiant soldier in labor's cause—Joe Hill,[2] the poet and song-writer of the I.W.W. who is in jail, sentenced to death, in Utah. You probably have already heard of the case. Judge O.N. Hilton[3] now has it in charge and is attempting to secure an appeal to the U.S. Supreme Court. I am enclosing data and a form of the appeal to the Governor that is being circulated widely in the East.[4] If you would write even a few lines to some of the Socialist press or to me to send copies to the Socialist press urging financial and moral support, the circulation of the petitions etc. it will help tremendously to stir up working class interest and co-operation for this almost unknown and very worthy comrade.

I wonder if The RipSaw would publish a form of appeal to the Governor to be filled out and sent in by the readers?[5]

I am sorry not to have met you on my Middle-West trip, but had a very pleasant hour with Kate Richards O'Hare.

With very best wishes and hoping to enlist your support and co-operation for Joe Hill, I am

Yours fraternally,
Elizabeth Gurley Flynn

ALS, InTI, Debs Collection.

1. Elizabeth Gurley Flynn (1890-1964) joined the IWW in 1906 and was for the

next decade deeply involved in most of that organization's major free-speech and strike actions. A founding member of the American Civil Liberties Union in 1920, Flynn was a leader in the effort to defend the many IWW and other victims of the post–World War I Red Scare. She later joined the Communist party (1937), wrote for the party's *Daily Worker*, and served a three-year sentence (1955-57) following her conviction for advocating force and violence in the overthrow of the United States government. In 1961, Flynn became the first woman to head the Communist party's national committee.

2. Joe Hill (1872?-1915) was born in Sweden, came to the United States about 1900, and in 1910 joined the IWW, whose journals, *Industrial Worker* and *Solidarity*, published his Wobbly songs, some of which—"Preacher and the Slave," "Casey Jones— The Union Scab," "There Is Power in a Union," and "Nearer My Job to Thee"— became permanent parts of labor-song history. In January 1914, Hill was arrested in Salt Lake City on a murder charge, in June of that year he was tried and convicted, and during the following seventeen months he remained in prison while a massive campaign to secure a new trial for him was carried forward. Eventually the Swedish government, Samuel Gompers, and President Wilson joined the campaign, but Utah authorities denied Hill a new trial and he was executed by a firing squad on November 19, 1915. His song "Rebel Girl" was dedicated to Flynn.

3. Orrin N. Hilton (1849-1932) practiced law in Denver for thirty years (from 1888 to 1918) and established a reputation as one of the West's leading criminal lawyers. He was counsel for both the UMW and the Western Federation of Miners in Colorado and was a Republican party leader in the state. His obituary in the *Denver Post* of December 16, 1932 described him as "nationally known in organized labor circles." Hilton was disbarred by the state of Utah because of his funeral oration for Hill in Chicago.

4. Flynn enclosed a printed petition to Governor William Spry of Utah and a form letter describing Hill's case and his need for support.

5. In "Plea for Joe Hill" (*Rip-Saw*, October 1915), Debs repeated much of the material in the petition to the governor of Utah, described the Hill case, and urged readers to write to Governor Spry and send money to Flynn.

EVD to Elizabeth Gurley Flynn

August 20, 1915
[Terre Haute, Indiana]

Dear Comrade Flynn:—

Your communication with printed enclosures in behalf of Joe Hill has just been received and I am glad to undertake without loss of time to comply with your request. When the life of a comrade is at stake all else must take second place. I have been interested in Hill's case but have had no chance on account of being so hard pressed to take any active part in his behalf. I have now written a letter to Governor Spry[1] of which you will find a copy enclosed.[2] You can use this in any way that will help. I have also written a brief appeal and mailed it to the editor of the American Socialist[3] and asked him to insert it in the next issue. You will find a copy of this enclosed also and you can use it in any way you may think best. As the A.S. is the party paper and all socialist papers receive it in exchange it is quite probable that a number of them will copy this article. Perhaps you would better send a copy of both the letter to the governor and the article to the A.S. to the Int. Socialist Review if you think it will help the agitation in Hill's behalf. I will gladly do anything more I can and I shall find other ways of getting publicity and reaching the people. Unfortunately the R.S. has gone to press and it will be a month before there is another issue and that will be too late.

I too am sorry to have missed you while we were in the middle states but am glad you had the visit with Kate Richards O'Hare. Earnestly hoping we shall be able to save Joe Hill and with all good wishes to you I remain,

Yours fraternally,

[Eugene V. Debs]

P.S. You will find my mite enclosed.

TLc, InTI, Debs Collection.

1. William Spry (1864-1929) was a two-term governor of Utah from 1909 to 1917 and head of the Farmers and Stock-Growers Bank in Salt Lake City. He rejected President Wilson's request for reconsideration of the case of Joseph Hillstrom (Hill's real name) as unwarranted interference.

2. See EVD to William Spry, August 20, 1915.

3. Debs's "To Save Joe Hill" (*American Socialist*, August 28, 1915) urged readers to write to Governor Spry and noted that "money is needed" for Hill's legal defense.

EVD to William Spry

August 20, 1915
Terre Haute, Indiana

Dear Governor Spry:—

Please allow me to say a word in behalf of Joseph Hillstrom (also known as Joe Hill). From the reports that have come to me from those in position to know the facts and whom I regard as entirely trustworthy, I am convinced that there is more than a reasonable doubt as to the guilt of this unfortunate brother of ours in the cause of labor. He was convicted upon circumstantial evidence, denied the right to choose his own counsel, while at the same time there was unquestionably a strong prejudice against him on account of his activity in the labor movement.

Joe Hill is a poet, a writer of songs, a man of soul, a tender and sympathetic nature and the crime of murder is as foreign to him and as unthinkable as it would be to any other man of like temperament. For this reason and others I will not trouble you with I beg you to give serious consideration to the case of Joe Hill and if you do I am confident you will grant him executive clemency. Joe Hill is not a murderer; he is a man and the great state of Utah where murder is so abhorred cannot afford to take his life.

Thanking you sincerely for myself and for the working people in whose behalf Joe Hill has labored and suffered and made many sacrifices I remain,

Yours very truly,
[Eugene V. Debs]

TLc, InTI, Debs Collection.

Elizabeth Gurley Flynn to EVD

ca. August 22, 1915
New York City

Dear Comrade Debs:—

I received your splendid appeal for Joe Hill and am trying to get same into N.Y. Call. Also received the enclosure of $2.00 which I have forwarded to the Defense Fund.

The latest advise I have received from the Salt Lake City Committee is that Judge Hilton (Hill's attorney, an exceptionally reliable lawyer who has defended many miners' cases—possibly you know him) decided that the only practical move now is to appeal to the Board of Pardons. So he will make another trip from Denver, where his office is, on the 3rd Saturday of Sept. for this purpose. It seems the first two lawyers Hill had did not register objections to points decided against him, so left very little technical basis for appeal to the U.S. Courts.

So we will continue circulating the petitions and having people write to the Governor, in hopes of a favorable effect.[1]

Thanking you for your co-operation, I remain, with best wishes,

Fraternally Yours,
Elizabeth Gurley Flynn

ALS, InTI, Debs Collection.

1. As noted, Hill was executed on November 19, 1915. In "Murder of Joe Hill" (*Rip-Saw*, January 1916), Debs accused Utah of having "committed murder in cold blood," adding that "this civilized and Christian commonwealth was not entirely void of charity: it gave its doomed victim the choice between hanging and shooting."

Victor G. Candamo[1] to EVD

August 24, 1915
Arecibo, Puerta Rico

Beloved and Distinguished Comrade: —

I am gratified to know that your health continues vigorous and strong, fortified by the enthusiasm and strength of your heart, always animated and encouraged by the knowledge that our great ideal holds you as one of its most fervid and heroic defenders. Yes, heroic and steadfast like Debs. Permit me, therefore, that with this motive, doubly grateful to me, I dedicate to you a copy of the Manifesto[2] which I have just issued here, addressed to the "Workers of America" as a means of propaganda and pledge of the conscience of the universal proletariat, and in order that I may contribute with my poor, weak efforts, although my desires are of iron and my enthusiasm is strong.

I pray you, therefore, that you translate it, and make it known to the American socialist press, not as written by me, which counts for nothing, but to further our great aims, for the great love we have for our ideals, for the great and redeeming principles of Marx, our great master and apostle of Socialism.

In doing this you would do a great service to our cause, and I would be most grateful and thankful to you.

It gives me great pleasure to respond to your courtesy with my photograph, in exchange for yours, which you have had the kindness to dedicate to me, some eight months since. As Spaniard and Socialist, I shall cherish all my life the honor which you have conferred on me, and you may be sure that I shall guard it and esteem it at all times and on all occasions. Yes, always it shall be a reminder of you in my home. I am proud of it, and in the breasts of my comrades and friends it shall be a reminder and example of a good citizen and a good socialist, which no one can deny, and whom I am one of the first to recognize and admire.

Finally, dispose of me as you may desire, and know that I have a home, which is yours, and a family which, though poor, will take pleasure in serving you.

Accept the greetings and sincere affection of one who claims to be your loyal comrade and admirer in truth.

                                                    Victor G. Candamo

ALS, InTI, Debs Collection.

1. Candamo's letter, in Spanish, was sent to the party's national office in Chicago, where it was translated by the executive secretary, Walter Lanfersiek, and forwarded to Debs. A calling card enclosed in the letter identified Candamo only as *Miembro del Partido Socialista de Estados Unidos.*

2. Candamo's "Manifesto" has not been found, but the *American Socialist* (March 11, 1916) printed "A Plea from Porto Rico," another letter from Candamo to Debs, which described "the hardships, persecutions, and suffering endured by our Porto Rican comrades."

William E. Sweet[1] to EVD

August 26, 1915
Denver, Colorado

Dear Mr. Debs:

I understand from father that you are comtemplating a trip to Denver next Fall. Would it be possible to make a date for the Mile High Club?[2] We have slipped up on this once or twice before.

With kind regards and awaiting your prompt advices, I am

                                                    Very truly yours,
                                                    Wm E Sweet

ALS, InTI, Debs Collection.

1. William Ellery Sweet (1869-1942) was the son of Debs's Denver friend Channing Sweet. An investment banker in Denver, Sweet was elected governor of Colorado in 1922 as a Democrat in a campaign in which his opponent attacked him as "a parlor socialist" (*Denver Post*, October 18, 1922). Sweet served one term as governor, from 1923 to 1925.

2. Founded in 1902, Denver's Mile High Club met monthly at the Brown Palace Hotel and was composed of the city's business and professional leadership. During 1915 the club heard lectures by Seth Low, Nicholas Murray Butler, Charles Evans Hughes, and Lincoln Steffens (Edward Ring, *Mile High Club*, n.p., n.d.).

EVD to William E. Sweet

August 28, 1915
[Terre Haute, Indiana]

My dear Mr. Sweet: —

Your note has just come and replying I have to say that I have not yet, so far as I am advised, any engagement in Colorado. All my dates, so far as the route sheet shows are in Oklahoma and Texas. It is possible however that negotiations are pending for dates in Colorado as the booking is done in St. Louis.

You know of course that {for} you personally I would gladly do anything but to be candid with you I do not think it would be well for you or for the Mile High Club or myself to speak before that Club at this time. I understand that the officials of the coal companies are members of the Club and if so I should certainly have to denounce them to their faces as arch criminals and conspirators, debauchers of the state's politics, committers of murder and of other crimes too numerous to mention. I am filled with the reports being issued by the Federal Board of Industrial Relations[1] exposing these rich men as the vilest criminals that ever went unhung and I could not be true to myself if I stood in their presence without telling them so. I certainly would not deliver myself of a lot of polished platitudes and go away from there with their applause ringing in my ears and despising myself for my hypocrisy. I assume that you are reading the reports being issued in installments by Frank Walsh and his Federal Commission and if you are you know beyond any question of doubt that these mine owners and their official hirelings are the coldest-blooded murderers, woman-ravishers and baby-roasters that ever figured in the annals of crime. They are wholly responsible and the Commission brands them for exactly what they are. Every drop of my blood is hot with indignation as I read the positive proof, the unimpeachable evidence of their crimes against the state and against the men, women and children[2] of the suffering poor who by their labor and sacrifice produced every dollar of their wealth. I cannot think of these crimes against the unfortunate and weak; I cannot think of the criminal conviction of Lawson, the passing of a measure through a rotten legislature at the instigation of these rich and respectable criminals to put a low shyster on the bench by special appointment of a degenerate governor,[3] the tool of these criminals, to send innocent men to the gallows; I cannot think of these brutal and disgraceful outrages upon civilization and humanity and everything of decent report among men without feeling every drop in my veins running hot and there is only one way I could deal with them and shall deal with them and that is to denounce them with all the passion that fills my soul and seek by all the means at my command to arouse the people against these modern pharisees and the corrupt and inhuman system that enables them to drink the life-blood of the toiling slaves and then despise them and shoot them down like dogs for protesting against conditions against which animals would revolt.

Allow me to thank you for the kindness intended which I appreciate fully and to subscribe myself as ever,

Very sincerely yours
[Eugene V. Debs]

TLc, InTI, Debs Collection.

1. The United States Commission on Industrial Relations published its *Final Report* in August 1915. That part of the document written by Frank Walsh and Basil Manly and approved by the labor members of the commission was a stinging indictment of unemployment, employer tyranny, and labor's inability to organize. The *Report* was particularly critical of the Colorado Fuel and Iron Company's role in the miners' strike in that state.

2. The commission's *Report* and Debs, in several editorials in the *Rip-Saw* ("Calumet and Ludlow," June 1914; "Lexington and Ludlow," August 1914; "The Ludlow Fiends Acquitted," October, 1914; and others), blamed the Colorado Fuel and Iron Company and the Rockefellers for the Ludlow Massacre of April 20, 1914, a pitched battle between striking miners and state militiamen that left two strikers, two women, and eleven children dead. The women and children died when the troops captured the miners' tent city and set it afire.

3. George Alfred Carlson (1875-1926) was the Republican governor of Colorado from 1915 to 1917 during the period of many of the trials growing out of the bitter and bloody miners' strike in Colorado (1913-14) against the Colorado Fuel and Iron Company. His appointment of a mining-company attorney, Granby Hillyer (1876-1942), to preside at the trial of John Lawson on a murder charge following the Ludlow Massacre and the life sentence given Lawson by Hillyer were bitterly denounced in the labor and socialist press. Debs's "John Lawson's Infamous Conviction" (*Rip-Saw*, June 1915) denounced the political leaders of the state and deplored the stupidity of Colorado workers who continued to vote for Republican and Democratic candidates. On August 17, 1915, the Colorado Supreme Court barred Hillyer from presiding at any future trials connected with the miners' strike (*New York Times*, August 18, 1915).

Julius Gerber to EVD

August 30, 1915
New York City

Dear Gene:

At last one of my wishes has been granted before my death; and that is, to have you with us for a week. Ever since 1900 I have tried to get you here for a week but failed; and now I have my wish.[1]

At this writing, we have not decided definitely on the meetings which we will hold. The possibilities are that you will speak on the 15th, 16th and 18th in New Jersey, as they have a special election on October 19th, on the question of woman suffrage,[2] and would like to have you. The places at which you may speak will be right in the vicinity of New York—such places as Newark, Elizabeth and Jersey City. I will not go farther than Elizabeth. This will leave the 17th, 19th, 20th, 22nd and 23rd for New York.

We had originally planned to have the meeting on the 17th in Carnegie Hall, but since we have the four additional dates I am considering cancelling Carnegie Hall (as the expense involved is very large—$500.00 hall rent alone); or change the date of the Carnegie Hall meeting from Sunday, October 17, to Saturday, October 23rd, so that we can close the series of meetings instead of opening them— with a large meeting at Carnegie Hall.

However, all these are matters which may not concern you much. We will work them out to the best advantage.

But to keep up the interest in the meetings, I would ask you to have five different subjects, one for each meeting—woman suffrage to be one of the subjects, as we are to vote on a constitutional amendment on the question this fall.

I am planning to use your presence in New York for a revival, to carry on an extensive organization campaign, and at the same time utilize your presence in our campaign for the election of assemblymen and aldermen to the State Legislature and Municipal Assembly. What the election of one or two assemblymen to our Rock-Ribbed Conservative, Republican State Legislature would mean for the workers of the State and the Socialist Movement, I need not tell you; and a few Socialist aldermen in the corrupt Tammany Board of Aldermen would work wonders; and we want your help in order to do it—and I feel that we will do it. (Remember, I wrote you last year that we would elect London to Congress, and we did.)[3]

Let me know as soon as possible the subjects for the meetings, as I want to start advertising. I will try and keep things humming.

My idea is to have two meetings every evening. You are to make a short address, and I will have an automobile to convey you from the hotel to meetings and back to the hotel. I can have two speakers at each meeting, so we can make the most of it.

We intend not to charge an admission at any of these meetings (except Carnegie Hall), so we can get the people out, and especially those who need Socialism most.

Let me know when you intend to arrive in New York and where you will stop, if you have any preference. If you will let me know the train on which you will arrive, I shall make it my business to meet you.

I will try and have a comrade with you during your stay in New York, if you want me to.

This is all for the present. I will write you later.

Let me have the subjects for the meetings soon, so that I can go ahead. We will try and do our best to make your week's stay here a memorable one, and hope that it will wake this town up as it never was before.

With best wishes to you and kindest regards to Theodore, I am as ever

Yours for the Cause,
Julius Gerber

TLS, InTI, Debs Collection.

1. In "Lecture Trip No. 18, October 1915," a typed copy of which is in the Debs Collection of Cunningham Memorial Library at Indiana State University, Debs was scheduled to be in New Jersey and New York from October 13 to October 23, 1915.

2. The woman-suffrage question was defeated in New Jersey on October 19 and in New York on November 2, 1915.

3. Abraham I. Shiplacoff was elected to the New York Assembly from Brooklyn in the 1915 election. No socialists were elected to the New York City Board of Aldermen.

John K. Hardy[1] to EVD

ca. September 18, 1915
Salt Lake City, Utah

Dear Sir:

Your communication, written on behalf of Joseph Hillstrom, has been received by the Governor, filed with the State Board of Pardons, which board, under the laws of Utah, acts upon applications for pardon and commutation.[2]

In order that you may be correctly informed as to the facts entering into the appeal of this case to the Supreme Court of Utah, I am enclosing a copy of the decision of the Court for your perusal.

Very respectfully,
John K. Hardy
Secretary to Governor

TLS, InTI, Debs Collection.

1. John Kay Hardy (1880-1930) served as secretary to Utah's Governor William

Spry throughout Spry's two terms (1909 to 1917). He later became an officer and director of a number of Utah banks and mining companies.

2. Hill's application for a pardon was turned down by the Utah Pardon Board on September 20, 1915. On September 30, President Wilson persuaded Governor Spry to grant a reprieve to Hill; it was terminated by the Pardon Board on October 16 and after further efforts by Wilson, which were, as noted, characterized by Spry as unwarranted interference, the execution was carried out on November 19, 1915.

Adolph F. Germer to Theodore Debs

September 21, 1915
New York City

Dear Theodore:—

No doubt, by this time you have been informed about the condition in the National office. As a member of the N.E.C. I have been put up against the problem of shaping the affairs whereby we can get down to some real work. We have finally come to the conclusion that a change must be had in the Secretary; that Lanfersiek, who is honest and all of that, has not the vision nor push that is required for the place. We have practically recommended to the N.C. that Lanfersiek be recalled and I believe he will. The next problem is to get a live man.[1]

You will recall that I spoke to you about accepting the place but could never induce you. The other day I received a letter from a comrade who had seen "Gene" and he said that you might accept the place. This news is almost too good to be true.

I am now writing you to satisfy myself of the correctness of the information.

Will you stand? I hope so for we need a real live wire for the campaign next year and I think you are the man for the job.

Let me hear from you so I can pass the word.

Yours in haste,
Adolph Germer
239 East 84th St.

ALS, InTI, Debs Collection.

1. Walter Lanfersiek was criticized for his abrasive manner and blamed by a number of party leaders for a decline in party membership and failure in elections, but the move to recall him failed and in the spring of 1916, Germer won a three-man race (against Carl Thompson and Lanfersiek) for executive secretary. *American Socialist*, May 27, 1916.

Theodore Debs to Adolph F. Germer

September 25, 1915
[Terre Haute, Indiana]

My dear Adolph: —

Your favor of the 21st. inst. is received and carefully noted. Believe me when I say that I am deeply sensible of your kindness and of the honor you do me in urging me to announce myself as a candidate for the office of national secretary of the party in case Comrade Lanfersiek is recalled, as you now seem to think he will.

Since receiving your letter I have given the matter the most serious thought of which I am capable but for reasons with which I will not trouble you I do not see my way clear to take the office, even if it was tendered to me unanimously. However, I feel none the less grateful to you and to other friends and comrades who would rally to my support and I trust that I may ever be worthy of this confidence and esteem which I hold above all price.

If the choosing of a man for this responsible position were left to me I am satisfied that I could pick a comrade that would measure up to the highest point of perfection. The man I have in mind has capacity, courage, integrity, organizing and executive ability, youth—well seasoned with experience, sound in his economics, holds membership in a trade union, understands the labor movement and is in every way qualified to fill the position in a way to do credit to the cause. And he is none other than Adolph Germer. You are the man, and you were never so badly needed as at present. I know of no one in the movement, and I know a great many, who is so well qualified by training and experience to take hold of the reins, reorganize the office and put it upon an efficient economic basis.

Gene is in Texas but I am sure he will endorse what I have written. I trust, my dear Germer, that you will not permit your well-known modesty to stand in the way, but that you will permit the use of your name, in case Lanfersiek is recalled, as his successor.[1]

With loving appreciation of your kindness and cordial good wishes I am,

Your friend and comrade,
[Theodore Debs]

TLc, InTI, Debs Collection.

1. As noted, Lanfersiek was not recalled, but Germer was elected executive secretary in the party referendum conducted in the spring of 1916.

Theodore Debs to Phil Wagner

September 30, 1915
Terre Haute, Indiana

My dear Phil:—

Gene is at home, in bed, where he has been since his return from Oklahoma. On the night of his return he was taken with a terrible nervous chill followed by a violent fever and is completely used up as the result of his last trip which was so booked as to deprive him of all needed rest and was finally capped by the worse than fool trip to O'Brien[1] at the expense of four days and nights and a continuous round of discomfort that amounted to torture. We have repeatedly cautioned Comrade O'Hare against this kind of booking and automobile connections and stated plainly that if this method of booking could not be changed Gene would have to give up his speaking under Rip-Saw auspices. You will find this clearly and repeatedly stated in the correspondence with Comrade O'Hare.

For the present you will please cancel Weston.[2] Gene cannot fill that on the next trip under any circumstances. At the very best he will not be half fit to do himself justice at the New York meetings. He has been set back more by this last trip and its killing routing, necessitating so much utterly useless travel, than he has gained in the last six months. It is not the actual platform work that did this but the booking of dates regardless of the speaker's health or comfort as if he were a cast-iron man. I have traced this last crazy routing on the map and I do not see how it could possibly have been worse, and not a single date was left open for rest. If Gene does not improve considerably in the next few days he will not fill the Eastern engagements and you will please be prepared to cancel them. I will advise you positively as to this within the next few days. I do not intend that Gene shall be completely broken down if I can help it. Gene has not made a single trip under R.S. auspices which has not had some kind of a "killer" in it. Against this we have repeatedly protested in vain.

Now it may be that the R.S. cannot do any better booking for Gene and that no one is personally to blame and if this is so then there is but one thing for him to do and that is to make other speaking arrangements. I know that I can book him from here so that he can do far better work, without wrecking his health and breaking down riding back and forth over railroads and putting in the time he ought to be at rest getting from point to point.

Please allow no Pacific coast booking to be done. Gene will undertake no such trip this season. This last experience has settled that.

As to any other booking, if there is to be any, please allow no trip to cover more than two weeks and at the close of every day's work there must be a night's rest and no racing away in sweat-soaked clothes or staying up until midnight or later to get to some junction to make the train for the next point.

If I have written plainly it is because I feel keenly and while not inclined to blame anyone unjustly I certainly have reasons, as you will surely admit, to take the stand I do in this matter.

At the time Gene made his arrangement with you it was understood that it could be terminated at the pleasure of either party and of course if the R.S. cannot book Gene without subjecting him to routing that utterly uses him up and breaks him down, and would break down anyone else, then, of course, you are at perfect liberty to dispense with his services.

I will write you more definitely as soon as I can do so and in ample time to enable you to take such action as may be necessary in regard to the Eastern engagements.[3]

Yours of the 29th. is received this day and I beg to thank you for pay check enclosed for week ending Sept. 18th.

With all kind wishes I am,

Fraternally yours,
[Theodore Debs]

TLc, InTI, Debs Collection.

1. O'Brien, Iowa. From September 6 to 23, 1915, Debs's speeches were in Texas and Oklahoma. O'Brien must have been added as a stop on his return from Enid, Oklahoma, where he spoke on September 23.
2. Weston, West Virginia.
3. As noted, Debs filled his "Eastern engagements" in October 1915.

Algie M. Simmons to EVD

October [14?], 1915
Milwaukee, Wisconsin

Dear Comrade Debs: —

Because I believe that after the long months of waiting there has at last come a time for action I am writing you to get your advice and cooperation if you agree with me, and if not, your advice and whatever else you choose to give me in place of cooperation. However I have no doubt that we will think alike and doubtless you are already at work. If so I want to know that so I can work with you.

The action that has aroused my interest is the International Socialist Conference that met in Switzerland[1] in the first week of September. I am enclosing for you a translation of the manifesto of the conference, from which you can determine its character. As I understand its intention, which I gather from the very extensive reports published in the Volkzeitung,[2] it is a move to line up the Socialists that have remained true to the flag throughout the war in each country and to get rid of the patriots, office-seekers, bureaucrats and similar trash.

I believe this will be the beginning of a "new International." I notice that Comrade Kollontay[3] takes a similar position in an article in the Volkzeitung, which I have translated for the "Socialist page" of The Leader for next Saturday. This is the only hope of getting back the old spirit. If we cannot do this then we may as well say good by to our lives and write them down as wasted, save as we sowed a little good seed that some other generation will reap.

I am writing you in the hope that you can take up this matter in as large a section of the Socialist press as possible,[4] with a view to having the Socialist Party give its adherence to this manifesto.[5] I have already written to Com. Lesueur[6] of the N.E.C. and Boudin[7] of the N.C. asking them to initiate such a move. I have also sent a very short communication to the American Socialist to start the discussion. You will recognize the importance of "getting a jump" on all opposition to such action. If we do this there will be no opposition, save from those of whom the movement can expect nothing.

This is the first "peace move" that does not bear the dirty finger marks of capitalist diplomacy. It is the first statement of the real proletarian attitude toward the war. It seems to me that it is up to us to give what help we can. The comrades who signed that put their heads in the lion's mouth. They risked life. We will risk nothing but a few votes (and I doubt if even that) by getting in with them.

Please let me know what you think.

Fraternally,
Algie M. Simons

Address:
    921 Bartlett Av.
    Milwaukee, Wis.

TLS, InTI, Debs Collection.

1. For the first time since the outbreak of the war, some forty socialists from twelve nations, including France and Germany, met at Zimmerwald, Switzerland, in September 1915 to discuss the war and its possible termination. The conference published a manifesto that described all wars as wars of aggression, called on socialists to wage "relentless opposition" in their respective nations to the continuation of

World War I, and urged them "to stand for the international solidarity of the working class."

2. The *New York Volkzeitung* was the largest German-language socialist daily in the country.

3. Alexandra Mikhailovna Kollontay (1872-1952) was an anticzarist Russian exile who attended the Zimmerwald Conference in Switzerland and was credited with shaping its manifesto. Joining the Bolsheviks in 1917, Kallontay became Soviet commissar of social welfare and later was Soviet minister to Norway (1923), Mexico (1926), and Sweden (1930) and ambassador to Sweden (1943). In 1915-16, Kollontay lectured, under Socialist party auspices, in more than eighty cities in the United States.

4. In "Reorganizing the International" (*Rip-Saw*, December 1915), Debs called the Zimmerwald Manifesto a "wise, courageous and inspiring document which should be read by every socialist" and urged the Socialist party of the United States to "get into harmonious and effective action" in support of the manifesto's goals.

5. The national executive committee of the party, on vote of three to two (Goebel and Seidel against), endorsed the Zimmerwald Manifesto at a meeting on October 21, 1915. *American Socialist*, October 23, 1915.

6. Le Sueur, James Maurer, and Adolph Germer voted for the manifesto.

7. Louis B. Boudin (1874-1952) came from Russia to the United States in 1891, graduated from New York University's law school in 1897, and set up his law practice in New York City. Boudin published *The Theoretical System of Karl Marx* in 1907 and *Socialism and War* in 1915 and was editor of the *New Review* from 1912 to 1915. At the party's emergency convention in St. Louis in April 1917, Boudin was a New York delegate and author of a minority report on the party's war stance. He left the Socialist party in 1919.

A. W. Ricker[1] to EVD

October 18, 1915
New York City

Dear Gene:—

I am enclosing you a press proof copy of my farmer pamphlet[2] not yet stapled. I shall be very much obliged if in some quiet moment— if you have such—you would look it over and drop me a line.

In considering what I have said about politics you will remember our conversation of yesterday. In view of the past history of farmer organizations I deemed it necessary to emphasize the necessity of steering clear of politicians. I sent the manuscript of the pamphlet to Comrade Thomson of Chicago and in his reply he urged me to recommend political action. I am certain in my own mind, however, that that would be suicidal and would defeat our object, so I took just the opposite course.

You will note from the correspondence that I have already made considerable headway. I shall value a criticism from you very highly.

I have hopes of doing something worth while along the lines indicated, and I am sure the effort will be well made even though I fail.

You may not have seen Russell's first article which started this whole thing so I am sending that along including a copy of the October and November issues of Pearson's.[3]

Fraternally yours,
A. W. Ricker

TLS, InTI, Debs Collection.

1. Formerly on the *Appeal* staff, circulation manager for *Party Builder*, and manager of the literature department in the party's national office, Allen W. Ricker was now editor of *Pearson's* in New York City.

2. In "Propaganda among Farmers" (*Party Builder*, September 27, 1913), Ricker argued that "the Socialist party has not given the farmers the attention they deserve" and blamed "our press, our literature and our organizers" for ignoring a huge potential socialist voting bloc.

3. In a series of articles in *Pearson's*—"The Revolt of the Farmer" (April 1915), "The Farmers' Battle" (May 1915), "Grain and the Invisible Government" (December 1915)—Charles Edward Russell described the "constructive radicalism" of northwestern farmers who were joining co-ops to defend themselves against "grain gamblers" and other predatory market interests.

EVD to Ida Husted Harper

November 12, 1915
Terre Haute, Indiana

My dear Mrs. Harper:—

It was with deep regret that I found myself obliged to leave New York without seeing you. I received your very kind letter and dropped you a hurried line of explanation after leaving the city. I was twice at the hotel, the second call being earlier than the appointed hour on account of another and unexpected engagement of an imperative nature being forced upon me. I knew how extremely busy you were and perfectly understood your situation and yet I cannot but regret being denied through adverse circumstances the pleasure of a visit with you.

You are having a great part in a great work[1] and I rejoice in all you do for the education of the women, for the awakening of the people, and for the coming of the better day.

Since my return I have met Mrs. Curry[2] and she has told me of her delightful visit with you and how greatly she felt herself benefitted by the interview.

Please remember me kindly to Winnifred and her husband[3] and believe me with all good wishes, in which Mrs. Debs cordially joins me,

Yours faithfully,
Eugene V. Debs

TLS, NN.

1. Author of a biography of Susan B. Anthony and co-author with Anthony of a history of woman suffrage, Harper was a leader of international prominence in the women's-rights movement.

2. Mabel Dunlap Curry (1869-1947) was the wife of Charles M. Curry, a professor of literature at Indiana State Normal School in Terre Haute. A writer and feminist lecturer, Mrs. Curry wrote a number of stories and poems about or dedicated to Debs, one of which, a poem titled "The City Beautiful," was widely reprinted in the socialist press. During or soon after Debs's unsuccessful campaign for Congress in 1916, the relationship between Debs and Mrs. Curry changed from that of neighbors who occasionally met socially to a strong bond of affection and love, the intensity of which can best be gauged by reading the letters of Debs to Curry and those of Curry to Rose Pastor Stokes, the latter of which are housed in the Yale University Library. During the years of Debs's imprisonment following World War I, Curry served as a volunteer in his Terre Haute office and was a tireless worker for his release.

3. George Eliot Cooley and Winnifred Harper Cooley. Like her mother, Ida Harper, Cooley was active in the women's-rights movement and wrote and lectured on that issue. Cooley wrote regularly, usually on feminist or nutrition subjects, for *Harper's*, *Independent*, and other magazines and for the *Minneapolis Tribune*, which carried her weekly column.

Leonard D. Abbott[1] to Theodore Debs

November 19, 1915
New York City

Dear Comrade Debs,

Your three recent letters, with inquiries evoked by Eugene's fine article on the Sanger case[2] in the November issue of the "Rip Saw," are received.

The Sanger pamphlet, "Family Limitation," is out of print. I have had to refuse to send copies in all cases. Even if I had it, I should think it wise to refuse. The Free Speech League is fighting for the right to distribute literature of the type of "Family Limitation," but it is not in the business of actually distributing or furnishing the pamphlet.

Margaret Sanger has distributed thousands of copies of the pamphlet at her own expense. That is another matter. She may decide to send out more, at her own risk. All letters that come to me are carefully preserved, and I shall turn them all over to Margaret. She talks of establishing a Birth Control headquarters in this city.

The League has collected something over $900 for the defense of the Sangers. All money left over after payments to Gilbert E. Roe[3] (the lawyer who represented Sanger for several months) has been handed over by me to the Sangers.

As you doubtless know, Margaret returned to this country early in October. When Eugene was in the city, she and I called on him. I am not sure that you have heard that since 'Gene's departure, Margaret's little daughter, Peggy, has died. Margaret has been sick. Bill Sanger, since he came out of jail,[4] is in bad nervous and physical shape. Altogether, the Sangers are having more than their fair share of trouble. They would not have had the money to cremate their little child had it not been for money that the Free Speech League was able to turn over to them out of moneys collected for the Sanger defense.

The federal authorities are handling Margaret very gently.[5] The Government lawyer is Harold A. Content,[6] Assistant United States Attorney. Mr. Content had a warrant for Margaret's arrest, but he has not used it. He could have put her under heavy bonds, but he did not do so. He acts as if he did not like to handle the case. He says that all he will ask for is a small fine, and he also says that he will do what he can to pave the way for a conference between Margaret and the postal authorities in Washington by which it is hoped that the Government may permit literature of the type of family limitation to go through the mails. Samuel Untermeyer,[7] and other lawyers, are working in Margaret's behalf, without pay.

Sincerely yours,
Leonard D. Abbott

Please send this to Eugene.

TLS, InTI, Debs Collection.

1. Leonard Dalton Abbott (1878-1953) emigrated from his native England to the United States in 1897 and soon joined the editorial staff of *Current Literature*, where he remained until 1925. A socialist in the early years of the party, Abbott was one of the founders of the Rand School and the Intercollegiate Socialist Society and in 1911 became president of the Free Speech League, which had been founded in 1902 as an organization devoted to preserving constitutional rights and privileges. Before the founding of the American Civil Liberties Union, the Free Speech League was the principal defender of such rights.

2. Margaret Higgins Sanger (1883-1966) left a career in nursing on New York's Lower East Side in 1912 to devote her life to birth control. She was a socialist and her articles appeared in the *New York Call*; in 1914 she founded *Woman Rebel*, which

was devoted chiefly to the birth control issue. In "The Conviction of William Sanger" (*Rip-Saw*, November 1915), Debs defended "Margaret Sanger's pamphlet on birth control for the working class" and denounced the New York City court that had fined William Sanger (Margaret's husband) $150 or thirty days in jail for distributing "obscene literature."

3. Gilbert Ernstein Roe (1865-1929) was an early supporter of Robert M. La Follette in Wisconsin politics, later counsel to a number of La Follette's United States Senate committees, and a director of La Follette's 1924 presidential campaign.

4. William Sanger rejected the $150 fine and accepted the thirty-day jail sentence imposed on him.

5. The case against Margaret Sanger for publishing obscene literature was dismissed before coming to trial.

6. Harold A. Content (1888-1944) was an assistant United States district attorney in New York from 1913 to 1918. During World War I he attracted national attention in the prosecution of subversives and radicals, including, among others, Emma Goldman and Alexander Berkman.

7. Samuel Untermeyer (1858-1940), one of the highest-paid attorneys in the United States at the time, was counsel for the Rockefellers, Hearst, and various banking firms and a strong critic of the banking trust and privately owned utilities. As counsel for the Pujo Committee investigating the nation's banking system, Untermeyer helped shape the legislation that created the Federal Reserve System.

Algie M. Simons to EVD

November 21, 1915
Milwaukee, Wisconsin

Dear Comrade Debs: —

You will undoubtedly receive hundreds of letters urging you to reconsider your refusal to accept the presidential nomination this year.[1] If I were only to write one more based on personal reasons it would be a waste of time.

This year there are reasons too big to be disregarded why you are the only possible candidate. At other times it would have been less important. This year any other candidate means trouble. The pro-German crowd are preparing to get control of the party — that means the end of the party. You have not made any public statement that the Kaiser-worshippers can use against you. Therefore they will not dare fight you if nominated. At the same time your nomination would make it impossible for them to claim control of the party in the campaign.

There is positively no one else on whom we can unite. Then we will need level heads to determine conditions at the close of the war. We either go up or down and out with this war. Do not let go now.

I could elaborate this line of thought to any extent. It would all end in the same story. You are needed on the ticket this year for national and international reasons bigger than any individual has a right to disregard.

Do not let anything prevent you from reconsidering at once.

Fraternally,
A. M. Simons

TLS, InTI, Debs Collection.

1. According to the party's constitution, ten nominations were required for the nominee to be placed on the referendum ballot (the party decided not to hold a nominating convention in 1916), and when Debs announced his declination, he had already received 105. In a telegram to the national office, Debs said he had "no special reason for declining other than that there are thousands of comrades who are at least as well qualified as I am for the nomination" (*American Socialist*, November 27, 1915). In the party's referendum of 1916, Allan L. Benson won the presidential nomination, George R. Kirkpatrick, the vice-presidential nomination.

George R. Lunn[1] to EVD

November 22, 1915
Schenectady, New York

Dear Comrade Debs: —

Thank you for your letter of congratulation. Steinmetz[2] and myself, as well as all other Socialists to be associated with us in the coming administration will do everything in our power to give such service as will make the mass of the people realize that the great big meaning of Socialism is above all Service to the people.

Trusting that I will be able to welcome you here during my term as mayor I remain,

Sincerely your comrade,
Geo R Lunn

TLS, InTI, Debs Collection.

1. George Richard Lunn (1873-1948) was a Presbyterian minister in Schenectady, New York, from 1903 to 1910, when he left that church to found the independent People's Church and, in late 1910, to join the Socialist party. He was the party's successful candidate for mayor of Schenectady in 1911, and his term (1911 to 1913) witnessed the introduction of a number of reform measures, some of which were defeated in the courts (a municipal ice and coal company) and others (municipal grocery stores and farms) abandoned after Lunn's defeat in the 1913 election. In the November 1915 election, Lunn was elected to his second term, during which a bitter controversy over his appointments led to his expulsion from the Socialist party in New York. Running as a Democrat, Lunn was elected to one term in Congress (1917-

19), two more terms as mayor of Schenectady (1919-23), and one term as lieutenant governor of New York (1923-25) under Governor Al Smith.

2. As noted, Charles Steinmetz was a member of the Schenectady Common Council and a close ally of Mayor Lunn.

Algie M. Simons to EVD

November 27, 1915
Milwaukee, Wisconsin

Dear Comrade Debs: —

I am certainly sorry that you cannot see your way to reconsider your position in regard to the presidential nomination, because of the special reasons that make your candidacy so essential this year. I will not urge further, for you know your own position and the party has no right to demand anything of you that you do not feel you can give, but if you should see your way clear to reconsider it would make the pathway of the movement much smoother.

We are in for troublous times. The wheels have been carefully greased to secure control of the party for a pro-German pro-officialism, anti-democratic faction. The letters now coming into the Socialist press urging the election of Berger, Hillquit and Kennedy on the N.E.C. and Thompson for secretary[1] is a part of this scheme. I am not blind to {the} ability of these candidates for the N.E.C. At another time I would favor their election, in which, perhaps, I would differ from you. But now they are part of a move to put the U.S. on the side of German pro-Kaiser officialism when the international is reorganized.

Unfortunately the opposition is in no way organized. I am, myself in doubt as to the best candidates. It seems to me that the best way to meet the move is to expose the fact of its existence, as shown by the letters referred to, and by demanding that all candidates show their hand. The vast majority of the party do not wish nationalism and militarism. If these candidates told where they stood they would be defeated.

If you could agree with me that such a demand should be made and should address a letter to the Am. Socialist simply urging the membership that does not wish to endorse nationalism and militarism not to vote for any candidate that refuses to say where he stands on these questions this would settle the matter.[2] I have already done this and expect to follow it up with further matter but the help of every comrade who sees the danger is needed.

If the S.P. is once tied up with the pro-Kaiser crowd then we are finished as a party. Fortunately the N.Y. Volkzeitung and the St. Louis Arbeiter-Zeitung have taken a splendid position so that the German party members are not entirely under the Kaiser crowd.[3]

If you can find the time I would be glad to get your opinion on these points.

Fraternally,
AM Simons

TLS, InTI, Debs Collection.

1. As noted, Adolph F. Germer was elected executive secretary of the party in the 1916 referendum. The five seats on the national executive committee were won by John Spargo, Morris Hillquit, Anna Maley, Victor Berger, and John M. Work.

2. In a series of issues in February and March 1916, the *American Socialist* printed the executive committee candidates' responses to questions on the war, militarism, preparedness, etc.

3. Living in Milwaukee, where he was editing the *Leader*, Simons was increasingly alarmed by that city's heavily German-American population's open support of and sympathy for the Central Powers. In December 1916, Simons resigned from the *Leader* and in a *New Republic* article, "The Future of the Socialist Party" (December 2, 1916), denounced the Socialist party as "a Socialist Tammany" that had ignored German atrocities—"the invasion of Belgium, the sinking of the Lusitania," etc.—abroad and its "classic mission" at home.

New York Sun to EVD

November 28, 1915
New York City

E V DEBS.

IN SPEECH AT PHILADELPHIA C E RUSSEL[1] SAYS ALTHOUGH A SO-CIALIST. HE BELIEVES WE CANNOT KEEP OUT OF WAR AND MUST PRE-PARE NOW QUESTION IS'NT WHO IS TO MAKE PROFITS WE MUST HAVE GUNS AND HAVE THEM NOW, WILL YOU WIRE OUR EXPENSE THREE HUNDRED WORDS YOUR VIEWS.

THE SUN

Telegram, InTI, Debs Collection.

1. In a speech at the convention of the Intercollegiate Socialist Society in Philadelphia on November 25, 1915, Russell said he "believed that America ought to be prepared to defend itself as the last bulwark of democracy." Debs disagreed, as his reply to the *New York Sun* makes clear, but in a letter to the *American Socialist* (January 29, 1916) he wrote that "it requires moral courage of the highest order to take the position [Russell] has taken . . . in the face of a hostile and overwhelming opposition."

Debs added that Russell had "forfeited the nomination for the presidency" by his statement. "Such men, however mistaken, are all too rare in the world."

EVD to *New York Sun*

November 29, 1915
Terre Haute, Indiana

NEW YORK SUN,

REPLYING TO YOUR INQUIRY, CHARLES EDWARD RUSSELL HAS HIGH STANDING IN THE SOCIALIST MOVEMENT, BUT IF HE IS CORRECTLY QUOTED IN HIS PHILADELPHIA SPEECH IN REFERENCE TO WAR, I DO NOT AT ALL AGREE WITH HIM, AND HIS VIEWS ARE AT VARIANCE WITH THE ATTITUDE AND PRINCIPLES OF THE SOCIALIST PARTY.

IT IS MY CONVICTION THAT WE CAN KEEP OUT OF WAR, BUT NOT BY PURSUING THE COURSE INDICATED BY MR. RUSSELL. EUROPE IS TODAY A FLAMING EXAMPLE OF WHAT PREPAREDNESS FOR WAR MEANS TO CIVILIZATION.

A LARGE STANDING ARMY, A POWERFUL NAVY, AND A STUPENDOUS MILITARY ARMAMENT SUCH AS PRESIDENT WILSON[1] WITH THE BACKING OF WALL STREET PROPOSES, MEANS A MILITARY AUTOCRACY AND IT CAN MEAN NOTHING ELSE, AND IF THE AMERICAN PEOPLE ACQUIESCE IN SUCH AN OBVIOUSLY PLUTOCRATIC PROGRAM THEY MUST NOT BE SURPRISED IF OTHER NATIONS TREAT IT AS A CHALLENGE TO WAR, AND IF THEY THEMSELVES ARE CONSCRIPTED TO FIGHT AND DIE TO MAINTAIN PLUTOCRATIC SUPREMACY IN THE UNITED STATES.

IF THE PEACE OF THE WORLD CAN BE MAINTAINED ONLY BY A RACE OF ARMED MURDERERS THEN THE RACE SHOULD PERISH FROM THE EARTH FOR IT IS NOT FIT TO SURVIVE.

SOCIALISM MEANS INTERNATIONALISM AND SOCIALISTS, IF THEY ARE TRUE TO THE FUNDAMENTAL PRINCIPLES OF THEIR CAUSE, ARE OPPOSED TO WAR AND TO "PREPAREDNESS" AS THAT TERM IS UNDERSTOOD IN THE PRESENT DISCUSSION. IT IS THE RULING CLASSES WHO INSTIGATE AND DECLARE WAR WITHOUT CONSULTING THEIR SUBJECTS, AND SO FAR AS THE SOCIALISTS ARE CONCERNED, THE ARISTOCRACIES, BUREAUCRACIES AND PLUTOCRACIES WHO ARE RESPONSIBLE FOR WAR MAY ALSO FIGHT THE BATTLES.

WE ARE LIVING IN THE TWENTIETH CENTURY BUT THE RULING CLASS STILL HAS THE BARBAROUS SPIRIT OF THE MIDDLE AGES. THE UNITED STATES GOVERNMENT IS TODAY IN POSITION TO STRIKE A DEATH-BLOW TO WAR BUT UNDER ITS PRESENT CONTROL IT MAY NOT AVAIL ITSELF OF THE SUPREME OPPORTUNITY.

IF IN THE PRESENCE OF THE APPALLING CONFLAGRATION THAT IS
NOW DESTROYING THE OLD WORLD THE GOVERNMENT OF THE UNITED
STATES WERE TO PROVE IN GOOD FAITH THAT IT IS OPPOSED TO THE
BARBARISM AND BUTCHERY OF WAR BY ISSUING A PROCLAMATION OF
PEACE, AND ITSELF SETTING THE EXAMPLE OF DISARMAMENT TO THE
NATIONS OF THE WORLD, ITS PREPAREDNESS WOULD BE, NOT ONLY IN
ACCORDANCE WITH ITS VAUNTED IDEALS, BUT A THOUSANDFOLD
GREATER GUARANTEE TO THE RESPECT OF ITS NEIGHBORS AND TO
ITS OWN SECURITY AND PEACE THAN IF IT WERE LOADED DOWN WITH
ALL THE IMPLEMENTS OF DEATH AND DESTRUCTION ON EARTH.

EUGENE V. DEBS

Telegram, InTI, Debs Collection.

1. In November 1915, President Wilson announced a preparedness program that
called for a building project that would add 156 ships to the navy, double the size of
the Regular Army to about 200,000 men, enlarge and bring under federal control
the National Guard, and strengthen the Merchant Marine.

Lucien Sanial to EVD

December 3, 1915
New York City

Beloved Comrade — dearest "Gene": —
    I received in due time your letter of Nov. 12th enclosing the booklet
entitled, "Danger Ahead for the S.P. in playing the game of politics."[1]
    Two days later I received from Comrade LeSueur a letter in which
he gave me his reasons for playing that game of politics and a statement
of his great expectations from that game.
    I have been, thus far, unable to answer him owing to the fact that
the little Northport[2] house owned by two of my daughters had to be
rented out and I had to move from it to our New York apartment a
stupendous mass of books, pamphlets, documents, manuscripts and
correspondence covering sixty years of my eighty and some of which
{may be} of historic value concerning the early days of the Socialist
movement.
    In that little house I did some of my best work, but since the death
of my wife it had become a burden as we could not occupy it except
during the two Summer months of school vacation, thereby invali-
dating the insurance for the other ten months. At my suggestion my
daughters rented it out at a nominal rate barely sufficient to cover
taxes and insurance and occasional repairs. Their tenant is a highly

esteemed Comrade—a wage worker with a large family and is, more-over, the indefatigable organizer of the Northport S.P. Local, which, through his efforts has trebled its membership and votes within the last twelve months. All the members he brought in are, like himself, wage slaves. No farmers for him; he knows them, body and soul, as well as he knows the skinning grocer and other members of the buffer-class. The land, he says, must not be "farmed"; it must be socially owned and socially cultivated. He has lived thirty years in Northport and can tell you, by names and figures, of all the farmers hereabout of the wages they pay to laborers, and of their passing from com-parative penury and indebtedness to actual wealth, not through their own labor but through the growth of population, which enabled them to sell a portion of their land, bought by them at the rate of $5.00 per acre, to city exploiters in need of fresh air during the canicule, or to {the still more} welcome planters of factories, at rates ranging from $200 to $2000 and even more, according to location. The original hut of the farmer has thus become a mansion. His son is a lawyer doing the dirty work of capitalists, or a reverend commending abstinence to the laborer. With a population of 2,300, the village has a national bank, a state bank and a trust company, with a total {of} capital and deposits amounting to $1,000,000, chiefly owned by farm-ers, while the earnings of the workers do not average $200 a year.

My friend could tell you all that and much more. He spells badly; his grammar is not orthodox; his tongue is not voluble; his voice never rises above a whisper, his science is {mere} common sense; but he looks straight at things and men, and {with} the facts which he has observed and stores in his well balanced brain he could quietly knock higher than a kite the fusion and confusion theories of our farming Comrade Arthur LeSueur.

It would not be proper for me, however, to delegate to my North-port Comrade the answer I owe to our learned but mistaken comrade of Fort Scott.[3] In a very few days I will be through with the preliminary sorting of all the stuff which has come from Northport, and I shall then take up his letter and send you a copy of it (if he has not done so) together with a copy of my reply, for I desire you to be fully acquainted with our correspondence.

In the meantime, next Monday (Dec 6th) I will mail you two booklets of mine; namely,

1. —one entitled, "General Bankruptcy—or Socialism" pub-lished in June 1914

2. —My report as a member of the Committee on Banking, etc., to the National Committee of the S.P., published in April of the present year.

Besides sending copies of these two pamphlets to each of the 68 members of the Bank Committee I sent to Comrade Lanfersiek 1,000 copies of the first and 300 copies of the second. What became of them I do not know. You should certainly have received one copy of each from the National Office.

Excuse this lengthy letter. I intended it to be very short but was carried away. I hope you will be able to read it. I cannot do so, — even with my magnifying glass. As soon as I will have done with this so-called "Money Question," I shall try another operation and then know whether I can still see or be blind for the remainder of my days

Affectionately yours,
Lucien Sanial

ALS, InTI, Debs Collection.

1. Debs's "Danger Ahead," which first appeared in the *International Socialist Review* in January 1911, was a warning to socialists against diluting their principles in order to win elective office.

2. Long Island.

3. Le Sueur had succeeded Christian Balzac Hoffman as president of People's College.

Frederic W. Raper[1] to EVD

December 5, 1915
Camp Hill, Alabama

Dear Comrade Debs:

I have just learned with deep regret that you have declined to be the Socialist candidate. Now, comrade, I hope you will reconsider that decision. I was quite a young man when I first began shouting for you, and now that my maturer judgment has vindicated my youthful enthusiasm I want an opportunity to prove it, and I can only prove it by voting and talking for you again. Four times I have shouted for you, but circumstances cheated me of my vote twice, so that I only got to vote for you twice. I was for you in Alabama in 1900; I voted for you in Ohio in 1904; I voted for you in Iowa in 1908, and I was for you in Alabama again in 1912. Of course, being a Socialist, I was not for you simply because you were Debs, but you yourself have been one of the strong sentiments of my life and I hate to give you up. I have taken all the ridicule that one must expect when one is for the candidate with ideals. Many a time have I been the goat at the boarding house table. And now I want that blessed privilege once again. I want to continue as a pioneer and continue to take all the inconveniences and pleasures that go with that condition. I want to say that here is the man I was for when I was a boy and here he is again and here I am again, and I ask all those who respect me to respect him.

Another thing—you are the only candidate they dare not persecute. You are the only one who can and will tell Judge Wright to go to hell,[2] and no corrupt judge dare lay his finger on you. When the polls close you will have the prestige of a man who has received from his fellow citizens several million votes.

Of course, if it is ill health that made you decline, your friends can have nothing to say, but I hope it is not that.

Very cordially yours,
Frederic W. Raper

TLS, InTI, Debs Collection.

1. Frederic W. Raper (1871-1941) published his poetry in a number of socialist papers and periodicals during the years before and after World War I. Probably his best-known one, "To Eugene V. Debs—In Prison," appeared in the *Liberator* in December 1919. After the war, Raper lived in Montgomery, Alabama, where he worked for the United States Engineers and during the Depression sought to collect Debs quotations for publication. See Raper to Theodore Debs, December 15, 1931; January 17 and 31, 1932. InTI, Debs Collection.

2. In "Go to Hell, Judge Wright" (*Appeal*, December 9, 1911), Debs attacked U.S. District Judge Daniel Thew Wright (1864-1943), who had, according to Debs, delivered a "diarrhetic diatribe" against the leaders of a strike on the Illinois Central Railroad.

Max Eastman[1] to EVD

December 8, 1915
New York City

Dear Mr. Debs: —

Would you mind writing me a short letter, not over two hundred words, answering the question "Do you believe in patriotism?" I want to publish a group of answers to that question from ten or twelve distinguished people of radical tendencies.[2]

Very sincerely,
Max Eastman

TLS, InTI, Debs Collection.

1. Max Forrester Eastman (1883-1969) was editor of *Masses* from 1911 to 1918,

when the magazine was suppressed for its strong stand in opposition to World War I. Along with John Reed and Floyd Dell and other staff members of *Masses*, Eastman was twice tried and acquitted of sedition under the wartime Espionage Act and in 1919 founded the *Liberator* as a successor to *Masses*. His many books included important works on Soviet Russia, collections of his poetry, and influential contributions in the field of literary criticism.

2. In its March 1916 issue, *Masses* printed the responses of Ernest Untermann, John Haynes Holmes, Charles Edward Russell, Elizabeth Gurley Flynn, and a half-dozen other "people of radical tendencies," but not one by Debs.

Lucien Sanial to EVD

December 8, 1915
New York City

Dear Comrade Debs: —

Confirming my letter of last week I enclose a copy of my Report of May 9th, 1915, to the N.C.[1]

I mail you also, under wrapper, a copy of my booklet, published in July 1913, entitled "General Bankruptcy — or Socialism," to which I refer in the first paragraph of my Report. But in order to save your precious time I would only call your Special attention to The Report itself, which is prefaced by a broad outline of the more voluminous booklet. Yet if perchance you had some leisure, you might find in it some interesting facts—even to this day "withheld from the public eye" and partly summed up in the 18 inch diagram at the end of it.

Now passing to another subject—a subject, this, of much importance to the Socialist movement—I may state that I was by no means sorry to hear of your emphatic declining of a fifth nomination for the Presidency. Leaving aside all other considerations I hold that your place {would} now {be} in Congress,[2] and while it is much more than a pity that you are not there at the present time, it would be still worse if you were not there next year, when a climax will be reached in the class struggle throughout the so-called civilized world. To the war to death now raging between the nations for capitalistic supremacy will inevitably succeed the war to death between the classes, and unless the earth perish the otherwise imperishable worker will in the end stand up alone, a victor, on the battlefield.

Affectionately yours,
Lucien Sanial

ALS, InTi, Debs Collection.

1. The "Report of the Committee on Banking and Currency," calling for a con-

tinuation of the committee's investigation of the nation's "banking, credit, currency, and monetary systems," was adopted by the national executive committee at its meeting on May 14, 1915. *American Socialist*, May 22, 1915.

2. Debs agreed to run as a congressional candidate in Indiana's Fifth District (Terre Haute) in 1916.

Ludwig Lore[1] to EVD

December 9, 1915
New York City

Dear Comrade Debs:

It is with great reluctance that I write to you in a matter that seems of the greatest importance to me at this time. When the call for nominations for our candidates on our national ticket was sent out our party members were practically unanimous in your favor as our standard-bearer. When you declined, we regretted your decision deeply, but refrained from pressing you because we were sure that only important reasons prompted your decision. Many of us hoped then that it would be possible to find a representative laboring man from among our party-membership who would measure up to the requirements of the hour and could be nominated.

We now learn that the only Comrades nominated are Charles Edward Russell, Fred Warren, Allen Benson and Emil Seidel. The two first named Comrades will decline and this for good reasons. The two remaining candidates—Benson and Seidel—are in the opinion of many not representative of our ideals, of the revolutionary working-class nor of the international Socialist movement. I believe, that the big majority of our party-membership would feel rather embarrassed if it had to choose between these two men.

It is therefore more than ever the conviction of many of the comrades from the rank and file, whose honest opinion I hereby voice, when I say that in this great emergency, when the world-wide war has crushed the International, when the hysterical preparedness campaign has sent good men like Russell into the camp of the enemy, it is your duty to the movement you served so well for so many years, to bear once more the brunt of the burden, and let your name go before the country as the rallying cry for all international revolutionists of this country.

This is no mere phraze, but it is the heartfelt desire of one who has no other interest than to see our American movement take its stand in the foremost ranks of the fighting armies of the proletariat and who knows that at this time it is most essential that you be our leader.

Assuring you that Comrade Schlüter,[2] the Editor-in-chief of the Volkszeitung, shares fully the opinion expressed in this letter, and hoping that you will reverse your decision,

I remain fraternally yours,
Ludwig Lore
Ass. Editor of N. Y. Volkszeitung

TLS, InTI, Debs Collection.

1. Ludwig Lore (1875-1942) was born in Germany, wrote and worked as an organizer for the German Social Democratic party, and emigrated to the United States in 1903. He was an early member of the IWW in Colorado and later served as executive secretary of the German Socialist Federation until 1919, when he left the Socialist party and joined the Communist Labor party. In 1917, Lore and Louis Fraina and Louis Boudin founded the *Class Struggle*, which became the leading journal of left-wing criticism of the war and reform socialism and of emphasis on the class struggle, not electoral politics, as the key to victory in the future. In 1919, Lore served ten days of a five-year term handed down in the Chicago trial of radicals caught in the Palmer Raids.

2. Herman Schlueter (1854-1919), emigrated to the United States from Germany (via Switzerland and England) in 1885 and in 1888 became editor of the *Volkzeitung*, called "the oldest Socialist paper in the United States." Lore succeeded Schlueter as editor of the paper at the time of Schlueter's death in January 1919.

EVD to Grace Keller

December 22, 1915
Terre Haute, Indiana

My dear Mrs. Keller:—

Returning from the West I find a letter here awaiting me from Mrs. Curry advising me of the illness of your daughter[1] and of your deep anxiety concerning your beloved child and I cannot resist tendering you such sympathy as fills my heart as I think of you and your loved one in this hour of trial and suspense. Most sincerely do I hope that the ordeal is passed ere now and that once more returning health to your dear child has brought gladness to your own heart.

Painfully am I aware of the weakness of words when it comes to expressing sympathy with loved ones in a dark and agonizing hour, but I would have you know that I feel deeply moved by your unhappy experience and that I shall feel relieved indeed to know that the shadow has been removed from your home. Please allow me in behalf of both Mrs. Debs and myself to assure you that our hearts are with you and that we would gladly if we could share with you as loving friends and comrades the burden of your anxiety and care.

We must all have our full share of life's sorrows and it is out of the depth of these that the sweeter virtues spring which bloom perennial in love and sympathy and compassion for our fellow-beings. Take heart of hope therefore for though the night be dark "joy cometh with the morning."

Yours faithfully,
Eugene V. Debs

TLS, InTI, Debs Collection.

1. Jean Keller (Bouvier) was born in 1899, at which time her parents, Grace and Eugene Keller, were living in Terre Haute. A graduate of the University of Minnesota, Bouvier taught for thirty-four years in the Los Angeles high schools and in 1981 published a memoir, *The Innocent Years*, in which several of Debs's letters to Grace Keller are reproduced.

Walter Lanfersiek to EVD

December 23, 1915
Chicago, Illinois

Dear Comrade Debs:

At the recent session of the Executive Committee, you were selected as one of a committee of three to request a public hearing of President Wilson on the Meyer London Resolution.[1] The action of the Executive Committee follows:

> "The National Executive Committee noted with pleasure the prompt introduction in Congress by Comrade Meyer London of a resolution providing that the President of the United States shall immediately call a conference of the neutral nations of the world with the purpose, if possible, to bring or hasten the coming of peace in war-distracted Europe. And be it further
>
> "Resolved, that we recommend the following line of action by all Socialist and labor union forces:
>
> (1) That resolutions and petitions be signed at mass meetings and otherwise in support of the Meyer London Resolution, such resolutions and petitions to be forwarded to Comrade London; that all Socialist papers be furnished simultaneously with matter for publication on the subject and that committees be organized at such meetings to further the proposed plan.
>
> (2) That official communication through our Executive and In-

ternational secretaries be opened with the Socialist Parties of the leading neutral countries with a view of having them introduce similar resolutions in the parliaments of their respective countries.

(3) That the National Executive Committee elect a committee of three to request immediately a public hearing of the President at which said committee shall urge the President to give the resolution his support as a matter of common decency and humanity. Our committee is further instructed that at this hearing, if granted, it shall voice the emphatic protest of the million Socialist voters against the entire so-called preparedness program of the administration as being in the interests of the munition manufacturers, bankers, certain business interests and other exploiters of labor, and which incvitably leads along the bloody path now being trod by our sister nations of Europe."

The other members of the committee are Morris Hillquit and James H. Maurer.

Yours fraternally,
Walter Lanfersiek
Executive Secretary,
Per B. H. B.

TLS, InTI, Debs Collection.

1. On the opening day of Congress, December 6, 1915, London introduced a resolution calling on Wilson to convene a "congress of neutral nations" that would "offer mediation to the belligerents . . . until the termination of the war" and for a "durable peace" based on freedom of the seas, disarmament, evacuation of invaded territory, liberation of "oppressed nationalities," and other goals. *American Socialist,* December 11, 1915.

EVD to Walter Lanfersiek

December 24, 1915
[Terre Haute, Indiana]

Dear Comrade Lanfersiek:—

Your communication of the 23rd. inst. advising me of the action of the National Executive Committee in appointing a committee to call upon President Wilson in the interest of the Meyer London peace resolution has been received and in reply I have to say that not being in harmony with the purpose of this resolution to call on the president, feeling convinced that it will be futile to do so, I am hardly qualified to serve on said committee and I prefer that some other comrade[1] be selected in my place who is in accord with the spirit and intent of the resolution and believes that some good will be accomplished by paying the president the proposed visit.

I am in perfect agreement with the Meyer London peace resolution and also with the action of the National Executive Committee in proposing nation-wide agitation in favor of said resolution but I can see no possible good in us as socialists calling on a capitalist president and asking him to do a thing he is committed not to do and has refused to others, and refrain from doing {another} thing which he has solemnly pledged himself and his administration to do.

Besides, I have a series of speaking engagements before me and I shall hardly be able to cancel these to accommodate myself to the purpose of the committee. Very fully do I appreciate the honor con- ferred upon me by the National Executive Committee in choosing me as a member of this committee but for reasons stated I feel that it will be better to have the committee consist {entirely} of members who are in full accord with its spirit and purpose. Thanking you for your kindness I am,

[Eugene V. Debs]

TLc, InTI, Debs Collection.

1. Meyer London joined Morris Hillquit and James Maurer on the committee, which on January 25, 1916, met with Wilson, who told the committee, according to Maurer's autobiographical *It Can Be Done* (p. 215), that "he had a somewhat similar plan in contemplation."

Basil M. Manly to EVD

December 24, 1915
Washington, D.C.

My dear Mr. Debs:
    Your very kind letter of December 21 reached me yesterday, and I immediately sent you 100 copies of the statement.[1] I shall be glad to send as many more as you think you can use.

The work is starting magnificently, and with the truly remarkable cooperation that we are receiving from every quarter I am sure that it will yield large results.

We are conducting a campaign to secure the printing by Congress, for *free* distribution, of 200,000 copies of the report and 10,000 copies of the complete testimony of the Commission. There is every reason to expect that we shall be successful. However, the matter is now before the Committee on Printing of the House, of which Mr. Henry Barnhart,[2] Representative from Indiana, is Chairman. The final success will in a large measure depend upon the character of the report of this committee. If you can bring any pressure to bear upon Mr. Barnhart it will unquestionably be of the greatest assistance.

With best wishes for the holidays and the New Year,

Faithfully yours,
Basil M. Manly

TLS, InTI, Debs Collection.

1. In "Important Notice" (*Rip-Saw*, February 1916), Debs summarized the appeal by Manly and Frank Walsh to secure publication of 200,000 copies of the *Final Report* of the United States Commission on Industrial Relations. It was seen as a body of evidence of employer tyranny and the deplorable conditions of American labor.

2. Henry A. Barnhart (1858-1934) was a Rochester, Indiana, newspaper publisher, telephone company owner, and banker who served in Congress from Indiana from 1908 to 1919. His committee, over the considerable opposition of employer groups that claimed the *Final Report* was biased, approved and Congress agreed to the publication of 100,000 copies of the *Final Report* and 10,000 sets of the eleven-volume *Testimony*.

EVD to Frank P. O'Hare

December 31, 1915
Terre Haute, Indiana

Dear Frank:—

I shall now try to answer more fully your favors of the 23rd. and 27th. inst. and when you have finished reading this please pass it over to Phil to save me the trouble of writing him also and covering practically the same ground.

First of all, I feel that I shall now have to make to the Pacific coast trip,[1] feeling that to cancel under the circumstances would be bad all around, especially in the cases of the points that were cancelled last year through no fault of their own. I did not intend to make this trip this year and was surprised to learn that you had booked these Pacific coast states. I note the letter from Theodore under date of May 19th. quoted by you and suggesting the postponement of the California trip to March or April but if you will look through your files you will find a letter under date of July 1st. {and} you will see that I enjoin against this kind of booking and I herewith enclose the copy of a letter written to Phil as late as September 30th. to make sure that no Pacific coast booking should be done this year. Please return this after you have read it and shown it to Phil. In addition to this I spoke to Phil particularly about this matter when he was here and he and Theodore and I talked it over and it was agreed that no trip should cover more than two weeks. It was explicitly understood at this meeting by Theodore and myself that there was to be no Pacific coast trip and I did not suppose for an instant that any booking was being done out on the coast until I began to get word from out there.

This trip cannot be made in two weeks, nor scarcely in a month and if it is made an easy trip as you suggest by leaving open dates between then I shall be gone away from home for a very much longer period that I want to be. All my life I have been an exile from home and I have been trying to so organize my work as not to be gone on any more of these trips that keep my away six weeks and more at a stretch, especially since I so narrowly escaped a complete breakdown, but it seems as if my efforts are in vain, and if I finally conclude to take the booking into my own hands it will be because I have been forced to do it in spite of myself.

You can book the date at Caldwell, Idaho, if you wish. Please do not make the trip any longer than you have to make it. According to your letter you have thirteen points booked with the prospects of adding two or three more and I think that will about complete the route. If it is necessary to add two or three points I do not object but I must have at least a day of complete rest in each week. I know this is not booking to advantage for the Pacific coast route to be what it should be should cover twice as many points but this is the best that I can do under the circumstances. I am being urged by some comrades not to give over fifty lectures a year and I have just received a letter from Channing Sweet in which he begs me under no circumstances to speak more than twenty times a year, declaring that I am deliberately killing myself doing what I am doing at my time of life.

Regarding Oklahoma[2] I note your explanation and it is entirely satisfactory and I do not know that anything need to be added regarding the situation there.

When we sat together at our last conference you remember my saying that I proposed quitting the lecture business. I am more and more determined to do this. The lecture business has gone to seed. Everybody has gone to "lecturing." It has become an old woman's business. I do not mean that I intend to quit the platform but I do intend to quit the "lecture" business, being tied up for weeks and months in advance in lecture tours organized on the basis of pay and not differing very materially from the lecture business in general which has about had its day. When I am mortgaged far in advance in this lecture business I become a cog in a wheel, a fixture, lose all inspiration and grow flat and stale, and when a strike breaks out and I am appealed to and ought to go to the front and help fight the battle of the workers, I am tied up in "lecture" engagements and I am almost ashamed to admit it and to offer that as an excuse to the embattled, half-starved suffering strikers. The garment workers appealed to me in their late desperate strike at Chicago[3] to give them a hand but my lecture engagements would not allow me to go to their rescue in their hour of sorest need and I could not but feel a sense of guilt for denying them even though I was powerless to set aside the meetings to which I had been committed.

Then again, the subscriptions scheme[4] in connection with the lecture business has been worked to a finish and is about played out. It is true that there are those who still adhere to it but the great majority turn from the scheme and will have nothing to do with it.

If I do my own booking from here I can make an appointment or two a week and then be free in case of some strike or emergency to take a real part in the class struggle where my heart is and help as I used to do to fight the battles of the working class, instead of "lecturing" my way into insanity.

Another thing that goes against my grain is the settle with the local and have them tell me how much they lost on the lecture. I would not take the money on my own personal account but I know of course that the Rip-Saw has to have the money to keep it going or quit business. In all the years that I was on the platform on my own account I never took a cent from a local or from an individual or from a society of any kind unless they came out whole on the lecture. I never allowed anyone under whose auspices I lectured to come out a cent behind, even if I had [to] leave without a dollar for my lecture. Innumerable times have I refunded or declined to take the full amount tendered to me when a loss had been sustained or when the net amount cleared was smaller than {it} should have been.

Of course I understand the absolute necessity of organizing the lecture business upon a financial basis but this does not relieve it of its most odious features to me. It is on this account that I have for years refused the Chautauqua booking agencies, notwithstanding they offered me $150. per lecture and as many dates as I was willing to fill. I have some times thought I ought to accept their proposition and make in a month more than I could make on the socialist platform in a year and then speak without money or price to the working-class and for the benefit of the socialist movement. To speak freely and without the taint of money is to speak from the soul and with the holy fire in one's speech instead of having the lips polluted and the inspiration smothered by speaking for pay, whatever form that pay may happen to take.

These are some of the thoughts that prompted me to say what I did at the conference about my determination to quit the "lecture" platform. I had no chance then to give my reasons on account of other matters that had precedence and so I concluded to set them down as soon as I had the necessary time.

But you will not understand me as proposing any immediate change or without due understanding far enough in advance to be satisfactory to all concerned. I have no complaint to make and never have had against the Rip-Saw. I have never been associated with a whiter, lot of comrades. Phil is the soul of honor and generosity and the more I have seen of him the more sterling has his worth become manifest to me. And all the rest of the Rip-Saw and Melting Pot comrades have been kind and generous and loyal and I love them all and shall always be happy to have been associated with them.

I am contemplating no change and I shall certainly do nothing in any definite way regarding these matters until we have had a personal meeting and have had the fullest opportunity of going over the situation together.

Most heartily do I wish you and all of you a New Year full of joy and of all that makes life rich in service and inspiring in example.

Yours always,
E. V. D.

P.S. Referring again to Theodore's letter of May 19th. when that was written I was expecting the Pacific coast to be covered and it was only after the horrible experience of the Okla. and Texas trip in Sept. that I called off the program and came near quitting entirely and would have done so but for abandoning the R.S. in a slump. The letters you have from me will show this.

TLc, InTI, Debs Collection.

1. Debs's tour in April 1916 took him to New Mexico, Arizona, California, Nevada, Utah, Idaho, Colorado, and Kansas. "Lecture Trip No. 22," Debs Collection, Indiana State University.

2. Debs spoke in seventeen Oklahoma towns and cities between February 26 and March 13, 1916. "Lecture Trip No. 21," Debs Collection, Indiana State University.

3. The strike of 200,000 members of the Amalgamated Clothing Workers of America in Chicago in the fall of 1915 and winter of 1916.

4. Part of Debs's fee for his lectures was in the form of blocks of subscriptions to the *Rip-Saw.* The same arrangement had been followed during his years on the *Appeal to Reason* lecture circuit.

Frank P. O'Hare to Theodore Debs[1]

[1916?]
St. Louis, Missouri

Dear Comrade,

Comrade Debs is now on the way and I wish to say one last word in regard to his personal care while he is in your charge. Someone ought to travel with Gene on this 8000 mile trip but as this is impractical I am appointing you Comrade Debs's right hand bower for the time being. The following recommendations are based on the experience 300 committees have had while I have been arranging his lecture tours.

First appoint a couple of *big husky comrades* and provide them with the following instructions:

Comrade Debs will reach town on the dot. He never misses a date. Meet him at the train and take him directly to the hotel and to his room so that he may remain there at his pleasure. No visitors should be introduced in order that Gene may rest, attend to the bulky correspondence that follows him or enjoy the luxury of stretching out and resting his travel-tired body.

Get him to the meeting a few minutes before the *moment* that he is to *speak*. Handshaking before the lecture has the effect of taking the fine edge off of his work and you are charged to keep him in the finest trim for his platform work.

At the close of the lecture be ready and merely kidnap him and rush him to his hotel. He will be completely soaked through with perspiration and should put on dry garments at once and have an hour to get back to normal conditions.

Comrade Debs may rebel at this program as he is eager to meet the many comrades and friends face to face but it is a sacrifice both he and the comrades must make. It is not the speaking, but the traveling and the meeting of many people that sends the traveling speaker to the hospital or causes physical breakdown. You realize the situation; just take him gently in hand and see that he does what you tell him to do regardless.

To your arrangement committee please say:

Kindly do not arrange for extra addresses, lunches, sight-seeing trips or other entertainment in advance. Comrade Debs will be travel-weary and will earnestly desire every possible hour that he can secure for quiet relaxation. We have declined many applications for dates on this trip to keep him in shape for your meeting. He is loaded full up with every bit of work that it is safe to require of him.

To your finance committee say:

I have told Comrade Debs that your committee will have ready for him a bank draft for the amount due which you will hand to him thus saving him the necessity of handling a large amount of currency of small denomination, saving an errand to the bank to buy a draft or the risk of carrying large sums on the train. Comrade Debs will have his report[2] for your meeting ready to mail home to St. Louis at the close of the meeting and your kindness in enabling him to merely enclose the draft and post the letter will be appreciated greatly by him. It is understood that extra cards can be settled for later.

To your program committee suggest:

Open the meeting at the advertised time; place written announcements in the hands of the chairman to be read when he opens the meeting. If a collection is taken and literature is sold have your ushers appointed in advance and fully instructed so that the entire audience can be canvassed in ten or twelve minutes. Music may be provided while the collection and literature is being attended to, after the chairman has announced the collection and literature. Do not hire brass bands, have as few preliminaries as possible and at the set time let the chairman introduce Comrade Debs. The chairman will make a hit with the audience by being real brief and not attempting to make a speech. One or two *minutes* will be long enough for the introductory remarks. The audience is there eager to welcome Comrade Debs. Make no attempt to hold the audience after the closing words, but let Comrade Debs know that he is to dismiss the audience and he will send them away with his last words engraved in their hearts. Let nothing mar this last impression!

Comrade Debs starts out on this trip in perfect condition. To see his youthful enthusiasm it is hard to realize that he has passed the sixtieth milestone.[3] He covers 8000 miles on this trip but with the good care that you will give him in co-operation with the other committees he will finish in fine fettle, ready for his succeeding campaign tours for the year. We want to save Gene to us for another twenty-five years and can do it by letting our love for him express itself by surrounding him with our thoughtful care. He is by no means to be handled like a decrepit old lady. He has a constitution like iron and the suggestions I have made should apply to every speaker who makes a similar trans-continental trip, sleeping on trains, changing beds every night, eating all sorts of food, missing meals, catching early trains, worrying about delayed trains.

I know that you will have a monster meeting that will forever be a source of happiness to those taking part and wish I could be with you to enjoy the jubilee. I thank you heartily for the comradely co-operation you have shown, the businesslike manner in which you have handled your end of the work and I send fraternal greetings to every comrade who has shared in any department of the work. I shall await the report of your success with the greatest interest.

Yours fraternally,
THE NATIONAL RIP SAW
F. P. O'Hare

TLS, InTI, Debs Collection.

1. This letter, addressed to Theodore Debs in Terre Haute, was obviously intended to be sent to the local arrangements committees on Debs's tour.

2. The Debs Collection at Indiana State University preserves a number of Debs's "Lecturer's Report Forms" for this 1916 western tour. Each report itemizes cash receipts, subscription sales, literature sales and expenses ("Hotel—$2.00" in Globe, Arizona) and usually includes Debs's comments on the weather, attendance, results ("good," "splendid," "excellent").

3. On November 5, 1915.

Gustav A. Hoehn[1] to EVD

January 4, 1916
St. Louis, Missouri

Dear Gene:—

Have just had a talk with Germer about Presidential nominations. We are agreed that under present conditions, with Russell gone the wrong way, you are the only proper candidate for president. It will be Militarism vs. Anti-Militarism and we need a strong fighter to lead.

Under ordinary conditions I should have accepted your reasons for declining, but at this time I see no other alternative for you but to accept.

Please act, and act promptly.

Yours in haste
G. A. Hoehn

ALS, InTI, Debs Collection.

1. Gustav A. Hoehn (1865-1938) was born in Germany, emigrated to the United States in 1884, and soon thereafter joined the staff of the *Chicago Arbeiter-Zeitung*, then being edited by August Spies and Michael Schwab, two of the Haymarket Massacre trial victims. In 1898, Hoehn founded the *St. Louis Arbeiter-Zeitung* and a year later *St. Louis Labor*, in which Debs's writings regularly appeared.

Sam T. Hughes[1] to EVD

January 4, 1916
Cleveland, Ohio

My dear Sir:—

From many sources there are beginning to come what apparently seem to be authoritative suggestions tending toward a peace in Europe. While most of these are said to have genesis in Teutonic quarters, nevertheless there is a growing peace sentiment in some of the allied countries.

America is the best informed country in the world in regard to all sides of the war and the great leaders of American thought are going to be the first to detect true signs of the coming of peace and, by saying so, aid in its realization.

May we ask you, as one of the 100 "first citizens" of the United States, whom we are addressing, to tell us briefly what hope you think there is for an early peace in Europe and what terms, in the main, the eventual peace treaty should embody?[2]

We are the editorial department of the Scripps newspapers and serve 117 daily newspapers in 117 American cities. These are read by over seven million persons.

Thanking you sincerely for your courtesy,

Very truly yours,
S. T. Hughes
Editor, Newspaper Enterprise Ass'n

TLS, InTI, Debs Collection.

1. Samuel T. Hughes (1867-1948) was born in Cleveland and spent his entire career in newspaper work in that city, first as reporter on the *Cleveland Press*, then as editor of the *Cleveland World* and managing editor of the Scripps-Howard Newspaper Enterprise Association.

2. Debs's "The Prospect For Peace," which was printed in the "Scripps League" papers and widely reprinted in the socialist press (*New York Call*, February 18, 1916; *American Socialist*, February 19, 1916), noted that "the lords of capitalist misrule are about ready to sue for peace" and cited the "ringing manifesto" of the Zimmerwald Conference as the "most promising indication of peace." Permanent peace could not come "until national industrial despotism has been supplanted by international industrial democracy."

Kate Barnard[1] to EVD

January 5, 1916
Oklahoma City, Oklahoma

Confidential

Esteemed Friend and Comrade:

Well, George Allen England has just written to say that he is tied up in a law suit involving $5000.00 and cannot help me on my Book before March 15th and possibly not then. He thought the case would be decided January 15th but the court moved the case sixty days further up on the docket and he is tied up nicely where he cannot do anything just as they wish him to be.

O This Capitolism is a wonderfully resourceful thing! I can get the Book published by Putnam Company or Ida Tarbell[2] but I must pull the teeth and fangs out of it and make a mollycoddle edition and my Message will be lost to the world. I inclose you herewith a rough draft of the Foreward which I forwarded to these people and they think it would sell well to their readers if I make it the rather sensational experiences of a woman novice in Politics. This makes me tired. Inclosed see also copy of a letter from the Redpath Chautauqua who are willing to absorb my efforts during the critical time when Socialism goes to a death struggle with capitalism in this state. Now what are you going to do about it?

Cannot you get Tichenor to come and handle it through the Ripsaw on a basis of Fifty percent for the Ripsaw and Fifty percent for me, the Ripsaw to bear Tichenor's expense. You and Kate O'Hare are both coming down here to campaign, I too will take the stump and Rose Pastor Stokes[3] says she will come and help at her own expense if I come out for the cause and all of us could push the Book and I believe it would sell to the extent of two hundred thousand copies. This would get me the money to enable me to take a years REST and if you all would push the book I would have something [to] foot expenses with while I get out another book on the terrible treatment of the Insane. Please take this up with Kate O'Hare at once if it appeals to you, and if not let me know at the earliest possible date.

I could clear $4000.00 on this Lecture tour but if the Book has all of us behind it it should turn twenty to forty thousand votes and make me comfortable beside. Remember I am not broke.[4] But property which was good income stuff a year ago is today in the heart of a red light district. This is part of the game to subjugate me, carried out by the Chamber of Commerce here who know I dare not and will not draw such rents so my houses are bringing less than the tax to poor who live there only because the rent is almost nothing. O God only knows the full horror of this story I have to unfold in which the whole power of the Democratic Machine backed by Organized Business of Oklahoma is combined to crush me because they cannot buy me scare me or bulldose me into a combination with their rotten Program. England is of course the man who should have handled this but he himself is caught in the web.

Something must be done IMMEDIATELY or it will be too late to write the book from the material I have collected and sorted.[5] At the State Socialist Convention the whole body of men rose and raised their horny hands and knotted fingers to me where I sat in the gallery and called "Kate, Come down." They wanted my help to save their homes and I am ready to come but I am bottled up here in the state and shut out of every avenue to reach the people and the only way I can come is to get a publisher who is in a position to PUSH the SALE of this Book.

I am a calm level headed woman. I have never made a mistake and have *carried down to defeat* every enemy I ever went after. All Oklahoma will tell you that. Very Well I am not coming out for Socialism unless I see the way open to get my message where it will WIN and this can only be when either the Appeal to Reason, The Ripsaw or the Kerr Company get behind it. I can string the Democratic Party higher than Hamen but I must have the Avenue open and all hands cooperating to get the Message to the Masses who love me and swear by me here and who think I am dead I have been shut off so completely by every newspaper in Oklahoma.

Red Revolt is in my veins but the world will never know it unless things move definitely and quickly for RESULTS. I will be no party to the fiasco of just going down to this little Socialist Local and TAMELY announcing I am a Socialist. WHO cares for THAT. It takes *FACTS* to cause REBELLION in OLD PARTY Democrats and Republicans.

I am able to give them unmitigated Hell but two things MUST first happen. I MUST have a writer to get the material in shape and I MUST have a publisher. I am willing to take Fifty percent of the sales for my share in order to get the Message over rather than a Cash sale to Conservative Publications.

This is January 5th. The Book must be on the market May 10th. IS there any time to lose? DESTINY is wrapped up in this letter.

Sincerely, and hurriedly,
Kate Bernard
Post Office Box 49—
Oklah City

If I were strong I could get the message over on the stump but I will only be able to make ten or fifteen speeches and I want a keen, analytical, forceful, class conscious, writer to take the physical burden off and get the Book out while I nurse my strength for a fierce personal clash with the "Opposition" on the Stump.

HURRY.

P.S. Creel[6] says I should ask for 25% instead of 50% for my Book. I therefore make this proposition as he is experienced in this line.

TLS, InTI, Debs Collection.

1. Kate Barnard (1875-1930) drew upon her youthful experiences with poverty and slum life in Oklahoma City to write and lecture in favor of a wide variety of reforms which were adopted by the Oklahoma Democratic party, incorporated in the state's constitution, and adopted in its legislation. She was credited with the acceptance of a full schedule of Progressive reforms in Oklahoma—compulsory education, abolition of child and contract labor, penal reform, and others—and with the popularization of such reforms throughout the nation through her lecture tours and writing, much of the latter in the *Daily Oklahoman*.

2. Ida Minerva Tarbell (1857-1944) was a leading muckraker of the Progressive period, a reputation based on her editorship of *McClure's Magazine* from 1894 to 1906 and *American Magazine* from 1906 to 1915. Her exhaustively researched articles for *McClure's* on the Rockefeller oil interests were collected in *The History of the Standard Oil Company* (two volumes, 1904).

3. Rose Harriet Pastor Stokes (1879-1933) was born in Russian Poland, lived in London's Whitechapel ghetto for nearly ten years, and was brought to America (Cleveland) when she was eleven years old. For a number of years she combined working in a cigar factory with writing poetry, some of which appeared in the *New York Jewish Daily News*, which Pastor joined as an assistant editor in 1903. In 1905 she married James Graham Phelps Stokes, a New York millionaire with socialist sympathies, and for the next twelve years Rose and her husband were among socialism's most active and prominent figures in the Intercollegiate Socialist Society, which James Stokes headed from 1907 to 1917, and in many other party enterprises. Rose Stokes and her husband left the Socialist party in 1917 in opposition to the party's antiwar stand, but she (not her husband) returned to the party in 1918 and then in September 1919 joined the Communist party. In 1918 she was indicted and sentenced to ten years' imprisonment for a violation of the Espionage Act, but the conviction was overturned in 1920. During the 1920s, Stokes remained active in the affairs of the Communist party by writing for *Pravda* and the *Daily Worker*, as a delegate to the Fourth Congress of the International in Moscow in 1922, and as a participant in many party-endorsed and -led strikes and political campaigns.

4. Barnard did not seek reelection as Oklahoma commissioner of charities and corrections in 1913 and retired from public life to spend her remaining years managing the rental properties her father left her in 1909.

5. Barnard's book was not published.

6. Herr Glessner Creel, who had served on the *Appeal to Reason* when Debs was on its editorial staff, joined the *Rip-Saw* in 1913.

Ernest Mills[1] to EVD

January 5, 1916
Denver, Colorado

Dear Sir and Brother—

The receipt which you called attention to in your communciation of December 31st was an old receipt, as John M. O'Neill is editing the Trinidad Free Press, Trinidad, Colorado, for the United Mine Workers of America, and we only wish financial circumstances were such that we could again have John M. O'Neill[2] with us, but such is not the case just at the present time.

After the hard struggle we fought out in Michigan,[3] the trouble in Butte, Montana, happened, and the venom of the fanatics spread to some of our other camps, and the effect of the trouble at Butte has very severely crippled the Western Federation of Miners.

The Arizona strikers[4] are undergoing great hardships just at the present time on account of our inability to furnish them with all the necessities of life, but we are doing the best we can and the strikers are determined to win and secure better conditions and maintain the organization.

Your wish to have the date of your subscription expire the first of next year will be complied with and I will credit the other fifty cents by sending the Miners Magazine to a worthy miner living down in the deserts of Arizona.

Trusting that you will enjoy good health during the present year and if you should be induced to again carry the Socialist banner in another Presidential election, I hope the vote will be greater than ever before anticipated and will at least double the records, I remain,

Fraternally yours,
Ernest Mills
Secretary-Treasurer
Western Federation of Miners

TLS, InTI, Debs Collection.

1. Ernest Mills was secretary-treasurer of the Western Federation of Miners.

2. O'Neill had formerly edited the *Miners' Magazine* for the Western Federation of Miners.

3. The Western Federation of Miners represented the Calumet copper miners in Michigan in a bloody strike that lasted from July 1913 to April 1914 and attracted national attention at Christmas 1913 when a fire in a miners' meeting hall took eighty lives. In April 1914 the miners voted to waive union recognition and return to work.

4. The copper miners' strike in Arizona in 1915-16 produced a union-recognition contract for the workers and was notable for the fact that Arizona Governor George

Hunt sympathized with the strikers and prevented the importation of strikebreakers into the state.

EVD to Upton Sinclair

January 12, 1916
Terre Haute, Indiana

Dear Comrade Sinclair: —

Your note of the 7th. inst.[1] enclosing a copy of your proposed military or anti-military program has been received and the latter has been carefully read. Replying, I regret not being able to sign the document as requested for the reason that I do not coincide with the views therein set forth. I appreciate fully the spirit and intent of your undertaking but I know of no reason why the workers should fight for what the capitalists own or slaughter one another for countries that belong to their masters. Any kind of an army that may be organized and any kind of a military establishment that may be instituted under the prevailing system and under the present government will be controlled by the ruling class and its chief function will be to keep the working class in slavery. I have not the least fear of invasion or attack from without. The invasion and attack I want the workers to prepare to resist and put an end to comes from within, from our own predatory plutocracy right here at home. I do not know of any foreign buccaneers that could come nearer skinning the American workers to the bone than is now being {done} by the Rockefellers and their pirate pals. The workers have no country to fight for. It belongs to the capitalists and plutocrats. Let them worry over its defense and when they declare wars as they and they alone do, let them also go out and slaughter one another on the battlefields.

I am with all kind regards,

Yours fraternally,
E. V. Debs

TLS, InU, Lilly Library, Sinclair MSS.

1. Sinclair's "Democratic Defense: A Practical Program for Socialism," which he enclosed in a January 7, 1916, letter to Debs, found "a difference . . . between democratic and autocratic governments," called for socialists to join in "the defense of the democratic principle throughout the world," and then for the "democratization" of diplomacy and military service.

Shubert Sebree[1] to Theodore Debs

January 13, 1916
[Terre Haute, Indiana]

Dear Comrade:—

Your kind letter received. Such generous sympathy as you express means more to me than I can tell. The knowledge that I have your sympathy and friendship in this time of sadness is most helpful.

My father[2] always loved Gene. When I purchased a copy of his "Life Writings and Speeches," it became my fathers favorite book.

Father did not often betray emotion, but I have often seen tears in his eyes when reading Genes writings and speeches.

To the world my fathers life would be adjudged a failure, but to those who knew him well, knew the burdens he had to bear and with what patience he bore them, They knew that fathers life was a success.

It is among socialists[3] that I have found this noble judgment and sympathetic understanding more than others.

The assurance of your sympathy will be treasured for all times.

Yours gratefully
Shubert Sebree
2436 Laf. Ave.

ALS, InTI, Debs Collection.

1. Shubert Sebree (1890-1980) was born in Mount Carmel, Illinois, and was brought to Terre Haute in 1897 by a father who was discharged and blacklisted as a railroad brakeman for his membership in Debs's American Railway Union and his participation in the Pullman Strike of 1894. From 1903 to 1918, Shubert Sebree worked in a Terre Haute glass factory, read all the socialist literature he could find, and became active in the Glass Bottle Blowers Association and in the Indiana AFL. In 1918 he was the Socialist party candidate for Congress in Indiana's Fifth District and soon thereafter lost his job. For many years Sebree lived in Chicago, where he helped organize carpenters' union locals, but he returned to Terre Haute during the Depression and was long known and respected for his active involvement in local social-justice causes.

2. Albert Austin Sebree.

3. The Sebrees' landlord in Terre Haute for a time was Stephen Marion Reynolds, who supplied Shubert Sebree with the *Appeal to Reason* and other socialist materials.

D. A. Bethea,[1] M.D., to EVD

January [16?], 1916
Terre Haute, Indiana

My Dear Sir:
    I want to thank you for that Masterly Article in the Post of last
Saturday.[2] It was grand and will do much good to Set people aright
on the Race question. I have sent marked copies to Colored Newspapers in New York, Chicago and Indianapolis.

Sincerely yours,
D. A. Bethea, M.D.

ALS, InTI, Debs Collection.

    1. Dennis Anderson Bethea (1878-1951) was a black physician in Terre Haute.
He was born in South Carolina, graduated from Jenner Medical College in 1907, and
practiced in Terre Haute from 1907 to 1923, when he moved to Muncie, Indiana.
In Muncie and later in Hammond, Indiana, Dr. Bethea wrote popular health articles
for newspapers in those cities. In December 1921, when Debs returned to Terre
Haute from prison, Bethea was a member of the welcoming committee at the Terre
Haute train station.
    2. In a letter to the *Terre Haute Post* (January 8, 1916), Debs denounced the widely
hailed motion picture *Birth of a Nation* as a "studied insult to the black race" intended
to "revive and intensify the bitter prejudices that grew out of the war" and added
that "for every white woman raped in the south by a black fiend a thousand black
women have been seduced and outraged by white gentlemen but no hint of this is
given . . . in 'The Birth of a Nation.' " Debs's letter was widely reprinted in the socialist
press (*American Socialist*, January 22, 1916; *Rip Saw*, March 1916; and elsewhere).

D. Jenkins[1] to EVD

January 16, 1916
[Terre Haute, Indiana]

Dear Sir;
    I have been trying for a week to get this opportunity to write a
few lines thanking you for your most excellent article in the Post
some days ago on the "Birth of a Nation."
    This film has been fought by Colored men and women all over
the country. When it first appeared in the East, about a year ago, the
colored people put up a fight that blocked it temporarily in New York,
Boston, and other cities. This was also the case in Chicago.
    We have been successful in defeating it in a number of places. The
Governor of Ohio has declared that it shall not show in that State

while he is Governor, this is also true in Kansas. Quite a number of cities have passed ordinances against such pictures.

I am giving you this little history of the colored people's fight against this play as I presume you may not have followed it as closely as we have.

Now when this photo play was advertised for Terre Haute, a few of us got together and took counsel. We noted that wherever the fight against this picture was a loosing one, it had served to advertise the play. So we decided not to make an open fight against this film, unless we had some assurance of winning.

We took it up with the Mayor and chief of police,[2] but nothing could be done. We were heart sick.

Imagine then our great joy when you came out in such strong language as you did. My wife telephoned me before I came home and I bought a copy of the Post and read it on the Car—unable to wait until I reached home.

I am utterly at a loss to find words to tell you how much we appreciate your words against this vicious play. We know it has done us much good in molding opinion. Assuring you that I shall never forget this kind act and holding you in very high esteem, I am,

Very truly,
D. Jenkins
501 Gilbert Ave.

ALS, InTI, Debs Collection.

1. David Jenkins is listed in the Terre Haute city directory for 1915-16 as a storekeeper gauger in a distillery.
2. Terre Haute's mayor at the time was James M. Gossom; the chief of police was Sylvester J. Doyle.

Charles A. Bailey[1] to EVD

ca. January 16, 1916
Connersville, Indiana

Dear Sir—:

I see in the Indianapolis Ledger, one of the greatest Negro journals of the United States, under the date of Jan. 16, 1916 a double header in large black a word of kindness from the famous Socialists orator Eugene V. Debs setting the famous play, "The Birth of a Nation," in its true light. I only wish that the speaker would allow that article to be published in pamphlet form that the twelve million Negroes in the United States could see for themselves a true and tried friend of the oppressed race of the United States. And if such a character was placed in the hall of Congress and by him being elected to that exalted position that the world could see the right man in the right place. Or if men of his caiber and his conviction speak the whole truth and all of the truth as our friend Eugene Debs did in his letter dated from Terre Haute, the prejudice against our people would melt as the frost on a May morning.

I have this day subscribed for, "The Appeal to Reason," as I hope the same will be done by every colored family in the United States.

This letter is only to show how the Colored people in this part of the state appreciate those sledge hammer blows from a free and fearless advocate of "Rights to the Many."

No more at present. May all your Efforts be crowned with success. I remain

Yours Truly
Chas. A. Bailey
Connersville, Ind.

ALS, InTI, Debs Collection.

1. Charles A. Bailey (1853-1934) was a banker in Connersville, Indiana, for more than fifty years and after World War I was head of a building and loan company for blacks in that city.

Ross D. Brown[1] to EVD

January 16, 1916
Muncie, Indiana

Dear Comrade

Perhaps you have forgotten me but four years ago I put in a week Lecturing around Terre Haute Brazil and Clinton. I also met and conversed with you upon your arrival to speak in Indianapolis. I see in this Weeks Indpls. Ledger an article on "the Birth of a Nation" that you wrote to the Post. this article is fine I prize it as highly as the recent article in the Melting Pot on Ingersoll[2] that was penned by you. I know you feel the pulsations of the Negro heart the best in my race are thanking you for your frank utterances. Hoping you may live a thousand times a thousand lives of usefulness I am yours for Socialism.

Ross D. Brown
1003 E. Jackson st
Muncie, Ind.

ALS, InTI, Debs Collection.

1. Ross D. Brown's letterhead described him as "The Unbleached Orator," inventor of the "Brown Automatic Glass Gathering Machine," and author of *Gems of the Class Struggle*. In 1918 he served on the Indiana Socialist party state executive committee and after the war worked as a party organizer in Ohio.

2. Debs's tribute to Ingersoll appeared in the April 1915 *Melting Pot*.

S. C. Garrison[1] to EVD

January 17, 1916
Montpelier, Indiana

Dear Comrade Debs

I take this means of expression to convey to you my Heart felt Gratitude and appreciation of your article in the Milwaukee Leader of Jan- 15

I am one of those 4,000,000 Mulattoes of whom you speak[2] I never had pleasure of knowing my father or my mother but there is one thing I do know—that it is Lovers of Justice like you and the Grand principles that you stand for—should be placed in the executive stations of Government—then we could have the principles of Human Justice applied to our Government

I know that the brainless aristocracy of dollars and their hirelings have all ways playd to the prejudices that ? they have instilled in the people as a member of the working class I have cought the rays from freedoms holy light which you so truly hold out to the down troden and the oppressed and if there is any life left in this old body of mine it Dedicated to the cause of and for the workers of the world—the Socialist Party I shall do all in my power to help here in Indiana to send you to Congress and I think that every member of my race in the 5th Cong- dist- should have a coppy of your article again sir I ask that you accept this feeble token of my gratitude I was borne in 1857 before the Klu Klux came but my face is yellow thomas dixson[3] has cap the work of John wilkes Booth for Dixson is an Assassin of

Jesus? whom he cliams to represent My heart it too full But I rejoice
to be a comrade on duty in the trenches of class consciousness

S. C. Garrison

L. Bx 655

Montpelier Ind.

TLS, InTI, Debs Collection.

1. A pamphlet, *Montpelier: Yesterday, Today, Tomorrow*, published in 1976, described
Stephen C. Garrison as a plasterer and janitor at a local bank who was "highly regarded
as a scholar and philosopher, . . . exceptionally well educated, . . . and a follower of
the doctrines of Eugene V. Debs."

2. In his comments on *Birth of a Nation*, Debs wrote that "there are 4,000,000
mulattoes in this country, most of whom were born out of wedlock, and all of whom
have a white father or grandfather, and these white gentlemen are ready to fight at
the drop of the hat for 'white supremacy' and against 'nigger equality.' "

3. Thomas Dixon (1864-1946) had built a fortune and national reputation as a
spellbinding Baptist minister in Boston, New York, and elsewhere before turning to
writing historical novels at the turn of the century. One of his novels, *The Clansman*
(1905), was adapted by D. W. Griffith for the film *Birth of a Nation*.

George R. Kirkpatrick to EVD

January 17, 1916
Peoria, Illinois

my dear Gene,

How are you?

Where are you?

Happy?

Here's lookin' at ye!

Some time ago I was homebound Memphis to New York via Effingham. I surely wished to be with you between ~~two~~ trains—but I
felt I had no right to call at 9 PM—perhaps to keep you up till 1
AM. and I was not sure you were at home. But down at Effingham,
Illinois, in the dinky hotel I had you in my mind and my heart—all
right.

I am both glad and sorry you are not to carry our banner the
coming Campaign—as our Presidential Candidate. Why am I glad?
Because the fierceness of the thing kills you too fast. You've sweat
enough blood of that sort, Dear Gene. The *fierce months push you
graveward* unmistakably—and I want *you* to live to see the foundations
of capitalism crumbling visibly—awesomely, refreshingly—*rejuvinat-*

ingly for your dear brave heart. *I do.* I want you to know the day when the dollar-marked crockodiles will shed a lot of genuine tears of fear.

Stay with us, dear good scout!

And I am sorry you are not our chief banner-bearer—because we *need* you, your size, vision, power and temperament. How nobly you have served us! And we still *need* you—no doubt of it.

I am hoping for Maurer.[1] Sincerely. I trust he looks good to you.

I am somewhat peculiarly interested in Goebel's election to the N.E.C.—I am emphatically interested. *He has courage!*

And as the possibilities now are ranged I'm distinctly in favor of Thompson. He has large equipment for the work; he is tirelessly industrious; he forgets wrongs of the personal sort; he would strive for harmonious activity all along the line; he is not bossy; he's strong {both} on details and on man's-size plans.

For a dozen years—since Thompson and I worked in Minnesota—I have felt he has not liked me—or had considerable prejudice against me, of a political {sort, I mean}. It has not mattered same as I regret to lose any measure of {political} fellowship, and now I am utterly indifferent as to what he may think relative to me. I *know* of his *efficiency* and heaven knows that is what we need now and in the coming campaign. I'm writing too much I fear—but I am keen for an *efficient* secretary. I trust Thompson looks good to you as secretarial timber.[2]

I surely was disappointed not to have you to luncheon when you were last in N.Y.—thoroughly so. Wife too. I was at the hotel "on the hour" and left you a note. I trust you had it.

Presently I shall presume to send you a "picter" of my wee man, George, the dearest {baby} Irishman ever!

Love to Theodore.

Love to Gene.

Always!

Most sincerely,
George R. Kirkpatrick[3]

Chicago next Sunday Omaha a week later

ALS, InTI, Debs Collection.

1. James Maurer of Pennsylvania, one of the nominees for the presidency in the party's referendum in 1916.

2. As noted, George Goebel was defeated in the election for membership on the national executive committee; Carl Thompson was defeated by Adolph Germer in the election of national executive secretary; Kirkpatrick was the party's vice-presidential candidate.

3. In "Kirkpatrick's Book" (*American Socialist*, September 11, 1915), Debs wrote that "no other book ever written on war" was more effective than Kirkpatrick's *War—*

What For in describing "not only the horrors of war but the causes of war and objects of war."

Ida B. Wells-Barnett[1] to EVD

January 17, 1916
Chicago, Illinois

Dear Sir:

As the president of the Negro Fellowship League[2] I desire to thank you for your splendid interview on the "Birth of a Nation." Of all the millions of white men of this country, you are the only one I know that has had the courage to speak out against this diabolical production as it deserves.

If you are likely to be in Chicago any time soon, the League would like the great pleasure of having you make an address for them.

Thanking you in advance, I am

Very truly yours,
Ida B. Wells-Barnett

TLS, InTI, Debs Collection.

1. Ida Bell Wells-Barnett (1862-1931), born of slave parents in Holly Springs, Mississippi, was educated in a freedman's high school and attended Fisk University in Nashville while teaching at a nearby rural school. As editor and part-owner of the *Memphis Free Speech* in the 1890s and later as a staff writer on the *Chicago Conservator* and *New York Age*, she attracted national and international attention to the issue of lynching in the United States, supported W. E. B. Du Bois's criticism of Booker T. Washington's policies of black compromise and accommodation, and joined in the founding of the NAACP in 1910 but stood apart from that organization on the grounds that it was insufficiently militant. Wells-Barnett's tireless work on behalf of Chicago's blacks was recognized in 1940 in the dedication of the Ida B. Wells-Barnett Public Housing Project in that city.

2. In 1910, Wells-Barnett founded the Negro Fellowship League in Chicago to maintain reading rooms, social centers, and dormitories for newly arrived Southern blacks.

EVD to Max Ehrmann

January 21, 1916
Terre Haute, Indiana

My dear Max:—

It was truly a wonderful meeting at Ann Arbor[1] and I thought of you and wished you could have taken it in. With your seeing eye nothing of its significance and portent would have been lost upon you. It was extremely cold, below zero, and yet the Auditorium was packed and overflowing and many had to be turned away. The faculty, the students and people of all kinds were there, but it was distinctively a university city audience. I spoke two hours and they seemed as eager and receptive at the close as at the beginning.

Thank you heartily for your very kind letter.[2] You are always generous and cheering and stimulating. I note particularly what you say about the biography. In the largeness of your appreciation you overestimate me. But when you get back you must come to see us and then we will talk it over. I am glad you are off for a bit of rest and change. You will come back refreshed and then we shall go over the plans you now suggest and for which you have my thanks and gratitude.

Hoping you will thoroughly enjoy your trip and return bouyant with youth renewed I am,

Yours always,
E. V. Debs

TLS, InGrD-Ar, Ehrmann Papers.

1. Debs spoke at a meeting of the University of Michigan chapter of the Intercollegiate Socialist Society on January 17, 1916.

2. Ehrmann's letter has not been found, but in his "Tribute to Eugene V. Debs" (*American Socialist*, October 21, 1916), Ehrmann "celebrated a living lover of men . . . before the tomb has canonized him." Debs's crime was that he "sought to make the dreams of poets a fact among men."

George D. Herron to EVD

January 24, 1916
Geneva, Switzerland

My Dear Brother,

I thank you most heartily for your words of greeting for the Christmas time and your wishes for the future. It is difficult to know what to expect, either for the world or for one's self, in this crimson time. The nations are drifting into the abyss. There is no sign that the war will end for two or three years yet, and I doubt if there will be peace in the world for a half generation. There will be, finally, a racial rebirth. But it will come after incredible and uncalculable universal suffering.

As to myself, I plan to close up all my affairs here and return to America in due time. But I can not tell how fast that will be accomplished.

My youngest boy has been very ill.[1] His lungs were much affected from having measles and whooping cough successively. He will have to live in the high mountains of Switzerland for a year, for at least most of the time. Then I must sell my home in Florence and that can not be done easily in such time as this. I hope then that I may give the rest of my years to the Rand School and the Socialist movement.[2]

I trust that you are opposing with all your power the development of militarism in America and all the compromises therewith on the part of the Socialist movement.

Even the so-called citizen-army will be used to destroy collective action on the part of the workers and to shoot them when they strike.

There is no more monstrous delusion than the idea that preparation for war is a preservation of peace. What kind of peace has Prussian military preparedness given to the world? If I were in America I should stand for unqualified disarmament.

With all love to you and Mrs. Debs.
George D. Herron

P.S. Until further notice, address me at: Les Falaises, 36, Chemin des Cottages, Geneva, Switzerland.

TLS, InTI, Debs Collection.

1. George Davis Herron, who was seven at the time.
2. Herron did not return to the United States, and in 1917 he broke with the Socialist party and published *Woodrow Wilson and the World's Peace*, an extravagant eulogy to the wartime president.

Theodore Debs to David Karsner[1]

February 8, 1916
Terre Haute, Indiana

My dear Comrade Karsner: —

You will permit me, I know, in my brother's absence, to acknowledge for him and in his name the receipt of your manuscript, "Horace Traubel, His Life and Work"[2] which has just come and to return his hearty thanks for same. I need not tell you that this manuscript will be of special interest and value to him and that it will have an honored place in his collection of personal documents.

It is exceedingly kind in you, and more than that, to thus favor my brother and you may feel assured that he will feel deeply sensible and gratefully remember this gracious act on your part. It is to be regretted that he could not comply with your wishes in the matter of the foreword but he has recently been so much absent and is booked for long tours in the future so that it has been a matter of physical impossibility for him to give personal attention to correspondence and to office affairs. I feel that my brother will agree with me when I say that there will be little room for suggestions after Mrs. Bain,[3] Dr. Wiksell,[4] Mrs. Traubel[5] and William Walling have gone over your work.

This work from your gifted pen is purely a work of love and you could not have bestowed this heart-tribute upon a more worthy soul, a finer, fitter lover of his fellows and comrade to all that breathe than Horace Traubel.

Believe me with affection and good wishes,

Yours fraternally,
Theodore Debs

TLS, NN, Kars.

1. David Karsner (1889-1941) was the author of two books on Debs, *Debs: His Authorized Life and Letters* (1919) and *Talks with Debs in Terre Haute* (1922), and as an editor of the *New York Call* he served as Debs's chief link with the Socialist Party and general public during the years of Debs's imprisonment following World War I. Karsner published a daily column in the Call, "Tho Jailed, He Speaks," excerpts taken from Debs's earlier speeches and writings, and the column was regularly reprinted in other socialist publications. Karsner's accounts of his visits to and interviews with Debs in the Atlanta penitentiary were another important link between Debs and the outside world.

2. Karsner's biography of Horace Traubel was published in 1919.

3. Mildred Bain was a regular contributor to Traubel's *Conservator*, the editor of *Five Traubel Songs* (1912), and author of her own biography of Traubel, which was published in 1913.

4. Gustav Percival Wiksell was a Boston dentist, a close friend of Horace Traubel, and like Traubel a collector of Walt Whitman material. Wiksell delivered the eulogy at Traubel's funeral in 1919 and in 1939 donated his collection of Whitman material to the Library of Congress. *New York Times*, August 21, 1939.

5. Anne Montgomerie married Horace Traubel in 1891 and served as associate editor of and regular contributor to the *Conservator* thereafter.

EVD to George D. Herron

June 3, 1916
Terre Haute, Indiana

My dear Comrade Herron,

The more than welcome letter from you has just come and I hasten to assure you that I shall be on the alert for the representative of the French Government who is to visit here and that I shall be glad indeed if I can be of any possible service to him.[1] I note carefully what you say of him and his mission and shall take pleasure in giving him such information as I have and putting him in touch with others who may be in position to be of service to him.

Since hearing from you last I have sent you two or three notes and some papers have been mailed to you from time to time but I doubt if you received them. The letters I receive from abroad, if they reach me at all, are censored and the papers are all examined and if they contain articles displeasing [. . . erased . . .] they never reach their destination, and so I conclude that the papers I sent you containing marked articles never reached you.

Thank you with all my heart for what you say about my nomination. I know how gladly you would help and how valuable such help would be but in your absence and under the circumstances the brotherly good will you express is immensely heartening and I am deeply grateful for it.[2]

We have thought of you many, many times and how you have suffered all these terrible months.

I hope your health, if not improved at least is good as usual and with all affectionate remembrances to yourself and your boys[3] in which Mrs. Debs and my brother join me I am always,

Your devoted brother and comrade,
EUGENE V. DEBS.

Transcript, CSt-H.

1. The visit, if it occurred, was not noted by the Terre Haute papers.

2. In a story, "Check from Switzerland," the *Terre Haute Tribune* (June 6, 1916) reported that Herron had sent to Noble Wilson, Debs's congressional campaign manager, a check for $100 "as a contribution to the campaign in this district." In "100.00 from Across the Sea," the *American Socialist* (June 24, 1916) announced Herron's gift and quoted Herron, in the letter accompanying the check, as saying: "If I were in America I should come to Terre Haute and give myself personally to the cause."

3. Elbridge and George Davis Herron, who were, respectively, twelve and five when their mother, Carrie Herron, died in 1914.

Mrs. Beatrice S. Thompson[1] and Miss L. Vanderberg to EVD

June 15, 1916
Los Angeles, California

Dear Sir:

We, the Women's Civic and Protective League, an organization of thinking Negro women, working and hoping for the betterment of our people, take this means to commend and thank you for the fearless stand you took against "The Clansmen," that gigantic thief of a race's prerogative to the right to the pursuit of happiness, and the maligner of a noble patriotism whose devotees died that all might share Freedom, the inalienable right of all mankind.

More words could no more adequately express our feelings.

We regret our tardiness in this expression but we are none the less sincere in our thanks and appreciation.

Hoping that you may have many more years of usefulness in your fight for humanity we are

Very sincerely
Women's Civic and Protective League[2]
Mrs. B. S. Thompson, Pres
Miss L. Vanderberg, Cor. Sec

ALS, InTI, Debs Collection.

1. Beatrice Sumner Thompson was a leader in the Los Angeles black community, secretary of the city's NAACP chapter, and an outspoken woman-suffrage advocate.
2. The Women's Civic and Protective League, according to D. Beasley's *Negro Trail Blazers in California* (1919), sought to teach women "the intelligent use of the ballot" and to secure passage of laws "for the protection of colored citizens."

EVD to Phil Wagner

June 24, 1916
Crystal Falls, Michigan

Dear Phil:—

Have just come back to hotel, sweat through, after making my speech under peculiar difficulties and extraordinary circumstances. Just after I arrived here, about 9 this A.M., strange rumors began to circulate and it was strongly intimated that something was to be pulled off that was not on the socialist program. You see this is an iron town, built entirely upon the iron mines located here, and the same abject slavery prevails here that characterizes all of Rockefeller's mining camps.

This town is near the strike zone where twenty thousand iron miners are on strike and where conditions are extremely critical and may cause a crisis at any hour. Then again, these iron towns have not yet gotten over the Calumet strike, fought so desperately on both sides, and in fact there is the most intensely bitter feeling in all these camps against socialism and organized labor. On account of its close proximity to the strike belt and on account of the bitter recollection of the previous desperate strike in the upper peninsula, this town is fairly shivering in its boots and all kinds of reports have been circulated as to what would happen when "Debs came to town." Well, the first thing they did this morning was to tear down all the red flags and talk loudly on the street corners about "Americanism," "Patriotism" etc. — They also rescinded the order of the school-board allowing our meeting on the school ground leaving us no place of any kind that could be obtained for the meeting. It was then decided to hold the meeting outside the city, and a bleak, barren hillside beyond the city limits was the only place that could be obtained and there the meeting was held. There was not a chair nor a plank nor a seat of any kind, and to make matters still worse it was a very ugly day, cloudy, cold and threatening, and the wind blew a perfect gale. But the crowd was there and it was a "corker" — almost wholly foreigners and mainly Finns, against whom, because of their manhood and loyalty to their class, there is the meanest, and most brutal prejudice and hate on the part of the American "patriots," spies, lickspittles, gunmen and dogs of all descriptions.

The crowd was honeycombed with spies, and surrounding the speaker's stand, (a mere box) when I mounted it, were the Sheriff and the Chief of Police and an army of deputies, sworn in for the occasion, and all conspicuously displaying upon the lapels of their coats the huge badges and stars of police authority. It was a sight to look upon. I was never in better form in my life to do justice to this particular occasion and I looked them all squarely in the eye before I opened my mouth, but unfortunately the wind howled so furiously that most of my strength (and I never felt stronger or fitter) was wasted in the desperate attempt to make myself heard, and I believe I succeeded, although I had to tear at my throat until it bled, and I am now quite content in the belief that I met the demand of the occasion in a way that will cause no socialist to blush in this corporation-ridden community.

If a single person left the crowd before I finished I did not observe the departure and believe me I gave those deputies with the big badges many a morsel to masticate before I got through. I told them who the thugs were and in whose service they did their dirty work for a few dirty dollars when honest men were fighting to put bread in the mouths of their starving children. I told them about capitalism and its army of mercenary hirelings that earned blood-money for their servility and lickspittlism that would outrage the conscience of a snake and drive a hyena to suicide. But I shall not attempt to report the speech—it could no doubt have been a good deal better, but I am willing that it shall stand for what it is worth and I hope that it met fairly well the demand of the occasion.

I have seen but one American socialist here who dares avow himself a party member—the rest of the Americans are all cowed and intimidated and afraid to join either a labor union or the socialist party. The despised "foreigners" are on the firing line here and have to bear the brunt of all the ignorant prejudice and bitter persecution of the corporations and the taunts and jeers of their retainers, mercenaries, pimps and lickspittles. But the Finns and other foreigners here are the true stuff and will fight to a Finnish(!) and win out in the end as sure as the sun shines.[1]

A report has just come that I must be on the lookout for trouble at Negaunee to-morrow. I don't know what's in the wind but I can pretty clearly anticipate the situation and I shall be on the alert for anything they may attempt to pull off for our benefit.

A prominent merchant here has just called to congratulate me on my speech—he told the comrades in my room that it had a powerful influence for good and that it had done more to remove the prejudice against socialists and their cause than anything that had ever happened here. He bought a couple of my books and expressed himself in the most enthusiastic terms about his "agreeable disappointment" in hearing so totally a different and loftier appeal than he had expected to hear from what he had been told of the speaker—and he said that others he had talked to, who were equally prejudiced and misinformed, also commended the speech and said the occasion would result in better feeling all around and in good to all concerned.

Well, I have felt the situation keenly and I earnestly hope that some good to the comrades and the cause may follow this day's work.

With love,

Yours always,
Gene.

P.S. As I have had to write this in great haste and you may have trouble to read it I am sending it to Theodore, who can read my Greek, and he will type-write it and put it in your hands.

TLc, InTI, Debs Collection.

1. A convention of some thirty Finnish socialist branches, meeting in Hibbing, Minnesota, in 1906 organized the Finnish Socialist Federation and the following year the Socialist party added a Finnish translator-secretary to its national staff. The federation grew to more than 12,000 members by 1913, lost membership in a bitter fight over political action and syndicalism in 1914-15, and, according to the *American Labor Year Book* for 1916, had 10,616 members in February 1916.

Bouck White to EVD

June 25, 1916
New York City

Dear Gene Debs:

Many thanks, comrade mine, for your handclasp. The letter brought a very clear and strong ray of sunshine into the prison cell.[1]

Certainly the Republic of these United States is moving into troublous waters. The thick-gathering storm across the ocean brine is making its thunders audible here; the masters are in frenzy, & are beginning to fear us.

The "Church of the Social Revolution" is putting a panic into their bones. Foreseeing the hurricanes that are {on} the way, & perceiving that this gospel of the social overturn in the name of the Crucified Carpenter is a true gospel & cannot be controverted, it is quite within the possibilities that they will seek to put me away for a long term; in order to get me out of action during the critical days that are before us, when the termination of the war in Europe will let loose the red thunders of revolt. Well, let them. We will take what comes, with a heart for any fate. The Overturn has God for its grand guarantee; & no prison gate was ever forged, to hold Him.

I wish for you, dear pal, many many years of strong health. We need you. A materialistic, cheap-reform vote is creeping into the Socialistic ranks. You have stood for the spiritual side, & accordingly for the uncompromising revolutionary side. Never were your words & works more necessary, than now.

Strength to your bow; & an ever more lofty platform to you, for your wholesome words.

Bouck White

ALS, InTI, Debs Collection.

1. On June 3, 1916, White was given a thirty-day sentence in New York for desecrating the flag, by burning an American flag during a sermon at the Church of the Social Revolution to demonstrate his opposition to preparedness and nationalism. *New York Times*, June 4, 1916.

EVD to Phil Wagner

June 26, 1916
Chicago, Illinois

Dear Phil:—

We had the greatest parade and meeting at Negaunee[1] yesterday ever held in that section and nothing happened to justify the rumors concerning which I wrote you from Crystal Falls. It began to rain on the immense crowd just as I began to speak—they were out in the open, under the blue sky, the thousands of men and women and children {and} they took their soaking without a murmur—they wouldn't budge until I got through and I poured myself into them in the effort to warm them up sufficiently to dry their clothes for an hour and forty minutes. They were mostly Finns and other foreigners and all hell and the arctic regions could not have dampened their ardor or quenched their revolutionary fire.

It's a good thing I have a day off for I'm hoarse down to my thorax and cawing like a crow, but otherwise I'm as frisky as a young colt and as lusty as a lion, and if Harry[2] happened to heave in sight just now I'd light on his ridge-pole, jerk out his rafters, and put out his lamps just for a bit of friendly and frolicsome exercise.

When the train I was on arrived at Negaunee yesterday noon a crowd was there of thousands and everything was red in all directions. They had heard of the red flags being destroyed at Crystal Falls and snatched from the leader of the parade in the strike zone and they made an immense red flag and had it at the head of the parade that was awaiting my arrival at the depot. They had an auto for me to ride in at the head of the parade but I declined and marched in the parade with the two magnificent Finnish girls who carried the Red Flag and the U.S. Flag through the principal streets and then three miles out in the woods to Cleveland Park. Believe me, nobody attempted to monkey with that flag, although many were itching to do so. Behind that flag were several thousand "Reds"—stalwarts of both sexes—and their almost endless procession struck the city like a thunderbolt from the clear blue. They did not dream there were so many socialists in the whole state. They came from Marquette, Gladstone,

Ishpeming, Ironwood, Escanaba,[3] etc. and I want to tell you that they were sure enough a red host to take off your hat to. I never saw a sturdier, cleaner, finer proletarian parade and I was prouder than a prince to have a place in it. When the parade marched through the streets where the "better claws" live it was to find their doors closed and their blinds drawn, while they withdrew from their porches and peered out upon the proletarian beast stretching himself out at full length from between their closed blinds. It was a beautiful sunny morning and the flags waved proudly in the breeze, held staunchly in the brave hands of the two proletarian Finnish women, while a Finnish band of 20 pieces, all trained musicians, filled the air with the stirring strains of "La Marseillaise." "We'll keep the Red Flag Flying" etc. Oh, it was a scene as dramatic as if the great stage had been set for it, and a demonstration of proletarian solidarity and enthusiasm never to be forgotten. You will soon get applications for dates from surrounding points. I urged them to get Kate[4] and they will do so as soon as arrangements can be made. The rain in the afternoon was unfortunate but the meeting was nevertheless a grand success.

With love to you all,

Yours always,
Gene

TLc, InTI, Debs Collection.

1. Negaunee, Michigan.
2. Henry Tichenor.
3. All in Michigan's Upper Peninsula.
4. Kate Richards O'Hare.

Murray E. King[1] to EVD

July 2, 1916
Salt Lake City, Utah

Dear Comrade Debs:—

Edna[2] and I cannot begin to express appreciation for your very kind letter regarding my poems and especially the one entitled, "Back to the Front."[3] Such words of praise and encouragement from you are worth more than we can express.

You spoke of having "Back to the Front" published in The Masses. I had already submitted this poem to The Masses months ago and have received word some time ago that they were considering it and intended submitting it to the board of editors at the next meeting.[4] This was about two months ago and I have not heard from it since. I would like to see it published for the publicity and recognition it would give me. If I can "break in" I intend to do much of this kind of work in the future, and if in the present situation there is any chance for you to influence the publication of this poem it will undoubtedly help me greatly.

Comrade Debs, we are praying, as only free thinking Socialists can pray, for your election to congress, because we recognize in you the typical voice of the toiler. We hope to contribute substanially before the end of the campaign to your election.

Fraternally,
Murray E. King

TLS, InTI, Debs Collection.

1. Murray Edwin King (1874-1941) was the Socialist party candidate for Congress in Utah in 1916 and one of the state's delegates to the party's emergency convention in St. Louis in 1917. One of his earliest published poems, "Debs," appeared in *Plain Talk* on October 29, 1910. King was a leader in the Farmer-Labor party in Minnesota after World War I and managing editor of the *American Appeal* in 1926.

2. King's wife.

3. King's poem "Back to the Front" was published in the *Rip-Saw* in September 1916; in the October 1916 issue of the *Rip-Saw*, Debs praised the poem, which dealt with "patching up" soldiers to be returned to the front, as "a terrible indictment of and pathetic protest against the war" and predicted that King's "name will one day shine resplendent upon the pages of revolutionary history!"

4. "Back to the Front" did not appear in *Masses*.

Jacob I. Sheppard to EVD

July 3, 1916
Fort Scott, Kansas

Dear Gene:—

Your kind and loving letter came this morning. It was, indeed, like a benediction. Your good, old, heart is so true, that you cannot say bad things about anybody. You overload your friends and enemies too with kind words and wishes. If all the men in the world were like you, this would indeed be "Heaven on Earth."

We did, indeed, win a great victory,[1] but think of what a pair of princes we had for clients and what a great cause we had to deal with through them. A lawyer who could not do well in such a case, should surrender his license to practice.

We have only just commenced the fight in the Howatt and Holt cases. We have a warrant out for the arrest of Hazen[2] for perjury and have sued Keith[3] and the other conspirators for Holt and also in another suit for Howatt. The law says that every man should have his day in court and we intend to see that the law is completely fulfilled in the case of these rascals. They shall have many days in court to their great dissatisfaction.[4]

Large sums of money have been used in an attempt to destroy Howatt and Holt but the thing has reacted upon them. Keith, the chief conspirator, is now where he hoped to put Howatt. He is disgraced and his associate scamps are going to depose him from the Presidency of The Central Coal & Coke Company and I think he will wind up in an insane asylum.

They had laid their plans well and had no mercy. The truth cannot be hidden if an honest effort is made to bring it to light.

It is, of course, a great pleasure to have your words of commendation. I value your good will more than that of any man in the world. All the good things you say about Frank Walsh are true. He is indeed a prince among men. His heart is true to the cause of labor and soon I intend to communicate with you upon a plan in which Walsh will lead for the establishment of a great Free Press in America. When you see the announcement, I am sure you will agree with me that it is a long step on the way to the emancipation of the workers. We must, if possible, make good use of the splendid work Walsh has done in his investigation. We must not allow the interest to die out and I believe we have a plan that will keep it always to the front and keep the rascals who live off the toil of others on the run.

Give my love to Theodore and when you have the time occasionally write me.

Your Friend,
JI Sheppard

TLS, InTI, Debs Collection.

1. Sheppard and Frank P. Walsh, in a jury trial in Kansas City in June 1916, successfully defended Alexander Howat and Fred Holt in a case in which the UMW officials were charged with and acquitted of accepting a $21,000 bribe from agents of the Arkansas Coal Operators Association. In a countersuit brought by Howat and Holt, the jury awarded them $7,000. Debs hailed the vindication of Howat and Holt and praised Sheppard and Walsh in the *Rip-Saw* (August 1916).

2. Joseph Hazen, an agent for the Arkansas coal operators, who charged that he had raised the $21,000 for use in the bribery of Howat and Holt.

3. Charles Keith, secretary of the Arkansas Coal Operators Association and president of one of the member companies.

4. As noted, the countersuit brought against Hazen and Keith, seeking $50,000

in damages, resulted in an award of $7,000 to Howat and Holt. *Appeal to Reason*, August 3, 1916.

Rose Pastor Stokes to EVD

July 22, 1916
Caritas Island, Stamford, Connecticut

Dear, dear Comrade Gene!

It was especially kind and sweet in you to send me greetings on the eighteenth, and I thank you warmly for remembering, or noticing, the accident.[1]

One forgets birthdays these terrible times—remembering days of world-wide death and the moaning of the women, who have lost. But sometimes, perhaps, it is well to remember—and remembering the struggle to which {we} are born—and dedicate, vow anew our allegiance to the cause of the People. Great leader of that cause, loving greetings to you

from
Rose Pastor Stokes

ALS, Debs Home, EVD Foundation.

1. Stokes was born on July 18, 1879.

EVD to Editor, *Weekly People*[1]

July 31, 1916
[Terre Haute, Indiana]

PLEASE ANSWER, MR. REIMER!

Editor Weekly People:—

In the debate between Arthur Reimer,[2] candidate of the Socialist Labor Party for president of the United States, and Martha Moore Avery,[3] as reported in the Weekly People of July 29th., in answer to a question by Mrs. Avery Mr. Reimer said:

"That question again implies the difference between the organizations that has already been raised. Debs has no definite principles from one time to another; the members of the Socialist party themselves have accused him of this. One of his lectures on industrial unionism is circulated now as Socialist Labor Party literature. In it he took the position that the republic to come would be an industrial republic; that presupposed the organization of industries and meant the death of the capitalist state. Since that time he has wavered around and nobody knows where he is at the present time. In Washington in 1912, during the presidential campaign, when a question was asked concerning industrial unionism, he waved it aside and said it had nothing to do with the question before him in that campaign. He is vacillating."

In reference to the foregoing statement I have some questions to ask of Mr. Reimer. First of all, was it Washington, D.C., or the state of Washington in which the alleged question was put to me to which the idiotic answer was made above reported? I wish Mr. Reimer to be specific. Who put the question and who besides Mr. Reimer will vouch for the answer he put into my mouth to serve his own purpose?

The fact is that no such incident ever occurred, in Washington or elsewhere; no such question was ever asked and I need not say, save for the benefit of Mr. Reimer alone, that no such asinine answer was ever given. The story is a pure fabrication; in plain words, a made to-order lie.

The statement by Mr. Reimer as above quoted boiled down amounts to this: Debs is a man of no principles; he is discredited and repudiated by even the members of his own party. This is the gist of Mr. Reimer's charge and the impression he sought to give his listeners. But like every other man who makes false charges against others he but succeeded in convicting himself.

For instance, he says that nobody knows where I stand. In this I presume he includes himself. Now if he does not know where I stand then by what right does he discuss me and attempt to discredit me? Why did he not say in the beginning that he knew nothing about me and stop at that?

Mr. Reimer does not know where I stand although I have stood for the working class probably since before he was born. I shall not attempt to enlighten Mr. Reimer as to where I stand but I can at least tell him where I do not stand—I do not stand for giving currency to lies and slanders about him because he belongs to the Socialist Labor Party instead of the Socialist party.

Mr. Reimer did not deceive Mrs. Avery by his false statement, nor did he add to his own credit or that of his party by making it. A candidate for president of the United States ought to be above making charges reflecting upon others unless he knows them to be true.

Now I wish Mr. Reimer to face me squarely and answer another question. When and where did the members of the Socialist party accuse me, as charged by him, with being destitute of principles? There is no chance for evasion here. Mr. Reimer will either produce his proof, make retractions, or stand convicted.

If such accusation was made Mr. Reimer will please specify the occasion and give the names of those who made it.

At the very time Mr. Reimer made this statement he knew (although protesting that no one knew where I stood) that I was the nominee by unanimous choice of the party to which I belong for a seat in congress. Was this proof, according to Mr Reimer, that the members of my own party regarded me as a man without principles? Was it convincing evidence to the mind of Mr. Reimer that the members of my own party had repudiated me because they nominated me, con- trary to my wishes, four times for the presidency of the United States?

According to the same logic he has been nominated as his party's candidate for the presidency because he is a man without principles.

Did the question of Mrs. Avery put Mr. Reimer in a hole he could only get out of by attempting to discredit me, and this by resorting to false and foolish statements?

Does not Mr. Reimer think that capitalists and their henchmen lie sufficiently about socialists without their spreading lies about one another?

Is this Mr. Reimer's method of illustrating the "difference" between the Socialist party and the Socialist Labor Party?

Mr. Reimer, if he is an honorable man, will either produce the proof to substantiate his charges or he will retract them and apologize for having made them.

Eugene V. Debs

TLc, WHi, Socialist Labor Party Papers.

1. Socialist Labor party paper.
2. Arthur Elmer Reimer (1882-1969), a Boston attorney, was the Socialist Labor party candidate for president in 1912 and 1916.
3. Martha Gallison Moore Avery (1851-1929) was born in Maine and in 1886 moved to Boston, where she joined, successively, the Bellamy Nationalist Club, the Socialist Labor party, and, in 1900, the Socialist party. After embracing Catholicism in 1904, Mrs. Avery joined David Goldstein in a crusade against socialism and in support of nonsocialist reforms. By World War I, Mrs. Avery's Catholic Truth Squad had become one of the best-known layman's apostolates in American Catholic history.

EVD to Daniel W. Hoan[1]

August 11, 1916
Terre Haute, Indiana

Dear Comrade Hoan:—

The press dispatches reported some time ago that you headed a military preparedness parade at Milwaukee. I denounced it at the time as a falsehood. Since then it has {been} repeatedly charged against you and I now drop you this line to get the denial from you direct. I simply cannot believe anything of the kind.

Awaiting your reply I am as ever,

Yours fraternally,
E. V. Debs

TLS, Milwaukee County Historical Society, Hoan Papers.

1. Daniel Webster Hoan (1881-1961) was attorney for the Wisconsin State Federation of Labor and city attorney of Milwaukee before being elected socialist mayor of that city in 1915. Hoan served as mayor from 1916 to 1940.

Daniel W. Hoan to EVD

August 15, 1916
Milwaukee, Wisconsin

Dear Comrade:—

I was very much pleased to get your inquiry of the 11th. In reply will state that I did parade here in what one or two of the newspapers continued to call a "Preparedness Parade" to the end. However, what the citizens committee in charge of the same and most of the papers here termed "A Patriotic Demonstration." At the outset the Security League[1] attempted to organize a regular preparedness parade, but thru up their hands in despair, consequently the Citizens Committee made an endeavor to hold a preparedness parade, but all of us socialists declined to participate, as did the federated trades council.

About three weeks before the parade was held, however, the committee saw perhaps that such a parade would be a fizzle and announced that the parade, which they would hold would not be a military preparedness parade, or for more munitions but merely a demonstration of national loyalty. It may not be easy to understand why the socialists should have anything to do with such a parade, but when the committee announced that the demonstration was not one in favor of militarism, the Caucus, with one exception, voted unanimously that I participate, and the County Central Committee as well, felt that while the socialists generally could remain out of the parade that for me to decline would be to deny any national feeling whatsoever, and probably cripple the party locally for years.

I will state, moreover, that all the documents which have been published, including the announcements of the committee, the letter of Mr. Potter,[2] inviting me to parade, my answer announcing my acceptance, and the proclamation declaring a half holiday, particularly the latter two, strongly emphasized that the parade was not military.

Anticipating some inquiries from the outside, I have requested Mr. Osmore R. Smith, a local comrade, on the staff of the Milwaukee Leader, to write up a history of the affair as he had learned it as a newspaper man and I am sending you herewith a copy of the article he wrote for the purpose of publication, if it were found necessary and and which you may use as you see fit.[3]

We appreciated fully just what the position was, and what the outside party members and others might think, but rather than set the party back a number of years and deny any loyalty to the American Nation what ever, it was agreed that I march. While demonstrations originating from capitalistic sources are hypocritical and more or less disgusting, I submit that careful thot will lead any thinking socialist to the conclusion that every socialist is imbued with a genuine patriotic spirit, and that we are devoting our lives to make this nation a better place in which the men who toil may live, as well as displaying an international patriotism. I feel that it is surely preferable, rather than scoff at the word patriotism, to seize upon it and make it a word to express our ideas and popularize our thots.

Yours fraternally,
Daniel W. Hoan
Mayor

TLS, InTI, Debs Collection.

1. The National Security League, headed by Theodore Roosevelt, was one of the leading preparedness organizations that sprang up around the country following the outbreak of war in 1914.

2. M. C. Potter was superintendent of Milwaukee's public schools and chairman of the parade committee representing the Milwaukee Citizens Committee, a Rotary Club group.

3. In a three-page typed statement by Smith, Potter is quoted as having said that "the participants will not be committing themselves to any specified kind of preparedness whatsoever," and Smith noted that Hoan had turned down invitations to march in preparedness parades in New York, Chicago, and other cities. InTI, Debs Collection.

EVD to Daniel W. Hoan

August 17, 1916
Terre Haute, Indiana

Dear Comrade Hoan:—

Your communication of the 16th. inst. with supplementary statement by Osmore R. Smith attached came to hand this morning and both have been carefully read.

I cannot but express my surprise and regret that you were placed in any such position by the socialists of Milwaukee, and I shall be mistaken if you do not find yourself under the necessity of explaining for a long time to come. I cannot at all agree to the views regarding patriotism expressed in your communication. Socialists are not required to demonstrate their patriotism for the benefit of the capitalist class and that class will not only not thank them for it but hold them in greater contempt.

The parade at Milwaukee from your own account of it was a capitalist parade and intended to serve capitalist ends and for myself I would have been eternally damned before I would have marched in it. The capitalist politicians were just a little too shrewd for the socialist politicians of Milwaukee and their press was not slow to spread the news over the country that the socialist mayor of Milwaukee had marched at the head of a preparedness parade.

The socialists of Milwaukee who are responsible for this perversion of principle may think it good vote-catching politics, but in my opinion it is an insult to militant socialism and it is just because of such vote-seeking, office-hunting political practices that hundreds of red-blooded socialists quit the party in disgust.

When we of the Socialist party have to march in capitalist parades to prove that we are patriots then I shall quit the party, and if that be a test of socialism then I shall deny that I am a socialist.

I can but repeat my surprise and regret, and if the socialists of Milwaukee expect to win for socialism by such methods they are doomed to bitter disappointment.

With all kind personal regards I am,

Yours fraternally,
[Eugene V. Debs]

TLc, InTI, Debs Collection.

EVD to S. M. Reynolds

August 17, 1916
Terre Haute, Indiana

My dear Stephen:—

I have just finished reading your letter and you are very near to me this morning. Thank you from my heart for each kind and loving word. You are always the same loyal, sweet-souled Stephen.

I knew that your heart would be in the campaign in this district and I need not say to you that your kindly interest is sincerely appreciated. The comrades are all working together earnestly and energetically and they seem to think that there is a chance for election. But whether it is or not we shall do our best just the same and when we do that for the cause we are winning even when we lose.

I note what you say in objection to the clause in the platform relating to health.[1] Upon every other point in your letter I am in hearty agreement with you, but I do not interpret that clause as you do. I cannot see why a department of health would not be in order and why it should not be organized and maintained upon a sound and scientific basis and do good work. Its control by the medical trust is another matter. I do not see why that should follow. As well might we assume the same in the case of every other proposition and refrain from creating a board for any good purpose for fear that it might be controlled by some private monopoly. But I am glad to have your views for your vision is clear, and when we meet, which I hope may be soon, we will go over the matter together.

I am sorry that I shall not be here on Sunday. I have already accepted an invitation which will take me away from here or I should be only too glad to see you. Perhaps you can come at some later time and I shall very likely be at Chicago soon.

You have had no letters from me lately because I have been too busy to write. But the hours are never so busy that I do not send you and Jessica and Marion my love-thoughts. We often regret that we cannot see you oftener. But you are not far away and we are always looking forward to seeing you again. Meanwhile the miles that lie between do not in the least divide us. You are always with us and we are always with you.

Katherine and her mother and Theodore and his family all join in greetings of love and good wishes to you all.
Ever faithfully,

Your comrade,
E. V. Debs

TLS, InH, Reynolds Collection.

1. Among its "Political Demands," the Socialist party platform for 1916 called for "the enactment of further measures for the conservation of health and the creation of an independent department of health."

R. F. Pettigrew[1] to EVD

August 24, 1916
Sioux Falls, South Dakota

My dear Friend:—

H. L. Loucks[2] of Watertown, S.D. could render you very valuable assistance among the farmers of your district. He has written you and you know of him. He was the author of the Populist platform of 1890 which declared for the public ownership of land and the means of transportation and communication.

He has just written a book on the money question[3] which is a very valuable contribution to the subject. He is an expert on that question and I am sure could give you great assistance in your district.

Yours very truly,
R. F. Pettigrew

C. S. Darrow[4] will come and help you if you ask him

TLS (with handwritten note), InTI, Debs Collection.

1. Richard Franklin Pettigrew (1848-1926) served as territorial delegate to Congress from Dakota Territory from 1881 to 1883 and was one of South Dakota's first two United States senators, serving from 1889 to 1901. Considered a radical by his Republican Senate colleagues, Pettigrew was a single-tax advocate, a free-silver supporter, and a strong anti-imperialist. His bitter opposition to World War I led to his indictment under the Espionage Act, but he was never tried.

2. Henry Langford Loucks (1846-1928) was a pioneer settler (1884) in Dakota Territory, publisher of the *Dakota Ruralist,* and leader of the National Farmers' Alliance and, after 1890, the Populist party, which he helped to organize. In 1892, Loucks was chairman of the Populist party convention at Omaha, which produced one of the most famous platforms in American history.

3. Loucks's *The Great Conspiracy of the House of Morgan and How to Defeat It* was published in 1916.

4. A number of prominent figures, including James Larkin, Madame Kollontay, Daniel Hoan, and Maynard Shipley but not including Clarence Darrow, campaigned for Debs in his 1916 congressional campaign.

Allan L. Benson to EVD

August 25, 1916
New York City

My Dear Debs:

I received your very kind letter yesterday, and am glad to know that what I am trying to do meets your approval.[1]

I don't know—but I strongly feel that this is America's critical year. Unless the people, this year, show some signs (by voting the Socialist ticket) of throwing off the gentlemen who are trying to throw and tie them, I feel that we shall probably go on to a period of semi-slavery which will ultimately be ended by physical revolution. I am therefore doing my best to awaken people to the fact that compulsory military service is coming if, indeed, it is not already here, and that our military appropriations—the greatest ever imposed upon a nation in time of peace—show that militarism is already here. Of course, I shall shoot full of Socialism everything I speak and write, but I am going to put the big danger signal over militarism. That, I think, is a danger so great that it can be seen, and so grave that it must go or all hope of peaceful evolution will go.

This is my last day but one before I start on my speaking campaign. For almost six months this has been hanging over me, and often I have dreaded it. Now that it is so near, I can hardly wait. I go with a feeling of sadness that, at first almost melts me—but it always hardens into an iron-clad resolution to bend every energy I have to the task. I know you must know how I feel. You have felt so four times.

I am sorry I am to have no part in your campaign. I had hoped that Comrade Wilson[2] might be able to use me this month before I went away. I suppose there was some reason why he couldn't.

Sincerely Yours,
Allan L. Benson

TLS, InTI, Debs Collection.

1. In his 1916 presidential campaign, much of which was conducted in the press, particularly in the *Appeal to Reason,* Benson stressed his opposition to preparedness, which he portrayed as a prelude to American intervention, and his belief that the

Democratic party slogan, "He Kept Us Out of War," was a cynical campaign deception. Suffering throughout the campaign from an invidious comparison with Debs's earlier campaigns, Benson received only 585,113 votes, about two-thirds as many as Debs had received in 1912.

2. Noble Wilson, Debs's congressional campaign manager.

Murray E. King to EVD

August 26, 1916
Castleton, Grand County, Utah

Dear Comrade Debs,

Another very gracious letter from you, that was forwarded to me here by my wife, reminds me that your comrade love and kindness is absolutely without reserve or bounds. You tell me of having forwarded to me 25 copies of the American Socialist with the poem in it, "Death-Dream"[1] and also of your having distributed copies for my benefit.

This, Comrade Debs, in the midst of the endless duty and work of your campaign, is more than any friend could have expected of you. Words cannot express my appreciation. I feel almost guilty in having already claimed your valuable time to such an extent. I cannot understand how with all your work and innumerable duties and burdens, you find time for so many kindnesses and courtesies. I will try at least to repay you by seeing that your kindnesses to me shall be the seeds of a harvest that will bear fruit.

In my last letter I said that I envied you and the comrades in the trenches. I, too, have since been conscripted. I was nominated for Congress from the Second Congressional district of Utah at the Socialist convention in Salt Lake a little over a week ago. I will make every effort possible to get away from here temporarily and help in the campaign.

I note that the reports from your district are most encouraging. Let us hope that your sixty years of service will at last place you in the position where you can teach and serve the nation, such as your election to Congress will do. I note your criticism in the Call of the proposed platform and agree with it.[2] Hope we can find a way to strike out those two false clauses without too long a delay.

Fraternally for the Revolution,
Murray E. King

TLS, InTI, Debs Collection.

1. An antiwar poem, "Death-Dreams" was published in the August 12, 1916, issue of *American Socialist.*

2. Debs's letter to the *New York Call* (August 11, 1916), criticizing the 1916 platform, was reprinted in the *Rip-Saw,* September 1916. Debs's "three objections" were that the "class struggle" was not "more emphatically declared," the qualification of the antiwar clause that would justify war "in case of invasion," and the failure of the platform to state "in unequivocal terms in favor of revolutionary economic organization."

Vittorio Buttis[1] to EVD

August 31, 1916
Chicago, Illinois

Dear Comrade:—

A comrade translated your letter to the American Socialist[2] in regards to our platform, and sent it to this paper for publication.

We have published it and in answer another comrade would like us to give your exact views on these three questions pertaining to the paragraph: *"If the Socialist Party is a revolutionary party, it is in logic and in fact bound to declare its recognition of and adherence to the revolutionary industrial union as against the reactionary craft union, and take its position accordingly."* TO WIT.

1st. DO YOU MEAN THAT THE SOCIALIST PARTY SHOULD RECOGNIZE AS THE "REVOLUTIONARY UNION" THE I.W.W.?

2nd. Or do you mean that the *Socialist Party* should agitate to form *ANOTHER* union along the lines you advocate.?

3rd Or do you mean that the Socialist Party should try to get its hold on the A F O L and conquer it to your point.?

Please remember that your answer might be used for the public, and therefore try to make it, therefore, as explicit and as brief as possible.

Fraternally yours.
Vittorio Buttis
Editor

TLS, InTI, Debs Collection.

1. Vittorio Buttis was editor of *La Parola Proletaria,* the weekly organ of the Italian Socialist Federation, published in Chicago.

2. Debs's "On the Proposed National Platform" appeared in the *American Socialist* on August 12, 1916. It was a reprint of the letter to the *New York Call* of August 11, 1916.

Eugene V. Debs on the stump (Eugene V. Debs Foundation)

Debs and Victor Berger (Eugene V. Debs Foundation)

Morris Hillquit (Cunningham
Memorial Library, Indiana
State University)

William F. Gable, Horace Traubel, and Debs (Eugene V. Debs Foundation)

Debs and Enos Mills at Estes Park, Colorado, in 1913 (Cunningham Memorial Library, Indiana State University)

Theodore and Gertrude Toy Debs, Katherine and Gene, and an unidentified younger man (Eugene V. Debs Foundation)

EUGENE V.
DEBS

"I know of no man living whose greatness of heart and mind is so generally conceded as is Mr. Debs."
—FRANK P. WALSH,
Chairman of Industrial Relations.

"Every Man that thinks a child is worthy of more consideration than a dollar, ought to vote for EUGENE V. DEBS for Congress."
—BASIL M. MANLY
Formerly Director United States Commission on Industrial Relations.

Go, search the earth from end to end,
And where's a better all-round friend
Than Eugene Debs? a man that stands
And jest holds out in his two hands,
As warm a heart as ever beat
Betwixt here and the Mercy Seat!
—JAMES WHITCOMB RILEY.

"Among all the Speakers I have ever heard there has not been one who came nearer my idea of Abraham Lincoln than Eugene V. Debs."
—REV. DEWITT TALMAGE

SOCIALIST CANDIDATE FOR
CONGRESS
Fifth District of Indiana
WILL SPEAK

AT _____

DATE _____

HOUR _____

Eugene V. Debs 1916 congressional campaign poster (Eugene V. Debs Foundation)

Debs in a characteristic speaking stance (Eugene V. Debs Foundation)

Debs's "Juno," Mabel Dunlap Curry
(Lilly Library, Indiana University)

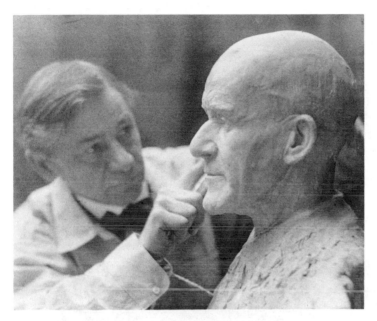

Louis Mayer at work on his bust of Debs, for which Debs sat at
the time of his trial in September 1918 (Cunningham Memorial
Library, Indiana State University)

Louis Mayer's bust of Debs
(Eugene V. Debs Foundation)

"Our Gene" at the start of his journey to Prison, from Cleveland, Ohio,
Sunday morning, April 13, 1919.

Debs en route to prison in Moundsville, West Virginia, 1919 (Amalgamated Meat
Cutters and Butcher Workmen of North America)

EVD to Vittorio Buttis

September 2, 1916
Terre Haute, Indiana

Dear Comrade Buttis: —

Your esteemed favor of the 31st. ult. has been received and I take pleasure in answering your three questions in reference to industrial organization as follows:

First, I do not mean that the Socialist party shall recognize the I.W.W. or any other organization as "the" revolutionary union.

Second, I do not mean that the Socialist party shall agitate to form ANOTHER union along the lines I advocate.

Third, I do not mean that the Socialist party shall get its hold on the A.F. of L. or any other particular organization.

I do mean that the Socialist party should declare itself unequivocally in favor of the principle of the industrial union or the revolutionary form of economic organization and that by education and all the influence at its command it should set itself the task of promoting industrial unionism among the workers and this it shall do within and without the present organizations until the task of organizing the workers along industrial and revolutionary lines has been successfully accomplished.

Hoping that I have made my position clear to you and with greetings and all good wishes to yourself and comrades I remain,

Yours fraternally,
[Eugene V Debs]

TLc, InTI, Debs Collection.

Arthur E. Reimer to EVD

September 9, 1916
Evansville, Indiana

Dear Sir;

On Friday Eve. Sep't 8, 1916, I visited the City of Terre Haute according to my schedule, as the Presidential candidate of the Socialist Labor Party, and held an agitation meeting. I have been informed by several workers in Terre Haute that one Maynard Shipley,[1] your assistant campaign manager, has been accusing me of being sent to Terre Haute by the capitalists for the express purpose of injury to your campaign. I met Shipley myself while at Terre Haute and asked him about this charge, and he admitted to me that he had made it and also admitted that he was in error and had gone too far.[2]

In as much as this statement or charge may be placed against me in the future and I have nothing to show whether or not this utterance by your assistant campaign manager was made with your approval, I feel that a statement by you directly repudiating this charge should by given to me. Awaiting your reply I remain,

Very truly Yours,
Arthur E. Reimer

ALS, WHi, Socialist Labor Party Papers.

1. Howard Maynard Shipley (1872-1934) had edited the *Everett* (Washington) *Labor Journal* and the *Northwest Worker* for several years before being sent by the national office of the Socialist party to serve as the associate manager of Debs's 1916 congressional campaign. An experienced speaker, Shipley worked throughout the Fifth District during the campaign and his accounts of the campaign in the *American Socialist* are valuable for their detail.

2. Reimer's letter to Debs was given to Shipley, whose answer was printed in the *American Socialist* (October 7, 1916). Shipley denied that he had "admitted he was in error," saying that he had admitted only lacking "legal proof" of the charges. Having talked with "all three" of the Socialist Labor party members in Indiana, Shipley said that he remained convinced that Reimer had come to Terre Haute "to divide the Socialists into warring camps."

John F. McNamee[1] to EVD

September 14, 1916
Indianapolis, Indiana

My Dear 'Gene: —

I have your kind and truly welcome letter of the 13th inst., with its enclosures.

It is unnecessary for me to say that it gave me real pleasure to let our readers of the present day know James Whitcomb Riley's estimate of you and also to publish your article "Publicity and the Income Tax"[2] for Gene every word you say in that article is the gospel truth and who dare question it.

It is a genuine gratification to me to read what you say as to how the Indianapolis boys feel towards me. Such a kindly feeling is an asset that all of the combined wealth of Rockefeller and all of the other labor crushers on earth could not buy and then those boys are

so sincere—men of progressive minds, intelligent and earnest think-
ers.

Note your request for extra copies of the September issue[3] and am
very glad to send you a half dozen which go forward by today's mail.
If you want any more say the word.

Many thanks for the autograph copy of "Labor and Freedom."[4]
Have glanced through it, it is surely fine. It states facts that are
incontrovertible. I will treasure it amongst my most valued possessions.
Your inscription on fly leaf enhances its value to me a thousand fold.

With every good wish, I am as ever,

Sincerely your friend,
John F. McNamee

P.S. In the first degree murder charge against Carlo Tresca and
the other strike leaders and the four strikers and that woman of which
you tell in your article in clipping you enclose,[5] I presume the same
brutal tactics will be employed to try to railroad the accused to the
gallows as were resorted to in the Moyer Haywood and Pettibone and
Lawson cases. J.F. McN.

TLS, InTI, Debs Collection.

1. John Felix McNamee (1867-1939) came to the United States from his native
Ireland in 1884, worked as a fireman during the years Debs edited the *BLF Magazine*,
and was elected to the BLF national executive board in 1898. In 1904, McNamee
became editor of the *BLF Magazine* and remained in that postion until 1924.

2. Debs's article "Publicity and the Income Tax" originally appeared in the *New
York Call*, July 25, 1916; Riley's most famous "estimate" of Debs appeared in "Terry
Hut," in which Riley described Debs as a man with "as warm a heart that ever beat
Betwixt here and the Mercy Seat."

3. "Publicity and the Income Tax" was reprinted in the September 1916 issue of
the *BLF Magazine*.

4. Debs's *Labor and Freedom* was a 176-page collection of his "stories, reminiscences, and sayings" that the *Rip-Saw* published in 1916 and sold for fifty cents a
copy.

5. Probably Debs's September 1916 *Rip-Saw* article, "Strike on the Mesabi Range."

Carlo Tresca[1] to EVD

ca. September 18, 1916
Duluth, Minnesota

Dear comrade Debs,

I have taken notice of your valuable, powerful, brotherless support
to my case with very much pleasure.[2] I am tankful to you. If, battling

for the liberty and the emancipation of our class, we expect any premium or rewards, I have the best anyone cant have because I have the support of Gene, the noblest, the greatest, the valiant leader in the field. Let your voice go, go everywhere, in every town and city, go to the heart of all the workers, calling, comrade Debs, not only for the necessary solidarity with all of us in jail, but, and most, for the necessity of uniting in one front only, in one army all the rebels of America for the coming great battle between the master and the slave, between the reactionarie force and the force of libertarian. We are at the point, right now: our banner most arised signifying our victory. Help, Gene! You are the heart, the brain of the worker in America and your voice is the voice of labor. Not make difference what well be, in this fight, the consequence for me and my felloworkers in cell, arise, comrade Debs, arise the workers and let them realize the necessity of the stand, one for all and all for one, unite against the Steel trust, the red blood thirsty monster.

Tank you, comrade! With greatest and heartest salutation.

I am, yours for industrial unionism

Carlo Tresca

P.S. Excuse me for writing with many mistakes this a first attemp for me to write in english.

ALS, InTI, Debs Collection.

1. Carlo Tresca (1879-1943) joined the socialist movement in his native Italy before emigrating to the United States in 1904, joining the Italian Socialist Federation in Philadelphia and becoming editor of its paper, *Il Proletario.* Increasingly recognized as the spokesman for immigrant Italian workers, Tresca joined the IWW and played a leading role in its most famous strikes in Lawrence, Massachusetts; Paterson, New Jersey; and, in 1916 in the iron miners' strike on the Mesabi Range in Minnesota. During the Mesabi strike, Tresca was arrested as an accessory to the murder of a sheriff's deputy, but the charge was later dropped. He was arrested under the Espionage Act in September 1917 and his paper, *L'Avvenire,* was banned from the mails, but he was never tried. After World War I, Tresca's association with Communists made him suspect among labor leaders and the non-Communist left, but his early and strong opposition to Italian fascism in the 1920s and his denunciation of Stalinism in the 1930s led Max Eastman to describe Tresca in the *New Yorker* (September 15, 1934) as, "after Eugene Debs, the most universally esteemed and respected man in the revolutionary movement."

2. In "Strike on the Mesabi Range" (*Rip-Saw,* September 1916), Debs denounced the capitalist, labor, and socialist presses for their silence about the Mesabi Range strike, which he called a fight for "industrial solidarity... against peonage," and praised the courage of Tresca and the "other honest and fearless men, lodged in jail and threatened with long sentences." Later, in "The Carlo Tresca Case" (*Rip-Saw,* December 1916), Debs asked readers for financial support for the legal defense of Tresca and other strike leaders who were being persecuted by "the most inhuman

ferocity of the steel bandits." The cases against Tresca and the others were dropped on December 14, 1916.

Theodore Debs to Alexander Trachtenberg[1]

October 2, 1916
Terre Haute, Indiana

Dear Comrade Trachtenberg: —

Your kind favor of the 22nd. was duly received as well as the copy of your "American Year Book"[2] and both would have had earlier acknowledgment but for the fact that both Gene and I have been out of the city and matters in the office have been sadly neglected.

Yes, I am quite sure that Gene would be glad to send you his opinion of this valuable book if he were here or had half a chance to go through it. But he is burdened far beyond his physical powers just at present. During the past two weeks he has spoken 55 times at different points, traveling from place to place in a Ford, often over very rough roads; and this has been only a part of his work. The daily demands are so numerous and the campaign is so exacting that with the very best of will it is utterly impossible for him to do the things which he would gladly do if he but had half a chance.

Gene is now in the Northwest on a speaking tour and he will not return to the Fifth District until about the middle of the month and he is already booked daily until the very close of the campaign for half dozen addresses each day.

But I will put the Year Book in his hands at the earliest opportunity. It is not necessary for me to tell you that Gene is heartily in sympathy with the work you are doing and you may be sure that if he can in any way help you in your splendid efforts it will be to him a real joy.

With all good wishes I am,

Fraternally yours,
Theodore Debs

TLS, NN, Rand School Records.

1. Alexander Trachtenberg (1884-1966) came from Russia to the United States as a revolutionary exile in 1906 and immediately became active in the socialist movement in New York City and in the Intercollegiate Socialist Society and the Rand School, where he taught courses in economics and history. Trachtenberg left the Socialist party in 1919 to help organize the Communist party, and in 1924 he founded International Publishers, which became a major publisher of translations of the works of Marx, Lenin, and Stalin and other Communist literature. Often brought before congressional committees investigating radicalism, Trachtenberg was twice convicted

under the Smith Act in the 1950s for advocating the violent otherthrow of the government, but both convictions were overturned.

2. The first edition (1916) of the *American Labor Year Book* was edited by Trachtenberg and published by the Rand School. During the years of its publication (1916-32), it was a valuable compilation of facts and information on labor and radical movements and groups.

J. E. Snyder[1] to Theodore Debs

October 5, 1916
Oakland, California

Dear Comrade Theodore:

I am enclosing a check for ($20.65) Twenty dollars and sixty five cents. One fourth of the collection at Gene's meeting at Idora park. The other three Fourths goes to the campaign here in Oakland and vicinity. Your share is for Gene's campaign.

The chumps down at Los Angeles got Gene all worn out and visited him to death. When I found him after his lecture in San Francisco he was all in and so we got hold of him and put Comrade A.K. Gifford with him on the rest of his dates in California. It rested him up and he left the state feeling fine so Gifford informs me. Gifford is a prince of good fellows. Gene fell in Love with him.

The place we held the meeting at here was misrepresented to us and so we did not give Gene a good chance. The noise was against him all the way through. No more amusement parks for me.

I wish you were here tonight. I wish that you could understand some things that are here in Oakland at this moment. I rapped my best up in The World for the past eight months and went against the traditions of building locals by merely getting in members. I thought to use the World to educate some people fit to be members before building up a local here. The local has about held its own. It is ahead of anything in the state for achievement and now a group of the old timers seem determined to wreck the whole business. They are taking the easiest way. The financial tack. They are using Comrade Tuck[2] as the lever to pry me loose from the town for it means that.

Read "The Master Builder" and you will see Comrade Tuck at present. No one can blame him. One just has to stand and look on and hope.

I realize that he has been superceeded. I didn't want to. I kept back but finally I got to putting in my best licks for I found myself being blamed by my coworkers for the shortcoming on the papers makeup etc. Tuck was taking it alright and urging me on until his old "friends" began to talk and they have all talked him into a state of mind that I am expecting every day now for an explosion. The old man, has, I'm afraid decided to climb the steeple once more. I am not going to fight for any position. I shall not allow others to do so for there are so many great fields to work in. I would however like to get located some time where I could stop a couple of years and live with my beautiful souled wife and baby.

I am hoping that the tide will turn and take away the damed thing that causes men to block instead of boost. That they will allow me to let myself out to my limit just for once.

You see Bogart[3] and Hibner[4] and others of my great companions are just getting warmed up through "The World." And now it looks as tho I am going to have to go on my journey which has been a joyful one in spite of all the hardships in the way. But I wanted to stay here and I am going to do so if possible.

My Lena and Grace are back in Iowa. Lena's brother Fred died three weeks ago and she was called back to take care of her mother. Maybe you noted the little tribute I paid him in the World about three issues back.

Well, I hardly know why I am writing this all to you but I guess it is because I Love You for the great Love You breath out of you for "our" big brother Gene.

I am your Comrade
J. E. Snyder

TLS, InTI, Debs Collection.

1. John E. Snyder (1870-1928), who worked on the *Appeal to Reason* during Debs's tenure on the editorial staff of the paper, was state secretary of the party in both Kansas and Oklahoma and a national organizer for the Socialist party in the southern states. He moved to Oakland in 1916 and the following year became editor of the socialist *Oakland World*.

2. Herman C. Tuck was a blind chair caner who founded the *Oakland World* in 1907.

3. Guy Bogart (1883-1957) was born in Terre Haute, where he was a neighbor of Debs and worked on the *Tribune* as a young man. In 1913 he moved to Los Angeles, where he served on the local Socialist party central committee and, as he told Theodore Debs in a letter on November 28, 1915, "specialized on propaganda work for the party." A poem by Bogart, "To Eugene V. Debs," appeared in the *World* on May 19, 1917. After World War I, Bogart became a public-relations expert and publicity agent for Hollywood film companies and chambers of commerce in various California cities and a nationally recognized authority on cats.

4. Another veteran of the *Appeal to Reason* during Debs's time on the paper, George F. Hibner served as the Kansas state secretary of the Socialist party, as a member of the party's national committee from Kansas, and as the party's candidate for Congress (1910) and governor (1912).

EVD to Grace Keller

October 22, 1916
Terre Haute, Indiana

My dear Mrs. Keller,

I drop you this line of greeting after seeing Mrs. Curry who advises, to my deep regret, that you have not been well, and I earnestly hope this may find you much improved, if not quite yourself again. We must all have our "day off" and when it comes we have to resign ourselves as best we can until the life-forces carry us out to the field of action again. Here we are engaged in a very exciting campaign and I am out speaking early and late and have but little chance to do anything else. Mrs. Curry, you will be glad to know, is in the fight with all her splendid ability and all her great soul and steadily winning her way to the front ranks of the revolutionary movement. She knows how completely your heart is in the cause and she speaks of you always with the tender devotion and fine appreciation and understanding one great soul always has for another.

Life would hold little worthwhile were it not for the service all may render, or at least try to render, to the suffering world. How deeply and tenderly both you and Mrs. Curry feel the heart-ache of the suffering poor I well know and it is this that brings to you the "dear love of comrades" in every hour of trial and darkness. Pardon these hurried lines and believe me with loving greeting and all good wishes to you and all your loved ones.

Yours faithfully,
E. V. Debs

ALS, InTI, Debs Collection.

Henry L. Slobodin to EVD

October 23, 1916
New York City

Dear Gene:—

Here is a mite to help your election. Have mislaid name and address of your Treasurer[1]—So you will excuse me for bothering you—

It is almost too good to believe that you really have a chance.— If only it should happen—It would act like a good, healthy storm— Purify the air in and revivify the Socialist movement. It would instill new life into the sluggish almost moribund Socialist party—Yours would be the true, trumpeting voice of the American working class—Good luck and good health to you—Elected or not, your every effort and every cent will be spent to spread the message of Socialism, the sort of Socialism which your life symbolizes, clean, robust.

Hope to see you some day, *Hon.* Eugene V. Debs. That would be great for a jail-bird.

Cordially yours,
Henry L. Slobodin

ALS, InTI, Debs Collection.

1. Debs's campaign treasurer was Luther R. Smyres, a Terre Haute insurance agent.

Peter Witt to EVD

October 27, 1916
Cleveland, Ohio

My dear "Gene":—

Through Frank Walsh who was here for a talk last week I learned of your candidacy for Congress. How I would like to be there giving you a lift; what a pleasure it would be, but circumstances over which I have no control makes it impossible for me to get away. Therefore, I am going to do the next best thing, by sending you a small contribution to help meet the expenses your fight will incur.

Oh, that the people of the district would only know of the glorious opportunity they have for putting Terre Haute on the congressional map, and what a magnificent chance for the workers down there to make a national contribution in the shape of "Gene" Debs as the people's tribune on the floor of Congress.

With hopes for your success I beg to remain

Yours as ever,
Peter Witt

TLS, InTI, Debs Collection.

Jack Carney[1] to EVD

November 5, 1916
Terre Haute, Indiana

My dear 'Gene Debs,

I am not going to come to your house, because I know perfectly well, that your are being deluged with visitors.

Words fail to describe the intense pleasure I have experienced, during my stay in Terre Haute. I have only one regret, and that is, that my friend Connelly[2] was not here to witness it.

Gene you are really fine, last night you took me back to the old days, when my dear old granddad used to take me around the old political meetings in Ireland.

Gene may God spare you to live for many more years, may the pleasure I have derived from working for you, be the chance of many more who have heard of dear old Gene Debs.

My kindest wishes go out to Mrs. Debs and yourself,

Yours for the dear old Cause.

Jack Carney

Would you send me an autographed photo to Liberty Hall, 2941 Indiana Ave., Chicago.

TLS, InTI, Debs Collection.

1. Born in Liverpool, Jack Carney worked with James Connolly and James Larkin in the Irish labor and socialist movements before emigrating to the United States. Carney edited the *Irish Worker* and later the socialist weekly *Truth* in Duluth, Minnesota. In 1919 he was among the foreign-born socialists who left the party to form the Communist Labor party.

2. James Connolly (1868-1916) was a founder of the Irish Socialist Republican party, and during his extended stay in the United States from 1903 to 1910 he was a popular figure on the socialist lecture circuit and an organizer for the IWW in New York. Returning to Ireland in 1910, Connolly became a leader of the Transport Workers Union in Dublin and in 1916 was one of the signers of the Proclamation of the Irish Republic. For his role in the Easter Week Rebellion in 1916, he was executed by a firing squad on May 12, 1916. In "James Connolly's Foul Murder" (*Rip-Saw*, July 1916), Debs wrote that "the British government has eternally disgraced itself" by executing Connolly and predicted that his death would "fertilize the soil" for a successful rebellion in the future.

Robert Minor[1] to EVD

November 6, 1916
San Francisco, California

My dear Comrade Debs:—

I have written the story of the prosecution of the five Labor prisoners[2] on the false charge of responsibility for the "preparedness parade" tragedy, for the Appeal to Reason.[3] I have received indirectly the assurance that Comrade Copeland[4] will give us a page, now that the election matter will be cleared out of the columns.

We intend to take many extra copies of the Appeal, to use in our publicity campaign,[5] and this, with the enormous normal circulation of the paper, makes the matter of great importance. It must be done exactly right. That means it must have a word by you.[6]

Enclosed is a copy of the story as I am sending it in. Also a record of the unsavory careers of the three "Harry Orchards"[7] that put Billings[8] behind the bars for life, and the additional one to be used in the Mooney trial.[9]

Could you write a short, snappy appeal to all the comrades to back up our {prisoners?} I'm sure you'll be tired out by your vigorous campaign, and (I hope) busy with your new duties as the American member of {the triumvirate} of great pioneers in parliament: Liebknecht,[10] Keir Hardy (whose spirit but waits for new flesh)[11] and— Debs. Yes, I hope you'll be busy at that congressional job when you get this letter,[12] but hope you can find time to give us a few words to go on the same page with the story.

Would you send it direct to the Appeal to Reason?

This story is, I believe strictly fair—not overdrawn. In fact, the nature of the matter concerning the state's witnesses, has forced us to rather understate it. The same in regard to prosecuting officers.

The question always arises, since the unfortunate McNamara affair, whether the prisoners are really innocent or whether we are sticking to them through loyalty alone. I want to give you my most sacred word of honor that this is a case of absolute innocence, even ignorance of the affair, on the part of our defendants. There is no danger of a "back-fire." I personally know all of the details.

With best wishes for your success, I am

Fraternally yours,
Robert Minor

TLS, InTI, Debs Collection.

1. Robert Minor (1884-1952) left his native Texas in 1904 to become a cartoonist

on Joseph Pulitzer's *St. Louis Post-Dispatch* and a few years later joined the Socialist party. By the time World War I broke out in Europe in 1914, Minor had become cartoonist for the *New York World* but was fired by that paper for his free-lance cartoons for the anarchist paper *Mother Earth*. In 1915 he joined the staff of the *New York Call*. With other writers, Minor helped to make the Mooney case—i.e., the arrest, conviction, and sentencing of Tom Mooney for murder following a July 22, 1916, bomb explosion at a San Francisco preparedness parade—a national and international cause célèbre. After World War I, Minor played an active role in the American Communist party as a writer for the *Daily Worker* and as a party functionary.

2. Tom Mooney; his wife, Rena; Warren Billings; Edward D. Nolan; and Israel Weinberg were charged with murder following the San Francisco preparedness-parade bombing.

3. Minor's "Graft, Dynamite, Stupidity" filled nearly half the space in the *Appeal* on December 2, 1916.

4. Louis Kopelin had served as editor of the *New York Call* and *American Socialist* and was Washington correspondent for the *Appeal to Reason* before becoming editor of the *Appeal* in 1914 when Fred Warren resigned. Under Kopelin, the *Appeal* rejected the Socialist party's antiwar stand in 1917 and Kopelin himself, who was conscripted as an army private, served on the government-endorsed Socialist Mission to Europe in 1918.

5. Minor was treasurer of the International Workers' Defense League, which raised funds for the defense of Mooney and the other radicals both before and after the Mooney trial.

6. Debs's "San Francisco Workers Victims of Capitalist Frameup" appeared in the December 9, 1916, *Appeal*.

7. In labor and socialist circles the name of Harry Orchard had been an infamous one since 1906, when Orchard's "confession" implicated and led to the arrest and trial of Western Federation of Miners officials Charles Moyer, William Haywood, and George Pettibone for the murder of Idaho Governor Frank Steunenberg. In his *Appeal* article, Minor described "the past criminal records of the state's witnesses" and identified them as Estelle Smith, Alice Kidwell, John M. Crowley, and John McDonald.

8. Warren Knox Billings (1893-1972) was convicted for murder on September 23, 1916, in a San Francisco trial growing out of the preparedness parade in San Francisco, and on October 8, 1916, he was sentenced to life imprisonment. Despite a generation-long campaign to secure his release, Billings remained in Folsom Prison in California until 1939. He finally received a full pardon from Governor Edmund G. Brown in 1961.

9. Thomas Joseph Mooney (1882-1942) was the central figure in one of the century's most celebrated cases involving the prosecution and imprisonment of radicals. Mooney was converted to socialism during a European trip in 1907, joined the IWW in 1910, and was an unsuccessful socialist candidate for several California state and local offices during the next few years. In 1913, Mooney was tried and acquitted of charges of using dynamite in a strike of electrical workers against the Pacific Gas and Electric Company. Following the preparedness-parade bombing in San Francisco in 1916, in which ten people were killed, Mooney was tried, convicted, and sentenced to death for murder, but his sentence was commuted to life imprisonment in November 1918 and in 1939 he was pardoned by the governor of California after two decades of agitation and legal efforts on his behalf.

10. Karl Liebknecht (1871-1919), son of pioneer German socialist Wilhelm Liebknecht, became a Social Democratic party member of the Reichstag in 1912 and was imprisoned for treason for his opposition to World War I. Released in 1918, Liebknecht

founded the Spartakus League and in 1919, following the abortive effort to found the German Soviet Republic, was shot, allegedly while attempting to escape from prison.

11. British socialist leader James Keir Hardie died in September 1915.

12. In the campaign in Indiana's Fifth Congressional District, Debs ran third with 8,866 votes behind winner Everett Sanders, the Republican candidate with 20,977 votes, and Ralph W. Moss, the Democratic candidate with 20,270 votes.

EVD to Daniel W. Hoan

November 7, 1916
Terre Haute, Indiana

My dear Comrade Hoan:—

It was certainly very kind of you to take the time out of your busy hours to come down here and make the splendid speech you did in behalf of the Socialist party and of myself as its candidate for congress in this district.[1] The comrades have told me that you made one of the most effective appeals of the campaign and that your coming here stimulated them to renewed activity in the campaign. Please accept my hearty thanks and the assurance of my sincere appreciation. I am exceedingly sorry and so is Mrs. Debs that we both happened to be out when you called. Mrs. Debs found your card on her return. I need hardly say that we should have been happy indeed to have had you break bread with us and visit our home.

I do not know what the outcome here will be but the comrades have all done their best and we shall be satisfied with whatever fate or fortune has in store and go on working with unabated energy for the cause.

If I had not been kept so extremely busy I should have looked you up but unfortunately there was not time enough to go around and some claims upon my attention had to suffer neglect. But you have been through all this and I am sure you understand. I only wish you to know that I am deeply sensible of your kindness and of your splendid service in our fight. Believe me with warmest wishes

Yours faithfully
Eugene V. Debs

TLS, Milwaukee County Historical Society, Hoan Papers.

1. Hoan was one of a score of nationally and internationally prominent socialists who campaigned for Debs during his 1916 congressional race. *Terre Haute Star,* September 15, 1916 et seq.

EVD to Grace Keller

November 11, 1916
Terre Haute, Indiana

My dear Mrs. Keller,

The dear, sweet, loving mother has gone out from you and you sit in sorrow in a world she left in darkness. Words are vain in such an hour but I would have you know that my heart is deeply touched and that I would if I could dull the edge of pain and share the burden of your sorrow.

Dear Mrs. Curry could not feel the anguish more keenly than if her own mother had been taken from her, and her eyes overflowed with tears as she expressed in broken words her tender, loving sympathy for you and the members of your stricken household.

Your dear mother lingered long and suffered much, as did my own mother, and yet the final hour, so welcome to the patient sufferer, was one of inexpressible pain to the loved ones left behind. But you will be comforted with the passing days. "Eyes that have been curtained by the ever-lasting dark never again know the burning touch of tears. Hearts of dust do not break. The dead do not weep." The hallowed memory of your beautiful mother will abide with you forever. With all loving sympathy.

Yours faithfully,
E. V. Debs

ALS, InTI, Debs Collection.

EVD to Horace Traubel

November 14, 1916
Terre Haute, Indiana

My dearest Horace: —

Both your messages are with me and my heart is full of them and of you. You make me rich and royal in defeat. You know I have never cared for office and that I stood as a candidate only from a sense of service, and so your words of comradely greeting and of congratulation fill me with rapture.

Your clear-seeing eye takes in the situation as it exactly is and your understanding of matters here is as perfect as if you had been through our entire campaign. You are a great comrade, continually rising above yourself yet never getting above the humblest that walks the earth. I salute, honor and love you!

Yours eternally,
Gene

TLS (with personal postcard), InTI, Debs Collection.

EVD to Peter Witt

November 14, 1916
Terre Haute, Indiana

My dear "Pete": —

You did not forget and your loyalty has not in the least diminished with the passing years. A thousand thanks! I should have made this acknowledgment long before but I have been away from my office and the campaign has exacted every moment of my time and every atom of my strength.

Coming from you, dear brother, this fine tribute and very liberal contribution touch me deeply. I know how willingly you would have entered the campaign had circumstances permitted and I know too that I feel as warm toward you and quite as grateful as if you had been actually with us over the entire district.

We more than trebled the vote of two years ago but we were up against all that the corporations and their minions could swing into line to beat us. We did not get office but we nevertheless achieved a notable victory and this entire section is now permeated with revolutionary sentiment.

I always inquire about you when at Cleveland. The last time I sent you my greeting through our mutual friend, Tom Moore,[1] great heart and loyal soul. It would give me very real pleasure to take you by the hand again.

Thanking you, dear old friend, again and again and with a thousand loving greetings and good wishes I am,

Yours always,
Eugene V. Debs

TLS, Western Reserve Historical Society, Cleveland, Witt Papers.

1. Tom Moore (1878-1946) emigrated from England to Canada in 1905, joined the Brotherhood of Carpenters and Joiners, and rose to the presidency of that union before becoming in 1918 president of the Canadian Trades and Labor Congress.

Thomas Van Lear[1] to EVD

November 16, 1916
St. Paul, Minnesota

Dear Comrade Debs:

Your favor under date of Nov. 11th was received and it gives me great pleasure to receive from you a letter that says so many kindly things.

Yes it was a splendid victory. We won over the powers of the public press and the slush fund created by special privilege, and I was elected to Mayor of the City of Minneapolis—a city of almost 400,000—by the largest number of votes ever given any candidate for Mayor in the history of this city, and I assure you I will give to the people while Mayor under my administration the best I have in me, and do all in my power to make the lives of the workers just a little brighter and just a little better. I will put forth all my efforts to give to the City a clean and honest administration, and I feel with the support I have had during this campaign, and so many loyal friends who believe in my ability that I can not fail.

Mrs. Van joins me in sending to you our hearty greetings and sincerely hope that in the near future you may have the opportunity to come this way and we may meet and again shake hands.

With kindest regards, I am,

Fraternally yours,
Thos Van Lear
Mayor elect Minneapolis.

TLS, InTI, Debs Collection.

1. Thomas Van Lear (1869-1931) was business agent for the Minneapolis local of the International Association of Machinists in 1916 when he was elected on the Socialist party ticket as mayor of Minneapolis. He served one term in that office (1917-19) and thereafter was a leader in the Farmer-Labor movement and editor of the *Minnesota Daily Star,* a Farmer-Labor paper.

EVD to George D. Herron

November 16, 1916
Terre Haute, Indiana

My dear Comrade Herron,

You will not think me remiss, I know, for not acknowledging sooner the very fine letter received from you in the early part of September and which I have taken occasion to read several times to friends and comrades, whose tear-filled eyes attested their heartfelt appreciation of its sad and pathetic contents. Your vivid description of the victims of war fills us with sorrow and we cry aloud in protest and horror against this shocking butchery of humanity.

How your great, tender, loving heart must be wrung daily, nightly, incessantly by the scenes of suffering you are fated to witness all about you! I can well imagine your own keen suffering and your outraged sensibilities as you medi[t]ate upon these awful crimes and the accursed system responsible for them. I am with you absolutely in the matter of militarism. I am opposed to any shadow of compromise with the God-damned institution and I would see myself in hell for all eternity before it should receive a word of encouragement or a particle of support in any form from me. Militarism has not a solitary redeeming feature and war is an unmitigated crime and I shall fight both un-compromisingly just as you are doing while there is breath in my body.

Well, our election is over and while we secured no office we won in every other way in this district. We more than trebled our vote and we now have an organization under way that promises much for the future.

The results of the national campaign as a whole are sorely disap-pointing to many of our comrades. For myself I never suffer myself to be disappointed or discouraged. Blessed are they who expect noth-ing for they shall not be disappointed. I simply do my little utmost as well as I can and take what comes without complaint and without regret.

I wish I could see you, dear comrade, and have a heart to heart talk with you over things in general. I would so love to counsel with you about plans for the future. Our party here needs to make some changes or it will certainly face deterioration if it has not already done so. There is too much time and effort given to vote-catching and office-seeking. If the politician can thrive in the Socialist party it is because its revolutionary spirit is dead and itself is doomed.

Pardon these incoherent lines. I am so far behind with my work in consequence of the campaign that I am unable to write you decently as you deserve. But you always understand and to you, beloved com-rade, I need never apologize or explain.

Theodore and I have sent you papers from time to time but I doubt if they were allowed to reach you. Our own matter has often been intercepted on account of the war and yours no doubt even more. We often, often think of you: we always love you.

We all unite in heartfelt greetings and most earnest wishes that your cruel banishment[1] may soon be ended.

Your brother in life and death,
(signed) Eugene V. Debs.

Transcript, CSt-H.

1. In 1901, shortly after his marriage to Carrie Rand in a New York City ceremony in which each simply chose the other as "companion" to dramatize their opposition "to all coercive institutions," Herron was bitterly attacked in the press, dismissed from the ministry, and fled to Italy.

Daniel W. Hoan to EVD

November 22, 1916
Milwaukee, Wisconsin

Dear Comrade: —

Yours of November 7th duly received, and it is needless to say that I was much pleased to receive it. I was quite anxious to meet you on my visit to Terre Haute, as I was convinced that should I have the pleasure of an interview I could convey some information which can hardly be expressed clearly by me in writing. I was fully aware of the fact that it would be asking too much to see you and therefore prevailed on the comrades not to bother you, especially at such a busy time.

I was indeed disappointed to learn that you were not elected to congress. After all these years of hard labor by so many noble comrades, success in your district would have been about the best news that could have been received. On my return from your city, I gave out an interview in which I stated if your votes are counted you will be elected; I fear I should have added if your votes are properly registered and counted you will be elected. I can remember many and many instances where the machine is used and the inspector enters a vote for a voter, that they deliberately pull the wrong lever. In the hurry and excitement of election-day, hundreds of workmen's votes are manipulated this way; where, moreover, the paper ballots are used and it is likely that many split the ballots, the inspectors will run thru the ballots hurriedly, at the opening of the ballot box, will deliberately, wherever they find a ballot marked with a cross at the top, place the ballot in the straight ticket pile. Just in the last election one challenger got a pile of straight ballots and looked them over a second time, and to his amazement out of a hundred ballots seventy-five were split on from one to more candidates on one ticket. At times we have found crooked work manipulated as follows: The man reading off the ballots will not read them off correctly or the fellows marking them down do not register them correctly. There has been more of this done here than we have discovered. I am satisfied that only the most pains-taking efforts of our boys on election-day and especially after the polls are closed, will result in a fair count.

I am enclosing herewith a copy of the speech I made in Minneapolis during the campaign, which was printed and distributed all over that city. With best wishes, I remain,

Fraternally yours,
[Daniel W. Hoan]
Mayor.

TLc, Milwaukee Country Historical Society, Hoan Papers.

EVD to Daniel W. Hoan

November 24, 1916
Terre Haute, Indiana

My dear Comrade Hoan:—

Thank you warmly and let me say that your kind letter is very much appreciated. I should certainly have enjoyed seeing you and should not have missed you but for the stress of the campaign. I shall not forget your kindness in coming here and the willing and valuable help you gave us.

I am not surprised that your speech at Minneapolis was widely distributed by the socialists. It is a powerful appeal, especially coming from you, for Van Lear and the socialist ticket.

I am sure you are right in your observation about our being cheated in the registration and count, and the characteristic and corrupt cap-italist method of it.[1] We were robbed in one way and another, largely by the means suggested in your letter, of thousands of votes and there is a wide and strong impression that if there had been a fair way for the people to express their preference and {an} honest count of the ballot so cast I would have been elected. It certainly seems so in this city to every one who witnessed the unparalleled parade and dem-onstration on the Saturday previous to the election.[2] But we shall profit by all these things and in due time we shall have a square deal and an honest count. Hoping to meet you again in good time I am

Yours always,

E. V. Debs

TLS, Milwaukee County Historical Society, Hoan Papers.

1. In "Right on the Job" (*American Socialist*, November 25, 1916), Debs claimed that "we lost many votes through the voting machines and many voted other tickets thinking they had voted the Socialist ticket," but he did not "think anything could be gained by petitioning for a recount" in the "capitalist courts."

2. The *Terre Haute Post* (November 4, 1916) reported that 10,000 Debs supporters from throughout the Fifth District and elsewhere would march in the final parade of the campaign in Terre Haute.

EVD to Horace Traubel

December 16, 1916
Terre Haute, Indiana

My dear Horace;

The writer of this editorial[1] evidently feels that he has a cinch of a case against us. He is too shallow to realize that if Belgium had been armed to the teeth and its people had been as warlike as Apache savages she would still have been crushed and desolated and that her fate would have been precisely the same. I agree with you absolutely. I am opposed to a nation carrying the weapons of murder about it as well as an individual. I am resolutely opposed to the whole damned infernal arming business and the whole diabolical program of human butchery. To hell with war and to hell with the system that breeds war and with the government that prepares for war.

Like you I yearn to see one nation have the moral courage, the common decency to be a coward nation, the first nation in history too cowardly to commit murder and to thrive in the fruit of massacre. Love and success to you now and always!

Yours right along,

E. V. Debs

TLS, InTI, Debs Collection.

1. Debs enclosed an editorial sent to him by the Argus Pressclipping Bureau in New York City. The source of the editorial was not given, but its argument was that Traubel was mistaken in a *Conservator* article in which he quoted approvingly Emerson's dictum that a nation which "embraces the doctrine of peace" is "one against

which no weapon can prosper." To support its position the editorial cited Belgium, "Quaker among nations," which had become "the most devastated and desolated among nations" in the war.

George D. Herron to EVD

December 19, 1916
Geneva, Switzerland

Dear Brother Debs:

It was good to get your ringing letter of six weeks ago. This time it came through without any erasure on the part of the censor.

I wish with you that we could have a heart to heart talk over the world's situation. Aside from yourself, none of the American socialists seem to have the least moral or intellectual understanding of what has happened and is happening. Perhaps a few have, such as Walter Kruesi,[1] English Walling and Carrie W. Allen,[2] but these are not in any official relation or leadership within the party. The party itself seems to be utterly subservient to the official German socialist leaders, who have now formed an alliance with the Prussian Jesuits. The degradation and betrayal of a great cause can go no further and deeper than it has gone at the hands of the German socialists. If American socialists imagine for one moment that the real socialists of Belgium and France, of Italy and England, will ever sit down together again in council with these pompous German traitors, or with any movement that they lead, then American socialists are as destitute of either intellectual or moral capacity as it is possible for human beings to be.

But I think the best expression I can give you of my own feelings is in a letter I wrote lately to Comrade Simons, who asked me to give him a view of the whole situation as I know it. I sent you a copy of the letter at the time, but I judge from your letter of the 16th of November that you never received it. I will enclose another copy with this.[3]

I have lately been getting very deep into the war. Quite unintentionally and unexpectedly, at the request of the editor, I wrote some articles under the general titles of "Le Complet Pacifist" for the well-known French weekly, "La Semaine Litteraire" of Geneva. I did this quite incidentally, and thought no more about them. But they were widely copied in all the leading papers of England and France and Italy, and they came to the attention of members of the government in the three countries. The result is that I have been drawn deeply and somewhat perilously into the whole controversy regarding a false peace, and have been bitterly attacked by Catholic and German organs. I have now written a little book, which will soon be published, entitled "The Menace of Peace."[4] I will send you a copy of it. This will explain my point of view better than anything else that I can send you.

With deepest love to you and yours,

Affectionately,
George D. Herron

Please note that the address of George D. Herron is changed from 36, Chemin des Cottages, Geneva, Switzerland to Hotel Beau Sejour, Champel, Geneva, Switzerland.

TLS, InTI, Debs Collection.

1. Walter Edison Kruesi (1881-1961) was a socialist at the time and superintendent of the Public Employment Bureau of New York City. In a long career of public service and humanitarian concerns, Kruesi worked and wrote in the fields of public health and hygiene, charitable and welfare agencies, and unemployment and relief policies.

2. Carrie W. Allen was described in a socialist biographical directory in 1912 as having "travelled from the theatrical profession to the university classroom" at Syracuse University. She was a national lecturer for the Socialist party, a member of the women's national committee of the party in 1913 and a socialist candidate for secretary of state of New York in 1912.

3. The Algie M. Simons Papers at the Wisconsin State Historical Society include a dozen letters from Herron to Simons, written between 1914 and 1917 and generally critical of the "diabolical Germans," but the letter referred to here has not been found.

4. Herron's *Menace of Peace*, which appeared in both French- and English-language editions in 1917, was an attack on "a peace that will leave the causes of war unknown" and on a "peace without victory." Such a peace would be a victory of "Prussian might and mastery" and would strengthen the Vatican, which depended upon "the subjugation of peoples" for its survival. On the other hand, an Allied victory would "lead to the banishment of war from our planet." *Book Review Digest* (1917), 262.

Duncan McDonald[1] to EVD

January 3, 1917
Springfield, Illinois

Friend Gene:

I read with considerable interest your editorial entitled "False Leaders of the Workers" in the January issue of the Rip Saw.[2] The article is so timely and appropriate that I am writing you to advise that I heartily agree with the sentiment expressed. The only regret I have is that the article does not go far enough in condemning the men who pose as true representatives of the working class but who turn turtle at every opportunity to get a smile from those in control.

I have been an official in the Miners' Organization now for fourteen years and practically ever since my connection with same I have been up against a "Gang" who have been more unscrupulous than the employers ever knew how to be, and after a many hard fought contest they have succeeded in stealing enough votes at our recent election to defeat me for this position.[3] I have always fared well with the individual members but the gangsters and crooks have fought me and are now gloating over their victory in defeating me for office—as if this petty office was all there was to life. But I find the same fight going on in every branch of organized labor, and when one has the courage to buck the Big Machine he is slated for retirement sooner or later.

The experience I have had in this work has been worth more to me than the few dollars I have received for my services, and some day I hope to be able to place this material in some publication, with a substantial circulation, so the workers may have the benefit of same.

Every Socialist, in the Labor Movement, who has the courage of his convictions is a target for these leeches, and there is little defense back of him so far as Trade Union Publications are concerned as they are in control of the other fellow. If we expect to retain any semblance of rights we must at least, have one organ that will go to the front for those who yet remain and want to perform their true mission as Leaders of the Workers.

No institution in America can be of more real service to the workers than a properly conducted labor union but there is no institution in America that can become more corrupt when used by a band of unscrupulous politicians to further their own interests.

Some time when you are going to be in St. Louis or near there I will be glad to arrange to meet you and talk over the entire matter.

With kind regards from Mrs. McDonald and myself, I remain.

Yours very truly,
Duncan McDonald

TLS, InTI, Debs Collection.

1. Duncan McDonald (1874-1975) held a number of positions in the UMW before World War 1, including those of president (1909) and secretary-treasurer (1910-17) of the Illinois UMW. McDonald was president of the Illinois Federation of Labor (1919-20) and in the postwar years a leader of the Farmer-Labor party, which nominated him for the presidency in 1924. McDonald withdrew in favor of Robert La Follette.

2. In the editorial, Debs denounced a number of "false leaders" of workers—including John H. Walker, president of the Illinois UMW—who had supported Democratic or Republican candidates in the November 1916 election.

3. As secretary-treasurer of the Illinois UMW.

George D. Herron to EVD

January 10, 1917
Geneva, Switzerland

Dear Brother Debs:

The chief of the Propaganda Bureau of the French Government has been to see me, and we have had three serious conferences concerning the situation in America and the advisability of a French Educational Agitation and Propaganda to bring understanding to the American people, and to counter-act the profound and wide pro-German influence. He has asked me if I would undertake a mission to America on behalf of France and I have replied in the negative, although I have placed myself at his disposal to render every possible service I can from here. I have told him frankly that I believe, both my past personal conflicts and revolutionary socialist attitude, would militate against my undertaking such a mission. It is possible that Bergson[1] will be persuaded to go. Indeed, he is now thinking quite favorably of it. But, in any case, there must be an American also. I have told the chief that I believe you are in a position to inform him, better than anyone else could inform him, of the common feeling of the people throughout all the interior part of the United States. He returns to Paris tonight, and will write to you at once.[2] Will you give him as complete a report as you can, of the pro-German influences at work, both in the general public and in the socialist party, and also as to what portion of {our} people, if any, understand the significance of this supreme human hour, and what it is the Allies are fighting for. You can render no greater service to the great Cause than this. For I can assure you, from personal knowledge as well as conviction, that the result of the victory of France and England will mean a speedy coming of the Co-operative Common-Wealth and the abolition of militarism in both countries.

I have just written a little book, entitled, "The Menace of Peace," which is being published simultaneously in London, Paris, Geneva and Florence. I think its appeal will interest you and I will send you an English copy as soon as it has appeared.

Please give my affectionate greetings to Mrs. Debs and to Theodore as well as take my eternal love for yourself.

Affectionately yours,
George D. Herron

TLS, InTI, Debs Collection.

1. Henry Louis Bergson (1859-1941), influential French philosopher and winner of the Nobel Prize in literature in 1927, arrived in the United States in February 1917 and spoke before a number of academic and cultural organizations, including the American Academy of Arts and Letters and the France-America Society, during the winter and spring of 1917.
2. Not found.

EVD to George D. Herron

January 23, 1917
Terre Haute, Indiana

Dearest of Comrades,

The letter from you under date of the 19th ult., enclosing copy of a letter from you to Simons, reached here this morning and both have been carefully read. It appears that a letter I wrote you about the holidays did not reach you. I do not remember the exact date nor have I a copy of it. I am sorry you did not get this letter, not that it was specially important, but that you might have known we were thinking of you and feeling for you and wishing ourselves able to share fully the terrible ordeal through which you of all others seems to have been marked by fate to pass through.

The letter from you just received arrived here cut open at the end by the censor, and not resealed, so that it came really open for the inspection of anyone that might choose to inspect its contents.

As I am just back from a speaking tour and am having to leave here soon again, with many matters here awaiting attention, I shall not attempt to review your letter to Simons which I am very glad you have allowed me to see. I share fully in your indignation but I fear that in the stress of the terrible position in which you have been placed, and with your keen sense of what should have been and your super-sensitive nature you have allowed yourself to become embittered and unduly pessimistic. All the vital and essential elements of the international movement are intact and I apprehend no such trouble about reviving the movement with all the cowardly and betraying elements eliminated. In the enclosed article from the current Rip-

Saw you will see what I think of Liebknecht and of the miserable traitors calling themselves socialists who are defaming him.[1]

There are some things in your letter that set me thinking seriously along new lines. I wish to feel as keenly as you do, though I fear that is impossible, the sense of shame and outrage socialists ought to feel for the failure of their movement at the time of its greatest opportunity and in the supreme crisis of the world. But is it not possible that too much was expected from the socialist movement under all the conditions that surround it? I am, like yourself, utterly opposed to excusing treason, but there are times when moral weakness is not a crime.

I cannot see my way clear to your view that the class-struggle is to be abandoned in the future realignment and program. I cannot imagine a socialist movement that does not incarnate the principles of the struggle, the warfare going on all about us and continuously between the exploited and exploiting classes of society.

But your views and opinions are always of the deepest concern to me and I need not say command in advance my most serious consideration. You write as does no other and if you are open to any criticism it is that you are what in capitalistic ethics is called "absurdly honest."

A thousand loving wishes!

Yours always,
(signed) E. V. Debs

Transcript, CSt-H.

1. In "Karl Liebknecht, Germany's Conquering Hero" (*Rip-Saw*, January 1917), Debs praised Liebknecht, who was imprisoned by the German government for his opposition to the war, as "the one Socialist leader in Germany who has stood boldly . . . for the true international position" of socialism and denounced "the Socialist dough-faces" of Germany who supported the war.

Theodore Debs to Alexander Trachtenberg

February 7, 1917
Terre Haute, Indiana

Dear Comrade Trachtenberg:—

Your note of the 3rd. was duly received. My brother has been ill with the grip or your request would have been complied with more promptly. I have just come from my brother's home. He dictated the enclosed in regard to your Year Book.[1] He wished me to say that if this will not serve he will try again. It is a matter of pleasure to him to be of any service to you and to the Rand School. Allow me in behalf of both of us to wish all success for the School.

Yours fraternally,
Theodore Debs

Gladly do I certify the value of "The American Labor Year Book" recently issued by the Department of Labor Research of the Rand School of Social Science. It is an invaluable volume not only for ready reference but for general information regarding socialism and the labor movement. It is gotten up in most convenient form and its contents are admirably classified for reference and other purposes. My copy is at my elbow and I have frequent occasion to consult its pages. Most heartily do I commend this very excellent work to readers of socialist literature and students of the labor movement.

Eugene V. Debs

ALS, NN.

1. The *American Labor Year Book* for 1917, edited by Trachtenberg.

O. B. Stephenson[1] to EVD

February 12, 1917
Chicago, Illinois

Dear Mr. Debs:

Our mutual friend, Mr. Bicknell,[2] was in the office this morning, and we discussed very thoroughly the future of your work with us. He is quite disappointed that you are unable to do any work at all this summer, as he had a number of prospects already outlined, as he has been on the road ever since meeting you. It is indeed quite a disappointment to both of us.

For 1918, we would like to use you, and would be pleased to have a definite understanding regarding the matter. Bicknell is of the opinion that we can secure good bookings for you, that all the committees are interested and that it would be a great deal for you. It actually costs us twenty-five per cent to transact business from this office, and when we charge you only twenty-five per cent commission for doing business we are doing you an honor that few people on our list receive. However, if you want to give us the last week of July and August for next summer, we will book you at $150.00, charging you twenty-five per cent commission. You of course, would pay your own railroads, your own expenses and furnish all necessary advertising, printing and cuts.

May we please hear from you at an early date regarding this proposition.

Yours very truly,
COIT-ALBER CHAUTAUQUA COMPANY,
O. B. Stephenson
Secty-Treas.

TLS, InTI, Debs Collection.

1. Orlistus Bell Stephenson (1867-1940) was at this time secretary-treasurer of the Affiliated Lyceum Bureaus of America, an umbrella organization for a dozen independently owned lyceum and Chautauqua bureaus, including the Coit-Alber Chautauqua Bureau. He later became owner of the Emerson Lyceum Bureau in Chicago.

2. George Bicknell, Debs's friend from Terre Haute.

George Bicknell to EVD

February 19, 1917
Indianapolis, Indiana

My dear Mr. Debs:

Your letter of Feb. 15, 1917. written to Mr. Stephenson in regard to your Chautauqua dating has been referred to me for reply. When Mr. Stephenson wrote to you "If you want to give us the last week of Aug. for next summer, we will book you at $150, etc" he meant the summer of 1918, not the summer of 1917. This was in answer to your letter saying you did not think you could do any work in 1917, and was preliminary to securing contract with you for 1918. What Mr. Stephenson meant to say was, we would book you for the last week in July and the entire month of Aug. 1918. Now all the agents are anxious to secure you as I have talked with a number of them and think it would be easy to sell you at $150.

Two bureaus that were booking on the 25% commission basis have gone out of business the last year because they lost money so Mr. Stephenson has made a resolution that he would not do any more booking on less than 25% basis, but will make an exception in your case, at 25%, but you would have to pay your railroad fare and your advertising expense. Now this advertising expense would not amount to more than $1.00 or $1.50 per town and that is not a big thing at all. We would take care at our main office of the sending out of this advertising matter and all we agree to furnish our committees is fifty window cards for each town and one small cut and they are to pay expressage on this material both ways. Of course the cuts would be your property and as I say all this matter would be attended to from our office but the cost of the making of the cuts and printing the window cards would be charged to you.

I am mailing you here a blank contract that we make to each individual committee for each date. I do this to show you how our contract reads with the committee.

Now as to booking any dates at all for this summer I think it is probably too late, however if I were able to secure a date or two for you sometime in Aug. simply to try out the proposition at $150 I think I shall go ahead and let the date be subject to your approval. If you want to cancel it is all right. But this is to show you that Mr. Stephenson's letter meant for the summer of 1918 and was in answer to a letter from you stating you did not think you would do any Chautauqua work in 1917.

I trust you and Mrs. Debs have waded entirely through your siege of grippe. I had a spell myself after I saw you in Chicago.

I have just read your Riley article in Pearson's Magazine[1] and I wish to say that I appreciated it very much. It might be of interest to you to know that I rode over from Terre Haute to Indianapolis last Saturday with Mr. & Mrs. Isaac Strauss of Rockville.[2] You will know Mrs. Strauss as the Country Contributer. They asked me if I had seen the Debs article on Riley and said they had a letter from Senator John Kern the day before from Washington calling their attention to the article and telling them to be sure to read it. I had a letter from Frank Harris[3] recently saying that in four months, or since he had taken the editorship of Pearson's its subscriptions had increased four-fold. Of course you do not want to go to New York without seeing Frank Harris. He is one of the very big men in America today and is a radical of long standing.

I am,

Very sincerely,
George Bicknell

TLS, InTI, Debs Collection.

1. Debs's essay, "Riley, the Hoosier Poet and Interpreter" appeared in *Pearson's* in March 1917.

2. Isaac Rice Strauss (1859-1934) was born in Rockville, Indiana, twenty miles north of Terre Haute, educated in its schools, and at the age of sixteen began work on the *Rockville Tribune*, of which he became editor and owner in 1883. In 1881, Strauss married Juliet Virginia Humphries (1863-1918), who joined the *Tribune* staff and in 1900 began writing a weekly column, "The Country Contributor," for the

Indianapolis News. The column brought Mrs. Strauss, a socialist, national recognition and she became a regular contributor to *Woman's Home Companion* and *Ladies' Home Journal* and enjoyed popularity on the lecture circuit.

3. Frank Harris (1856-1931) came from Ireland about 1872 and worked in a variety of unskilled jobs in Chicago and, according to his account, in Texas. He worked his way through the University of Kansas, which awarded him a law degree in 1875, before returning to Europe for further study and to England, where he edited several English magazines, including *Saturday Review* and *Vanity Fair.* Harris's biography of Oscar Wilde was considered too frank for English publishers to risk, so he returned to the United States, where he printed and sold it himself. Similarly, his *My Life and Loves* was at first turned down by both English and American publishers and printed in Germany. Harris bought *Pearson's* in 1916 and, despite government harassment during the war and chronic financial troubles, made it a leading literary journal during the next half-dozen years.

J. E. Snyder to EVD

February 24, 1917
San Francisco, California

EUGENE V DEBS

TOM MOONEY SENTENCED TO HANG MAY SEVENTEENTH   HE IS DOOMED UNLESS LABOR ORGANIZATIONS AND SOCIALIST PARTY ACT AT ONCE   THE VERDICT IS ABSOLUTELY AN OUTRAGE   MOONEY URGED ME WIRE YOU AT ONCE   WE ARE COUNTING ON YOU GENE[1]

J E SNIDER[2]

Telegram, InTI, Debs Collection.

1. Debs's editorials in the *Rip-Saw* and articles in *American Socialist* and *Appeal to Reason* helped to create the national interest in the Mooney Case. As noted, Mooney's death sentence was commuted to life imprisonment.
2. John E. Snyder at the *Oakland World.*

EVD to Charmian London[1]

February 25, 1917
Terre Haute, Indiana

My dear Comrade London: —

Thank you warmly for your very appreciative letter just received. I can only regret that it is not better deserved. I have been suffering with the grip these several weeks past and my work has been but poorly done during that time.

Your beloved husband[2] was very dear to me as he was to many thousands of others who never had the privilege of laying their eyes upon him. I often wondered why I was among the unfortunate who were never permitted to see him. I felt the great heart of him, loved him, read nearly everything he wrote, and rejoiced in applauding his genius. But I never happened to be in the same place with him at the same time and I hoped that some good day in the future I might meet him and have the chance to tell him how much I loved him and how glad I was that he was in the world. But the chance never came, and there is not another in all the world to take his place.

Mrs. Debs and I thought of you with the deepest sympathy when the painful and shocking news came and we wished ourselves near enough to speak to you our word of loving sympathy. But you did not want for friends and comrades in that solemn hour and I hope that by this time you have become reconciled and that the sun again shines into your life.

Our dear Jack is with you and us still and will abide with us for the great soul of him cannot die.

Thank you for the very excellent picture you were so thoughtful as to enclose. It is just what I wished and I prize it far more than could be expressed in words.

Mrs. Debs joins me in affectionate greetings and warmest wishes and I am always,

Yours faithfully,
Eugene V. Debs

TLS, CSmH, London Papers.

1. Charmian Kittredge London (1877-1955) wrote a number of books on Hawaii, Australia, and other countries; completed and published in *Cosmopolitan* in 1924 Jack London's *Eyes of Asia;* and regularly contributed to American magazines articles on travel, biography, and fiction.

2. Jack London committed suicide on November 22, 1916.

EVD to Theodore Debs

March 3, 1917
Buffalo, New York

Dearest old Pard:

Never was such a Socialist meeting in Buffalo. The great Music Hall crowded to the doors—over 5000 paid admissions. They took collection & sold literature to amt. of nearly $600.00 & took nearly

300 subs to the local socialist paper. They're wild with enthusiasm over results. My speech—well, I wish you had heard it—they said I never made such a speech in my life. Billy Sunday[1] is here & I took him down the line—stripped him stark naked & the great crowd went wild as I showed him up for the fraud & charlatan he is. See papers. They give fair report for a capitalist paper. Feel fine as a bear—all the "grip" is out of me & I could throw a buffalo, knock out a steer, trim the claws of a wild cat, and eat a skinned moose. Love & kisses to you all.

Your old pard
Gene

I'm giving war hell & peeling the hides of the "patriots."[2]

ALS, InTI, Debs Collection.

1. William Ashley Sunday (1862-1935) was the best-known American evangelist of his era, a foe of socialism (or, for that matter, any form of political liberalism), and often the target of attack in the socialist press. In "Billy Sunday" (*Melting Pot,* March 1916), Debs argued that the legal logic used in the Haymarket trial should be used against Billy Sunday, one of whose sermons was allegedly responsible for the murder of a Syracuse, New York, woman by her son, who, having listened to Sunday, went home and killed his mother "to send her to heaven."
2. In "Making the Fur Fly" (*American Socialist,* March 24, 1917), the paper described Debs's "tour through the eastern states" as "attracting considerable attention from the press generally" and quoted him as saying at Canton, Ohio, that he "wished for one coward nation, a nation too cowardly to commit murder."

EVD to Theodore Debs

March 7, 1917
Boston, Massachusetts

My dear old Pard:
    Terrific snow-storm struck this section yesterday—a fearful blizzard. My train got stuck but I got here finally at 8—just in time. It was a fearful night. I expected an empty hall but to my surprise a grand audience was present. Had it been but half decent the vast temple would not have held half the people. The papers all gave fine reports—will try to get one & send it to you. Have been up since 5 this AM. Went to bed at 12.30—a dozen are now waiting for me. Have engagement at 11 with Nora Connelly, daughter of Jim Connelly,[1] the Dublin martyr & also with Margaret Haile[2]—she came to hotel with me. Sends you love, so does Jim Oneal[3] & so does "Eddy."[4] Too damned busy to write. Recd 2 bndls papers here from you & 1

from Phil.[5] My grip is loaded with stuff—may have chance to look at it tomorrow. No chance here. Roy Goodwin[6] was in audience at Buffalo. Did not get to see him after meeting as I was hustled out through back door. Great meeting last night & I made 'em a speech that stirred 'em to the depths & you ought to have seen & heard their approval & applause.

Eugene V. Debs

ALS, InTI, Debs Collection.

1. Nora Connolly came to the United States following her father's execution. In "James Connolly, Revolutionist" (*Call*, June 8, 1919), she explained her goal of "making plain the puzzle of James Connolly's action in the Insurrection of 1916," a goal she pursued on the lecture circuit and in her writing.

2. Margaret Haile was a pioneer socialist in the Boston area, one of the founders of the Social Democratic party at Chicago in 1898, and a delegate from Massachusetts to the party's 1900 convention in Indianapolis, which nominated Debs as its presidential candidate.

3. James Oneal left his position as state secretary of the Socialist party in Indiana in 1913 and in March 1915 assumed the same postion in Massachusetts.

4. A fruitless search for an Eddy among Boston socialists of the period raises the possibility that in this Debs was facetiously sending along a greeting from Mary Baker Eddy.

5. Phil Wagner at the *Rip-Saw*.

6. Roy Goodwin, one of the directors of the American Railway Union, who was jailed with Debs following the Pullman Strike.

EVD to Robert M. La Follette

March 7, 1917
Providence, Rhode Island

HON ROBERT M LAFOLLETTE

LET THE WALL STREET WOLVES AND THEIR PROSTITUTE PRESS HOWL.[1] THE PEOPLE WILL SUSTAIN YOU AND HISTORY WILL VINDICATE YOU.

EUGENE V DEBS

Telegram, DLC, MSS, Division, La Follette Family Collection.

1. For his leadership of the filibuster that prevented the passage of the armed-merchant-ship legislation in Congress's short session, which closed on March 4, 1917, and for his vote against the declaration of war the following month, La Follette was bitterly denounced in a broad spectrum of the press as pro-German and lacking in patriotism. In time, his position on the war led to an unsuccessful attempt to expel him from the Senate, almost incredible charges by patriotic organizations, and censure by the Wisconsin state legislature and the faculty of the University of Wisconsin.

Ludwig Lore to EVD

March 9, 1917
New York City

My dear Comrade Debs:

Comrade L.B. Boudin and I tried very hard yesterday and to-day to see you. We intended to lay before you a proposition that, we were quite sure, would interest you and whose purpose would find your support.

The whole story is in short as follows:

A group of Socialists who indorse the position of the Zimmerwald and Kienthal Conferences has decided to start a new Socialist periodical, whose task shall be mainly to educate the intelligent rank and file of the Party.

The publication which shall appear, for the first time, on April 15th., dated May 1st., is intended, at least for the near future to be a bi-monthly of about 96 magazine size pages.

We have decided to publish a number of articles, each about 8 pages in length, which appear in the regular issue of the periodical, as propaganda pamphlets, which, as we hope will help us to reach a considerable part of the membership with our message, and will support us in our primary purpose, the influencing of the Party in the direction of that wing of the Socialist movement that maintained, throughout the war, its international and social-revolutionary character.

The financial basis of this new publication is secure. But we hope soon to raise enough funds to be able to publish it monthly.

The Editorial Committee hereby asks your co-operation and urges you to send us an article for the first issue if at all possible.[1] To give you an idea of the tentative program mapped out for the first issue[2] we add hereto the list of articles that have been secured or promised:

Socialism and Pacifism by Leon Trotzky.[3]

The Condition of the Socialist Party by Louis B. Boudin.

Problems of State Socialism by L.C. Fraina.[4]

What the War is doing to America by A.M. Simons (promised)

Militarism and educational problems by William Bohn[5] (promised)

American Trade Unionism and Imperialism by Ludwig Lore.

The International Socialist Movement

Editorial Department under the editorship of L.B. Boudin.

We hoped that you probably might consent to write an article on "The Defense of the Fatherland," a subject that could be treated by no other pen as well and powerfully as yours and that undoubtedly could and would find a very large circulation as a separate pamphlet.

If you could find time to call up Comrade Boudin (Teleph. Worth 1173) tomorrow morning, he could, I am sure, give you any further information you might desire. That such a magazine for the enlightenment of our intelligent Party-workers is an urgent necessity, nobody can doubt. Your assistance would assure its success.

Fraternally and cordially yours,

Ludwig Lore

Ass. Editor N.Y. Volkzeitung.

The Editorial Committee consists of:

L.B. Boudin.

Leon Trotzky.

L.C. Fraina.

M. Burgin[6]

L. Lore Secretary, 15 Spruce Str., N.Y.C.

TLS, InTI, Debs Collection.

1. Debs's first article in *Class Struggle*, "The Day of the People," did not appear until the February 1919 issue, in which he is also listed as editor, along with Lore and Louis Fraina.

2. The first issue of *Class Struggle* was for May-June 1917.

3. Leon Trotsky (1879-1940) was hailed as the author of the antiwar Zimmerwald Manifesto when he arrived in New York on January 13, 1917. During the following two and a half months he watched the early stages of the Russian Revolution, lectured on the subject to scores of rallies in New York, and frequently wrote articles on the war and the revolution in *Novyi Mir* (*New World*), a daily published in New York by Russian émigrés. Trotsky left New York on March 27, 1917, before *Class Struggle* was well under way, but his article "Pacifism in the Service of Socialism" appeared in the November-December issue of the magazine. As noted Debs's Cooper Union speech was given in New York during Trotsky's stay there and the future leader of the Bolshevik Revolution and the Red Army, who thought most American socialists were "Babbitts," admired Debs's "quenchless inner flame of socialist idealism" and claimed that "whenever we met, he embraced and kissed me." Quoted in Isaac Deutscher, *The Prophet Armed: Trotsky, 1879-1921*, 243.

4. Lewis Corey (1892-1953) was born Luigi Carlo Fraini near Naples, Italy, and was brought to the United States in 1895. Best known as Louis C. Fraina during his long career in American radical movements—the Socialist Labor party, the left wing of the Socialist party, the Communist party (which he left soon after it was launched), and "independent socialism"—he began to write under the name Lewis Corey in 1926 and it was under that name that his major work, *The Decline of American Capitalism*, was published in 1934. During the last two decades of his life, he worked on the non-Communist American left as a writer, teacher (at Antioch College from 1942 to 1951), editor (for the International Ladies' Garment Workers' Union and the Amalgamated Butcher Workmen's Union publications) and organizer (in 1940, the Union for Democratic Action, which became Americans for Democratic Action; in 1946, the National Educational Committee for a New Party; and other groups), but he was nonetheless

a target of the McCarthy era's vigilance and was scheduled for deportation under the McCarran Act when he died in September 1953.

5. William E. Bohn (1877-1967) earned a doctorate in English at the University of Michigan in 1906 and taught in the English department there until 1910, when he was "eased out of his job," as he described it in his autobiographical *I Remember America* (1962), for spending his weekends giving lectures on socialism in the towns around Ann Arbor. Bohn wrote regularly for socialist publications, especially the *International Socialist Review*, which he edited for a time. He taught courses at the Rand School and was educational director there from 1929 to 1940; in 1941 he became editor of the *New Leader* until his retirement in 1956. Bohn's "Educational Experiment" appeared in the May-June 1917 issue of *Class Struggle*.

6. Burgin was a regular contributor to *Class Struggle*.

Ludwig Lore to EVD

March 19, 1917
New York City

My dear Comrade Debs:

Your very kind letter was thankfully received. Comrade Boudin and myself regretted very deeply our inability to speak to you for a few moments, for we feel sure that we could have succeeded in interesting you in this new venture, "The Class Struggle," a bi-monthly magazine to be published in the interest of the revolutionary international wing of our movement.

But we do not give up hope yet. We are, of course, very well aware that you are overworked, and that it will be more than difficult for you to write lengthy articles. Nevertheless we once more urge you to write for us a short contribution that will, at least, show that you are with us, that your sympathies are on our side. This means much to us, because the cry will be raised, as soon as we begin to criticize the movement, that we intend to split the Party. As soon as you, who are recognized everywhere as one of the most loyal and at the same time one of the most critical Socialists of this country, are with us, this ridiculous cry would become nonsensical.

Hoping to hear from you soon and wishing you, dear Comrade Debs, good health and double strength for your noble work,

I remain fraternally and most cordially yours,

Ludwig Lore
243—55. Str. Brooklyn.
(or 15 Spruce Str., N.Y.C.)

TLS, InTI, Debs Collection.

Fred D. Warren to EVD

March 22, 1917
Madison, Wisconsin

Dear Gene:—

Here's a little clipping that perhaps will interest you. It is "my bill"[1] finally introduced, or rather proposed, into congress. It has taken me three years of pretty hard work, single handed, and the expenditure of a considerable sum of money to get it this far. About a million copies were printed and distributed and some of the friends bombarded congress pretty vigorously in its behalf.

The original proposal was that all congressmen and senators who voted yes on the declaration of war should be drafted into service; also all newspaper men and stockholders in munition factories who sold war supplies. But I had a lot of fun out of the thing, and it's all in the game, anyway.

My original bill was more modest than the one herewith proposed. This one provides that ALL the income of the rich over $100,000 shall be taken by the government.[2] I only asked for 90%!

Hope you are well and happy, and that Mrs. Debs is in good health. We are spending the winter in Madison where the boys are going to school—Glenn in the university and the other boys the public schools.

Sincerely Yours,
Fred D. Warren

TLS, InTI, Debs Collection.

1. In 1916, Fred Warren's "bill . . . relating to military service of all persons instrumental in bringing about war and profiting by the sale of munitions of war to the United States government" was widely reprinted in the socialist press (*Rip Saw*, April 1916; *American Socialist*, April 6, 1916; and elsewhere). It called for drafting of senators and congressmen who voted for war; editors who supported war; "preachers or priests who asked God's blessing on war"; stockholders "supplying munitions of war"; etc. "Funds to pay such soldiers" would be raised by "a tax of 90% against all incomes over $3,000 per year."

2. In the congressional debate on financing the preparedness program—by the sale of bonds or through increased income taxation—a number of proposals were introduced that would have sharply increased taxation on large incomes, including several that would have imposed a 100 percent tax on incomes over $100,000.

EVD to Fred D. Warren

March 23, 1917
Terre Haute, Indiana

My dear Fred:—

I am glad, real glad, to hear your chirp again and to find you in the same chipper mood you always were when we did things together out in Kansas. I note the administration bill as reported in the Tribune to which you call my attention and its likeness to the bill you drafted covering the same proposition a long time ago. I remember your bill very well and the comment it excited and the ridicule it met, the common fate of every new idea, and now it is seriously proposed by the powers that be to incorporate it in the law of the land. That's the way it goes and that's the story of human progress. You now congratulate yourself that the wise capitalist solons are beginning to browse over the soil you made fertile years ago.[1]

We have all had the grip down here, victims of an epidemic, but we are pretty well over it and trying to get things under way again. I have just concluded an eastern trip and will soon be leaving for California. I met Brewer at Pittsburg the other day and we jointly and severally sent a few rockets in your direction. I have thought of you and Mrs. Warren and the boys many a time since last we met. The golden hours at Girard, especially those spent at your happy home can never be forgotten. I hope Mrs. Warren is well and that the boys are getting along famously at school. Mrs. Debs joins me and so does Theodore in greetings of love and warmest wishes to you all. I am in the same old way,

Yours in the cause,
E. V. Debs

TLS, CtU, Fred Warren Papers.

1. In March 1917, Congress passed and Wilson signed the Emergency Revenue Act, which was intended to raise an additional $200,000,000 annually through a 50 percent increase in the estate tax and a new excess-profits tax.

Bruce Rogers[1] to EVD

April 1, 1917
Seattle, Washington

Dear Eugene Debs:—

Your thoughtfulness in letting us have copy of NY Times with excerpts from your memorable address.[2]

I am entirely with you and I favor definite action *in time:* but I have a like interest in the Everett Matter.[3] Five workers in pursuance of an orderly purpose were most wantonly shot and 74 are on trial for their lives. Knowing your broad guage, your continued aloofness to IWW conflicts is most puzzling to me.

Letter you wrote me at Spokane never cleared it up. Am not anxious to revive the bitter correspondence we had here but intimate contact with three acute IWW struggles have been justified in my own knowledge. I wonder why you stay away from them and why you stay so long out of the action of the movement which so much needs you.

It is not for me to urge you but I do and must feel that history, by withholding your leadership from the Revolution's physical phenomena, is being cheated.

In all devotion and Loyalty,
Bruce Rogers
1433 Lakeside

Write me in advance of your visit here if there is any demand you may have for me while in the state.

ALS, InTI, Debs Collection.

1. Bruce Rogers (1870-1934) had worked in Girard with Debs on the *Appeal to Reason* and other Wayland publications. He wrote the foreword to Debs's *You Railroad Men*, a 1908 campaign pamphlet, and edited *Debs: His Life, Writings and Speeches* (1908). Rogers moved to the Seattle area from Kansas and became a leader in that city's IWW and other radical movements.

2. Debs's Cooper Union speech in New York (*New York Times*, March 7, 1917) blamed the "war agitation" on Wall Street and called for a strike if war were declared.

3. On November 5, 1917, five IWW members were killed and scores wounded in the Everett Massacre, in which a county sheriff and several hundred special deputies attacked a boatload of Wobblies from Seattle who had gone to Everett to aid in an anti-open shop, free-speech campaign. Debs denounced the episode in "The Shame of Everett" (*Rip-Saw*, January 1917).

EVD to Bruce Rogers

April 9, 1917
Terre Haute, Indiana

Dear Bruce Rogers: —
Your letter of the 1st. is at hand and coming from you I am surprised at it not a little. Since when have you discovered that I have done nothing for the Everett victims? You are the only one I know to lay

claim to that distinction. I have appealed in their behalf in nearly every speech I have made, have appealed in their behalf for funds and support through the Rip-Saw and other papers, in my correspondence and every other way I have known how, and I have their grateful acknowledgment of my fealty to their cause and the service I have rendered them.

You think me slow to help them because they belong to the I.W.W. I have good reason not to feel kindly toward some of them but I have never in a single instance refused them aid and support and it seems strange to me that you appear to be in utter ignorance of this fact. So far as I know you are the only one to bring this complaint against me.

Who was the first man appealed to by the I.W.W. victims at Lawrence and especially the leaders on trial? And who was the first to respond? Ask Ettor, ask Giovannitti.[1] They know.

I raised more money than anyone else to defend them and have the written expression of their thanks and gratitude. The same is true of the Paterson strike and its arrested leaders.

Who issued one of the first appeals for funds to save Joe Hill, wrote personal letters to the governor and did everything in his power to save his life?

To whom did the Mesabe strikers turn first when they were arrested and who issued the first appeal for funds and support in their behalf? Ask Ettor, ask Carlo Tresca. If you do not know they can tell you.

I fought for them to a finish through the papers and in every way I knew how and I have letters from both of them[2] expressing the deepest thanks and sincerest gratitude in their own behalf and in behalf of their organization and the cause they were fighting for. I even had myself bitterly criticised in socialist circles for charging in some of my articles that the strike on the Mesabe range was not being supported because it was led by the I.W.W.

You seem to mourn over the alleged fact that I am withholding myself from the "Revolution's physical phenomena." I challenge you to name a single instance in which your I.W.W. has fought a fight of any account in which I have not given encouragement and support by all the means in my power. I have been trying for years to keep {up} with all the demands that have been made upon me and so often have I exceeded my physical strength that twice recently I have been on the verge of a complete nervous and physical collapse from overwork, and at this writing I am barely able from the same cause to stand on my feet and yet Bruce Rogers thinks the revolution is being "cheated" out of my services. In the name of God, what do you want? I have given my life to the working class and its struggles drop by drop, and almost to the last atom of my strength, and if this is not enough to satisfy you then I have absolutely nothing more to offer or to give.

Yours fraternally,
[Eugene V. Debs]

TLc, InTi, Debs Collection.

1. Joseph James Ettor and Arturo Giovannitti, leaders of the 1912 textile strike in Lawrence, Massachusetts, were charged with murder, and spent nearly a year in jail before their acquittal.

2. See Carlo Tresca to EVD, ca. September 18, 1916.

EVD to Adolph F. Germer

April 11, 1917
Terre Haute, Indiana

Adolph Germer,

Greetings of love and loyalty to my comrades in convention[1] assembled. I had intended being with you but am too ill to leave home. You have met at the most crucial hour in history. The future of our party, the hope of the workers is in your hands. I have full faith that you will rise to the demand and declare to the world in clear and unmistakable terms the attitude of the party toward war and toward the ruling class system which has forced this frightful catastrophe upon mankind.

Now is the time for the Socialist Party to prove itself and to make revolutionary history for the working class. There must be no fear, no evasion, and no compromise. The crisis forced upon us by the ruling class must be faced squarely by an aroused and determined working class. Our enemy is not abroad but within our {own} borders. The American plutocracy with its prostituted press and pulpit, wrapped up in the stars and stripes, and hypocritically proclaiming its hostility to Prussianism in Germany is at this very hour straining all its mighty energies to Prussianize the United States. Its program for the future is one of absolute military domination.

Conscription, enforced military service, a rigid censorship, espionage, military training of children in public schools, the guarding of industrial plants by federal troops, compulsary arbitration, the penalizing of strikes are all embraced in this arch-conspiracy of capitalist preparedness, which must be exposed, denounced and resisted to the limit if every jail in the land is choked with rebels and revolutionists.

The Socialist party as the exponent of international working class solidarity can have no concern in any ruling class war. To be consistent with its revolutionary character and true to its international principles and pledges it is morally bound to stand squarely against every war save and alone the war against war, the war of the world's enslaved and exploited workers against the world's enslaving and exploiting masters.

The convention, I feel confident, will not fail to give all possible consideration to the case of Tom Mooney and his associates and to the victims of the Everett massacre[2] now on trial at Seattle. I beg that no measure of sympathy or support to these outraged workers be overlooked. The infamy of the conviction of Mooney and his associates and of the cold-blooded murder of the union workers at Everett at the behest of the Lumber Trust must stir to hot resentment the blood of every delegate who sits in a socialist convention. Everything within the power of our party and our press must be done in behalf of these martyrs to our own class. To them we owe all loyalty and all support, but not one particle to the brutal exploiting class of which they are the victims.

Praying devoutly for the success of your deliberations[3] and the future of our party, I am with heart and soul

Yours for the Revolution,
Eugene V. Debs

TLc, InTI, Debs Collection.

1. The emergency convention of the Socialist party held in St. Louis from April 7 to April 12, 1917, was the most significant convention in the party's history. Called to determine the party's course in the event of the United States's entry into the war, the convention opened just one day after Congress's war declaration and the strong antiwar position it adopted was eventually seen as a turning point in the party's history.

2. Resolutions demanding a congressional investigation of the Mooney case and a federal investigation of the Everett case were passed on April 10, 1917. *Proceedings Emergency Convention of the Socialist Party . . . 1917*, 26-27.

3. The majority report, adopted by the emergency convention and subsequently by the membership in a referendum, called for, among other things, "unalterable opposition to the war," the refusal of workers to support it, "public opposition to the war," and propaganda against military training.

Bessie M. Womsley[1] to EVD

April 11, 1917
Pittsburgh, Pennsylvania

Dear Comrade Debs:

The enclosed will enlighten you regarding the situation here. There is little to be said, as the occurrence is a logical result of any, even passive opposition to the ruling powers.

If Comrade Prosser[2] has violated the law, it has been violated many times before by others, but, naturally, some one must pay the penalty. It has been said that Mr. Prosser ought to be starved out of Pittsburgh. He is strong politically, religiously, economically. The working class know him as a brother; he has the power to convince religious people that socialism and christianity are in harmony; and he is well known to be politically clean. Yesterday evening at the County Detective's office, where he was lodged until we secured the necessary bail, Chief of Detectives, Clark, said to him: "Too bad, Dr. Prosser, you were counted out at the election of County Commissioner." This is a pure and simple frame up. U.S. Assistant District Attorney told us this morning that not one attorney out of a hundred in the State knew of the existence of this law until war was declared. There are hundreds of others who could have been taken on this charge, but this one is a force in the community.[3]

I hope you will have good meetings that will arouse the people as never before. The rulers are chagrinned at the lack of recruits and are going the limit in oppressive measures against the people. None knows who will be the next victim.

"Be brave!"

Fraternally,
Bessie M. Womsley

TLS, InTI, Debs Collection.

1. Bessie M. Womsley is listed on the letterhead as secretary of the United People's Church in Pittsburgh. The city's directories during the period list her as either a secretary or a stenographer.

2. William A. Prosser (1868-1936) was the socialist pastor of the United People's Church, which he founded in 1913 following his dismissal as pastor of Ames Methodist Church in Pittsburgh. A delegate to and supporter of Charles Edward Russell at the Socialist party's 1912 convention, Prosser wrote to Debs on March 26, 1917, to tell him that he had dedicated "a little pamphlet" to Debs and to thank him "for your work for the cause of Social Democracy." Prosser had attended Debs's speech to a lyceum meeting in Pittsburgh on March 11, 1917.

3. Prosser's imprisonment for making an "anti-war speech" in Pittsburgh on April

7, 1917, and the public-nuisance law under which he was charged were described in
American Socialist, April 21, 1917.

Theodore Debs to George Bicknell

April 13, 1917
Terre Haute, Indiana

My dear Mr. Bicknell: —

Yours of the 7th. inst. has been received and carefully read. Gene
has just had to cancel every speaking engagement including his California trip on account of a threatened breakdown from long years
of overwork. We are now arranging for him to leave here, first to a
sanitarium and next a period of retirement that may cover a year.
The doctors have insisted that any further delay would be fatal and
Gene's present condition clearly indicates this to be the fact. He will
probably also resign his editorial position and everything else connected with it.

At this writing Gene is confined to his bed, utterly exhausted. I
have read your letter to him and talked over the matter of the date
at St. Peter[1] upon which so much seems to hang. Gene, as you well
know, would leave nothing undone to be of any service to you and
he feels as if to save you and Mr. Stephenson and your company from
embarrassment he should make a special effort to fill the St. Peter
engagement. He will therefore so shape his program that, unless
something untowardly should occur, he will fill that date. This will
be the only date that Gene will fill during the coming months. He
will have to make a special trip to do it and of course it is not now
known from what point he will have to travel to get there. As to the
exact date let it be July 4th. as originally scheduled. That will no
doubt suit the local people best of all and help them to make it a big
day and to realize hoped for results.

The local people or the Bureau will have to furnish the advertising
matter and do the advertising as we have had nothing to do with that
part of it under our present arrangement and have nothing in that
line on hand.

Another point that must be understood is that Gene will make his
speech and express his views upon the questions he discusses. The
need of saying this is suggested by the statement which appeared
recently, intended as a rebuke to La Follette, that from now on the
Chautauqua companies would only book "patriotic" speakers. Gene
is not of that stripe. He is patriotic alright but not of the kind of

lickspittles that bark obedience to the Wall Street masters. His kind of patriotism has brought upon him the charge from various sources that he is a traitor and he has made no attempt to deny it. That is the only way the gang that calls him that can compliment him. I do not doubt however that his speech will satisfy if not all at least the great bulk of the audience.

I hope we have met your desires and interests in the matter and that what is here suggested will be entirely satisfactory to you. Please let me know as soon as possible as we are to leave here at an early day. I am sending a carbon copy of this letter to Mr. Stephenson.

Affectionate regards to you and the warmest wishes for your success in all things.

Yours as ever,
[Theodore Debs]

TLc, InTI, Debs Collection.

1. St. Peter, Minnesota, where Debs was scheduled to speak at the Chautauqua on July 4, 1917. Juliet Strauss, "The Country Contributor" from Rockville, Indiana, was scheduled to speak at the same Chautauqua on "How Mother Gets Her Halo." *St. Paul, Minnesota Chautauqua, July 1-7, 1917,* brochure.

Jim Larkin[1] to EVD

April 13, 1917
St. Louis, Missouri

EUGENE DEBS
    PROMINENT OFFICIAL OF PARTY IT IS ALLEGED SAID IN COMMITTEE YOU ADVISED LEAVE MOONEY CASE ALONE KINDLY REPLY VITAL
JIM LARKIN

[EVD reply]
    ABSOLUTELY FALSE. HAVE ISSUED STRONG TELEGRAPHIC APPEAL TO CONVENTION TO DO EVERYTHING POSSIBLE IN SUPPORT OF MOONEY AND HIS ASSOCIATES. PLEASE ASCERTAIN IF THIS TELEGRAM WAS READ TO CONVENTION.[2]

E. V. DEBS

Telegram (with note by EVD in hand of Theodore Debs), InTI, Debs Collection.

1. James Larkin (1876-1947) came to the United States in 1914 following a stormy career in Ireland, where he had organized the Irish Transport and General Workers Union and in 1913 led the union in an eight-month strike against a lockout in Dublin. In the United States, Larkin sought funds for the TGWU, "Larkin's Union," as editor

of the *Irish Worker*, which was published in Chicago. After World War I, Larkin was sentenced to a ten-year prison term in New York for criminal syndicalism but served only three years before being released by Governor Al Smith.

2. Debs's telegram "sending greetings to the Convention and urging action against war" was read on April 11, 1917. *Proceedings . . . 1917*, 8.

Jim Larkin to EVD

April 13, 1917
St. Louis, Missouri

EUGENE DEBS

THANKS CLEARS AIR YOUR MESSAGE DELIVERED TO CONVENTION INSPIRATION RESULTS GLORIOUS

JIM [LARKIN]

Telegram, InTI, Debs Collection.

Claude G. Bowers to EVD

May 16, 1917
Fort Wayne, Indiana

My Dear Mr. Debs:—

I only learned of your illness and presence in Terre Haute an hour before time for the train and stopped at the house just to shake hands and say "Howdy." I was glad to find that you were able to get down to the office. I had intended sending you a copy of my story about you but had neglected it in the multiplicity of things here. A funny thing—my editorial page[1] has actually created something of a furor here and while I have been here but six weeks I am swamped with speaking engagements which together with the work on the paper— which I easily do in four hours daily—keeps me busy. It seems some one here sent you a copy. The demand for the Sunday papers on account of the "Kabbages and Kings" and the Lay Sermon[2] makes it impossible to keep copies in stock and we had to send to a village near by to get these four copies. If you ever get up here I want you to take dinner with me and see Pat—that's the kid. I hope you will

devote yourself to resting for a year. It will pay. With regards to Mrs
Debs and Theo.,

Cordially,
Claude G. Bowers

TLS, InTI, Debs Collection.

1. Bowers joined the *Fort Wayne* (Indiana) *Journal-Gazette* in March 1917.
2. "Kabbages and Kings" and "Lay Sermon" were two feature columns written
by Bowers for the Sunday edition of the *Journal-Gazette*.

Clarence A. Royse[1] to EVD

May 21, 1917
Terre Haute, Indiana

Dear Gene:
   I am sending you a copy of the book by Andre Cheradame[2] entitled
the "Pan-German Plot Exposed," which I have just finished reading.
It is a book of the utmost significance to my mind, and brings together
a lot of evidence which has been drifting into our minds gradually.
There is another book written by Naumann[3] entitled "Mitteleuropa,"
by an authoritative German, which sets forth the plot again. There
can be no possible question that this plot, complete as to all details,
was conceived many years ago in the minds of the German authorities,
and is now in process of fulfillment, and will undoubtedly be carried
out, and will place the German autocracy in absolute control not only
of Europe, but of America, and the rest of the world, unless by sheer
brute military power, her steps can be stayed. The profound danger
which attends a premature peace is clearly set forth in this book. No
matter how much any of us may hate war, we are bound to choose
between the sacrifice of war and the utter sacrifice of the principle
of democracy and the rights of man.
   It may be that you have already read this book, but if not, please
take time to do so, and then I trust that you will add your voice to
those of Russell, St. Clair, Ghent[4] and other American Socialists, in
an appeal to the Russian Socialists to stand fast in the struggle for
universal liberty.
   With most sincere regards, I am,

Yours very sincerely,
Clarence A. Royse

TLS, InTI, Debs Collection.

1. Clarence A. Royse was a Terre Haute attorney whose friendship with Debs dated back to the days of the Terre Haute Literary Society, of which both men were leading members.

2. André Chéradame (1871-1948) published a number of books on Pan-Germanism, including *The Pan-Germanism Plot Exposed*, which was published in 1917.

3. Joseph Frederick Naumann (1860-1919) was a German Protestant theologian, one of the founders of the National Socialist party in Germany, and a member of the Reichstag from 1907 to 1918. His book *Mitteleuropa*, which looked toward a Central European empire for Germany, was published in 1915.

4. Charles Edward Russell, Upton Sinclair, and William James Ghent were among scores of socialist intellectuals who repudiated the antiwar manifesto of the emergency convention in St. Louis.

Tom Mooney to EVD

May 21, 1917
San Francisco, California

EUGENE V. DEBS

SAN FRANCISCO AGAIN OUTRAGES JUSTICE   RENA MOONEY TRIAL[1] STARTED TODAY   CRIMINAL SCOUNDRELS EYCKERT[2] CUNAH[3] STAFF PROSECUTING INNOCENT WOMAN AND DEFENDING PERJURER OXMAN[4]   TAKING WARNING MORE UNDERWORLD PERJURY JURY BRIBING WILL TAKE PLACE TO SAVE THEIR POLITICAL SOCIAL STANDING   CHAMBER COMMERCE SOLIDLY BEHIND PROSECUTIONS   RAILROADING CONSPIRACY AGAINST LABOR   REAL FAIR TRIAL IMPOSSIBLE UNDER THESE CIRCUMSTANCES   MONSTER DEMONSTRATIONS PROTEST MEETINGS SHOULD ORGANIZE IMMEDIATELY   EXERT BEST EFFORTS TO PREVENT FURTHER PROSECUTIONS OUR CASES BY THESE CRIMINALS   NEW TRIAL FOR MYSELF YET UNDECIDED IN SPITE GLARING PERJURY EXPOSURE   THERE IS REAL DANGER AHEAD FOR DEFENSE   ENLARGE EDITE[D] TELEGRAM   GIVE SAME WIDEST POSSIBLE PUBLICITY[5] POSSIBLE.

TOM MOONEY

Telegram, InTI, Debs Collection.

1. Rena Herman Mooney (1878-1952) was a music teacher in San Francisco who was arrested with Tom Mooney and charged with complicity in throwing the bomb in the 1916 preparedness parade in San Francisco, which killed ten and injured scores of people. She was acquitted in her San Francisco trial, which ended on July 25, 1917, but under other murder indictments she spent altogether twenty-two months in jail before her release, after which she was a leader in the Mooney defense campaign.

2. Charles Marron Fickert (1873-1937) was the prosecuting attorney in the Mooney trials.

3. Edward A. Cunha was an assistant prosecuting attorney in Fickert's office.

4. Frank C. Oxman, the key prosecution witness in the Mooney trials, was tried in September 1917 for perjury in his Mooney-trial testimony and was acquitted.

5. In *Social Revolution* (successor to the *Rip-Saw*), Debs wrote editorials and articles on the Mooney case. "The Mooney Frame-Up Collapses" (May 1917); "Tom and Rena Mooney" (August 1917); and "They Shall Not Murder Tom Mooney" (October 1917) defended the Mooneys and called for financial aid for their legal defense.

Major General George Barnett[1] to EVD

May 29, 1917
Philadelphia, Pennsylvania

EUGENE V. DEBS

MAJOR GENERAL GEORGE BARNETT COMMANDING UNITED STATES MARINE CORPS ASKS YOUR GENEROUS SUPPORT OF MARINE CORPS NATIONAL RECRUITING WEEK JUNE TENTH TO SIXTEENTH AND THE CALL FOR FOUR THOUSAND ENLISTMENTS IN THE MARINES BY SATURDAY NIGHT AND REQUESTS FROM YOU A RINGING PATRIOTIC MESSAGE TO THE PEOPLE IN THE MARINE CORPS THE SOLDIER BRANCH OF THE NATIONS FIRST LINE OF DEFENSE THE AMERICAN MILITARY FORCE THAT HAS SHOWN THE WAY TO FIGHTING MEN SINCE SEVENTEEN HUNDRED NINETY EIGHT THAT HAS UPHELD THE HONOR OF THE FLAG THE WORLD OVER THE MINUTE MEN OF TODAY   WILL APPRECIATE YOUR MESSAGE BY WIRE TO U S MARINE CORPS PUBLICITY BUREAU   117 EAST 24 ST   NEW YORK

Telegram, InTI, Debs Collection.

1. George Barnett (1859-1930) was commandant of the U.S. Marine Corps from 1914 to 1921. Considering Debs's often-stated views on war in general and on the United States's entry into World War I in particular, the request for a recruiting message from him seems facetious or bizarre.

EVD to Clarence A. Royse

May 31, 1917
Terre Haute, Indiana

My dear Clarence Royse: —
    Absence from the city has belated my acknowledgment of the book you were kind enough to send me, with its friendly personal inscription, and the personal note that came with it. I shall be glad to give

the book careful reading and when we meet again I hope we may
have time to talk it over.

I may say in response to your suggestion that I have not one particle
of fear that German autocracy will ever destroy what little there is
of liberty and democracy in this country. Our own Rockefellers and
Morgans and their Roosevelts and Roots and other vassals too numerous to mention constitute the only menace to the liberties of the
American people.

Autocracy is autocracy and there are others besides that which
bears the German brand, and we do not have to go three thousand
miles away from home to fight it. If the German "barbarians" have
perpetrated any more brutal outrages upon the innocent than Rockefeller has upon the women and babies of Colorado I have yet to be
advised of it. And when it comes to brutal exploitation, England's
ruthless slaughter of the Boer farmers and the utter dispossession and
spoliation of these industrious and inoffensive people, to say nothing
of her unspeakable atrocities in India and Egypt, and Belgium's hellish
crimes in the Congo under the degenerate Leopold, and all for cold-
blooded robbery and plunder, will match anything that can be justly
charged against the "Pan-German Barbarians."

It seems strange to me that it should not appear strange to you
that the people here are all wrought up over the suffering children
in Belgium when thousands of babies are literally perishing from
starvation at their own doors. Let anyone come with me to the East
Side of New York and look upon those little living skeletons, thousands
of them, the products of our own beautiful democracy and "Christian"
civilization, and then tell me why they are so profoundly stirred about
the suffering of the little ones in France and Belgium and yet are
absolutely unconcerned about the starving children here at home.

According to the U. S. Government's own reports two-thirds of
the American people are today below a standard of decent living,
underfed, starved, body and soul in this, "the richest country on
earth," and to fight this monstrous wrong under our own flag is in
my opinion far more patriotic than to cross the Atlantic in the "pomp
and circumstance of war" for the alleged purpose of destroying the
"PanGerman Autocracy."

The "patriotic" American food pirates and their ilk, all of whom
are frantically for conscription and war and not one of whom will
take a chance of having his own paunch filled with leaden slugs,
constitute the "autocracy" which concerns me far more directly than
does the PanGerman. The utter infamy of the latter I do not for a
moment deny or attempt to extenuate, nor do I doubt that its fate
is sealed, but when it goes down it will be because it has been put

down by the German people and not because it has been destroyed by the no less autocratic powers and personalities represented by such servile tools and arch-enemies of the people as Elihu Root.

Thanking you warmly for your kindness and with all loving personal regards I am always,

Yours faithfully,
[Eugene V. Debs]

TLc, InTI, Debs Collection.

Herman Hulman[1] to EVD

[June 1917?]
Terre Haute, Indiana

Dear Mr. Debs—

I am sending you the letter you read last night. As a friend please read it again and later return it to me.

I would not feel I had done my duty to you as a friend with out this "final effort" to urge on you an open mind.

Your wonderful power will be for naught unless you "get in tune" with the world.

Your wonderful power will be unleashed for the good of mankind if you "get in tune" now.

Next week—next month will be too late.

Do not let that Convention[2] put you on record for Treason in this great crisis.

Mr. Bryan[3] was as strong against war as you were. He has lined up for our flag—so will every other open mind do the same.

Buy a liberty Bond—send word to our government that you offer your service, "in an open letter"—help Russia to brace up and consolidate her present position and then in your new gained sympathy and power you would really be of value to mankind.

With out that Community sympathy you are hopeless in your cause.

As a friend please accept my sincere respect and best wishes— please bear with me for it has taken courage to speak my mind. For your welfare and honor I have risked a great deal but I am sure our friendship will be strengthened through this interchange of mind & that you will honor, regardless, my sincerity as I do you.

Herman

You said last night, "if this war were a clean cut fight between

Autocracy and Democracy" that you would on the moment jump in and help.

My dear friend, this is a clean cut case between German autocracy and United States Democracy—no more & no less. Do not let the fact, that other nations, (both autocratic and Democratic), are also at war with the Autocracy we are fighting, confuse your mind. For get the details and accept the one Big thing—"We are at war with Autocracy."

Going along a little farther suppose Autocratic Germany should defeat England France Russia Italy and Japan. That then would leave Autocratic Germany fighting Democratic America *alone.* That would then be a clean cut case, with out the details—but then your help would *be too late.*

It is now or never for all of us. If we waver untill the guns are roaring around Terre Haute *We lose.*

Self preservation is the first law of nature—*do it now.*

ALS, InTI, Debs Collection.

1. Herman Hulman (1852-1922) succeeded his father in the operation of Hulman & Co., one of Terre Haute's major employers, for which Debs had worked as a clerk as a young man. As noted, Herman Hulman, Sr., who died in 1913, was a close friend of Debs and the author of an appreciative essay on Debs that was distributed during Debs's 1912 presidential campaign and 1916 congressional campaign.

2. The Socialist party emergency convention in St. Louis.

3. William Jennings Bryan, Wilson's secretary of state, resigned in 1915 following the sinking of the *Lusitania* to protest what he considered to be Wilson's unduly strong note to Germany and his lack of commitment to genuine neutrality. When the United States entered the war, Bryan announced his support of Wilson's policy.

Herman Hulman to EVD

June 13, 1917
Terre Haute, Indiana

My dear Debs
In conclusion let me say the experience of our conference has been pleasing. I am confident you understand my motive even though your convictions may yet stand. Let me again, tell you my motive was to advise you not to close the door against the American people. That was my motive, so that you might have a future life to work according to your light and reason for the welfare of mankind. To keep the door open you must accept the American flag and pledge Allegiance to it, and to the Republic for which it stands, indivisable, with liberty

and justice to all. I am not advocating any creed nor religion nor doctrine—the future will solve all that for us, if we but stand by this present symbol of liberty which is the best so far to be had.

We have not yet achieved freedom according to an Editorial in the T.H. Star[1] of this morning. We have not yet perfected democracy. But the nations now allied against the Central Empires are laboratories in which the problem may be solved, workshops in which the several parts of a better social structure may be fashioned. For the worlds sake liberals and democrats and socialists—all of them experimenters—must be free to go on with their great task. All the great minds we can get should remain in that general workshop or laboratory, to aid in the eventual perfecting of this great social & Economic machine, but remember the [that] our card of admission is the American flag. If you have that in your heart you may enter and remain at work. With out the American flag you may not enter. I want you to stick to the Ship. Henry Ford thought he could end the war with a peace mission of love and good will and failed.[2] He now has offered his factory to the U.S. Government for war purposes.

The German Kaiser has the hallucination that he is by devine right empowered to rule the world by force of arms. Others in the past have accepted love—good will—charity—as a devine right to obtain peace.

All such must fail because of the presumption of devine right in a mortal being. Such can not be. Only our Redeemer has come from God and He only that the sins of men should be forgiven because they know not what they do. Any further conception is sacriligious and not for mortal man to assume lest he seek the wrath of a just God.

My dear friend these are facts. To go away from facts leads as in the case of the German Kaiser into the life of a dreamer of and for Ideals impossible for mortal's to achieve—then on to hallucinations as to Devine power and then on to Eventual Weakening of mind & reason—the end of the German Kaiser. You have been frank with me and you have given no offense to me, personally. All you said is sacred with me as coming from friend to friend. I have been frank with you and I know I have given no offense to you personally.

Our convictions stand. Time will show who is right.

Your Friend
Herman

ALS, InTI, Debs Collection.

1. The editorial, "Stating the Issue Clearly" (*Terre Haute Star*, June 13, 1917), quoted at length Algie Simon's explanation of his decision to support the war on the

grounds that, while the Allies were not "perfect democracies," it was nonetheless necessary to support them against "German militarism."

2. With William Jennings Bryan and Thomas Edison waving from the pier, Henry Ford's peace ship, called variously *The Ark of Peace, Ship of Fools*, etc., sailed from New York on December 5, 1915. The 150 passengers, including Ford, hoped to bring the war to an end and "get the boys out of the trenches by Christmas." Ford's disappointment in the failure of the mission was compounded by the ridicule it met in the press.

EVD to Horace Traubel

June 27, 1917
Terre Haute, Indiana

My dear Horace:—

At the time you handed me the personally inscribed copy of that fine little work of Walling's on you and "Old Walt"[1] you intimated that you would like to have a word concerning it. At least I so understood you. I meant to have let you have this before now but have been sick and weak from overwork most of the time and much of my work has had to be neglected on that account.

I now take pleasure in enclosing what I hope may in some measure meet with your wishes. It is not well done, not nearly as well done as it ought to be, but it is about all I am capable of doing at this time. I have been away and have been picking up some but when one is sixty past and has been battered all his life he does not recover so readily from threatened nervous collapse. I shall soon be gone and when I return I hope to be fit to take hold again. I am going up into the pineries to run wild for awhile and see if I can't get some of the effects of civilization out of my system.

We received with emotions of great joy the announcement of Gertrude's[2] marriage. She is a wonderful girl and a daughter to be proud of and we are hoping that her wedded life may realize all her fondest dreams and her dearest aspirations.

Take to yourself and to Mrs. Traubel the full measure of our love and continue to remember me as

Yours always,
E. V. Debs

P.S. Of course you are at liberty to use this in the Conservator[3] or in any other manner that you may wish.

TLS, InTI, Debs Collection.

1. William English Walling's *Whitman and Traubel* was published in 1916.

2. Gertrude Traubel, who married Arthur C. Aalholm in July 1917, had as a young girl served as associate worker and later as associate editor of the *Conservator.*

3. Debs praised *Whitman and Traubel* as "a masterly review" of the work of the two men and said the book "should be read by every friend and admirer of these two eminent lovers of men and servants of humanity." *Conservator,* July 1917.

J. A. Poetz[1] to EVD

July 9, 1917
St. Peter, Minnesota

My dear Mr. Debs:

As President of the St. Peter Chautauqua, I wish to write an explanatory letter in regard to our cancellation for you to speak here on July 4th. The people of St. Peter and vicinity looked forward to your coming and your message with no small degree of satisfaction when, at the last moment, a few citizens, who are troubled with hysteria rather than patriotism, threw their hands in the air and protested against a Socialist performing on a Chautauqua platform. The decision of the Chautauqua Committee, backed up by assurances that a man of your prominence and distinction would not do or say anything to offend the most loyal American, would not satisfy them. They appealed to the State Safety Commission and that omnipotent body agreed that it would be dangerous to have you speak here. We argued with them that they had no constitutional right to deny free speech, but rather than subject you to any unpleasantness, we gave way in humble submission to their decree.

We all regret the incident very deeply, not so much on our account, but because of the injustice done you, namely — convicting you before you were heard. I heartily agree with one of your admirers who said that some people are so narrow that a German sharpshooter could not hit them ten feet away.

Dr. Bradley[2] spoke here today to a large audience and he paid you a fine tribute. It would have done your heart good to have heard the ovation the people gave you in spite of the fact that they have never seen nor heard you.

No doubt there will be an invitation extended to you to speak at

St. Peter some time in the future,³ and in justice to yourself and those
who want to hear you, I sincerely hope that you will come.

With kind regards and best wishes, I am

Yours truly,

J. A. Poetz

Pres. of St. Peter Chautauqua

TLS, InTI, Debs Collection.

1. Joseph A. Poetz (1869-1948) was a distinguished local druggist in St. Peter,
Minnesota, from 1896 to 1942, often referred to, according to his obituary (*St. Peter
Herald*, August 6, 1948), as "the dean of southern Minnesota pharmacists."

2. Preston Bradley (1888-1983) was an ordained Presbyterian minister when in
1912 he withdrew from that church and the following year founded the People's
Church, which met in various Chicago theatres until 1926, at which time the People's
Church building was completed. His lecture subject at the St. Peter Chautauqua, "Mist
and Marble," dealt with "the lasting worth of music, art, literature and religion." *St.
Peter Chautauqua 1917*, brochure.

3. In "Debs and Public Safety," the *American Socialist* (July 28, 1917) described
the cancellation of Debs's lecture in St. Peter and printed a letter from the St. Peter
Chautauqua to the Coit-Alber Chautauqua Bureau in Chicago requesting a speaker
who "will deliver Simon pure patriotic Americanism on July 4th."

EVD to Theodore Debs

July 11, 1917
[Green Lake, Minnesota]

My dear old Pard:

Could not have come to a finer place.¹ It's ideal, glorious & I
already feel like a new man. We're on the edge of a grand lake in a
fine cottage in a beautiful grove. We sleep outdoors in a screen ver-
anda. We fish & row & go bathing morning & evening. Mrs. Odell²
& her daughters cook everything I like & they are fine cooks. We
can't eat half the fish we catch. Lord, how I wish you & Gertrude &
Marguerite were here. We're outdoors all day long & when I get back
I'll be strong as a lion & active as a wild-cat—& then we'll make up
for lost time. Don't look for many letters. There's no P.O. & no railroad
here & I'm glad of it. The Odell family are God's own people—you'd
love them all on sight & they all send you their love. I'm going to do
no writing here except what is absolutely necessary—I'm going to
stay outdoors & get well.

It's cool here—cold in fact. Last night I slept under three blankets.
Give my love to Gertrude & Marguerite. Hope you're all chipper.

Don't write unless you have to. Give yourself to the outdoors all you can.

Rec'd bdle papers from you to day—Thanks!

Eugene V. Debs

ALS, InTI, Debs Collection.

1. On Green Lake, near Spicer, Minnesota, where Debs vacationed en route to the sanitarium at Boulder, Colorado.

2. Spurgeon Odell was president of a bank in Marshall, Minnesota, and was a longtime friend of Debs. During Debs's imprisonment after World War I, Odell attracted the attention of the War Department Military Intelligence Division, one of whose agents reported that Odell had "started a series of lectures all over the western country in Debs's behalf, for the purpose of collecting funds to be used in a campaign for the release of Debs from the federal prison." The agent added that "up-to-date Odell has been spending his own money." National Archives, Records of the War Department Military Intelligence Division, Record Group 165.

EVD to Theodore Debs

August 4, 1917
Denver, Colorado

My dear old Pard:

Your notes recd—also letters, papers etc. Will answer the letter from St. Peter Minn.[1]

Shall be here with the Sweets till Monday AM—then Comrade Sweet will go to Boulder with me. He knows the head doctor there & is confident I'll be greatly helped & in time fully restored!

I'm already improved, but my breathing is still difficult & my heart weak & that is what I'm expecting Boulder to correct for me & then I'll be myself again. Hope you & Gertrude & Margeurite had a fine time. I had a lovely time at the lake with the Odells. It is hot here but the nights are cool. I shall see Ed & Ranita[2] to-morrow. Love & kisses to you all.

Your loving old pard
Eugene

The Sweets send loving regards. My address is Genl Delivery Boulder Colo

ALS, InTI, Debs Collection.

1. See Joseph A. Poetz to EVD, July 9, 1917.
2. Edward and Ranita Toy, Gertrude Debs's brother and sister-in-law.

EVD to Theodore Debs

August 5, 1917
Boulder, Colorado

My dear Kude:
Arrived here 11 A.M. Sunday. Comrade Sweet came with me &
introduced me to the Sanitarium people & they are doing everything
possible for me. The place was crowded, not a room to be had, but
the Mgr. soon had a nice room for me. The weather here is ideal. I
slept under two blankets last night. It's just as high as Denver—about
5200 ft.
Am being thoroughly examined & it will take a week to complete
it. The Doctor put my heart under the X-Ray & said all my trouble
originates there. He found my heart dilated & a "leak" in it that is
small & he expects {it} will yield to rest & treatment. I'm on a special
diet—the doctor prescribes each meal each day & his wife sees that
it is served exactly according to directions. The doctor is giving me
the most careful attention. He says I'm a "strong man for 61" & he
expects to put me in shape to be of some use again. I could not have
come to a better place.
Address all mail to me *Care Sanitarium   Boulder   Colo.*
Pls. drop a few lines to *M.A. Enger*[1] *402 Ann St.   Willman   Minn.*
& say to him that his letter to Spicer reached there after I had left
or he would have heard from me—& that you are sorry I could not
comply with his request to address the Willman comrades. Send best
wishes etc. & some printed matter.
Called on Ed & Ranita at their lovely home Saturday P.M.—Missed
Ed, but {had} a delightful visit with Ranita. Will try to see them both
on the return trip. Ranita is certainly a fine soul—insisted on my
staying with them & resting for a month. This is a beautiful little
city—wish you were all here with me. Have not smoked since I've
been here.

Love & kisses to you all!
Gene

ALS, InTI, Debs Collection.

1. Martin A. Enger (1867-1943) was born in Toten, Norway, and emigrated to
the United States in 1889. A machinist, he worked for more than forty years on the
Great Northern Railroad. *Willmar* (Minnesota) *Weekly Tribune,* June 16, 1943.

EVD to Grace Keller

August 9, 1917
Boulder, Colorado

My dear Comrade:

You will understand, I am sure, with what deep regret I left your beautiful home[1] and the fine souls I met there to start on my Westward journey. Never can I forget those golden hours.

A thousand thanks to you, my dear comrade, for the loving kindness and sympathy and understanding which made possible the beautiful visit and the joyous hours which will linger in my memory "until it empties its urn into forgetfulness."

A few souls enoble a generation and glorify the whole race. You and Mabel[2] are pre-eminently of these as all must realize who come within the range of your fine influence. You have the spirit of the future. You have the vision of the coming day, and in your souls there is the radiance of the dawn.

It is at once your misfortune and your glory to have come into the world centuries in advance of your time. Many and severe are the penalties you will have to pay, but the service you render, the hopes you inspire, the promise you give to the future compensate a thousand fold for them all. May health and strength abide with you and may you live to completely realize your fondest hopes and dreams and aspirations.

Pardon these poorly written lines. Words can express but little of what is in my heart. You will know, I feel confident, how deeply grateful I am for your kindness and with what loving appreciation it will be remembered, and if I can ever be of service to you or reciprocate in any way I shall be happy indeed to have you command me.

I am improving here and believe I shall be greatly benefited if not entirely restored at this wonderful mountain retreat.

I hope this finds you and your loved ones well and joyful. The thought of you is always sweet and inspiriting to me. Happy am I to know that there are such hale and noble souls in the world.

Remember me kindly to Mr. Keller and to your beautiful daughter[3] and believe me with all love and good wishes

Yours faithfully
E. V. Debs

ALS, InTI, Debs Collection.

1. In St. Paul, Minnesota.
2. Mabel Dunlap Curry and Grace Keller became friends in Terre Haute before

Keller moved to St. Paul. In her memoir, *The Innocent Years*, Jean Keller Bouvier recalls her family's spending a year at Oxford with Charles and Mabel Curry and their family.

3. Eugene A. Keller and Jean Keller.

EVD to Theodore Debs

August 11, 1917
Boulder, Colorado

My dear old Pard:

Papers recd. OK—Thanks! Channing Sweet is coming to see me {early} next week. Had so many telephone calls & visitors that doctor {has ordered} that no one can see me. I'm sorry to deny myself but it has to be done. Had 15 visitors one day—some wanted me to make speeches, others to take drive with them etc etc.

I like this place more & more. I'm getting along slowly but nicely. My heart has subsided & I can now lie down & sleep. The first few days I couldn't lie down without choking. The course of treatment here is certainly building me up & I can feel the red blood getting back into my veins. I never knew until my examination was complete how near a dead man I really was. Had I waited any longer I would certainly have been beyond hope. The doctor here has brought this home to me as I never could see or understand it before.

I'm following the treatment to the letter & putting every atom of my willpower behind the treatment. The air, the diet, the massages, the electric bath, & rub-down & everything else combine to put me in the running again & I'm coming. I can feel that the tide has turned & that life is now coming instead of going.

Pls. send me an extra copy of the *August S.R.*[1]—You will find some stamps enclosed. Enclosed from Phil is answered. Put it in wastebasket. It is only for your information. I shall send him the Editorial matter direct from here & have so written him. Mrs. Clenenger[2] is still here & sends love to you all.

Shall beat you up on sight.

Love & kisses!
Gene

ALS, InTI, Debs Collection.

1. Debs continued to write editorials for *Social Revolution*, which succeeded *Rip-Saw* in March 1917.
2. Belle C. Clenenger, an adopted sister of Gertrude Debs.

EVD to Theodore Debs

August 12, 1917
[Boulder, Colorado]

My dear old Pard:

Your letter of the 9th came this morning. It is all to the good &
my heart is full of the sweetness & devotion of it. Each word touches
me & I'm filled and thrilled with the fine spirit of it.

Yes, I'm in the right place for once. I'm going to come as near
getting well & strong here as I could anywhere on earth. The Doctor
allows no one to telephone me or see me without first passing through
his hands. Otherwise I'd be swamped. The air is cool & bracing. Have
on my winter underwear & slept under heavy blankets. Take 75 drops
of Digitallis daily & a cup of special oil at night. That's all the medicine
I take. The rest is scientific treatment, diet & nature. Treatment three
times daily—every kind of bath, massage, electric accessory imagin-
able. The diet is meatless,—the doctor prescribes in detail *each meal
I eat each day.*

The examination is now completed. My blood is nearly normal—
all my organs are perfectly sound except my heart & that's dilated &
has a small leak due to strain & exhaustion—& that is what the doctor
is concentrating on. He gives me full encouragement & says I'll come
out OK but I must have rest & quiet & food & treatment & stick to
the program till we get the results. And so I'm following instructions
in every detail with the resolute will & determination to win the fight
& I'm going to do it, & when I do, old pard, get a steel armor for
your beak.

Ranita is dead anxious that I shall spend a month with them before
I return—she just begged me to rest with them & promised everything
if I would. She's a fine soul, a sweet & loyal girl you can't help but
love and I may spend a day or two or more with Ed & Ranita when
I leave here. Mrs. Clenenger wants me to go visiting with her to some
folks 8 miles from here on Tuesday but I'll have to decline for I've
made up my mind to stick to my treatment in every detail & not
depart from it if I can possibly help it. If I make an exception I'll
make another. All the points around here want me to visit & dine etc
etc & I've refused them all. Mrs. C. is a lovely woman & I see her &
chat with her everyday. She always sends all of you her love.

I most enjoyed the letter from Ryan Walker—he's a dandy good
scout.

Old man, I'm going to get on my pins right this time & when I do & get back we'll set things humming & make up with interest for lost time. Only wish you were here with me.

Love & kisses to you all.

Your old pard to a finish
Gene

ALS, InTI, Debs Collection.

EVD to Grace Keller

August 18, 1917
Boulder, Colorado

Dear Comrade Keller:

My heart opens to receive your message of love and cheer. A thousand thanks!

Happy memories cover a multitude of cares and vexations and happy anticipations give us wings and light up the skies of the future.

I can already see the log-cabin in the Northern woods, catch the odor of steak and onions, and hear the voices of sweet content mingling with the myriad melodies of the primeval wilderness. Spurgeon will certainly have to be one of the tribe. Love to you and a thousand happy wishes!

Faithfully,
E. V. Debs

ALS, InTI, Debs Collection.

EVD to Mabel Dunlap Curry

August 1917
Boulder, Colorado

Sayings of Great Women
Buck Up!—Juno[1]
    x x x
Give me liberty or take the consequences—Tail-Wagger
    x x x
Let me *rise* to the level of the Bottom dogs—Mrs. Wilson
    x x x
    I am laughing all to myself this morning as I hear you say, "I must

buck up." It used to be "perk up" but under the Junoistic revision it's "buck up," which is far more proletarian and expressive, and far better suited to the B. D. *Vocab.*

In the name of Juno and her iconoclasts image-smashers, convention-killers and rebels.

"*Let us 'buck up'* "!

We get mail here twice daily—8 AM & 4 PM—I'm all eyes when my letters are handed out to me. Wouldn't you be?

x x x

Through this black ink I can see pink.

x x x

You are hereby authorized to bid in every available share of the J.J. Light, Heat and Power stock. It's a great plant and I wish, if possible, to control the entire output.

x x x

Daily I take 75 drops of Digitallis & that's all the medicine there is in my treatment. The rest is nature and science. I was never more kindly treated than here. I was given one of the best rooms in the house at a time when not a room was to be had in main building or any of the many cottages, and the manager is *confidentially* making me a weekly discount of $10 on my bill.

The people here are mostly middle class, a few poor & a few rich, but they are all as kind as they can be and all want me to speak to them about socialism as soon as the doctor will consent to it.

I am now waiting for a "general statement" from the pink despot.

August 24th—First anniversary at the "*Grand.*" I'll be there with all my heart. Vividly is every minute detail of the day recalled. It's all golden in my memory—the sweetest, fairest, most radiant vision that ever filled the heart with reverence and rapture and exalted and glorified the soul of man.

x x x

Wednesday 2 PM

Two weeks ago to-night—10.30 Ah, me, "I hear intoned in every chime" etc.—At 10.30 I'll send my message of love across the intervening miles.

x x x

I have to prepare my copy for the September issue of Social Revolution this week.[2] Am now at work on it & must mail the last of it from here not later than Saturday. My copy to Pudgy, however, has precedence and must get to press on time.

Don't trust Walker.[3] He'll throw you when you least expect it. I know him & he knows me. He knows enough to be a Socialist, but lacks the man-hood to *be one*. He flukes at every crucial test. At last election, although a member of the Socialist party, he went over to Wilson and was kicked out of the Danville local as a traitor. He's plausible but utterly unreliable — has some brains but little conscience & no spine. He stuck to Mitchell to the very last because they are of a feather. I'd rather deal with a straight out crook or an avowed enemy.

x x x

There is a typical Texan here, tall, courtly, fine-looking. He has his beautiful wife and little daughter with him. He and I have taken a great liking to each other. He is an ex.-senator & a thoroughly fine fellow. At noon to-day while we were waiting for the elevator to take us up to dinner he whispered in my ear: "My dear Debs if this were not a bone-dry proposition, you and I would have a little good red *Lickaw* together, by Gad suh!" It required a genuine Texas gentleman to smack his lips and put the eloquent meaning into it he did. He says when I come to Houston next time he will see to it, *by Gad suh,* that nothing is lacking. But there'll be nothing from the bottle because I'm on the aqua chariot for good.

x x x

Joke on me: There's a double row of booths here where we undress for bath & massage. After I was served this P.M. I got into the wrong booth got into another man's underwear & was about to get into the rest of his clothes when I was halted by a roar of laughter from several onlookers who were "wise" to my mistake but said nothing until I was well into the other fellow's clothes. They insisted that my "break" called for a lubricant of the nature my Texas friend described as "good red *lickaw.*"

x x x

The enclosed cartoon from the Globe Democrat would doubtless have Clarence's[4] hearty approval. We just smile & wait.

x x x

My dear old friend Ma Lovejoy[5] of Girard, Kas has gone to her reward. My heart is deeply touched. She was 97 — born in the same year as my father. She was a pioneer abolitionist & suffragist — a grand, heroic soul. She loved me and I loved & venerated her. We had many a beautiful hour together at Girard. She called me her sweetheart & was never so happy as when we walked together arm in arm as we did as often as we had the chance. She kissed and blessed me a hundred times and her sweet memory will be sacred to me forever.

Love eternal!
Gene

ALS, InU, Lilly Library, Curry Papers.

1. In his extensive correspondence with Mrs. Curry, beginning at Boulder and continuing through his imprisonment following World War I, Debs addressed her as Juno and often signed his letters Ura, a reversed spelling of ARU, the American Railway Union.

2. In the February 1917 issue of *Rip-Saw*, Phil Wagner announced that, beginning with the March 1917 issue, *Rip-Saw* would become *Social Revolution*, "a name that is more suited to what the *Rip-Saw* really stands for."

3. John H. Walker, UMW leader in Illinois.

4. Possibly Clarence Royse, Debs's Terre Haute friend who disagreed with Debs on the issue of America's entry into the war.

5. F. Lovejoy, who served as a socialist deputy clerk in Crawford County (Girard), Kansas during Debs's tenure on the *Appeal* staff.

EVD to Mabel Dunlap Curry

[August 1917?]
Boulder, Colorado

Dearest Comrade Curry   Friday AM

The doctor has just examined my heart & pronounced me 100 per cent better than when I came.

I've just read your "playlet" with exceeding interest. It's a burning satire on the "culture" clubs & it would also fit the Red Cross to perfection. The characters are admirably drawn & there's no trouble to find their counterpart in real life. There's great suggestion of your versatile genius in this little farce—it amazes me. You're a dramatist & playwright as well as poet orator and literateur. In this "farce" you hit off a Rabelasian style the vast self-conceit and insanity which plume themselves on their "culture" in so many of the pompous little "clubs" that infest modern society.

By even mail I'm returning the M.S. Thank you so much for letting me see this choice bit of interest.

Have read with delight the fine report in the Plymouth paper of your brilliant success there. You certainly have captured the Plymouth people & they are yours in increasing numbers & devotion for the future. Be sure to save this for future reference—also the two clippings enclosed, one of which has you in glowing terms on both sides.

Hearty congratulations! This is but the beginning of the great things you are slated for, & with all my heart I am wishing you the completest realization of your rosiest dreams.

I do not suppose you saw my friend Charley Kellison[1] at Plymouth. He's a fine fellow & a particularly bright & progressive one, & I wish he might have come in personal touch with you.

Channing Sweet of Denver was here to see me yesterday & I had a very pleasant hour with him. He's coming again next week.

x x x

That "look" will never be given, nor that "word" ever spoken. Know, therefore, by these presents that your fate is sealed.

x x x

No, I do not wish you to be one bit less plain. I want you to write & say just what you have in your heart—& I shall always fully understand & perfectly appreciate your frankness.

x x x

My Texas friend who has a faculty of knowing all that goes on here has just given me in confidence a bit of information. The day I came here there was no room to be had—I am told—& I was not assigned a room until toward evening. Well, my friend informs me that after I came a meeting of the board of trustees was hastily called to see if I should be received as a guest & patient on account of my *irreligious views*. What do you think of that! You see this is a Seventh Day Adventist institution & prayer is uttered in the dining hall before every meal. You ought to have heard my Texas friend's comment. Well, it's different now & they couldn't possibly be kinder or treat me with greater consideration.

There's but one man here who don't speak to me—a would-be-plut who swells out & looks the other way when he sees me. It's quite amusing but he takes it very seriously.

The enclosed letter from Theo. you can destroy, so also the one from Philadelphia.

There are about 150 people here—they keep coming & going & there are some very fine men & women among them.

There's a woman just arrived—almost your exact figure & carriage. I sat on the lawn as she passed and from a rear view I would have declared it to be Juno—it startled me for a moment. I shall have to tell her that she reminded me of the most beautiful woman in the world—& that will probably not displease her.

That "limerick" on Adam was simply "erful." How could you! I never had any use for Adam but this made me feel sorry for him. Adam woke me up in the middle of the night & with tears in his voice

& quivering lip he asked, "What have I done to her?" It's certainly a "hum-dinger" of a limerick.

I'm so glad it has gotten cool at T.H. & hope most earnestly that you will be well rested before you enter upon your fall campaign.[2]

No, I don't see our love through "glasses any less rosy." On the contrary it grows sweeter, diviner with the passing days. July in the perspective is still more beautiful and sustaining and fills my heart with peace & my soul with rapture.

For all you have been to me through all these days & nights of trial I thank you with all my heart. Never can I forget your loyalty, your devotion, your love, which to me have been a source of unceasing inspiration.

Note that you now have a pair of desk scissors & you may look for me to present myself for surgical attention if I find myself the sudden victim of a gum-shoe conspirator.

Can fully appreciate your indignation at the cowardice & hypocrisy of the "patriots" who howl with the majority because they lack the backbone to stand alone. Your comment upon your visit to Mrs. Ruttgers [?] is to the point. Yes, you may well congratulate yourself upon your escape. You have at least the *spirit* of freedom, the essence of womanhood, & that is of priceless value.

I had my first war discussion here this morning. In the bathroom at the morning spray one of the gentlemen told of having been at a picture show in Boulder the night before & seeing "The Slacker"[3] presented. Then he went on to say that it was a *disgrace* to the country that 75 per cent of the drafted men had applied for exemption. I could not keep still. I asked him if he was going to war. He said no. Then I had a few swift jabs at him & the discussion ended. He will not come to me again about the "slacker."

The "King of the Pachyderm" will never relax his grasp. Have no fear—or rather entertain no hope. He will hold on with a relentless grip to the end. He has never been known to let go & he will certainly not in this case. Wisely submit, therefore, to the fates of the Pachyderm world.

My heart is touched by each loving word in your beautiful letter. You have been and are more to me than can ever be expressed in words. I wish it were in my power to be of some small service to you in return for all you have been to me.

I have a deep sense of you and your wonderful ability—your considerable mental, moral and spiritual endowment—your noble personality,—your superb worth and works—and with all my heart

I send you love and devotion and sincerest wishes for the complete fulfillment of your happiest dreams and your highest aspiration.

E. V. Debs

ALS, InU, Lilly Library, Curry Papers.

1. Charles Kellison (1850-1923) was a Plymouth, Indiana, attorney who had served with Debs as a Democratic member of the Indiana General Assembly in 1885. In a letter to Theodore Debs, February 14, 1920, Kellison described himself as "a friend of Gene's for over 30 years."

2. Curry was a leading organizer and speaker in the Indiana woman-suffrage campaign.

3. One of the chief goals of the film industry in World War I was to incite public opinion against men who failed to enlist or sought to evade the draft. An early example was Christy Cabanne's *The Slacker* (1917), a Metro film starring Emily Stevens and Walter Miller.

EVD to Mabel Dunlap Curry

August-September 1917
Boulder, Colorado

Dearest of Comrades: 5:30 AM Wednesday

How I wished your here this morning, this perfectly glorious morning is the sun-lit mountains! I'm just leaving for a walk up the canyon as far as the second ranch-house, about two miles, and I'll walk leisurely and commune with the peaks, and pick wild flowers, and think of the day near when I shall again have the joy of seeing your dear face and hearing the melody of your sweet voice.

Last eve at precisely nine I received a message that warmed my heart and I was made happy by the sweet serenade of "The Dance of Love."

You must try your very best to be strong these terrible days for we shall soon be needed when the madness is over—needed in all our strength as we never have been before. Go to see Theo. as often as you can for you are necessary to each other in these darkest and trying hours.

As for me, I'm dutifully taking Juno's prescription and shall soon be ready for the fray
for with both hands I'm stowing away.
Three marvelous B.M. every day.
With all my heart

Your loving comrade
Gene

ALS, InU, Lilly Library, Curry Papers.

EVD to Mabel Dunlap Curry

August-September 1917
[Boulder, Colorado]

My dear Comrade,   Thursday A.M.

You are a wonderful letter-writer. You put life and meaning in all your words—and they all blossom and are fragrant. Not a line of commonplace—there is none in your lofty, poetic soul. You think and feel and express yourself in terms of your own exaltation—and hence your sweet humility, your utter freedom of vanity and self-conceit.

So they smile at your "assiduity" at the writing table! I must confess that I do too and where you say so cheerily, "leave it to me," I smile again, and with all the confidence in the world in your {bland} assurance. And once more I smile as you tell me how closely you buzz about the mail-box at the evening hour—like the hornets here about their nests in the trees.

You remind me that I made no reference to what you said in the event of something happening to me. No, I did not, but it is not because I am insensible to its import. On the contrary, I was almost stunned by it, and have thought of it a hundred times since. I took it too seriously to write about for I know that you meant it, and the very thought of it pained me more than you can well understand. I meant to recall it to you on my return when I could express myself more fully and clearly than I could do by letter. You must not for a moment permit your thought to run in that channel and if you knew how it pained me I know you would not.

You do yourself and your destiny great injustice when you say that your future is largely behind you. How can you! Why, you are still in your girlhood. You have just years enough behind you to give you your "ripening," and all the beautiful rich, mellow years that are to come to glorious fruition are still before you and hold out to you lovingly their outstretched hands. And you will realize and fulfill your higher self in noble achievement that will inscribe your name where it will forever remain.

I have to report here weekly to Mrs. Wade, the lovely wife of the Doctor,[1] who is also Dietitian here, as to my increase, if any, in weight, and when I told her I had taken on four pounds she seemed as happy as Charlotte[2] building her raft on Buck [?] Lake.

Channing is frowning on my being indoors so much. "Cut out the letter writing and stay outdoors in the air and sunshine" is his imperative command, but I have succeeded in persuading him that certain matters (without indicating their specific nature) were too important to be neglected.

I would love to go to Mills,[3] as you suggest, after leaving here, and spend a few days with him, and see once more the "Honeymoon," the dear little cabin in which I lived and dreamed and greeted the sun and the peaks and the pines, but I fear that I shall be too "restless" by that time and eager to take the first train for home. Don't you think?

I note with joy that you had such a beautiful letter from Spurgeon and that he is to see Grace. These two fine souls will recognize themselves in each other the very instant they touch hands and look into each other's eyes. Congratulations to them and also to you. You are a great general and as such an adept in strategy.[4]

Those "heart-symptoms" disturb me. Can it be that you are the victim of psychic transferance? I hope not, but in any event you must not ignore these symptoms. They are the warnings of Mother Nature and you {must} try to keep calm (not easy for one with a soul these terrible days) and not allow your emotions to interfere with the functioning of that great, warm, wonderful heart.

The embargo goes off "fried chicken" the hour I leave here I know how gladly you'd cook with your own dear hands the welcoming dinner and from my heart I thank you for your kind thoughts and your sweet solicit[at]ion.

Don't allow your "enemies" to disturb the serenity of your mind a single moment. Please don't. That's one thing you are *too poor* to afford. They are too small and you are too big — you tower above them too far to even see them. Don't do yourself the injustice to hate them — they can't help it & they are, God knows, sufficiently punished. Think for a moment how favored you are of the gods, how infinitely rich you are, and you will pity the insects that true to their nature, buzz out to you the tribute of their envy and malice.

Your confidential whisper to "Mr. Debs" that you suspect that you are about to fall in love is certainly a matter of grave concern and a serious menace, I do not doubt, to your happiness and peace of mind. As to the remedy, I can not feel myself qualified to prescribe but it may be that "Junkintan" would relieve the more disagreeable symptoms and possibly restore you to a normal state.

Be wise and emulate the parrot. It is so much cheaper & pays so much better to whistle than to whine — to carol than to croak. Your life was made for music and mirth — for love and laughter and never should despondency or despair be allowed to distort or disfigure them.

I shall be glad to let you know as soon as I get the first word as to the probable time of my leaving here. I am steadily improving but

I still lack flesh and strength & these will come with the passing days and when you see me again you will see me whole and sound and ready for action.

Glad you stick to the swimming schedule. Don't let go of it Just what Juno needs & am sure the girls are right in observing Juno's "cuteness" in her bathing suit. By the way, where do you swim, at Branson's? I used to go there quite often.

I'm meditating to-day upon the problem of coast-wise navigation— and eager to pursue explorations into uncharted regions. I'm getting "restless," in fact, and may soon have to resort to a "general state- ment"—I realize the wisdom, however, of going slow and "feeling my way," and in this you may not disagree with me.

July: Elysium—First week in August: Gethsemene.

Some things would make it very uncomfortable for me if I'd let 'em. To eat three meals a day & sleep in a good bed at night & have everybody serve you & be kind to you, and do absolutely nothing in return, goes against my grain & makes me feel like a thief. My con- science stabs me every time I allow myself to think of it. Then it's hard for me to rest. I've never known how. God never intended that I should.

I can see the dawning of a glad New Way
Since I'm eating "Three Big Meals a Day"

Recd enclosed pathetic letter from dear Dague.[5] He's the most heroic soul I know. He's a veteran of the civil war & there he lost health & has been a ruined man ever since. But he keeps sweet as "The Dance of Love"—For 10 years he's been a *skeleton*, propped up in bed & yet he sends his wonderful messages to the world. You have no doubt read his writings. He has a popular style & is so sweet & persuasive that he's widely quoted. He's 77—his wife 78—both invalids, bedfast, & yet full of hope & cheer. Think of them & of us! How we are blessed! When the cloulds hang low let's think of them & take fresh heart.

Love and life and blessings manifold!
E. V. Debs

ALS, InU, Lilly Library, Curry Papers.

1. The letterhead of the Boulder Sanitarium listed L. H. Wade as a member of the medical staff.

2. Mabel Curry's daughter.

3. Enos Mills, at Estes Park, Colorado, where Debs had sought to recover his health in 1913.

4. Spurgeon Odell and Grace Keller were married in October 1922.

5. Robert Addison Dague (1840-1919) was for forty years editor and publisher of a series of radical papers in Creston, Iowa, and a frequent contributor of articles

and essays to the socialist press, particularly in *Miners' Magazine*, the *Milwaukee Leader*, and the *Melting Pot*. Debs praised one of Dague's booklets, *The Twentieth Century Bible*, in the *Melting Pot* of March 1918 and in the *Eye-Opener* on February 2, 1918.

EVD to Mabel Dunlap Curry

September 1917
Boulder Colorado

My dearest Comrade,   Wednesday P.M.

The muses were clustered about you and had you in full control when you penned the beautiful Sunday morning letter which reached me this morning. There are parts and passages and paragraphs as sweetly poetic as ever flowed from the inspired souls of "the masters." You have the divine afflatus and your winged steed has drunk deep at the Pierian springs. I hung entranced on your rhapsody to the "Black Currant Pie"—as sweet in sentiment as the pie is in fact. And that particular chef d'ouevre! "The past rises before me like a dream." No wonder your muses were captured and enraptured and have poured out their very souls in poetic panegyric. Like Pandora the gods and goddesses are now beginning to lavish their gifts upon Juno to make her immortally complete.

Bravo, Purdue letter! Just what I would have expected from you. They will "count you out" but they will respect you a thousand times more than they will the meek mercenaries who are counted in after receiving their orders and obeying them like trained spaniels.

You are *exactly* right also about New York. A month ago I said, go! Now I say, No! You have it all as clear as daylight. The campaign will be a frost and a fizzle like the one in Maine.[1] The war lords & their vassals have the floor—let them have it along with the "Conservative" and "respectable" leaders of the "suf." movement who stand in with the plutes in New York and the politicians in Washington, and who will not tolerate militancy, without which a movement such as the women's is as dead as a mummy. The press is already denouncing Dudley Field Malone[2] because he had honor enough to insist upon [one word illegible] the pledge made to the women instead of violating it once more as it has been violated since the days of Susan B. Anthony and Elizabeth Cady Stanton before the civil war.

It's alright for Jenne McGehe[3]—she's a militant socialist and they engaged her to appeal mainly to the socialists—she can say what she pleases and it will be charged to the socialists, so that they will get all the benefit {of} and none of the blame for her agitation. She will make her own speech & she may be arrested, but it's different, entirely different with you. You are supposed to be first & last a "suf" & {to} plead with the regulation meekness & mildness for "votes for women," but you would not be permitted to offend the war lords, the "*bellicose*" profiteers, or Wilson and the politicians. Let the Mrs. Stimsons and the Mrs. Coxes and Mrs. Coopers[4] and their stripe of both sexes, including the Stitt Wilsons[5] et al, run that campaign. It is their kind of campaign & you could not figure in it except through your emasculation and discredit it. The N.Y. campaign is dead from the start this year[6] — it will attract little attention & arouse no enthusiasm. You would be as sadly out of place in it as I would be in a Coca Cola campaign for the national beverage. Let the women who denounce the pickets & pander to the politicians, let them and their "patriotic" bunch have full control of that campaign and then take a snap-shot at them when the returns come in.

By the way, I sent a little message to you and Mrs. Ragsdale[7] through Art Baur.[8] Have you been in the drug store & has Art told you about it?

The sweetest & fattest & happiest little woman you ever saw has just come. I've named her Juno III. She's all dimples & diamonds & the best-natured little dumpling you ever saw. She's a perfect blond — combs her hair just like you, is just a shade shorter & several shades plumper, in fact plump enough to be called fat. Curiously she and Juno II and her sister have already become quite "charming" & form quite a vivacious group. The sister of Juno II is a striking beauty of a very rare type. She has titian hair, the softest brown eyes, clearest-cut features and perfect complexion with rosy red cheeks — she dresses in exquisite taste and is most gracious & charming in manner. They are all Southern women with conservative opinions but as sweet and gracious in manner as any I've ever met. But what are they all compared to the only Juno who o'erarches and outshines them as the azure skies do the haunts of hornets!

Note all you say in encouragement of my seeking companionship here among the ladies and appreciate it all, but I've no heart for it. Yes I did not even take that walk I wrote you about and now the dear lady is gone. I have not taken a walk with other than men since I've been here — *not once,* unless with some man & his wife. There has been and are lovely women here and I've met and chatted pleasantly with them and that is all. I've spent my time in my room and on the lawn alone or chatting with some "male" friends. But by far I've spent most of my time alone, keeping aloof as far as I could, writing and dreaming of the loves that fan my heart and that I'm yearning to see with an insistance [?] that {has} admitted of no other companionships.

My, but your personal orders as to the program for the return trip are rigid and fierce! I'm scared, I am, clean through & I confess it. I never before saw the smoke of wrath issuing from Juno's nostrils. Ye gods, save the poor Vagabond from his alleged Victim! Let him be burned in a seething lake of Coca Cola or drowned in a foaming torrent of Bero, but in Mercy's name spare him the fury of a bellicose suffragist scorned.

Junk and fiz—take out my soul and loaf,
and lead the orchestra at the Kaiserhof.

Please address me *here to and including Monday 24th*. On 25th, you can address me c/o Channing Sweet   1445 Gaylord St   Denver. After that (O.L.W.) *general delivery*   Chicago.

My love to you, my dearest comrade, and to all you love. I'm feeling fine to-day & getting better every day. The weather, day by day, is perfect, ideal, glorious. All the peaks are in full regale & I love 'em all & we smile back at each other every time we pass.

Faithfully & always yours
E. V. Debs

ALS, InU, Lilly Library, Curry Papers.

1. The woman-suffrage amendment was defeated in Maine, approved in New York in 1917.

2. Dudley Field Malone (1882-1950) was a leader of the anti-Tammany Democratic forces in New York; a close ally of Woodrow Wilson, who made Malone collector of the port of New York; and an early supporter of the NAACP, the woman-suffrage movement, and the American Civil Liberties Union. In 1917, Malone served as an attorney for sixteen militant suffragists who were jailed for picketing the Wilson White House. Although Wilson pardoned the women, Malone resigned his post as collector in New York in September 1917 in protest against the continuing arrest and imprisonment of other militant suffragists.

3. Jennie McGehe was a socialist organizer and writer from Denver who served as the *American Socialist* correspondent from Colorado before World War I and was a Colorado delegate to the Socialist party's emergency convention in St. Louis in 1917. Many of her articles in *American Socialist* dealt with the suffrage issue.

4. Kate Meehan Cox, wife of an Indiana State Normal School professor, and Stella C. Stimson, wife of a Terre Haute judge, were leaders of the Equal Franchise League of Terre Haute.

5. Jackson Stitt Wilson was the former socialist mayor of Berkeley, California, who left the Socialist party in 1917. He was an early supporter of the woman-suffrage movement.

6. After turning down the suffrage movement in 1915, New York voters on November 7, 1917, approved it with a 100,000-vote majority.

7. Nora B. Ragsdale was a reporter for the *Terre Haute Tribune*.

8. Debs's brother-in-law.

EVD to Ryan and Maude Walker

August-September 1917
Boulder, Colorado

My dearest "Ryanie" and "Maudie":

So glad to get that dear message from you even though it bore the inevitable pictorial libel that Ryanie's malicious devotion can never overlook. A thousand thanks! The very thought of you warms my blood and brightens my skies. I appreciate & love you more and more with the passing days and years.

Spurgen Odell is one of the very finest souls on earth. When I first met him at the close of a meeting I addressed he was President of the First National Bank at Marshall Minn. He and his beautiful wife and two lovely daughters are now members of the Socialist party. You and the Odells must meet and know each other and when you do you will all be infinitely the richer.

I'd love to see the new house—the creation of "Maudie's" artistic intellect and soul. I'll bet it's a dream and I can rest my tired body looking at it & into its cosy crannies even from here.

With all my heart I hope your brother will not have to go to the front—to hell. Gods, it boils my blood to think of it.

That's a *great* cartoon you have on the Red Cross.[1] *Great!* ! Your genius is at high tide in that bit of wonderful work. Bravo!

I'm here under treatment—the doctors don't want me to write but I can't resist you. I'm run down from overstrain & I've had to let go for a while. It's hard to be silent these fearful days & harder still to keep my blood cool. But I've got to or give up the ghost.

I'm getting along finely at this beautiful mountain resort & I'm going to get back my strength so I can go back into the fight where I belong.

Love eternal to you Dear Comrades!
E. V. Debs

ALS, TxU, Holl MSS.

1. Ryan Walker was cartoonist for the *New York Call* at the time. His "Henry Dubb" cartoon in the *Call* (July 29, 1917) portrayed the Red Cross aiding "Science" and a "Doctor" in their work of "patching up" wounded soldiers who were then "sent out to get killed again."

EVD to Theodore Debs

September 20, 1917
Boulder, Colorado

My dearest old Pard:

Yrs. 17th at hand. You're sound in every bit of your advice & I'm taken it to heart. I'm answering little correspondence & taking all possible rest — & *I'm getting along finely.* Feel better to-day than I have for five years. That's a fact. Thank you, my dear old pard, for each beautiful word. You're dear to me in the core of my heart. You've never flickered — don't know how, & old man I'd shed my last drop for you just as you would for me.

Gompers — Spargo — Simons! You have it right. Your picture is from life. Whew! And Bouck White![1] Jesus Christ! What next. But we'll stand all the stauncher — and to a finish if it's in hell!

Please strike from your memo the articles that appeared in Sept. S.R.[2] & make a new Memo. to add to the "Left-overs" the list enclosed. Don't address me here *after 24th.* Send me everything *to & including 24th* — then I'll advise you.

Love & kisses!

Yours eternally
Gene

ALS, InTI, Debs Collection.

1. John Spargo, Algie Simons, and Bouck White had either been expelled or resigned from the Socialist party to support the war; Samuel Gompers, of course, was labor's chief spokesman in the mobilization of labor for the war effort.

2. In addition to his editorials, Debs wrote "A Plea to Our Friends" for the September 1917 issue of *Social Revolution.* The plea was for additional financial support and new subscribers for the monthly.

EVD to Morris Hillquit

September 21, 1917
Boulder, Colorado

Dear Morris,

Congratulations upon your nomination![1] Wish I could lend you a hand. I'm keeping up with you through the press and need not say that my heart is with you and the comrades in New York in that splendid fight you are making to maintain our principles and our cause against the powerful opposition of the enemy.

These are trying days for socialists but there is nothing to despair of—on the contrary, the fiery ordeal through which it is now passing will be the making over of our movement.

Like Job's war-horse I can smell the battle from afar, and it distresses me not a little not to be on the firing line where I belong. But for a while yet I must remain in the "hospital camp" until I am whole again.

With socialist greetings and all good cheer I am

Yours for victory
Eugene V. Debs

No answer!

ALS, WHi, Hillquit Papers.

    1. As the Socialist party candidate for mayor of New York City in 1917, Morris Hillquit polled 21 percent of the votes in the November election on an antiwar platform.

Morris Hillquit to EVD

September 24, 1917
New York City

Dear Gene:

Notwithstanding your strict injunction of "No answer!" I could not resist the temptation of saying a few words in reply to your fine letter of September 21st. With the many thousands of your other comrades in the Socialist movement I am sincerely grieved that you should be temporarily unable to make your powerful voice heard just at this critical time. But I know that there are yet many important struggles ahead of us and that the most important service you can render the movement at this time is to take good care of yourself and to return to us strong, hale and hearty as soon as possible. In the meanwhile you may find comfort in the knowledge that the great mass of militant American Socialists are still inspired by your writings and that their hearts beat in unison with yours.

With kindest regards and affectionate greetings,

Faithfully yours,
Morris Hillquit

TLS, InTI, Debs Collection.

EVD to Robert M. La Follette

October 15, 1917
Terre Haute, Indiana

My dear Senator LaFollette:

Several times I have been at the point of writing or wiring you but hesitated knowing how completely engrossed you were and what little time your enemies left you to yourself. I only want to say to you, and that as briefly as possible, what is in the heart of millions. You have had the central part in the great drama of the past few weeks[1] and you have borne yourself with absolute rectitude, such uncompromising courage, such lofty bearing as to win the admiration and love of the honest people not only of your own country but of the whole civilized world. It is to your glory that the plutocracy of Wall Street is seeking to oust you from its senate and if it succeeds your triumph and vindication will be complete and your political immortality secure. All honor to you for your courage, your manhood and your devotion to the cause of the people in the face of the bitterest and most brutal persecution to which the lawless looters of this nation and their prostitute press ever subjected a faithful public servant.

The people are with you in every hour and every moment of your trial and history will do you justice.

Believe me with all loyal appreciation and unfaltering devotion,

Yours for the people,
Eugene V. Debs

No answer!

TLS, DLC, MSS Division, La Follette Family Collection.

1. As noted, La Follette's opposition to the war and his defense of free speech during wartime and of Congress's right to control war policy led to a massive attack upon him, including an effort to remove him from the Senate, but he became at the same time a hero in the socialist press, which reprinted his speeches and his editorials in *La Follette's Weekly*. *American Socialist*, July 28, 1917; September 1, 1917.

Scott Nearing to EVD

October 18, 1917
New York City

Dear Comrade Debs:

Do you know of anyone prominent among the railroad workers who would be willing to act on our committee? We need a transport

worker and do not know exactly where to lay our hands on one.
With best wishes, I am,

Yours truly,
PEOPLE'S COUNCIL OF AMERICA.[1]
Scott Nearing[2]
Chairman   Executive Committee.

TLS, InTI, Debs Collection.

1. At a conference in Chicago on July 7 and 8, 1917, the People's Council of America for Democracy and Peace was launched to preserve democracy during the war, guarantee public voice in the terms of peace, and bring the war to an end at the earliest possible time. With headquarters in New York City, the People's Council became a national umbrella for local councils that were formed in scores of cities by 1918.

2. Scott Nearing (1883-1983) taught economics at Swarthmore and the Wharton School at the University of Pennsylvania until 1915, when he was dismissed for his radical views. One of Nearing's pamphlets, *The Great Madness*, published by the Rand School in 1917, led to his indictment for conspiracy to cause insubordination in the armed forces, but he was finally acquitted. During his long career, Nearing was the author of dozens of books on socialism, economics, the Soviet Union, and back-to-the-land issues and topics, and of several autobiographical volumes, and in his later years he became a symbol of the back-to-the-land movement.

William D. Haywood to EVD

November 2, 1917
Chicago, Illinois

Dear Comrade: —

We are soliciting your active co-operation in regard to the defense of our many class war prisoners, 116 men being under arrest at this time.[1]

Anything you may be able to do in the way of organizing a Non-partisan Defense League will be greatly appreciated. The idea is to have this Nonpartisan League work in conjunction with the General Defense Committee[2] of the I.W.W., here in Chicago.

Anticipating your support, and with best wishes, I remain

Yours for Industrial Freedom,
Wm D Haywood
J. A. L.

TLS, InTI, Debs Collection.

1. In September 1917 a federal grand jury in Chicago returned an indictment against 114 members of the Industrial Workers of the World, charging them with

nearly 10,000 specific crimes as part of a conspiracy to interfere with the war program. Their trial, presided over in Chicago from April to September 1918 by Judge Kenesaw Mountain Landis, resulted in 93 convictions and sentences ranging up to twenty years' imprisonment for some of the defendants, including Haywood. While free on bond in 1921, Haywood escaped to the Soviet Union, where he remained until his death in 1928.

2. The General Defense Committee in Chicago attempted to coordinate the legal defense in the various trials of "over one thousand members of the IWW who are in jails across the country." *International Socialist Review,* February 1918.

Pervuninsky Feodor[1] to EVD

November 5, 1917
16th Siberian Battery

Willing to get more acquainted with the revolutionary movement in 1905–6 (in Russia) and having no means for that I beg to ask the Committee of Russian Socialists in America to send suitable books to my detention camp or notify the Russian organization (in Russia) for the relief of war prisoners.

Pervuninsky Feodor
Germany War Prisoner #13318

ALS (with translation), InTI, Debs Collection.

1. Written in Russian, Pervuninsky Feodor's note was addressed to "Hon. Eugene V. Debs, National Secretary North American Socialist Party, Omaha, Nebraska, USA."

Amos R. E. Pinchot[1] to Theodore Debs

November 8, 1917
New York City

My dear Mr. Debs:

Let me thank you for your very kind letter of November 2nd. I am very glad to send you four additional copies of my letter to the Conference Committee of the Senate and House,[2] gratis. Will you please acknowledge receipt of same, as the mails are very irregular.

With kindest regards, I am

Sincerely yours,
Amos Pinchot

TLS, InTI, Debs Collection.

1. Amos Richards Eno Pinchot (1873-1944) became active and interested in politics in 1909 when his brother, Gifford Pinchot, who was chief of the United States Forest Service, accused Secretary of the Interior Richard A. Ballinger of favoring corporate interests at the expense of the government's conservation program. The Ballinger-Pinchot Controversy, which resulted in Gifford Pinchot's removal from office, was the beginning of a controversial public career for Amos Pinchot, who sought to break the power of industrial monopolies in America, first as a Theodore Roosevelt supporter in 1912, then as a Wilson supporter in 1916, and finally as a supporter of Morris Hillquit's bid to become mayor of New York as the Socialist party candidate in 1917. Opposed to the war and its accompanying suppression of civil rights, Pinchot was a founder in 1917 of the National Civil Liberties Bureau, predecessor of the American Civil Liberties Union, of whose executive committee he remained a member until his death.

When Debs's conviction was upheld by the United States Supreme Court in 1919, Pinchot wrote "Debs Sent to Prison to Protect Present System" (*Appeal*, April 26, 1919), in which he described Debs as "a patriot in the highest sense, a man of marvelous courage, unselfishness, and purity of courage" who was being imprisoned because he was "a dangerous agitator" who demanded more justice than "the ruling classes are willing to concede."

2. Written in his role as chairman of the American Union for a Democratic Peace, Pinchot's letter urged "a peace . . . without annexations, indemnities, or economic reprisals following the war." *New York Times*, November 13, 1917.

Theodore Debs to Joseph E. Cohen

November 12, 1917
Terre Haute, Indiana

My dear Joe: —

As Gene is not yet able to take up his correspondence I am having to acknowledge your very kind letter which I do with exceeding pleasure. Gene has been in a sanitarium for some time, slowly improving, but as the threat of nervous prostration and a physical breakdown was the third one and also the most serious, it is taking considerable time to recover sufficiently to enable him to take up his work again. You can well imagine that no one regrets this more than he at this particular time when all his heart has been at the front with the comrades who are bearing the banner through these trying days, but it could not be helped and for a time yet he is compelled under strict orders from his doctors to keep quiet and free from excitement so that he may finally recover his strength and vigor and resume his activities in the movement. At the time he let go he was pretty nearly sapped of his vitality and the wonder to me now is that there was enough recuperative energy left to bring him back to himself again.

It is with deep interest that I note your suggestion that Gene write his "Reminiscences." Coming from you this suggestion has peculiar appeal to me as it will also have to Gene. I know he has always been averse to writing about himself believing as he does with Ingersoll that "a life should not be written until it has been lived." In other words, Gene's feeling is that if he has done anything worth writing about he prefers leaving it to some one else to write after his work is finished.

Still I can appreciate your suggestion as I can also the object you have in view and the motive which inspired the suggestion. An interesting volume or two could doubtless be written of Gene's experiences in the movement and your suggestion is certainly worthy of the consideration I am sure he will give it when I bring your letter to his attention. Let me thank you as warmly as may be for the warm personal feeling which prompted you to make this comradely suggestion. I need not assure you that it will be fully appreciated by Gene.

When you see or write to George please remember us to him with affectionate regards and kindly extend the same to your father and all of your household.

Yours loyally,
Theodore Debs

TLS, NNU Tam, Debs Collection.

EVD to Secretary, People's College[1]

November 13, 1917
Terre Haute, Indiana

Dear Comrade: —
For some time, owing to ill health, I have been unable to keep up my regular work, and while I am improving and expect to recover fully and resume my former activities, for the present I am obliged to withdraw from official service of every kind and I therefore tender my resignation as president, chancellor, and member of the Advisory Board of the People's College, the same to take effect at once. Please see that this resignation is placed in the proper hands for action.

It has long been a matter of regret to me that I have been unable to give the College in which I have felt so deep an interest the personal attention due it but I have been so constantly overburdened with other duties that with the best will I have found it impossible to do so. Under these circumstances I feel that I can no longer in justice to the College or to myself withhold my resignation, and that it is my duty to sever all official connection with the College.

Allow me to take this occasion to thank all the comrades at the College for the kindness and consideration they have always shown me and earnestly wishing for the College a future of increasing usefulness and success I remain,

Yours fraternally,
[Eugene V. Debs]

TLc, InTI, Debs Collection.

1. The *People's College News* for October 1917 listed Laura L. Reeds as secretary of the college.

Adolph F. Germer to Theodore Debs

November 19, 1917
Chicago, Illinois

Dear Theodore:

I am glad to know that Gene is on the road to recovery. I know his restless nature and I hope you will succeed in "taming him" until he is himself again. When we were in West Virginia several years ago, he used to sit up and read all night and be on his feet all day. I tried to send him to bed in order to get some rest, and I always got his faithful promise to do so, but whenever I would wake up at night, I would find him still reading. As you say, he is not as young as he was and does not possess the vitality of years ago.

I saw the two articles he sent in and I know he will not recognize them when he finds them in print.[1] The scalping of those articles is not due to our disagreement with what Gene has to say. I agree to every word and nothing would give me greater pleasure than to publish them just as they were sent in, but since we are making the world safe for democracy, the editor in chief of the Socialist Press, is a fellow from Texas, A.S. Burleson.[2] Whenever a Socialist editor prints anything that is distasteful to the fancy of the Texas landlord, the paper is put out of commission. In order to obviate that we are obliged to get out a sort of milk and water sheet.

We have only a few copies of the "Call-to-Action"[3] left. Under separate cover, we are sending all we can spare. We are preserving this little choice bit of history and oratory for the next congressional campaign. If I have my way, we will have millions of copies printed and sent to every corner of the United States. As per your request, we are also sending you what copies we can spare of "Woman and War."[4]

We are still working on the Stanley Clark case,[5] but so far have met with no success, I was in hopes of hearing from his Texas friends offering to furnish the security for the bondsmen, but to date no word has been received. One of Clark's friends has been in the City for some time and he drops in to see us several times a day. I ought to get some word one way or the other from Texas in the next few days.

With all good wishes, I remain,

Fraternally yours,
Adolph F. Germer
Executive Secretary.

TLS, InTI, Debs Collection.

1. Debs's "Criminal and Cowardly Capitalism," which appeared in the party paper *Eye-Opener* on November 24, 1917, was a blistering attack on "the lynch fiends and mob leaders" set loose by wartime passion; in "Socialist Election Returns" (*Eye-Opener*, December 1, 1917), he claimed that important socialist gains in the November 1917 elections had been "suppressed by the capitalist press."

2. Albert Sidney Burleson (1863-1937), who served as Woodrow Wilson's post-master general from 1913 to 1921, interpreted the wartime statutes to ban from the mail and withdraw mailing privileges from scores of socialist publications, many of which never resumed publication.

3. "Call to Action" was sold by the party as an "organizational leaflet" in its "Seed Catalogue." *Eye-Opener*, November 17, 1917.

4. Debs's "Woman and War," another "organizational leaflet," originally appeared in *Rip-Saw*, November 1914.

5. In "Stanley J. Clark's Arrest" (*Social Revolution*, January 1918), Debs described Clark's arrest and imprisonment in Chicago for "seditious utterance against the government" and asked readers to send contributions to Germer for "the Stanley Clark Defense Fund."

EVD to Robert M. La Follette

November 26, 1917
Terre Haute, Indiana

My dear Senator La Follette: —

Please have your secretary send me, if entirely convenient, half a dozen copies of your speech in the senate on "Free Speech and the Right of Congress to Declare the Objects of the War." I could use a dozen copies to good advantage and am quite willing to remit for them. If the supply is limited I should at least like a single copy for my library.

Permit me to congratulate you heartily upon this supremely patriotic and masterful expression. It is one of the few really great speeches ever made in congress and will take its place among the classic orations of the age and one of the most eloquent, fearless, forceful appeals ever made for human rights and human freedom. The facts you marshalled in deadly array, the historic precedents you cited in support of your convincing, conclusive argument and your masterly, incisive logic made your speech absolutely unanswerable, and it is not at all strange that it has been tabooed and as far as possible suppressed by the prostituted sheets of the Wall street robbers.

The very kind and appreciative letter from you in answer to mine touched me deeply and I thank you from my heart for each word it contains.

Today begins, according to the press dispatches, the investigation by the senate of your alleged "treasonable" utterance at St. Paul[1] which still rings in the hearts of millions. Be proud of this exceptional distinction. It is the only possible tribute the arch-tratiors to the nation could pay you. If you needed to be sustained from without in this hour of trial you would surely find sufficient encouragement and support in the fact that the hearts of the liberty-loving millions are with you.

If the plutocratic profiteers, the most shameless robbers in history, are "patriots" under their own regime then can you well afford to be branded as a "traitor" and be proud of it.

The impudent, insulting investigation of which you are the intended victim is discredited in advance, bearing as it does upon its very face the stamp of robber-class persecution, and its only effect will be to re-act with deadly effect upon its criminal authors and add fresh lustre to your honor and fame.

Please do not take the time to answer this. You need every moment for the hounds that are baying at your heels.

Believe me, dear senator, with every good wish,

Yours faithfully,
Eugene V. Debs

TLS, DLC, MSS Division, La Follette Family Collection.

1. La Follette's statement in a speech before the Non-Partisan League in St. Paul, Minnesota, on September 20, 1917, that the *Lusitania* was carrying munitions of war at the time of its sinking was the basis of an investigation by the Senate Committee on Privileges and Elections of La Follette's loyalty and the various demands for his

expulsion. After more than a year of hearings (and acknowledgment by the press services that La Follette had been misquoted), La Follette was exonerated on January 17, 1919. *New York Times*, January 18, 1919.

EVD to William F. Gable

December 8, 1917
Terre Haute, Indiana

My very dear Gable: —

It is a matter of wonder to me that you, one of the busiest of men I know, with every moment mortgaged far in advance, can still find time to write the beautiful messages which come to me bearing your loving remembrance. The one just at hand by you and Horace jointly brings joy to my heart and the mist to my eyes. I can fancy you and Horace in a conspiracy of love, with Shollar[1] a willing accomplice, and see the sparkle in your eyes and the smile in your faces as you hit upon the surest way of sending a thrill of joy to the heart of your intended victim.

I caught the full import of your loving communion and feasted with your royal quartette in love and fellowship. In these days when humanity has reverted to savagery and men's ruling passion is to cut one another's throats, widow one another's wives, and convert the blooming earth into a hideous shambles, it is a blessed relief, a balm to the soul to think of you and Horace and other actual human beings who dare to stand erect and fearless with the threatening multitude raging about you and to affirm and re-affirm your faith in the divinity of human nature and in the ultimate triumph of love in the world.

My brother joins me in reciprocating with our hearts in our words the precious greeting you send and in wishing for you and yours the complete fulfillment of life's rosiest dreams.

Yours always,
Eugene V. Debs

TLS, CtY.

1. Frederick J. Shollar was a Philadelphia socialist, friend of Horace Traubel, and Socialist party candidate for governor of Pennsylvania in 1914.

Harold L. Varney[1] to EVD

December 12, 1917
St. Louis, Missouri

Fellow Worker, —

I am sure that you will be surprised at what I, a stranger to you, am about to write, but I feel that it will not be wholly without interest and effect.

I am a member of the I.W.W. of some six years standing and a National Organizer; One of the only two National Organizers in fact, who were not included in the indictment. I have often regretted that you were not with us, in the I.W.W. as I have felt that you possess the personality which could make the I.W.W. a titanic force in this country. But I have been able to realize that perhaps the time was not ripe. Our membership and activities have been primarily directed toward the migratory workers and it requires a peculiar psychology to successfully lead such a movement. This personality, Haywood possesses and, as our General Secretary he has certainly made good.

A great crisis has suddenly engulfed us, a crisis which cancels all our previous attitudes. The persecutions, the suppression of constitutional rights and the developments in Russia are all challenges for each of us to act in this crisis to the full extent of our powers and to leave all past prejudices and differences behind us. We must act or socialism will be beaten to death. We must act or our Russian comrades will be annihilated.

In the labor movement, the I.W.W. is the backbone of the revolution. I do not say this on account of any superiority of their theory or tactics. What I mean to imply is that the I.W.W. has the real men in it. Men who fear nothing. Men who know no limit of sacrifice. Roughly speaking, there are probably 100,000 of us. If anything, more. I believe that if the I.W.W. will step forward at this time, this 100,000 will grow into an army. There is a certain magic in the name which commands the loyalty of the brave and rough element of labor.

The government realized the menace of the I.W.W. and concentrated its attacks upon us. The result is well known. Haywood and 165 others in prison. All the old time leaders who could command the support of the membership, locked up. Many hall[s] closed. In spite of that fact, new members have been rushing into the I.W.W. by the hundreds. Much of this increase is from the S.P. There are thousands on the outside waiting for a psychological moment to throw in their lot with us. The old scissor bill element,[2] driven to desperation by the war, would act if the I.W.W. showed the qualities of leadership, but in this emergency, we are without a leader. Haywood is in jail and there seems little hope for his release. And the mass are so composed, as you full well know, that they will not act without a leader.

Fellow Worker Debs, I have talked this over with many of our men. They agree with me. We want you to come back into the I.W.W. It is the greatest opportunity of yours and our lives. I believe we can make history. With you at our head, the workers will rally to us by the thousands. You have the power to cement us together with the radical Hebrew Trades of N.Y.[3] There are great things which we can do among the U.M.W. of A. And then, there is always the chance of a sudden crisis arising when that group will assume the leadership which is prepared to snatch it. Fellow Worker Debs, will you consider this. I am speaking to you out of my full heart. I love the I.W.W. and thousands more like me do. I have given to it the best that is in me and I don't want to see it crushed. I believe you are the man who can save us. If you will come in, I will make every arrangement with the volunteers who are now in charge in Chicago. Will you let me know your decision soon?

Yours for the One Big Union,
Harold L. Varney
2512a Prairie Ave.
St. Louis, Mo.

TLS, InTI, Debs Collection.

1. Harold Lord Varney was described, in an agent's report to the War Department Military Intelligence Division dated January 2, 1918, as "organizer of the People's Council" in St. Louis, a "soap-boxer, organizer, and agitator," who was converting southern Illinois miners to the People's Council antiwar position. Varney's novel *Revolt*, described in the *New York Call* (May 25, 1919) as "a pen picture of the American Labor Movement," was published in 1919.

2. In Ryan Walker's popular cartoon strip "Henry Dubb," a "scissor bill" was a worker who agreed that workers should "get guns and learn to shoot for the good of the boss." *American Socialist*, December 11, 1915. In Wobbly slang, the "scissorbill" was either a person whose income was not from wages or, more commonly, a worker who lacked class consciousness or would not join a union.

3. Founded in 1888, the United Hebrew Trades Union in New York was composed chiefly of Jewish garment workers. The union was strongly socialist in leadership and membership.

EVD to Ruth Le Prade[1]

December 13, 1917
Terre Haute, Indiana

My dear Comrade Ruth:—

Very sorry am I to note in Guy Bogart's column in the World[2] your illness and I feel that this word of sympathy and cheer and love must go from my heart to yours in this hour of your affliction. I am not surprised to learn that you have for the moment succumbed to the overwhelming forces of hate and destruction which have been beating relentlessly upon your great and tender soul these many months past. With your infinite capacity for sympathy and suffering, equal to your capacity for love and tenderness, your comrades may well imagine how your frail body, in spite of your wonderful poise and moral heroism, has finally given way to the cruel shocks it has sustained in these frightful days when humanity has seemed bent upon brutalizing itself to the last degree and annihilating itself from the face of the earth.

But you will and must grow better and soon be your whole precious and promising self again. Please do allow yourself the necessary time. There is so very much waiting for your soul to vision and your hands to do. You are the inspiration and hope of thousands upon thousands who love you and look to you and yet may never see you.

I am indebted to dear Comrade Guy for the privilege of sending you this missive of affection and good cheer. He too is a gifted and beautiful comrade and we love him well. He was once our neighbor[3] but though he is miles away he is still and always will be near to our hearts.

Mrs. Debs and my brother and his family and all of our household join in love and a thousand prosperities to you and to all you hold dear and I am,

Yours always,
Eugene V. Debs

TLS, CLSU, Poets Garden Collection.

1. Ruth Le Prade (1895-1969) was a Los Angeles poet, described by Harold H. Story in his *Memoirs* (UCLA, Oral History Program, 1967) as a protégée of Edwin Markham, and Socialist party activist who assembled and edited the materials for *Debs and the Poets*, a collection of poems and prose tributes to Debs by many of the leading poets and writers of the time. Upton Sinclair provided major financing for the pub-

lication of the volume. Le Prade and Harold Story married in 1919 and were divorced
in 1930. Their son was named Eugene.
    2. *Oakland* (California) *World.*
    3. In Terre Haute.

EVD to Louis Kopelin

December 14, 1917
Terre Haute, Indiana

Dear Comrade Louie: —
    I refuse to believe the press dispatch in three lines announcing that
the Appeal had become a capitalist war organ. The current issue of
the Appeal[1] just received confirms the report. The news to me is
shocking and incredible but I am not altogether unused to such practices. J.A. Wayland would, I think, sit up in his grave if this report
came to his ears.
    You have been kind enough to send us weekly a dozen Appeals to
use in connection with our correspondence and we have been trying
to make each copy serve the paper and the cause. Please discontinue
these. We will have no use for a so-called socialist paper that becomes
a capitalist war organ.
    You begin your statement and your attempted justification with an
absolute falsehood in the opening paragraph. It is not true that President Wilson has espoused the democratic peace formula and you
know it. But I am not going to argue the question.
    For obvious reasons it is with profound regret that I bid good bye
to you and the Appeal. You will not have to live long to see that the
Appeal has committed suicide.

                                              Yours fraternally,
                                              [Eugene V. Debs]

TLc, InTI, Debs Collection.

    1. The *Appeal to Reason,* changing its name to the *New Appeal,* announced in the
December 15, 1917, issue that it supported the war effort as a means of securing a
socialist victory in the postwar period. Thereafter, until he was drafted in May 1918,
Kopelin strongly supported Wilson "in carrying out the great principles which he
had announced as America's aims in the world conflict" (*New Appeal,* June 1, 1918).

Frank P. O'Hare to EVD

December 27, 1917
Ruskin, Florida

Dear Gene—

It is tragic to read the stories in the Socialist press regarding Kate[1] at this time. The sample from the Dec 22 issue of St L Labor will illustrate.

We are not afraid of prison, but to have Kate reported by our own press as a foul mouthed virago is beyond toleration. And why in hell can't Hoehn,[2] who knows Kate, forget his animosity long enough to phone to Phil[3] to get the facts?

And the RS running THREE stories about Bigelow[4]—who is *out of* jail, in the same issue in which Kate had the privilege of stating her own case herself[5]—without one comradely word from her "associate" editors. I do not blame Phil—he was overwhelmed with troubles at the time—but what were the rest of the bunch doing—

And the Jan. issue—{what was} preferred for that?[6]

The February issue—will it be handled with any sanity? will it, perhaps not even be TOO LATE! Suppressed may be!

I almost believe that Kate is right. For years she has told me of the snubs and scorn and jealousy of the kumrid leaders toward her as a WOMAN. I have laughed it away—but why laugh at facts? Thank the gods, the rank and file love her in spite of her being a woman.

Suppose it had been Comrade ********, former {Executive Com. man and} former international secretary—who had made the one and only brave tour this summer and fall and had fallen afoul of the star chamber bunch—would it have been from JULY till DECEMBER before a word would have gotten to the public regarding the facts, or the life, or the work of the said male *******, and would the publicity in the Socialist press have then been of the same libellous character as the present output? Would he have been on the defensive *alone* all this time, accused by the capitalist press with Socialist press acquiesence?

And the trip to Gethsemane—would he have made it *alone*—would he have had his lawyer wish the job on HIM of chasing all over ND for witnesses—blizzard drives of 200 miles each way from Bismark to Bowman—and then to face a jury Thursday with thirteen hours sleep since the preceding Sunday—the intervening time spent in travel and work from Fargo to Bowman and back to Bismark—or would some one have been along—Kate's lawyer—a democrat—what did he care or know, and how should he feel that her poise concealed a stunned and bleeding heart? Her letters to me—meant to be reassuring, tore my heart—almost made me insane—perhaps did—and it was too late and to far for me to fill the breach!

She will be home tomorrow—I cannot keep her here—it is true—but it will break the fearful three months since she started away.

And from her "comrades" in the movement just one letter has come—yours!—at least to this place. But the rank and file have filled every mail {to me} with their offers of loyal service and devotion.

Phil writes me that he is on the job. to the last ditch. I do not blame him—I know his circumstances—he has stood by loyally to the best of his ability. But he can't handle it alone. You know the former mess. He means well—his heart is right and he will do what is right with the right help and advice.

I am here to make a home and a living for my family.[7] I cannot do that and take care of anything else. I had expected that this year would have closed Kate's field work? She cannot keep up. She is approaching that time of life—it may even be on her—when peace and rest and loving care must be hers. Perhaps she will have the peace and rest in prison—it may be God's way to save her life. The question with me is: Shall I scatter the little squad among those who will give them physical care and sympathetic love—to take up the fight for my wife—or can I hold the squad together and attend to my business and thus keep her heart from completely breaking? Is there enough competent and willing cooperation among the so-called "leaders" to handle the fight intelligently without me—or shall the punishment meted out to her extend to the point of the destruction of our family life while I do for my mate what {my} comrades should be willing to do?

We did not seek martydom—we do not avoid it. I knew, when at the convention,[8] just what would happen. It has happened. We have no regrets. To me Kate has written her name among those of the immortal by her heroism and fortitude. On this one trip her experiences make your own, bitter enough, sink to the level of a petty pleasure picnic. And because she seemed to be brave, tireless and self reliant—she was allowed to almost be killed by the fiendish labors exacted of her in North Dakota. Her lawyer "caved" and got "buck ague" when he really found the crux of the case. She had to sustain *him*.

I want you to find out from the so-called leaders of the party just what in hell they are going to do and to report to me. I will then decide what I shall do about it. I am used to fighting my fights without them, and don't need them much now. Only in this way—to keep Kate from being crucified through her loved children? The rank and file are ready and willing and eager and are asking what to do next. Who shall organize them? I can do it if necessary.

This {letter} is to you and you alone and not for anyone else to see or to know of. If you say you are satisfied that action will be taken, proper action, and that Kate and I shall be exempt from the details, through intelligent action of the others—so it shall be. But I shall not sit here and see another six months go by as the past irrecoverable six months have slipped away.

Frat
F.

TLS, InTI, Debs Collection.

1. On December 14, 1917, Kate Richards O'Hare was given a five-year prison term by a federal judge in Bismarck, North Dakota, for having "obstructed and interfered with recruiting and enlistment" in a speech she gave in Bowman, North Dakota, on July 17, 1917. Mrs. O'Hare served thirteen months of the sentence at Jefferson City, Missouri, before her release in May 1920.

2. Gustav Hoehn, editor of *St. Louis Labor.*

3. Phil Wagner, publisher of *Social Revolution*, which O'Hare continues to call *Rip-Saw.*

4. Herbert Seely Bigelow (1870-1951) was pastor of the People's Church in Cincinnati and an outspoken critic of the war. In August 1917 one of Bigelow's sermons, in which he prayed for the "moral improvement of the Kaiser," was interpreted as being pro-German and he was taken by a mob across the Ohio River to Kentucky, where he was stripped, beaten, and left for dead. Debs wrote three editorials on the incident in the October 1917, January 1918, and February 1918 issues of *Social Revolution.*

5. Kate Richards O'Hare's "Waiting," an account of her fight at Bismarck, appeared in the December 1917 issue of *Social Revolution.*

6. Debs's "Conviction of Kate O'Hare," in which he denounced her conviction and sought funds for legal expenses, appeared in the January 1918 issue of *Social Revolution.*

7. In the December 1917 issue of *Social Revolution*, Frank O'Hare ran an advertisment of "Ruskin, Florida Farms," 4,000 acres to be sold in small plots to "successful farmers" who believed in "practical cooperation."

8. Kate O'Hare headed the war and militarism committee, which drew up the Socialist party's antiwar resolution at the emergency convention in St. Louis in 1917.

Theodore Debs to David Karsner

December 29, 1917
Terre Haute, Indiana

My dear Karsner:—

The very beautiful letter from you addressed to Gene is in my hands and my heart is full of it. Every line is pregnant with the fine

thought and noble spirit so characteristic of you. Let me thank you
from the heart for both Gene and myself. In these dark and tragic
days the thought of such a soul as you and Horace and Gable[1] and
your kindred has comfort in it to the troubled mind and balm to the
sad and suffering soul.

I am glad you are editor of the Call Magazine.[2] You are the very
man. You put the spiritual note in your columns that is so much
needed to touch the heart and stir the emotion of the people and
rouse them to enthusiasm without which so little is possible. Cold
logic has its place but it is not all by a very great deal.

We have read with real joy of the dinner[3] to our beloved poet and
prophet of the coming day. Gene was touched indeed to hear that he
was remembered in that soulful gathering. What a privilege to breathe
if but for a moment an atmosphere redolent of such high spiritual
emanation! Allow me to congratulate you all even at this late day. I
am sure we can at least catch a breath of the inspiration way out here.

Gene, I am glad to say, is improving. He has been having a trying
time of it but he is now picking up his strength and we feel confident
that in a few weeks more he will be himself again and ready to take
up his work.

I was certainly fine in you to treat Gene's article on Jesus[4] so
generously. Please accept this word of thanks and appreciation. The
Art Young[5] conception of Jesus is superb. When you see or write to
Art please say to him that Gene and I think it is a master conception
of the master revolutionist and that there is genius in it of the highest
order. Gene thinks and so do I that this ought to be enlarged and
given place and publicity in everything socialists have to say and do
in connection with Jesus.

You have been extremely kind to send some copies containing this
issue. If by any chance you have three of four more copies you can
spare I should very much like to have them. But only if you can spare
with perfect convenience, not otherwise. If they do not come I will
understand. You need not take the time to answer this for your hours
are busy ones. Gene wishes me to say that your Labor Day monograph
on and tribute to Labor[6] was quite the finest thing of the day, a perfect
prose poem. Best love and all the season's joy and blessings in which
we all join.

Yours heartily,
Theodore Debs

TLS, NN Kars.

1. Horace Traubel and William Gable.
2. Karsner was actually editor of the *Call Sunday Magazine*.

3. The Whitman Fellowship Dinner, held annually in November in New York City.

4. Debs's "Jesus, the Supreme Leader" was the lead article in the *Call Sunday Magazine* on December 22, 1917.

5. Arthur Henry Young (1866-1943) was a news illustrator and cartoonist for scores of newspapers and magazines and a co-editor of *Masses* from 1911 to 1919. His cartoons appeared regularly in socialist publications, including the *Appeal, American Socialist,* and the *Call,* and he ran as a socialist candidate for a number of offices in New York and Connecticut. A collection of his cartoons, *The Best of Art Young,* appeared in 1936.

6. *Call Sunday Magazine,* August 25, 1917.

EVD to Frank P. O'Hare

January 2, 1918
Terre Haute, Indiana

Dear Comrade Frank: —

Your letter of the 21st. in answer to mine in regard to Comrade Kate's cruel sentence and your later letter of the 27th. ult. have both been received and carefully read.

First, let me express the hope that Kate reached home well and is now safely in the bosom of her family. I shall rejoice to think so.

Next, let me tender to you and Kate and your little brood in behalf of Kate and myself and our family all loving wishes for a joyous and fruitful New Year. This may seem like sarcasm after your heartbreaking experience and in the light or rather the darkness of the present situation, but I prefer to think of the year before us in terms of cheer and confidence and to preserve inviolate the faith that we are bound to conquer in the end and safely reach the promised land.

Now in answering your last letter which is filled with reproaches, all written between the lines however, I am going to be entirely frank with you. Why did you write me such a letter? I resent both the spirit and the method of what you have to say to me. I object to having you strike me over the shoulders of others or to striking others over my shoulders. If you mean me, or to include me in your bitter censures, why do you not frankly say so? That is the way I deal with a comrade when I have anything to say to him and that is the way I expect you to deal with me.

I have nothing to apologize for in your indictment for I have been remiss in no particular whatever toward Kate or you in this ordeal or at any other time. I have always stood by and for you and never more than now when trouble is upon you which I realize it is my duty to share and not to shirk.

In the first place, I should not be editor of Social Revolution at this time at all, and I would not be except for Phil Wagner. For several months I have been literally fighting for my life and at one point I came near passing over. For the third time I am suffering a physical and nervous breakdown, the result of thirty-seven years of almost continuous strain and overwork. This time the recovery is slower than ever and although I have been picking up and expect to be restored fully so that I can continue my work, there are days when I can barely stand on my feet from sheer physical weakness. In this condition I have been entirely unfit for mental work and when Phil came here to see me I tendered my resignation and urged him to accept it which he would not do, feeling that my connection with the paper would be of some use to him in his struggle to keep it alive. Of course I would not desert Phil who has been so extremely kind to me and to us all, and whom I regard almost as a brother, and this is the only reason I am connected with Social Revolution today. I well know my work has been poorly done but poor as it is I have yet the satisfaction of knowing that it was the best I could do under the circumstances. When my health and strength are restored, as I am confident they will be, I shall then do my best to make up for lost time.

You complain about the Bigelow articles taking up so much space in the December issue to the exclusion of Kate's case. I did not know all these articles were to appear. You must know that I had nothing to do with making up the issue. I sent my own article which did not occupy much space, not knowing that any others were to appear. But as Kate had a full page in that issue with her portrait as the centerpiece, and this the opening page, I don't see what ground you had for complaint. You say she was left to state her own case. Why not? Could anyone do it better? Hundreds of others have been arrested and were in jail with no publication in which they could exploit their case to the public. At that time Kate had only been arrested among hundreds of others and I knew absolutely nothing to write about the case {except} that she had been put under arrest and I think I treated this fairly in my editorial in the October issue in which I did not stint my praise even if I did not use a page to express it. Kate is fortunate to have an organ and unlimited space and genius for expression so that she can tell her story and keep telling it to the world. There are hundreds of our comrades lying in jail, suffering their martyrdom in silence, with no one to write their story and no one to exploit their persecution, or even to concern themselves in their wretched fate.

Let me see if you have any real ground for complaint against me as one of the "associates" of Kate you sneeringly refer to. The very moment I read of her arrest I wrote Phil asking for particulars. I followed this closely with a second letter and a third. I also wrote to Kate expressing my sympathy and assuring her of my support. This letter I sent in care of Phil who informed me that it had not been received but later acknowledged that it had come to hand. I wrote Kate a second letter the moment I heard of her sentence. Meantime I could get no information in regard to the case other than the bare announcement of the arrest in the first instance and later the sentence. Not only did I write to Kate when I saw the report of the sentence but I also wrote to you and busied myself otherwise in getting action. I wrote to Germer declaring that it was the duty of the national office and the executive board to take up her case, issue an appeal in her behalf, raise funds for her defense, and do everything else possible to secure a reversal of the infamous verdict. I wrote two editorials for S.R. which you will see in the January number.[1] Read these and then tell me if I could have said more to prove my fealty as one of the recalcitrant "associates." I think I did not stint in what I had to say in behalf of Kate in these articles. Now please tell me what else you expected me to do to win from you anything but sneering insinuation.

I do not blame you for feeling as you do but you will have to get it out of your head that Kate is the only martyr in the revolutionary movement. My heart has ached for her and I have felt all my blood boil in resentment of her persecution, but there are scores who have suffered far more than she whose names have not even found their way into print. Kate was not stripped stark naked, lashed with a whip until her flesh was ribbons and then had hot tar rubbed into the wounds as were the poor fellows in Oklahoma,[2] some twenty in number, who were guilty of absolutely no offense, not even of making a speech alleged to contain seditious utterance. Hundreds of our comrades have lain in jail, abused, starved, beaten and then sentenced to from one to fifteen years in the penitentiary without anyone to make a fuss over their brutal persecution. The I.W.W. prisoners at Chicago, most of them perfectly innocent of any offense whatever, are having the hose turned on them in their cells, as I am reliably informed, when the mercury is at zero and then left to spend the night half-frozen in their wet clothes. These poor wretches have a thousand times more cause than you to complain that they are being neglected yet I have heard not one of them utter a word of complaint. These nameless ones are and always have been the real martyrs in every cause in history. I have letters from some of these prisoners but not one of them contains a word of complaint.

You say that the mail is loaded with letters to you expressing sympathy for and loyalty to Kate and you. Then what more do you want?

Is it not a privilege to serve, even to go to jail, when a million hearts turn to you in love and gratefulness?

I am as much in favor of all proper publicity in Kate's case as you are but I don't propose that so far as I am concerned it shall be degraded into an advertising campaign, and this reminds [me] of what they used to tell me at the Rip-Saw office about your proneness along that line.

You complain that Kate is being discriminated against and suffering injustice in the Socialist party solely because she is a woman. That is pure bosh. She has many advantages over men and is shown considerations men do not receive for the very reason that she is a woman. You speak particularly about the party officials in this connection. Well, she was a high party official herself for quite awhile and I don't remember that she was any different than the rest.

Let me tell you something or rather remind you of something in this connection that you must well know. You know that for years the national office, under Berger, Spargo and Hillquit, the ruling trinity, was deadly opposed to me, that not a clerk who was friendly to me could stay in the office, that not an organizer who had a friendly word for me could stay on the road, that at the conventions of 1908 and 1912 the whole national executive committee, the whole of high officialism, including the clerks and the working force, were all on the ground to defeat me for a nomination I was not a candidate for and did not want. Everything possible was done for years by the national office and everyone connected with it to discredit me, to defeat me in all my endeavors, but I made no complaint of it to anyone, and do not now, and I never dreamed of charging that this malicious and under-handed opposition, prompted as I believe by mean and narrow jealousy, was due to the fact that I was a man instead of a woman. But I do not see why Kate should object to the disfavor of officialdom when in the next breath you tell me that the mails that come to you are loaded with evidences of love and fealty of the rank and file of the party. I should think this would be enough to satisfy the most exacting.

You are kind enough to say that on this one trip alone out West Kate suffered more than I did in all my experience and that compared to her torture and crucifixion my bitterest experience was, to use your words, "a pleasure picnic." Well, I grant that millions of poor souls have suffered more and sacrificed more than I have. My claim for myself in this regard is modest enough, I hope, but to save me I cannot understand wherein Kate suffered so fearfully when at the time you tell me that she was surrounded and supported by loyal and loving comrades every step of the way. There are plenty of fine comrades out in North Dakota and how they utterly deserted Kate in the hour of her need and left her to her fate is utterly beyond me.

As for myself, for thirty-seven years I have been doing my little best, beginning at a time when an agitator was kicked out everywhere and under conditions and hardships of which you do not even dream. Later on I have lain in jail, covered with lice, with hundreds of hungry, squeaking sewer rats for bed-fellows. I have been two weeks in the broiling heat of mid-summer without my clothes off, followed by detectives without number, scarcely eating enough to keep me alive. I have for weeks at a time received from thirty to fifty threats of assassination from all parts of the country by every daily mail and I have been followed by hired assassins who only waited for a chance to put a knife into my vitals. I have had a jailer come to me when I sat in my cell with a blood-stained rope in his hand with which a poor wretch had been executed a few days before and sneeringly tell me to get ready for my turn. I have for weeks fully expected that I should be hanged. The papers in Chicago were demanding it and the most prominent lawyers there predicted that I would certainly go to the gallows. I could if I was so disposed tell enough more to make a large volume but I only wish to suggest that if Kate suffered more on one short trip to North Dakota than I did in all my life and that all my bitter experience, compared to her martyrdom, is but "a pleasure picnic" you need to have something done to restore your mental balance before you venture further comparisons.

I am writing frankly but without the least bitterness. You wrote me with bitterness but without frankness. I have always had an affectionate, loyal regard for you and Kate and your family and I have always shown it and tried to prove it. Never once have I mentioned either of you except in praise and approval, and so it should not seem strange that I should feel sensitive, indeed hurt by such a slurring, accusing letter, filled with vicious innuendo, without a shadow of justification, as that received from you.

I am closing as I began with the greetings of the New Year and with love and all good wishes to you and to all of your family.

Yours fraternally,

E. V. Debs

P.S.

There is a point in your letter I overlooked. In the closing paragraph you demand of me the assurance that the national office and those connected with it officially shall take what you call proper action, that you and Kate shall be exempt from details etc. You issue this in the form of a command, judging from the tone and letter of it, to which you add the following peremptory order: "I want you to find out from the so-called leaders of the party just what in hell they are going to do and to report to me. I will then decide what I shall do about it."

To which I have to say in answer that whatever else may ail you there is nothing the matter with your gall. I would ask nothing of the kind from "the so-called leaders" for myself and I certainly would not stultify myself by presuming to issue, or to be used by you to issue your orders to them. I am no more responsible for what the "so-called leaders" do than any other private member, and if you want to know what they are going to do in Kate's case you are at perfect liberty to write to them and find out for yourself. I will do my part as best I can in the present circumstances and this I will do entirely as a matter of duty to myself and the cause; I will use any influence I may have to secure all the favorable action possible bearing on the case but I will not undertake to issue orders to the national office and discredit myself by appearing as a petitioner in the ante-room of those from whom I would under no circumstances ask anything for myself.

It may interest you to know that I have just received a ten page letter from Chicago and another of less pages both complaining bitterly that the whole of Social Revolution is given up to Bigelow and other so-called martyrs and that not even a mention has been made of Stanley J. Clark, the brave and eloquent Texas revolutionist who has been lying in jail at Chicago for weeks without anyone to even procure bail for him. I think he has good ground for complaint after all he has done for the cause. His mail is not loaded with letters and he does not get a full page in any socialist paper exploiting his persecution. Not even a mention of it has been made until the little ed appeared in the January issue.[3] I did not ignore or forget Clark but I could find no way of having published what I wrote about the case. I think he is just as much entitled to consideration and to space and defense as anyone in the whole movement.

The thought of Rena Mooney also comes to me. For a year and half she has been standing on the trap-door of a gallows-tree with a halter about her neck and the other end in the hands of leering, blood-thirsty devils. She has been locked in a water closet all night with a male brute, she has been manhandled, third-degreed, called a "damned dirty slut" and "damned dirty bitch," this fine, sensitive, noble little woman, but I have not heard that she has made any complaint that she was not getting space enough in the papers. The sufferings of Kate O'Hare were bitter enough in North Dakota, God knows, and I felt for her with all my heart, but there is nothing in her case in point of cruelty, outrage, suffering, torture, to be compared one moment with that of Rena Mooney. Did you write to Rena Mooney or did you write to any paper about her and her case and complain that she was not getting space enough in socialist prints nor support enough from the national office and the "so-called leaders?"

I am trying to think not of one alone but of all the brave victims of the hellish persecution of these murderous days. I am thinking most of all of the nameless ones of the rank and file who never get into print, who are never lauded and glorified, but who suffer and die unknelled and unknown. They are in my opinion the greatest sufferers and sacrificers and martyrs of all.

The 1,600 and more poor devils who were torn from their homes and lodgings, many from their wives and children, at Bisbee[4] by a gang of armed vigilantes, deported and dumped on the desert of New Mexico and warned that if they attempted to return they would be murdered, could each of them, I do not doubt, tell a tale of horror at least the equal of that of any of the more prominent ones whose cases have been exploited and who have been lionized through the press for their part in the revolutionary struggle.

Referring once more to S.R. and its columns and what appears therein instead of what should appear, I have only to say that Phil has repeatedly warned me to tone down my writings or S.R. will be suppressed entirely. The P.M.[5] at St. Louis is especially hostile toward anything written by me. The fact that I write it is enough to condemn it in his eyes, and he is the censor. I have therefore had to write under this difficulty, a very great one to me, and even then my articles after they reached the office have been revised, cut down and the vital passages cut out entirely, to which I have had to submit for the sake of keeping S.R. from being killed. You may be sure that I would not have submitted to this under any other circumstances.

Let me say finally in regard to Kate's case that she has not yet been in jail and in my judgment she will never go to Jefferson City for an hour. If the war were over today her sentence would virtually be annulled. The case will probably hang fire in the courts until the war is over and either the higher courts will reverse the lower one or there will be a pardon granted. I am not a prophet but I will venture to predict this to be the outcome and I hope it will come true.

TLc, InTI, Debs Collection.

1. "The Conviction of Kate O'Hare" and "Kate O'Hare's Defense" appeared in the January 1918 *Social Revolution*.

2. On November 9, 1917, seventeen men, thought to be Wobblies, were taken

from the custody of the Tulsa police and after being whipped and tarred and feathered were driven from the city and warned not to return.

3. Debs's "Stanley J. Clark's Arrest" appeared in the January 1918 *Social Revolution*, and his plea for funds for Clark's legal defense, "To Our Comrades and Friends," appeared in *International Socialist Review* in February 1918.

4. On July 12, 1917, some 1,200 workers in the Bisbee, Arizona, copper mines were rounded up by a "Loyalty League" force and "deported" to New Mexico.

5. Colin McRae Selph (1864-1929) was a St. Louis lawyer and Democratic party leader who was appointed postmaster in St. Louis in 1913 and served in that position until 1921.

EVD to Stephen Marion Reynolds

January 3, 1918
Terre Haute, Indiana

My dear Brother Stephen: —

There is always a note of gladness and serenity in your messages and the one of loving remembrance just at hand is especially bright in all its lines and sweet in all its sentiments. You and Jessica radiate cheer and comfort as naturally as the sun does warmth and life.

It is a great thing to have overcome the impediments and obstacles which clog the pathways of so many poor plodders and to stand upon the shining heights where you do, "o'er all the ills of life victorious." I am not so fortunate but I can at least flatter myself upon the privilege of drawing upon your sunshine, as I have often done in the past, when the clouds hang low and threatening in my skies.

Kate and I are delighted to hear of your perfect health and your calm and composure in these harrowing days. It is not easy to keep sweet and to breathe out love in a world made fierce and mad and hateful in the red carnival of self-slaughter which rages all about us. But we can keep the faith within us strong until the tide turns and humanity becomes sane again and lifts up its eyes to the beautiful comrade-world that is to be.

I am sure there was mutual mirth and perfect enjoyment during the evening that your spent with Mrs. Brandt and the Baurs[1] and they spent in your lovely circle. I can well imagine the picture and the spiritual vision of it is good to the soul. Kate and I and all of our tribe send love to you and Jessica and Marion and a thousand good wishes.

Yours always,
Gene

TLS, InH, Reynolds Collection.

  1. Possibly Debs's brother-in-law, Arthur Baur.

Dora Merts to Theodore Debs

January 6, 1918
Chicago, Illinois

Dear Comrade,

I have been rushed awfully this week and have delayed longer than I wished answering your dear letter. Stanley[1] sent to me the letter that you wrote him. I am hoping that your efforts have had some effect. For Comrade Loe[2] got a summons to meet Seymour Stedman[3] at the Federal bldg tomorrow (monday) on the matter of the Clark bond.

I am sure some pressure has been brought to bear in some direction and I know of no other influence that has been at work. I can hardly dare to hope that it will amount to anything, yet it is impossible not to hope. I am sending you a copy so you can see what use we made of your plea and we have sent it to any number of little local papers of mush-room growth in Okla and Texas that we have been so lucky as to receive a copy of. They are best for the reason that they are not so likely to be "Burlesoned" as some of the others and I think Loe is sending some to some of the larger Socialist papers.

I want to thank you for writing the article that you wrote for Social Revolution and also for the one you sent to us and for your dear kind letters to myself and Clark, also for the work you have done on the National office. Whatever can be said of the officials it is certain that You and Gene have left nothing undone, and if Clark is free tomorrow I will cherish a heart full of gratitude to you, but I am afraid I have hopelessly lost faith in the good intentions of the National office that has to be driven to work for a comrade only through the persistent effort of a comrade known to have a greater influence than themselves. I mean you and Gene.

Yours Loyally and gratefully
Dora Merts
341-349 E Ohio St.

TLS, InTI, Debs Collection.

1. Stanley Clark.
2. Caroline Lowe, who was assisting in the defense in the Chicago IWW cases.
3. Stedman was a Chicago attorney and longtime friend of Debs who served as Debs's counsel in his trial and appeal in 1918-19 and as his vice-presidential running mate in 1920.

Guy Bogart to EVD

January 8, 1918
Llano, California

Dear Gene, —

Your letter of the second received. I shall be glad to act as your representative in the matter of the lot in Long Beach deeded to you by Comrade Mrs. S.M.J. Craven. Shall write to the state secretary of the S.P., Mr. Cameron H. King[1] of San Francisco, tonight, and shall see the attorney sometime this week. Today I showed your letter to Secretary M.C. Stewart of Local Los Angeles, who has had considerable Court House experience as a civil service man. He said he would try to look up the records and see the standing of the property in the records.

Ever did your noble soul think only of the class to which we belong. In a thousand ways have you shown your appreciation of the dawning Humanism when man shall take the free gifts of nature without price.

I am sure Mother Burt and Nellie[2] were delighted to have met you and Theodore. The dual ties of neighbor and comrade have endeared both of you to them and to us. I miss the old visits to your office on my rounds of newsgathering.

Thanks for your kind remarks about my reviews and other writings. There is no danger of my saying more concerning you and your work than you merit. I am sorry my typewriter functions for so unworthy a brain to write of your loyal comradeship to the world. You and

Theodore are two men, to have known whom it were worth a lifetime of trial and effort.

We feel keenly the lack of harmony in the world, but are by no means discouraged, for we know it is thru this that the world-harvest of spirituality and Humanism is to spring. I hope Kate O'Hare will not have to suffer in the meantime.

Lucy and Robert[3] join me in loving wishes to you and Theodore and families. May you grow strong again—and then be careful not to waste your strength by such prodigality of effort.

Yours as ever,
Guy Bogart

TLS, InTI, Debs Collection.

1. Cameron Haight King (1877-1947) was an attorney in San Francisco who served as chairman of the Socialist party in California from 1918 to 1924 while editing the *Labor World,* a socialist weekly published in San Francisco.
2. Bogart's mother-in-law and sister-in-law, Flora A. Burt and Nellie Burt.
3. Bogart's wife and son.

EVD to Frank P. O'Hare

January 12, 1918
Terre Haute, Indiana

Dear Frank:

I have just finished your letter. There is no answer beyond saying that I am entirely satisfied. I have not a particle of feeling. Malice I never had a trace of in my nature toward you and could not have.

As you referred specifically and with bitter reproach to Kate's "associates" in one of the opening paragraphs of your previous letter and charged that not one comradely word had been spoken in her behalf by her "associates" editors, how could I help taking your rebuke to myself? If I felt unduly sensitive upon the point it is simply because of my conception of comradely duty, for if I felt myself guilty for a moment of ignoring or deserting a comrade such as Kate when she was attacked while she was fighting our battle and attacked in the most cowardly and brutal way, I would feel myself to be the meanest and most contemptible of creatures, and it is in that light that your letter placed me according to my interpretation of it. This may account for the spirit in which I resented the imputation so clearly implied in what you wrote. In your accusation of neglect and desertion against Kate's "associate" editors you made no exception, and I as the chief among them could not but feel in the face of such a plain and direct charge that the entire burden of it was meant for me, notwithstanding I had done all I could, little enough, God knows, to help Kate under the circumstances. Had you known how keenly I felt the outrage perpetrated upon her, how deeply I sympathized with her in the hardships she had to bear, and how gladly I would have shared it all with her if I only could, you would never have written as you did and you would not blame me for answering as I did. You were particular {to say} in your letter that you did not blame Phil but you were not so particular to say that you did not mean me. Your whole bitter tirade was directed against Kate's "associate" editors and party leaders to which you made Phil the sole exception. I was glad at the time, and still am, that you were at least just to Phil. But I had rather you had accused me outright of almost any infamous crime than to have charged me with the base betrayal and desertion of a loved and loyal comrade such as Kate has always been to me and I have always tried to be to her. But let it all pass and be forgotten. There is nothing that rankles here. Nothing. Your letter just received wipes it all out. Perhaps I should have made more allowance for your over-charged feelings. You had all the reason in the world to be super-heated with indignation and resentment.

But let us now deal with the present and the future. I am only sorry not to have the physical strength to do what I would like to do as my share in Kate's behalf. I believe I know what my duty is and I want to come as near as I can doing it. The Feb. S.R., chiefly through Kate herself, will give her story to the world.[1] The readers will want this from her and from no one else. The rest of us will help as best we can. I only want to say in closing that I am at your service. If you have any suggestion let me have it; if you know of any way in which I can help command me. With all love and loyalty to you and Kate and to the four dear little O'Hares I am,

Yours always,
Gene

TLS, MoH, O'Hare Papers.

1. Virtually the entire February 1918 *Social Revolution* was given over to the Kate O'Hare situation, including "The Speech Delivered in Court by Kate Richards O'Hare," a long article by Kate O'Hare, "Guilty," and a Debs editorial, "Our Duty to Kate O'Hare."

EVD to Katherine Metzel Debs

January 13, 1918
Terre Haute, Indiana

Kate is my sweetheart and the idol of my heart,
Faithful, loving, kind and true is my darling wife;
Thanks to God that she is mine, may he bless her noble life,
I will worship at her shrine till in death we part.

Eugene V. Debs

Poem (in hand of Katherine Metzel Debs, signed by EVD), EVD Foundation,
Debs Home, Katherine M. Debs Scrapbook No. 3.

EVD to George D. Herron

January 26, 1918
Terre Haute, Indiana

My dear Comrade Herron,
    The beautiful and touching holiday greeting from you was placed
in my hands by the postman this morning. The fine sentiment it
contains, fine as the soul that sent it forth on its mission of love and
greeting, should be graven on the hearth of all mankind. That in the
midst of the tragedy of horrors which surrounds you such a divine
message is possible is proof of your own divinity and insures the
triumph of your soul over all that now so cruelly oppresses it.
    I am glad, more than glad to know that you have had the strength
to survive the fearful anguish you have had to suffer through these
weary, agonizing years just passed, and with all my heart I hope that
the power which nerved you for many a trial in other days may sustain
you and keep your faith and fortitude unshaken to the end.
    Your message brings your beloved mate near to us this morning,
and the sweet memory of her is sacred to us beyond words.
    Mrs. Debs and Theodore and all of our family unite in loving
greeting to you and your dear boys, and with all my heart I am,

Yours always,
(Signed) EUGENE V. DEBS

Transcript, CSt-H.

Harry W. Laidler[1] to EVD

January 29, 1918
New York City

My dear Comrade Debs:

Thank you so much for your manuscript on the Negro Problem. We shall be very glad to print it in the Spring issue of the Intercollegiate Socialist. Unfortunately, the Feb.-Mar. issue has now gone to press, and it is impossible to include it in that number. However, we will be glad to place it in our succeeding number, and thank you so much for sending it to us.[2]

With kindest personal regards and with best of Comrade greetings, I am

Sincerely yours,
Harry W. Laidler

TLS, InTI, Debs Collection.

1. Harry W. Laidler (1884-1970) helped to found the Intercollegiate Socialist Society in 1905 and was associated with the society and its successor, the League for Industrial Democracy, until 1957. He was the author of some fifty books and pamphlets, mostly on democratic socialism, and his *History of Socialism*, published in 1968, became a standard in the field.

2. Debs's "The Negro: His Present Status and Outlook" appeared in the April-May 1918 issue of the *Intercollegiate Socialist Review*.

EVD to Ralph Korngold[1]

January 30, 1918
[Terre Haute, Indiana]

Dear Comrade Korngold:—

Your favor of the 28th. inst. in regard to your proposed co-operative undertaking is with me[2] and has been carefully considered. I am in hearty accord with the project and hope you will get the good work going without unnecessary delay. I fully appreciate the necessity of the co-coperative movement you outline and have often regretted that it had not been undertaken long ago as it has in all other countries and brought into harmonious and effective co-operation with the economic and political movement.

I believe the plan you propose for the beginning a wise one and I believe you to be the very man to set it going. I have full faith in both your integrity and capacity and if I can be of any help to you I am at your service but you will understand that for the present on account of my physical condition I shall not be able to take any active part in the work. I have been for some time trying to recover from physical and nervous exhaustion and it has been rather slow, especially at a time when it is even harder than the hardest kind of work to have to remain inactive. But I am slowly recovering my strength and in good time expect to be fully restored and ready to take up my work again.

I am willing you shall have the use of my name as requested on condition only that the men who are to be in charge of the enterprise are of unquestioned integrity of character. Those you mention are of that type with the single exception of John Walker. I cannot consent to have any responsibility for any trust committed to his keeping. He is a trimmer and a traitor and his record proves it. If you doubt it ask Adolph Germer {who} knows him well. He is the kind of a low politician who pretends to be a socialist that he may steer his misguided followers into the democratic party. He was expelled for such treason by the Socialist party. Just at this time he is a war boomer for pay. The report in the Mooney case[3] which he had a hand in investigating and which gave him an opportunity to show what he is is a sufficient index of his character. It is a weak milk and water return, cowardly and evasive, fearing to give offense to those rich criminals on the coast who should have been shown up as the conspirators and murderers they really are. That kind of a man is not to be trusted with the interests of the working class. I far prefer an open enemy who cannot do the harm a Walker can who is smooth enough to pose as the champion of labor and betray it from the inside.

Duncan MacDonald is the kind of a man you can absolutely trust and I am glad you are to have the benefit of his aid and support.

Wishing you all success I remain,

Yours fraternally,
[Eugene V. Debs]

TLc, InTI, Debs Collection.

1. Ralph Korngold (1886-1964) was born in Poland and came to the United States in 1909 as a correspondent for the *Daily Telegraf* of Amsterdam. Korngold's articles on socialist issues were regular features in the socialist press, he edited the *Chicago Daily Socialist* for a number of years, and he was a national lecturer and organizer for the Socialist party before World War I. After the war, Korngold was best known as the author of popular biographies of Thaddeus Stevens, Robespierre, Wendell Phillips, and others.

2. On January 28, 1918, Korngold wrote Debs to describe and ask his moral

support for a "mail-order house that is genuinely co-operative" and would serve the demand of "the radical workingmen and farmers in the United States."

3. In October 1917, President Wilson appointed a mediation commission to investigate the Mooney case in California and report back to him. John H. Walker, head of the UMW in Illinois, was a member of the five-member commission, whose legal counsel was Felix Frankfurter. In its report to the president the commission cited the "dubious character of the witnesses, the subsequent revelations against them, and the conflict in their testimony" as the basis for its recommendation that Wilson "use his good offices" to secure a new trial for Mooney.

EVD to Phil Wagner

February 1, 1918
Terre Haute, Indiana

My dear Phil:—

Since receiving the February issue I have checked the editorials which appeared therein from the list sent you and I now find that the following editorials sent you still remain unpublished:

Let us Fight Our Own Battles   They Go Scot Free
Reactionary Unionism   The Wall Street "Alliance"
The Lying Capitalist Press   Prest. Wilson on Censorship
"The New Freedom"   Law and Order "Smashers"
Strangling Democracy   Good and Bad Socialists
Plutocrats, Patriotism and Prices   Gompers and His Social! Root and the Russian Revolution Friends
We Protest Plutes, Pimps and Prostitutes   The Crime Against the Mooneys
The Boston Outrage   Socialism Is Spreading
The Press Censorship   Winning for Social Revolution
Arrest of Socialist Speakers   Sowing the Seed of Socialism

There are 22 of these editorials. In addition to these you should have the following two signed articles:

Where We Stand and Why   Kate O'Hare & Her Sentence

Now I wish you to let me know which of these editorials and signed articles you have on hand whether in type or still in manuscript.[1] I want to find out exactly what articles have been lost. Please check the editorials and signed articles you have on hand by the above list and then let me know the result.

Please let me know also as nearly as you can on what day you returned those articles you feared would not pass the censor. Let me know how they were sent, in one or more envelopes and any other particulars you may remember. I propose to write to Postmaster General Burleson and demand the return of those articles if they were picked from the mails by his secret service agents. I am going to make the demand and later on I will find some way of following it up if I do not obtain satisfaction. Some of these editorials and articles would have been worth while to save for I put in my best at them. But aside from that I am going to find out if the mails can be picked with impunity and I am going to make an issue of it, a public issue in some way I shall find.

Kindly reply at your convenience, giving me the information desired and oblige.

Yours
Gene

TLc, InTI, Debs Collection.

1. "Socialism Is Spreading," "Plutes, Pimps, and Prostitutes," "Sowing the Seed of Socialism," and "Kate O'Hare and Her Sentence" appeared in the March 1918 *Social Revolution;* "President Wilson on Censorship," "Winning for the Social Revolution," and "Good and Bad Socialists" appeared in the April 1918 issue of the magazine, the last issue published under the name *Social Revolution.* The *Social Builder,* which was the successor to *Social Revolution,* was published in May 1918 for one issue only, and none of the editorials or articles in the above list was included.

Mary Marcy to EVD

February 18, 1918
Chicago, Illinois

Dear Comrade Debs:—

May we ask if you have a copy of an article by you appearing in TRUTH published in Duluth on The Rising Sun,[1] or something like that? {And if you will send us a copy?} By Government order we are prohibited from mailing or expressing copies of any magazine now. We shall publish a Labor Scrap Book within two weeks and something (at same price as Review)[2] every month or two—BOOKS. In the next one we shall publish the greatest article we have ever received—almost—by Herman Cahn on the Collapse of Capitalism in which he proves why this system must utterly COLLAPSE withing 18 months, or {18 weeks}.[3]

Comrade Debs—I never have thought that going to jail, or even fighting the class struggle; or even EDUCATION was going to greatly help the Revolution because I thought it would come only when the workers had no other way out than ACTION in the industries, than in taking control of production—{when Capitalism collapsed} and this article by Cahn simply keeps me in a fever—he adds the utter collapse of the financial system to what I already had seen. I feel utterly worn out to-day from the emotion of seeing Dreams Come True—as I believe we surely are to-day. I think capitalism will collapse absolutely—money will be repudiated at once, with titles, etc. etc. deeds and other capitalism bulwarks. THAT WILL BE OUR DAY.

Our stenographer is sick and I am doing double work—so this must be short. I liked your article and we may run it in the Scrap Book. We may make it a symposium of ideas on the present situation— the TREND to-day. Chas. Schwab said[4]—what he said because he sees there is not enough gold to back up the paper money. The capitalists are doomed. Only by taking control can labor save the world from ruin and starvation. And Labor will HAVE to take hold and we shall have production for USE at last.

Yours for the Glad Day,
Mary Marcy

TLS, InTI, Debs Collection.

1. Probably "Toward the Sunrise," one of Debs's most-often reprinted essays.
2. *International Socialist Review,* which was published by Charles Kerr and edited by Marcy in Chicago.
3. Cahn's *Collapse of Capitalism* predicted that "the capitalist system of production is proceeding to its breakdown and the tendency is accelerated by the accumulation of war loans in the leading nations." *Book Review Digest* (1918), 75.
4. Charles Michael Schwab (1862-1939) was one of America's leading industrialists and financiers who parlayed his early career as a Carnegie lieutenant into the presidency of United States Steel Corporation and later the ownership of Bethlehem Steel Corporation, the latter a major arsenal for the Allies during World War I. Marcy apparently refers to a January 24, 1918, speech given by Schwab in New York City in which he predicted that labor would rule the world in the postwar period. *New York Times,* January 25, 1918. In "Schwab's Palace and Preparedness" (*American Socialist,* March 4, 1916), Debs criticized the luxury of Schwab's New York mansion as a product of the "profits of neutrality."

Lena I. Jaffe[1] to EVD

February 20, 1918
Philadelphia, Pennsylvania

Dear Comrade Debs,
    The Socialist Party, Socialist Literary Society, Jewish Daily Forward and other radical organizations calling themselves 'Friends of Russian

Freedom' (as Socialism and Socialists are taboo in Phila.) are going to hold a celebration of the first anniversary of the fall of Russian Czardom, on March 23rd.

We want to make this the biggest thing Phila. has ever done and toward this end have gotten the biggest hall, splendid speakers, inspiring Russian Revolutionary music and moving pictures of the 'Revolution in Action' taken in Petrograd and elsewhere by Col. Thompson.[2] A really wonderful set of pictures.

In connection with this we are getting out 'A Brief History of the Russian Revolution 1905-1918. Beside the history we intend to have several short contributions that will help make the book very valuable. And we therefore beg you to contribute a short article on the 'Soul or Spirit (or call it what you will) of the Russian Revolution.[3]

We are going to sell the booklet for 25 [cents] and the profit of this and the entire proceeds of the meeting will go for the defense of our Local Secretary and the Executive Committee who are under indictment for distributing a leaflet called 'Long live the Constitution.'[4]

As our booklet must be ready for the meeting March 23rd. (and as I need not tell you how long it takes for setting up, printing, etc.) we would deem it a great favor if you send article as soon as possible.

Trusting that you are enjoying good health, I am

Sincerely and fraternally
(Mrs.) Lena I. Jaffe (Secy.
526 N. 4th. St

ALS, InTI, Debs Collection.

1. Lena I. Jaffe and her husband, Jacob K. Jaffe, a physician, were leaders of the Socialist Literary Society in Philadelphia before World War I and of the Philadelphia Jewish Socialist party after the war.

2. William Boyce Thompson (1869-1930) built a fortune in Arizona copper-mining enterprises before World War I, during which he greatly enlarged his fortune as a leading war contractor. In 1917, having offered to pay the expenses of an American Red Cross mission to Russia, Thompson was sent with the mission as business manager and later became head of the mission. Thompson hoped that the photographs he took in Russia would stimulate general American sympathy for the revolutionary government there, but the chief audience for their exhibition was among small, radical groups whose Bolshevik sympathies came under growing attack.

3. In a letter to David Karsner at the *New York Call* dated March 30, 1918, Debs asked Karsner to print "The Soul of the Russian Revolution" in an upcoming edition of the *Call*, adding that the article "was written for the Philadelphia comrades . . . for the benefit of the defense of the comrades under indictment at Philadelphia." The article appeared in the *Call* on April 21, 1918. InTI, Debs Collection.

4. Charles T. Schenck, secretary of the Socialist party in Philadelphia, and Elizabeth Baer, member of the party's executive committee, were sentenced to six- and three-month prison terms, respectively, for mailing to men about to be drafted a leaflet headed on one side "Long Live the Constitution of the United States" and

on the other "Assert Your Rights." Schenck appealed his case to the Supreme Court and in March 1919, Justice Oliver Wendell Holmes, Jr., delivered the unanimous opinion of the court, which held that the leaflet constituted a "clear and present danger" and therefore affirmed the judgment of the lower courts.

Margaret Sanger to EVD

February 20, 1918
New York City

Dear Comrade Debs: —

I have been wanting to write to you for a long time, but heard that you were coming East to be at this National Conference[1] and I waited in the hopes that I might see you then.

As you did not come, I am now writing you to ask if it would be possible to have an article from you for the May number of the Birth Control Review.[2] I would like, if possible, to make this number a woman's number, using a great many articles that you have written on many women.

I think the last one I have read of yours was in the New York Call on "Fantine"[3] which was most excellent. I am going to reprint that and also the article of yours on Susan B. Anthony[4] and I wonder if you could tell me any others that you have written of women and where I could get a copy of them. I think that your expressions of woman and your whole interpretation of womanhood is the finest of any of our living men today.

I am sending you under separate cover the three last issues of the Review and I note upon looking over our files that in some way your name has been missing. Dr. Blossom[5] has left the birth control movement, so we have just been getting ourselves to office work and the routine of getting out a magazine.

I am now trying to combine the magazine with the birth control and feminist movement, for I feel it is not only necessary to have birth control knowledge but also the goal that woman should strive for that they have personal and political freedom.

I hope you are well and will be able to give the time to an article of a thousand or twelve hundred words on any subject that you wish to write about concerning woman or woman's future.

All best wishes to you, I remain

Yours fraternally in the cause,
Margaret Sanger

TLS, InTI, Debs Collection.

1. Socialists and other radical groups against the war met in Bryant Hall in New York City on February 16 and 17, 1918, to formulate a peace program and organize support for the "Trotzky-Lenine regime in Russia." *New York Times*, February 17, 1918. In a telegram from Scott Nearing dated February 3, 1918, Debs was invited to address the convention, but he did not attend. InTI, Debs Collection.

2. In "Freedom Is the Goal" (*Birth Control Review*, May 1918), Debs argued that as part of woman's struggle for freedom "she shall have sole custody of her own body" and "perfect sex-freedom as well as economic, intellectual, and moral freedom."

3. In "Fantine in Our Day," which appeared originally in *International Socialist Review* (March 1916), Debs dealt with the "fallen women of our day" who were driven to prostitution by the capitalist system and compared them with Hugo's "sublimest of martyrs" in *Les Miserables*.

4. Debs's reminiscence of Anthony originally appeared in *Socialist Woman* in January 1909.

5. Frederick Augustus Blossom (1879-1974) was, with Sanger, a pioneer in the American birth-control movement and a founder of *Birth Control Review*. For a time before World War I, Blossom was a member of the IWW (said to have been its only Ph.D.) and played an active role in the Paterson, New Jersey, silk workers' strike. Later in his career he established a national reputation as a translator and librarian at the Library of Congress and as a leader of the Southern Conference Education Fund.

A. Sussman to EVD

February 20, 1918
Philadelphia, Pennsylvania

Dear Comrade:

The capture of Jersualem by the English expeditionary forces, the declaration of the English Government for a Jewish State in Palestine and the indorsement of the English Labor Movement and other Socialist and Labor Bodies of Europe has revived the hopes of the Jewish people for their Home Land to such an extent that the Jewish Labor Organizations throughout the country felt the need to lay aside their indifferences to the Zionist movement and as a result of that, the question of taking an active part in this movement is now the topic of the day.

The question now discussed in our Labor Press and Organizations is whether a class conscious Socialist can conscientiously endorse and give his moral and financial support to a movement of that sort and so help the national interest of this people.

A number of organizations have already decided in favor of that movement, others are still discussing the matter.

You as one of the leading spirits of the Socialist movement of this country, will do a great service to the Jewish comrades who are still seeking an answer on this question by giving your opinion on same.[1]

Hoping to hear from you in the very near future, I remain yours for Socialism.

A. Sussman
LABOR EDITOR
"THE JEWISH WORLD"
per R.B.

TLS, InTI, Debs Collection.

1. Debs's response to the *Jewish World,* which was "the only Jewish daily published in Philadelphia" and was printed in Hebrew, has not been found, but in a letter dated April 10, 1918, H. Ehrenreich, secretary of the Jewish Socialist Labor party, Poale Zion, in New York City, described Debs's "communication of the 26th of February to the 'Jewish World' of Philadelphia setting forth your opinion of Zionism" as "a source of great pleasure to us" and added that "we feel we have found in you the greatest and noblest champion of our cause in this country." InTI, Debs Collection.

EVD to Frank P. O'Hare

February 22, 1918
Terre Haute, Indiana

Dear Frank:—

Your note of the 17th. at hand. Surprised to find you in Gotham. Just the very place for you at this time. Wish only I could be there with you. I am sure that with your clear understanding and your great organizing capacity you will be able to start something worth while.

I see no reason why you should encounter any opposition from national headquarters as intimated in your letter. There is every reason why you should be backed up in every effort you make to get action in behalf of Kate and the rest of the indicted, convicted and imprisoned comrades.[1] Command me in anyway I can possibly help you. I am with you heart and soul in behalf of all these comrades.

Yours always,
E. V. Debs

TLS, MoH, O'Hare Papers.

1. O'Hare was in New York City helping to organize the Liberty Defense Union, whose stated goal was to create "popular support in behalf of persons prosecuted for the exercise of their constitutional rights of free speech and free press." Debs was listed as a member of its "emergency committee." *Social Revolution,* April 1918.

Frank P. O'Hare to EVD

February 28, 1918
New York City

Dear Comrade Debs: —

Enclosed please find a copy of a letter which I received today from Comrade Germer.

At this writing a defense committee has been organized, and the final meeting to conclude the preliminary organization will be held tomorrow (Friday) morning. Charles W. Ervin will be the chairman of the executive committee; Amos Pinchot treasurer, and Roger Baldwin[1] secretary. On the committee will be Helen Phelps Stokes,[2] Theresa S. Malkiel, Frederick A. Blossom, Scott Nearing, and others of like type. Office space at the above mentioned address[3] has been donated by Nearing.

The purpose of the organization will be to raise the necessary funds and to promote the necessary publicity for the defense and succor of all the comrades who are being prosecuted for the exercise of the rights of free speech, free assemblage and free press.

When I got deeper into the problem here, I found that the support was so warm, universal and liberal that we could proceed to the support of all the comrades as well as of Kate; and at this writing I am glad to be able to say that the defense organization will be able to assume all of the expenses which have been advanced by Comrade Wagner in Kate's case.[4] Several hundred dollars in cash have been collected, and $2000 in $1 pledges is in the hands of the committee, of which the collections will probably run 90 per cent.

When I came to New York I had a two-minute interview with Comrade Hillquit. He told me to telephone him for an appointment, which I did on Thursday; and he told me that he would be able to see me on the following Tuesday. This was not possible on my part, and by that time the preliminary committee had been organized. Due notice of the two following meetings of the committee were sent to him, but he was unable to attend either of them. The nominating committee has placed his name on the list of the executive committee.

In addition to the work of the executive committee in New York City, there will be a committee of 100 representative persons throughout the United States who will be asked to lend their names to an advisory committee of 100. You are to be one of these, if you will. An effort will be made to establish in 100 cities autonomous groups of 10 persons, both in and out of the Socialist Party, to act in their individual capacities in raising funds.

On February 23rd I wrote to V. R. Lovell,[5] at Fargo, N. D., Kate's attorney, in reply to a letter which had been written to her on February 18th. He wrote as follows:—

"I do not want you to ask Mr. Stedman to act in a subordinate capacity. While I appreciate your loyalty and confidence, I do not doubt he is much more capable than I am for briefing and arguing before the Circuit Court of Appeals the questions involved in your appeal. As you are aware, he has been engaged in this class of cases all over the country. I told him I wanted him to brief your appeal independently and to present an argument before the Court of Appeals upon the hearing, and he promised to do so. He is, of course, interested in a number of other appeals of the same class now pending. He seemed to approve of the various suggestions made by me regarding time and place where your case could be presented most advantageously."

I wrote to Mr. Lovell on February 23rd as follows:—

"We have personal reasons why we do not wish you to withdraw from this case. Mrs. O'Hare has positively not constituted Mr. Stedman her attorney to represent her in the Court of Appeals; and in case you wish to retire from the case it will be necessary for her to secure another attorney to represent her. There are reasons for this that I do not care to explain in this letter."

Personally, I am rather in a quandry as to what to do. My business venture in Ruskin Plaza is hanging fire at present, as I have made to the owners of 3700 acres of land an offer to buy them out, and have not yet received their acceptance of my terms. If I do receive a favorable reply from them, I have a business organization here in New York, with a very capable and loyal Comrade who is a lawyer, to handle the proposition in a first-class and straightforward manner. But all bets may be off in regard to Ruskin, as I cannot tell anything about Miller, and he is a man who is impossible for me to work with.

Ever since I discovered the gravity of the case (which was only four or five weeks ago) I have not been able to put my mind on ordinary business affairs. Otherwise, I would secure employment here in New York, in order that I might be near the scene of action and in touch with what is going on; but I feel now that the only thing that I can do whole-heartedly is to devote all my efforts to the work on behalf of Kate and the other Comrades who are in danger.

I should be very glad to have you send me your frank and explicit advice and comments, which I will await with eager interest.

I hope that you are steadily improving in health and strength, and assure you that I am grateful to you for the many kindnesses that you have done me and mine.

Yours fraternally,
FPO

TLS, InTI, Debs Collection.

　　1. Roger Nash Baldwin (1884-1980) earned a master's degree in anthropology at Harvard in 1905; moved to St. Louis, where he taught and worked as a probation officer; and in 1912 published *Juvenile Courts and Probation*, which was based on his St. Louis experiences. During World War I, Baldwin worked with the American Union Against Militarism, and after the United States entered the war in 1917 he helped organize the National Civil Liberties Bureau, forerunner of the American Civil Liberties Union. Baldwin spent a year in prison for his refusal to be drafted and following his release in 1920 became director of the ACLU, which thereafter involved itself in most of the major struggles for civil liberties in the United States and abroad.

　　2. Helen Olivia Phelps Stokes (1887-1970) served on the executive committee of the Intercollegiate Socialist Society from its founding in 1908 through its reorganization as the League for Industrial Democracy in 1921. A portrait painter, Stokes was active in the Socialist party, the New York and national consumer league movement, and the American Civil Liberties Union, for which she served as treasurer.

　　3. 138 West Thirteenth Street, New York City.

　　4. *Social Revolution* solicited funds for Kate O'Hare's defense in each issue.

　　5. Verner R. Lovell (1863-1937) received a law degree from the University of Iowa in 1886 and two years later set up practice in Fargo, North Dakota, where he served as a Democratic city attorney and mayor.

EVD to Frank P. O'Hare

March 2, 1918
Terre Haute, Indiana

Dear Frank:

　　Your communication of the 28th. ult. with enclosure from Germer under date of the 25th. has been received and I have just finished reading both carefully. I can tell you what I should do in a few words. If I were you I should take the first train for Chicago and have an understanding with Germer. You cannot arrange matters by correspondence and there is a possibility of friction that ought to be avoided. Adolph will do the fair thing, I am sure, if he properly understands your undertaking.[1]

　　I was under the impression that you had a working understanding with Germer and the national office, especially as you had informed me that Hillquit was co-operating with you in the work you were doing in New York.

Now if I were Germer I would place this matter before the N.E.C. and ask them to commission you as the representative of the board for the special purpose of organizing the financial side of the defense of Kate and the rest of our comrades. You are exactly suited to this work and no one could do it better and it can never be made a thorough success unless a special department is organized for it under the direction of a comrade who is fitted for that kind of work and can and will put his whole heart and energy into the work, organize the defense committees throughout the country and raise funds enough to thoroughly defend all the comrades under arrest and indictment and have a fund on hand kept standing for the same purpose in the future. This committee need not consist wholly of socialists, or members of the party, and I think you are right in enlisting influential liberals and radicals to co-operate with you in the work. You are the comrade for the job. I know that you have ability for that sort of thing amounting to genius. With you to give this matter your whole attention it is bound to be a success, all the necessary funds will be supplied and legal defenses will be made that will compel the powers that be to sit up and take notice. All of this should be done with the assent and co-operation of the national office and if you make a personal visit there this ought to be arranged with little loss of time and without trouble. You can be no more anxious even as the husband of your beloved Kate than I am as her comrade to see her defense made complete in every particular as well as the defense of all other {persecuted} comrades who have been arrested and made to suffer for our sake. It is our fight and we have got to put our hearts into it if we are worthy of the sacrifices these splendid comrades have made in our behalf.

I note what you say about your personal interests and can sympathize with you in having to let everything go by the board to follow your duty in the cases which have been forced upon you and your family by the enemy. But I know you will not lose cheer and I am sure there are brighter days ahead and that there is compensation in some form for every wrong now endured and every seeming loss now sustained.

Thank you warmly for your kind words and with love to you and Kate and the dear little ones I am,

Yours always,
E. V. Debs

TLS, MoH, O'Hare Papers.

1. The Germer-O'Hare correspondence has not been found, but Germer apparently viewed O'Hare's Liberty Defense Union as encroaching on the work of the

Socialist Party Liberty Defense Fund, which the national party had launched and which soon would make Debs's defense the center of its campaign to raise funds. *Eye-Opener,* December 29, 1917.

Klarenc Wade Mak[1] to EVD

March 4, 1918
Kansas City, Missouri

Dear Komrad:

We wud like to hav yu kum here and help us out with a speech during the last week ov the Kampane if you kan du so. I am the editor and publisher ov The Fool Killer, and wen yu ran for kongres twu years ago I did al I kud thru the magazene and utherwize for yu, and now yu hav a chanc to get even if yu want to. Wot wil be the least it wil kost us to get yu to kum here and giv us wun addres? We wud prefer to hav yu the last week ov the kampane, but if yu kud not kum then we mijht arranjc for a datc to suit your time, etc.

I am the nomine for mayor[2] and we opend our kampane yesterda with a big meeting. Everything looks good for a viktory, and the old parties ar so skared tha have united with the fake labor element on a kombinashun tiket, entiteld, "The Citizens-Labor Tiket."

Tha nominated an atturny for mayor. I hope yu ar wel, komrad, and that yu kan slip over into Missouri and help us sho them. Kind regards to Mrs. Debs and your bruther, Theodore,

Yours Fratrnaly,
Dr. K. W. Mak.

TLS, InTI, Debs Collection.

1. Mak's letterhead identified him as a "Helth Speshalist, Author & Publisher of his own Books, Magazene, Post-Kards & Songs." Among his books, published "by himself," were *Ekkoes from the Hart* (1900), *The Fool Killer* (1918), and *The Laws of Health* (1918). In a phonetically spelled article in the *Rip-Saw* (July 1913), Mak wrote that "I have bin a Sochalist for 25 years" and offered to "surkulate" socialist books. At the time of Debs's death in 1926, Mak, who had moved to Fond du Lac, Wisconsin, published a poem, "In Memory of Debs," a copy of which, in traditional spelling, is in the Debs Collection at Indiana State University.

2. On March 19, 1918, the Kansas City election commissioners "rejected the entire Socialist ticket" because the "signers to the petitions for the Socialist party nominees," including Mak, "lacked the required number." *Kansas City Times,* March 20, 1918.

Frank P. O'Hare to EVD

March 4, 1918
New York City

Dear 'Gene: —

I am just in receipt of your splendid letter of March 2nd, and you have grasped the whole situation perfectly and laid down a course of action which I can follow with the utmost enthusiasm. I have not written to Comrade Germer, hoping that Comrade Hillquit would find time to attend the committee meetings here, and thus be put in touch with the whole situation.

I have tried to keep you and Phil posted, but each day has been a turmoil of events, and it has been only within the last few days that I have had the opportunity or facilities to write at length.

I also received today a letter from Kate which had been sent to her by Phil, and a carbon copy of her reply to Phil. I am sending both on to you, knowing that you will be able to say six words that will clarify matters both for Kate and Phil. I will say, however, that I assume personally all responsibility for what has been started here, as Kate was in absolutely no condition to think when I left her in Ruskin. I do not {know} whether I will be able to get over to Phil what a big and spontaneous movement this is getting to be, and that {he needs} a man there in St. Louis (like George Goebel) to pilot the ship {(the S.R.)}[1] through this particular storm.

The Rip Saw organization as it stands is all right for fair weather; but the ordinary routine won't work now. Brilliant executive work must be done; and Phil has got to get somebody to do it.

I think many of the suggestions in Kate's letter are very good. The rank and file of the comrades all over the country will get up protest meetings in connection with Rip Saw subscriptions, if the campaign is properly handled from St. Louis.

One reason why the prominent Socialists are "backward in coming forward" in this case is because they don't want to feel that this occasion is being used as a circulation opportunity for any privately owned periodical. This is something that cannot be removed from their minds by reasoning. The experience with certain other Socialist papers is not forgotten.

Kate will be in New York City on the 11th and 12th, and I think there will be a committee meeting[2] at that time, especially to confer with her. It would be the best thing possible if Phil were also here to consult with that committee.

As I write this, my attention is called to the fact that the committee will probably meet with Kate on *March 8th.*

You will be on the mailing list and get everything that goes out from the committee.

Again thanking you from the bottom of my heart,

Fraternally,

F. P. O'Hare

Carbon copy to Phil Wagner
     "   "   " Kate O'Hare

TLS, InTI, Debs Collection.

1. *Social Revolution.*
2. Liberty Defense Union.

Margaret Sanger to Theodore Debs

March 4, 1918
New York City

Dear Comrade Debs: —

Your very kind letter of the 25th of February has been received also the literature and the book with Gene's inscription which touched me deeply and for which I thank you highly.

I have heard from time to time that he has not been well and I am hoping, as everyone is, that he will soon be strong again.

I should, of course, love to have an article from him, but do not worry him over it unless he should feel urged or inspired to write something he should not be troubled about it.

I am so glad to have the various articles that he has written and I am sure we can make the issue a very splendid one.

It is with great pleasure that I read your encouraging words in relation to the support that the Socialists and radicals should give, and I am glad to say that I have had in the majority of cases their whole-hearted support. It is because of the radicals and their splendid and courageous stand with me that I have been able to do even the little bit that has been done.

I hope you are getting the magazine regularly, for I have Gene on the subscription list.

Again my best wishes to you both and my thanks, I remain

Fraternally yours,

Margaret Sanger

TLS, InTI, Debs Collection.

EVD to Upton Sinclair

March 5, 1918
Terre Haute, Indiana

Dear Comrade Sinclair:—

Your note is at hand and with it the initial copy of Upton Sinclair's,[1] the contents of which I have examined with special interest. Your introductory message makes strong appeal to thinking people at this critical hour and I hope there may be a sufficient number of these to give you the support you need to make a permanent success of your laudable undertaking.

Upton Sinclair's is clean and attractive in appearance, all that could be expected of paper and type; it is admirably put together and its contents from the first page to the last are of a character and variety to interest and benefit every intelligent reader.

In declaring the mission of your magazine you have sounded the clear note of Social Justice and you have amply and brilliantly sustained your claim in all the pages of your opening number. Very earnestly do I hope that you and your talented wife may be substantially encouraged and supported in your labors by the wide and sympathetic response of your many friends and of alert and thinking people generally throughout the country.

Upton Sinclair's has the distinct personality of its gifted and energetic author and will create if it does not find its own field for the propaganda of industrial freedom and social justice.

Allow me at this late day to thank you for the copy of "King Coal"[2] which I have read with inexpressible satisfaction. I have not been well lately or this acknowledgment would have been sooner made.

"King Coal" is a great book—in some respects greater even than "The Jungle." I marvelled as I turned its pages at your mastery of the subject to its minutest details. Having served as special organizer for both the United Mine Workers and the Western Federation of Miners, and having been warned, threatened and actually driven out of mining camps for attempting to organize the slaves of the pits, I am in position to appreciate fully your graphic, fearless {and} startling exposition of the horrors of slavery as it exists in the mining industry under private ownership to the utter degradation of the working class and their families and the shocking disgrace of civilization.

"King Coal" ought to be in every public library. A hundred thousand copies should be spread over the mining regions and a million copies more among the people.

I have read with particular interest the flattering review of and comment upon your work by Frank Harris in Pearson's. I have great regard for Harris' literary judgment and he certainly places a high estimate upon your work, and I feel assured that his confident prediction of your future will be brilliantly fulfilled.

With socialist greetings to you and Mrs. Sinclair and all wishes for your success in all things I am,

Yours fraternally,
Eugene V. Debs

TLS, InU, Lilly Library, Sinclair MSS.

1. The first issue of *Upton Sinclair's Magazine* was dated April 1918.
2. Sinclair's *King Coal* was published by Macmillan in September 1916.

Mary Marcy to EVD

March 6, 1918
Chicago, Illinois

Dear Comrade Debs: —

We received the Terre Haute Tribune, containing the interview[1] with you and wish to tell you that it has pleased us very much. We feel just as you do and have been asking ourselves how much we were going to endure before we spoke out in meeting.

In New York they have held several meetings {for the Russians with} packed houses, at one of which the collection was $560.00. Women and men took off their rings and watches to throw in the baskets to help Russia fight against the invading Germans. Our New York friends have written us asking if we could not organize meetings for the benefit of the Russian Government. They are also planning to organize volunteers who are willing to fight with the Russians *against invasion*. The enthusiasm is simply wonderful and we may help to organize something of that sort here.

Of course, the aid we will hope to give will be to help Russian Socialism in maintaining its freedom and *not* to help wage war for *any* capitalist government.

If we can get these meetings reduced to a practical basis and find we are allowed to hold them, we will write you again on this subject, as we believe you could be a very important factor at meetings. Of course, all this is uncertain yet, but it seems to me the Socialists ought to take some position in this matter.

Everyone in the office joins me in sending you all good wishes.

Very cordially, yours,
Charles H. Kerr & Company
Mary Marcy Sec'y

TLS, InTI, Debs Collection.

1. The interview, "Debs Rejects Socialists of the Kaiser Brand," appeared in the *Terre Haute Tribune* on March 2, 1918.

EVD to Frank P. O'Hare

March 6, 1918
Terre Haute, Indiana

Dear Frank:—

I was never more surprised. I supposed there was a perfect understanding and not only this but the deepest and most binding mutual sympathy between you and Phil and Kate in the development of your present plans. I am seriously disappointed and distressed to note the cross purposes revealed in this correspondence. Go to Chicago to see Germer and wire Phil to meet you there and come to an understanding with both. If this is not done there is serious trouble ahead and Kate's interests will suffer along with all the rest.

With love,

Yours,
E. V. Debs

TLS, MoH, O'Hare Papers.

Henry M. Tichenor to EVD

March 8, 1918
St. Louis, Missouri

My Dear 'Gene:

Your timely contribution in the Terre Haute Tribune[1] deserves nation-wide publicity. The murderous action of Prussian Junkerdom, backed up as you say by the political majority Socialist traitors of Germany, punctures my natural peace instincts. I want to see Kaiserism wiped off the earth. We can then wage our fight against international capitalism, but not until then. The attempted strangling and slaughtering of our comrades in Russia commands the rallying of all reds on earth to the support of the first Socialist Republic in history. We should make it a life and death fight, giving our lives freely, if necessary, to hurl to hell the Hohenzollern highwaymen.

I shall use your article in my next issue[2] — that is, if the fates provide a way to get it out. There will be some delay, caused by financial difficulties, but I hope to be able to win out. I am going to make a change and issue a $1. a year publication, as the 50c proposition, with no advertising, and the paying of one-cent postage, is impossible.

Love to you and Theodore from Mrs. T, Mary,[3] and yours always

Harry

TLS, InTI, Debs Collection.

1. "Debs Rejects Socialists of the Kaiser Brand," *Terre Haute Tribune*, March 2, 1918.
2. Tichenor was publishing *Pro-Humanity*, "A Twentieth Century Magazine For the Complete Freedom of the Human Race," in St. Louis at the time.
3. Mary E. Tichenor, Henry Tichenor's daughter, was business manager of *Pro-Humanity*.

EVD to David Karsner

March 18, 1918
Terre Haute, Indiana

My dear Dave Karsner: —

You are kind and gracious in every thought and breath. The trifle I sent you merited no such generous expression of appreciation as you have given it.[1] I can but wish my simple offering more worthy of you.

A thousand thanks for the generous treatment the contribution is to have at your generous hands in the Call Magazine! I am delighted to hear that Ryan Walker has consented to illuminate the story with his genius. That will surely atone for what is lacking in the way of literary merit. Ryan is a dear soul, as you know. He and his wife are a twain of the sweetest, finest mortals on earth. Such as these are the savor of life, and verily, such as these and you and Horace[2] are the kingdom of heaven. Love always!

Your comrade,
E. V. Debs

TLS, NN Kars.

1. In a letter to Debs dated March 16, 1918, Karsner praised Debs's "great soul" and thanked him for "The Story of a Convict," Debs's account of an ARU man who was imprisoned in Utah for his participation in the Pullman Strike and whose pardon Debs secured after a long battle with the authorities in Utah. The story, illustrated by Ryan Walker, appeared in the *Call Magazine* on March 23, 1918. InTI, Debs Collection.
2. Horace Traubel.

Mary Marcy to EVD

March 19, 1918
Chicago, Illinois

Dear Comrade Debs: —

You are kind again to help us out with the article on The Bluff that Failed.[1] Our SCRAP BOOK (copy of which was mailed you) is going very well and we hope to be able to get out another booklet for May Day—but I am so worn out and Comrade Kerr is so ill, having been sick, though at work, for nearly two months that Mr. Marcy and Comrade K and I are going to get away for a ten day vacation. Comrade Kerr may be away a month if he is not in improved health. So we are not quite sure what we will bring out next time. But we are going to plan to use your article unless we find it necessary to print only ONE VITAL one. We believe you will permit us to hold this until we KNOW, when, if we have to compromise again—we will write you at once.

You will note that we printed half of Herman Cahn's new book in the Scrap Book. It sounds very encouraging to me. As you know, Marx said that money has now to be WORLD money. Gold serves not only as a measure of value to-day but also as a means of circulation of commodities. It still (according to Cahn) serves as a measure of value, but the needs of expanding capitalism require about thirty-five times as much gold for the circulation of commodities as there is gold—with the ratio increasing rapidly.

So the capitalist class print unbacked paper money, which causes a rise in prices—and higher wages; which in turn requires more money (which they print) and which again causes a rise in prices—and around and around they go in a circle. Personally I can see no way out for capitalism. The question is when will they reach the limit? It looks as though the war were making the situation for the ruling class more acute every day.

Dear comrade—perhaps the system we have fought so long and you have suffered so in opposing may collapse. Then surely will be OUR day. I believe it is coming. Take good care of yourself the very best care of yourself—for you MUST live to take part in the New Era. Can YOU see any lasting way out for the capitalist class? I read the financial news—every word I can find. It all bears out Cahn. And, thank the Gods—Germany is in no better condition—in a worse in fact—than any other country. Besides—how can ONE endure with capitalism ruling—if one or more other countries fail on a gold basis? What can they substitute! I just have a haunting fear that the German Imperialists might try actual slavery—but I don't think that would work out. There must be some international basis of exchange—UNLESS THE Germans are able to enforce some sort of feudalism.

I will have to confess that I am fearful of the Germans.

We will be glad to hear what you think of the Cahn article in the Scrap Book.

Yours for the Glad Day,
Mary Marcy

TLS, InTI, Debs Collection.

1. "The Bluff That Failed," published in the *Call Magazine* on August 25, 1918, was Debs's recollection of an 1894 speaking tour in the South and of the large crowds of railroad workers who turned out to hear him in spite of threats by Louisville & Nashville Railroad officials to fire any L&N employees who listened to "the criminal and anarchist."

Alexander Trachtenberg to EVD

March 20, 1918
New York City

Dear Comrade Debs:

The Rand School of Social Science has moved to its new quarters, having acquired a fine six-story building at 7 E 15 St., which was formerly occupied by the Y W C A. In this fine new house, the Rand School has been given the opportunity to expand and to reach with its activities a large number of persons among the workers of the city. There are now about 4,000 men and women, predominantly members of various labor organizations, attending courses at the School.

The People's House was built for school purposes, and besides the auditorium and classrooms, we have a library with all the facilities for about 50,000 volumes. It is our aim to build a library which should become in time a storehouse of literature to which students of the labor and Socialist movement may turn for information and study. We are already in possession of a great number of invaluable pamphlets which are now out of print, and we are planning to reach a large number of older members of the Socialist and trade organizations who have collected various pieces of literature dealing with the beginnings of the movement in the hope that we may enrich our collection with the contributions of these persons. There are also a great number of organizations which have small libraries of valuable material and which will be glad to deposit them with us for preservation and for wider use.

I am writing to ask whether you would allow the use of your name for an appeal to be sent in behalf of the library to various individuals and organizations throughout this country for donations of material on labor and Socialism. I am sure that such an appeal, sent out broadcast among sympathetic groups, will result in an aggregation of invaluable contributions to the library, thereby making it a central labor library in this country.

Thanking you in advance for your generous co-operation,[1] and hoping to hear from you soon, I remain

Fraternally yours,
Alexander Trachtenberg
Director

TLS, InTI, Debs Collection.

1. In 1923-24, Debs donated a large volume of materials—books, bound volumes of the publications he had edited or for which he had frequently written over forty years, pamphlets, scrapbooks, etc.—to the Rand School.

William F. Kruse[1] to EVD

March 22, 1918
Chicago, Illinois

Dear Comrade Gene:

Will you please write me a special little article for the May Day— Marxian Centenary special edition of the YOUNG SOCIALIST MAG-

AZINE? It will be a special edition in every way, 20 pages instead of 16 and goes to press exceptionally early, April 8th, so as to reach its readers for the first. It will not be complete without something from your pen, and I am not forgetting your promise made while on your way West to get well, when I had the great pleasure of riding from Terre Haute to Chicago with you on the fine July afternoon.

Counting on your response[2] and hoping that our grand old man will soon be back stronger than ever on our firing line, I am

Yours for comradeship,
Wm. F. Kruse

TLS, InTI, Debs Collection.

1. William F. Kruse was national secretary of the Young People's Socialist League, director of the young people's department of the Socialist party, and editor of *Young Socialist Magazine*. In February 1918, Kruse and Victor Berger, Adolph Germer, J. Louis Engdahl, and Irwin St. John Tucker were indicted for conspiracy to obstruct recruiting and enlistment, among other things. All five were convicted and sentenced to twenty years' imprisonment by Judge Kenesaw Mountain Landis, but they were released on bail and their sentences eventually were overturned on appeal.

2. Debs's "Marx and the Young People" appeared in the May 1918 *Young Socialist Magazine*.

Tom Mooney to EVD

March 23, 1918
San Francisco, California

Dear Comrade,—

Now that the Supreme Court of California has decided that the program of hanging me must be carried out,[1] our fight has been brought to a clear-cut issue. This is only what I expected, from the night of our conviction; and I said then, that our hope was in the organized labor movement, and not in the courts of California. That statment has proven true.

Your splendid efforts in our behalf during these past twenty months, make me feel almost selfish in asking you to do anything further in that regard;[2] but, under these trying circumstances, a man in my predicament perhaps is justified in doing almost anything, as a matter of self-preservation, to say nothing of the great principle involved in this struggle.

Although Weinberg[3] has been taken out of the clutches of the law-and-order gang of the Chamber of Commerce, and although it is very improbable that the prosecution will venture any more "trials," still, by the time this letter reaches you, it is possible that I may have been taken away to San Quentin.[4] Still, I have no fear as to the ultimate outcome of our case. I am absolutely confident that ultimately we shall all be vindicated. That result can only be brought about by the united and determined action of the entire working class in this country, because the forces opposed to us are so powerful, and are still audacious and determined to go as far as they can with the "frame-up."

I wish at this time, to appeal to you to try to interest friends in our behalf, who will contribute to a fund that will enable me to liquidate a debt to my printer, of about $3000. This was incurred for 100,000 copies of "Justice Raped in California," distributed, free of charge, in the city of San Francisco during the recent attempt to recall Fickert. This transaction was a dead-weight expense to me, no returns coming from it; but the work had to be done in our defense, and I undertook it. So far, in spite of all my efforts, I have been unable to meet the obligation. I am sending a copy of this letter to a number of our friends throughout the country. My hope is that, after I am incarcerated in San Quentin, my committee will be able to continue the work of sending out this literature, which has done so much toward bringing our defense to its present wholesome position. If it were not for the publicity that has been secured throughout the entire world, we should all be rotting in a bed of quicklime by this time. Publicity is the weapon that must be used to rouse the workers to the point where they will DEMAND justice for us.

I wish to thank you from the bottom of my heart, for your past support in this splendid, though severe, struggle.

I believe that Rena also will be admitted to bail during the coming week.[5] She joins me in kindest regards and best wishes to you.

Yours,
Tom Mooney

TLS, InTI, Debs Collection.

1. On March 1, 1918, the California Supreme Court reaffirmed Mooney's conviction and death sentence. In early June the death warrant, specifying August 23, 1918, as the date of execution, was signed but, as noted, the sentence was commuted to life imprisonment.

2. Debs published "Tom Mooney Sentenced to Death" in the April 1918 *International Socialist Review* and "Tom Mooney's Appeal" in the June 2, 1918, issue of *Eye-Opener*, the official party paper at the time. In both he sought financial aid for Mooney.

3. Israel Weinberg, a San Francisco "jitney cab" driver, was one of the original five defendants in the Mooney case. He was acquitted of the charge of murder on November 27, 1917.

4. Mooney entered San Quentin on July 17, 1918.

5. After raising $15,000 cash bail, Rena Mooney was released on March 30, 1918.

T. H. Robertson[1] to EVD

March 23, 1918
Canton, Ohio

Dear Comrade;

I am instructed by our Local to invite you to Canton on June 16th.[2] Our state convention meets here June 14th & 15th, followed by a state picnic on Sunday the 16th. Our comrades Ruthenberg, Baker and Wagenknecht[3] are confined here in the County Workhouse, and we expect to make our state meet a big one.

The speaking program will take place in a park during the afternoon.

Please Come.

State terms, etc

I am Yours for the Revolution
T. H. Robertson
832 Rex Av   NE
Canton, O

ALS, InTI, Debs Collection.

1. Robertson was secretary of the Socialist party local in Canton, Ohio, and editor of the *Torch of Reason*, a monthly published in that city.

2. Debs's speech at Canton on June 16, 1918, one of the most famous of his career, was the basis of the government's case against him for violation of the Espionage Act.

3. Charles Emil Ruthenberg (1882-1927) joined the Socialist party in Cleveland in 1909 and became an organizer for and secretary of the Cleveland branch of the party and a perennial candidate for local and state office as a socialist before World War I. A delegate to the emergency convention in St. Louis in April 1917, Ruthenberg was a vocal opponent of the war, and on July 25, 1917, he and Charles Baker and Alfred Wagenknecht were sentenced to one year in the workhouse at Canton for encouraging draft resistance. After the war all three men played leading roles in organizing the Communist party or the Communist Labor party (1919) and the successor Workers party (1921).

Lena I. Jaffe to EVD

March 27, 1918
Philadelphia, Pennsylvania

Dear Comrade Debs,

It grieves us deeply that we are unable to use your most inspiring and wonderful contribution[1] as we had to abandon the celebration of the Russian Revolution. Most people here are heart-sore with conditions in Russia and are not in the mood for celebrating, and then again all large halls were closed to us for the purpose.

But that did not deter us, as we camuflagued a Recital for this coming Friday eve, and expect to realize about $2500 for the defense fund of our comrades anyway.

We want to thank you for your prompt and generous response and I assure you that it has inspired all of us to push along with a better will and a lighter heart.

Again thanking you sincerely and trusting that you may be spared to us for many, many years, we are

Sincerely,
The Committee
Lena I. Jaffe sec'y
526 N 4th St

ALS, InTI, Debs Collection.

1. Debs's "Soul of the Russian Revolution," which, as noted, was originally written at Jaffe's request for the Philadelphia "Friends of Russian Freedom" and also sent to the *New York Call*, where it appeared on April 21, 1918.

EVD to Frank P. O'Hare

April 1, 1918
Terre Haute, Indiana

Dear Frank:—

Your circular letter in behalf of the Liberty Defense Union[1] with your appreciative personal note attached is with me. I congratulate you upon this evidently splendid piece of work and can only regret that I have so insignificant {a} part in it. You certainly have succeeded in presenting a formidable array of revolutionary and progressive men and women to the country, and if their appeal is not fruitful of results it would be vain for any others to try in the name of the same worthy cause. There are millions and millions for war and destruction, including the destruction of liberty, but pennies only and few and far between for defense. It's sad but true and out of this truth, sad as it is, we get our chief inspiration. We couldn't and wouldn't work and risk everything except under just such conditions as crush and break the lives and spirits of all but the unvanquishable minority.

You have chosen wisely for each of the important positions[2] and you are fortunate in having such a combination of high-souled men and women united in such a perfectly laudable undertaking.

Let me suggest that you send a copy of this circular letter, if you have not already done so, as I suppose you have, to Phil and ask him to reproduce it in full in the R.S., M.P. and Paladin.[3] I can and will comment on it editorially.[4] If you have any suggestions please let me have them.

I hope you and Kate are holding up and not venturing too near the brink of over-doing and risking the grave consequences I have had to suffer to bring me to my senses. Socialists have less sense than any others I know about keeping within the bounds of their physical capacity and endurance. They simply do not think about it until something breaks and then when they lie helpless in a heap they wonder how it happened to happen. Kate and you have both had {a} sample of the real thing and let me warn you, especially Kate, to keep your eye on the speedometer often enough to avoid the inevitable disaster. It doesn't pay either from the personal standpoint or that of the cause. It is better to conserve a bit as the years speed by and stretch out the service as far as it will go.

With affectionate good wishes to you and Kate and kindest greetings to the comrades about you I am,

Yours always,
E. V. Debs

TLS, MoH, O'Hare Papers.

1. The two-page typed letter described the work and identified the officers and committee members (including Debs) of the Liberty Defense Union. InTI, Debs Collection.

2. Charles W. Ervin, managing editor of the *New York Call*, was the LDU executive committee chairman, John Haynes Holmes and Helen Phelps Stokes were vice-chairmen, Harry W. Laidler was treasurer, and Roger Baldwin was secretary.

3. *Rip-Saw (Social Revolution)*, *Melting Pot*, and a new Wagner publication, the *Paladin*, which was edited by Walter Hurt.

4. Debs's "Liberty Defense Union" appeared in *Social Revolution*, April 1918.

Everett Sanders[1] to EVD

April 1, 1918
Washington, D.C.

My dear Mr. Debs:

I was able, the other day, to get a bound set of "Industrial Relations," being the final report and testimony submitted to Congress by the Commission on Industrial Relations, created by the Act of August 23, 1912.

It occurred to me that you might want a set of these books in your library, and I have accordingly sent them to your Terre Haute address, and it will probably reach you in a few days. If it happens you have another set, you can give this set I am sending you to some friend.

If at any time you are interested in any Government publications that are available for distribution, it will be a pleasure for me to obtain them for you.

Very cordially yours,
Everett Sanders

TLS, InTI, Debs Collection.

1. Everett Sanders (1882-1950) practiced law in Terre Haute from 1907 until 1916, when he was the successful Republican candidate for Congress in Indiana's Fifth District in the race in which Debs ran a distant third. Sanders served in Congress from 1917 to 1925 and, after declining his party's nomination in the 1924 election, as President Coolidge's secretary from 1925 to 1929, and as Republican national chairman from 1932 to 1934.

EVD to Frank P. O'Hare

April 2, 1918
Terre Haute, Indiana

Dear Frank:—

Your favor of the 31st. ult. with copy of your letter and enclosures to Clore Warne has been received. As it is a rather voluminous {writing} I am taking the whole of it home with me so that I can go over it carefully tonight undisturbed.

I note what you say about the personal expense you had to raise on your insurance. I would gladly, if my own pockets were not depleted, send you a check for at least half the amount. But I have not earned or received a dollar from any source for a good many months.

However, we shall tide over and if I get a dollar or two ahead and you are still in hock I shall be glad to share it with you.

You have done a really great work in organizing the Defense Union. I can only hope the machinery will all work perfectly in accordance with your plans and realize all hoped-for results.

I can realize your predicament about the Florida business but I can't advise or help you. Wish I could. If you take hold of the work for the Call and the Rand School I believe you can relieve them of their chronic financial deficitation.

Yours,
Gene.

TLS, MoH, O'Hare Papers.

EVD to Frank P. O'Hare

April 4, 1918
Terre Haute, Indiana

Dear Frank:—

Have your letter to Phil[1] of the 2nd., or rather copy of it, and it has given me great satisfaction. I am sure it did Phil good in a real way and he certainly deserves the fine compliment you paid him. This appreciative expression from you at this time will have a happy effect. I am fully repaid if my very small part in the April S.R.[2] contributed in any degree to bringing about this result. This is the relation that should exist and the spirit that should prevail between us at all times.

I am glad you enclosed the statement just issued by the L.D.U.[3] setting forth the measures taken for the defense of Scott Nearing[4] and emphasizing the importance of the case. Nearing is one of our biggest and best performers and his indictment and its meaning should be made clear so as to arouse the people as far as possible as to the vital issue it involves.

Wishing you continued and unbounded success in your labors

Yours always,
Gene

TLS, MoH, O'Hare Papers.

1. Phil Wagner.
2. *Social Revolution.*
3. Liberty Defense Union.
4. As noted, Nearing's pamphlet *The Great Madness,* was the basis of his indictment

for draft obstruction and encouraging insubordination. He was acquitted, but the Rand School, which had published the pamphlet, was fined $3,000. The fine was overturned on appeal.

EVD to Thomas H. Uzzell[1]

April 6, 1918
Terre Haute, Indiana

Dear Mr. Uzzell: —

Your favor of the 3rd. inst. has been received and I take pleasure in giving you my view as to the present political outlook of the Socialist party in the United States. From the reports I receive from day to day from various sections of the country I am convinced not only that the Socialist party as a whole is in a better condition than ever before but that the outlook this year is more promising and that we may confidently expect a decided increase in the socialist vote in the congressional and state elections this fall.

There have been but few defections from the party due to the war and to make up for these there has been a large increase in the party membership, and I am advised by the national secretary of the party that the growth of the party at this time is more rapid than ever before and that the party is in excellent condition to wage an active political campaign.[2]

It is true that the war has interfered with certain activities in the socialist propaganda but it is also true that the war has furnished many object lessons in the way of nationalizing industry to show the people the necessity for as well as the praticability of organizing the industrial life of the nation upon a social and democratic basis, in consequence of which socialism is being discussed as never before and the vote this year will eclipse all previous records.

Very truly yours,
[Eugene V. Debs]

TLc, InTI, Debs Collection.

1. On April 3, 1918, Uzzell, who was a writer and later a literary critic and lecturer at Columbia, wrote to Debs to ask for "a very brief statement of opinion . . . as to the prospects of the Socialist Party in the coming fall national election." The material gathered was to be sent to Russia and other countries to inform them "as to the more radical movements in the United States." InTI, Debs Collection.
2. The results of the 1918 campaign for the Socialist party were mixed but generally disappointing. Victor Berger was elected to Congress in Milwaukee; Meyer London was defeated in New York. Socialists ran well in state and local elections in

Minnesota, Iowa, Michigan, and South Dakota, but in many states the wartime defections and government and public attacks took their toll and resulted in losses in both city and statewide elections.

EVD to Adolph F. Germer

April 8, 1918
Terre Haute, Indiana

My dear Adolph:—

For some time I have been thinking there should be a special convention of the Socialist party to re-state the attitude of the party toward the war and its policy and purpose when the war is over, in the light of present conditions.

To enter the national campaign this year on the war platform adopted a year ago would be a colossal blunder and make of our campaign a losing one from the start.[1] We cannot go before the country in the present state of affairs on that platform. A year ago when that declaration was adopted, barring certain unfortunate phrasing, it was alright. Today it is flagrantly wrong and it will not do at all. You cannot defend it nor can I or anyone else in its entirety.

The Russian revolution and Germany's treatment of Russia, especially her ruthless invasion and attempted dismemberment of that country and the reduction of its people to a Hohenzollern vassalage has created a tremendous change of sentiment throughout the world which we cannot afford to ignore.

Another matter of which we must take cognizance is the recent conference of the Inter-Allied Labor and Socialist forces held in London[2] for the formulation of the "Labor War Aims" of the labor and socialist movement. You have no doubt read the proceedings of this conference and its report. After going over this report carefully I find myself almost wholly in accord with it. It expresses the conviction and declares the attitude of practically the whole labor and socialist movements of England, France, Italy and Belgium, and I feel that the Socialist party of America should at this time make a similar declaration, defining clearly its present attitude toward the war and the policy it proposes shall be pursued in the making of the peace and in the reconstruction era that is to follow the war. We should have the courage to face the situation exactly as it is and make our declaration as socialists {and} representatives of the Socialist party of America without evasion or equivocation to the world.

If you are in agreement with me I wish you would confer with the

members of the national executive committee regarding the matter
and see what can be done to have a special convention called to deal
with this overshadowing question of the day. I feel that the necessity
for action is urgent and imperative.

Please drop me a line and let me have your views.

Yours fraternally,
[Eugene V. Debs]

TLc, InTI, Debs Collection.

1. In "The Socialist Party and the War" (*Social Builder*, May 1918), Debs published
his ideas regarding the need to revise "the St. Louis platform" in the light of "the
most extraordinary and unexpected developments since that time," particularly the
Russian Revolution, which had "changed the face of Europe." At a national conference
of the party held in Chicago on August 10, 11, and 12, 1918, Debs agreed with the
conference decision not to alter its opposition to the war and in a speech on August
11 said it was "not for me to outline what should be the purpose or the policy of
this conference"; he urged the delegates to remain "true to the principles of international Socialism." *St. Louis Labor*, August 24, 1918.

2. The Inter-Allied Labor Conference, held in London in late February 1918,
called for, among other things, a league of nations, disarmament, the prevention of
war in the future, and territorial changes "based on justice and right." *New York Times*,
February 24, 1918.

Daisy C. Millard[1] to EVD

April 10, 1918
Cincinnati, Ohio

Dear Comrade; —

May I inquire if you are filling any Lecture dates at this time? Local
Cincinnati is very anxious to have you come here for May 5th, either
a Sunday afternoon or evening lecture, if you are speaking.

We have opened or will open at that time a new headquarters,
seating capacity about 1000. The comrades are working day and night
to have it finished for May Day week.

I am quite sure that your presence here at this particular time and
occasion would renew our faith and give us more courage to go on
with the struggle.

Will you kindly advise me, Comrade, at your earliest convenience
and oblige[2]

Sincerely,
Daisy C. Millard.

Comrade Debs, I know you will forgive me for this personal note but because of your love for Walter you will understand. We are passing through a crisis in our own personal life. Walter seems to be lost in the face of this world war and is flying away, leaving us to crash on the rocks. But I love him and will hold fast.

Dear Comrade—am most sorry I write this, for surely I should be able to carry this alone, but—Will you kindly write me what you think we should do (I don't mean personally) about the stand of the party on the war and Wilson statements? You realize it is on this point that Walter and I are divided. My faith in him makes me hesitant to think he is swayed by a spirit of nationalism. I am willing however, to compromise to some degree, but am at sea just how far to go.

Comrade Debs, if you have the time to answer this you need not remember the personal, just advise me as secretary For even now, I have covered it all up and I smile.

Sincerest love to all those you love.

Always
Daisy Millard.

Walter is now in Nebraska., for the Proportional Rep. League.

TLS, InTI, Debs Collection.

1. Daisy Conklin Millard (1875-1956) was listed in the Cincinnati city directories of the period as a secretary or stenographer. Her husband, Walter J. Millard (1870-1951), at the time a writer and lecturer for *Social Revolution*, was later a national leader of the American Proportional Representation League.

2. Debs spoke on May 5, 1918, at Canton, Ohio. Theodore Debs to William H. Henry, April 22, 1918. InTI, Debs Collection.

Carl D. Thompson to EVD

April 12, 1918
Chicago, Illinois

Dear Gene;—

I do not know how you may feel, but it seems to me that we are up against a very serious situation in the matter of our St Louis war program. Whatever may have been the justification for the position taken by the party at the time of the St Louis convention it seems to me that the program there laid down is now absolutely impossible, unworkable, and, in view of recent developments, unscientific unso-cialistic and wrong.

I felt, at the time, that the St Louis resolutions were a serious mistake. I have never felt anything that has happened so deeply, and

I have grieved over it ever since.[1] But I have stuck to the party and tried to my utmost to be loyal to a program that it has seemed to me was murdering the party. I realized, of course, that I might be wrong. All of the comrades seemed to be so absolutely, so positively sure of their position. But as time has gone on, as events transpired, and now with the tragic invasion of Russia, after the splendid stand of our comrades of the Bolsheviki government, after Brest-Litovsk,[2] and the annexation by German militarism of nearly one-third of the territory of Russia, one third of her railroad mileage, 73 percent of her iron production, 89 per cent of her coal, and 56,000,000 of her population,—AND THE GERMAN ARMIES STILL GOING—what now can we say,—what is left to us to say? Shall we lie down while the first socialist Republic that has ever been established upon the earth is being strangled?

It seems to me for these and many other reasons that I cannot go into in a brief letter, that we are in an absolutely impossible position. I want to see the Party get right. I want the program changed. I want it to be a consistent and a socialist position. And it seems to me that the nearest approach to a rational, well considered, well balanced and at the same time consistent position that is at the same time in accord with socialist principles is the program of war aims laid down by THE INTER-ALLIED SOCIALIST AND LABOR CONFERENCE held in London in February last. It represents, it seems to me, the last and the best thought of the socialist world on this problem.

Something like that, it seems to me, should be the position that the American Socialist Party should take. That is what I would like to see us do. How do you feel? Do you not agree with me? Can we not get action along this line that will release us and the Party from this impossible position that we are in? If you will, let me know your mind, and what you think.

Here in my ward in Chicago, the 27th, (400 members,) we have started the discussion and consideration of this problem. We have arranged for a special meeting for the consideration of this problem. It is the purpose of those of us who are pressing the matter to see if we cannot persuade our membership to adopt a restatement of our attitude on the war along the general lines of the Inter-Allied Socialist and Labor program. We are re-writing the statement so that it will be thoroughly American and will apply to our situation here, but we wish to follow the general lines laid down there. And then, if we can get this adopted here, we propose to send it out to the comrades elsewhere, and if possible thruout the country and ask for support so that we can get the matter to a general referendum vote of the membership.

It seems to me that we do not need to wait for a conference in this case, but that we can save the expense and the time of the delay by going at once to referendum. But whether this be true or not, at least we wish to get the matter before the comrades for earnest consideration. It will be a difficult task now in view of the limited circulation of our papers and the innumerable restrictions upon our means of communication. There is a grave danger of misunderstanding and of poorly considered action.

If I am right in believing that your judgment will coincide with mine in this matter then I am hoping that you may see your way clear to help us in this crisis. A word from you will help immensely.

May be I am presuming too much, but someway, it seems to me that you must be with us in the feeling that a situation now has arisen that calls for definite and perhaps heroic action in order to put our Party in the right position. At any rate, if you will, drop me a line, and shake out your heart to me on this matter.

I WANT TO SEE THE MOVEMENT GO FORWARD INTO THIS WONDERFUL, IF TRAGIC COSMIC CRISIS AND BE GLORIFIED IN THE FIGHT IT MAKES AND THE VICTORY IT WINS.

As ever, your comrade,
Carl D. Thompson,
4131 N. Keeler Ave.

TLS, InTI, Debs Collection.

1. Thompson was not a delegate to the emergency convention in St. Louis in 1917.

2. The Treaty of Brest-Litovsk, signed on March 3, 1918, between Germany and its allies and the Soviet Republic, called for full demobilization of the Russian army and losses to the new Russian government of 34 percent of its population, 32 percent of its farmlands, 54 percent of its industrial plant, and 89 percent of its coal mines. The treaty is considered to represent the lowest point in Russian national power, the highest point of German ascendancy in Eastern Europe, in modern times.

David Karsner to EVD

April 13, 1918
New York City

Dear Comrade Debs:—

I think I see the reason why your eloquent essay on the Russian Revolution was not printed in my absence. There are just two lines in the paragraph I will quote that it would seem to me would arouse the ire of Mr. Burleson and cause him to stop the whole national edition. Your paragraph reads:

> All the forces of the world's reaction, all its dynasties and despotisms, all its kingdoms and principalities, all its monarchies and republics, all its capitalism and imperialism, all its ruling exploiting classes and their politicians, priests, professors and parasites of every breed, all these are pitted openly or covertly against the Russian revolution and conspiring together, *allies cheek by jowl with the entente powers,* for the overthrow of the victorious Russian proletariat and the destruction of the new-born Democracy.

The censor would doubtless see in the passage I have underscored "aid and comfort to the enemy"—they have done more stupid things than this, believe me. If you would allow me to delete the passage underscored I will rush the essay into print next Saturday. It is without a doubt the finest appreciation of the Russian revolution I have read, and could have come from none other than your inspired pen. I will have the essay put into type and will await your word.[1]

Love to you always,
David Karsner

Could you not write something for Marx's hundreth anniversary?[2]

TLS, InTI, Debs Collection.

1. With Karsner's suggested deletion, Debs's "Soul of the Russian Revolution" appeared in the *Call* on April 21, 1918.
2. Debs's "Marx the Man: An Appreciation" was published in the *Call* on May 4, 1918.

Caroline A. Lowe to EVD

April 14, 1918
Chicago, Illinois

Dear Comrade Debs—

I'm so glad to hear from you again—you didn't say so, but I'm hoping you are greatly improved and that you are entirely your old self once more. There comes such a feeling of *relief*—a sense of security, some way—when I know you are well and within call when a crisis arises in the affairs of the party. And it may be that a crisis in the revolutionary movement is nearer than we think. Sometimes I feel it is rapidly approaching and that there is no conscious, organized preparation being made to meet it. At the last meeting of the N.E.C. I said something to this effect. Comrade Hillquit said that plans were futile when the crisis arises, it will bring with it its own solution. Perhaps he is right—but someway it seems to me that *some* sort of preparation can be made. At least a warning sent out to be *ready* to handle any situation. For instance—Suppose millions of leaflets be published—*Short*—one page—and addressed to the key industries— the organized workers. Saying just this—"To the Members of the United Mine Workers of America. Should a crisis arise in this country, such as arose in Russia—is your organization prepared to handle the production of coal without chaos or confusion? If not—perfect your organization until it can do so. You *miners*—not the mine owners— are responsible to the nation for this necessary coal. Prepare yourself through your organization to do your duty." Then another sent to the Railway Workers—asking if their industry is so organized as to be able to handle the distribution—etc etc. Make no attempt to dictate—*how* but start the thought of the workers in line *with* the change that should come. Then *also*—Get a few—as many as pos- sible—of the leading spirits in various organizations Socialist Party— I.W.W. Non-Partisan League, People's Council U.M.W. of A.—etc.— to come to *this one* understanding *should* a crisis arise these organi- zations would immediately hold a conference and act in unison in response {to} *that* particular situation. In this way we can prepare to *reach* a common basis. Don't you think? Or is this idea absurd? *Surely* now is our time if we fail to grasp it generations may pass before our fight is won.

But I *meant* to tell you about the trial'—Isn't it wonderful that I am permitted to have a part in it? I'm not doing the real court room work—I'm getting the evidence in readiness—the papers—bulletins etc. And I conducted an investigation of the industries in Chicago— garment workers, car factories, stores, etc. where women are em- ployed. This to lend human interest and local color. A corp of women— about a dozen—went to work as employes and then reported con- ditions.

There is really nothing to this jury sensation. We had the co- operation of the Socialists—and were getting the best of the situation because of our fund of information about the Venire men. The pros- ecution had used three out of the six preemptory challenges—and not one juror sworn. We had offered four to be sworn—one a Socialist and another a *near* Socialist. Others would have necessitated the pros- ecution using two more challenges—leaving but one to be exercised on the remaining eight—While we had used but one. At this point the prosecuting attorney made his charges. Judge Landis[2] inquired of some of the Venire men and found that they had been asked over the phone to vote for the Socialist candidate and interrogated respecting their opinions on Socialism and the I.W.W. He then dismissed everyone and instructed a new Venire be drawn. This has proved quite satisfactory thus far for the proportion of workingmen on the new list is far greater than on the old. So we begin all over again tomorrow.

Remember me most kindly to Mrs. Debs and to Theodore. If either of you come to Chicago be sure to look me up. I'm enclosing my card—so you'll know I'm really a sure-'nuff "lady lawyer." At least on paper. It takes *practice* to be one in court.

I told you about how good Dr. Mayo was to Comrade Owens,[3] didn't I? He took him in and gave him a *thorough* examination told him what to do—and never charged a cent. Altho' he pronounced him incurable.

Dearest love to you, Comrade Debs and a heart full of good wishes for you all. Believe me ever—and *more* than ever

Yours for the Revolution
Caroline A. Lowe

Read the enclosed editorial Comrade Debs—My attention was just called to it since closing my letter—*They're* expecting it, too, aren't they? Praises be!

C

ALS, InTI, Debs Collection.

1. Lowe was assisting in the defense of the 101 IWW members whose trial opened in Chicago on April 1, 1918.
2. Kenesaw Mountain Landis (1866-1944) attracted national attention for the superpatriotic manner in which he presided (and imposed jail sentences) at the IWW trial and the trials of other radicals during and after World War I. His later fame rested on his role as baseball commissioner from 1920 until his death.
3. Edgar Owens was a former state secretary of the Socialist party in Illinois and an Illinois delegate to the emergency convention in 1917.

EVD to David Karsner

April 15, 1918
Terre Haute, Indiana

My dear Comrade Dave:—
A thousand thanks! Did not know you had returned to Gotham. Had hoped for the passing glimpse you thought possible on the return trip.

Please find article enclosed with some corrections noted.[1] I am wondering how the type-setter came to leave out the engineers and their chief official at two very important points in the opening. It is a serious misstatement of facts which results from this omission, and engineers who see it will no doubt resent it. I hope this was caught in the proof for otherwise a note should appear in an ensuing issue making the correction. I know it was not your fault. You have treated the article in your usual magnanimous manner and I am deeply sensible of your kindness.

Your I.W.W. article I will take home with me to read tonight. It will be doubly interesting because it is your picture and has in it the coloring of your brush.

Your letter of the 13th. inst. in regard to my article on the Russian revolution is at hand this instant. I note reason for delay in publication. Thank you, dear comrade, for your suggestion as well as your precaution. You are of course at liberty to omit the words underscored in the paragraph you quote, the words being as follows, "allies cheek by jowl with the entente powers." Kindly see that the proof is carefully read to avoid error.

I feel flattered by your more than generous and enthusiastic estimate of this bit of writing.

I have written two Marx articles which are supposed to have gone to the socialist press, one on "Marx the Man" and the other on "Marx and the Young People." The first went to the Socialist Times of Minneapolis with the understanding based on their own suggestion that it was to be sent to all socialist papers for general use. If you have not received this please drop a line to Georgian[2] the editor of that paper and ask him to send you a copy. Kruse, secretary of the Y.P.S.L., will no doubt be glad to send you the other article if you wish that also. I would gladly write something special for you if it were physically possible but I am so far behind with demands coming in by every mail that I am unable to do it, and I am working a good deal more than I ought to be doing in my still weak condition.   /

My love to you, dear comrade, with all my heart.

Yours in all things,
Eugene V. Debs

P.S. Kindly send a dozen copies of the Magazine containing my article[3] if you have them to spare.

TLS, NN Kars.

1. Debs's "The Strike That Should Have Won" (*New York Call*, April 13, 1918) was his account of the Burlington railroad strike of 1888 and of the scabbing by the conductors against the engineers, firemen, and switchmen during the strike.

2. Alexis Georgian (1891-1940) edited and published the *Minneapolis Socialist Times* and for twenty-five years operated a "radical book store" in Minneapolis. In 1919, Georgian was rounded up in one of Attorney General Mitchell Palmer's raids and sentenced to deportation to his native Russia (Georgia), but the sentence was never executed, largely on the technical grounds that the United States had no formal diplomatic ties with the Soviet government. Georgian's appeal, which went to the United States Supreme Court in 1921, successfully argued that "he could not be deported to a country the United States did not recognize." *Minneapolis Times,* November 14, 1940.

3. "The Strike That Should Have Won" appeared in the Sunday edition of the *Call,* April 13, 1918.

EVD to Lena Schuhardt[1]

April 16, 1918
Terre Haute, Indiana

My dear Comrade Schuhardt:—

The morning paper tells the story of your persecution and I drop you this line not so much of sympathy as of congratulation. The silly, trumped-up charges upon which you were dismissed in that farce of a trial deceived no intelligent person in this community. Every one who knows you knows how conscientiously and with what exceptional ability and faithfulness you have done your work, and every one will also know before the matter is over with that the charge of disloyalty is a falsehood and calumny and that you were driven from the service because as a socialist you were persona non grata with the capitalist masters who rule in our schools as they do in their factories and stores.

Your dismissal under such circumstances is to your credit and honor and only those who are responsible for thus attempting to smirch you will ever have cause to blush for it.

You refused to pollute the mind of childhood by glorifying human butchery and national massacre; you refused to degrade yourself by inoculating the youth in your charge with the poison of militarism, and for this we love and honor you and for this you will be remembered when those who hurled the contumelious stone are forgotten. I know you will be patient and I know too that in good time justice will come to you and that the temporary sacrifice {will} bring you the merited compensation.

Mrs. Debs and all of our family join in greetings of affection and assurances of loyal devotion to you, and I am always

Faithfully your comrade,
[Eugene V. Debs]

TLc, InTI, Debs Collection.

1. Lena Schuhardt had been a teacher in Terre Haute's public schools for seventeen years when, in April 1918, she was dismissed by the school board for failure "to correct unpatriotic ideas expressed by her pupils," "opposition to the war," teaching that "the war is capitalistic and economic," and failure "to teach her pupils the proper respect for the Star Spangled Banner." *Terre Haute Tribune*, April 16, 1918.

Adolph F. Germer to EVD

April 18, 1918
Chicago, Illinois

My dear Gene:—
I just returned from Colorado and found your letter of the 15th inst. On April 9th I wrote you as follows:

"My dear Gene:
This morning's mail brought your letter of yesterday and I note with interest what you say about holding a special convention of the Socialist Party to re-set our war aims and peace terms.

We have received several suggestions along similar lines and something will have to be done before we open the campaign. While a convention would perhaps be the most advantageous method of getting a new program, the cost of it is prohibitive in view of the fact that we have not yet paid last year's convention expenses. To elect delegates in the regular manner would take from two to three months so that the convention could not be held until sometime in July.

The National Executive Committee will have a meeting the first week in May. Under the new constitution, a conference of State Secretaries is to be held once a year. What I have in mind is to have a joint session of the State Secretaries and the new National Executive Committee, which will be composed of fifteen members and let that gathering formulate a program for the period of the war and for the reconstruction era.[1]

I don't think the invasion of Russia will in the end be as fatal to us as it now seems. The other day I was speaking to a comrade who is closely in touch with the Russian situation and he is firmly convinced that the German autocracy is digging its own grave by its treatment towards the Russian government. He says first of all that the further the German army gets into Russia, the more will the German military power be weakened on the Western front. In addition to this, he contends that while the German autocracy is conquering Russian territory, it is by no means conquering the

Russian revolutionary spirit and that with the territorial conquests, the German autocracy also inherits the Russian revolution, which will eventually force its way into Germany and Austria. The more territory Germany conquers, the more soldiers will be needed to keep that territory in check and correspondingly, the more soldiers will be taken from the Western front.

I can subscribe in the main to the program of the Inter-Allied except where they call for a support of the war. In view of what the Democratic Administration has done, to the members of the Socialist Party all over the country, and in view of the merciless suppression of the press and the interference with our general propaganda, I don't see how we can consistently support the policy of the Democratic Administration.

It seems that we are all agreed that a re-statement should be made of the Socialist Party position but there is difference of opinion as to the best course to pursue. The sentiment created by the German invasion of Russia is in a measure being offset by the Japanese and British invasion of Siberia and of course, here it must be said to the credit of Wilson, that he has so far refused to give his approval of that policy. Ramsey MacDonald,[2] in an article published in Pearson's Magazine for April struck the key note when he said: 'If a different Government now spoke for England—not a Government of surrender, but a Government of clearly defined democratic aims, a Government ready to seize such openings as Count Czernin[3] gave, and to remove suspicions from the minds of the peoples of the Central Powers—Europe could have peace.' Here MacDonald points out that the people of the Central Empires are just as suspicious of the Allied Governments as the people of the Allied Governments are suspicious of the Governments of the Central Empires. In my opinion we should formulate a policy that will command the confidence of the working class of all the country, a policy of clearly defined Democratic aims and then insist that the Allied Governments adopt them as a basis for peace negotiations at the earliest possible moment. If the governments adopt such a policy, then we will have something to get into the war for. If they refuse, we have a right to be suspicious of them and to refuse our support.

Berger is in town this morning and tho I talked the matter over briefly with him yesterday, I am to have another conference with him this afternoon.

I will be glad to hear from you further in connection with this all important matter for we want the benefit of other comrades' views.

With all good wishes, I am as ever

Fraternally yours,
Adolph Germer,
Executive Secretary."

Evidently like a lot of other mail, this letter has gone astray. I hope it has done some good wherever it went.

There is a growing feeling in favor of changing the Party position. Here and there we receive a letter opposing any radical change but the bulk of the correspondence on the subject, and most of the members with whom I have come in personal contact, favor a change. However, I am not enthusiastic over a convention. We still owe about $7,000 on last year's convention and the fact that we have not been able to pay that bill will cause a lack of enthusiasm for a convention. I suggested to the National Executive Committee that we advance the date of the joint meeting of State Secretaries and the new National Executive Committee, which is composed of fifteen members, to June 1st. Stedman comments as follows:

"I believe it is advisable to hold a meeting of State Secretaries and the new National Executive Committee, and we should welcome assistance from States which are able to send representatives at their expense. This conference might issue, subject to a referendum, a re-statement of the present attitude of the Party."

I favor this conference in preference to a convention for three reasons. First, it is a conference that must be held anyhow in accordance with our constitution. Second, it will be less expensive than a convention and third, it can be held at a much earlier date than a convention.

It is quite probable that I will be in Indianapolis on May 5th when we can talk this matter over in person.

The other day while out in Denver, I met our mutual friend and comrade, Channing Sweet and I had quite an interesting talk with him. Of course, he inquired about you and when I told him that my information was that your health was rapidly improving, he was very much delighted. He is a great old fellow and I wish we had a million more like him.

With every good wish, I am as ever

Fraternally yours,
Adolph Germer
Executive Secretary.

P.S. Let me know whether this reaches you.

TLS, InTI, Debs Collection.

1. As noted, the national conference of the national executive committee members and state secretaries was held in Chicago in August 1918.

2. James Ramsay MacDonald (1866-1937) was a leader of the British Labour party who opposed England's entry into the war and its wartime policies. He lost his leadership role in the party and his seat in Parliament during the war but regained both in 1922 and served as Labour prime minister in 1924 and 1929-31 and as head of a coalition cabinet from 1931 to 1935.

3. Count Ottokar Czernin (1872-1932) served as the Austro-Hungarian foreign minister from December 1916 to April 1918, during which period he urged peace upon the German leaders and Emperor Charles, even if it included Germany's loss of Alsace-Lorraine and the restoration of Belgium, and climaxed his career as foreign minister by negotiating peace treaties with the Ukraine (February 1918), Russia (March 1918), and Romania (April 1918).

J. A. Phillips[1] to EVD

April 21, 1918
St. Louis, Missouri

Dear Comrade Debs:

For many moons I have wanted to write to you but it seemed to me presumptious, and you may deem it unwarranted that I should unload on you any criticisms of our party.

The position taken at the St. Louis convention on the war question was a suicidal one from my viewpoint, and I have been hoping our leaders would see the situation in that light and come out openly with it. I love the Socialist Party for the good it has done, and in spite of its many mistakes. I shall continue to support it in every way possible, regardless of my opposition to its war policy. I will stick with the ship even tho it is not piloted as I wish, but I MUST unload on some one so here goes.

Our mistaken policy has resulted in imprisonment for some of as good comrades as ever lived, and persecution for many others. It has given the Reactionary element an opportunity long wanted to get even on old scores, and they have been busy at the job. It was neither the *right* stand nor the *political* one.

Every other Socialist party in the world has stood with their governments against German invasion led by German Junkers and German Socialists vigorously supporting the World conquest of their ruling class. What would have been the fate of the World had the Socialists in Belgium, France, Italy, and England taken our position with regard to war?

One thing is sure: If the working class in Germany support their war mad rulers there can be no peace neither in Europe nor elsewhere. And they have so far supported every thing done by the Kaiser and his Military Machine. They did not even *protest* when Belgium was invaded, or when France was invaded without cause. They have not protested against the double dealing of their Diplomats with stricken Russia. They had not the courage to protest when unrestricted Submarine warfare was announced, and they would not do so if the Kaiser ordered them to violate every law of humanity and justice. They have never been Internationalists, therefore do not deserve our consideration as such. Yet that is exactly what we have given them.

Every other group of Socialists have taken their stand openly against the war mania of Germany, and at the same time have opposed their own master class in the manner of conducting the war and have profited by it. For any policy which serves and helps the working class is bound to increase the power of the party responsible for it. Here we have only opposed the war. Instead of openly supporting the war until a just and honorable peace can be made   and that will not be until Germany is exhausted, at the same time conducting an active agitation against the way war has been conducted, we stand up and try to repeal Conscription. We should have been busy last winter holding mass meetings demanding Government ownership of the Coal Industry, likewise the Packing Industry and all others that are ripe for it. Instead we were busy denouncing the Government and the war. What a tragedy.

The German Socialists *support* their Government in *every* act. We on the other hand, *oppose* our Government in its *every* act. Both positions are wrong. Ours as much as theirs, and particularly on account of theirs. For with Germany *united* and all others *divided* it takes no seer to predict the future for the world.

When I see Gompers able to make almost any charge against the Socialist Party, and know that it is not guiltless as charged, it is enough to make an Angel go to war. We will never get from where we are to where we want to be until we learn that TACTICS are necessary to move in the right direction. Theory is fine but it breaks down under fire. Jaures was against war, and could not see that his every word and act met the approval of both German Kaiser and German Socialists, for he helped hold back the French Nation from getting ready to meet the Invaders until the Germans were almost upon them—losing his life as a result. With all his wisdom he let his love for Internationalism get the better of his knowledge of FACTS, for he certainly should have known the psychology of the Germans well enough to know they would follow their teachings for war and force.

Now Gene here is where you fit into this letter. I have been watching your articles in all our publications, hoping and hoping you would lead the way and light the road for the rest of us. We look to you for leadership, and you cannot escape that responsibility. If you continue to stand against the war you may and no doubt will hold the party in that road, but I am hoping you will come out openly and put the party and some of our lop-sided leaders in the right way.

We have everything to gain by getting on the right road and we have everything to lose by continuing to follow the wrong one. Either the party is wrong or *I AM*. If I am not right I want to be set right. And I know you can do either job—for the party or me. Its up to you.

Yours ever,
J. A. Phillips

My Love to Theodore and All, and pardon my pestering you in this moment. *But you need it.*

TLS, InTI, Debs Collection.

1. James Andrew Phillips (1873-1949) worked through the ranks of the Order of Railway Conductors to become general chairman of the union's Chicago, Rock Island & Pacific Railway line in 1918, vice-president in 1919, and president from 1934 to 1941.

EVD to Frank P. O'Hare

April 26, 1918
Terre Haute, Indiana

Dear Frank:—

Sorry I was obliged to leave you before your train time. Should not have done so except for illness at home.

Theo. has just handed me the very happily posed family group with Kate's autograph and greeting for which I thank you. It is a lovely grouping, so very expressive of family love and life at its best, and I need not say that it will have a permanent place in our little emporium of art where the near and dear are ever with us.

Please do not have the L.D.U. send those envelopes to the different points I am booked to cover in Indiana,[1] nor arrange to handle the matter as you indicated while here. I do not think that under the circumstances the thing can be successfully done that way. There are several reasons for this.

Of course no one but Kate herself can begin to handle that particular matter in that particular way with the results she has obtained. People go especially to hear her story and it naturally and appealingly unfolds into the collection for the defense. [two illegible words] personal appearance commands the success that [two illegible words] appeal for the defense of her comrades and herself [two illegible words] aside from this there are other matters connected with the meetings I am booked to address which make another plan preferable. First of all, it is not at all certain that these meetings will be permitted to be held. I should not be at all surprised if as has been already intimated the authorities followed the lead of the Council of Defense of Minnesota and issued an order prohibiting me from addressing these meetings and probiting the meetings from being held. Just what I should do in that case I do not yet know but I should certainly not tamely submit. You doubtless know that the comrades in Minnesota wanted me to address some meetings in that state but that the Council of Defense and the governor decided that I could not speak in the state during the term of the war and the comrades were forced to abandon the meetings because they could secure no places in which to hold them.[2]

In the next place, these meetings, if held, will be under the auspices of the state committee and for the special purpose of opening the political campaign in the several cities where they are held. The state office is furnishing the printing and advertising and will of course expect some return, while the local at each point is counting on taking up a collection in addition to the admission fee to start its campaign with. Besides all this I shall want to do something for Phil and the Social Builder[3] to help them out of the hole, and under these circumstances it is not at all probable that the plan of distributing envelopes and calling for dollar subscriptions would pan out in very satisfactory results. I think it better, therefore to make a general appeal for such funds as may be secured for the defense fund. Of course I shall discuss Kate's case and make such an appeal for her as I can and show the absolute necessity of raising funds for the legal defense of herself and other comrades under indictment for serving the cause.

I believe this will have a better effect and secure better results than to attempt the other method at these particular meetings. I am wishing you all success in every effort and every undertaking in behalf of Kate and the [two illegible words] the comrades threatened with the vengeance of the ruling [two illegible words].

Yours fraternally,
E. V. Debs

TLS (with typed signature), MoH, O'Hare Papers.

1. In a letter (April 22, 1918) to William H. Henry, state secretary of the Socialist party in Indiana, Theodore Debs listed seventeen "points in the state" at which Debs was scheduled to speak between May 13 and June 28, 1918.

2. In 1920 the *American Labor Year Book* (p. 90), reviewing the attack on civil liberties during the war, noted that "Minnesota appears to have been the state most vigorous and thorough in its sweeping abolition of all freedom of opinion."

3. In May 1918, *Social Revolution* (formerly the *Rip-Saw*) "metamorphosed into the *Social Builder*," with Phil Wagner as "Superintendent of Construction" and Debs one of the "Foremen."

EVD to Max Ehrmann

April 27, 1918
Terre Haute, Indiana

My dear Max:—

You have no doubt seen the current issue of Pearson's which contains your beautiful and, I fear, too generous appreciation.[1] I did not know of its appearance until advised by a New York friend who wrote to pay you a fine compliment and to tender me, as well he might, his congratulations upon being the recipient of so flattering a testimonial at your hands. I wondered how Pearson's came by the paper, whether through the biographical people for whom it was prepared or direct from you, and I concluded that it had been sent by you. Of course this is of little consequence but I should be glad to be advised if I am not right.

The tribute reads even more beautifully than when I heard it read by you from the original manuscript which you afterward very critically reviewed and revised. It is an extraordinarily fine piece of writing and reflects the highest order of literary craftsmanship. It is indeed a classic and will stand as such entirely apart from the large and generous personal estimates which perhaps not many will give assent to.

I will not attempt to thank you. Words are entirely too blank and meaningless. I shall do the very best I can, vain though it be, to live up to the flattering likeness your generosity has made of me.

Love to you, dear friend, and my heart's warmest wishes!

Yours always,
Eugene V. Debs

TLS, InGrD-Ar, Ehrmann Papers.

1. In "Eugene V. Debs" (*Pearson's*, May 1918), Ehrmann compared Debs with Socrates, Luther, Voltaire, Wendell Phillips, and Susan B. Anthony, calling Debs "the travelling college professor of the masses, their lecturer on economics, their stirrer-up, their provoker."

EVD to Max Ehrmann

April 30, 1918
Terre Haute, Indiana

My dear Max:—

Thanks to you for the cordial and appreciative message from you just at hand.

It appears once more that "great minds" run in the same channels. I had already thought of putting the Pearson's articles[1] in a book after suggestions of the sort had come to me, and I had already applied for and secured permission for Pearson's to use them for that purpose. And now comes your happy suggestion with the generious offer of your inspired appreciation for the introductory. Just the thing! If all these writings had conspired to compliment and complement each other a happier result could not have been achieved.

Wagner, St. Louis, will gladly publish the book and he has facilities for giving it considerable advertising. Any other publisher you may suggest or prefer will have precedence. I hope we may talk it over soon and shall be glad to see you any time after this week at your own convenience.

Yours always,
E. V. Debs

TLS, InGrD-Ar, Ehrmann Papers.

1. Debs's reminiscences of James Whitcomb Riley, Robert Ingersoll, and Wendell Phillips, which had appeared in *Pearson's* in March, April, and May 1917. The project of putting them in a book did not materialize.

Jack Carney to Theodore Debs

May 8, 1918
Duluth, Minnesota

My dear Comrade Theodore,

Thanks very much for your postcard, by this same mail I have sent you ten copies of the paper,[1] more if you want them.

Working up here is the very exciting task. The Commercial Club have formed four committees and they are doing their damdest (is that grammatically correct.) to stop our advertising. They have also formed another committee to get me and tar and feather me. The latter only makes [me] homesick, because we have that every day of the week in Ireland. It is a hard fight, and unfortunately some of our comrades are getting nervous. I am not in favor of ALL that the I W W do, but by God I want them to have their Constitutional rights. Comrades object, and even the I W W go out of their way at times to call me a middleclass intellectual. All this makes it hard, but we should worry, the fight is a good one and the Cause is a better one.

I do not want to worry 'Gene, but a line from Gene for the paper,[2] would do a whole lot in this benighted burgh. I am just all my lonesome. I am getting into a rotten way of looking at things. You sit all alone in the office, expecting every minute some gunman or thug to go for you, and so you cannot be too open with your own comrades, because some of them are strangers to me. So you will readily see how things go. But I am not giving up. The Dept of Justice had me grilled for ninety minutes, tried to scare me. But Theodore I am just one bit more revolutionary, every time they go for me.

Gee but it is good to be a Socialist these days, we are coming into our own, so we should worry.

Give my love to 'Gene and his dear wife and all of your family. Guess Gene is my real guide, when I feel blue I just think of dear old Gene and I start all over again and receive new inspiration.

With all the love of comradeship.

Always smiling and keep old RED FLAG flying,

Yours in REVOLT.

Jack Carney

TLS, InTI, Debs Collection.

1. *Truth*, "the official organ of the Socialist Party of Duluth and Superior."
2. During the month following this letter, Carney published a series of Debs's articles in *Truth*: "Debs's Tribute to Women" (May 10, 1918); "Stand By Your Ground" (May 17, 1918); and "Farewell, Capitalism!" (May 24, 1918).

Phil Wagner to EVD

May 17, 1918
St. Louis, Missouri

My dear Gene:

Your letter of a few days ago at hand and contents carefully noted.
I decided to suspend publication[1] after viewing the matter from all
sides as I found it impossible to continue under the heavy burden
that I was under. I can assure you that I am sorry that I was compelled
to give up the big fight but the odds were against me. Possibly later
on we will again be able to resume.

Words fail me at this time to tell you how I appreciate your loyalty
to me in past years and I hope that some day I may be able to repay
you in part at least, for the many kindnesses shown me.

Kindly give my kindest regards to Mrs. Debs, your mother [sic],
and also to Theodore and tell him I will write him at my earliest
opportunity.

With best wishes and hoping that this finds you enjoying the best
of health and hoping your lecture trip[2] will not be a hardship on you,
I remain

As ever yours,
Phil

TLS, InTI, Debs Collection.

1. *Social Builder* (formerly *Social Revolution* and *National Rip Saw*) suspended pub
lication after one issue (May 1918).
2. Debs's two-month lecture tour in Indiana in May and June 1918.

EVD to S. M. Reynolds

May 25, 1918
Terre Haute, Indiana

My dear Stephen:—

Your messages are always sweet to me and the one that came in
my absence is now in my hands and its loving assurance touches me
deeply. But I am not entitled to your felicitations. I have not changed
in regard to the war. I have simply been lied about by the capitalist
press as I have been many times before.[1] My position has been and
will continue to be that of an internationalist. I cannot be pro-war in
any war capitalist nations make upon one another. The spirit of the

lying press is made manifest in the editorial abuse I am getting for having, as alleged, "changed in the last hour and now come cringing to the band wagon." They need not lay that flattering unction to their deceitful and malicious hearts. I can if necessary stand alone and I certainly would not change my position to be popular or because of threats or intimidations. This is a trying ordeal for us all. We have simply to be true to the light within and all will come well in the end.

We are all loving you and all of you in the same way. There can never be any change. Out on the road many inquire about you and always in the fondest terms. All inquirers are also your lovers. I am just leaving on another speaking tour.

Loving remembrances to Jessica and Marion.

Yours always,
E. V. Debs

TLS, InH, Reynolds Collection.

1. In "Debs Issues Statement Correcting Lie Spread by Capitalist Papers," which appeared in the *New York Call* (June 4, 1918) and several other socialist papers, Debs denied that he had been "whipped into line" regarding the war and was now "humbly clambering aboard the band wagon" but repeated his call for a special convention to revise the "St. Louis platform."

Job Harriman to EVD

June 3, 1918
Leesville, Louisiana

My dear Comrade Debs,

I am writing to you at the request of the associate editor, Comrade Sessions,[1] to see if you will consent to writing a series of articles on the social revolution for THE INTERNATIONALIST.[2] We do not care particularly what phase of the movement you wish to handle, just so you do not subject us to any danger of suppression. We would, of course, reserve the right to edit your copy a little, and, if need be, expunge what seemed to us dangerous.

We shall be glad to pay you ten to fifteen dollars or more for every 1500-word article that you would send us. In answering, kindly state what you consider a reasonable compensation for your time. We are not in the healthiest financial condition as far as paying contributors is concerned, but we realize that your time is worth a great deal, and we would like very much to pay you something.

I read with interest you recent editorial in the SOCIAL BUILDER advocating a re-statement of the Socialist Party position on the war. You are right. Conditions have arisen which make it imperative for us to take another and more constructive stand. Personally, I believe that the Majority Report was a mistake; that it could have been so worded that we would not have brought the wrath of the powers that be down upon us to such an extent as prevails, and that would have made us the rallying point of the nation's constructive forces. At present, we are but easy prey.

I would like very much to talk this question over with you. At any rate, I would appreciate your writing me a letter.

Trusting that you will reply soon to our request, and with best wishes, I am

Sincerely and fraternally,
Job Harriman

TLS, InTI, Debs Collection.

1. Alanson Sessions was a regular contributor to the *New York Call* and other socialist publications before World War I and editor of *Kern County Union Labor* in Bakersfield, California. He was a leading figure in Upton Sinclair's End Poverty In California movement in the 1930s.

2. *The Internationalist* was the official publication of the Llano Colony, which Harriman founded in California's Antelope Valley in 1914. In "Co-operative Colony a Success," an article in *American Socialist* (January 27, 1917), the enterprise was said to be "preparing for ten thousand residents in a few years," but according to Harriman's letter to Debs on July 24, 1918 (below), it moved to Louisiana in December 1918 "because the soil would not yield the crops desired."

Alanson Sessions to EVD

June 3, 1918
Leesville, Louisiana

DEAR Comrade Debs,

I am writing to you to ask you to kindly contribute a series of articles to the column of THE INTERNATIONALIST. As you probably know, our magazine is now considered the leading Socialist monthly journal in America.[1] Its editorial policy, determined largely by Job Harriman, is thoroly constructive and yet revolutionary. And as our magazine is read by over 10,000 subscribers, we are sure that you here have an excellent opportunity to get your interesting ideas across to a large group of careful readers.

Could you send us 1500 to 2000 words every month, commenting on current events much in the same style as your editorials in THE

SOCIAL BUILDER? We have a good cut of you and will run that also. If you consent to this, we will make the announcement in this month's magazine.[2]

We have made arrangements with Comrade Phil Wagner to buy the mailing list of the SOCIAL BUILDER and we are endeavoring to carry on the good work where Phil had unfortunately been compelled to stop.

Kindly let us hear from you at an early date. I am sure that we may co-operate to great mutual advantage.

Very cordially,
Alanson Sessions
THE INTERNATIONALIST

TLS, InTI, Debs Collection.

1. The *Internationalist*'s letterhead identified it as "formerly *The Western Comrade*" and "The Most Constructive Socialist Magazine in America."

2. Debs's decision not to join the *Internationalist* was probably dictated by his preoccupation with his own arrest, trial, and conviction, which followed his Canton speech of June 16, 1918.

Tom Mooney to EVD

June 4, 1918
San Francisco, California

Dear Friend Gene:—

I feel as though I should say a few words to you, along with a number of other friends, prior to my being taken away from this jail to San Quentin.

In spite of all showings on the surface (and I hope that I am greatly mistaken), it is in my opinion, judging from every act of Governor Stephens in connection with developments in our case, that he will not do anything as suggested by the President, toward seeing that I get another trial.[1] I base my belief in this matter, on the ground that every single statement given out by the Governor has a tendency to show that he is not in the slightest degree favorably disposed to do the right thing in this case. Every important communication—such as telegrams from the President of the United States on three different occasions, and a letter on one occasion; cablegrams from the London Trades Council, and many others—after they have reached the Governor, have been withheld from publication by him. This fact leads me to believe that he is trying, as much as possible, to bury all matter that would have a tendency to justify him in the public eye, in doing something to straighten out this vile mess of Fickert's. Judge Griffin last week wrote the Governor a letter I presume in support of his former request to the Attorney General and the Supreme Court; viz., that I should receive a new trial, and saying that, had the Oxman letters been before him at the time of his passing on my motion for a new trial, he would have unhesitatingly granted it. The Governor refuses absolutely, to make any statement as to the contents of Judge Griffin's letter.

There are some people in this town, who are close in political circles to the Governor; some of them are actually holding office under him. A member of the Pardon Board (Mr. Neumiller, of Stockton[2]) told a friend confidentially, and it came to us indirectly, and confidentially—that Governor Stephens would not do anything in the Mooney case.

A very influential man in the commercial life of San Francisco— the owner of the largest shoe store; a man who was a member of the grand jury that whitewashed Frank C. Oxman—has declared that Governor Stephens will not do anything in behalf of Tom Mooney. This man has further said that nobody with any sense believed Mooney guilty, but that the "s— o– b—— should get it, anyway."

In my estimation, these things speak volumes. In such a moment, I believe that I am as calm and cool as any man might be; and I am reserving my judgment, publicly, until a decision has been made. Then we can see whether my reasoning was correct or incorrect.

I hope that you will do all in your power to bring about publicity[o] and action on the part of all the progressive element in the country, and the labor element in particular, to the end that, unless justice is done in this case, there shall be drastic action taken by the President of the United States, in support of his request. At this time, a definite plan is being put on foot by the International Workers' Defense League, and I hope that you will give it every aid possible in furtherance of its success. That is, they propose that the American Federation of Labor, and all of its affiliated bodies, request the President to take the whole matter out of the State's hands and see that a new trial for me is had, to determine the validity of the evidence presented against the defendants in the former trials, and in the new trial. This, to me, looks like the only possible solution, because Fickert is determined; and we get it now that, on the low down, the Chamber of Commerce is determined, and they are going to "stay put," and let the whole program go through—no question of commutation of sentence, but let it stand just as it is. It is time that we speak of these matters frankly, and understand ourselves and the situation that confronts us. Of course, if the American Federation of Labor, and the progressive element of the country, are willing to say Amen to a court's decision that holds, if the district attorney can hire perjury enough to hang a man on, there is no remedy—if the A. F. of L. acquiesces in that sort of thing, there is nothing to be done, only to let the hangman proceed. But I feel keenly, that the rank and file of the labor movement in this country will not stand for a man being hanged, when they know that that man is the victim of a conspiracy of anti-union-labor forces,—that his conviction was brought about by perjury, as well as a "jury" well fixed by its foreman and by the prosecutor in the case.

I have declared myself absolutely, to be uncompromising in the final outcome of this matter. My innocence has been proven beyond a doubt, and I will not accept anything short of absolute vindication of this dastardly charge; and every effort that is made in my behalf, must be to that end. I hope that you will keep this point uppermost in mind, in any action that you invoke for me.

Now that the A. F. of L. convention is about to convene at St. Paul, it strikes me this is the logical time for them to declare a policy, in pursuance of a successful termination of the issues involved in this scandalous and outrageous attack upon organized labor. *There never will be another trial in connection with these cases, unless it is had by the Federal Government;* and this can only be undertaken, not as a legal matter, but as an extraordinary procedure, justifiable only as a war measure and emergency. The President is commander-in-chief of the army and navy, in time of war; and in that capacity, he can do almost anything if it becomes a war measure. If this case is permitted to drag along, and injustice is done to the individuals involved, I am inclined to believe that many unions will not hesitate to go on strike. I am forming this judgment from the communications that I have received by the hundred, from unions all over the country, declaring that they will take such action; and many of them had already voted to do the same, but my letter to them, asking them to call off the strikes, had a tendency to stay action for the time being, at least. I am inclined to think that, if these circumstances confront me, I will be absolutely justified in permitting the workers to follow their inclination, because my life is not the real issue involved in this struggle. There is a great principle, far more important and more valuable to preserve, than the life of one man; and that is, the right of every working man to a fair and free trial; and at the same time, the right of Labor to organize without being victimized by powerful, criminal, plotting, anti-union-labor employers' organizations.

The London Central Labor Council (representing more than 100,000 trade unionists have sent resolutions protesting vigorously against the sentences imposed upon Billings and myself, and in the strongest possible manner, appealing to the American ambassador in London,[4] the President of the United States, and Governor Stephens, for a new trial. They also sent a cablegram of their protest to the Governor, asking him to stay the execution until another trial could be had. They sent a copy of this cablegram to the S.F. Labor Council, and to the S.F. Daily Bulletin. The British Labor Party has gone on record, declaring itself unequivocally in favor of fair play in this matter, and endorsing the decision of the American Federation of Labor, in its request for a new trial. These matters, in my judgment, if properly crystalized by the American Federation of Labor and the progressive element of the country, can be placed in the President's hands, and be justified in taking the necessary action to straighten out this whole, reeking, Chamber-of-Commerce mess.

I have tried in the foregoing, to give you an idea of my personal opinion in the matter, and what I think ought to be done. If you can be of any assistance in furtherance of this plan, I hope that you will proceed immediately, as the issues in this case have now reached a crisis. I feel keenly, that the final decision will be reached, one way or the other, within the next nine or ten weeks.

With kindest remembrances and best wishes to you,

I am,

Very sincerely and fraternally yours,
Tom Mooney

TLS, InTI, Debs Collection.

1. As noted, California Governor William Denison Stephens (1859-1944) rejected several of President Wilson's appeals for a new trial or pardon for Mooney before commuting Mooney's death sentence to life imprisonment in November 1918.

2. Charles Louis Neumiller (1874-1933) was a member of the California Prison Board from 1912 until his death and a nationally recognized figure in the field of prison welfare and reform.

3. Debs's "Tom Mooney's Appeal" appeared in the June 22, 1918, issue of the *Eye-Opener*, the Socialist party's official publication. It called for the unconditional release of Mooney, who had been convicted on "perjured evidence," and asked readers to write Governor Stephens and demand that he do his duty.

4. Walter Hines Page (1855-1918) was United States ambassador to Great Britain from 1913 until poor health forced him to resign in August 1918.

Oliver C. Wilson[1] to EVD

June 5, 1918
Chicago, Illinois

Dear Comrade: —

I would very much like to know if it will be possible for the national office to enter into a contract with you to fill 40 speaking engagements in the campaign this fall during September and October. If this is possible I would like to visit you at your home in the near future and ~~make~~ go over the details of the tour.

I realize that your health will make it impossible and inadvisable for you to work this fall as you have in the years gone by. On the other hand the very life of the Socialist Party is at stake and the one thing that will do more than any other thing to put courage in the movement will be a tour of the country by you during the campaign.

It will take some time under prevailing circumstances to arrange such a tour and I desire to get started as soon as possible. I wish you would consult with your physician and then notify me if you can undertake this task.

Of course the tour would be arranged in such way as not to over tax you physically and you could be accompanied by your brother. We would also have a representative along to look after some special work we have in mind.

Trusting that I may hear from you in the near future and that it will be possible for you to comply with this request, I am

Fraternally yours,
O. C. Wilson
Campaign Manager

TLS, InTI, Debs Collection.

1. Oliver C. Wilson was financial director of the Socialist Party and head of the party's 1918 campaign effort.

EVD to Bolton Hall[1]

July 6, 1918
Terre Haute, Indiana

Dear Brother Bolton Hall: —

Thank you warmly for your kind and sympathetic message. I am expecting nothing but conviction under a law flagrantly unconstitutional and which was framed especially for the suppression of free speech.[2] I shall make no denial of a word I uttered and it is only for the sake of the party and the cause that I have consented to any defense at all and this only as a means of resisting the attempts now being made to entirely suppress free speech and crush every radical and progressive movement. I am simply one of thousands who have the privilege of doing a bit of extra service for the cause in these days of madness and destruction. Believe me always,

Yours fraternally,
Eugene V. Debs

TLS, NN, Bolton Hall Papers.

1. Bolton Hall (1854-1938) came to the United States from his native Ireland in 1868, graduated from Princeton in 1875 and the Columbia law school in 1881, and thereafter combined the practice of law with a consistent advocacy of workers' rights. A disciple of Henry George and one of the nation's leading single-tax exponents, Hall published a number of books on taxation, back-to-the-land programs, and land-for-the-poor projects, and his poetry appeared frequently in the radical and socialist press.

2. Debs's speech at Canton, Ohio, on June 16, 1918, in which he set forth ideas and opinions on the war made repeatedly during the preceding four years—the relationship between capitalism and war, the uneven burden of the war on capitalists and workers, the injustice of the convictions and imprisonments being carried out under the wartime Espionage Act—was the basis of his indictment, conviction, and imprisonment for violation of the Espionage Act.

EVD to James Oneal

July 8, 1918
Terre Haute, Indiana

My dear "Jim":—

I have your splendid letter and the copies of the Call containing your kind, generous and loyal tribute. A thousand thanks. Your letter has the exceptional note in it that rings clear and true and your article puts the World critic to shame and gloriously vindicates his would-be victim.[1] You have only been too generous, my dear boy, and given me so much more than is coming to me. The older I grow the smaller I feel my part has been in the cause in which I would gladly have endured anything to render service of some actual account. Thousands of others have gone to jail and my going there is but an incident. If but the cause is served the jail is preferable to the fireside at home much as we may be devoted to the loved ones there.

Let me thank you right warmly for both your beautiful letter and your generous and inspiring article. The latter, aside from all personal consideration, is an exceptional bit of logical reasoning and a piece of really fine writing. I am glad you are on the Call.[2] I feel that you belong there at this particular time. You and Ervin and Karsner and Wanhope make a great combination. Theodore and my wife join in love to you and yours.

Always loyally,
Eugene V. Debs

TLS, NNU Tam, Debs Collection.

1. In a *Call* article, "The 'Erratic' Debs" (July 4, 1918), Oneal quoted a *New York World* editorial that described Debs as "an erratic person given to violence" and then acknowledged that Debs was erratic in the same way that "Bruno, Huss, Brown, Phillips and Garrison were erratic."

2. Oneal resigned as state secretary of the Socialist party in Massachusetts to join the *Call* staff in March 1918.

EVD to John Edwards[1]

July 9, 1918
Terre Haute, Indiana

Dear Comrade Edwards:

Very fully do I appreciate the nomination for Congress tendered to me by my comrades, especially under the circumstances in which the nomination came to me, and very gladly would I accept the honor if I were able to do so. But there are reasons in my present situation, physical and otherwise, which make this absolutely impossible. The coming months promise to be very busy ones for me and I have already more in hand than I can well manage, and am therefore compelled, much to my regret, to decline the nomination.

Under all ordinary circumstances I realize it to be my duty to serve the cause in any way my comrades may think best and to yield willing obedience to their wishes, but my situation at present for obvious reasons forbids this and I am reluctantly obliged to inform you and through you the District Committee and the comrades of the Fifth District in general that greatly as I appreciate the honor they have conferred upon me and the confidence it implies, I cannot possibly in justice either to the party or myself accept the nomination.

Allow me to express to your committee and to each comrade in the district my hearty thanks for the kind partiality and generous consideration shown me. I need not assure you that I am with you and shall be with you in all things that may be undertaken to vitalize the socialist propaganda, wage a successful working class campaign, and spread the light of socialism among the masses.

What is now needed above all things is sound education, the kind that clarifies the minds of the workers and enables them to see the international struggle of the working class against their exploiters and oppressors, and teaches them to organize their industrial and political forces and develop their power as a class that they may abolish the prevailing capitalist system of exploitation, emancipate the toiling masses of all nations, and bring democracy and peace, freedom and self-government, brotherhood and love to a war-torn, blood-drenched and distracted world.

Yours fraternally,
[Eugene V. Debs]

TLc, Int'l, Debs Collection.

1. John W. Edwards was a Terre Haute coal miner and chairman of the Socialist party in the Fifth Congressional District in Indiana. Debs's letter to Edwards was summarized in the *Terre Haute Tribune*, July 10, 1918.

EVD to James Oneal

July 9, 1918
Terre Haute, Indiana

Dear "Jim": —

The issue of the Call Magazine of the 7th.[1] inst. containing your "portrait" of me is at hand and I wish to thank you very heartily for this more than generous tribute which I fear is but scantily deserved. Your gifted pen has made this a really vital sketch and I feel especially flattered to have this fine offering come from you, a typical young proletarian, in whom I have always had a special interest and for whom the personal attachment has grown stronger with the passing years.

You have certainly made me the subject of a fine piece of personal writing and if I do not remain in the literature of the movement it will not be because you failed to place me there. Thank you, my dear young comrade, for this service of love which touches me to the heart and which does me honor in far greater measure than I deserve. When I look back over the trail it seems to me that the things which may be credited to me are all small and paltry and I cannot understand by what magic except by that of your love and devotion these things could have been magnified sufficiently to be made to appear as actual achievements as they do in your beautiful and appreciative sketch.

You have always been to me one of the brightest and most promising of {young} revolutionists and I have always been certain of your self-fulfillment. With the little advantage you had in youth you have actually accomplished wonders. That history of the working class by you, written under the most embarrassing restrictions and limitations and with all sorts of difficulties to overcome, is still a masterly work and in all its pages it is written that you are destined to be the historian of the movement. Your extraordinary faculty for historical research and analysis is in evidence in all the chapters of this chronicle so long and so shamelessly neglected of the workers in American history.

And so I have good reason to feel that I have been thrice complimented by having this eloquent testimonial, this loving tribute come from you, and how deeply sensible I am of the loyal devotion which inspired it no words of mine are sufficient to tell.

I can only thank you and love you and I do both from the depths of my heart, and most earnestly do I hope to see you advance step by step to larger usefulness and a loftier plane, and finally to see the hopes and dreams, the ideals and aspirations of your youth triumphantly realized.

As always in the past I am,

Your loving comrade,
Eugene V. Debs

TLS, NNU Tam, Debs Collection.

1. Oneal's "Eugene V. Debs," which appeared in the *Call Magazine* on July 7, 1918, recalled Debs's role in the Pullman Strike and his reception in Terre Haute following the strike and predicted that his indictment in Cleveland for the Canton speech would be "as important as his former arrest 24 years ago."

Adolph F. Germer to EVD

July 15, 1918
Chicago, Illinois

My dear Comrade:

I am herewith transmitting a letter just received from J. Ramsey MacDonald, with a note not to be published.[1] I am sending it to you for your personal information.

The information contained in this letter is of such a nature that I think it should be brought to the attention of the American working class, but in justice to Comrade MacDonald, we must withhold it until we get his consent. I am writing him asking that he give this consent, or that he supply us with a statement for publication. In the meantime, I request that you regard this letter as strictly personal.

With best wishes, I am

Fraternally yours,
Adolph Germer
Executive Secretary.

TLS (with two-page copy of letter to Germer from J. Ramsay MacDonald), InTI, Debs Collection.

1. In his letter to Germer, dated June 5, 1918, MacDonald described the American Federation of Labor as "hopelessly out of date" and was particularly critical of the United States government-sponsored "Labor Mission," which was composed of Algie Simons, Louis Kopelin, Frank Bohn, John Spargo, Charles Edward Russell, and others sent "to represent American labour" in various European labor and socialist meetings held in 1918. MacDonald felt the mission had made no positive contributions to the meetings held in England and claimed to have been told that the members were "even more aloof in Paris than they were in London."

Tom Mooney to Theodore Debs

July 17, 1918
San Francisco, California

My dear Comrade; —

Your kind letter of recent date received and contents carefully noted. I appreciate your words of kindness in acknowledging my brief, and I want to assure you that I am in hearty sympathy with your brother, who finds himself at the present time in a similar predicament.[1]

I dictate this letter to you on the eve of my departure for San Quentin, there to be placed in the death cell, to await that terrible fate unless I am rescued by the hands of Labor. When this letter reaches you, I shall have been in San Quentin for almost a week, as I leave tomorrow morning. Convey to Gene my kindest regards and best wishes. I am confident that, with the aid of Labor, we are bound in the end to be vindicated. The organized-labor movment will not permit this dastardly plot; and I know that yourself and Gene are doing all in the world to stop it.

With best wishes, kindest regards and fraternally greetings to you,
I am,

Yours,
Tom Mooney

(Dictated July 16th.)

P.S. Tom was taken across to San Quentin this morning, as he
expected to be.

[illegible initials]

TLS, InTI, Debs Collection.

1. Debs had been free on $10,000 bond (provided by Marguerite Prevey and a
Cleveland tailor, A. W. Moskowitz) since his indictment in Cleveland.

EVD to Claude G. Bowers

July 18, 1918
Terre Haute, Indiana

My dear Friend Bowers:—
    Mrs. Debs and I are both very sorry to have missed you when you
called at our home. Had we only known of your coming you may be
sure that we would have been only too glad to make you welcome.
Your call and the kindness intended are fully appreciated by us both
and the next time we hope to be more fortunate and to have you as
our guest. Please commend us to Mrs. Bowers and with all kind regards
and good wishes to you both I am always

Yours faithfully,
Eugene V. Debs

TLS, InU, Lilly Library, Bowers MSS.

Theodore Debs to William F. Gable

July 19, 1918
Terre Haute, Indiana

Dear and Loyal Friend Gable:—
    There is a wealth of soul in the brief writing from you at hand
this moment. How can you, the busiest of men, find time on every

occasion, and even without occasion, to inquire into and look after the possible needs of so many others? It is a wonderful thing and one of the supreme things that stamp you as a wonderful man.

Answering your inquiry, Gene has certainly been through hell during the last three weeks. His mail was intercepted for some days but is now apparently coming along alright. For the past few days he has been suffering with acute lumbago and confined to his bed. This, it seems, to cap the climax. But his spirit remains unbroken. Like Henley his "head is bloody but unbowed."

What can you do for him? What have you not done and what are you not now doing for him? I wonder if you can imagine how much your friendship, confidence and love mean to him and how rich he feels and actually is in possession of such priceless treasures! So give yourself no thought of concern about Gene. He is sure of his ground and the enemy will only help him to win out the more certainly and the more triumphantly in the end. Let me thank you, dear brother, for the loving thought of my brother your precious message has brought to my heart and will bring to his when it comes into his hands. He is now up again and has gone away for a brief period to escape the many demands and importunities that are now made upon him. He is slowly recuperating but it will be some time yet before he will have entirely recovered from his attack of nervous and physical exhaustion due to many years of strain and overwork.

Let me say as a final word that, loving and honoring you as Gene and I both do, the one thing above all others you can do for him in this hour of trial is to love him as you have always done, and sustained as he will be by such love I am sure that our dear Horace[1] will agree, that the gods are with him and that he is bound to conquer in the struggle to banish autocracy in every form from the earth and bring freedom and peace and the love of comrades to all mankind.

The greetings of the day to you and yours and all loving wishes from

Yours always,
Theodore Debs

TLS, CtY.

1. Horace Traubel.

Theodore Debs to Oliver C. Wilson

July 19, 1918
Terre Haute, Indiana

Dear Comrade Wilson: —

Your telegram of the 17th. directing that no booking be done save through your office was received. It said "letter follows." But no letter has yet come.

Your telegram from Cleveland came at 5 this A.M. Gene is not in the city. He has been in bed during the past five days with an acute attack of lumbago and has now left the city, it being impossible for him to get any rest here.

I must now come to a distinct understanding with you in regard to Gene's booking. You remember that when you were here he had it understood that everything would depend upon his health and strength. He made you no positive promise and I wish to say now that you are not to count on him, for the present, for a single speech. He has one engagement only and for the present no more will be made. He will speak at Akron, O., on Labor Day and until the condition of his health is definitely determined there will be no further booking. In this I speak not only for myself but for comrades here and elsewhere who are urging that Gene give first consideration to his health. And I am going to see to it that this is done. It will be the first time since his connection with the socialist movement that he has paid any attention to his health until he was ready to drop in his tracks from overwork.

In past campaigns for twenty years now he has invariably been driven to exceed his strength and three times he has come to the very edge of a breakdown and the doctors have now warned him flatly that if he has a relapse this time he will die.

In your circular letter to the party recently issued you announce that Gene is in perfect health.[1] I am sorry you made any such statement. It is not true. If it were I would not now be writing this letter. He has been in bed suffering the acutest pain these last several days, a condition brought on by his nervous and physical exhaustion. The trouble is that he is never permitted a chance to rest. Day and night, every day in the week, he is being sought and besieged and called upon to render service {of one kind} and another which he has always tried to do even to the point of breaking down physically at the task.

It is true that Gene is slowly improving but he has been through a great strain during the last three weeks for one in his condition. He has been hunted early and late and the letters and telegrams have been coming from all direcions. In such a situation you will see that not only is rest impossible but it {would} be only a question of time until something would snap and he would then be totally unfit to do anything, and perhaps it might mean his end.

Gene has been advised by Comrade Stedman[2] that he will not be needed until the time for his trial approaches. The demurrer can be filed without him.

Now let me say to you frankly, knowing better than you just what Gene's condition is, that he is not to be promised for any meeting until we have been consulted. If Gene is no better than he is now he will do absolutely no speaking during this campaign. If he improves, as we believe he will, provided he is given a chance, it will be different, but there must be no booking through your office or elsewhere until you have been advised from here that Gene is in fit condition to fill the engagements. In all previous campaigns Gene has been booked with utter disregard of his health and he has been made to speak from five to a dozen times a day every day in the week and for weeks at a stretch, and it is a wonder that he is alive at all and he would not be if he had not had a constitution of steel. I have been with him and I know whereof I speak. I have protested at times but have submitted to campaign managers and committees for the sake of the party. But a point has been reached in Gene's life when I am not going to see him killed. I want him to serve the party and the movement to his fullest possible capacity and to the latest day of his life and this can be done only at his age if he is conserved and if his engagements are made according to his health.

There is ample time to decide what engagements, if any, Gene can fill. It is certain that he will fill none before his trial on September 9th., except the one at Akron.

I have written you plainly and I hope there may be a perfect understanding. I appreciate your zeal and energy and your desire to push in every possible manner the work you have in hand. I appreciate all of this as fully as any comrade can but I have also a duty to my brother and I am going to see that for once his campaign efforts are confined to the limits of his strength. No comrade can say that he has ever in the past shirked any duty to the party and if he has wronged the party in any way it is by having impaired his health and undermined his strength in its service.

With all greetings and all wishes for your success in all things I am,

Yours fraternally,
[Theodore Debs]

P.S. On July 11th. Gene sent you an article entitled "The Fight for Liberty," over his signature.[3] Did you receive this? And if so, did you send copies of it to the socialist papers? Gene wished this statement to go out to the party and he wrote you to that effect. No acknowledgment of the article was received from you. Please let me know about this. I have a copy of the article and if you have not handled it I will handle it from here.

TLc, InTI, Debs Collection.

1. The circular letter has not been found. Its content was apparently in sharp contrast to Wilson's letter to local secretaries, dated July 14, 1918, in which he described Debs as "62 years old, broken in health, and without funds."
2. Seymour Stedman was one of a battery of socialist attorneys who defended Debs in his trial in Cleveland, set for September 9, 1918.
3. In *The Fight For Liberty*, which was published as a campaign pamphlet by the national party in 1918 and widely reprinted, Debs discussed his Canton speech and his indictment and told readers that "if my friends and comrades would help me they can do it in but one way and that is to stand by the Socialist Party." His own defense would be "managed entirely by the national office of the Socialist Party" and "all funds for this purpose should be sent to Comrade Wilson at the national office."

Clarence Darrow to EVD

July 20, 1918
[En route to New York]

My dear Debs

I am on my way to England & France & will be gone about two months. I want to send you this line from the coast to say, that I know I do not need to say, that I am sorry for your indictment & that you now as always have my deepest love & sympathy & that if I can ever be of any assistance to you I will give all the aid in my power. I know you always follow the right as you see & no one can do more

With love always
Clarence Darrow

ALS, EVD Foundation, Debs Home.

Job Harriman to EVD

July 24, 1918
Stables, Louisiana

Dear Comrade: —

I know that you will be somewhat surprised at my writing you along the line that I am about to suggest.

I have wrestled with this Colony for four years now and feel that we are in a way to make a permanent success. We have had a lot of trouble, of course, but it has been no greater than you or I have had in the ordinary local. You find all sorts of positive, pessimistic and optimistic minds in the Socialist movement and it is very hard to handle them.

We were compelled to leave Llano, California, because the soil would not yield the crops desired. We came here last December and have put our crops out and will raise enough this year to keep us.

We are now in shape to finance this enterprise by borrowing money and giving absolutely good security. What I want to do is to borrow enough money—$150,000. or $160,000, for a long term of years, so that we will have nothing in the way to cripple or interfere with our development. We can give a first mortgage on our land and would be willing to borrow of one person or several persons. We have 20,000 acres of land under contract of sale and if we could arrange this loan, would pay the present owners of the land, thus enabling us to give first mortgage on the land as security for the loan.

I wonder if you know any wealthy person in our movement who might be induced to investigate the feasibility of such a loan? I am not asking him to investigate the feasibility of the Colony, but the feasibility of a loan on good security. Perhaps you can put me in touch with one or more persons who might have the money to loan. I wish you would write and tell me if you can suggest any one.

The Government is loaning one-half of the value of similar land to ours, but we do not want to divide our land into individual holdings.

I want this to be a practical business proposition between the person loaning and this Company. If they are Socialists all well enough and good, but whoever they are, they cannot lose.

You doubtless have received many letters adverse to the Colony enterprise. This is perfectly natural. Some people come, stay a month or two, become dissatisfied without a reason, want their money back, and want to go—a thing that is impossible in any capitalist organization and no Socialist would even expect it, but they do expect it of this corporation. This gives rise to some difficulty. Nevertheless, we feel confident that, by making this loan, we will have no difficulty in putting our proposition over and in a way that all Socialists will be proud of.

I want to say something to you and that is this: there is a whole lot more to the social problem than the bread and butter question. It is up to us to develop a social spirit, a spirit of fellowship, a spirit of give and take, and we are doing it in this Colony and doing it magnificently. However, I do not wish this to be the consideration for the loan. I only mention this that you may see how hard we are trying and with what we have to contend.

Thanking you in advance for a reply to my letter and for any favor you may confer, in suggesting persons whom we might interest in this loan, I am

Yours fraternally,
Job Harriman[1]
President.

TLS, InTI, Debs Collection.

1. In 1919, Harriman, disillusioned with the Louisiana Llano Colony, which had suffered from poor crops, isolation, sickness, and poverty and had declined from fifty enthusiastic families to fifteen dispirited ones, returned to California, where he died in 1925.

Morris Hillquit to EVD

August 5, 1918
New York City

Dear Comrade Debs:

At the request of Mr. Joseph W. Sharts[1] I enclose herewith the papers on the motion to quash the indictment against you. Please sign the affidavit towards the bottom of the third page of these papers and have your signature sworn before a Notary Public and then mail these papers as soon as possible to Morris H. Wolf,[2] attorney at law, American Trust Building, Cleveland, Ohio.

Fraternally yours,
Morris Hillquit
AL

TLS (signed by Alexander Levine for Morris Hillquit), InTI, Debs Collection.

1. Joseph William Sharts (1875-1965) graduated from Harvard Law School in 1897, served in the Spanish-American War, and opened a law practice in 1899 in Dayton, Ohio, where he became a leader of the local Socialist party. Sharts served

as counsel for Debs at his trial in Cleveland in 1918 and edited the *Miami Valley Socialist* in Dayton after the war.

2. Morris Herbert Wolf, another of Debs's attorneys, was born in Russia, came to the United States in 1906, and practiced law in Cleveland throughout his career.

EVD to Oliver C. Wilson

August 7, 1918
Terre Haute, Indiana

Dear Comrade Wilson:
Have just returned and Theo. has put yours of 3rd. before me. Yes, I can fill a few engagements before the trial begins on the 9th. prox, but a few only. These can be made between the 1st. and the 9th. excepting the 2nd., Labor Day, on which I am booked to speak at Akron. You can notify Buffalo, Rochester and Detroit accordingly, but please do not assign them definite dates until I see you. I will be at Chicago on Sunday to attend the conference and we can then arrange our program and assign the several points their dates. I am feeling better but this tropical heat almost saps me of vitality. But I shall be strong by the time the trial is over and hope to be of some service in the campaign.[1]
Loving regards to you and the comrades with you, and the very best of wishes!

Yours always,
Eugene V. Debs

TLc, InTI, Debs Collection.

1. On August 22, 1918, Wilson sent Debs a letter laying out a schedule that called for Debs speeches in New York, Ohio, Michigan, Pennsylvania, New Jersey, Massachusetts, Rhode Island, Indiana, Illinois, Wisconsin, Minnesota, Missouri, Kansas, Colorado, California, and Washington, in thirty-five cities, between September 1 and November 4, 1918.

EVD to Shubert Sebree

August 21, 1918
Terre Haute, Indiana

My dear Comrade Sebree:—
Please accept hearty congratulations from Theodore and myself upon your nomination for congress.[1] A better selection could not

have been made. I need not say to you that you will have all the support we can possibly give you. You are a true representative of the class and the cause which the Socialist party represents and your nomination is alike creditable to yourself and the party.

With all affectionate personal regards and good wishes I am,

Yours fraternally,
Eugene V. Debs

TLS, InTI, Debs Collection.

1. Sebree was nominated as the Socialist party candidate for Congress in Indiana's Fifth Congressional District after Debs declined the nomination. Sebree ran third behind the Republican incumbent, Everett Sanders, and the Democratic candidate, Ralph Moss. Debs's 17 percent of the total vote cast in 1916 dropped to less than 2 percent in 1918.

Orlando F. Ryerson to EVD

August 23, 1918
Alameda, California

Dear Comrade:—

The very nice things, like sweet bouquets, thrown at you in the columns of "The World" of Oakland and your own congratulatory words in the same number,[1] this week's, give me courage to add my mite and my hopes for {the} success of your wish that the enemies of free speech may be overthrown.

I will, if I live, be 63 years of age on Nov. 26th next, and yet I do not look that old nor feel that old and I am hoping that the love of your comrades and the happy things you hear and read about your work and yourself will buoy you up and rejuvenate you so that you may not fail physically any more than you do in spirit.

A few years ago {(in 1912)} I wrote the enclosed poem: "Columbus." When you had recited Joaquin Miller's[2] poem on the same subject in Piedmont Pavillion in Oakland about 3 years {since} a friend of mine said: "I wish he could have recited yours." I answered: "My time has not come yet."

In this crisis in our evolution when the whole world is rent assunder and no one knows what dire calamity may befall the true friends of true freedom I offer this poem[3] for your personal use. If you like it well enough you may publish it as much and as often as you wish to do so. I should feel well repaid if it encourages any weary comrades and feel honored if you ever recite it anywhere.

Comrade Tuck asked me once how it was that I could sell Debs tickets, when I never seemed able to sell other tickets. I told him that question was easy to answer. "Debs tickets sell themselves."

Anything I have to "*boost*" never gets sold by me.

I hope that this letter will be handed direct to yourself, even if it waits for you to come home from a trip. I should feel disappointed if you did not see this letter and get the poem.

Yours For Socialism
Orlando F. Ryerson.

P.S. We have no local here now (in Alameda) but there are some true blue comrades here who may yet revive the organization. R.

ALS (with poem), InTI, Debs Collection.

1. "Gene Debs Ready for Free Speech Struggle," *Oakland World*, August 14, 1918.

2. Cincinnatus Hiner ("Joaquin") Miller (1839-1913) lived in "The Heights" above Oakland, California, during the last thirty years of his life. His "Columbus" was written in 1892 to commemorate the four-hundredth anniversary of the discovery of America. A handwritten copy of the poem was sent to Debs in prison at Atlanta by "a comrade from Warren, Ohio."

3. A clipping of Ryerson's "Columbus" was enclosed and is in the Debs Collection at Indiana State University.

J. B. Salutsky[1] to EVD

August 26, 1918
New York City

Dear Comrade Debs:

A committee formed under the auspices of the Jewish Federation, Socialist Party, with Comrade Winchevsky as treasurer and a number of Jewish Socialists of renown on its Executive Board, is preparing in the Yiddish language a book on "Debs, His Life and Works."[2] The publication will contain a short sketch of your public activities as seen by men active in the movement, and extracts from a number of your articles and speeches as published in the volume of the Appeal to Reason.

The committee would very much appreciate a contribution by yourself in the form of a special preface to the Yiddish edition.[3]

The Comrades on the committee are convinced that the book will have considerable success and that not a small sum will be realized towards the defense fund in your impending trial. In fact, rendering possible assistance for your defense work was the original cause for forming the committee and publishing the work at this time.

You are of course at liberty to choose any particular form for your contribution to the book, but at any rate, we shall appreciate your early reply to this request.

We shall be glad to submit any further information in case you care to know more about this undertaking.

Fraternally yours,
J. B. Salutsky
Editor of the Yiddish Edition
"Debs, His Life and Works"

TLS, InTI, Debs Collection.

1. Jacob Benjamin Salutsky (Hardman) (1882-1968) came to the United States from his native Russia in 1909, served as secretary of the Jewish Federation of the Socialist party from 1912 to 1921, when he joined the Workers party and, about the same time, became educational director for the Amalgamated Clothing Workers of America.

2. J. B. Salutsky, *Yudzkin Victor Debs: Zayn leben, Schriften, un Redes* (New York, 1919).

3. The Yiddish edition carried an autographed picture of Debs and his "special preface."

Caroline A. Lowe to EVD

August 28, 1918
Chicago, Illinois

Dear Comrade Debs:

We all of us appreciate the encouragement you send us. We need it. Truly, I was never more disheartened in my life than over the verdict.[1] We were not expecting it; we were all of us confident that the very worst we might expect was a hung jury. It was foolish of us, no doubt, but we had put up such a good fight and it seemed to us the message had been made so clear that even the most prejudiced jury must be won by it.

Almost without exception the boys made wonderful witnesses fearless and outspoken, kindly and generous in every way.

I can see nothing now except that you, too, and Scott Nearing and Comrades Berger, Engdahl, Germer, Kruse and Tucker[2] and the many hundreds of comrades and fellow workers over the United States are doomed to serve prison sentences. There is absolutely no hope, and jury trials are but a farce. I suppose we must go through with them, but it seems to me to be so much time and money wasted.

Last night I read your article in the Chicago Socialist.[3] I wish all the world could read it; and all the world would love you for the great spirit and unselfishness expressed in it. It makes me sick at heart to think of your going to the Penitentiary, but I have no hope of anything else now. 28 boys were arrested in Butte yesterday and the day before 29 in Spokane; also 20 yesterday in San Francisco, and so it will continue. We, who have been in the revolutionary movement for years, should expect nothing else, but it is heart-breaking just the same. As I mingle with all these splendid boys now about to be sentenced here and realise that all over the country the finest souls in the world are being imprisoned, it fills me with hot rebellion. But things will be worse before they are better and we may as well prepare for it.

I wish I could be present at your trial on September 9th. If I could possibly afford it I would go, but you will know that my heart is with you, that the love and admiration of not only your comrades but of thinking men and women all over the world will be following you, and when you, too, are sentenced to imprisonment, as you say about our boys here, "the sacrifice, bitter and tragic, will not be in vain."

With sincerest love to you and Theodore and the other members of your family whom I have not met, tho I hope to do so some time, I am

Ever your comrade,
Caroline A. Lowe

TLS, InTI, Debs Collection.

1. The guilty verdict handed down by the jury in the IWW trial in Chicago on August 25, 1918. On August 31, 1918, Judge Landis sentenced thirty-five Wobblies to five years in prison, thirty-three to ten years, and fifteen to twenty years, the legal maximum.

2. Not previously identified, Irwin St. John Tucker (1886-1981) was ordained an Episcopal minister in New York City in 1909 and after moving to Chicago became associate editor of the *Christian Socialist* and founder of a "hobo college" for migrant workers. As head of the Socialist party's literature department at national headquarters in Chicago, Tucker was indicted with Berger, Germer, Engdahl, and Kruse for obstruction of recruitment and enlistment; convicted; and sentenced by Judge Landis to twenty years in prison. The verdict and sentence were overturned on appeal. In addition to his many works on socialism, Tucker wrote a number of books on poetry and history and was for thirty years religious editor of the *Chicago Herald-American*.

3. Debs's "Hail To The Comrades," *Chicago Socialist*, August 27, 1918, expressed his feeling of comradeship with "all the sons and daughters" of the "proletarian revolution" who had been "loaded with fetters and bowed to the earth."

EVD to Morris Hillquit

August 29, 1918
Terre Haute, Indiana

My dear Morris:—

Very deeply touched am I by the beautiful and appreciative message which came from your heart to mine this morning. It is so very much more than I deserve. A thousand loving thanks!

I am not going to write. You need rest,[1] perfect rest as far as that is possible with your temperament, and not letters. I know. The comrades can now serve you best by allowing you to give yourself wholly to yourself until your are wholly yourself again. Write me only if there is anything I can do to help in the least to make you comfortable. My wife and my brother and all of us send you love and greeting and fondest wishes.

Yours always,
Eugene V. Debs

TLS, WHi, Hillquit Papers.

1. Hillquit was attempting to recover from another attack of tuberculosis at Saranac Lake in northern New York.

Theodore H. Lunde[1] to EVD

September 13, 1918
Chicago, Illinois

Dear Mr. Debs:

Thinking of you, while still in bed, this morning, I formulated a telegram which, on second thought, I feared would not be allowed to pass, in consequence of which I enclose it herewith.

It is refreshing to observe the courage with which you have made a stand on your principles as well as your Constitutional rights,[2] and little by little, it is to be hoped, more will follow until there be a revulsion of opinion in favor of putting a stop to the infernal conditions which now prevail on earth.

I sincerely hope a new trial may be granted, and that it may result in a verdict through which you may retain your freedom and assist us in the biggest fight which has ever engaged humanity.

Unfortunately there are few who can see beyond the mere superficial aspect of a controversy between two alliances of political powers, whereas, in the last analysis, it is a struggle between the International Money Trust and the Human Race.

Sincerely yours,
Theo. H. Lunde

TLS, NNU Tam, Debs Collection.

1. Theodore H. Lunde was secretary and later president of the American Industrial Company, a piano hardware firm in Chicago. Lunde served as treasurer of the Peace Council in Chicago during the war and was active in the amnesty movement in the postwar period. *American Monthly,* May 1921.

2. At his trial for violation of the Espionage Act, held in Cleveland from September 9 to 14, 1918, Debs personally addressed the jury, which found him guilty, and Judge David C. Westenhaver, who sentenced him to ten years in prison. His "Address to the Jury" and "Statement to the Court," along with his Canton speech, which had led to his indictment and conviction, became three of his most famous speeches and were widely reprinted. In his speech to the jury Debs admitted "having delivered the speech," which he insisted was protected by First Amendment rights, said that he "would not take back a word of it," and warned that "if the Espionage law finally stands, then the Constitution is dead." To Judge Westenhaver, Debs acknowledged that he was "opposed to the social system in which we live," predicted that the world's "sixty millions of socialists" would "sweep into power to inaugurate the greatest social and economic change in history," and asked for "no mercy . . . no immunity."

Otto Branstetter[1] to EVD

September 13, 1918
Chicago, Illinois

EUGENE V. DEBS

THOUSANDS OF US SAD BUT PROUD THIS MORNING. YOUR ATTITUDE AN INSPIRATION YOUR CONVICTION A CHALLENGE WHICH WE ACCEPT.

OTTO BRANSTETTER.

Telegram (copy), Collection of Mrs. Philip Taft.

1. Otto Branstetter (1877-1924) became state secretary of the Socialist party in Oklahoma in 1906 and during the next decade created one of the party's most successful state organizations. Branstetter and his wife, Winnie, were two of the party's most popular speakers and effective organizers, and Otto Branstetter served as national secretary of the party from 1919 until shortly before his death.

EVD to Otto Branstetter

September 18, 1918
Terre Haute, Indiana

Dear Comrade Branstetter:—
    A thousand thanks! your message has inspiration and strength in
every line and word of it. I have but done a very small part in a very
large work and my one regret is that I cannot do more for the cause.
    I had looked forward to the New York meetings with eager antic-
ipation but the order of the court will prevent me from attending
them.[1] I know how hard you have worked in the field and I am
earnestly hoping that the results may not fall short of your expectations. With all loving greetings to you and the comrades about you
I am,

                                                    Yours always,
                                                    E. V. Debs

TLS, Collection of Mrs. Philip Taft.

    1. The terms of Debs's release during the appeal of his case to the Supreme Court
restricted his movement to Terre Haute and the Northern District of Ohio. He had
planned to speak at party rallies in New York in support of Scott Nearing, Meyer
London, Morris Hillquit, and other candidates for congressional and state offices.
New York Times, September 12, 1918.

EVD to Upton Sinclair

September 19, 1918
Terre Haute, Indiana

My dear Upton Sinclair:—
    I have just finished reading the first installment of "Jimmie Higgins"[1]
and I am delighted with it. It is the beginning of a great story, a story
that will be translated into many languages and be read by eager and
interested millions all over the world. I feel that your art will lend
itself readily to "Jimmie Higgins" and that you will be at your best
in placing this dear little comrade where he belongs in the socialist
movement. The opening chapter[2] of your story proves that you know
him intimately. So do I and I love him with all my heart, even as you
do. He has done far more for me than I shall ever be able to do for
him. He is in fact, though but few seem to know it, the actual maker
of our movement the wide world over. He more nearly than any other

is the actual incarnation of the social revolution and he works unceasingly in and out of season to bring it about. He is scarcely ever seen above the surface. He modestly remains at the bottom where the real work is done and there is no task, however disagreeable, that does not find his heart and his hands ready for it.

"Jimmie Higgins" is the chap who is always on the job; who does all the needed work that no one else will do; who never grumbles, never finds fault and is never discouraged. All he asks is the privilege of doing his best for the cause where it is most needed. He expects no thanks and feels himself embarrassed if by chance his zealous efforts attract attention. The pure joy it gives him to serve the cause is his only reward. What a fine example of humility, unselfishness and consecration "Jimmie" sets us! I have often in my communion with "Jimmie" envied him and wished I might exchange places with him.

Almost anyone can be "The Candidate," and almost anyone will do for a speaker but it takes the rarest of qualities to produce a "Jimmie Higgins." These qualities are developed in the "lower class" only. They are denied those who know not the trials and privations, the bitter struggle, the heart-ache and despair of the victims of man's inhumanity to his less fortunate fellow-man.

You are painting a superb portrait of our "Jimmie" and I congratulate you upon the progress and promise of your very laudable undertaking.

There is in my heart much that I should like to say to you about your generous and sympathetic treatment {of} "The Candidate" but for obvious personal reasons I shall for the present have to forbear. I need not say that "The Candidate" feels himself highly honored by you to occupy the center of the stage in company with his beloved "Jimmie" in the opening scene of your drama. It is really "Jimmie" who is the central and commanding figure and deserves all the recognition and applause, "The Candidate" serving only as a background to bring "Jimmie's" noble personality into sharper relief.

Allow me to return my personal thanks for your kindly interest in behalf of comrades who have been sentenced to prison on account of their opposition to war.[3] I have read with special interest your correspondence with the president and members of his cabinet and while I expect, for my own part, no personal consideration at their hands I appreciate none the less the comradely, humane motive which actuated you to make this plea for convicted socialists and others who face prison sentences for refusing to support the war or for asserting their constitutional right of free speech. You have always taken an active part in helping comrades in trouble and in going to the rescue of those in distress, no matter whom they might be, and for this I have always had for you a strong personal attachment.

Allow me in closing to thank you warmly for the place of honor you have given me in the story of dear "Jimmie Higgins" and for the comradely consideration you have always shown me, and with all cordial greetings and good wishes to you and Mrs. Sinclair I am,

Yours always,
Eugene V. Debs

TLS, InU, Lilly Library, Sinclair MSS.

1. Sinclair's tribute to the Socialist party's "Jimmy Higginses," the members of the party who "do the hard work and get none of the glory," as Sinclair described them in *New Appeal*, August 24, 1918, appeared in *Jimmy Higgins Goes to War*, which ran serially in *Upton Sinclair's* from September 1918 to February 1919 and was published by Boni and Liveright in 1919.

2. Chapter 1 of *Jimmy Higgins* was titled "Jimmy Higgins Meets the Candidate," who strongly resembled Debs. The candidate "had been Candidate for President so often that every one thought of him in that role."

3. Sinclair's "An Appeal to President Wilson" for the release of "political prisoners" appeared in *Upton Sinclair's*, September 1918.

EVD to Morris Hillquit

September 20, 1918
Terre Haute, Indiana

My dear Morris:—

We all love you and we are all with you. We are all sending our vitalizing currents in your direction and you are sure to get well.[1] Be patient, forget everything except that our hearts are with you, and give yourself wholly to rest and recreation that you may come back to us in the full panoply of health and vigor again. We can spare you now but the future will need you as never before and we will welcome you back with loving hearts and open arms. Do not dare to answer this under penalty of a longer sentence than has just been *bestowed* upon me.

As ever and always,

Your loving comrade,
Eugene V. Debs

TLS, WHi, Hillquit Papers.

1. His attack of tuberculosis in the summer of 1918 did not force Hillquit to withdraw as a congressional candidate in the fall election in New York City.

EVD to Shubert Sebree

September 20, 1918
Terre Haute, Indiana

My dear Comrade Sebree:—

Thank you heartily for your fine message! You can hardly know what this loving and loyal expression from you means to me.

I am more than sorry but not a bit surprised that you have been hounded out of town.[1] It is the fate of such true souls as you and I know you can bear it. You were too good and real a union man to last among these miserable pretenders. But your day will come as sure as the truth prevails.

I know how gladly you would serve my sentence and my heart goes to you in love and gratitude. Theodore and I and all our family send affectionate greetings to you and your loved ones and I am,

Yours always,
E. V. Debs

TLS, InTl, Debs Collection.

1. Sebree's refusal to purchase Liberty Bonds at the Terre Haute glass plant where he worked and his lunchtime speeches as the Socialist party congressional candidate delivered at the plant led to his dismissal from his job in August 1918. Finding himself blacklisted in Terre Haute, Sebree moved to nearby Danville, Illinois, in search of work.

EVD to John Reed[1]

September 21, 1918
Terre Haute, Indiana

My dear John Reed:—

I have read and have been deeply moved by your fine article in the September Liberator.[2] You write differently than anyone else and your style is most appealing to me. There is a living something that breathes and throbs in all you say.

Please let me thank you, dear comrade, for the fine and generous spirit in which you have written of me and of my humble service in the cause. I have done so little to deserve so much. It is the bigness of you to which I am indebted for this flattering testimonial which, coming from the heart of John Reed, touches me more deeply than can be told in words. Please extend my thanks to dear Art Young[3] for his fine part in the story. This paltry expression is but a poor return but both of you must know that I love you very much and that I am with you in all things that strengthen our cause and make for the revolution.

My only regret is that I saw so little of you two royal comrades. I shall hope to see more of you in the future. I had a delightful little visit with Max Eastman[4] in Cleveland. He is certainly one of the gods' annointed.

Success to the Liberator![5] It is a flaming evangel of the revolution and deserves the loyal support of every socialist and every radical and progressive.

My love goes to you all, to you and Art and Max and Floyd Dell[6] and Crystal Eastman[7] and every blessed one of you, and I am

Yours always,
Eugene V. Debs

TLS, MH.

1. John Reed (1887-1920) graduated from Harvard in 1910 and in 1913 joined the staff of *Masses*, where he established a reputation as a leading left-wing journalist for articles on Pancho Villa, the war on the eastern front in Europe, and the Russian Revolution in 1917. His most famous book, *Ten Days That Shook the World*, was one of the most widely read accounts of the Bolshevik Revolution. In 1919, Reed was expelled from the Socialist party, led in the formation of the Communist Labor party, and edited its journal, *Voice of Labor*. Indicted for treason in 1920, he fled to Russia where he worked for the new Soviet regime until he was stricken by typhus and died in Moscow on October 17, 1920.

2. Reed's "With 'Gene Debs on the Fourth of July" (*Liberator*, September 1918) was an account of his and Art Young's day with Debs in Terre Haute on July 4, 1918. Reed reported that, despite his arrest and the charge that he was a traitor, Debs remained firm in his opposition to the war.

3. Art Young illustrated Reed's article with profile drawings of Debs and Seymour Stedman and a drawing of "Debs's Hands."

4. Max Eastman reported Debs's trial for the *Liberator*.

5. Following the suppression of *Masses* in 1918, Eastman, Dell, Young, and others launched the *Liberator* as "A Monthly Magazine of Revolutionary Progress."

6. Floyd Dell (1887-1969) was an editor of *Masses* from 1914 to 1918 and of its successor journal, *Liberator*, from 1918 to 1924. Thereafter he was better known as a novelist and playwright and in the 1930s as a publicist and speech writer for various New Deal agencies.

7. Crystal Eastman (1881-1928), Max Eastman's sister and co-editor of *Liberator*, was a nationally known authority on workmen's compensation legislation and was a leading feminist writer whose feminism embraced suffrage, birth control, the Equal Rights Amendment, and opposition to war. Much of her writing after World War I was devoted to the interrelationships among pacifism, feminism, and socialism.

EVD to David Karsner

September 26, 1918
Terre Haute, Indiana

My dear Comrade David: —

I have just returned from Ohio to find your kindness here awaiting me. The page you have made up in the Call,[1] of which you send me advance copies is a very beautiful and flattering one, so very much more than is coming to me. You are more than kind and generous in all you have to say of me and in all the many things you feel moved to do for me and if they are but ill deserved I am sure you understand I am {at least} not wanting in appreciation of the great heart and noble soul in which they are inspired.

Thank you a thousand times for the Call page, filled in all its lines with your touching partiality, and for the beautiful letter with its message of affectionate devotion that goes straight to my heart.

I am so glad you have seen our dear Horace.[2] I am sure the touch of you was tonic to his blood and brought gladness to his eyes. Give him my love with your arms about him for us both and say to him for me that he must become whole again for the still greater work awaiting him and which no other on earth can do.

Yes, we still wish you to write that introduction and I will let you know about this as soon as the speeches are ready. I believe the intention of the committee is to publish the Canton speech and the jury speech and the speech before the judge all in one. The one last named I have not yet received.[3]

No one could more fittingly render this service than you, nor one whose loving kindness in so doing would be more fully appreciated.

Theodore and all of us unite in love to you and to all the comrades about the Call and I am,

Yours always,
E. V. Debs

TLS, NN Kars.

1. In the *Call Magazine* (September 22, 1918) Karsner printed "Praise from Persons in All Walks of Life," a collection of some thirty articles praising Debs, written by Edwin Markham, Robert Hunter, Basil Manly, and others.

2. Horace Traubel, whose *Life and Work* Karsner published in 1919.

3. As noted, Debs's Canton speech and his addresses to the jury and judge at his trial were widely reprinted. Karsner wrote the introduction to the edition of the speeches published by the Socialist party national headquarters.

EVD to Editor,[1] *Weekly People*

September 27, 1918
Terre Haute, Indiana

Dear Comrade:—

Please let me express my appreciation of your editorial[2] in the current issue of the Weekly People which I have just read with much satisfaction. The differences there have been between us to which reference is made in the article make the spirit of fairness in which the article is written all the more commendable.

With comradely greeting and all good wishes for your success I am,

Yours fraternally,
E. V. Debs

TLS, WHi, Socialist Labor Party Papers.

1. Arnold Peterson, who was also national secretary of the Socialist Labor party.
2. In "Eugene V. Debs" (*Weekly People*, September 21, 1918), the paper acknowledged that it had had "serious disagreement" with Debs in the past but added that in his trial at Cleveland Debs had "taken a position that is worthy of all men's admiration."

EVD to James Oneal

September 28, 1918
Terre Haute, Indiana

My dear "Jim":—

A thousand thanks! Your fine letter is filled with inspiration. Coming from you this message has special meaning and touches me to the heart. I need not say that each inspiriting word and each loving expression is warmly reciprocated.

I note what you say about the infamous Sisson forgeries[1] in connection with the infamous conspiracy to throttle the noble Bolshevik under pretense of saving the Russian nation. I cannot believe that that criminal crowd will get wholly {by} with that flagrant piece of fraud and false pretense. But if they succeed in perpetrating that crime against humanity that the crushing of the Russian revolution would mean it will be all the same to them what means were employed to accomplish their infamy.[2]

Enclosed is a copy of the poem of Edmund Vance Cooke[3] which you may want to publish in the Call. He lives in Cleveland and was present at the trial and was moved to write this poem notwithstanding he is on the other side so far as the war is concerned. If you publish the poem let me suggest that you place a paragraph in parenthesis under the title explaining when and where and under what circumstances the poem had its origin.

You comrades on the Call are doing heroic work these days. I am very glad you are on the staff and glad Charley Ervin is at the helm. You and he, I know, work admirably together. What a fine thing it would be if Ervin could be elected to congress![4]

My love goes to you all.

Yours always,
E. V. Debs

P.S. Jud[5] was in the other day. He is looking fine. Jud is a loyal soul. We love him. None better anywhere.

TLS, NNU Tam, Debs Collection.

1. Edgar Grant Sisson (1875-1948) was an editor of the *Chicago Tribune* (1903-11), *Collier's* (1911-14), and *Cosmopolitan Magazine* (1914-17) before becoming associate chairman of the Committee on Public Information during World War I. In September 1918 the Wilson administration published Sisson's *German-Bolshevik Conspiracy*, in which he claimed to produce documents, brought to the United States by a former Russian army officer, proving that "Bolshevik leaders . . . were being paid by Germany." *New York Times*, September 9, 1918.

2. Oneal printed much of Debs's opinion in "The Sisson Documents," *Call*, October 6, 1918.

3. Edmund Vance Cooke (1866-1932) was a native of Ontario, Canada, whose father, a Methodist preacher, brought him to Minnesota and then to Cleveland, where he spent his adult life writing poetry, children's books, and social criticism. Soon after Debs wrote this letter to Oneal, a number of Cooke's poems appeared in the *Call* "Pals," October 3, 1918; "The Seas of Sleep," October 14, 1918—but, curiously, not the poem dealing with Debs's trial in Cleveland. A poem "written in the courtroom by Edmund Vance Cooke, at Cleveland, Ohio," and titled, "Our Gene" was reprinted in *Debs's Magazine*, January 1923.

4. Charles W. Ervin, editor of the *Call*, was the Socialist party candidate for governor of New York in the 1918 election, in which he got nearly 100,000 votes. The Democratic candidate, Al Smith, won the election.

5. James Oneal's twin brother, Judson (1875-1919), worked as a "heater" in Terre Haute, where he remained active in the local Socialist party and wrote occasional articles for the state party's *Bulletin*.

EVD to Ruth Le Prade

September 30, 1918
Terre Haute, Indiana

My dear Comrade Ruth: —

It would be vain for me to attempt to tell you how deeply I am touched by your beautiful letter and your inspiring poem which are now in my hands and fill me with rapture. Each word is precious to me and each sympathetic, cheering, loving thought inspirits and enriches me.

A thousand thanks, my beloved young comrade! you have compensated me in full and overflowing measure for all it has ever been my privilege to do for the cause. You have been too generous and you have bestowed upon me honors but ill deserved since my contribution in service, compared to some others, is so paltry that at times I am almost ashamed of it. My one regret is that I have not had more to give to the cause.

That in the recent trial I stood where every loyal comrade was in duty bound to stand entitles me to no such generous recognition, such magnanimous and flattering consideration as your beautiful letter and your wonderful poem have brought to me.[1]

Coming from you, dear comrade, who have given your health and all but your life to the cause of humanity, this tribute you have paid me moves me to tears. You are very near to me at this moment. I can almost feel your hand-clasp and look into your sweet face.

How could anyone fail to be true with such faithful, devoted, consecrated comrades to sustain one!

Your fine soul shines in all the lines of your poem and I am heartened and inspired by it more than these poor words can express. It is a characteristic production, so like you, "Our Ruth," and breathes the spirit of the glad new day now dawning.

You are endowed with a marvelous gift. Your name is destined to be known in many tongues and climes for the gods have placed you among the immortals. That you may have health and strength to sustain you until the day of complete fulfillment of all your beautiful dreams and noble aspirations is my most ardent wish and hope.

Since the day the sad news of your illness came I have been thinking of you and, in my way, praying for your restoration. You are so precious to us and the cause. The future holds so much in store for you. You must get well and strong for the great work awaiting you and which no other can do. And you must allow yourself time enough in all patience to make the recovery complete so there shall be no possibility of relapse.

And now, my dear young comrade, thanking you again and again in the name of Mrs. Debs and for myself and all our family, and with all love and greeting and good wishes to you and yours and to all for whom you have so freely given yourself in devoted service, I am always

Faithfully yours,
Eugene V. Debs

TLS, CLSU, Poets Garden Collection.

1. Le Prade's poem, "Eugene V. Debs" (*Protest*, May 1919), urges Debs to "Go take your place with Socrates and Christ."

Marguerite Prevey[1] to EVD

October 7, 1918
Akron, Ohio

Dear Comrade Gene:

Just this morning I received a list of your dates in this district, I am sending you a copy, the State Secy[2] may have already done so but I'm not sure, we should have some good meetings on this trip.

I hope the arrangement of dates meets with your approval, the State Secy did her best to follow your wishes in the matter, I enclose a letter from one of the Canton comrades, it will give you an idea of the arrangements there, I told them if the Banquet was arranged they must excuse you by eight thirty,

Kindly let me know where we may expect to find you for the Canton meeting (it is in the afternoon)[3] If you come on Saturday better come to Akron, our little crowd will be on hand for the Canton meeting,

I spent yesterday at the Lake with Davy and Emma,[4] we read the story "Jimmy Higgins Meets The Candidate" we enjoyed it immensely, it would not surprise me if that Candidate did take a bath in the river, "Barbarian Instincts" crop out in Saints as well as Sinners, It occured to me it might be well to ask you where we should find you, after reading that story.

I hope Kate is feeling rejuvenated after the little trip to Chicago, poor soul she probably worries a great deal when you are gone, it is hard for the loved ones at home, but the world must be saved.

The War news is exceedingly interesting this morning, Now that the Germans are willing to accept President Wilson's Peace proposals, something in the way of a conference should happen in the near future, let us hope our boys will be back on American soil before the New Year, how happy the poor Mothers Wives and Sweethearts would be. As usual I am optimistic, I feel the worst will be over soon, the German people can hardly stand another winter of this awful torture.

The Little Indian sends love, says he will be with you on your trip, hope you are feeling quite well,

Love to Theodore, Yourself and all The Family,

Faithfully Yours,
Marguerite

TLS, InTI, Debs Collection.

1. Prevey, Debs's longtime friend from Akron, Ohio, and A. W. Moskowitz, a Cleveland tailor, supplied Debs's $10,000 bond at the time of his arrest on June 30, 1918.
2. Alfred Wagenknecht's wife, Hortense, was serving as state secretary of the party in Ohio.
3. Debs spoke at Canton on October 13 and at Akron on October 27, 1918. A manuscript, "Debs Dates in Ohio, October 13 to November 5th, 1918," listing a dozen dates in the state, is in the Debs Collection at Indiana State University.
4. Prevey's children.

EVD to Algernon Lee

October 10, 1918
Terre Haute, Indiana

My dear Algernon Lee:—

The beautiful letter from you, fine and touching and inspiring in every line and word, has just reached me, and my heart is full of it and of you and your beautiful wife.

A thousand loving thanks to you both! Words are too weak and cold and formal to express my appreciation.

I am wondering constantly as dear comrades write to me in such loving and sympathetic terms what on earth I could have done to merit such lavish praise and commendation. As I see it I did my simple duty to the party, and that in a small way, almost comtemptible compared to the heroic services rendered by Lenine,[1] Trotzky, Liebknecht, Rosa Luxembourg[2] and numerous others, not overlooking those here among us who have been lynched, tarred and feathered, manhandled, deported and outraged in every other conceivable manner. It is true that I have been threatened with all these things but I have somehow contrived to escape all but the minor ones. As for my conviction to prison I have given little thought to that and if I go there I shall find comrades there and may perhaps be able to make more comrades out of my fellow-convicts.

For all the little I have ever been able to do for the movement I have been compensated a thousandfold. This kind, generous, touching expression from you is of itself more than sufficient to balance the account of a prison sentence.

Yes, we are well rid of those who have "lied their souls away," as you so aptly put it, to betray the party, and loyal comrades who have stood the test now measure up and stand forth with a majesty with which they were never clothed before.

Well do I remember the Minneapolis meeting and dear old "Bill" Erwin,[3] but I had no idea that Algernon Lee was there. Those were stirring days and I was just beginning to have my eyes opened to what is now to me the greatest thing in all the world.

What would I not give to have an hour with you dear comrades and the other fine souls I met with you at the Rand School! I very often think of Bertha Mailly and always as the incarnation of the finest idealism of our movement. Please give her my kindest remembrances.

There is a good deal more I would like to talk over with you but the letters are many and I am soon having to leave here. I speak at Canton, where the trouble began, next Sunday and I am booked in Ohio until election day. Under the terms of my parole I can speak within the jurisdiction of the court but not outside of it. Of course I am not permitted to say anything that will "hurt the war" and I will therefore have to make all my drives against the system. We are going to cover the district thoroughly and do our best to send Ruthenberg, now serving his sentence at the workhouse in Canton, to congress, and I believe we shall do it. On the 22nd. ult. I spoke at Cleveland and the demonstration was a most extraordinary one. All things are coming our way. We have but to keep cheerful and put the best we have and all we have into the work.

Thanking you again and again for your loving, loyal remembrance, which enriches me beyond words, and with all affectionate greetings and good wishes to you and Mrs. Lee I am,

Yours always,
Eugene V. Debs

TLS, NNU Tam, Debs Collection.

1. Nikolai Lenin (Vladimir Ilich Ulyanov, 1870-1924) was the leader of the Bolshevik faction of Russian socialists and father of the revolution that overthrew the

Kerensky provisional government in 1917 and established a dictatorship of the proletariat in January 1918.

    2. Rosa Luxemburg (1870-1919) was a German socialist agitator, called Red Rosa,
who shared with Karl Liebknecht leadership of the Spartacus party and with him was
arrested and killed while being taken to prison in January 1919.

    3. William W. Erwin, a Minneapolis (later St. Louis) attorney who represented
workers during the Homestead Strike in 1892 and the ARU in the Pullman Strike
of 1894.

EVD to Morris Hillquit

October 14, 1918
Terre Haute, Indiana

My dear Morris:—

    A thousand thanks! Your appreciative words touch me deeply. If
the speeches[1] met with your approval nothing more need be said in
their favor. I am only sorry they went out before I had a chance to
go over them as there are a number of errors in the stenographic
report which should have been corrected. For the present it is impossible to circulate them as the court has given orders that inasmuch
as the speeches are seditious they must not be permitted to go through
the mails or be otherwise circulated. But perhaps this may add to the
interest of the people have in seeing them and will help to increase
their circulation later on when the embargo is removed.

    I am more than gratified to hear of the improvement in your health.
This is even better to me than the best that could be said about the
speeches. You are surely on the way back to yourself and in due time
will be at your post again. If my lips were not gagged by the court
order nothing would give me greater joy than to speak for you in
this campaign. You must and shall go to congress. I wish it were to
the senate and your election certain. In congress you will make a
record we shall all be proud of. From the reports I get your election
is assured.[2] Hurrah!

    With all love,

                                                    Yours always,
                                                    E. V. Debs

TLS, WHi, Hillquit Papers.

    1. Probably Debs's Canton speech and his addresses to the jury and judge at
Cleveland.

    2. Hillquit was defeated in his race for Congress in 1918 by Isaac Siegel, a Re-
publican-Democratic fusion candidate.

EVD to Lena Morrow Lewis[1]

October 18, 1918
Terre Haute, Indiana

My dear Comrade Lewis:—

I have just read with real interest and appreciation your good letter of the 12th. inst. and I thank you warmly for your kindness and thoughtfulness in writing it. Coming at this time such sentiments as it contains from a loyal comrade such as you have always been are precious to me and heartening and sustaining beyond words.

I am glad you were with dear Comrade Ruth[2] and that she flattered me by letting you see my poor letter to her, and I especially appreciate the beautiful, touching compliment you pay to her, the tribute of one fine soul to another. Ruth is indeed a sweet soul, a tower of strength in the cause to which she is consecrated, and an inspiration to us all. May her frail body which has suffered so much from the cruelties of capitalism her delicate nature could not withstand grow strong again and may all good influences combine to restore her physical vigor and energy that she may realize in fullest measure her noble aspiration to serve the cause of freedom and humanity!

Yes, I had already seen the Times editorial but I am glad to have this additional copy and thank you for sending it. Otis and his heirs and descendants never, never forgave or forgot the flaying I gave Otis in a great meeting packed to the doors at the old Hazzard Pavilion in Los Angeles, since destroyed by fire, in 1894. It was following the A.R.U. strike. I was out under bail. The Times attacked me foully in a column editorial following my speech there. When I concluded the tour I went back there to make reply. Otis himself, driven by curiosity, was there, expecting to be unnoticed. He got caught in the center of the jam and could not back out or get away. I was told he was there and invited him to come to the platform and face me before the people of Los Angeles. Of course he didn't dare to come. The crowd began to yell for him but he made no attempt to defend himself. I then exposed his editorial lies and calumnies and tore his dirty scab sheet to tatters and flung them into his face. I denounced him as a coward and literally flayed him before his own people. The great crowd hooted him and his mortification, if he had one particle of shame, was complete. From that time to this Otis and his Times have missed no opportunity to attack me, and I don't blame them in the least. I settled my account with them almost 25 years ago and they are not apt to ever forget.

It has been a long time since I have had the pleasure of seeing you but I have partly at least kept up with your work through the socialist papers. And you have been doing good work, dear comrade, and you have stuck to it without a flicker. It has seemed to me that the national office had sent you to the remotest regions and assigned some of the toughest jobs to you, a compliment that only a loyal comrade such as you deserves or can appreciate.

I am not a bit surprised about Stitt Wilson[3] and the rest you name. Let them do their worst. Little do they dream that they are discrediting themselves instead of the party. I do not doubt your work just now is hard but it will be all different when the war is over. Then the last shall be first.

With all love and good wishes I am,

Yours always,
Eugene V. Debs

TLS, NNU Tam, Debs Collection.

1. Lena Morrow Lewis (1862-1950) was the Socialist party's leading organizer and lecturer in Alaska from 1912 to 1917, when she returned to Los Angeles to edit *New Justice* and, from 1925 to 1930, *Labor World,* in which she promoted the causes of socialism and feminism. In 1914 and 1916 she was the party's candidate for delegate to Congress from Alaska.

2. Ruth Le Prade.

3. Jackson Stitt Wilson, the former socialist mayor of Berkeley, California, who left the party in opposition to its antiwar policy.

Horace Traubel to EVD

October 24, 1918
Norwich, Connecticut

Dear Gene:

You are a ray of light in a dark place.

You are a great sea on which the biggest ships may sail.

You are a ripe harvest field that no mortal eye can see the end of.

Gene, you are something big without a name, and I can't think of you without thinking of measureless expanses and oceans and skies.

Horace Traubel

Transcript of ALS, NN Kars.

EVD to Upton Sinclair

October 28, 1918
Terre Haute, Indiana

My dear Sinclair:—

Just a word of suggestion which needs no answer. I am going through your "Profits of Religion"[1] a second time with keen interest in every page. It is one of those books that grows greater with re-reading. You have packed a lot of the most vital stuff into this little volume and a million copies at least should be in the hands of the American people. Let me congratulate you especially upon your courage in unmasking hypocrites in high places and telling the naked truth about the superstitions, frauds and false pretenses which masquerade in the name of religion and which serve now as in the days of Christ to buttress tyranny, fatten insolent parasites, leeches and the whole foul brood of ruling class blood-suckers, {while} keeping their mass of victims exploited to the marrow of their miserable bones, in ignorance and slavery.

You made a very proper example of that arch-hypocrite, that pious, shameless pretender, Lyman Abbott,[2] who prates about "Christian Ethics" while he reeks with the filthy subsidies of his filthy masters.

The suggestion I wish to make is that you put pages 92 to 109 inclusive in a 16 page pamphlet and make a rate on them per 100 and per 1,000 so that this particular expose and eye-opener may be distributed by hundreds of thousands.[3] Every wage slave in America ought to have one of these put into his hands, and if possible into his gray matter to dislodge the superstition placed there by priestcraft which keeps him in bestial subjection to his capitalist master and his mercenaries, the priests and professors and politicians and editorial hirelings.

Yours always,
E. V. Debs

TLS, InU, Lilly Library, Sinclair MSS.

1. Sinclair published *The Profits of Religion* serially in *Upton Sinclair's Magazine* between April and September 1918, and the book appeared in October. Debs called the book one that "must be read and studied to understand the significance of churches founded on the plutocratic idea of exploitation." *New Appeal*, November 16, 1918.

2. Lyman Abbott (1835-1922) was for many years a close associate of Henry Ward Beecher as editor of *Christian Union* (after 1893, the *Outlook*) and at Plymouth Congregational Church in Brooklyn, where Abbott succeeded Beecher as pastor in 1890 and served until 1899. In *Profits of Religion*, Sinclair devoted a long section to Abbott, whom he accused of having "traduced and betrayed [Jesus Christ] by the most amazing piece of theological knavery that it has ever been my fortune to encounter."

3. In November 1918, Sinclair published, "at the request of Eugene V. Debs," a twenty-page pamphlet, *The Profits of Religion*, which reproduced pages 92-109 of the book. The section dealt with the "Fifth Avenue clergy" of New York and "the Corporation of Corruption" that sustained them.

John F. McNamee to EVD

October 30, 1918
Cleveland, Ohio

Dear Sir:

It is with regret that I find myself obliged to discontinue sending you our Magazine[1] complimentarily. This has been made necessary by instructions of the War Industries Board, which is fully explained in the enclosed leaflet, same being a reproduction of a notice appearing in our October 1st issue.[2]

It is very much against my personal wishes that I find it necessary to have your name taken from our complimentary list.

Very truly yours,
JOHN F. MCNAMEE,
Editor and Manager.

TL (form letter), InTI, Debs Collection.

1. *Locomotive Firemen and Enginemen's Magazine*, successor to the *Brotherhood of Locomotive Firemen Magazine*.
2. The notice in the October 1, 1918, issue of the magazine quoted a War Industries Board regulation prohibiting "giving free copies; except for actual services rendered."

William F. Kruse to EVD

October 31, 1918
Chicago, Illinois

Dear Gene:

I understand that next Tuesday is your birthday,[1] and hasten to send in my congratulations. Since it is also Election day I hope and trust that the vote cast for our candidates will be a monumental natal gift for you.

Under another cover a present is being sent you. No, it is not from myself, tho there is nothing in the world you might need that I would not send you, were I able to do so. It is a silver plated coffee service, the gift of the Douglas Park Jewish Branch, which, as a campaign fund raising stunt was "auctioned off" to the most popular socialist in the world at so much per vote. Needless to say, you won.

The engraving on the front is in the nature of hieroglyphics that I defy anyone to decipher. No, it is not Hebrew—it consists of good old English letters. The top line is "Pr," meaning "Presented." The second line is "B.D.P.," meaning, they assure me, "By Douglas Park"; the third line is "J.B.S.P.," meaning Jewish Branch Socialist Party." The acknowledgement should be sent to the Secretary, Albert Albert, 3203 Douglas Park Boul., Chicago, Ill. As I attended their meeting to line up some watchers for next Tuesday, they asked me to serve as their shipping clerk, which I am glad to do.

Next month is December and in it is Christmas. That means a Christmas number of Y.S.M. Will you write a little message to our young folks for it—preferably Christmas and New Years greeting—something inspiring and yet SAFE enough for a little harmless paper like mine to go thru the mails? I am sure I can depend on you for it.[2]

My heartfelt love and comradeship to you, especially on this your birthday, and here's hoping that we get out of jail together (if we ever go there)[3] in time to see a free American working class take its place beside its comrades from the rest of the world.

Your loving comrade,
Wm. F. Kruse

TLS, InTI, Debs Collection.

1. Debs's sixty-third birthday was November 5, 1918.
2. Debs's "To Our Young Socialists" appeared in the December 1918 issue of *Young Socialists Monthly*.
3. As noted, Kruse and Berger, Germer, Engdahl, and Tucker were found guilty of obstructing recruitment and other violations in January 1919 and sentenced to twenty years in prison by Judge Landis. Their conviction was overturned on appeal, but Berger was refused his seat in Congress because of his conviction.

Jeannette D. Pearl[1] et al. to EVD

November 1, 1918
New York City

My Dear Comrade Debs,

We have received your letters re Lehane[2] and the letter you re-addressed to him at the Call office I gave him today. We are all very

sorry to have had to trouble you in this matter as we in the east here
well know the trouble you have been having and our hearts are with
you through it all. However all the trouble we have caused you has
borne fruit and it is due to your letter to Larkin[3] more than {any}-
thing else that Lehane was finally bailed out. The fact that Lehane
was "in bad" with certain members of the party through his attack
on some prominent comrades was used in every conceivable way to
turn off the aid that one Socialist naturally gives to another. We, here,
argued along the lines that you used in your letter (that all differences
between comrades were our own concern and that we should settle
them ourselves without any help from the outside) but it was not until
your voice was added to ours that the appeal carried weight.[4]

We naturally turned to you as the affair was urgent and we knew
that you would view it in the light that you did. We enclose a copy
of the resolution that was passed by the State Committee of Connecticut and Local New York has also endorsed the case {a copy of
which was sent under separate cover} nevertheless we have no funds
money is very tight here and we really feel that in this case we are
entitled to the same proportion of the Million Dollar[5] fund as anyone
else. We do not desire any money from you personally as we are well
aware of the circumstances we only desired your endorsement and
your good offices. These you have given readily as we knew you would
and we send you the data so that you may be able to answer the
arguments that you meet. Lehane did not accuse the party of anything
but he did accuse individuals some of whom have left the party, and
of course neither did Larkin ever accuse the party of selling out.

We appreciate all your work in this connection as we appreciate
your work in the wider field and your magnificent stand at Cleveland.
You have stood as a beacon light in a very dark period and our hearts,
like the hearts of our comrades all the world over and not the least
in Ireland, are with you

Yours for the cause
Jeannette D. Pearl
E. W. MacAlpine[6]
Mrs. K. Buckley Withrow
Joseph R. Brodsky[7]
Morris Samuels
Members of the Defense Comm.

TLS, InTI, Debs Collection.

1. Jeannette D. Pearl, a writer, was secretary of the Socialist party in New York
County. One of her short stories, "Pride," appeared in *Masses* in June 1917. Pearl

left the Socialist party in 1919, joined the Communist Labor party, and wrote regularly, usually on women's issues, for the *Daily Worker* in the 1920s.

2. Called "the Ambassador of the Irish Republic," Cornelius Lehane (1870-1918) was a pioneer of the labor and socialist movements in Ireland and England before coming to the United States in 1914. During the next four years, Lehane became a leading speaker on the socialist lecture circuit and in April 1918 launched a new socialist journal, *World Republic*. During the 1916 congressional campaign, Lehane gave a dozen speeches in Indiana's Fifth District on Debs's behalf. In June 1918 he was arrested in Connecticut for a violation of the Espionage Act and his trial, first set for November 7, 1918, was set back to January 1919, but Lehane died of pneumonia in New York City on December 31, 1918.

3. James Larkin and Lehane had worked together in Ireland and England before both came to the United States.

4. In a letter from Adolph Germer, national secretary of the Socialist party, to Debs, dated October 14, 1918, Germer acknowledged receipt of a letter from Debs of October 9, 1918, in which Debs had discussed "the Lehane case." Germer said that he was reluctant to use funds from the party's Million Dollar Defense Fund for Lehane's defense because he was "not so sure that Lehane's activity was entirely of a Socialist nature" but that he would be guided by "members near the scene of Lehane's recent activities." In a letter from the "Lehane Defense Committee" dated October 26, 1918, Pearl reported that the "National Executive Committee [has] contributed to the defense." In Lehane's December 1918 letter to Debs, Lehane suggested that Germer's reluctance to support him was the result of Germer's belief that Lehane had charged that the American Socialist party had "sold out to the British govt." InTI, Debs Collection.

5. The effort to accumulate a million-dollar defense fund" was begun by the party's national executive committee in the fall of 1917. Funds collected (which, of course, never approached a million dollars) were to be used for both the fall 1918 campaign and the legal defense of socialists tried for violation of the various local, state, and federal espionage, sedition, and syndicalist laws. *Eye-Opener*, December 29, 1917.

6. Eadmonn W. MacAlpine was a leader of the Boston left wing, which left the Socialist party in 1919 to form the Communist Labor party. He served as managing editor of *Revolutionary Age*, the group's chief journal, and wrote regularly, often on the "Irish Question," for that journal.

7. Joseph R. Brodsky (1890-1947) was born in Kiev, brought to the United States in 1897, and graduated from New York University in 1912. In his thirty-five-year legal career in New York, Brodsky specialized in labor law and served as counsel to various Communist party leaders, including William Z. Foster and Earl Browder. He was one of the attorneys for the defendant blacks in the Scottsboro case.

Theodore Debs to Upton Sinclair

November 6, 1918
Terre Haute, Indiana

Dear Comrade Sinclair:—

Your favor of the 1st. to Gene has just been received. Gene is away at present and I do not know how long he may be gone. I will see to it that your communication reaches him, but I fear that for the present at least he will be unable, glad as I know he would be under other circumstances, to take the matter of the pamphlets which he suggested in hand. I am sure that nothing would please him better than to have the pamphlet published as suggested and push it with all possible energy, both on account of the pamphlet itself and the good it would undoubtedly do as propaganda and at the same time to comply with your wishes and aid you in your work, but he is himself so much overworked at present and there are so many demands upon him from all directions that I fear that with the best will he will not be able to carry out your suggestion.

To explain more fully, my brother has but recently been recovering from a nervous and physical breakdown, the third one, due to years of strain and overwork and some how the work seems to be forced upon him and he is not given much chance to recuperate his health and strength. But for some time now he has been slowly gaining and we believe that if he does not overdo himself again he will quite recover his former self in the near future. This may account for his inability to do a good many of the things he has been asked to do by comrades, such as your own request which of itself is of a small matter but is only one of a great many which combined make a great demand.

Possibly at a later time when the circumstances are more favorable Gene may be able to help you to get out the pamphlet[1] and to push the circulation of the whole excellent book[2] and I need not assure you that it will give him pleasure to do so.

As to our correspondence list, I fear that there are not enough addresses available to make it worth while to copy the same for the purpose suggested. First of all, we have been expecting our office to be raided ever since the war was declared and our files are scattered about and it would be a difficult matter to go over them in their present shape. Then again many of our letters have been destroyed as we do not have room nor facilities to keep complete and up-to-date files. Another bit of explanation may be necessary.

You see our office here is almost like a national office on account of Gene having been four times the candidate for president. It is safe to say that 95% of our correspondence and other work is for the party and the movement and yet we pay the entire expense out of our personal pocket, and since the war and the suppression of the papers with which we were connected[3] we have had no income and have had to go into debt to keep our office going and to pay our living expense. We do not sell any leaflets, pamphlets or other printed matter but give them away free in connection with our correspondence. This we have been more than willing to do as long as we had any income to draw on but at this time we have had to go into debt to the extent of over a thousand dollars without income in sight. You know, of course, that under Gene's parole he was prohibited from speaking outside of the jurisdiction of the court, the north-eastern part of Ohio. He arranged to cover about 20 points in that district hoping to raise some revenue and do some good for the party but the influenza broke out and all the meetings had to be cancelled. I only make this explanation that you may understand the state of affairs here, our lack of facilities to do the work that should be done and the unsatisfactory condition under which our work has now to be done. We shall pull through and we are not going to halt or hesitate any more than we are compelled to. The war will soon be over and then we can get a fresh grip on ourselves and the situation.

Now Comrade Sinclair I have tried to make clear to you why we cannot now do the things that are requested in your letter and I am quite sure you will understand.

Please let me thank you sincerely for your proposed address to President Wilson pleading for amnesty for political prisoners.[4] I know that Gene will appreciate fully your good intention and whether you succeed or not it is certainly a highly commendable and unselfish undertaking on your part.

With all wishes for your success I am,

Yours fraternally,
Theodore Debs

TLS, InU, Lilly Library, Sinclair MSS.

1. As noted, Sinclair published the pamphlet, *The Profits of Religion*, in November 1918.
2. In "Debs' Favorite Passage from Sinclair's New Book" (*New Appeal*, November 16, 1918) Debs called attention to the material that Sinclair abstracted for the pamphlet and urged readers to get copies of both the book and the pamphlet.
3. The *Rip-Saw, Social Revolution*, and *Social Builder*.
4. Sinclair's letter to Wilson, "Amnesty for Political Prisoners," signed by both Upton and Mary Craig Sinclair, was published in *New Appeal* on November 23, 1918. Sinclair wrote regularly on the subject in *Upton Sinclair's Magazine* and the *New Appeal*.

EVD to Ruth Le Prade

November 15, 1918
Terre Haute, Indiana

My dear Comrade Ruth: —

Returning home after several days absence I find myself reading the beautiful letter, the wonderful letter from you written on my birthday. What shall I say, what can I say in answer? You have enriched me beyond measure and if my birthday had been remembered by no one else and been honored in no other way your noble tribute, so characteristic of you, would of itself have honored me as greatly as if I were among the foremost in the files of time instead of a mere comrade who is trying as best he can to do his small part in the great cause in which we are all enlisted.

Dear Ruth, you have eyes as generous as your heart is tender and your soul great. You see in your comrades the riches of spirit you yourself possess and you give them full credit for the lofty motives which animate you and the loving services you yourself render as freely and unconsciously as the flower gives its fragrant breath to the air and sunshine.

You have on many occasions given evidence of your precious and inspiring comradeship and I would be ungrateful indeed if I had not a deep sense of what you have been to me, especially in the hours that were dark when the thought of a loved and loving comrade comes to one as a ray of light in a dungeon cell. If I have been of any real help to my comrades in this great crusade for a better day it is due entirely to what I have drawn from themselves, and though they may not know it they have been to me & are to me infinitely more than I can ever hope to be to them. Among these helpful and inspiring comrades, you, dear Ruth, have a place all your own and when at times the outlook seems dark I can always turn toward you and see the light. And so if you find in me anything which serves to brighten our sky in the least you may feel that you are well entitled to it, for since I have known you and of you every hour of your consecrated life and every aspiration of your soulful being has been to brighten the skies of others.

I should have deemed it a privilege to remit for the copy of your precious poems[1] sent at my request to Mrs. Baur but since your generous partiality has forbidden this I shall venture to hope that some good day I may in some way reciprocate your kindness. Let me thank you with all my heart for the very gracious manner in which you responded to this request and which I shall always gratefully remember.

And how very, very thoughtful and generous you were to send me the additional autographed copies! Your kindness blossoms perennially and your generosity has no bounds. Thank you and bless you over and over again. I shall place each copy in the hands of a comrade who will read our beloved Ruth with sympathy and understanding.

Mrs. Debs and Theodore and all of us are one in love to you and all the good wishes in the world.

Yours always,
Eugene V. Debs

TLS, CLSU, Poets Garden Collection.

1. In *Social Revolution* (March 1917), Debs wrote that "every person who loves real literature and genuine poetry" should read Le Prade's collection of poems, *A Free Woman*.

EVD to Louis N. Morones[1]

November 16, 1918
Terre Haute, Indiana

LOUIS N. MORONES,

BE NOT DECEIVED BY MOYER'S STATEMENT.[2] HE IS NOW TRAINING WITH THE FEDERATION FAKIRS THAT WANTED HIM HUNG TWELVE YEARS AGO AND MALIGNING THE MEN THAT SAVED HIS LIFE. IF YOU WANT THE TRUTH I CAN FURNISH IT AND I DARE GOMPERS[3] TO FACE ME AND DENY IT.

EUGENE V. DEBS

Telegram (draft), InTI, Debs Collection.

1. Morones was secretary-treasurer of the Mexican Federation of Labor; he was attending the Pan American Labor Conference, which was being held in Laredo, Texas.
2. Charles Moyer, who, along with William Haywood and George Pettibone, had been strongly defended by Debs and acquitted in their trial in 1906-07 for the murder of former Idaho Governor Frank Steunenberg. In 1911, Moyer led the Western Federation of Miners (the Mine, Mill and Smelter Workers after 1916) into reaffiliation with the AFL. In a speech at the Pan American Labor Conference (*New York Times*, November 16, 1918), Moyer declared that the AFL had "poured out its money" in the defense of Moyer, Haywood, and Pettibone and that "Bill Haywood is in prison, a fate he richly deserves. I warn you against him and his propaganda."
3. Samuel Gompers headed the American delegation to the Laredo conference. He defended the AFL's role in the war, cited instances of its support for Mexican workers, and joined the attack on Haywood and others "who would destroy the only real labor movement in the United States." *New York Times*, November 16, 1918.

EVD to Jack [Carney]

November 18, 1918
Terre Haute, Indiana

My dear Jack:—

I wish you to be kind enough to give space to the enclosed communication.[1] It explains itself. I think you will agree that it is of interest to union men and socialists. You can headline it as you think best. You will know after reading it how to handle it. Perhaps a brief introduction by you would be proper. Use your own judgment. It was the socialists who began the agitation and kept it up persistently that saved the lives of Moyer, Haywood and Pettibone while Gompers and his crowd were not only indifferent but hostile. Moyer seems to have forgotten this and he now ignores the socialists while he fawns at the feet of the labor misleaders who would have rejoiced in his hanging, and I do not propose to see this falsification of the facts go into the labor record.

I wish you to be kind enough to send me 25 copies of the issue containing this article with bill for same. You must allow me to remit and I will gladly do so. Please read the proof over carefully yourself if not too busy so the article will appear free from error. I am going to have it reproduced as widely as possible with due credit given to Truth.[2] This has not yet appeared in print. You will be the first to publish it.

Love to you, my lad! I am,

Yours always,
E. V. Debs

TLS, InH, Reynolds Collection.

1. In the November 22, 1918, issue of *Truth*, Carney published "Debs Challenges Chas. Moyer," a letter from Debs to Moyer in which Debs declared that "Gompers and his gang wanted you and Haywood and Pettibone hung twelve years ago" and that "the socialists and the loyal men in the labor movement" had saved their lives.

2. Debs's letter to Moyer was reprinted in *Revolutionary Age*, December 7, 1918, with no credit to *Truth*.

Seymour Stedman to EVD

November 20, 1918
Chicago, Illinois

Dear Sir: —
     I am enclosing a copy of ~~the enclosed~~ letter to Judge Westenhaver[1]
and will forward to you a reply immediately upon receipt.
     Please hand Theodore one wallop from me. Love to all of you
from us.

                                                            Steddy

My dear Judge: —
     In view of the fact that an armistice has been signed would you
entertain a motion to modify the territorial restriction placed upon
Mr. Debs by the terms of the bond for supersedeas executed by him.
     The prosecution of the war having ended it does not seem to me
that the condition of the bond referred to can any longer answer a
war purpose. I remain

                                          Sincerely yours,
                                          [Seymour Stedman]

TLS (with one-page copy of letter from Stedman to Judge D. C. Westenhaver), InTI, Debs Collection.

     1. In February 1917, President Wilson appointed David C. Westenhaver (1876-
1928) judge of the federal district court in the Northern District of Ohio. He presided
at Debs's trial in Cleveland in September 1918 and handed down Debs's ten-year
sentence. Westenhaver refused Stedman's request to change the terms of Debs's bond.

EVD to Theodore Debs

November 24, [1918]
Cleveland, Ohio

My dear old Pard:
     Arrived here in good under. We will have a great meeting here
tonight. To-morrow we're to plan a thorough canvass of the entire
district.[1] We shall cover every important point in it. Shall arrange to
have the rest of the meetings (after this trip) covered after Jan. 1st
as you & I agreed, so we'll have the rest of the month, after I get
home, for corduroys & Babe[2] and bucks.
     Feeling fine & ready for the work ahead. Would love to have you
here to practice on—to expend my excess energies on. Can't write

much for the room is full of comrades. Marguerite[3] is here & sends love — Says it's a shame you're not here — & so say I. You shall be soon — When we're hooked up, again as I hope we shall be after this trip, & then we'll organize things so that we can go together as we used to do in other days. All the comrades send love — they all know "Theodore" & Marguerite has just told them that "Theodore is the silent power behind the throne." Then she added: "He does his work so quietly & modestly that nobody sees or hears him but all the same there's only one of Theodore & he's one of the biggest, finest, truest men in the whole movement — and he's so unselfish that he wants Gene to get all the credit without ever being seen or known." And that's the fact, old pard, and I'm glad that there are others as well as myself who know it.

If I had ya here a love-swish would light on your beak — but it will keep till I get home.

Love & Kisses to you & Gertrude & Marguerite — You all seem even dearer to me when I'm away & I hunger to get back and be where you are.

Forever, old pard, forever & ever

Yours
Gene

ALS, InTI, Debs Collection.

1. A letter from Hortense Wagenknecht to Debs, November 19, 1918, listed ten speeches for Debs in northeastern Ohio between November 24 and December 8, 1918, and expressed the hope that "two dozen dates" could be filled before Christmas. InTI, Debs Collection.
2. Theodore Debs's hunting dog.
3. Marguerite Prevey.

EVD to Cornelius Lehane

November 30, 1918
Terre Haute, Indiana

Dear Comrade Lehane: —

Your very kind letter is received and I am glad to know that the misunderstandings that have heretofore existed between you and other comrades are being cleared away. If we have been helpful, even in a small way, in calling attention to your case and having you properly defended in court we are much gratified. We did only our duty and for this we are entitled to no credit. But I must be frank enough to say in this connection that I have no time for bickering, unraveling misunderstandings or the settling of personal differences between comrades. There are still in jail and under indictment hundreds of our comrades unable to furnish the exhorbitant bail bonds demanded; many have been convicted who now languish in foul dungeons for the lack of bonds until their cases can be heard by a higher court. And there are few, if any of these, that are not appealing to us for one thing or another. Among the heaps of unanswered letters on my desk is one from a young woman comrade, a school teacher,[1] tubercular, who has been in a filthy Texas jail for months, for weeks held incommunicado, saw no living person but the white-livered brute that threw in a hunk of sour bread, a dish of tainted beans and a little water, with a ten year sentence upon her head, as noble a soul as ever lived in this world, and as heroic, who almost apologetically asks what, if anything, we can do for her! To these comrades we owe everything, every moment of time and every atom of strength, and God knows there is not enough of either to meet the daily demand. If I can be helpful to you in other ways I shall be most happy to serve you.

With cordial good wishes and hoping that the best of success attend your efforts I am,

Fraternally yours,
[Eugene V. Debs]

TLc, InTI, Debs Collection.

1. Flora I. Foreman was tried in federal court at Amarillo, Texas, in December 1918 for a violation of the Espionage Act centering on the charge that she had publicly refused to join the Red Cross and had told her audience they could "go and tell the little school teacher in Washington" how she felt. She was found guilty and given a five-year sentence; President Wilson reduced the term to two years and Foreman was released from the Colorado state prison on May 28, 1920. *Toiler*, December 10, 1919; *New Day*, June 1, 1920.

EVD to Tom Mooney in Care of John Snyder, Editor, *World*

November 30, 1918
Akron, Ohio

TOM MOONEY

"Tear up that commutation[1] and fling the scraps in the brazen face of the corporation hireling that insulted you and the working class by that infamous act. Let Patrick Henry once more speak through you: 'Give me liberty or give me death.' There must be no compromise. You are innocent and by the eternal you shall go free. The working class is aroused as never before in history. They will tear the murderous clutch of criminal capitalism from your throat. All hail the general strike! If they insist upon war let it come. We have nothing to lose but our chains. God loves justice and hates cowards. Stand by your colors and the workers of the world will stand by you to Victory or Death."

Now is the time for the workers of America to prove themselves. Tom Mooney and his Comrades cry aloud to the Proletariat of the world. Arouse ye millions, for whom he risked his life and save that life for the future of his class and for the vindication of right and justice and all things of good report in the civilized world.[2]

EUGENE V. DEBS

Telegram draft, AS, InTI, Debs Collection.

1. On November 28, 1918, Mooney's death sentence was commuted to life imprisonment by Governor Stephens of California. Mooney wrote Governor Stephens on November 29 to "refuse to accept the commutation," placing his "hope . . . in the solidarity of organized labor," but the general strike called for by the Workers Defense League and by some local unions to protest Mooney's life imprisonment was opposed by the AFL leadership, notably Gompers, and resulted chiefly in alarming public opinion. A general strike in Seattle from February 6 to 10, 1919, combined with the call for a general strike by Mooney supporters, helped prepare the public mind for the excesses of the Red Scare of 1919-20 and its aftermath.

2. Debs's telegram to Mooney, the draft of which was written on the letterhead of Marguerite Prevey, "Optometrist and Optician," appeared in the *Oakland World*, the *New Appeal* (December 14, 1918), and other socialist and radical publications.

Theodore Debs to Seymour Stedman

November 30, 1918
Terre Haute, Indiana

My dear "Steddy":—

Yours of the 27th. inst. containing communication from Westenhaver[1] is received and I will hand same to Gene when he returns to the city. According to the press dispatches the authorities are still on his trail, having taken and forwarded a full report of his Toledo speech to Washington,[2] so this dispatch says. Well, let 'em do their damndest and their dirtiest it will not influence Gene in the least.

Sincerely yours,
Theodore

TLS, NNU Tam, Debs Collection.

1. Judge Westenhaver's letter has not been found, but Stedman's November 27, 1918, note to Debs described it as "tantamount to refusing our request." The United States district attorney for the Northern District of Ohio, Edwin S. Wertz, reported to Attorney General A. Mitchell Palmer that he "opposed the application and the court refused to permit Debs to leave the jurisdiction of this court." Wertz to Palmer, January 23, 1919, National Archives, Records of the Department of Justice, Record Group 60, File 77175.

2. An eighteen-page typed copy of "The Speech of Eugene V. Debs, Palace Theatre, Toledo, Ohio. November 27, 1918" is in ibid. In it, Debs defended Tom Mooney and argued for "the use of force—the force of education."

Cornelius Lehane to Theodore Debs

(December 1918)
New York City

Dear Comrade Debs,

This is to thank you for your very kind letter and for the interest you and your brother have taken in my case. The misunderstandings are clearing away and in the end will all be cleared up.

If the National Office insists that I stated the Socialist Party of America had been sold out to the British Govt or any other govt. I think it only fair that they should be asked to submit the evidence on which they base the charge. I deny that I stated anything of the kind. Surely if you wrote a letter to Comrade Germer and asked him in common fairness to quote to you the verbal or written statement of mine which has been used as the basis of the allegation against me, you would not be asking too much? Is it not due to you, to Eugene and to all who supported me while I am in the clutches of the govt. that the National Office should be if necessary *compelled* to make good THEIR statement that I charged the National Socialist Party with having sold out?

If you put that point to Germer it will finally clear the air.

Meantime I wish to thank you and Eugene for your support, and to assure you that I am with you in every effort you make for the advancement of the cause we all have at heart.

Yours for the cause,
C. Lehane

TLS, InTI, Debs Collection.

EVD to Rose Pastor Stokes

December 5, 1918
Sandusky, Ohio

My dear Comrade Rose;
    A thousand thanks for the beautiful letter from your hands which came to me here! Each word from you has cheer and strength and inspiration, and how deeply I am touched and how gratefully I appreciate your continued kindness and devotion I shall not attempt to tell you.
    I have heard of your wonderful meetings[1] and your inspiring picture of the trial, including your precious personal tribute, and while deeply, tenderly sensible of it all, I wished some one inspired like yourself had been there to tell of the truly heroic, noble and overshadowing part Rose Pastor Stokes had in that trial.[2]
    I'm very, very sorry to hear of the sad end of your faithful little pet but glad indeed that you [one word illegible] the danger — you who mean a world to us who know and love you and a world to our great movement.
    I am just leaving for Cleveland — there's no chance to write. You will understand. They still follow me & report my speeches to the Dept. of Justice (!) Let them. We have nothing to fear. The comrades everywhere ask about you — they all love you and well they may.
    With all my heart

Yours
E. V. Debs

ALS, CtY.

    1. Following Debs's trial in Cleveland, Stokes, who attended it, spoke at meetings and rallies in New York City on "Debs's Trial as Witnessed by Rose Pastor Stokes" (*New York Call*, September 21 and October 15, 1918).
    2. Stokes was threatened with contempt of court by Judge Westenhaver for leading applause during Seymour Stedman's outline of Debs's career to the jury. In his Canton speech, Debs cited Stokes as "an inspiring comrade" who "had her millions of dollars" but "went out to render service to the cause" for which "they sent her to the penitentiary for ten years."

EVD to Theodore Debs

December 6, 1918
Akron, Ohio

My dear old Pard:

Just returned here from Sandusky. Marguerite is still in bed with "Flu." The damned thing seems to be getting worse. It has certainly knocked us in the head good & hard, but we're used to it & it can't knock us out. Recd. your letter & papers here. Have written Ellis Jones[1] & Horace Traubel. Will to-day write & forward appeal requested by Jack Carney—we can't go back on him. I've sent a red hot telegram (paid $3.00 for it) to Tom Mooney—you'll see it in Socialist papers—the World of Oakland. Am having to write a couple of articles & editorials for Ohio Socialist.[2]

I speak at Ravenna Saturday if "Flu" don't knock us out—& I shall probably speak at Cleveland again on Monday night. They are urgently requesting another speech & I shall make it if "Flu" don't cancel the arrangement. Everything is uncertain—can't tell from day to day what the devil is going to happen & at every point the secret service agents are on deck—but I'm onto them & give them no chance to get the better of me. Personally they treat me very decently because they respect me—they've got to do that at least.

This will be my last note till I see you. Shall be home Monday night or Tuesday afternoon.

Have been kept in hot water all over this trip but am feeling fine & frisky—in first class fighting fettle—& for this at least I am thankful.

We'll win out yet old man!

Love & kisses to you all!
Gene

ALS, InTI, Debs Collection.

1. Ellis O. Jones (1874-1967) was a poet, songwriter, and journalist whose works appeared regularly in the socialist press before World War I; he was an Ohio delegate to the party's national conventions. As chairman of an antiwar demonstration in New York's Central Park in December 1918, Jones was arrested and charged with sedition but released after eleven days in Bellevue Hospital. During World War II, by which time Jones's political loyalty had moved to the right, he was arrested, tried, and convicted of violation of both federal and California state laws for activities that were alleged to have been pro-Nazi and designed to disrupt the war effort. As one of thirty alleged seditionists tried in Washington in 1944, Jones was convicted of plotting to overthrow the United States government and establish a Nazi state, but the case was dismissed in 1946.

2. Debs's "To Our Russian Comrades" appeared in the *Ohio Socialist*, January 1,

1919; followed by "The Situation in Ohio," January 8, 1919; "Mooney Telegram,"
January 29, 1919; and "Youngstown Speech," February 5, 1919.

EVD to Horace Traubel

December 6, 1918
En route in Ohio

Horace Dearest:

Your note and statement have just reached me. My heart aches.
It's a damned burning shame. You, dear, beautiful brother, above all
others! I'd give the last shred of my garments to be of any real use
to you at this trying moment.[1]

For the second time the "Flu" is cancelling my speaking engagements and the secret service agents are doing the rest. You know that
under my parole I can only speak within the jurisdiction of the court
and here the "Flu" has cancelled my arrangements and sealed my
lips. I've had no income for a long time and have had to go deeply
into debt to keep up my office and pay living expenses—otherwise
you would have had a check from me long ago. I know, dear Brother
mine, without a word from your patient and uncomplaining lips, for
you're next to my heart and I feel all you suffer and regret only that
I can't bear it all. The secret service agents follow me everywhere
and the people are so largely intimidated, that my work is made the
more difficult and the returns the more meager and fruitless on that
account. But we'll not yield, we'll not weaken, we can't—No one
knows this better than you.

But you! I'm almost bitter when I think of all you are, all you have
been to all, all you have braved and borne, all you have dared and
done—and have the great, white, fine soul of you insulted for the
want of a few dirty dollars that you wouldn't defile yourself by touching, if the world about you were only half-civilized. But you'll not
despair and the Conservator will not succumb.[2] Out of the loves you
have fed and of your own great love, help will come and strength
and victory. So when I can breathe again I'll gladly share my all with
you. Love always and always.

                                                                    Gene

Love to the Leslie's and Murphy[3] and all the dear ones of your
comrades.

Transcript T, DLC, Traubel Papers.

1. In the fall of 1918, Traubel suffered a stroke and heart attack from which he never fully recovered before his death in September 1919.

2. Traubel published the last issue of the *Conservator* in June 1919.

3. Traubel was visiting William and Anna Leslie in Norwich, Connecticut, at the time of his heart attack. William Leslie was secretary-treasurer of a textile firm in Norwich, and during Debs's imprisonment after the war he occasionally sent checks for $100 to Debs. A document listing such contributions, in the Debs Collection at Indiana State University, notes smaller contributions from "M & K Murphy," possibly Mary and Katherine Murphy, Norwich teachers and friends of Traubel and the Leslies.

EVD to Jack [Carney]

December 7, 1918
Akron, Ohio

My very dear Jack:

Here it is![1] God bless you! Make any change you wish—so it will serve. If it will not do tell me and I'll try again. You are entitled to my very best. I'm so deeply in debt myself or you'd had a check long ago. Hoped to raise some money on this trip enough to pay some loans—but the "Flu" has cancelled meetings & the secret service agents are at my heels. But we'll not give up—that's one thing we don't know how to do.

How I'd love to send you a check! Maybe I can a bit later.

Thank you a thousand times for your big & generous treatment of the Moyer article! My hands are across the spaces. Command me in any way I can serve you. Your kindness, generosity and love enrich me beyond measure—I love you!

Yours always
E. V. Debs

ALS, InH, Reynolds Collection.

1. "We Must Now Organize," *Truth*, December 14, 1918.

James L. Wallace[1] to EVD

December 10, 1918
Missoula, Montana

My dear Sir:—

I just finished reading your challenge to Chas. H. Moyer as to his statement at the Pan-American Labor Conference at Laredo, Texas.

For 50 odd days I was present at the trial of Haywood at Boise and am familiar with some of the circumstances and happenings in connection therewith. Speaking of what Pettibone said on his death bed,[2] I am reminded of what one of his nearest and dearest friends told me in regard to the thing which hastened his death. This friend told me that the fact that {when} Moyer accepted bond and went out to his liberty on bail, instead of remaining in jail until Pettibone too was released on bail or had been given bail, was the poisoned arrow that broke his heart and brought on his death. To be left alone in the prison cell to take the "gaff" and his associate out on bond, he considered the "unkindest cut of all," and I am told that he begun to fail rapidly from the day his friends and associates departed from Boise. This may be of interest to you. You can get much information from his former wife if you can get in touch with her, if you desire more information.

Sincerely yours,
James L. Wallace

TLS, InTI, Debs Collection.

1. James L. Wallace (1863-1930) was born in Whatcheer, Iowa, graduated from law school at the University of Nebraska in 1894, and practiced law in Missoula, Montana, from 1907 until his death. In 1907, Wallace was a witness in a trial in Boise, Idaho, in which Harry Orchard, the state's chief witness in the Haywood-Moyer-Pettibone case, was charged with the murder of thirteen miners in a Colorado mine explosion. *Daily Missoulian*, May 6, 1930.

2. In his speech at the Laredo conference, Charles Moyer claimed that "on his deathbed George Pettibone blessed the [AFL] for what it had done for him." *New York Times*, November 16, 1918.

EVD to Frank X. Holl

December 13, 1918
Terre Haute, Indiana

My dear Frank: —
    Your beautiful letter is with me and I feel deeply touched this morning as I recall the past and see you and Mrs. Holl way back younder when we were still in the early morning of life. The devotion of you two dear souls has never wavered for one moment. We have not always seen things just alike but we have always had perfect faith in each other and the years have but served to strengthen that faith.
    I am deeply pained to hear of the protracted illness of your dear daughter Frances. I remember her since her beautiful babyhood and

when I last saw her I was so impressed by her sweet manners, so very like her mother, and her lovely young womanhood. Please give her a loving greeting for me and say to her that I hope that soon, quite soon, she may recover from her illness and be quite her dear self again.

A thousand thanks, my beloved old friend, for your contribution. You need not have sent me a cent and I almost wish you had not done so. I need no assurance of that sort of your loyal devotion. I can always count on that and there has always been sweet comfort and sustaining influence in it far beyond the power of dollars. Nevertheless I thank you with all my heart and I beg of you to return my thanks to each of the contributors with a warm greeting from me as well as the hope that some time I may be of some loving service to them. This particular contribution from you carries with it the spirit that makes every dollar worth ten thousand.

I am just back from Ohio and am having to leave for there again. I can still speak in that state, within the jurisdiction of the court, but not outside of it.

The Minneapolis convention of 1886 comes back to me this morning. I can see you as you were then, working like a young trojan and with all the fire of youth to make the convention a success. And then I recall the convention at Atlanta two years later[1] and the first time I met the lovely young woman who later became Mrs. Holl. It is all beautiful in memory but there is a touch of the pathetic in it when one recalls those scenes, those sweet scenes of life's morning that are now with the vanished years.

And now hoping once more that dear Frances may soon be completely restored and with all loving greetings and good wishes to yourself and Mrs. Holl I remain as always,

Yours faithfully,
Eugene V. Debs

P.S. Kindest remembrances to our old friend Calcutt if he is still there.

TLS, TxU, Holl Manuscripts.

1. The Brotherhood of Locomotive Firemen conventions.

Theodore Debs to Thomas A. Hickey

December 13, 1918
Terre Haute, Indiana

Dear Tom: —

Thanks and congratulations! Your letter and announcement come like a sunburst. Gene is still filling speaking engagements in Ohio. Under his parole he can speak in the jurisdiction of the court but not outside of it. He addresses a mass meeting at Akron on Sunday. I need not say that he will be deeply interested in your new undertaking and that both of us will wish you and Covington Hall the largest measure of success.[1] You two warriors will make a great team. All you want is the second class mailing right and you will do the rest. Better than any others do you know what the dispossessed farmers and the impoverished proletariat of the South need at this time. Your paper will be launched at the very time it is needed for the biggest work yet undertaken by the workers.

We have often thought and spoken of you. Never for one moment did our faith in you falter. We always knew that though they might hound you relentlessly they could not break your spirit and that in due time you would be on the job again. And here you are! And here's a hand and a hearty good wish for your success.

Thank you warmly for your generous words to Gene. He will appreciate this expression of confidence from you more than any amount of gold.

With all greetings to yourself and family,

Yours in the same old way,
Theodore Debs

TLS, TxLT, Hickey Papers.

1. Covington Hall (1871-1952) was a Mississippi-born poet, a member of the IWW, and a leader in the Brotherhood of Timber Workers and the Socialist party in Louisiana. At the time, Hall and Hickey were planning to resurrect the *Rebel*, which had been suppressed during the war, as the *Voice of the People*, but the plan never materialized. James R. Green, *Grass Roots Socialism* (Baton Rouge, 1978), 382. In April 1915, Hall sent Debs an autographed copy of *Songs of Love and Rebellion*, a collection of his poetry. EVD Foundation, Debs Home.

EVD to Horace Traubel

December 19, 1918
Terre Haute, Indiana

My dear Horace:—
   Please find remittance enclosed for which extend my subscription to the Conservator to cover the year ending December 31st., 1919. My present subscription expires with the calendar year. I have just returned and am having to leave again. The present indications are that I will be in the penitentiary in the early part of January.[1] But wherever it may be it will be for the cause and there will be no lowering of the colors and no departure from principles or desertion of ideals. I earnestly hope your health is better and that you may soon be your perfect self again.

Yours fraternally,
E. V. Debs

TLS, DLC, Traubel Papers.

   1. Debs was imprisoned at Moundsville, West Virginia, on April 14, 1919.

EVD to William F. Gable

January 2, 1919
Terre Haute, Indiana

My dear Brother:—
   The sweet message from you to my wife and myself this morning comes to us like a greeting from the gods. You are a right royal soul and you never forget. With all our hearts we reciprocate your loving salutation and wish for you and Mrs. Gable and all of your beautiful household a New Year laden with blessings manifold.
   Need I say that we often, very often, think and speak of you and hold out our hands to you in benediction? How could we ever forget you? I am just leaving for Ohio. Pardon this very hasty note. There are several miles of writing I would love to inflict upon you.
   It would be the joy supreme to see you here and have you with us. Let us hope. The prospect of seeing you anywhere stirs the blood and makes the heart beat faster.
   I learn that our dear Horace is steadily improving. Thank all the gods at once. May his recovery come soon and be complete.

My wife, my brother and all of us, jointly and severally, send love and blessing to you all and I am always,

Yours without variation,
Eugene V. Debs

P.S. Since writing the foregoing the joint note from you and Horace with enclosure from Herman Kuehn[1] has been received. The two photographs referred to have not yet come but will doubtless follow by a later mail. As soon as these reach me I will with pleasure autograph them as requested and send them on to their destination. Kuehn is a fine fellow and so is Luke North and what you say in regard to the great fight they are making out on the coast to kill off the land sharks and transfer that part of the earth to the people who inhabit it has my unqualified approval. Upon receipt of the photos I will promptly advise you. Am writing Horace at Camden as I presume he is home again by this time. Once more best love to you both.

TLS, CtY.

1. Herman Kuehn (1853-1918) was the author of a number of books and pamphlets on economic and social issues. In 1905, Charles Kerr published Kuehn's *Shoes, Pigs and Problems,* a collection of essays on socialism in the United States, written under the pseudonym Evelyn Gladys. Other Kuehn essays were collected under the same pseudonym in *Thoughts of a Fool* (1905) and *The Problem of Worry* (1909). At the time of Kuehn's death, Debs wrote a tribute to him, "The Passing of a Man," which appeared in Luke North's *Everyman* in April 1918.

EVD to E. B. Ault[1]

January 15, 1919
Terre Haute, Indiana

E.B. AULT, SECRETARY MOONEY NATIONAL LABOR CONGRESS,[2]

A THOUSAND THANKS TO THE CONVENTION FOR ITS KIND INVITATION. NOTHING WOULD GIVE ME GREATER PLEASURE THAN TO APPEAL TO THE DELEGATES IN BEHALF OF MOONEY AND BILLINGS, BUT I AM IN THE CUSTODY OF FEDERAL COURT OFFICIALS AND NOT PERMITTED TO GO TO CHICAGO. FREE SPEECH PREVAILS IN RUSSIA, BUT IS DEAD IN THE UNITED STATES SINCE WORLD HAS BEEN MADE SAFE FOR DEMOCRACY. THIS MORNING I WIRED DELEGATE WAGENKNECHT[3] A FULL EXPRESSION OF MY VIEWS RESPECTING THE PURPOSE OF THE CONVENTION. THE CONSERVATIVE ELEMENT HAS THE UNQUALIFIED APPROVAL AND SUPPORT OF THE CAPITALIST PRESS, WHICH CAN ONLY MEAN THAT THE CONSERVATIVE ELEMENT IS TRUE TO THE CAPITALIST

CLASS AND FALSE TO THE WORKING CLASS. I AM WITH AND FOR THE
RADICALS. THE HOUR HAS STRUCK FOR ACTION. LONG-WINDED RES-
OLUTIONS AND HUMBLE PETITIONS TO CORPORATION TOOLS IN PUB-
LIC OFFICE AND CORRUPT POLITICIANS ARE WORSE THAN USELESS.
MOONEY IS INNOCENT AND THE WORLD KNOWS IT. THIS IS ENOUGH.
THE CONVENTION CAN DO NO LESS THAN DEMAND HIS UNCONDI-
TIONAL RELEASE AND ISSUE AN ULTIMATUM TO THAT EFFECT, GIVING
DUE NOTICE THAT IF THAT FAILS A GENERAL STRIKE WILL FOLLOW
AT A SPECIFIED TIME AND INDUSTRY PARALYZED THROUGHOUT THE
LAND. APPEAL HAS BEEN MADE TO THEIR CONSCIENCES IN VAIN, AND
NOW LET THE BATTERIES OF LABOR BE OPENED ON THEIR PROFITS.
THERE IS NO HALF-WAY GROUND. EVERY EXPEDIENT HAS BEEN TRIED
AND FAILED AND NOW THE WORKING CLASS MUST COURAGEOUSLY
PROCLAIM ITS PURPOSE AND ASSERT ITS POWER IF THE AMERICAN
LABOR MOVEMENT IS NOT TO STAND CONVICTED OF COWARDICE AND
TREASON BEFORE THE WORLD. THE CAPITALIST CLASS AND THEIR OF-
FICIAL HIRELINGS HAVE UTTERLY FORFEITED THEIR RIGHT TO COUN-
SEL OBEDIENCE TO THE LAW. THEY, THEMSELVES, HAVE TRAMPLED THE
LAW IN THE MIRE IN THEIR COLD-BLOODED DETERMINATION TO MUR-
DER LABOR LEADERS TOO RIGIDLY HONEST TO SELL OUT AND TOO
COURAGEOUS AND SELF-RESPECTING TO BE BROWBEATEN AND INTIM-
IDATED. LET THE ULTIMATUM BE THE UNCONDITIONAL RELEASE OF
OUR FELLOW WORKERS OR A GENERAL STRIKE. IF THE SILK HAT CON-
SPIRATORS AND WOULD-BE LYNCHERS OUT ON THE PACIFIC COAST AND
ELSEWHERE INSIST UPON WAR, LET IT COME. WE HAVE NOTHING TO
LOSE BUT THE GAGS UPON OUR LIPS AND THE CHAINS ON OUR BODIES.
NOW IS THE TIME TO PROVE THE SOLIDARITY OF OUR CLASS THE
PEOPLE ARE WITH US IN THIS FIGHT AND WILL STAND BY US FROM
COAST TO COAST IN OUR DETERMINATION TO REBUKE CAPITALIST
CRIMINALS AND MAINTAIN OUR RIGHTS AS AMERICAN CITIZENS.

(SGD) EUGENE V. DEBS

TLc, InTI, Debs Collection.

1. Erwin Bratton Ault (1883-1949) was born in Newport, Kentucky, and as a
young man moved to Seattle, where he joined the Socialist party and edited and wrote
for a number of socialist papers in the Northwest until 1912, when he became managing editor of the *Seattle Union Record*, a paper that he made into a leading supporter
of Tom Mooney and one that regularly reprinted Debs's articles and editorials.

2. Officially called the National Labor Congress on the Mooney Case. Delegates
from more than 1,000 union locals, without the blessing of Gompers, met in Chicago
January 14-17, 1919, to draw up a program intended to free Tom Mooney and Warren
Billings. Among other things, the congress called for a referendum among constituent
unions on a general strike in support of Mooney and Billings.

3. See Debs to Wagenknecht, January 16, 1919.

EVD to Alfred Wagenknecht

January 16, 1919
Terre Haute, Indiana

GREETINGS TO THE RADICALS, THE TRUE FRIENDS OF MOONEY AND THE REAL REPRESENTATIVES OF THE AMERICAN LABOR MOVEMENT. STAND BY YOUR PROGRAM. THE ORGANIZED WORKERS MUST NOW SHOW THAT THEY ARE MEN AND WOMEN TO BE RESPECTED AND NOT SYCOPHANTS AND SLAVES TO BE SPAT UPON WITH CONTEMPT.

THE CAPITALIST PRESS IS FULL OF PRAISE FOR THE CONSERVATIVE ELEMENT. THIS OF ITSELF IS PROOF OF THE COWARDICE OR TREASON OF THAT ELEMENT.

DOWN WITH THE COWARDS AND TRAITORS WHO IN THE NAME OF UNION LABOR WOULD CRUCIFY MOONEY AND BETRAY THE LABOR MOVEMENT! THEY WEAR UNION BADGES BUT THEY ARE EVEN LOWER AND VILER THAN THE PLUTOCRATIC PIRATES AND THEIR SERVILE TOOLS WHO FRAMED UP MOONEY AND HIS ASSOCIATES.

MOONEY'S WORST ENEMIES ARE THE TREACHEROUS UNION MEN WHO HAVE THEIR THIRTY PIECES FOR THEIR PERFIDY AND WOULD {NOW} MAKE A FARCE AND FAILURE OF THIS CONFERENCE.

MOONEY AND BILLINGS ARE INNOCENT AND WE KNOW IT. THE WHOLE WORLD KNOWS IT. THAT IS ENOUGH. LET THE CONFERENCE ISSUE ITS ULTIMATUM. WASTE NO TIME ON CAPITALIST COURTS, LEGISLATURES, OR POLITICIANS. GIVE THE CAPITALIST CONSPIRATORS SO MANY DAYS. UNCONDITIONAL RELEASE OR GENERAL STRIKE.[1] NO COMPROMISE. UPON THAT ISSUE WE CAN FACE THE WORLD. IF THE CAPITALISTS MUST HAVE WAR LET IT COME. THE PEOPLE ARE WITH US. WE HAVE ALL TO GAIN AND NOTHING TO LOSE BUT OUR CHAINS.

DO NOT CRAWL AND BEG BUT STAND ERECT AND COMMAND. THE HONEST WORKERS OF THE NATION WILL BACK YOU UP TO THE FINISH. ALL THEY ASK IS BOLD AND FEARLESS LEADERSHIP. NOW IS THE TIME FOR LABOR TO REBUKE CAPITALIST CRIME AND STRIKE A HISTORIC BLOW FOR INDUSTRIAL FREEDOM AND SOCIAL JUSTICE IN THE UNITED STATES.

EUGENE V. DEBS

Telegram (transcript), NN Kars.

1. The public's fear of a "Mooney General Strike," which was widely believed to be planned for July 4, 1919, but never materialized, was successfully exploited by Wilson's attorney general, A. Mitchell Palmer, in launching the Red Scare of 1919-20.

Phil Wagner to EVD

January 17, 1919
St. Louis, Missouri

My dear Gene

Yours of the 15th at hand, sorry that I did not give you the information you asked for in your previous letter, the binder's name is Kampmeyer & Wagner—4th & Locust St.

As I wrote you last fall the plates of your "Life & Writings"[1] have been unfortunately destroyed, but the binder has quite a few on hand, which I agreed to give to you for the asking.

We never had plates made of "Labor and Freedom"[2] but there are quite a lot of them on hand, also some of the pamphlets, you can have everything I have on hand, if you will pay the binder for what work he has done on the books, such as folding, storing etc.

I read with considerable interest your telegram to the Labor Congress at Chicago and I want to say amen.

as ever
Phil

ALS, InTI, Debs Collection.

1. In 1916, Wagner and the *Rip-Saw* reprinted "from the original plates and with all the original illustrations" *Debs: His Life, Writings and Speeches*, which was first published during the Red Special campaign of 1908. *Rip-Saw*, April 1916.

2. *Labor and Freedom*, also published by Wagner in 1916, was a collection (176 pages) of Debs's "miscellaneous writings as well as four complete orations."

Raymond Wilcox[1] to EVD

January 23, 1919
New York City

Dear Comrade Debs:

A dream of several years is about to become a reality. For almost eleven years The New York Call has issued every day from the press of a private printer. Every year thousands of dollars have been paid him in profit and thousands more have been wasted through capitalist inefficiency. Each year, too, the Socialist movement in this great city has paid out hundreds of thousands of dollars for printed matter, paying the printer lords thousands of dollars in private profits.

But this is all to end; a great Party printing plant is to be established which will turn back into service and education these thousands of hard earned dollars of the workers.

Two years ago the Socialists of New York raised money to buy the great Peoples House, the home and heart of a greater movement, a regular bee-hive of Socialist and labor activity.[2]

A new company, The New York Call Printing Co., Inc., has just been chartered to install and operate a complete and up-to-date printing plant to print The Call and the books and pamphlets with which the workers of the new world's greatest city will be won to Socialism. We must raise $100,000. to complete this great undertaking. We want everyone whose heart beats for Socialism to be represented as a stock holder.

We want you, dear Comrade Debs, the most loved among those who are giving their best for our great cause, to be the first to call upon the workers of New York and the entire country to raise this money.[3] It must be done within sixty days; we can do it with your wonderful help. We need a good letter from you to blaze the trail.

With personal greetings and all good wishes,

Sincerely yours,
Raymond Wilcox
Business Manager.

TLS, InTI, Debs Collection.

1. As business manager of the *New York Call*, Raymond Wilcox launched a campaign in February 1919 to raise $90,000 for the purchase of a printing plant for the paper, labor unions, and "other working class organizations" (*New York Call*, February 17, 1919). Debs, Algernon Lee, and others solicited funds for the project (*Call*, February 18, 1919), and on May 29, 1919, the paper announced its "day of victory," on which it moved into "a five-story building at 112 Fourth Avenue . . . owned by The New York Call Printing Company."

2. In 1917 the Rand School purchased from the Young Women's Christian Association a building at 7 East Fifteenth Street and renamed the building People's House, which thereafter housed the school, a socialist bookstore, a theatre, auditorium, library, gymnasium, and the party's state, local, and county offices.

3. In "Chains" (*New York Call*, February 14, 1919), Debs warned readers that "the capitalist press" was "determined to destroy the Call" and urged them "to furnish the money to shelter the Call . . . so that we can have at least one English daily in the American metropolis we can call our own."

[Roger N. Baldwin] to EVD

February 5, 1919
New York City

My dear Mr. Debbs,

On or about Lincoln's Birthday, there will be mass meetings to demand the release of political prisoners in nine or ten cities across the country. Won't you send to our New York office[1] a message which can be read as coming from you at all these meetings?[2]

Cordially yours,
[Roger N. Baldwin]

TLc, NjP, Mudd Library, ACLU Archives.

1. National Civil Liberties Bureau, predecessor of the American Civil Liberties Union.
2. Debs's response, if any, to this letter has not been found, but he is not mentioned in the *New York Times* coverage (February 17, 1919) of the New York City Civil Liberties Bureau meeting, which was held on February 16, 1919, and heard speeches by John Haynes Holmes, Owen Lovejoy, and Dudley Field Malone, all of whom demanded the release of political prisoners and the repeal of the wartime Espionage Act.

EVD to Frank X. Holl

February 6, 1919
Terre Haute, Indiana

My dear Frank:—

On my return from Ohio I learned through Theodore for the first time of the death of your dearly beloved daughter Frances[1] and was inexpressibly pained and shocked by the news. It seems utterly unbelievable that this beautiful child has been taken from you and yet the report in the newspaper sent by you places the solemn fact beyond all doubt. To you and Mrs. Holl my heart goes out in loving sympathy and in this Mrs. Debs and Theodore and his family all join sincerely.

I have known from your previous correspondence that Frances was ill but had hoped and believed she was improving and would soon recover her health. But alas! We can never say what may happen in this uncertain world. We only know that our loved ones are taken from us when least expected and that sometimes the young with all their years before them are summoned to the unknown land before their lives on earth have fairly begun.

As I knew Frances from her babyhood, her sweet disposition, her gentle manner, her tender heart, I feel pained beyond expression to think of her bright and promising young life being ended when she had just begun to realize herself and fulfill the hopes and dreams of her loved and loving parents. But after all, it may be better so. Who can tell? There is so very much in life to pain and shock a tender soul and to cause grief and anguish that there may be some comfort in knowing that dear Frances has been spared these bitter and harrowing trials and experiences.

May you bear your bereavement with strength and fortitude and may you find comfort in the blessed memory of the dear daughter who has gone before. We all send you our love and sympathy and I am as always in the past,

Yours faithfully,
Eugene V. Debs

TLS, TxU, Holl MSS.

  1. Frances Love Holl (1901-19).

Adolph F. Germer to EVD

February 7, 1919
Chicago, Illinois

Dear Gene: —

I received your letter of the 4th inst. regarding the French Federation.[1] Comrade DesChamps[2] and I have exchanged several letters on the subject. In the last one he assured me that the re-affiliation with the party would only be a matter of time. I shall keep after them for I am more than anxious to get the French comrades back into the Party.

Good luck old man, I am glad you are having those whales of meetings.

I am enclosing some figures on Party membership. If we are dead, we are a pretty darn alive corpse.

As ever

Yours,
Adolph Germer

[enclosure]
NATIONAL OFFICE SOCIALIST PARTY

To the National Executive Committee   Chicago, February 5, 1919
Dear Comrades:—

This year started out in splendid style in point of membership. The dues stamp sales were 108,106, the exempts 1,480, making a total of 109,586. This is the highest since April 1914, when 110,782 stamps were sold. The following are the figures for the last two months of 1917 and the first month of 1918 and the last two months of 1918 and the first month of 1919:

November 1917—86,570	November 1918— 56,644
December 1917—73,341	December 1918— 84,495
January 1918—86,650	January 1919—109,586

TLS, InTI, Debs Collection.

1. The Confédération Générale du Travail, France's major labor body, which officially supported the government during World War I. Its large socialist membership was bitterly divided over the confederation's war policy and the Socialist party itself declined in membership from 92,000 in July 1914 to 17,000 in December 1915 and then began a slow recovery to 36,000 in December 1918, followed by a dramatic increase to 102,000 by August 1919. *American Labor Year Book 1920*, 344.

2. Florent Deschamps, editor of *Le Socialiste*, which was published by the French Language Federation in Johnson City, Illinois. Deschamps was the author of "L'Organisation et Le Cas de Debs" (*Le Socialiste*, March 1919), which argued that Debs's conviction and imprisonment would fuel a rapid growth of the Socialist party in the United States and abroad.

Raymond Wilcox to EVD

February 10, 1918
New York City

EUGENE V. DEBS

LETTER RECD   SITUATION GETTING MORE SERIOUS   TENDANCY TO BRING PRESSURE TO BEAR UPON PRINTERS BY THESE OPPOSED TO RADICAL PUBLICATIONS   WE ARE ASKING ALL PROMINENT SOCIALISTS FOR AN ARTICLE ON THE POWER OF THE PRESS AND NECESSITY FOR MAIN-

TAINING IT AT ALL COSTS AND MUST HAVE YOURS[1] AMONG THE
FIRST   WE ARE HOLDING UP PLANS AWAITING YOUR MESSAGE   PLEASE
WIRE COLLECT

RAYMOND WILCOX
NEW YORK CALL

Telegram, InTI, Debs Collection.

1. Debs's editorial "The Power of the Press" first appeared in the *Rip-Saw* in
November 1916. "An Ideal Labor Press" appeared in the *Call* on April 16, 1919.
As noted, Debs's "Chains" (*Call*, February 14, 1919) also dealt with the need for a
socialist press.

Theodore Debs to David Karsner

February 12, 1919
Terre Haute, Indiana

Dear David: —
   Your telegram to Gene last night did not get into his hands until
today. He at once dictated a statement in compliance with your request
and this statement I have filed with the Western Union as a night
rate message. It is rather long and I sent it night rate to make it a
little more economical for you assuming that it would reach you in
time tomorrow morning to serve your purpose. Nothing could be
more infamous than the policy of deportation[1] which the plutes have
now inaugurated. We must fight it tooth and nail.
   Kindly send me two or three copies of the issue containing Gene's
statement.[2]
   Always glad to think of you. Best love to you now and always.

Theodore Debs

TLS, NN Kars.

   1. One of the phenomena of the Red Scare was the public and congressional
demand for, and the federal government's implementation of, a program for the
deportation of radicals, Bolsheviks, aliens, etc. The most dramatic episode growing
out of the fear was the deportation in December 1919 of 249 men and women from
New York on the *Buford*, an army transport called the "Soviet Ark." Perhaps the best
known of those deported on the *Buford* were Emma Goldman and Alexander Berkman,
longtime leaders of America's anarchist movement.
   2. In his telegram (*Call*, February 13, 1919), Debs described the deportation policy
as "the crime of crimes and the infamy of infamies," which he blamed on "Chief
Gompers, the scabbing and strikebreaking craft unions, . . . and the Wall Street power"
who were eager to get rid of those "charged with being anarchists, Bolsheviks, and
IWW."

EVD to Theodore Debs

February 17, 1919
Akron, Ohio

My dearest old Pard:

A perfectly wonderful outpouring at Lorain yesterday—never addressed a more marvelously responsive & sympathetic audience & that's where they made their threats, raided socialist headquarters etc etc but a week ago.

Marguerite's sister & brother[1] brought me here, got me a fine supper & then put me to bed with hot water bottle at my feet. Marguerite is at Toledo where she spoke last night. To-night I'm at Cleveland & to-morrow I'm to meet with Committee to arrange to cover the whole month of March. They're all wild with enthusiasm over our meetings. I'm going to stop a day at Galien to see the Bishop[2]—have word from him—he wants to see me very much & I'm sure I can put Hollingsworth[3] in this field through the Bishop. Feel finer than a young colt. Shall probably be home Thursday—may be not till Friday.

Love & Kisses to you all
Gene

ALS, InTI, Debs Collection.

1. May and John Deibel, Marguerite Prevey's sister and brother.

2. William Montgomery Brown (1855-1937) was an Episcopal bishop who was deposed in 1925 following a widely publicized heresy trial, about which Brown wrote a book, *My Heresy* (1926). One of Brown's heresies was his support of communism, which was reflected in such books as *Communism and Christianism* (1920) and *Teachings of Marx for Girls and Boys* (1935). In a letter to Theodore Debs (November 11, 1919), Brown offered "on behalf of Mrs. Brown and myself" to send "a check for $50.00 per month for a year a least" so that Theodore could "continue to do the work which is required of you by the socialist public." InTI, Debs Collection.

3. Probably James L. Hollingsworth, Debs's Terre Haute friend, Methodist minister (whose economic and political views offended several midwestern congregations during his long career), and editor of *What Debs' Neighbors Say About Him*, the pamphlet used in Debs's 1912 presidential and 1916 congressional campaigns.

EVD to Jean Keller[1]

February 17, 1919
Akron, Ohio

Dear Jean,

Through the kindness of our dear Mrs. Curry I was permitted to see your wonderful story[2] in the Minnesota Daily of Dec. 17th. Mrs. Curry, an eminently fine critic, exclaimed with enthusiasm, "It's literature!" And so it is, real literature, rarer than ever these Days when all the arts are vanished for fresh sources of material profit.

I read the story, coming from a child of your years, with astonishment and delight. Young as you are you have already visualized the things that have filled history with tragedy—the things that will one day break all fetters and burst with the glories of a new free day for all the race.

Your story might well have been a chapter in Dickens' "Tale of Two Cities." He wrote nothing finer, more touching, or gripping and appealing. Please let me tender my hearty congratulations!

The future, all aglow with promise, holds out to you, dear child, its outstretched hands. How very proud your parents must be of you! Your beautiful mother's eyes will fill and overflow often in the sweet, mystic process of your fulfillment.

My love to you and to all of your dear household, now and always!

Faithfully,
E. V. Debs

ALS, InTI, Debs Collection.

1. Jean Keller (Bouvier) was the daughter of Grace Keller, who had lived in Terre Haute at the turn of the century and was a close friend of Mabel Dunlap Curry.

2. Keller's story, "A Flicker of the Candle," appeared in the *Minnesota Daily*, a University of Minnesota campus paper, on December 17, 1918.

Raymond Wilcox to EVD

February 20, 1919
New York City

Dear Comrade Debs:

Thank you for your good message contained in your recent telegram, and also for your good letter of February 11th which I have not answered before for the reason that I have been detained in court much of the time.

A good, frank, straight from the shoulder letter like yours is a great help to us here in the office. Although I cannot help but feel that your opinion would be somewhat different if you were located in New York, yet I know there is a great deal of truth in what you say in regard to the policy of The Call, and although I am in no way responsible for the editorial or news policy of The Call, I have to stand my share of criticism.

I have shown your letter to Comrade Ervin,[1] and no doubt he will write to you, too.

It seems necessary that we should have our periods of criticism and marked differences of opinion such as the one that we are passing through at the present time. We generally come out of them much the better for the experience. We here in The Call are striving to produce the kind of paper that the Party want to have, and make it of the greatest possible service to the Party.

Again thanking you for you kind letter and your good message which has helped materially in our campaign, I am, with warmest personal regards to a good comrade who has given so much to the Movement,

Fraternally yours,
Raymond Wilcox
Business Manager.

TLS, InTI, Debs Collection.

1. Charles W. Ervin, editor of the *Call*.

EVD to Morris Hillquit

February 26, 1919
Terre Haute, Indiana

My dear Morris:

This will reach you through the hands of L.P. Benedict, of Montana, a particularly warm friend of mine, who desires to consult with you regarding some matters having a legal aspect which he will explain to you. Mr. Benedict and I were associated together officially and personally during the A.R.U. strike. He had charge of my correspondence, both official and private, and in our intimate relationship I came to love him as a younger brother. He is pure gold. You can trust him absolutely and any service you can render him, or any favor you can show him, will be appreciated as fully and remembered as gratefully as if conferred upon

Yours faithfully,
(Signed) EUGENE V. DEBS

TL, WHi, Hillquit Papers.

EVD to Julius Gerber

February 27, 1919
Terre Haute, Indiana

My dear Comrade Gerber:—

I have been in Ohio and your letter came in my absence. I am soon having to return there and have but little time here for the many letters that demand attention. I have committed myself not at all in the direction of your inquiry. I have not even read the manifesto.[1] I have been taxed to my capacity these past days and beyond it and there have been many things that have come in here to which I have been unable to give personal attention.

I am in sympathy with the radical tendencies in our party.[2] There needs to be a change in many things, especially in our attitude toward the Gompers scabbing and strike-breaking unions. Thousands of our members are disgusted by this. We have got to take a clean cut stand in favor of revolutionary industrial unionism. We have got to get completely away from Scheidemannism[3] and what it stands for and plant ourselves squarely on uncompromising ground both economically and politically.

I thank you for thinking I have a "good heart" but you need have no fear that that that [sic] heart is going to mislead me as to the essential facts of the situation. I have plenty of sentiment but I do not allow sentimentality to befog my vision or weaken my resolute determination to take my stand where duty demands that I take it regardless of consequences {to} myself.

But the changes that are necessary can all be made and should be made within the party. I am opposed to splitting the party and I refuse to get into any squabble the New York comrades may have between themselves. I have no time for that sort of business.

If I may venture a bit of advice, a thing I rarely indulge in, it is that the leaders of these opposing tendencies in the party in and about New York get together and talk matters over in the true socialistic spirit[4] and endeavor to make a program to which all can subscribe and in accordance with which all can work along their own lines. There ought not at this time be dissension and factional quarrelling. The situation in New York just now is serious enough and if the comrades can do nothing

TL (transcript, first page only), NNU Tam, Debs Collection.

1. On February 8, 1919, *Revolutionary Age*, edited by Louis Fraina, published the "Manifesto and Program of the Left Wing," which was adopted a week later by the "Left Wing Section of the Socialist Party in New York," which quickly became a party within the Socialist Party of America, with its own officers, press, and program. The manifesto denounced the leadership of the Socialist party for its failure to transform World War I into a proletarian revolution and to create a government of "Federated Soviets" on the Russian model. The manifesto documented the growing split between the old leadership of the party and the new radicals, which by the late summer of 1919 led to the formation of the Communist party and the Communist Labor party.

2. *Class Struggle*, which, beginning in February 1919, listed Debs as an editor, along with Louis Fraina and Ludwig Lore, published the "Manifesto and Program" in its May 1919 issue.

3. Philipp Scheidemann (1865-1939) was a leader of the German "war socialists" during World War I and in February 1919 was elected first chancellor of the Weimar Republic, a post he held only until June 1919, when he resigned. His ardent support of the war was for Debs symbolic of the failure of socialist internationalism.

4. After the publication of the manifesto in February 1919, "meetings of Socialist locals [in New York] became little more than squabbles between the Left Wing and the regulars." David A. Shannon, *The Socialist Party of America* (Quadrangle Books, 1967), 132.

EVD to John Haynes Holmes[1]

February 28, 1919
Terre Haute, Indiana

My dear Mr. Holmes: —
The very kind and beautiful letter from you has come into my hands since my return from Ohio and I beg you to believe that it has touched me deeply and that words are inadequate to express my appreciation and gratitude.

I feel myself indebted to our dear friend Mayer[2] for many favors, not the least of which is his generous commendation to his friends among whom I know you to hold first place. During our sittings at Akron he spoke often of you and always with love and reverence so characteristic of the man. He is one of the really fine souls who grows upon one with contact and becomes nearer and dearer with association.

During my visits to New York during the last few years I heard of you very often through mutual friends and admirers. I also read and was greatly interested in some of your eloquent and appealing addresses and have hoped that it might some time be my pleasure to take you by the hand. I was particularly impressed by your courageous and altogether noble attitude at the beginning of the war, an attitude of moral loftiness and genuine patriotism which you have maintained with unfaltering rectitude and devotion ever since.

Thanking again and again for your very kind and appreciative and inspiring letter and with all good wishes to you I am,

Yours faithfully,
Eugene V. Debs

TLS, DLC, Holmes Papers.

1. John Haynes Holmes (1879-1964) graduated from Harvard in 1902 and was ordained a Unitarian minister in 1904. From 1907 to 1949 he was pastor of the Church of the Messiah (Community Church of New York) in New York City and a leader of countless reform organizations and movements, including the National Association for the Advancement of Colored People and the American Civil Liberties Union. Holmes was an outspoken critic of World War I and of the government's wartime legislation and policies, particularly the hysteria created during the Red Scare of 1919-20. In his Community Church sermons, which were published annually, and as editor of *Unity* from 1921 to 1946, Holmes was a voice of liberalism from the Red Scare to the Cold War.

2. Louis Mayer (1870-1969) was a sculptor who did a bust of Debs in Akron, Ohio, in the fall of 1918 following Debs's trial in Cleveland. He recounted the experience in "A Real *Brüderschaft* Drink with Debs" (*Papers of Eugene V. Debs*, microfilm edition) and recalled their frequent visits to a nearby "bar room" for drinks during the several days Debs sat for the bust.

Jim Larkin, Rose Pastor Stokes, John Reed, and Maximilian Cohen[1] to EVD

February 28, 1919
New York City

Dear Comrade Debs,

The revised Manifesto and Program of the Left Wing Section, Local Greater New York has been forwarded to you under separate cover for your perusal and we hope, acceptance. It is already for publication in pamphlet form. We urgently desire a foreword from you as an introduction to be published along with the Manifesto.[2] Will you therefore let your statement range from 100 to 200 words suitable for the purpose.

You are no doubt aware of the progress of the Left Wing all over the country. We in New York find it ever so much harder to reach the rank and file because of party conditions peculiar to our city. Our opponents attempt to discredit us by claiming that we are disrupters and secessionists and even worse. So you can see what an uphill battle we have on our hands.

Awaiting an early reply, we are,

Your Comrades,
Jim Larkin
Rose Pastor Stokes
John Reed
Dr. Maximilian Cohen,
Secretary.
100 Sixth Ave., N.Y.C.

P.S. Manifesto has been officially adopted and endorsed by: Local Boston; Local Philadelphia; Local Essex County, N.J.; and Jos. Coldwell,[3] State Secretary, Rhode Island.

TLS, InTI, Debs Collection.

1. Maximillian Cohen was a Brooklyn dentist who served on the New York Left Wing committee that drew up the manifesto and program. In September 1919, Cohen was a leader at the Chicago meeting that launched the Communist Party.

2. The manifesto was widely reprinted (in *Class Struggle*, May 1919; *Truth*, April 23, 1919; and elsewhere), but without an introduction by Debs.

3. Joseph Maurice Coldwell (1870-1949) was a pioneer socialist and labor organizer in New England and the Socialist party candidate for a number of local, state, and national offices in Massachusetts and Rhode Island over a period of forty years. His opposition to World War I led to his imprisonment in 1919 in the Atlanta Federal Penitentiary, where Debs was a fellow prisoner. Both were released at Christmas 1921.

Ludwig Lore to EVD

March 3, 1919
New York City

My dear Comrade Debs:

It is rather late for your co-editor[1] to come to you now with plans for the next issue that is to appear at the end of March. But since we are agreed that you must be bothered as little as possible and since our general policy has been determined by the contents of our first two volumes,[2] it seems hardly necessary to trouble you with incidentals and details.

But can we count on you for an article on some American topic for this number?[3] I suggest an American subject, because I sometimes fear that The Class Struggle is rather in danger of treating too exclusively with the revolutions of Russia and Germany, without sufficient application to conditions at home.

Your first article[4] met with such wholehearted appreciation everywhere, that we have decided, at the suggestion of a number of comrades, to print a first edition of 200,000 copies of it in leaflet form.

There is one other matter that I should like to discuss with you. You know, of course, that "Left Wing" organizations are springing up everywhere in the Party. Although I am in full agreement, as you know, with the fundamental principles that prompt these organizations, I personally feel that, at this time they constitute a grave danger, not only to the Party, but to the very cause for which they are being created. So far as I have been able to discover, the membership of our Party is radically inclined and will support a revolutionary position. But the propagation by organizations such as these within the Party must inevitably, I feel, bring about a split in the movement. A split that will, moreover, not strengthen, but weaken revolutionary socialism in America by driving the rank and file into the arms of right wing leaders as a protest against the methods of the more radical minority.

Our co-editor, Louis C. Fraina, has become one of the leading spirits of the new movement. The Socialist Publication Society will hold a meeting in a few days to decide its position and to determine whether The Class Struggle shall take a definite editorial stand on this question.[5] A brief statement of your attitude would, I am sure, be more than welcome.

Hoping you well, I remain with cordial and fraternal greetings to Comrade Theodore Debs, to Mrs. Debs and to yourself,

your devoted and admiring comrade
Ludwig Lore

TLS, InTI, Debs Collection.

1. As noted, Debs was listed as an editor of Class Struggle, beginning with its February 1919 issue.

2. The first issue of Class Struggle was dated May-June 1917.

3. Debs did not send an article for "this number" (May 1919), but in a Lore editorial, "Eugene V. Debs, a Revolutionist," he was described as "foremost among . . . the best the international socialist movement has produced" and his impending imprisonment was cited as proof that Debs was "made of sterner stuff."

4. "The Day of the People," Class Struggle, February 1919.

5. As noted, in its May 1919 issue, Class Struggle printed the "Manifesto and Program of the 'Left Wing' Section Socialist Party, Local Greater New York." In an

editorial in the same issue, Louis Fraina concluded his discussion (and praise) of the Left Wing with the call, "On with the war against moderate Socialism in our party! Turn to the 'left'!"

Louis C. Fraina[1] and Charles E. Ruthenberg to EVD

March 6, 1919
Cleveland, Ohio

EUGENE V DEBS

HAVE YOU ACCEPTED NOMINATION INTERNATIONAL SECRETARY   IF NOT WE URGE YOU TO   STRONG SENTIMENT EVERYWHERE THAT YOU SHOULD BE OUR INTERNATIONAL SECRETARY   THE PARTYS FUTURE DEMANDS IT AND YOU CAN ALSO SERVE THE RADICALS

C E RUTHENBERG

LOUIS C FRAINA

Telegram, InTI, Debs Collection.

1. Louis Fraina as secretary of the Left Wing socialists in Boston, Charles Ruthenberg as secretary in Cleveland, and Maximilian Cohen as secretary in New York sought Debs's election as the party's international secretary in "Referendum A, 1919," in which three national executive committee members, four international delegates, and the international secretary were chosen. *Eye-Opener,* January 1919.

H. Wagenknecht to EVD

March 6, 1919
Brecksville, Ohio

Dear Comrade Debs: —

The Lima meeting is not to be held on the 9th, so the routing is off for a while. Cleveland has decided definitely on a meeting for the 12th and we are trying to get more right after that, but nothing is certain as yet.

Be sure to make Cleveland on the 12th tho.[1]

I will let you know in a couple of days what you can expect. Halls are the problem the locals have to face, rather the absence of those halls.

Please pardon this hastily written note. Will let Marguerite know that Cleveland is your first date.

Yours,
H. Wagenknecht
State Secy.

TLS, InTI, Debs Collection.

1. Debs's speech in Cleveland was his first speech following the Supreme Court's decision, announced on March 10, 1919, upholding his conviction and ten-year sentence. Writing for the majority, Justice Holmes found that "the verdict . . . for obstructing and attempting to obstruct the recruiting service of the United States must be sustained." In the Cleveland speech, which was printed as a leaflet and widely distributed, Debs said that "in my dreams, I did not think of going to the penitentiary [but] I had a thousand times rather go there and spend my remaining days there than betray this great cause." National Archives, Records of the War Department Military Intelligence Division, Record Group 165, File 10110-559.

Helen Keller to EVD

March 11, 1919
Forest Hills, New York

Dear Comrade,—
Of course the Supreme Court has sustained the decision of the lower court in your case. To my mind, the decision has added another laurel to your wreath of victories. Once more you are going to prison for upholding the liberties of the people.

I write because my heart cries out, it will not be still. I write because I want you to know that I should be proud if the Supreme Court convicted me of abhorring war, and doing all in my power to oppose it. When I think of the millions who have suffered in all the wicked wars of the past, I am shaken with the anguish of a great impatience. I want to fling myself against all brute powers that destroy the life, and break the spirit of man.

In the persecution of our comrades there is one satisfaction. Every trial of men like you, every sentence against them tears away the veil that hides the face of the enemy. The discussion and agitation that follow the trials define more sharply the positions that must be taken before all men can live together in peace, happiness and security.

We were driven into the war for liberty, democracy and humanity. Behold what is happening all over the world today! Oh where is the swift vengeance of Jehovah that it does not fall upon the hosts of those who are marshalling machine-guns against hungry-stricken peoples? It is the complacency of madness to call such acts "preserving law and order." What oceans of blood and tears are shed in their name! I have come to loathe traditions and institutions that take away the rights of the poor and protect the wicked against judgment.

The wise fools who sit in the high places of justice fail to see that in revolutionary times like the present vital issues are settled, not by statutes, decrees and authorities, but in spite of them. Like the Girondines of France they imagine that force can check the onrush of revolution. Thus they sow the wind, and unto them shall be the harvest of the whirlwind.

You dear comrade! I have long loved you because you are an apostle of brotherhood and freedom. For years I have thought of you as a dauntless explorer going toward the dawn, and, like a humble adventurer, I have followed in the trail of your footsteps. From time to time the greetings that have come back to me from you have made me very happy, and now I reach out my hand and clasp yours through prison bars.

With heartfelt greetings and with a firm faith that the cause for which you are now martyred shall be all the stronger because of your sacrifice and devotion, I am,

Yours for the Revolution, — May it come swiftly, like a shaft sundering the dark.

Helen Keller

> Stand up! ye wretched ones who labor.
> Stand up! ye galley-slaves of want.
> Man's reason thunders from its crater
> 'Tis the eruption none can daunt
> Of the past let us cleanse the tables
> Mass enslaved, fling back the call;
> Old earth is changing her foundations
> We have been nothing, now be all
> 'Tis the last cause to battle!
> Close the ranks, each in place,
> The staunch old International
> Shall be the Human race.

ALS, InH, Helen Keller Collection.

Adolph F. Germer to EVD

March 19, 1919
Chicago, Illinois

My dear Gene:—

I am herewith enclosing a copy of a letter that has just been mailed to the *Appeal to Reason*.[1] This outfit betrayed us once and we will not give them an opportunity to do it again. They are totally without conscience and will take advantage of everything to enrich their coffers. I think a statement similar to this ought to come from everyone whose case they use to exploit unsuspecting Socialists and sympathizers.

The United States Supreme Court did what I expected it would do in your case, but I feel confident that you will never serve your ten years or any great portion of it. Enough hell will break loose in the next year or so to tear the prison bars open and liberate those who have fallen victims of the war insanity. The only regret I have is that you are not to join us in Leavenworth. I have time and again more than enjoyed your company while at large, and I know I would equally enjoy it in the bastile.[2]

With every good wish, I am always

Faithfully yours,
Adolph Germer
Executive Secretary.

TLS (with one-page letter from Germer to *Appeal*), InTI, Debs Collection.

1. In his letter to the *Appeal*, dated March 19, 1919, Germer recalled the *Appeal*'s support of the war and its attacks on antiwar socialists and said he scorned the *Appeal*'s call for a $30,000 legal fund to be used in defense of Germer, Berger, Tucker, Engdahl, and Kruse, who, as noted, had been sentenced to twenty years' imprisonment in January 1919.
2. Freed on bail, the "Chicago Socialists" appealed their conviction and in 1921 the Supreme Court overturned the Landis sentence.

Alfred Wagenknecht to EVD

March 19, 1919
Chicago, Illinois

Dear Comrade Debs;—

We intend to launch an organization campaign together with our call for 5,000 meetings on May 1st. We want to print enough application blanks to supply all places holding meetings.

Toward this end we feel that we MUST get out something new and a bit different in an application blank.

We decided that an invitation issued by you to all who attend the May 1st meetings would be just the thing.

We have worded an invitation, and we enclose you a copy.[1] May we use your name in its circulation as it appears in the enclosed copy.

If you can write a STRONGER letter than that which we have attempted to write for you, then PLEASE DO SO.[2] We want a letter that will go right to the HEARTS of all who attend these May 1st meetings.

Wire your O.K. if the enclosed is O.K. If it is not O.K. then wire night letter of whatever change you desire to make. All at our expense—for the printer is waiting for the copy and we dare not delay if these meetings are to be made successful.

Yours in Comradeship,
A. Wagenknecht
Director.[3]

TLS (with one-page appeal letter), InTI, Debs Collection.

1. A revised copy of Debs's "personal invitation to you to join the Socialist Party—and after you have joined—STICK" appeared in the *Socialist Party Official Bulletin*, March 24, 1919.

2. Debs's membership letter, perhaps reflecting his concern over the growing left-right split in the party, seemed to stress unity: "Let us unite as we have never united before. Let us build in unison the Socialist Party."

3. Wagenknecht had become director of the party's department of organization and propaganda.

Theodore Debs to Helen Keller

March 21, 1919
Terre Haute, Indiana

Dear Comrade Helen Keller:—

Allow me in behalf of Gene to thank you with all my heart for your beautiful and inspiring letter just received. Gene is in Ohio where he is still permitted to speak under his parole and where he will fill engagements until the mandate is issued by the court which takes him to prison.

I will see that my brother receives your letter and I need not say that it will touch him to the heart and that he will feel as I do that to have served sufficiently to receive such a testimonial from such a source is certainly worth going to prison for. I know {with} what a sincere regard and admiration and with what loving tenderness my brother regards you and I am sure that he will treasure this fine characteristic message from you as one of the most precious he has ever received. Going to prison is not the least punishment to him so long as the cause is served. You understand this, I am sure, for if it had fallen to your lot you would have gone in the same spirit.

Please pardon this brief and inadequate acknowledgment of your fine letter. Gene will write you if he has the chance. He may be called upon to go to prison any day now and I do not know what liberties, if any, will be allowed him once he is behind the walls.

The revolution, as you say, is upon us and with you I also say, let it come, the speedier the better.

Yours for the better day,
Theodore Debs

TLS, American Foundation for the Blind, Keller Collection.

EVD to Theodore Debs

March 23, 1919
Akron, Ohio

My dear old Pard:

Canton has cancelled—just recd. the word—the "authorities" wouldn't allowed. Had Marguerite & I only known it in time we would have gone there anyway & held the meeting in the streets & defied them—as we did at Lima. I shall go to Canton later & speak there— but not on this trip. Just recd. telephone message from Cleveland that they would probably make up for Canton & they will probably arrange a meeting for Friday evening. They are having a monster mass Debs protest demonstration on the public square today. Ten thousand reds at least will be there & there'll be no interference.

The meeting at Girard last night was a record-breaker—greatest *ever* held there. The house was jammed & hundreds unable to get in & the enthusiasm was frenzied almost beyond imagination.

Send the mail here *Care Marguerite* to & including *Thursday morning*. Weather fine. Feeling like a young wild cat. Marguerite & Mae & John & Emma all send love

Your old pard
Gene

ALS, InTI, Debs Collection.

Theodore Debs to David Karsner

March 25, 1919
Terre Haute, Indiana

Dear Comrade David: —

Copies of your beautiful editorial,[1] the Lovejoy letter[2] and the news story[3] of the decision have all been received. Your well of kindness, often as we draw upon it, seems inexhaustible; and how much it is appreciated cannot be told in mere words. Gene wished these copies for a special purpose and as he is now in Ohio I will hold them until his return. I assume he will return, even if the mandate is received, as they will probably allow him sufficient time to come home to close up his affairs.

I am glad the little tribute to Jud Oneal pleased Jim.[4] Jud deserved it and much more. His whole life was a tragedy and I often marvelled at his fine courage and infinite patience. He was a fine soul, pure gold, crucified by the fates.

Gene will, I know, be glad to have you accompany him to Moundsville. I know of no one he would rather have as a chaperon.

Love always to you and yours,
Theodore Debs

TLS, NN Kars.

1. In "Debs Goes to Jail" (*Call*, March 11, 1919), Karsner recounted Debs's Canton speech and his trial in Cleveland and claimed that "he must now go to jail for having had the temerity and courage to stand by his right of sovereign citizenship."

2. Owen Reed Lovejoy (1866–1961) was a pastor of Methodist and Congregational churches in Michigan and New York until 1904, when he joined the National Child Labor Commission, which he served as assistant secretary from 1904 to 1907 and general secretary from 1907 to 1926. In "Good Night, Comrade—and Good Morning" (*Call*, March 12, 1919), Lovejoy wrote that Debs had been convicted . . . of hating war [and] I think you are guilty," that the "trouble with [Debs]" was that he "came on earth too soon," and that "while you are in prison we are not free."

3. On March 11, 1919, the *Call* gave front page coverage to the Supreme Court decision and to a "Special Telegram" from Debs in which he argued that the issue in his case was "the fundamental right of free speech" and that the decision had made "the constitution another 'scrap of paper.' "

4. In "Farewell to Judson Oneal" (*Call*, March 23, 1919), Theodore and Eugene Debs praised Judson Oneal, James Oneal's brother, as a man who "had but one purpose in life, and that was to serve the working class."

EVD to Theodore Debs

March 28, 1919
Akron, Ohio

My dear old Pard:
    Your letter recd—so glad to have a chipper chirp from you—all
the papers have come OK. Meeting at Youngstown[1] last night broke
all records. *Thousands* couldn't get in. Marguerite addressed them on
the public square. I spoke to the overflow 5 minutes. They were in
a frenzy of enthusiasm. Feeling fine as a young buck. So many callers
I have no chance to write.
    A thousand loving greetings to you old pard & to Gertrude &
Marguerite from
                                                    Yours forever
                                                            Gene

ALS, InTI, Debs Collection.

    1. "Debs' Last Words at Youngstown," as reported in *Melting Pot* (June 1919),
dealt chiefly with a defense of the Russian Revolution, the United States courts ("they
can go to hell with their courts"), and Debs's prediction that he was "about to go to
prison for the rest of my life."

Theodore Debs to EVD

April 14, 1919
Terre Haute, Indiana

EUGENE V DEBS
    THEY HAVE YOUR BODY BEHIND PRISON WALLS[1] BUT YOUR UNCON-
QUERABLE SPIRIT, RADIANT AS A SUNBURST, SOARS HUMANITY'S LU-
MINOUS HEIGHTS A MILLION MILES BEYOND THE FOUL TOUCH OF
FILTHY HYPOCRITES AND THEIR PROSTITUTED MERCENARIES. YOUR
UNWAVERING FIDELITY TO PRINCIPLE, YOUR UNFALTERING LOVE AND
DEVOTION TO THE CAUSE OF THE CRUSHED AND OPPRESSED WILL BE
AN UNCEASING INSPIRATION. I WAS NEVER SO PROUD OF YOU. MY ARMS
ARE ABOUT YOU, OLD PAL, AND WILL BE THROUGH TIME AND ETERN-
ITY.
                                        YOUR LOVING BROTHER,
                                            THEODORE DEBS[2]

Telegram, InTI, Debs Collection.

1. Debs left Terre Haute on April 12, 1919, reported to the federal marshal in Cleveland the following morning, and was taken to the Moundsville, West Virginia, penitentiary to begin serving his ten-year sentence.

2. Theodore Debs's telegram was widely reprinted in the socialist press (see, e.g., *New York Call*, April 22, 1919).

Theodore Debs to Helen Keller

April 15, 1919
Terre Haute, Indiana

Dear Comrade Keller: —

Your beautiful message to Gene inspirited him and warmed the hearts of us all.

It is the sympathetic touch and the loving greeting of such souls that make these dark days bearable and I wish to thank you in the name of Gene and on behalf of all suffering humanity for your deep understanding, your loving heart, your tender words of comfort and your stupendous courage.

Your letter could only come from the luminous soul of a great woman! a woman who has caught the vision and walked the heights and to whom the new Kingdom of Brotherhood is not a far off illusion but a loving reality.

Gene went to his new task sent him by the capitalist courts with his head up and his spirit unbroken. They have but given him a new weapon and a new audience.

Your loving message helped to make us feel the triumph of his going and I am wondering if you would consent to its being used by the press and in this way pass the inspiration to the countless friends who grieve for Gene.

If for any personal reason there is the least objection I shall fully understand and commit it to our treasure chest.

Its loving benediction has served us greatly for which accept the undying gratitude and affection of Gene and of us all.

Fraternally
Theodore Debs

P.S. Kindly wire decision[1] as to letter at my expense.

TLS, InTI, Debs Collection.

1. See Keller to Theodore Debs, April 17, 1919.

EVD to Theodore Debs

April 16, 1919
Moundsville, West Virginia

My dear Theodore:

Received your telegram and need not say that it did me more good than words can tell. Arthur[1] has probably told you that the trip here was made without special incident. Marguerite Prevey and her sister and her husband, Fred and Moskovitz[2]—and the rest were all as kind as they could be to the very last. Karsner, Wagenknecht & Engdahl,[3] along with Arthur, attended me all the way & did all they could to make the trip a pleasant one. Marshal Lapp & his deputy Mr. Walsh[4] treated me with all kindness & consideration.

Since I had to be imprisoned I congratulate myself upon being here for it is in all regards the best {prison} I have ever seen. The Warden, Mr. Terrell,[5] is a gentleman in the true sense of that term and everyone here without exception respects & loves him. He maintains discipline mainly through kindness and the prisoners with rare exceptions behave themselves accordingly. It is a great institution—almost 900 prisoners & capacity for at least 600 more. Mr. Terrell has given me every privilege consistent with the prison rules & I was never treated more considerately in my life. I have a delightful room on the ground floor of the hospital bldg & the liberty of the vast court-yard. In front of me is a spraying fountain & about me the green lawn & the beautiful flowers. The meals are excellent & everything is scrupulously clean.

Pls. hand enclosed note to Mary & ask her to kindly hand it to Mrs. McGregor[6] when she calls. Pls. don't send me any letters except the really important ones. I do not wish to write or receive an unnecessary one. Mr. Terrell has been more than kind & I do not want to abuse the privileges he allows me.

Don't worry about me in the least. I'm alright. Love to Gertrude & Marguerite.

Your loving brother
Gene

Love to John and Mary

ALS, InTI, Debs Collection.

1. Arthur Baur, Debs's brother-in-law, who accompanied him from Terre Haute to Moundsville.
2. As noted, Marguerite Prevey and A. W. Moskowitz, a Cleveland tailor, posted Debs's bond following his arrest in June 1919.

3. David Karsner, who published a small (fifty-eight pages) booklet, *Debs Goes to Prison,* an account of Debs's trip from Terre Haute to Cleveland to Moundsville; Alfred Wagenknecht; and Louis Engdahl.

4. Charles W. Lapp, United States marshal, and Thomas E. Walsh, deputy marshal, of the Northern District of Ohio.

5. Warden Joseph Z. Terrell, in whose "Imprisonment of Eugene V. Debs," a typescript recollection of Debs's two-month stay at Moundsville (Archives and Manuscripts Section, West Virginia University Library), Debs is called "a man of character, courage, integrity, and intelligence." Terrell recalled that he was "criticized by some people and, also, by some newspapers" for his lenient treatment of Debs at Moundsville, but he "paid no attention to either" and felt "vindicated" in 1921 when Debs was permitted to travel without guards from the Atlanta Federal Penitentiary to Washington for a meeting with Harding's attorney general, Harry Daugherty.

6. Possibly Orientha A. McGregor, a longtime friend and neighbor of Debs's parents and Mary Baur, Debs's niece.

Helen Keller to Theodore Debs

April 17, 1919
Richmond Hill, New York

THEO DEBS
YES USE LETTER   MY HEART GOES WITH IT[1]

HELEN KELLER

Telegram, InTI, Debs Collection.

1. Keller's letter to Debs appeared in the *New York Call* (April 24, 1919), *Appeal to Reason* (May 17, 1919), and other socialist publications.

EVD to Theodore Debs

April 21, 1919
Moundsville, West Virginia

My dearest Theodore:

By even mail I send you a package of letters, cards & telegrams. None of these has been acknowledged. You will know how to handle them. Pls. acknowledge their receipt. There are so many that you will have to be brief. Three or four lines of thanks & appreciation on a half sheet will do. Tell them I can not write. The Warden, Mr. Terrell, could not be more kind, but at the same time he is expected to enforce prison rules *impartially* & you know there are many who would protest at once if he showed me any special favors. He is the very kind of a man I would not embarrass & so I must keep myself within bounds. Do not let any {more} letters come to me from comrades than are absolutely necessary. You will understand. The prison rules are strict but Mr. Terrell is doing the best he can & all he can for me & I don't want to be the means of subjecting him to any embarrassment. Pls. say to Mabel[1] that I recd her letters & thank her with all my heart. What a dear, devoted, brave and loyal soul she is & who could help but love her! The courage & fidelity of her is wonderful & she is the very soul of nobility. Pls. let her see this & tell her that no words can express my appreciation and love. I shall write her soon. When I read that she was now your office "devil" I had to laugh for a moment & then I could have wept when I thought of what an angel she is, & how she has proved herself & shines [one word illegible] with a heavenly radiance in this hour of trial. Be good to her in every way you can.

Tell dear Marguerite her dear little Easter card sweetened the day for me & the "cute" little elf is now tacked up on my chamber wall.

Kate writes me in such good cheer & I'm so glad she bears the separation so bravely. Wish you & Gertrude & Marguerite would see her as [often as] you can conveniently & ask Mabel to see her often as she can. I know you're very busy, but you'll be of good cheer & it's all the world to me that *you are*. God never made a nobler soul than you, dear boy, & I love you in my heart of hearts forever.

Marguerite Prevey & her sister have just been here—so glad Marguerite will speak at T.H. May 4[2]—they sent me a big box of candy from Wheeling. They are the dearest [one word illegible].

I love all these poor souls here & I believe they all love me.

Rec'd 8 boxes of flowers, potted plants in full bloom, 2 boxes cigars, fruit & letters & telegrams without number for Easter remembrance. I give all my flowers to patients in the tuberculosis hospital.

P.S. All the letters I send you I wish you would pass over to Mabel & let her read them & after you have answered them give them to Kate to read & save.

AL, InTI, Debs Collection.

1. Mabel Dunlap Curry, who worked as a volunteer in the Terre Haute office throughout Debs's imprisonment.

2. The *Terre Haute Tribune* (May 5, 1919) described the "orderly parade" and speeches given by Seymour Stedman and Marguerite Prevey and noted that "about 500 marched in the parade" and that "since no red flags appeared and the speeches were considered mild there was no public demonstration against the socialists."

EVD to David Karsner

April 22, 1919
Moundsville, West Virginia

My dear Comrade David:

A thousand thanks! You can never know how very much I appreciate all your kindness. Your coming here with me was so good of you, and the many fine things you have said and written in your splendid articles[1] will abide with me for all time.

I wish you could have been here long enough to know the Warden, Mr. Terrell, as I have learned to know him. I say this because of a reference to him of a questioning nature in one of your articles.[2] I know you would not intentionally do him the least injustice. He occupies a very trying and difficult position and my being here under the circumstances does not make things any easier for him. He has certainly treated me as well as he possibly can under the rules of the prison which, as you know, he is expected to enforce *impartially*, and there are not a few who would be glad to see him subject me to the severest discipline and set me at the hardest task. Mr. Terrell has had all regard for my health and has in every other way treated me not only humanely but kindly, and I am sure he has the welfare of all the prisoners at heart and does the very best he can by them all. But after all, it's a prison, and I am sure there are many things he would do differently if he were free to carry out his own individual wishes. Please thank all of the *Call* staff for me for their beautiful devotion and support. I can never repay them. My love and gratitude goes to you all.

Kindly send me a copy each of the *Call* of April 13th, 14th, 15th, 16th, 17th, 18th, 19th and 20th. I have given my copies to the Warden's clerks who want the articles for their scrap books.

Believe me always, always

Yours in loving comradeship,
Gene

P.S. Tell the comrades they must not worry about me in the least. I am all right. There is nothing to regret, nothing to fear—there is everything to hope for & to live and work for.

Hundreds of letters, telegrams etc are here. I could not begin to answer them even if it were not for the rules. I appreciate each loving word—each touch of comradely kindness.

ALS, NN, Kars.

1. Karsner's *Call* articles were collected in *Debs Goes to Prison* (New York: Irving Kaye Davis & Company, 1919).

2. In a *Call* article on April 16, 1919, Karsner quoted Warden Terrell as saying that "the Soviets might be all right in Russia but in Moundsville I am the supreme dictator."

Morris Hillquit to Theodore Debs

April 27, 1919
Saranac Lake, New York

Dear Theodore,

Will you please use the enclosed cheque[1] to procure for Gene some little comforts and pleasures to help while away the heavy hours of his confinement. I have been intending to send him some books, cigars and other trifles direct from here, but in the first place I can get nothing in this remote village, and in the second you know his needs and tastes so much better than anybody else. I sincerely hope you will take the offer in the spirit in which it is made—as a slight tribute of a true friend and good comrade.

My congratulations upon your message to Gene. It was fine and worthy of both of you.

With cordial good wishes

Sincerely and fraternally yours
Morris Hillquit

ALS, InTI, Debs Collection.

1. For $100. See Theodore Debs to Morris Hillquit, May 5, 1919.

Rose Pastor Stokes to EVD

April 30, 1919
New York City

Gene, dearest Comrade:

I have been yearning to write you since that day you entered the Gates of the New Day. I am sure that all is well with you, yet it is but natural that we outside, should feel imprisoned while you are where you are, though we know that you are free even though your body is robbed of liberty.

I too have been hard pressed and therefore my delay in writing.

Only yesterday, when I told myself that I must put all other matters aside and write you, I sat down instead to write to Emma.[1] I thought: I have not written *her* since her entry in the State Penitentiary of Missouri, though I have often wanted to. Now I know that 'Gene would wish me to write her *before* writing him. We differ, but she is one of the most courageous spirits in the ranks of the struggling workers. I wrote her yesterday that she might know how often I have thought of her and her courage. Tomorrow, I was to write you, so that you might have a message—a May Day message from me too among the many that will pour in on you. But all the things I meant to say I cannot here. Instead I shall say them to my comrades and fellow workers throughout the city on Thursday, beginning at ten in the morning and ending up some time late in the evening according to the present schedule. There is so little time. My own appeal[2] is to be heard on May 12, in St. Paul in the Circuit Court, and though my case legally is a monstrosity of injustice, still we are hardly sent to prison these days for anything, in the last analysis, save for our devotion to the cause of the working class, and I expect to get news of an adverse decision. Thank heaven, there is a growing consciousness on the part of the workers—indeed a phenomenally growing consciousness—that that is the true reason for these prosecutions and imprisonments. In this one fact alone we should, and do, feel our strength. The future (and not the distant future) belongs to us, and we can afford to bear out our confinement and be even joyful in our imprisonment. The Comrades, many of them, do not understand how it is possible to take the matter so calmly and even gladly. How shall it be otherwise when the Rising Sun of the Day of the People throws a roseate light and warmth upon our countenances the very moment we face the prison gates! This must comfort even the uncomprehending. For us, who know—and see—, there is blessedness even in the darkness of the dungeon.

Dearest Comrade, of course I understood! Indeed, I felt remiss for not writing again at once; and felt too that *you* would understand why *I* did not. I even dreamed of coming out to see you, but that the material situation is such at present I am not able to realize my dream. But we are not greatly in need of communion on the plane that is so manifestly essential to most of our human kind. To all those who draw their sustenance and strength from things spiritual, neither space nor time nor matter intervenes.

I think we understand each other well, and actual sight of, and nearness, to each other is not necessary to have a good understanding. The other day a beautiful thing happened, when a young woman Comrade, who had been saving up her pennies for a trip to Moundsville offered me the money because as she put it, "it is more important for you to see him than for me." You will conceive how touched I was. Of course, I refused to take it, but before we left the meeting she assured me that the money would be there for me to use, whenever I was ready to go! And how eager she is herself to see you! and how much sacrifice of necessary other things the sum represents! It is wonderful. I shall never forget this act of devotion. And the name of Rose Spanier[3] will always be enshrined in my memory. She is a wonderful little woman with a big, big spirit, who issues a very good paper — a weekly. One that brings her nothing and for which she must give up money and the recreation-hours of a worker.

I meant to write to M.[4] again this week, but oh, the work and the brief while to work in! And what among other things do you think I am doing now? launching a dramatic movement — The People's Playhouse is giving a first performance of three proletarian plays for the first time on any stage, and the players young workers all of them, are also to be "for the first time on any stage." I am the dramatic director and the author of one of the plays.[5] The other two are also written by Comrades. I am going to be oh, so proud of the accomplishment! We must prove the high as well as the vital art that resides in the common people — the Jimmie Higginses. I wish you could see the players — The burning sincerity, the subtlety, the tragedy, the humor. We shall have a great time evening of May 7, when we face an audience and "put it over" . . . .

So, you see, dear Comrade, life is made up of a number of things. If we stand in the shadow of the bastille, we still serve the people and art joyously — aye, even *gaily*. Behind it all love, like a great sun, warms and illumines the way — and if it be the Way of Sorrow, why — if love be shining there, our feet go gladly and with out stumbling even though our shoulders bear the burden of the Cross.

Yours with the dear love of Comrades,

Rose Pastor Stokes

TLS, InTI, Debs Collection.

1. Emma Goldman (1869-1940) emigrated from Russia to the United States in 1885, joined a socialist group in Rochester, New York, soon thereafter, and, influenced by Alexander Berkman, Johann Most, and others, in 1889 determined to join the anarchist movement. As a public lecturer and in her writings, in *Mother Earth*, which she edited from 1906 until it was suppressed in 1917, and in tracts and books, Goldman became one of the country's best-known and most-feared anarchists and radicals, and her opposition to World War I led to her conviction in 1917 for obstruction of the draft law for which she spent two years in the Missouri state prison at Jefferson City. Soon after her release in September 1919, Goldman's citizenship was taken from her by a federal court and, as noted, she was deported on the *Buford* in December 1919.

Her original support of and disillusionment with the Russian Revolution are recounted in *My Disillusionment in Russia* (1923), and her early career and postdeportation exile in Europe, where she established a reputation as a major literary and dramatic critic, are described in her autobiography, *Living My Life* (1931).

2. As noted, in May 1918, Stokes was convicted and sentenced to ten years' imprisonment for violation of the Espionage Act. She was free on bail at this time and her conviction was overturned in March 1920 by the Court of Appeals in St. Louis.

3. Rose Spanier was identified in *Revolutionary Radicalism* (Lusk Committee Report), I:677, as "financial secretary of the Left Wing of the Socialist Party" in New York City.

4. Probably Mabel Dunlap Curry, whose extensive correspondence with Stokes during the period of Debs's imprisonment is preserved at the Yale University Library.

5. Stokes's announcement of the launching of the People's Playhouse at the Rand School appeared in the *Rand School News*, February 1919. Her own play, *The Woman Who Wouldn't* ("marry a man merely because he was the father of her children") was on "the first bill of one-act plays."

EVD to Helen Keller

April 30, 1919
Moundsville, West Virginia

My dear Helen Keller:

You will, I am sure, excuse my seeming remissness. My brother, in my absence, acknowledged the receipt of your beautiful, cheering and inspiring letter, and I meant to write and thank you soon after it came into my hands., but I was kept so busy and in such a state of uncertainty on account of daily expectation of arrest & incarceration that I was unable to give attention to my correspondence. Permit me, my dear comrade, to say to you at this late day that no letter I ever received touched me more deeply or afforded me greater satisfaction. Coming from you this fine, appreciative, characterisic expression compensates in full for a life-time of service.

You have always been to me, since first I knew of your heroic struggle and your incomparable attainment, the most wonderful of women, and your bold, fearless, uncompromising espousal of the cause of the workers won at once my admiration and respect and endeared you to me beyond words. You have used all the power you have won and all the success you have achieved to confer power upon the workers, aye, "the least of these," that they might win the world for the freedom and happiness of all. You have never faltered, never doubted, and never compromised. You are the incarnation of the revolutionary spirit now conquering, freeing, and humanizing the world. You combine all that is fine and brave, sweet and strong, ennobling and inspiring in your contribution to the cause, and I thank you with all my heart, and with love and all good wishes to you, I am always

Yours faithfully
Eugene V. Debs

ALS, American Foundation for the Blind, Keller Collection.

EVD to Morris Hillquit

May 3, 1919
Moundsville, West Virginia

My dear Morris:

You can hardly know how deeply your fine, cheering letter touched me, nor how much of light and joy and inspiration it brought to my prison chamber. A thousand loving thanks! I wish I could feel myself but half worthy of your generous praise—it seems to me I have done so little to deserve it. Hundreds and thousands of others who are scarcely known, or not known at all, have been far more cruelly persecuted and suffered infinitely more in the service of the cause. To me it is all privilege and no punishment, so long as the great purpose is served, and after all, it is my flesh only that is confined within these walls. The spirit soars above and beyond all prison limitations and mingles with the comrades beloved in the great free world.

I am glad, more than glad to have this beautiful and generous personal expression {from you,} and I am especially interested in your legal view of the case, but had you not written a line I would still have understood perfectly that your heart was with me and that your fealty in the hour of trial was unquestioned. I read your more than beautiful printed tribute[1] with tears in my eyes, and my wife saved it and laid it away with her little treasures.

Along with countless thousands of your comrades *I want you to get well* and you must and shall get well. We command it. I would gladly share my red drops with you. Give first care to *yourself* if you love us, as I know you do.

I am alright, and Tomorrow is already dawning.

Always, Your loving comrade
Eugene V. Debs

ALS, WHi, Hillquit Papers.

1. In the April 14, 1919, *Call,* Hillquit wrote that "with Eugene Debs goes to jail all that was best in America—her liberty and democracy, her justice and fairness."

EVD to Upton Sinclair

May 4, 1919
Moundsville, West Virginia

My dear Upton Sinclair:
I have just finished reading your stirring appeal in my behalf and in behalf of political prisoners in general,[1] and I want to thank you with a deep sense of the noble spirit which has moved you to put forth your best efforts to secure the liberation of the victims of the espionage act, so-called, which still operates to deprive men and women otherwise good citizens of their constitutional rights. You perceived the injustice of this from the beginning and protested with such persistency and forcefulness as made itself felt in high official circles, and when this wrong is finally righted, as it certainly will be, you will be entitled to a larger measure of credit than any other for opening the prison doors of your unjustly convicted comrades and fellow men. And so I thank you for the masterly article and for the more than kind and generous tribute it contains, only wishing I were more worthy of such high praises, and with all loving greetings and good wishes, I am

Yours always
Eugene V. Debs

I have about 900 fellow-prisoners here and there are as fine souls among them as may be found anywhere. The Warden is a fine man [illegible words follow].

ALS, InU, Lilly Library, Sinclair MSS.

1. "Upton Sinclair on the Debs Case," *Appeal to Reason,* March 22, 1919. The entire issue of the March 29, 1919, *Appeal* was given over to the "political prisoners" amnesty demand.

Theodore Debs to Morris Hillquit

May 5, 1919
Terre Haute, Indiana

Your very beautiful letter with a check for one hundred dollars is received. What can I say? I don't know. I am overwhelmed with a feeling of gratitude that I cannot express. There are times when the heart is so full that anything that might be said falls so far short of what we feel as to seem cold and almost contemptible. I can but tell you that my heart is overflowing with your loving kindness which I can never forget.

But it is too much, especially at this time when you are yourself burdened by obligation, and I should be tempted to return at least a part did I not fear to give offense to the tender and loving spirit which inspired your more than generous offering. Gene will be touched, as am I and all our family, to the very depths of his being, and I am quite certain that when he learns of your great kindness his eyes will be filled with tears and his heart with affection and gratitude.

We have often spoken of you and of how freely you gave yourself to the cause—even to the last ounce of your vitality. With thousands of other comrades we are hoping that your enforced rest[1] will bring back to you health and strength—and that in the very near future.

With all my heart I thank you for your words of personal kindness which are precious to me beyond words, and with love and thanks and the very best of wishes to you and yours I am,

Your comrade ever,
Theodore Debs

TLS, WHi, Hillquit Papers.

　　1. As noted, Hillquit was recovering from an attack of tuberculosis.

Louis Mayer to Theodore Debs

May 5, 1919
New York City

Dear Comrade & friend:

Your kind letter of Apr. 19th overflowing with warm appreciation for my effort to hold for future generations the aspiring and inspiring features of your much beloved brother should have received a much earlier reply. But these are busy days. With troubles all about, and a desire to do a days work inspite of them, it is a difficult task to get to letter writing.

There is no reason that Gene should have my letter in preference to the {other} thousands. He knows that he has so endeared himself to me that I shall be with him in my thoughts always.

The cast made at Akron from the modelled bust was defective in many ways. I have had to work over the greater part of it. A few days ago I finished and sent you the first photo which, however, shows the discoloration on the top of the head, due to the straw packing. After I have other casts made from this model the first shall go to you—a gift to Gene upon his return home which cannot be far off. Another I will present to the Rand School.[1]

If not before, I know you are coming to N.Y. with Gene upon his release. I am anxious to become better acquainted with you, for you must be much like Gene.

In the meantime my loving greetings go to you as they shall always go to him.

Sincerely yours
Louis Mayer

Started bust of Scott Nearing last Friday.

ALS, InTI, Debs Collection.

1. In a letter to the EVD Foundation, dated June 12, 1962, Mayer wrote that his bust of Debs "was never cast in bronze" but that he had "several plaster casts made and presented one to the Rand School and sent one to Kate." InTI, Debs Collection.

EVD to Madge Patton Stephens[1]

May 7, 1919
Moundsville, West Virginia

My dear Comrade Stephens:

You have been so loyal and unflinching in your devotion to the cause during these trying days, and you have been so very kind to me in so many ways, that I respond with joy to the suggestion of Mrs. Curry that I drop you a line of appreciation. Mrs. Curry has been writing to me of your wonderful fidelity, courage and energetic activity, which does not surprise me, knowing from intimate personal contact how whole-heartedly and unreservedly you have given yourself to the cause through all these years.

Theodore has told me that not only would you accept nothing in payment of your services to me but you were almost offended when he asked for the bill. You are more than kind, dear comrade, you have a nobility of nature which all appreciate who come to know you, and I certainly feel touched by what you have done for me and shall in the days {to come} strive all the more faithfully to serve the cause and realize the ideals to which you have given your life, and your fidelity to which you have sealed with your consecration.

Permit me to thank you with all my heart for all your splendid services and for your personal kindness and devotion, the thought of which gives me fresh strength and inspiration.

My love goes to you and your good husband.[2] (Theodore thinks him the finest man he knows) and to all the dear comrades at Terre Haute, and with a heart brimful of good wishes for you all, I am always

Yours faithfully
Eugene V. Debs

ALS, EVD Foundation, Debs Home.

1. Madge Patton Stephens (1869-1954) was born in Sullivan, Indiana, graduated from Indiana Medical College in 1895, and practiced medicine in Terre Haute from 1897 until her death. The deep-seated prejudice against female physicians (especially in the profession), her use of unorthodox treatment (including, in the 1920s, the Abrams Electronic Reaction Machine), and her aggressive support of radical causes— socialism, birth control, pacifism, women's rights—made Dr. Stephens a controversial figure in Terre Haute and a frequent irritant to the city's medical establishment. She campaigned for Debs during his 1916 congressional campaign, worked tirelessly for his release from prison, and served as his physician in Terre Haute following his release.

2. Stephens's husband, Wallace W. Stephens, is listed in the Terre Haute city directories of the period as an undertaker and real estate agent.

EVD to Morris Hillquit

May 9, 1919
Moundsville, West Virginia

My dear Morris:

In a letter just received from Theodore he tells me of your very generous gift. It is too much. You should not have done it. You are yourself entitled so much more, in your impaired health, to the generous, self-forgetting consideration you bestow upon me. My heart is touched and the mist is in my eyes. Who am I and what have I done to merit such riches of kindness and love? The check is large, too large, too liberal—the spirit in which it was written and tendered is beyond estimate, converting the hundred dollars into countless millions. That is how you have enriched me, my dear comrade, and with my brother and our wives and families, I thank you with a deep sense of your precious personal devotion and your noble generosity in the present hour of trial, in which such devotion and such loyalty to the cause which inspired it mean the fulfillment of prophecy and the realization of Humanity's noblest dreams and loftiest aspirations.

The time may never come when you shall need it, but if it does the last biscuit in our cupboard and the last penny in our purse is yours.

And now *get well*, beloved comrade, and make us all happy! That's all I ask.

Your loving comrade
E. V. Debs

Please don't answer!

ALS, WHi, Hillquit Papers.

EVD to David Karsner

May 15, 1919
Moundsville, West Virginia

My very dear Dave:

Your loving letter of the 11th filled my heart and made me very happy. Every word from you is a gleam of light in my prison chamber. Thank you, my beloved young brother, with all my heart! I can not tell you what riches you have brought into my life, nor how dear the very name of you is to me. The mail has just been delivered to me and in it I find your beautiful booklet "Debs Goes to Prison"[1] and the advance sheet of the Call Magazine containing your sweet, poetic piece of writing "While Debs Prepared for Prison."[2] You overwhelm me with your kindness and I do not half deserve it. In your own generous soul you are prompted to magnify my paltry services which do not begin to compare to those deserved by many a brave and modest soul whose name is scarcely known.

Your little book is a real masterpiece. You have put into every line of it the art of the craftsman, the soul of the poet, and the love of a noble Comrade. You have honored me beyond words—you have touched the very heart of me and I can answer only with my tears. The article in the Magazine (Call) is another characteristic piece of your beautiful work with the real heart of you pulsing in all the loving lines.

To-night I shall read carefully and enjoy with all my heart both the little book and the article. Meantime my arms are about you and the love of you enriches me beyond dreams. Theo. & the folks at home have written about your visit there — they all see how noble you are and love you dearly. Thanking you with my heart and my life for your measureless kindness and hoping that some day I may in some small way serve you I am in life & death

Your loving, grateful comrade

E. V. Debs

[enclosed note]

My loved Davy:

I'm always asking you for something. Pls. send me, if convenient, an extra copy of your article on "While Debs Prepared for Prison" — just the 2 pages containing the article — also the sheet in Call Mag. of *May* 4 containing the little poem by Joshua Kuntz,[3] also the sheet (Page 4 Call Mag May 11) containing the 3 poems by Macy, de Witt & Winston.[4]

If you can send me the 3 sheets above referred to I shall be so glad to have them & if you could send the same 3 sheets to Theo. he would feel grateful — but *go to no trouble.* You are kept very busy & if you can't do it conveniently pls. dont do it at all. The mail comes in a flood. I'm busy, in fact rushed, from 6 AM to 9 PM every day. I know every prisoner here. We all love each other mightily. I visit them & they come to see me & it is wonderful what help we can be to each other.

I boiled in every drop in every vein, when I read of the attempted lynching of the Call.

P.S. Have just read the three beautiful and truly wonderful poems on pg. 4 of Call *Magazine* of May 11th by John Macy, S.A. de Witt and Alvin Winston. They are all perfectly fine & so very noble in spirit. Can you do me the kindness to thank these three beautiful poet-comrades for me & give them my love — Tell them how very deeply I feel touched by their flattering tribute — also in the Call *Magazine* of May 4th there is a wondrous poetic tribute by Joshua Kunitz. It is a perfect gem of poetic art & a great soul stirs forth from it. Do you know him? If so, will you not kindly thank & love him & tell him I feel touched to the heart by his beautiful little poem.

ALS, NN Kars.

1. As noted, Irving Kaye Davis & Co. of New York published Karsner's *Debs Goes to Prison.* Karsner's acknowledgment in the booklet was dated May 1, 1919.

2. *New York Call,* April 27, 1919. The article was illustrated by a photograph of Louis Mayer "at work in his New York studio on the bust of Eugene Victor Debs."

3. The poem "Debs — America's Soul," by Joshua Kunitz, was one of many that compared Debs with Christ. *New York Call,* May 4, 1919.

4. The poems of John Macy, Samuel A. De Witt, and Alvin Winston were all dedicated to Debs, "the dauntless leader of the Socialist movement" (*New York Call*, May 11, 1919). In January 1920, Samuel De Witt was one of five socialists expelled from the New York state legislature on the grounds that he had opposed the war and given aid and comfort to the enemy during the war. Finally given his seat in September 1920, De Witt resigned in protest the continued exclusion of two of his colleagues and was reelected in November 1920.

Theodore Debs to Rose Pastor Stokes

May 16, 1919
Terre Haute, Indiana

Dear Comrade Stokes:

Your good letter, with scores of others, came to Gene on May Day and helped in great measure to make happy for him the day of all days, even behind prison walls. The influx was so great that even if there was no restriction placed upon his letter writing it would still be physically impossible for him to handle this correspondence and so he has sent it all here.

Gene wishes you to know, however, that he read your letter, each word, each line, with sincere appreciation and the greatest of satisfaction. Had the written word not come he would still have known that your fine spirit was ever near to comfort, strengthen and inspire in every hour. It is the love and confidence of the many beautiful souls in the movement that sustain him, strengthen him, and fill him with hope and cheer.

He is hoping, as are we all, that the court will reverse the infamous and outrageous decision rendered in your case and that you will not have to enter prison. I know we have nothing to expect from capitalist courts and yet I cannot make myself believe that this rape of justice is to stand. It is in such flagrant violation of all law and decency as to make the most hardened capitalist blush with shame at its infamy.

Gene wishes me to send you his greeting, his love and his thanks for all you have done and are doing to bring light and peace and happiness to a struggling world.

Fraternally yours,
Theodore Debs

TLS, NNU Tam, Stokes Papers.

EVD to Marguerite Debs [Cooper]

May 27, 1919
Moundsville, West Virginia

My dearest Marguerite:

The box of kindness from your dear hands came in perfect order on your birthday,[1] and it would be naive for me to try to tell you what emotions possessed me as I read your sweet note and saw the abundance of cakes, cookies and candies—all prepared by you—your thoughtfulness has provided for my enjoyment. Thank you, dear Marguerite, with all my heart. You are a dear girl, and I can not tell you how much I love you. The little cakes and the home-made candies are perfectly delicious, and the patients here in the hospital who are sharing these delicacies with me, join me in hearty thanks and appreciation.

Accept my loving congratulations upon your birthday! How very swiftly the years go by! It seems to me that it was just the other day that you were a little girl at your mother's side, and I can still see that same little girl as if it had been yesterday. I hope the day was a happy one for you and that all your birthdays not only, but all other days may be happy and fruitful ones, and that all your girlhood dreams and plans may be fully realized.

Kate has written me about the lovely time you all had together on Sunday and it makes me very happy to think of you all gathered together and making each other glad {and} loving each other in our beautiful family. Kate is very proud of you and loves you very dearly, as she told me when she was here last week.

I am getting along as well as anyone possibly could in my situation. I have no regrets and am sure that everything will come out right in the end.

Give your dear Mother and Father my love and with a heart-full of love for you and kisses for you all I am always

Devotedly yours
Gene

I hope "Babe" is well and prosperous.

The little Daisies were so sweet. They are now on my table and whisper lovingly of you.

ALS, InTI, Debs Collection.

1. Debs's niece, Marguerite, was born on May 25, 1894.

EVD to David Karsner

May 29, 1919
Moundsville, West Virginia

Beloved Comrade Dave:

You are the very dearest, sweetest, finest of comrades, and you have proved it times without number since first you came, as if by special providence, into my life. I find myself so often under the necessity of thanking you for some past kindness that I have come to realize how little of what sings in the heart and sighs for expression can be transferred to the written page. Please give the "youngster" in the office my love for his kindness in helping you to furnish me with the *Call* files and clippings as requested, a service on the part of you both that I gratefully appreciate. You were not in the least to blame about the lawyers—nor were they. No one was to blame. It just happened so. No one could suppose that they would rush me off with such indecent haste, especially as I had voluntarily surrendered myself. But they were excusable on the ground that they were scared— As to notifying Stedman, Theodore had wired to National Office & supposed they had notified Stedman and that was the information {you received} that prompted your statement. But I'm glad the objectionable paragraph is to be eliminated, & there should now be good feeling all around.[1]

Dear, beautiful wonderful Horace![2] Put your arms around him and kiss him for me until I can do so myself. The Almighty never made but one of him. Tell him for me to cling to the willows and live— he cannot otherwise, for he's immortal. The Whitman Fellowship Banquet of the Gods[3]—will revive, restore and re-inspire him—How I'd love to be with you & put my arms about you all—I'm busy here, every minute. All's well within my walls—if only the {same} were true without!

My heart will be with you at the Call Anniversary Celebration![4]

I've been reading the reports of your speeches in the Call & other papers and my heart has so expanded lovingly and gratefully to each kind word in your stirring appeals. You are the very soul of loyal devotion.

My love to our dear Horace, Ann Montgomerie, your sweet Rose, the Aalholms[5] and all the comrades at the Call!

Yours until the last sunset.

Gene

Warden Terrell has inquired about you—He thinks very kindly of you as you do of him.

ALS, NN Kars.

1. In *Debs Goes to Prison* (pp. 33-34), Karsner claimed that in Cleveland after Debs had voluntarily surrendered himself, none of his attorneys was notified in time to be there to represent him in the service of the Supreme Court mandate calling for his imprisonment. The proceeding was irregular, Karsner said, and "the greatest figure in the American labor movement was kidnaped by deputies through extra legal proceedings and with no one to interpose objection, save a woman, Mrs. Prevey, one of Debs's bondsmen."

2. Horace Traubel moved to Karsner's home in New York City in early May 1919.

3. The Walt Whitman Fellowship celebrated the Whitman centenary at the Brevoort Hotel on May 31, 1919.

4. The *Call* celebrated its eleventh anniversary in May 1919.

5. Arthur and Gertrude Traubel Aalholm, Traubel's son-in-law and daughter, who lived near Karsner in New York City.

Theodore Debs to Upton Sinclair

June 2, 1919
Terre Haute, Indiana

Dear Comrade Sinclair:—

Only today I came to your letter to Gene under date of May 13th. which came many days ago with scores of others. The letters are so many that we are unable to keep apace. Gene cannot answer these letters on account of prison restrictions which limit his writing. But he is none the less thankful for your kindness. He wishes me to tell you that he has "The cry for Justice" and also "King Coal" and will of course be glad to have "Jimmie Higgins" when it comes from the press.

Gene bears no grudge to the Appeal[1] nor is it in him to harbor malice. He is looking forward and not backward. What is past is past. The Appeal has certainly done and is now doing splendid work for amnesty[2] and for the cause and he appreciates it for what it is now doing, rather than to condemn it for what it has done in the past, but under prison rules he can write nothing of a party or propaganda nature and *nothing* for publication. There have been many requests for articles, statements etc. but Gene has had to decline them all.

With all good wishes I am,

Fraternally yours,
Theodore Debs

P.S. This very moment comes a note from Gene saying that the copy of "Jimmie Higgins" has been received and for which he returns his very warmest thanks. He is deeply grateful for this volume, made priceless by its loving inscription, and which will be a precious prison companion to him as long as he is in Moundsville.

TLS, InU, Lilly Library, Sinclair MSS.

1. As noted, the *Appeal to Reason* supported the government during World War I, changing its name temporarily to the *New Appeal* in 1917 and back to the *Appeal to Reason* on March 1, 1919. "Upton Sinclair's Page" was a regular feature of the paper during the war and early postwar period.

2. The *New Appeal* launched its "general amnesty" campaign on November 16, 1918. In "Debs Thanks Sinclair" (*Appeal*, May 24, 1919), Debs praised Sinclair's efforts on behalf of "political prisoners in general," congratulated him for having "perceived the injustice" of the government's wartime restrictions "from the beginning," and thanked him for the "kind and generous tributes" that Sinclair had paid him in "Spirit of Debs Cannot Be Shut Up Behind Walls of Steel or Iron" (*Appeal*, April 26, 1919).

EVD to Theodore Debs

[June 4?, 1919]
Moundsville, West Virginia

My dear old Pard:

Your chipper letter of the 2d gave me several thrills of joy. I only want to know that all is right at home—*that's all*. The rest does not trouble me. I know that everything is working to a good end & that everything is bound to come right. There's never anything the matter with me. I'm always in tune with the vibrations of the infinite. I'm getting along the best in the world & my spirits are as vocal as the springtime. The comrades could not be more loving & loyal, & what else could I desire or expect? The prison is just now my part and I'm taking it just as calmly & serenely as if it were staged in some delightful retreat for my special delectation. At 63 I take what comes with smiles, be it what it may, especially if it is the enemy of smiles & would banish smiles from the eyes & souls of men—*& that's victory*, the kind of victory that drives away fear, keeps the heart warm, the spirit young, & fills to the brim the cup of life with the sparkling nectar of love and joy. And *them's my philosophy*, old pard, as a prison convict at 63.

AL, InTI, Debs Collection.

EVD to David Karsner

June 5, 1919
Moundsville, West Virginia

My dear "Davy"

Will you kindly send me by return mail a copy of the Call of *May 31st* and much oblige me. Give my love to Comrades Ervin, Gerber, Oneal and all at the Call office. And our beloved Horace! Great, wonderful, illuminated soul! How I'd love to put my arms about him once again! Do this for me, Davy, and some time I'll do it for you. Love to you all!

Yours always
E. V. Debs

My heart is with you all the time.

How the Anniversary[1] must have touched and thrilled Horace! It certainly honored and vindicated him above all others. The next Century will be celebrated by the whole world and Walt and Horace will be crowned and canonized together.

Pls. send me 2 copies of May 31st if you can spare them.

ALS, NN Kars.

1. The one-hundredth anniversary of Walt Whitman's birth on May 31, 1919.

Louis Mayer to EVD

June 5, 1919
New York City

Dear Gene:

While I have not written you directly you know that I have remained close to you in spirit and that my love for & devotion to you has only grown by your present fate. The enclosed photos[1] show you that the "meditations of my heart" have found, to some extent, expression through the work of my hands.

From your brother Theodore to whom I sent the {first} small photo taken from the bust, (discolored as it arrived from Akron) you may have heard of its final completion. Had the bust and also the medallion on exhibition at the Call bazaar.[2] Next week the finished bust goes to the Rand School—and another intended for you, also a medallion. I will try to get off to your brother's address.

I also want to get a reduction made of the medallion—one that can be struck off in metal, and so I must also make a reverse side, for which I want some terse sentence (not too many words)—a motto that stands for you and your aims.

Nearing suggested: As long as there is a lower class I am of it . . . As long as there is one man in prison I am not free"—That is plenty long but I think I could manage to place it without crowding. However when I spoke to Mrs. Malkiel of The Call this morning she suggested: "I sould rather be jailed a thousand times, than betray the working class once." Probably you or Theodore would have still other suggestions. Most of all I would like you to choose the words. Wish you would write them to your brother Theodore who could forward them to me.[3]

It is comforting to know that things are made reasonably bearable for you—yet for the sake of all who love you, you too must seek to make your seclusion as short as possible.

I and my family are looking forward to the time when you shall visit us here. You will be no stranger to Mrs. & the boys.

Isn't it a queer incident that in the latest exposure of the bust the words 'Liberty' should be so prominent on the paper on which the bust stands? May it be a good omen.

Always lovingly yours,
Louis.

ALS, InTI, Debs Collection.

1. Mayer enclosed photographs of his busts of John Haynes Holmes and Debs and one side of a Debs medallion.

2. As part of its eleventh-birthday celebration the *Call* held a four-day bazaar—May 29 through June 1, 1919—at the New Star Casino in New York.

3. Theodore Debs's letter to Mayer, July 1, 1919, praises Mayer's bust as "a wonderful piece of work" but does not include a suggested medallion text. Mayer's medallion, with Debs's profile, has "Socialist Party" on one side, "Workers of the World Unite" on the other.

EVD to David J. Douglas[1]

June 10, 1919
Moundsville, West Virginia

My dear Comrade Douglas

A thousand thanks! You are more than kind to me in inscribing to me that inspiring poem from your gifted pen and in sending me those sheets of thrilling music with their flattering personal tributes. The poem is a masterly production and I feel greatly honored to have been made the subject of such an inspiring protest and prophecy — far more so, indeed, than if it had been penned by the author of "Danny Deevers" himself.

I agree with all my heart with all you say about Music and the vital mission of Music in the world movement. The soul-stirring appeal of Music arouses, animates, thrills and inspires when all else fails. Let the swelling anthems of the Glad New Day now dawning ring out joyously through the land and throughout the world.

You will find autographed copy of your splendid poem[2] enclosed.

Most heartily do I wish you success in fullest measure in the work you have undertaken at International Song Publishers.

Please give my love and thanks to comrades Liebich, Gallagen and Biedel,[3] and with all affectionate devotion to you I am

Faithfully your comrade
Eugene V. Debs

ALS, CU, Gallagher Collection.

1. As head of International Song Publishers in Chicago, Douglas described (*Eye-Opener*, August 15, 1919) his plan to publish "a new revolutionary song each month . . . to arouse the class consciousness of the workers of this country."

2. Douglas's song "Eugene V. Debs" was copyrighted in 1919. Each of its eight-line refrains ended with "We are takin' Debs to prison in the mornin'."

3. Rudolph B. von Liebich, a musician and composer who provided music for socialist picnics and rallies in the Chicago area, and Richard Beidel, listed in the Chicago city directories of the period as either music teacher or musician. Liebich later (1931) provided the music for Michael Gold's *Proletarian Song Book of Lyrics from the Operetta The Last Revolution*. On August 27, 1922, when Debs was at Lindlahr Sanitarium in Elmhurst, Illinois, Douglas, Liebich, Beidel and Mary E. Gallagher (whose poem, "Child Laborer's Spring Song," was recited) provided a program of entertainment "for their friend and Big Brother, Eugene V. Debs." Typescript program, Debs Collection, Indiana State University.

EVD to Theodore Debs

June 11, 1919
Moundsville, West Virginia

My dear Theo:

Pls. write a nice letter to *Ralph Korngold   2444 Leland Ave. Chicago* & thank him warmly for a box of very fine cigars just recd. from him — tell him how grateful I feel for his generous remembrance & send *him & his wife*[1] my loving greetings, my deepest thanks & warmest wishes.

Write, please, to *Miss May Lane, R #1   Calumet   Okla* & thank *her and her mother* for the beautiful little boquet they sent me & which now sheds its fragrance in my prison chamber. Send 1 Hurt & 1 Dist.

David Karsner, Mahlon Barnes & W. Blenko[2] were here today. They all send you love. Barnes brought me a very fine, warm-hearted letter from our old friend Barney Berlyn[3] with his picture in it. Please write Barney a nice letter & tell him his message went straight to the heart & that his picture rests on my table. Tell him how deeply I appreciate his loving remembrance & that I send him my love & best wishes. His address is *Barney Berlyn, 6002 Prairie Ave. Chicago Ills.*

Tuesday AM It has rained here & is now very cool and comfortable—am feeling better right along—I keep quite busy from the time I get up in the morning, usually at 5 or 5 30 until I retire at 9.

I notice that the Typographical Union at T.H. passed some fine resolutions which were published in the Post—Kate mailed me the clipping—It is a clear, fine, strong expression of sympathy & support.[4]

I get the papers you send right along & stacks of others besides—I can hardly keep up with them all. You need no longer send the *Appeal* as they have put me on their list & send it to me here.

I'm in the very best of spirits—could not be better. My *morale* needs no tonic—I keep myself in tune—my mind clean, my conscience clear, & true to my best. I care absolutely nothing about what petty people say or think. I'm true to myself & my own soul & absolutely unafraid—& that's what counts & wins in the end.

Love & kisses to you & Gertrude & Marguerite

Your own old pard
Gene

ALS, InTI, Debs Collection.

1. Janet Fenimore Korngold.
2. William Blenko (1854-1933) emigrated from his native England to the United States at the turn of the century, settled in Kokomo, Indiana, and tried unsuccessfully to establish a glass factory for the production of decorative glassware and stained-glass windows. Blenko went back to England for a time, returned to the United States, and in 1922 founded the Blenko Glass Company in Milton, West Virginia, a firm that eventually became world famous in the specialized field of decorative glassware and stained glass. When Blenko died in 1933, his wife, Sarah Blenko, wrote Theodore Debs that "I'd like to have Dad's ashes scattered on [Debs's] Grave." In reply, Theodore Debs said that he would "be happy to meet your wishes" but that "the complete estrangement between our family and Gene's wife" made it impossible. Sarah Blenko to Theodore Debs, December 10, 1933; Theodore Debs to Sarah Blenko, December 12, 1933. InTI, Debs Collection.
3. Bernard Berlyn (1843-1931) was born in Holland and was brought to America in 1850. During the Civil War he helped organize the Cigar Makers' International Union in New York City and after the war settled in Chicago, where he was a founder

and lifelong activist in the Socialist party as a candidate for various offices, delegate to national conventions, editorial writer for the *American Socialist* and *Chicago Daily Socialist*, and leader of the party's Seventh Ward organization. Berlyn traveled widely as a party organizer before World War I, and his command of English, Dutch, German, Hebrew, and Yiddish made him especially valuable in that role.

4. The resolution, which was sent to President Wilson in a letter dated July 5, 1919, described Debs a "a man whose character heretofore has been above reproach," noted that "the war is over and the victory has been won," and asked Wilson "for the immediate and unconditional pardon of our neighbor and fellow townsman." National Archives, Records of the Office of Pardon Attorney, Record Group 204.

EVD to David Karsner

June 14, 1919
Moundsville, West Virginia

My loved "Davy"

Please let me ask you to serve me again. I call on you, I confess, without hesitancy because you always make me feel that I am serving you instead of your serving me. I have just finished reading John R. McMahon's wonderful dream picture in the Call Magazine of the 8th inst.,[1] and I wish you would kindly see that good comrade, if you can, or drop him a line or two if he's not there, and tell him how very deeply touched I was by this bit of real literature from his gifted pen. Please say to Comrade McMahon that my tears dropped on the tender and heart-gripping lines of his sweet and pathetic story as my dimmed eyes passed over them. If McMahon were not a Lincoln himself he had never produced this exquisite bit of spiritual psychology. Please say to him that he has honored me a thousand times more than I deserve and that I send him my love and my deepest thanks.

Your last visit is not yet ended. You still linger here. I can see and hear & feel you and draw infinitely upon your precious stores. Love to you and your dear Rose!

Always yours.
E. V. Debs

Love to all the Call comrades — Ryan Walker and all.

If you can send me an extra page or two of the Call Magazine of the 8th containing the McMahon article I should like to have them. But go to no trouble.

When you see dear Horace love him hard for me—embrace him savagely—without mercy—he'll know me.

ALS, NN Kars.

1. John Robert McMahon (1875-1956) was a New York journalist and author whose "Lincoln Visits Debs's' (*New York Call*, June 8, 1919) portrayed Lincoln as passing on to Debs "an earth title that was bestowed on me—The Emancipator."

Index